D0573844

Major World Religions

An essential introduction to the study of religion, this book is designed to answer the perennial questions about the great religions (Hinduism, Buddhism, Judaism, Christianity and Islam). Each chapter describes the fundamentals of the religion it discusses, but more specifically, includes *modern* developments and understandings of religion.

Today, we are witnessing the development of secularism on the one hand, and the revival of religious sentiment on the other. This necessitates a discussion of modernity and postmodernity – ideas which have had a significant effect on religious understanding – and of fundamentalism, and these topics form the basis of the final two chapters.

The reader is brought up to date with recent developments and commentaries on religious thought, theology and religious-political movements. The contributors to the book are recognized as experts in their fields, and also write with the benefit of a great deal of teaching experience, thus making the volume highly suitable for the undergraduate student of religious studies.

Lloyd Ridgeon teaches Islamic Studies at the University of Glasgow. His main areas of interest include Sufism, modern Islam and contemporary Iranian politics and culture. Previous publications include *Persian Metaphysics and Mysticism* (2002), *Islamic Interpretations of Christianity* (2000) and *'Aziz Nasafi* (1998).

Major World Religions

From their origins to the present

Edited by Lloyd Ridgeon

RoutledgeCurzon
Taylor & Francis Group
LONDON AND NEW YORK

G

First published 2003
by RoutledgeCurzon
11 New Fetter Lane, London EC4P 4EE

Simultaneously published in the USA and Canada
by RoutledgeCurzon
29 West 35th Street, New York, NY 10001

RoutledgeCurzon is an imprint of the Taylor & Francis Group

Typeset in Garamond and Frutiger by Keystroke, Jacaranda Lodge, Wolverhampton
Printed and bound in Great Britain by TJ International Ltd, Padstow, Cornwall

British Library Cataloguing in Publication Data
A catalogue record for this book is available from the British Library

Library of Congress Cataloging in Publication Data
Major world religions : from their origins to the present / edited by Lloyd Ridgeon.
      p. cm.
   Includes bibliographical references and index.
   1. Religions—History. I. Ridgeon, Lloyd V. J.

BL80.3 .M35 2003
200′.9–dc21   2002032642

ISBN 0–415–29768–0 (hbk)
ISBN 0–415–29796–6 (pbk)

Contents

LIST OF CONTRIBUTORS

Jeff Haynes is Professor of Politics in the Department of Politics and Modern History at London Guildhall University, where he teaches a variety of courses concerned with politics in 'Third World', international and religious contexts. His books include *Religion in Third World Politics* (1993), *Religion in Global Politics* (1998) and *Politics in the Developing World: A Concise Introduction* (2002).

Joseph Houston was educated at the University of Edinburgh and the University of Oxford, where his DPhil was gained in Philosophical Theology, on referring to God. Since 1966 he has taught at the University of Glasgow, at present in the Department of Theology and Religious Studies. He is Director of the Centre for Philosophy and Religion. His books include *Reported Miracles: A Critique of Hume* (1994) and *Thomas Reid in a Nutshell* (2000).

Alastair Hunter is Senior Lecturer in Hebrew and Old Testament Studies in the University of Glasgow. He teaches and researches in the fields of the Hebrew Bible, Judaism and literary and cultural studies. His most recent book is a study of the Psalms published in 1999. He is currently working on a commentary on Jonah.

Alison Jasper gained her PhD from the University of Glasgow. With a background in Christian theology and philosophy she has published in the area of feminist biblical hermeneutics, most specifically on the Gospel of John. Recent work has focused on the broader question of whether women can continue to find significance in the religious legacy of the West, looking particularly at the categories of body and embodiment as they are viewed by contemporary women scholars, writers and artists. She is a Lecturer in the Department of Religious Studies at the University of Stirling. She is married with three daughters.

David Jasper is Professor of Literature and Theology in the University of Glasgow. Educated at the Universities of Cambridge, Oxford and Durham, he was the Director of the Centre for the Study of Literature, Theology and the Arts at Glasgow from 1991 to 1998. The founder Editor of the journal *Literature and Theology*, he has written six books, and most recently has edited *Religion and Literature: A Reader* with Robert Detweiler. He is currently writing a book on contemporary desert theology.

Dermot Killingley retired in 2000 as Reader in Hindu Studies in the University of Newcastle upon Tyne. He studied at the University of Oxford and at the School of Oriental and African Studies, London, and taught previously at the University of Malaya in Kuala Lumpur. His books include *Rammohun Roy in Hindu and Christian Tradition*, *Hindu Ritual and Society* (with Werner Menski and Shirley Firth),

Approaches to Hinduism (with Robert Jackson) and *Beginning Sanskrit* (two volumes, with a third in preparation).

Lloyd Ridgeon lectures in Islamic Studies at the University of Glasgow, and his research focuses primarily on various aspects of Iranian studies. His books include *'Aziz Nasafi* (1998), *Islamic Interpretations of Christianity* (ed.) (2000), *Makhmalbaf's Broken Mirror: The Socio-Political Significance of Modern Iranian Cinema* (2001) and *Persian Metaphysics and Mysticism: Selected Treatises of 'Aziz Nasafi* (2002). He is currently working on a book about the Iranian intellectual Ahmad Kasravi.

Kiyoshi Tsuchiya was born in Takatō, Japan. He gained his MA from Shinshu University, Japan, 1989 and his PhD from the Centre for the Study of Literature, Theology and the Arts, University of Glasgow, 1995. He has been Deputy Director of the Centre since 1995, and Lecturer in Religious Studies since 1997. His books include *The Mirror Metaphor and Coleridge's Mysticism: Poetics, Metaphysics, and the Formation of the Pentad*, and 'Noh and purification: the art of ritual and vocational performance', in *Studies of Literary Imagination* (2001).

Studying religion

Joseph Houston

WHY STUDY RELIGION(S)?

That is a question which you would expect to see considered in a book like this. Let us consider it by focusing particularly, if not at each stage exclusively, on each of the three words expressing the question.

Why study religion(s)?

The 'why' may suggest that anyone who becomes a student of religion(s) will have considered the matter at length and made a careful, thoroughly informed rational choice. That is an ideal; and the existence of this book, it is confidently hoped, will enable more people to approach the ideal. But, often, less than ideally reasonable factors take students into their subject area, whatever it may be: maybe it fitted a timetable slot, or was not at 9 a.m., or was gushingly recommended by the only student from your school to go to your university shortly ahead of you, and who may just have been swanking seniority. Most of us make such decisions partly on somewhat reasonable grounds, partly on non-rational motives and partly because of accidental factors, which are causes rather than motives of ours.

Among the most obvious and entirely legitimate reasons we might have for taking up religious studies will be curiosity about the nature and value of religion(s), religious discourses and practices. Perhaps you or your family have a religious background of some sort: it may be mixed or uniform/unanimous, and either way you may be prompted to try to understand better what these religious commitments and activities are or were, what were their origins, what were the inspirations, teachers, scriptures, organized institutions, thoughts, feelings, rituals, morality, and the difficulties, of these believers.

Maybe, whether because of family religion, or because of friends or reading or music or striking experience, you are trying to *evaluate* some particular versions of religious life and faith with a view to rejecting, or going along with and making your own, its vision, its claim or its way of life. You may be more or less deeply committed, and are studying the better to understand, in the ways religious studies can make possible, the way you have begun to walk in.

Many religious studies students have had *no* such personal involvement with religions, but have had an awareness of the part(s) religion plays in the history, literatures, institutions and practices (such as the family, or education), philosophies, science or morality of cultures and civilizations. So, as one way of gaining insight into a great range of human life and experience, they study religion(s), usually in due course narrowing their focus so as to achieve a deeper understanding of particular times, places and people: Islamic Persian mysticism, religion in nineteenth-century English literature, politics and twentieth-century Buddhism . . . So, religion is treated as an important human phenomenon. If you are to understand it well, that will require that you also have a good grasp of some more particular phases and/or competencies of human beings. Often studies of humankind by humankind are said to belong to 'the humanities', which saw a great revival at the Renaissance (literally 'rebirth'); and the slogan of humanities' people is 'I consider nothing which is human to be alien to me.' It is commonly in this spirit that religious studies is pursued, intertwined with e.g. history, sociology, language-study, literature, philosophy – and studied with at least some of them to their mutual illumination.

Since religions are professed, and professedly (if inconsistently) acted upon, by human beings, religions are in (at least) that respect human. But are they only, or most significantly, human? Many religious devotees hold their religion to be much, and very significantly, more: to be in fact God-given, God-prompted, of divine origin, or something such. Of course, such claims are contentious. But, by the same token, so also is it contentious to maintain that religions are, essentially or principally, human quests – for God, for significance, human attempts to give meaning to human life. Neither the view that some religion is (God-given) revelation nor the view that it is a mode of human perception, a meaning-giving take on our life, can reasonably be assumed without argument. Of course, either can be, and either sometimes is, actually argued for in the religious studies world. Often the issue is left on one side while the phenomena (i.e. the obvious appearances) are investigated, and their human significance pursued.

People who take up religious studies simply, and properly, as humanities students may be content enough to leave aside, bracket off, questions about the reality or non-reality of God, or 'the transcendent' as people say, in a way that could stand some clarification. But students who come to this academic area certainly with the intention to understand a religion (or religions) in its (their) significance for human life, but also, and importantly for them, to assess whether some religion is god-given, in some way to be considered, should attempt to check out how far these latter questions are actually explored in the department they consider joining, and in the courses they select. Theology or philosophy options are most likely to help here. (If, decades ago, religious studies courses may have been presented on an assumption that some supposedly basic religious claims are true, it is more common now to find them presented on an explicitly, sometimes assertively, secular basis.) Where these issues are well treated, as they should be in universities, arguments from different sides will be presented.

I have been talking as if we *can* bracket off the attempt to grasp a purely human significance of religion, and properly study just this, from questions about the reality or truth of that, beyond the this-worldly to which a religion claims to point – so that we can leave the latter alone and attend to the strictly human. But even this can be questioned. After all, whether there is a god who makes godself known will affect what is the significance for humans of the religion with which they have to do: either the religion is an illusion, helpful or damaging, or a bit of both, or it is humans' destiny. Equally, and from the other side it can be, and is, questioned whether religious truth or reality are actually conceptions which have any content.

You can, at least, leave these questions in the background, and, to good effect, pursue what may be your own very various immediate interests (as it might be Hindu architecture and ritual, the poetry of the mystics, new age religion, old time religion, Christian social action, Qu'ranic studies, New

Testament Greek . . .); these will present their own questions, challenges to understanding, of very different sorts.

The exciting variety of questioning and enquiry calls for and develops skills and disciplines, and calls for relevant information, of correspondingly varied kinds. Hence a religious studies student requires to bring together a range of competencies in dealing with each particular issue. Not for her the one-eyed treatment of all subjects by the one method. And that ability to treat problems by employing an appropriate battery of disciplined resources is of value to employers, because most problems which are encountered in practical life also require to be coped with, in the round, by an appropriate assortment of approaches and methods.

Religious studies, then, is a good general preparation for employment, and can easily be presented as such. Naturally, it can equip people more specifically to work, for example, either in contexts where cultural and racial awareness may be paramount – in most modern cities, and for many modern businesses or other providers of public services such informed awareness is valuable and valued – or with better understanding in contexts which have a religious basis. Accordingly, the usefulness of religious studies as a preparation for work yields another sort of answer to the 'Why'.

Why *study* religion(s)?

Already we have begun to touch on some characteristics of the *study* of religions; a repertoire of skills and competencies will be necessary even for most specialisms, let alone for the more general, wider-ranging collection of interesting courses available in religious studies departments.

Sometimes, though, some one expertise will be *the* vital central discipline in a student's equipment. Specific linguistic ability will commonly be needed if you are to master texts, historical sources or scriptures, for example. Arabic, Greek, Hebrew, Latin or Sanskrit might any of them be a basic competence for someone. (Few people will have more than one of these.) Most students will read texts, for which these were the original languages, in English translations, and will then be able to engage in discussions e.g. of the likely contexts in which, and underlying purposes for which, the texts might probably have been used. But the person who has the original language will be less at the mercy of what established experts say, better able to exercise independent critical judgement about the text's most basic sense (on which all else depends). And in a university, learning to develop and exercise your independent critical judgement is of first importance.

Any university course must aim to make you more capable than you were before you took the course – more capable of understanding the course's subject matter and, relatedly, more capable of soundly making your own interpretations and assessments. Naturally, you may begin to study a topic from rather a low level of information about it, and possibly handicapped by some misinformation. Before you can gain understanding and ability to make good judgements for yourself, you need simply to find out more. Even this is seldom a simple matter of assembling, or having someone else assemble, some hard facts. Often there are few quite uncontested and uncontestable known facts to be used by everyone as fixed points, let alone as foundations on which an agreed structure of understanding can be raised up. Even while you are discovering or being told what has at least seemed to be the case, or what has been thought, you usually need to be asking which version of the matter in hand looks, so far, most convincing. The pursuit of understanding involving the exercise of judgement starts early; and as you go on you can expect to get better at it. All of this is an exciting liberation from mere information-grubbing; it is no burden-to-be-feared but an opportunity to hold people responsible for what they tell you. Authors of books have to explain and justify themselves on the printed page. Lecturers and tutors are there with you in classroom and seminar to be challenged.

The more disciplines you can exercise competently the better. Language is just one sort of discipline. Knowing how to handle historical evidence, or spot the common lack of it, is another. Seeing how a context, social or political or ritual, can give a text its peculiar occasion so as to yield a particular force, is another. Ability in philosophical argument is a further competence, important in religious studies. As you study, you build up your powers for making the relevant judgements well, enabling you to study even more fruitfully.

I have been emphasizing the openness to question and debate of very much of religious studies' subject matter. This questioning seems to some people inappropriate in the more advanced stages of education: surely *knowledge* is the output of education, and (perhaps it may even be said) the knowledge economy is what it serves? Certainly, knowledge is what we aim at; I shall say more on this in the next section. But knowledge is hard to come by. In physical science, which is nowadays thought of so highly, it is plain that, on any question, the currently held view replaced an earlier view which people (reasonably up to a point) trusted, in its time; and that replaced an earlier view still, and so on backwards. Science has been progressive, we believe; why should we suppose it to have *arrived* finally now, 'on any question: to have attained knowledge? And so also it is in historical understanding, political theory . . . and most areas within religious studies. We can claim better understanding, often, even though knowledge cannot confidently be claimed, and even when we seem far from it. Still further *understanding* emerges out of questioning and open discussion. We do have knowledge of many particular facts: 'information'. But that is (at best) data, raw material for understanding, and then, maybe, for the knowledge we aim at in advanced education or research.

From the difficulty of acquiring deep knowledge, some people have concluded that there are no truths to be known. That does not follow. Consider some examples.

There is a famous mathematical theorem called, after its apparent author, 'Fermat's Last Theorem'. Fermat (d. 1665) said he had a proof, but he did not say what it was. For centuries people tried to find a proof for it; in the last decade Andrew Wiles did so. But suppose that neither he nor anybody else ever found a proof, or a refutation for the theorem, that failure would have had no tendency to show that the theorem is neither true nor false, i.e. that there is no truth of the matter and nothing to be known. *We* do not know whether Caesar ate breakfast the day he was assassinated; that does not show there is no truth of that matter, nothing to be known. Again, historians dispute the origins of World War I, and after much debate and millions of printed pages, the issue is not settled. That does not show there is no truth, and so nothing to be known about this issue. So difficulty in arriving at well-founded conclusions in so many of the discussions involved in religious studies does not give any reason to think neither truth nor knowledge exists where such issues are concerned.

Quite often (as often in pubs as in purely academic settings) argument of the shape I've just criticized is employed with reference to the claims made by religious systems themselves (e.g. that Jahweh is creator of the universe and protector of his people Israel, or that Allah is merciful), as well as statements *about* religions (the Buddha taught indifference to the world, Christians practise baptism). So the long and unresolved debates between religious communities are said to show that the claims made by the religions are neither true nor false: hence there is nothing here to be known. But, once more, because after long enquiry we cannot determine who the 'dark lady' of the Sonnets (i.e. of Shakespeare) was, nor who Jack the Ripper was, nor who killed J. F. Kennedy, it does not follow that there is no truth about these issues to be found. (For example, it does not follow that there is no one who is Kennedy's killer.)

Some students *will*, and quite properly, be interested in the grounds for, and the strength of, claims made about the world and its destiny and that of humankind by major religions: questions of religious truth. But other students will in practice mostly set aside questions of religious truth and concentrate only on matters of historical and human significance, textual interpretation, 'cultural' interaction, sociology, ethics.

That last section, especially in light of what went before it, not only points towards what *studying* religion may involve; it also begins to indicate what the *religion* is which is studied. But there is more to be said on that, next.

Why study *religion(s)*?

Plainly, from what has been said already, religion which is studied is rarely, if ever, studied unconnected with literatures, histories, societies, cultures, philosophical movements, ritual, morality and much else. Hence, you have (at least a bit) to handle texts, acquire historical understandings, gain a sense of how societies worked and work, how art and ideas contribute, and how practices and doctrines that relate can (if at all) interact; at least you require some of the foregoing as they and religion mutually relate. Religion as studied is thus not pure religion, religion unrelated to any other discipline or concerns. How could it be when it is the religion of particular people who are set in their personal and social contexts and who participate in religions in ways that have a history to be understood, using discourse we can examine, acting in ways we can scrutinize and try to understand?

Someone may say: 'There can be pure science and pure maths. Might religion not be studied, like them, in ways which make no reference to, and no connections with, history, culture or action? Could a religion perhaps be studied in that way? Maybe this would be most likely if it was something like an austerely mystical or philosophical type of awe-struck contemplation of the Perfect Good?'

Here we need to distinguish two sorts of intellectual activity which may be confused with one another. The austerely mystical/philosophical (and admittedly rather a-typical) religious person contemplating the Perfect Good and becoming aware of the character and demand of the Perfect Good is not studying religion, but participating in it, in a somewhat reflective way – albeit religion of a historically rare, and rarefied, sort. The *intellectual* component of this person's religiousness (as distinct, say, from *feelings* of awe or unworthiness, and from resultant *resolutions* about lifestyle and behaviour) will be a sort of *theology*, a contemplative study of the Perfect Good (aka God?). The analogy suggested above between pure maths and pure religious study will be better understood as being between pure maths and pure theology. Theology aims to establish what can be known, what should be said about God; and our austere mystical or philosophical contemplator of God, when she attempts to express or state what she contemplates, is a mystical and/or philosophical theologian. (Most theologians consider a God who is to be known in ways not so exclusively contemplative.) Generally, then, theology students aim to focus their study on God, whereas religious studies students look at religious people in their varied contexts, describing and interpreting religious systems of belief and practice, religious communities and their histories. Where there can be and should be an overlap is on the question of whether there is indeed such a God as believers say there is.

We saw that religious studies students do not necessarily pursue that question, being content rather to study what the human implications have been of particular people's believing as they do; but they may and often do pursue (such) questions of religious truth. Whereas the theologian is primarily concerned to discover what is true about God because of interest in God, interest in Godself, the religious studies student is, rather, interested in what the implications of holding particular religious beliefs are for human believers and their lives, together and in society.

Religious studies belongs in the humanities, as one of the species of the study by humans of humankind (in respect of its religious aspect). Theology aims to be about God.

It may be asked: 'What difference can it ever make to religious studies work whether the beliefs of the religious people studied are or are not true? If these people believed them, and their having their beliefs have the same implications and effects whether true or false, why should a religious studies student ever care about the truth or falseness (or the impossibility of deciding which) of the beliefs or doctrines?'

Often, and for many kinds of religious studies, it indeed will *not* matter what truth there is in the religious doctrine in question. So, when Max Weber tells us that the origins of modern Western capitalism lay in the terrors of Protestant, especially Calvinist, believers, who wanted some sort of assurance that they were of the elect, chosen for salvation, so that they worked and reinvested their gains, to their utmost ability in order to maximize the good condition of society as willed by God – when Weber tells us this, it may well not matter for the truth of *his* thesis whether the Calvinists were correct in their beliefs, or reasonable in their fears. All Weber requires is that they did have such beliefs and anxieties.

But in at least two ways the question of religious truth can matter in religious studies. First, it is surely of importance whether people who treat their religious commitments as more important than any other, whose lives and the lives of their communities and cultures are shaped by their religious beliefs, who some of them risk or give up their lives from loyalty to their God – it is of importance whether such people are in error, even putting their whole trust in an illusion.

Second, and important for work in modern religious studies, are the relations between people of differing religions. Most of the world's large cities have substantial groups of people who profess a religion different from that of other substantial bodies of fellow citizens, each such body professing its religion. Easy transport makes migration, business, intermarriage and holidaymaking common, so that people of different faiths make significant contact. Encounters of such sorts lead to mutual awarenesses, and sometimes dialogue or debate (as well as less constructive interactions). The character of dialogue will depend on questions which we must notice. (1) Are religions actually the sort of thing, activity, that really makes claims about the truth? That is: are religions true or false at all? They might not be saying how the world *is*, but rather purely be expressing emotions or complex attitudes to the world. If you say 'Life's a bitch', you are not claiming to say what is true; rather, you are giving expression to an attitude, or just to a passing emotion, letting off steam; and it would be inappropriate for someone to say 'I don't think you are quite correct there', any more than it would be appropriate to say that in response to your saying 'Ouch', or 'Whoopee' (very simple expressions of emotion and attitude). Perhaps a religious stance is a complex attitude, or set of attitudes, or maybe emotional responses. If so, religions do not seek to describe how things are: they do not lay claim to the truth. (2) If religions do make claims to have truth, about God, gods, or the world, do the claims of different religions exclude one another, so that if one is correct another, or others, must be wrong? Or may reconciliation in the truth be possible? Let us address these two questions, in turn.

1   Expressions of attitude or emotions *are* certainly involved in religious discourse: praising God or confessing in despair or expressing hope, for instance. But when a Jewish believer affirms that Jahweh has made a covenant with his people, or the Christian that God is three in one, or the Hindu that humans are *atman* rather than body, she is surely claiming to say what is true, and is not just expressing an attitude. If not, then interreligious exchange will not have to cope with factual disagreements, disagreements about the truth. Differing attitudes, and emotional responses, may of course make it harder for those who have them to enjoy, or tolerate, one another's company or understand one another's inner life, but they need not. People can happily differ, and perhaps should

simply do so without further negotiation, where they find one another to have merely attitudinal/ emotional disagreement. Much more is properly called for where there are factual differences, i.e. differences as to the truth, about issues which both sides regard as enormously important. Interreligious 'dialogue' will have a very different character if differences about the truth have to be addressed. Careful definition, explanations, efforts at mutual understanding, and then debate to try to approach the truth in respectful argument, will be called for. Such a programme will require many years. Mere differences in attitude and emotion do need to be grasped and understood; but after that, after they have been noticed and respected, whatever else may be helpful, debate and argument is not. Hence, people who propose or engage in interreligious dialogue need to have a view on this question (1) in order to shape and conduct their project appropriately.

2   However, even if religions do make factual claims, truth claims about the world, perhaps these claims are compatible, consistent with one another? On the face of it religions seem to make exclusive truth claims which, if accepted, effectively consign other religions to (at best) an inferior status: a confused and partly erroneous fumbling after the truth, perhaps. But some writers have claimed recently that when the major religions are properly interpreted, and distortions or inappropriate additions to the basic true faith have been eliminated, the different religions can emerge as different more or less successful attempts (different because they emerged from different cultures and are expressed in different conceptual schemes) to speak of the one Reality on which the universe depends, by which it is loved. On this controversial but widely discussed account (of which John Hick is the best-known exponent) the truth claims of the major world religions, properly understood, will constitute a basis for a coming-together, rather than a reason for separation and mutual condemnations.

That conclusion may be hard to maintain, e.g. as between people who say that there have been and are many instances of divine incarnation, those who say there is one unique incarnation, and those who say God cannot be incarnate at all. Or again as between those who say God is One, those who say God is three-in-one, and those religious people who say there is no god. If such claims are not reconcilable by the Hick programme of the previous paragraph, religious dialogue should consist in important part in debate, reasoned argument, to establish, if possible, which worldview if any is true.

Hinduism

Dermot Killingley

1 WHAT IS HINDUISM?

The introductory chapter has discussed religion, but we now turn to particular religions. While the study of religion and the study of religions are related and support each other, they are different kinds of study. When we study religion we deal with questions which cannot be answered satisfactorily by examining a particular religion, such as: 'Is religion a necessary part of being human, or is it something that some people opt into and others opt out of?' 'How is religion related to society?' 'Are religious claims in principle verifiable, or falsifiable?' When we study a religion, we deal with related but different questions. For instance: 'How many adherents has this religion?' 'How is this religion related to the society in which those adherents live?' We may also judge whether the claims made by this religion are true or false, or we may deliberately avoid such judgements. But whatever our findings about this religion, they are not directly related to what we may think about some other religion, or about religion in general. Thus the questions we might ask when studying a particular religion are different in kind from those we might ask when studying religion. Religions and religion are two different things, and we study them in different ways.

To make this clearer, we can observe that the word *religion* has two uses which are grammatically different as well as different in meaning. English has two classes of nouns: countable (or count) nouns and uncountable (or mass) nouns. A countable noun *x* occurs in either singular or plural form, in phrases such as *an x*; *the x*; *these xes*; *another x*; *three xes*. An uncountable noun *x* can occur by itself (without a word such as *a, the, this/these*) as the subject or object of a sentence, e.g. *x is useful*; *we all need x*; it does not occur in the plural. For instance, the noun *pebble* is countable: you can say *a pebble*; *these pebbles*; *another pebble*; *three pebbles*, but it would be grammatically odd (leaving aside the question of what it might mean) to say *pebble is useful*; *we all need pebble*. The noun *oxygen* is uncountable; you can say *oxygen is useful*; *we all need oxygen*, but it would be odd to say *an oxygen*; *these oxygens*; *another oxygen*; *three oxygens*.

Some nouns occur in both classes: you can say *three coffees*, and you can say *we all need coffee*, without sounding odd. Some nouns, such as *iron* or *lamb* or *curiosity*, occur in both classes but with a distinct difference of meaning; consider the difference between *you need an iron* and *you need iron*, or between *I like lambs* and *I like lamb*. Other examples of nouns which occur in both classes, but with different meanings, are *religion* and *language*. The difference between the countable and the uncountable sense of *language* is well known: when we study a language (countable) we are concerned with its grammar, pronunciation, vocabulary, and so on, which are noticeably different from those of other languages. When we study language (uncountable), we are concerned with questions such as whether language is a universal feature of humankind, or how it is related to the structure of the human mind. French has two nouns: *la langue* (countable) and *le langage* (uncountable), and linguists writing in English sometimes use these nouns, rather than the ambiguous English noun *language*, to make it clear which they mean.

The difference between the countable and the uncountable sense of *religion* is less well known, but similarly important. The uncountable sense has a long history, going back to the Latin noun *religio*, which refers to something within a person that governs their actions and makes them inclined to revere the gods or God. The countable sense is much more recent; it dates from the seventeenth and eighteenth centuries, when English-speaking people (and people using similar words to English *religion* in other languages) began to study and write about 'the religion of the Mohammedans' (meaning Muslims), 'the religion of the Hindus', and so on (Smith 1978). Note that in these contexts there is no grammatical indication whether the noun *religion* is countable or uncountable; it is ambiguous in the same way as 'the lamb on the table' is ambiguous. An eighteenth-century writer might therefore write of 'the religion of the Hindus', meaning the various rituals which Hindus perform, the norms of behaviour which they follow, the way they worship gods, and so on, using the word *religion* in the uncountable sense. But the phrase could easily be understood differently, using *religion* in the countable sense. 'The religion of the Hindus' would then be a system of religion which Hindus follow, which differs from the religion that Christians follow or the one that Muslims follow.

To avoid confusion between the two senses of *religion*, some scholars speak of 'religious traditions' rather than 'religions'. This helps us to remember that the religions, or religious traditions, of the world do not exist as self-perpetuating entities, but depend on being handed down and received by individual men and women, and thus are liable to change. It may also help us to see that the religions, or religious traditions, of the world are not a number of discrete entities, like so many pebbles or lambs. We talk about Hinduism, Islam, Christianity, and so on, and call each of them a religion, as if each of them was equally a specimen of a species called religion; but that is merely one of the ways in which we mentally simplify the world around us, so that we will not be totally bewildered by its complexity, and so that we can talk about it coherently to each other. Some such simplification is always necessary, but it is often misleading. In this case it disguises the fact that each of these religions or religious traditions is a bundle of traditions: Islam includes the Sufi and Ismaili traditions and many more, while Christianity includes the Maronite and Calvinist traditions and many more, and so on. Some of these traditions are highly organized and others not, while each of them is in turn divisible into smaller traditions. When we consider this fact, we may question whether our habit of bundling certain traditions together and calling them a religion is not arbitrary, resulting from historical accident rather than from the nature of the case.

1.1 In what sense is Hinduism a religion?

It is useful to begin an account of the major religions of the world with Hinduism, because the example of Hinduism shows how misleading our habit of cataloguing the religions of the world can be. It has been argued that what is called Hinduism is not one religion but several, related to each other as Judaism, Christianity and Islam are, though in a more complex way whose history is harder to trace (von Stietencron 1991: 20f.). For various historical reasons, many different traditions have come to be regarded (at least by non-Hindus) as sects within one religion called Hinduism. For other historical reasons, Jains and Sikhs have been counted as followers of religions distinct from Hinduism, though they can as reasonably be called Hindu as Lingayats, for instance, can.

The word *Hinduism* is an extreme case of a term which disguises the multiplicity of an indefinite number of religious traditions, and appears to include some traditions which might have been excluded, and exclude some that might have been included. However, it is not a unique case. In describing Hinduism we have to make general statements for the sake of simplicity, or to avoid a bewildering complexity. We should therefore remember that when we are talking about Hinduism, general statements are always subject to exceptions. This, indeed, is the only reliable general statement that can be made. But when we look at other religions we should still be prepared for dodgy generalizations and fuzzy boundaries, because in the last analysis we are dealing with countless individuals whose religious experiences are different from one another, and whose responses to the traditions they have received are not uniform. The extreme case of Hinduism should put us on our guard against the falsehoods inherent in the construction of entities called religions.

1.2 The term 'Hinduism'

It is often said that Hinduism is very ancient, and in a sense this is true, as we shall see in the next section of this chapter (pp. 15ff.). Yet when we use the word *Hinduism* we are using a word that dates only from the late eighteenth century, and became generally current in the early nineteenth. It was formed by adding the English suffix *-ism*, of Greek origin, to the word *Hindu*, of Persian origin; it was around the same time that the word *Hindu*, without the suffix *-ism*, came to be used mainly as a religious term. This is not just a matter of the history of the English language: there was no word for 'Hinduism' in Indian languages either. But once the word *Hinduism* became current, it influenced the thinking of people who spoke or read English, including the growing number of Hindus who did so.

The name *Hindu* was first a geographical name, not a religious one, and it originated in the languages of Iran, not of India. It is used in inscriptions in the Old Persian language, which list 'Hindu' among the countries ruled by the Persian emperor Darius around 500 BCE (Kent 1953: 136f.). It is also found in the Avesta, a collection of ancient ritual texts in another Old Iranian language, related to Old Persian but distinct from it. In the Avesta and the Old Persian inscriptions, the name *Hindu* referred to the land around the great river Indus, and was also the name of the river itself. (In Sanskrit and other Indian languages the river is called *sindhu*, which is also used as a common noun meaning 'river' or 'ocean'. Iranian languages are closely related to Sanskrit, and have many words in common with it, but regularly have the sound *h* at the beginning of a word where Sanskrit has *s*, e.g. Persian *haft*, Sanskrit *sapta* 'seven'.) The name *Hindu* as the name of the river was adapted into ancient Greek as *Indos*, and another Greek name *India* was formed for the adjacent land. These two names were in turn adapted into Latin as *Indus* and *India*; these are the names we still use in English, and similar names are used in many other modern languages. In time, the name *India* has come to be applied to a far larger territory than the Indus region to which it originally referred; moreover, since the partition of India in 1947 the Indus region has not been part of India, but of Pakistan (pp. 14, 30).

In Persian, the name *Hindustan* 'the country of the Indus; the Hindu country' is applied to northern India, or to the whole of India. The name *Hindu* continued to be used in Persian for the people of the region; originally a geographical name, it had become an ethnic name. Persian was the language used by the various Muslim powers which had great political and cultural influence in India from the eleventh to the eighteenth century CE, though many of them were not of Persian origin, but Afghan or Turkish (p. 25ff.). Muslims in India, descended from immigrants or from indigenous converts, became a substantial part of the population (22.2 per cent according to the 1931 census). They referred to the non-Muslim majority, together with their culture, as 'Hindu'. In time, both Muslims and non-Muslims came to refer to certain people, families, ways of dress or diet, and so on, as Hindu, in contrast to others which were Muslim (O'Connell 1973; Wagle 1991). Since the people called Hindu differed from Muslims most notably in religion, the word came to have religious implications, and to denote a group of people who were identifiable by their Hindu religion. In this way, the word has passed into English as a religious term.

Even in English it was not always used in this way, but remained an ethnic term in some contexts. Sir William Jones (1746–94), who went to India as a judge in 1784 and was one of the pioneers of Western scholarship on ancient India, wrote an important essay 'On the Hindus' in 1789 (Marshall 1970: 246–61). In this essay Jones writes of the Hindus not as a religious group but as a people, particularly an ancient people, to be studied in the same way as the ancient Greeks and Romans. Even in the nineteenth century, *Hindu* could be an ethnic term without religious implications, so that it was still possible to speak of a 'Hindu Christian', or even a 'Hindu Muslim', meaning one who is Hindu by ethnicity and culture.

However, it is as a religious term that the word *Hindu* is now used in English, and *Hinduism* is the name of a religion, although, as we have seen, we should beware of any false impression of uniformity that this might give us. The word *Hinduism* became current in English in the late eighteenth century, as a shorter term for what had hitherto been called 'the religion of the Hindus' or 'the Hindu system of religion' (Sweetman 2001: 219 n. 4). Probably the first Hindu writer to use it was Rammohun Roy (pp. 27).

If a word denotes a group of people, it means one thing to members of that group and another to outsiders. To the former it refers to 'us', and implies familiarity, reliability, normality. To the latter it refers to 'them', and implies something strange, unpredictable, and calling for explanation. It also calls for evaluation, whether 'we' think of 'them' as wicked, miserable and ignorant, or as better, happier and wiser than 'we'. One of the most knowledgeable and perceptive outsiders ever to write on Indian culture, Al-Biruni (973–1048), a Muslim from Uzbekistan writing in Arabic, leaves his readers in no doubt about the otherness of the Hindus: 'For the reader must always bear in mind that the Hindus entirely differ from us in every respect' (Sachau 1888: 17).

Some Western writers of the eighteenth century greeted the otherness of the Hindus with enthusiastic admiration. Voltaire (1694–1778) believed that India was the home of a primordial rational religion, which was the source of all true religion (Halbfass 1988: 57f.). Sir William Jones also admired the ancient culture of the Hindus, though in a much better-informed way. In the sphere of religion, he thought that the Hindu idea of rebirth in accordance with one's deeds was preferable to the Christian doctrine of eternal punishment (Mukherjee 1968: 119). A far more hostile reaction to the otherness of Hinduism came from Christian missionaries. To them, the religion of the Hindus was a system of error, the more monstrous for being the product of a learned tradition and not of mere ignorance. Alexander Duff (1806–78), the first Church of Scotland missionary to India, wrote: 'Of all the systems of false religion ever fabricated by the perverse ingenuity of fallen man, Hinduism is surely the most stupendous' (Duff 1839).

The word *Hinduism* thus had connotations of otherness for its first users, whether the other was to be admired or shunned. But in the early nineteenth century there was a growing number of Hindus using English, and for them *Hinduism* did not connote otherness. They were, however, aware of British views on Hinduism, and this influenced their own views. Rammohun Roy used the word in two contrasting ways. In 1816, he wrote: 'The chief part of the theory and practice of Hinduism, I am sorry to say, is made to consist in the adoption of a peculiar mode of diet' (Roy 1906: 73). In the following year, he wrote: 'The doctrines of the unity of God are real Hinduism, as that religion was practised by our ancestors, and as it is well known at the present day to many learned Brahmins' (Roy 1906: 90).

In the first quotation, Rammohun deplores the concern with rules of food and purity into which he believes Hinduism has degenerated. In the second, he claims that, despite its many gods, Hinduism contains an ancient tradition, still surviving but insufficiently known, of belief in one God. He thus divides Hinduism into two: a false Hinduism which he condemns, and a true Hinduism which he seeks to promote.

This double view is found among other Hindu writers who are concerned with the definition of Hinduism. Bankim Chandra Chatterjee (1838–94), another Bengali brahmin, wrote of a 'false and corrupt Hinduism' and the 'true Hinduism' (King 1978). During the nineteenth and twentieth centuries, Hinduism was exposed to the criticism of the English-speaking world, and Hindu thinkers reacted to this criticism by rejecting as 'false Hinduism' those parts of their tradition which were most open to objection, and upholding as 'true Hinduism' those which they thought the objectors had ignored or misrepresented. Hindu writers did not all agree on what to uphold or reject, but 'false Hinduism' often included the elaborate rules of purity decried by Rammohun; Gandhi similarly complained that 'unfortunately today Hinduism seems to consist merely in eating and not eating' (Killingley 1993: 64). 'False Hinduism' also often included the worship of many gods and the oppression of women and low castes, while 'true Hinduism' often included belief in one God as the source of the universe, and an ethic of universal love.

It would be an oversimplification to conclude that Hinduism is an eighteenth-century Western construct. Hinduism is several constructs, some of which are indigenous and some Western; some, too, are products of the composite indigenous and Western culture which dominated Indian political and intellectual life from the mid-nineteenth century to the late twentieth. Long before the word *Hinduism* was formed, there already existed a vast literature in Sanskrit, which embodied many of the beliefs, values and practices that are now recognized as typically Hindu: an indefinite number of gods; rebirth according one's deeds; a hierarchical social order, in which the hereditary class called brahmins have authority in religious and legal matters; rituals involving service to images; and so on. This literature represents a construct which would later be called Hinduism. But the Sanskrit texts vary enormously in the rules they give for acts of worship and for the social order, and above all in the myths they narrate about the gods.

Accounts of Hinduism that have been written since the word was formed vary also. There is the Hinduism attacked by Duff and other nineteenth-century missionary writers: idolatrous, irrational and cruel, especially to women. There is also the Hinduism vindicated by James Stuart, a British military officer in India, who protested against the missionary view with *A Vindication of the Hindoos*, published in 1808, claiming that the Hindus had an exalted idea of God and a pure system of morality. There is Rammohun Roy's monotheistic 'real Hinduism', and the many real Hinduisms constructed by others who looked into the scriptural tradition as Rammohun had done, selecting various texts and interpreting them in various ways. There is also the mass of food rules and caste rules which Rammohun and others dismissed as false Hinduism.

It is useful to think of the meaning of the word *Hindu* as a matter of contrast with what is non-Hindu, which varies in different contexts. Thus we can speak of Hindu rulers in India as opposed to Muslim ones (pp. 25f.), and in earlier periods of history we can speak of Hindu rulers as opposed to Buddhist ones (pp. 18f., 21–3). We can also speak of Hindu deities and forms of worship as opposed to Vedic ones (pp. 17, 20f., 23). The phrases 'Hindu Christian' and 'Hindu Muslim' imply a contrast with people whose culture is more typically Christian or Muslim.

Twentieth-century Hindu writers have presented various views of Hinduism. Many of these are based on the school of Advaita Vedanta, which teaches that all reality is one, and the world is (in a special sense) false (Radhakrishnan 1960; Mahadevan 1956). Others protest against this view and claim that the true Hindu approach to the world is positive and pragmatic (Chaudhuri 1979). Some Western writers have based their views of Hinduism on a body of textual tradition in Sanskrit going back to the Veda (e.g. Zaehner 1966), while others have started from their observation of the practices of Hindus who know little or nothing of such texts (Babb 1975; Fuller 1992). Some have traced a coherent pattern underlying the diversity (Zaehner 1966; Biardeau 1989). Others have explicitly rejected the search for a single essence of Hinduism, and avoided presenting it as a unity (e.g. Jackson and Killingley 1988; Lipner 1994; Knott 1998). This can be seen as an attempt to atone for the sins of a colonial past when the British imposed their own concepts on the people of South Asia, classifying them as Hindus, Muslims, and so on; but it can also be seen as a neo-colonial attempt to deny the right of Hindus to their own definitions of Hinduism, at a time when such definitions are being more aggressively asserted (Smith 1998).

To say that the word *Hinduism* is of recent origin is not to say that the concept is invalid, or to question the right of millions of people to identify themselves as Hindus. But the concept is a complex one, and one of the purposes of this chapter is to explore that complexity. 'There are Hindus, but there is no Hinduism' (Smith 1978: 65). This means that what we should be studying is not a Hinduism constructed from preconceived notions, but what Hindus think, say and do. But it then follows that if Hindus think and say that there is Hinduism, and act to uphold it, then there is a Hinduism, or more probably several Hinduisms.

So what is the Hinduism we are talking about in this book? First of all, we must recognize that any description of Hinduism cannot be exhaustive; it is limited by the writer's knowledge, and selects what seems to be typical and to form a coherent picture. Second, since there is no single authority that can tell us what is true or false Hinduism, we should avoid setting up one kind of Hinduism as normative or authentic, and rejecting others as inauthentic, whether by preferring the ancient to the modern, the elite to the majority, the learned to the illiterate, the indigenous to the Western-influenced, or vice versa. We should be open to the diversity of Hinduism, even when we are looking at those Hindus who promote a monolithic form of Hinduism. Material will be drawn from many sources. Much of it is from ancient Hindu texts, and much is from modern descriptions, some referring to different parts of India and some to Hindus elsewhere.

2 HINDUISM IN HISTORY

The name *India* has a different meaning now from the one it had before 1947. When British rule ended on 15 August 1947, India was partitioned into two countries: India, with a Hindu majority, and Pakistan, with a Muslim majority. While India inherited the name *India*, Pakistan inherited the river Indus. Pakistan consisted of two territories, one centred on the Indus basin, and the other in eastern Bengal, with about a thousand miles of Indian territory between them. In 1971, the eastern portion separated to become Bangladesh.

When the name *India* refers to ancient India, or British India, it includes what are now India, Pakistan and Bangladesh. These countries are all included in the term *South Asia*, which also includes Afghanistan, Bhutan, Nepal, Sikkim and Sri Lanka. Another term covering approximately the same area is *the Indian subcontinent.*

South Asia is separated from the rest of Asia by mountains. Leaving aside Afghanistan, which is the threshold between South Asia and Central Asia, it measures about two thousand miles from west to east and from north to south, and is divided into two roughly equal parts. The northern part is bounded by mountains but flat in the interior, and watered by three great rivers: the Indus, the Ganges and the Brahmaputra. This part is known as the Indo-Gangetic plain. The southern part of the subcontinent is a peninsula, mountainous in the interior and bounded by sea to the west and east. Rivers have played an important part in the history of northern India, and many of its historic cities are inland, on rivers. Peninsular India, separated from the north by the Vindhya and other mountain ranges, is open to sea routes linking it to Arabia, Africa and Southeast Asia; many of its historic cities are on the coast.

External natural boundaries – mountains and sea – have given South Asia a cultural unity, while internal boundaries – mountains, forests and deserts – have helped to maintain the cultural distinctiveness of its regions. It has never been a political unity, though the ambition of ancient India kings was to rule an empire from the Himalayas to the eastern and western seas. Some powers have ruled most of this area, but not all of it: the Maurya dynasty in the third century BCE, whose greatest emperor, Ashoka, is remembered as a patron of Buddhism; the Guptas in the fourth to sixth centuries CE; the Mughals in the seventeenth century; the British in the nineteenth and twentieth centuries; and the present state of India.

Within this area live people of diverse cultures but having some traits in common: loose, unsewn clothes, though sewn garments are also known; a concern to avoid pollution, and a respect for water, the sun and cattle as means of purification; a view of society as divided into hereditary groups, each with its own way of life and rules of purity; a belief that after death people are reborn in other bodies, according to their previous deeds; a way of worshipping by placing offerings of food in front of images or other objects representing gods. These people are Hindus. A Hindu anthropologist has written: 'while it is not possible to define a Hindu, it is not very difficult to identify a person as a Hindu' (Srinivas 1962: 150). However, not all Hindus fit the above description: both in South Asia and elsewhere, there are Hindus who wear suits, seek hygiene rather than ritual purity, and do not worship gods. If it is impossible to define a Hindu, it is harder still to define a lapsed Hindu.

As a very rough guide, we can divide the history of South Asia into the following periods. The dates, except 1947, are arbitrary approximations which do not refer to any specific events, and the dating of the first two periods is contested.

Harappan period	3000 BCE	to	1500 BCE
Vedic period	1500 BCE	to	500 BCE
Period of north Indian empires	500 BCE	to	600 CE
Period of regional kingdoms	600 CE	to	1200 CE
Period of Muslim rule	1200 CE	to	1800 CE
Period of British rule	1800 CE	to	1947 CE
Post-independence period	1947 CE	onwards	

2.1 The Harappan period: 3000 BCE–1500 BCE

The Harappan or Indus Valley civilization has been known to archaeologists since the 1920s. Its main sites are Mohenjo-daro, in the Indus valley, and Harappa, 350 miles to the north-east. Sites have now been identified over an area about 700 miles from north to south and from east to west, with outlying sites at even greater distances. The sites are the remains of brick-built cities, showing a remarkable uniformity in the size of bricks and the width and geometrical layout of streets. The most remarkable artefacts are steatite seals, depicting human figures, plants and animals, and inscribed with characters. There have been many attempts to decipher the script and identify the language, but none has convinced all scholars. The antecedents of this civilization can be traced back to the seventh millennium BCE, and its mature period is about 2300 to 2000 BCE. It declined between 1800 and 1700 BCE, probably as a result of climatic and geological change.

As for the religion of the Harappan civilization, there is little evidence and much speculation. The large baths in the cities may have been for ritual bathing, like the pools known as tanks adjoining Hindu temples. The numerous exaggeratedly female clay figurines may be connected with the mother goddesses worshipped by Hindus in village shrines (pp. 51f.). A figure on one of the seals appeared to Sir John Marshall, the pioneer of Harappan archaeology, to show features of the god Shiva; he tentatively identified it as 'Proto-Shiva'. Further examination makes this identification less likely (Srinivasan 1984). Many writers on Indian religion have said that the Hindu belief in rebirth was inherited from the Harappan civilization, but this is only conjecture. It rests on a mistaken view that the doctrine of rebirth appears suddenly in the Upanishads without any precedent in the earlier parts of the Veda (Killingley 1997: 1; Tull 1989).

2.2 The Vedic period: 1500 BCE–500 BCE

The Harappan civilization presents us with a mass of material remains, much of them datable by radiocarbon and other techniques, but no literature. The Vedic period, on the other hand, is known from a mass of literature which carries no dates, and is difficult to match with any archaeological record. This literature was not written down for some centuries, but was memorized and handed down orally with great exactness. The word *Veda* means 'knowledge', and the Veda is a collection of the knowledge which was preserved by a class of people called Brahmins, who needed it for the rituals they performed.

The Veda is a very large and varied collection of texts, composed over a long period, perhaps even a thousand years. The oldest part, known as the hymns of the *Rig-Veda*, may itself span some centuries.

These hymns are poems addressed to various gods, and less commonly goddesses, spoken by a priest as part of the ritual. Modern scholars usually date them to the second millennium BCE. However, there is no direct way of dating the Veda; according to Hindu tradition it is eternal.

Vedic rituals became very elaborate, requiring a staff of priests with different specialisms. Some of these rituals are described in texts called *Brahmanas*, which discuss their meaning and purpose. These texts are part of the Veda, as are the *Upanishads*, which also discuss the meaning and purpose of rituals, but often reach the conclusion that nothing of lasting value can be achieved by them. The *Upanishads*, which reject ritual, have proved the most influential part of the Veda. Among their key ideas is the contrast between the many things of this world of impermanence, and the One which is the origin and goal of all existence. Rituals, which are performed for goals such as long life, wealth or security after death, are concerned with the many; infinitely more valuable than knowledge of rituals is knowledge of the ultimate truth, or *brahman,* to be found in the cave of the heart (pp. 53f.).

From the geographical names they contain, the hymns of the *Rig-Veda* appear to have been composed in the northern Punjab. In the later parts of the Veda the geographical horizon is extended eastwards along the Ganges and southwards towards the peninsula. Much of the territory known to the hymns is the same as that of the Harappan civilization, but city life is unknown, and the main form of wealth is cattle. The composers of the Veda referred to their own people as *Arya*, and despised the non-Arya peoples, regarding them as enemies to be conquered.

The language of the Veda is an early form of Sanskrit, the classical language of Hinduism. Languages of the same family are now spoken over most of northern and central South Asia, including Hindi, Bengali, Gujarati and Marathi. Together they are called the Indo-Aryan languages, after the name *Arya* by which the Vedic people referred to themselves. These languages are closely related to the Iranian languages. The ancient Iranians, incidentally, similarly called themselves and their language *Arya*; they also referred to *Aryana Vaeja*, 'the Arya country', and this is the origin of the name *Iran*. The Indo-Aryan languages are also related, though less closely, to most of the languages of Europe, forming the Indo-European language family.

Since all the other branches of the Indo-European family were spoken outside South Asia, and since the river-names in the hymns of the *Rig-Veda* indicate that the hymns were composed in the Punjab, it seems that the Indo-Aryan branch came into South Asia from the north-west and subsequently spread over most of the subcontinent. This inference from the linguistic and literary evidence, which was well established by the middle of the nineteenth century, is a very reasonable one. Unfortunately, however, it has been associated with much misunderstanding and controversy.

It was generally assumed in the nineteenth century that a language was intimately connected to a people and its culture. Indeed, this assumption was a driving force behind research on the Indo-European language family at a time when the Romantic movement, especially in Germany, encouraged ideas of the nation as a spiritual entity. If, therefore, the Indo-Aryan language in which the Veda was composed came into South Asia from the north-west, it was thought that the Aryan people must have come from the north-west, bringing their culture with them. The many references in the hymns to warfare against non-Aryas were worked up into a scenario in which the Aryans, seeking pasture for their cattle, and given superior mobility by their horse-drawn chariots, descended on the fertile plain from the mountains of Afghanistan, and conquered the indigenous people. This scenario, summed up as 'the Aryan invasion', was taken as a key event in Indian history, happening around 1500 BCE.

The hymns do not mention an invasion or a previous Aryan homeland, nor do any other Hindu texts. It is now recognized that a language can move geographically without a great movement of population, through being adopted by a group of people who had not used it before; so can a feature of material culture such as a form of pottery or the use of the horse (Renfrew 1987: 120–44). However, in the nineteenth century and much of the twentieth, prehistory was understood in terms of peoples, each with its material culture and its language. Kinship of language was taken to mean kinship of peoples, so that the word *Aryan*, which was often applied to all the Indo-European languages, was understood as referring to a supposed Aryan people. Different branches of this people were thought to have invaded not only India but Greece, Italy and all the other places where Indo-European languages are spoken. In a development of this idea which reached its culmination in Nazi ideology, the Aryans were portrayed as a master race whose destiny was to conquer and rule inferior races. Partly for this reason, many scholars now avoid the word *Aryan*. However, we still need to use the Sanskrit word *Arya* because it has a distinctive meaning. As we shall see, in post-Vedic literature it refers to a hereditary group in Hindu society which has certain ritual privileges (pp. 44–5).

The idea of the Aryan invasion conflicts with a Hindu tradition that the Indo-Gangetic plain is and always has been Aryavarta, 'the country of the Aryas' (*Manu* 2.22). Some Hindus see it as a colonialist attempt to claim that the origin of Hindu culture came from the West. In the late twentieth century, there have been many attempts to revise the history of the Vedic and Harappan cultures in the light of accumulating archaeological evidence, new theories of cultural and linguistic history, and new interpretations of the texts. The origins of Vedic culture remain obscure, but it may have been formed in north-western South Asia from indigenous as well as imported elements, rather than being imported in its entirety.

While this culture differed in many ways from the Hindu culture of the past two thousand years, its legacy remains. Though full Vedic rituals are little practised today, verses from the Veda are still recited as *mantras* (p. 51). Though most of the gods and goddesses named in it are little known today, some important Hindu ideas can be traced to it. Foremost among these is the idea that the many things we see in this world are reflections of one ultimate reality, and the rejection of worldly things in search of this reality which we find in the *Upanishads*. Another is a theory of society which divides it into four classes: brahmins, who have ritual and intellectual functions, a ruling and fighting class (*kshatriya*), an agricultural and commercial class (*vaishya*), and a servile class (*shudra*); members of the first three classes are Arya, but *shudras* are non-Arya (pp. 44–5). The sanctity of cattle for Hindus can be traced partly to the importance of cattle in Vedic culture, although the Vedic people, unlike Hindus today and for many centuries past, killed cattle in sacrifice.

The spread of Aryan culture from the north-west is recorded in Hindu tradition. The Veda itself describes the god Agni, whose name means 'fire', burning his way eastwards through the lands of the Ganges basin, which may refer to the clearing of forests by fire, or the establishment of the Vedic ritual centred on fire, or both. One of the two great Sanskrit epics, the *Maha-Bharata*, tells how the Vedic sage Agastya subdued the Vindhya mountains, and the other epic, the *Ramayana*, describes him as having made the forests of the south fit for Aryas.

At the same time as this geographical change, perhaps from around 1000 to 500 BCE, there was a change in political and economic structures. The king, who had been a war leader elected by a tribal council, became a monarch. Whether his claim to kingship rested on heredity or interpersonal struggle, it had to be legitimated by rituals which were in the hands of brahmins. While the king depended on the brahmin for ritual legitimation and sanctification, the brahmin depended on the king for patronage. In the *Brahmanas* and *Upanishads* we read of ritual experts who are sought after by kings, as well as poor, obscure brahmins who turn out to possess transcendent knowledge.

This relation between temporal power and spiritual power, the king and the brahmin, recurs in many forms throughout Hinduism. Its development in the Vedic period depended on an accumulation of wealth in the hands of the king, which Marxist historians especially have attributed to material developments such as the iron-tipped plough, which enabled the land to produce a surplus which could be appropriated by the king. The king could then support a host of retainers who did not work the land: jewellers, artists, soldiers and others, including brahmins, who were valued not only as ritualists but as advisers in worldly business as well as spiritual matters. Power and wealth were concentrated in cities. Wealth was no longer counted in cattle but in money.

Some of these trends can be seen in a story in an early *Upanishad*. Janaka, king of Videha in the lower Ganges basin, one of the more recently Aryanized areas, invites the brahmins of the Kuru and Panchala countries further west, where Aryan culture has been long established, to perform a great sacrifice. When they are assembled, he offers a thousand cows to the best brahmin among them. Cows are a traditional reward for brahmins; but these cows have ten gold coins tied to their horns, marking a transition from a barter to a money economy. The prize is immediately claimed by the great ritual theorist Yajnavalkya, and he upholds his claim by answering the questions of the brahmins who challenge him (pp. 48f.). He out-talks them all; the questions use ritual terms and concepts, but are not so much on the ritual itself as on cosmology, the nature of a person, what becomes of a person after death, and the nature of ultimate reality (*Brihad-Aranyaka Upanishad* 3).

2.3 The period of the north Indian empires: 500 BCE–600 CE

The concentration of power and wealth in cities, and the symbiosis of the king with the brahmin who provided religious legitimation for his power and worldly advice on how to augment it, led to the ideal of the *chakra-varti*, literally the 'wheel-turner': the emperor who conquers all neighbouring kings and makes the whole world revolve round the hub of his capital. No ruler in Indian history ever quite achieved this aim, but several came close to it, basing their power in the northern plains and extending it into the peninsula.

In the fourth century BCE the short-lived Nanda dynasty, with its capital at Pataliputra (modern Patna), conquered the Ganges basin and parts of the peninsula; it was overthrown by Chandragupta Maurya. Chandragupta's grandson Ashoka, who reigned from 268 to 232 BCE, ruled northern India and parts of the peninsula. Ashoka patronized Buddhism, and the Buddhist community may have helped to consolidate his power. The extent of the Maurya empire decreased after Ashoka, and in 185 BCE the throne was seized by Pushyamitra Shunga, a brahmin; the Shunga dynasty lasted till about 73 BCE. The most successful north Indian empire, again based on Pataliputra, was that of the Guptas, from the middle of the fourth century to the middle of the sixth. This was a period of prosperity, when the arts flourished, and Indian culture spread to parts of Southeast Asia. The earliest surviving temples date from this period.

The expansion of kingdoms was made difficult by natural barriers, especially in the south, and by the resistance of rival powers. These included invaders from the north-west, the usual route for invasion from outside India. In the second century BCE kings of Greek descent, or at least with Greek names and Hellenistic culture, from Bactria (now northern Afghanistan), occupied territories in India and may even have conquered Pataliputra. In the last century BCE Shakas, of Central Asian origin, conquered Bactria and north-western and western India. They were invaded in turn by Parthians, from northern Iran, but some Shaka rulers retained power in parts of western India. Another group of invaders from Central Asia, the Kushans, established an empire which extended over most of northern India and across the mountains into Central Asia, around the second century CE. In the fifth century the Huns, also from Central Asia, invaded the north-west, and during the first half of the sixth century they commanded a large part of western India.

With the exception of the Huns, these rulers from the west integrated themselves into the Indian cultural world. The Kushan kings patronized Buddhist monasteries, and their empire facilitated the spread of Buddhism into Central Asia and thence to China, but they also identified themselves with Hindu gods. The earliest of the many Sanskrit inscriptions in literary style was put up by a Shaka king in 150 CE. One monument of Greek presence in India is an inscribed stone column at Besnagar, in central India, set up by Heliodorus, an envoy from a Greek king in Taxila (near modern Islamabad) to a Shunga king. Heliodorus calls himself a Bhagavata, meaning a devotee of Vishnu.

The growth of empires in northern India during this period is linked to an ideal of kingship, and to the concept of *Bharata-varsha*. *Bharata-varsha* is an ancient name for the known world as it appears in traditional Indian accounts: bounded on the north by mountains, and on the east, west and south by sea. Beyond these boundaries lie outlandish places, including Meru, the vast mountain beyond the Himalayas at the centre of the earth. Within them are the rivers, cities and mountains of what is now called South Asia, where the ideal *chakra-varti* rules. *Bharata-varsha* is named after an ancient hero Bharata, the ancestor of most of the heroes in the great epic of the sons of Bharata, the *Maha-Bharata*. This epic says that the hero Bharata himself became a *chakra-varti*, after a hundred royal consecrations and hundreds of horse sacrifices. *Bharat* (a shorter form of *Bharata-varsha*) is now the Hindi name, sometimes also used in English, of the present country of India; the use of this name is often taken to imply (and is often intended to imply) that India is a holy land in Hindu terms, dedicated to upholding Hindu ideals of polity.

The duties of a king are discussed at length in the *Maha-Bharata*, in the other great Sanskrit epic, the *Ramayana*, and in *The Laws of Manu* and other Sanskrit books on law. *Manu*, named after an ancestor of humankind, was composed around the second or third century CE; the two epics evolved between 400 BCE and 400 CE. The word *law* in this context translates *dharma*; we shall discuss this term later (pp. 40f.). The king is concerned to increase his power by going to war or forming alliances with neighbouring kings, and also to extract wealth from his subjects. But he is also responsible for their happiness. 'A king who protects creatures in accordance with the law, and strikes down those who deserve it, offers sacrifices with gifts of hundreds of thousands every day' (*Manu* 8.306) – that is, he earns as much merit as if he offered such sacrifices. 'A king who receives excise, taxes, tolls, tributes and fines without protecting will quickly go to hell' (*Manu* 8.307). To perform these duties the king needed advice, and his advisors were expected to be brahmins.

Under the patronage of kings, brahmins developed and preserved a body of learning in many fields besides ritual and statecraft. Ancient Indian phonetics and grammar show amazingly acute observation and abstract thinking, most notably Panini's grammar of Sanskrit, composed in the fifth century BCE. Mathematics and medicine were also advanced, and most of the achievements in all these fields were the work of brahmins. Poets wrote plays and other literature for court entertainments, and eulogies of the king and his ancestors. At the same time as this highly elaborate literature, the more relaxed tradition of the epics was continued in a class of texts called *Purana* (meaning 'ancient'). *Puranas* tell stories of gods, and also give accounts of dynasties of kings and their conquests. Like the epics and the *dharma* books, they contain teachings on kingship, ritual and related matters.

Some time during this period, though when is not clear, were composed some of the fundamental texts of Hindu theology. Some of them were incorporated in the *Maha-Bharata*, including the *Bhagavad-Gita*, which is at once a devotional poem, an account of the world and its relation to God, and a lesson in the moral and physical discipline known as yoga (Johnson 1994). It has been interpreted in various ways by countless commentators in Sanskrit, in other Indian languages and in English (pp. 29, 33). Another text which has received many interpretations is the *Vedanta-sutra* or *Brahma-sutra*, a set of brief notes on the interpretation of certain passages in the *Upanishads* (pp. 53f.).

All this literature was composed in Sanskrit, which, after being standardized by Panini's grammar, hardly varied from one part of India to another, and remained largely unchanged while the various vernacular languages – those spoken by ordinary people – changed through the centuries. The authorities on Sanskrit language and literature, known as *pandits*, were generally brahmins. Sanskrit was the language of diplomacy, since each king could be expected to have *pandits* at his court who could understand and reply to letters in Sanskrit, whether or not the king himself could.

At the beginning of this period a variety of doctrines flourished, some of them based on the Veda and others openly opposed to it. The best-known teacher is known by his family name Gautama, but much better known by his title *Buddha*, meaning 'aware', which indicates that he has reached perfect knowledge of the nature of phenomena and of personality. Gautama the Buddha came from the aristocracy of a small state on the northern fringe of the Ganges basin, near the present borders of Nepal. Estimates of his dates vary, but he probably lived in the fifth century BCE, when the Ganges basin was being transformed by urbanization, the concentration of wealth in the city, and the alliance between king and brahmin. Some modern interpreters see his teachings as a reaction to these changes (Ling 1973). The Buddhist practice of maintaining monks (and a smaller number of nuns) through voluntary donations, to follow a discipline of meditation and study, allowed them to develop a well-structured body of ideas which was independent of brahminical thought, and eventually prompted the brahmins to construct counter-arguments. While Buddhism was a powerful religious and intellectual force in South Asia in the first millennium CE, it did not survive there long in the second millennium, except in Nepal and Sri Lanka. However, it established itself in Central, East and Southeast Asia, and in the nineteenth and twentieth centuries was hailed by Indian intellectuals as one of ancient India's gifts to the world.

Another teacher of about the same time was Maha-vira, known by the title *Jina*, 'conqueror', because like the Buddha he had overcome the limitations of human existence. His followers are called Jains (meaning 'belonging to the Jina'), and whereas they did not carry his teachings outside South Asia, they survive there today, especially among the commercial class of Gujarat in western India. Mohandas Gandhi, who belonged to this class, was influenced by Jain teachings of non-violence.

Buddhists and Jains reject the authority of the Veda. However, they agree with the Vedic schools that after death a person is reborn in a human, animal or other form according to their previous deeds (pp. 34f.). Another school who originated at about the same time were the materialists or Lokayatas, founded by Charvaka, who denied any sort of existence after death. Their writings do not survive, but something is known of them from hostile accounts by Buddhist and brahminical writers. Twentieth-century Indian materialists have taken an interest in these ancient predecessors.

Urbanization and the rise of kingship may help to explain the emergence of holy places in the geography of South Asia. The Vedic ritual was performed on ground ritually marked out and consecrated for the occasion; there is no indication of temples in the Veda. But permanent holy places may have been known in the Harappan civilization, and they are a feature of Hindu life today, whether in the form of a stone in the open air or a great temple. Many of the pilgrimage centres are also centres of commerce, such as Varanasi on the Ganges; they may have started as simple shrines which grew as the trade routes brought worshippers to them. According to the *Artha-shastra*, a treatise on statecraft written around 300 BCE, temples owned property including land, gold and cattle, and were a source of revenue for the king. It is further suggested that a king may raise revenue by setting up a new temple or holy place overnight (*Artha-shastra* 5.2.39).

The deities worshipped in temples are not all the same as the ones mentioned in the Veda. Indra, the god most frequently worshipped in the Vedic hymns, remained as king of heaven but had little to do with this world, though his name is often used as an element in the names of kings. Vishnu, who rose to prominence as lord of the sacrifice in the later Vedic period, became widely worshipped as supreme God. This position is also claimed for Rudra or Shiva, who in the Veda is a god of the wild, isolated from other gods. Goddesses, who are little mentioned in the Vedic hymns except as the wives of gods, were common in this period, as in India today. These differences, together with the importance of images and temples, mark the Hinduism of the past two millennia as substantially different from the religion of the Veda. It is thus possible to describe certain deities and rituals as 'Hindu' as opposed to 'Vedic'.

Some modern scholars, especially in the nineteenth and early twentieth centuries, marked these differences by separating 'Hinduism' from what they called 'Vedism' or 'Brahmanism'. But such labelling gives a misleading impression of distinct systems succeeding each other, and raises the unanswerable and unprofitable question of when Vedism or Brahmanism ended and Hinduism began. It is more helpful to think of a great number of different religious practices which come into prominence at different times, and are recorded in different kinds of sources. The Veda, for instance, is concerned mainly with a particular group of rituals performed by brahmins for their patrons, in an expanding but limited geographical area, and cannot be taken as evidence that other kinds of ritual, such as worship of images in temples, did not take place outside, or even within, that area. Thus goddess worship, rather than an innovation, is probably a feature of Hindu life that went unrecorded for centuries, apart from archaeological evidence, but first appears in texts in the last five centuries BCE. Vedic ritual, on the other hand, continues to be practised in attenuated forms. Some elements of it occur regularly as part of Hindu marriage and death rituals, and large-scale Vedic sacrifices are occasionally performed. One of these, in 1975, was filmed and used as a basis for descriptions and theoretical discussions by modern scholars (Staal 1983).

Temples, and also Buddhist monasteries, depended largely on the patronage of kings; so did brahmin *pandits*. Particular kings favoured Buddhist, Hindu or Jain institutions, but not exclusively; South Asian states were not like European states after the Reformation, each supporting one form of religion and more or less forcibly suppressing others. Thus Ashoka favoured Buddhism, but also patronized Hindu temples, as did the Kushans, while the Guptas favoured Hinduism but also patronized Buddhist monasteries.

2.4 The period of regional kingdoms: 600–1200 CE

No later Hindu empire covered as much of South Asia as that of the Guptas; instead, the subcontinent was shared between a number of powers based in different regions. The regional distribution of power helps to account for the growth of regional cultures and literatures, and also for regional varieties of Hinduism. Dynasties rose and fell, but four regions remained important: the land around the upper Ganges and its tributary the Yamuna, known as the Doab (from Persian *do-ab* 'two waters', like *panj-ab* 'five waters'); Bengal, around the Ganges delta; the plateau to the west of the centre of the peninsula, known as the Deccan (from Sanskrit *dakshina* 'south'); and the far south, where the Tamil language was spoken, approximately Tamil Nadu and Kerala.

Literature in Tamil goes back at least to the first century CE. The language is unrelated in its origins to the Indo-Aryan languages such as Sanskrit, and Tamil culture is in many ways separate from that of north India. However, the early literature mentions brahmins, and early Tamil kings were influenced by northern ideals of kingship, performing Vedic rituals and claiming to rule as far as the Himalayas. Gods of the Tamils came to be identified with gods known in the north: the mountain god Murugan was identified with Shiva's son Skanda.

There were three ancient Tamil dynasties: Chera, Chola and Pandya. These declined around the fifth century CE, and in the sixth century another dynasty, the Pallavas, emerged as the supreme power in the south. The Pallavas built temples on a larger scale than hitherto, setting the pattern for the distinctive South Indian style of temple building. While the typical north Indian temple consists of a hall with a small shrine at the east end, with a peak surmounting the shrine and an entrance at the west end, the great South Indian temples surround these with subsidiary shrines, courtyards, outbuildings and gateways. A feature which appears first in the Pallava temples is the *go-puram* (literally 'cow-castle'), a tower built over a gateway, covered with statuary. As the South Indian style developed, the *gopurams* were multiplied, each overtopping the peak of the shrine.

Pallava power declined in the ninth century, to be succeeded by a resurgence of the Cholas of Tanjore (Thanjavur) which continued until the thirteenth century when the Cholas were eclipsed by the Pandyas of Madurai. The Cholas built some of the largest and finest South Indian temples, each with several courtyards, with high *gopurams* facing north, south, east and west. It was under the Cholas, too, that the art of casting sculpture in bronze was brought to perfection. The bronze images of the dancing Shiva, associated with the great temple of Shiva at Chidambaram, south of Madras, became in the twentieth century one of the best-known visual symbols of Hinduism.

Further north, in the Deccan, the Shatavahana dynasty ruled from the end of the last century BCE to the beginning of the third century CE, its northward expansion checked by the Shakas and Kushans. In the Doab, a new empire arose under Harsha, who ruled from 606 to 647 at Kanauj on the Ganges. He was a notable patron and author of Sanskrit literature, and had Buddhist monks as well as brahmins at his court. Kashmir was the major power in north India for part of the eighth century, until a new empire was formed in Kanauj by the Gurjara-Pratiharas, who claimed descent from Lakshmana, brother of the hero Rama. They belonged to the group of tribes called Rajput (from Sanskrit *raja-putra* 'king's son'), a title used by several ruling families in the western part of northern India. Their claim to the title rests on their success as fighters and rulers rather than their ancestry.

The Gurjara-Pratiharas were confronted by the Rashtrakutas in the Deccan, and in Bengal by the Palas, who flourished from the mid-eighth to the mid-twelfth century. The Palas favoured Buddhism; and by their support of the long-established Buddhist university of Nalanda, and their own foundation Vikramashila, they facilitated the development of Buddhist learning and art in Tibet and in Southeast Asia. They were overtaken by the Sens, who were Hindus; Ballal Sen, in the twelfth century, is credited with having established a system of precedence among the brahmins of Bengal. In the peninsula, the main rivals of Rashtrakutas were the Chalukyas, the Pallavas and the Cholas.

Conquered kings in this period were often restored or retained on their thrones as vassals of the conqueror (Kulke and Rothermund 1998: 122). This reduced the centralized bureaucracy of the earlier empires, but it also meant that the vassal could in turn seize power from the paramount king. The ebb and flow of empires helped to distribute ideas, styles of art and architecture, and so on through the subcontinent. At the same time, through the system of vassalage, and because certain regions remained prosperous and powerful while dynasties changed, each region developed a distinctive culture. While the use of Sanskrit throughout South Asia for ritual, diplomatic and literary purposes continued or even increased, regional languages were also written. This had been the case for centuries with Tamil, with its rich literary heritage. The use of regional languages for literature is closely bound up with the development of devotional poetry, which will be discussed later.

The instability of power influenced the pattern of kingship. Conquest and marriage alliances were the usual devices for acquiring power, but they were not sufficient to secure it; power once gained had to be legitimated. Gopala, the founder of the Pala dynasty in Bengal in the eighth century, is said to have been chosen by the leading members of the people: a form of legitimation suited to the dynasty's

Buddhist ideology. A more typically Hindu way of legitimating kingship is through the support of brahmins, and the Vedic ritual which only they are entitled to perform. Many kings claimed in their inscriptions to have undergone the Vedic royal consecration, and even to have performed the horse sacrifice which makes a king into a *chakra-varti*. They also claimed close connection, or even identity, with particular gods. The Pandyas, for instance, claimed descent from Shiva and his wife Parvati.

To provide for their ritual requirements, and to show their piety, kings invited brahmins to live in their realms, giving them grants of land so that they could live on the revenue which otherwise would have gone to the king. Remoter regions have traditional accounts of brahmins being brought there from the old centre of sanctity in the Punjab and Doab. In Bengal, for instance, the semi-legendary king Adishura is said to have brought brahmins from Kanauj, while the brahmin priests of the temple of the dancing Shiva at Chidambaram in Tamil Nadu are said to have come from the north. The Pandya and the Chola kings both claimed the support of the Vedic sage Agastya, the legendary bringer of brahminical culture to the peninsula.

Though *Manu* (2.22–4) says that Aryas should live in the Indo-Gangetic plain, the boundaries of the Aryan country are elastic. In the ninth century, a commentator on *Manu* reconciled the text with current practice by explaining that any territory could become suitable for Vedic ritual if a righteous king conquered the barbarians and established the system of four social classes there (Halbfass 1988: 178). Aryavarta remains the holiest territory, and the Ganges is the holiest of rivers, but this does not mean that other places are unholy. Later, we shall see more examples showing that *dharma* is a matter of better and less good, not of absolute good and bad (p. 42). Moreover, a holy river in the peninsula, for instance, can be identified with the Ganges.

Another example of changing values concerns Vedic ritual and temple ritual. Temple ritual and the worship of images are disparaged in the *dharma* texts, yet in this period they were more commonly practised than Vedic ritual. This was justified by saying that Vedic ritual was appropriate for an earlier age, but temple worship is right in the present fallen age of the world (the Kali age, pp. 39, 47). The terminology and symbolism of Vedic ritual were transferred to the temple; a text of the sixth century says building a temple earns the same merit as Vedic sacrifices (*Brihat-Samhita* 55.2).

Each large temple had its staff of brahmins, to perform rituals and to manage the temple and its lands. Temples could act as banks, financing agricultural projects (Kulke and Rothermund 1998: 129). The great temples are highly visible displays of the recognition and ritual support which kings received from brahmins, and their munificence towards them. Less visible, but no less present to the minds of local people, are the myths about the temple's origins recorded in the local *purana* (*sthala-purana*). At the great temple of the goddess Minakshi in Madurai, Tamil Nadu, it is said that the goddess was a Pandya queen who defeated Shiva's army in battle and then became his bride; the temple and its ritual celebrate this marriage (Fuller 1984: 1).

Conquest, the business of the king, was closely linked to sanctification, the business of the brahmin. A good example is the exploit of Rajendra Chola when he defeated Mahi-pala of Bengal in 1023. To commemorate his victory he built a new capital to the north of Tanjore, naming it *Gangai-konda-chola-puram*, 'Ganges-conquering Chola city'. According to his inscription, he compelled the princes of Bengal to carry water from the Ganges to fill a tank in the new city (Kulke and Rothermund 1998: 115). Thus he simultaneously brought the purifying and sanctifying power of the Ganges into his own country, and humiliated the Palas by making them his water-carriers.

It was during this period that the form of devotion known as *bhakti* took shape. In Sanskrit this word can refer to devotion of various kinds, such as a warrior's to his king, or a lover's to his or her beloved, or a worshipper's to a god or goddess; it is in this last sense that the word is used in English. It is already used in this sense in the *Bhagavad-Gita*, one of whose central themes is devotion to God, who appears in the poem as the warrior prince Krishna. However, what is often called 'the bhakti movement' began later, around the seventh century in the far south; its founders are poets who used the Tamil language, and are revered as saints by Tamil Hindus today. They used the poetic devices of the Tamil literary tradition to express intensely emotional devotion to Shiva or Vishnu (Peterson 1989; Ramanujan 1981). The longing of a girl for her absent lover, a common theme of Tamil poetry, was used to represent the devotee's longing for God. This theme was especially appropriate to the worship of Krishna, who is said to have grown up in a community of cowherds, inspiring ecstatic love in the local women (p. 53).

Tamil, unlike Sanskrit, is a vernacular language, spoken in a particular region of South Asia, and it is during this period that the regional vernaculars came into written use, fostered by the regional bases of political power. The bhakti movement broke the brahmin monopoly of communication with the great gods; many bhakti poets were non-brahmins or even people of very low caste. It also broke the monopoly of men, since some of its saints were women.

The practice of composing devotional poetry in vernacular languages spread northwards from Tamil Nadu. In the twelfth century, short poems to Shiva were composed in the Kannada language (Ramanujan 1973); they are still recited by the Virashaiva or Lingayat sect, in the south-west of the Deccan (Schouten 1991). Like other bhakti poems, they scorn distinctions of caste and gender, the only valid distinction being between devotees and others; but the Lingayats went further than many bhakti sects in carrying the principle of equality into social practice. Further north, poems to Vishnu and Krishna were composed in Marathi from the fourteenth century, and in Hindi and Bengali from the sixteenth. These poems, like those of the Tamil saints, are still used in temple worship and popular devotion. Krishna worship in Bengal was shaped by the followers of Chaitanya (1486–1533), who expressed his devotion in singing and dancing, often identifying himself with the love-sick cowherd girls whose longing for Krishna is a favourite theme of bhakti poetry.

The word *sect* requires some comment. When used with reference to Hinduism, it does not imply rebellion against a church, as it may with reference to Christianity. Nor does it imply deviance from the norms of society. Though bhakti sects often reject particular traditions such as the ritual exclusiveness of brahmins, it is often they who uphold the social norms of the region in which they flourish. In a Hindu context, a sect is what is called in Sanskrit a *sampradaya*, literally a 'handing-on': a tradition of teachings, often embodied in a text composed by a historical teacher, together with the succession of teachers who hand them on and the body of people who follow them. Membership of this body is in principle a matter of personal commitment, but in practice it is largely hereditary, and particular sects flourish in particular regions. Membership may be marked by a ritual of initiation, and often by something members wear: Lingayats, for instance, wear a silver capsule on a string round their necks, containing a miniature linga, the form in which Shiva is worshipped. Worshippers of Vishnu or of Krishna, known as Vaishnavas, may wear a fork-shaped mark on their foreheads, and worshippers of Shiva, known as Shaivas, may wear three horizontal white lines; the form of these marks varies with particular Vaishnava and Shaiva sects.

Sects are not necessarily exclusive; the same person or family may follow the teachings and go to the temples of more than one sect. It has been said that Hinduism is polycentric (Lipner 1994); that is, it does not have one source of authority but many. This polycentrism is seen in the way different sects hand on related but different traditions, and in the number of local, regional and global places of pilgrimage. One of the reasons for it is the development of regional powers, each promoting a distinctive culture, but united by a network of communication that included merchants, pilgrims and pandits.

2.5 The period of Muslim rule: 1200–1800 CE

No single event established Muslim power in South Asia, and no part became completely Islamicized. Sind (now southern Pakistan) was conquered by Arabs in 711. Their power was checked by the Chalukyas, Rashtrakutas and Gurjara-Pratiharas, and the Muslim princes took their place among the competing dynasties. From 1000 to 1025, Mahmud of Ghazni (south of Kabul, in Afghanistan) repeatedly raided India, sacking Kanauj and other cities, and looting temples. Mahmud, whose empire extended into Central Asia, was the patron of Al-Biruni (p. 11), but did not share his enquiring attitude to Hindu culture.

Ghazni was sacked in 1151, and Ghur, further west, became the ruling power in Afghanistan. In 1175 Muhammad of Ghur conquered the Punjab, and subsequently most of northern India, but was checked in the east by another Muslim dynasty, the Khaljis, who had displaced the Sens in Bengal. Muhammad was murdered in 1206, and his viceroy in Delhi, Qutb-ud-din Aibak, became an independent ruler. Qutb-ud-din's successor Iltutmish, of Turkish origin, was created Sultan of Delhi by the Caliph of Baghdad, and the Delhi Sultanate became the major power in the north. Delhi, which stood approximately on the site of Hastinapura, remembered in the *Maha-Bharata* as the capital of the Bharata kings, had been one of several Rajput strongholds. It now became the capital of a Muslim empire, and remained so until the eighteenth century. Around 1300, Sultan Ala-ud-din extended the empire into the Deccan, subduing Rajput and other Hindu rulers. In the far south he conquered the Pandyas of Madurai, and the Hoysalas of Dvarasamudra (also called Halebid), former vassals of the Cholas who had become an independent power. However, Muslim expansion was resisted on the east coast by the kings of Orissa, who built the great twelfth-century temple of Jagan-nath (Vishnu as 'lord of the world') at Puri and the thirteenth-century temple of the sun at Konarak.

The Delhi sultanate collapsed in the fourteenth century, after an attempt to replace vassalage with rule by centrally appointed Muslim governors. The governors of Madurai in the south and Bengal in the east declared themselves independent sultans, and the Bahmani sultanate was established in Gulbarga (Karnataka), which in turn split into four around the end of the fifteenth century. A new Hindu kingdom in Vijayanagar (further south in Karnataka) dominated the south until the sixteenth century. Two remarkable brahmins flourished under the early Vijayanagar kings: Vidyaranya and his younger brother Sayana. Vidyaranya wrote several works supporting the theology of Shankara (pp. 35f., 53f.), and is also credited with reconverting the founders of the dynasty who had been converted to Islam. Sayana wrote the standard Sanskrit commentary on the *Rig-Veda*. Both the Hoysalas and the Vijayanagar kings built magnificent and elaborately carved temples, which helped to consolidate their power by attracting the loyalty of brahmins and others (Kulke and Rothermund 1998: 183).

The last and greatest of the Muslim dynasties was that of the Mughals from Samarkand in Uzbekistan, descendants of Timur, who himself had pillaged Delhi in 1398. The Delhi sultanate was re-established by the Lodi dynasty from Afghanistan, but was conquered in the sixteenth century by a Mughal ruler, Babur, who took the Persian title of Padishah. The Mughal empire extended over north India and for a time over most of the peninsula, and influenced Indian culture even more profoundly than the preceding Muslim dynasties. It was confronted in the Deccan by the Muslim sultanates of Bijapur and Golkonda, and by the last Hindu empire, founded by the Maratha chieftain Shivaji, who was consecrated with Vedic royal rituals in 1674. The Maratha empire enjoyed the support of a school of Vishnu-worshipping saints who composed poems in the Marathi language. One of these, Ramdas, was Shivaji's personal guru, and hailed him as the protector of gods, cows and brahmins.

This period overlaps with the preceding, since the interplay of regional powers continued, with the difference that some were Hindu and some were Muslim. The practice of retaining conquered kings as vassals also continued. Foreign powers from the north-west were nothing new; indeed, Hindus referred to the Muslim invaders by the same name, *Yavana*, which they had used for the Greeks. (*Yavana* is derived from the ancient Greek form of *Ionian*, which refers to the Greeks of the coast of Asia Minor; similar names are used in other Asian languages for the Greeks in general.) This new use of the name *Yavana* implies that, like the Greeks, the Muslims were respected for their tradition of learning and material culture, which distinguished them from mere barbarians (*mleccha*).

It would be a mistake to think of a simple opposition of Hindu and Muslim rulers, since Muslim powers often fought each other, as did Hindus. Muslim rulers employed Hindu military and civil officers, and Hindus employed Muslims. The Mughal emperor Akbar took an interest in Hindu culture, and commissioned Persian translations of the *Maha-Bharata* and *Ramayana*; his great-grandson Dara Shikoh commissioned a Persian translation of the *Upanishads*. Persian culture flourished, particularly under the Mughals but also under the Deccan sultans, who were Shi'-ites as the Persians were. While Persian remained the language of government, literature was developed in Urdu, a language like Hindi in its grammar, but taking much of its vocabulary from Persian, Arabic and Turkish.

The Mughals also introduced European innovations, from the muskets and cannon which blasted Babur's way to Delhi, to the perspective in Mughal paintings. At the same time, European powers were attempting to control the sea trade routes around the peninsula: the Portuguese in the sixteenth century, and the Dutch and British, and later the French, in the seventeenth. They established coastal trading bases, but had no territorial ambitions.

Large numbers were converted to Islam, so that in the twentieth century over a fifth of the South Asian population was Muslim. However, many of these Muslims retained elements of Hindu culture. Within Islam, the Sufi tradition was particularly congenial to Hindu religious ideas, since it sought knowledge through discipline and meditation under the guidance of a master. A new form of bhakti emerged, which rejected not only rituals and the authority of brahmins, but the mythological attributes and images through which deities were known to earlier bhakti poets. Kabir, in the fifteenth century, composed poems in Hindi, ridiculing both Muslim and Hindu religious practices and asserting that God is neither in the mosque nor in the temple but in the heart. Nanak (1469–1539) proclaimed a similar message in the Punjab. His followers were known as Sikhs, this being the Punjabi form of the Sanskrit word *shishya* 'pupil'. Nanak is remembered as the founder of the Sikh community.

2.6 The period of British rule: 1800–1947 CE

In the eighteenth century, when the Mughal empire was in decline, Britain and France competed for power in India. Each of these countries operated through a trading company, which became a military and political power by forming alliances with Indian rulers and raising its own Indian army. By 1760 the British had emerged as sole European power in India. The East India Company, founded in 1600, had bases in three seaports: Calcutta (now Kolkata), Bombay (Mumbai) and Madras (Chennai). These were known as 'Presidency towns' because in the eighteenth century their governors were called 'presidents'. Each became the centre of an expanding territory called a 'presidency'. The largest of these territories was Bengal, which the Company administered as the agent of the Mughal emperor. By the middle of the nineteenth century, British India had acquired the shape which it retained, with some changes, until 1947. About two-thirds of the subcontinent was under direct British rule. About one-third was under Indian rulers, some Hindu and some Muslim, who were bound by treaties requiring them to accept the advice of British officials. The Maratha empire, last of the regional powers and last Hindu empire, had been defeated in 1818 and divided between Bombay Presidency and a number of indirectly ruled states. There also remained some small enclaves of Portuguese, Dutch, French and Danish power, on or near the coast.

The Company was headed by a Court of Directors in London, but the three governors could not always wait for instructions from the directors, and made their own policy. From 1773 the Company became increasingly under the control of Parliament, until in 1858 the Company was abolished and the government of India was placed directly under the Crown. The Regulating Act of 1773 provided for a Governor-General based in Calcutta, which thus became the capital of British India until 1911, when the capital was transferred to Delhi.

The Company had a policy of not interfering with Indian society and religion, though this was modified in the course of the nineteenth century. Even before then, the British presence in India made religious and social change inevitable. The increasing use of English, and of printing in English and in Indian languages, together with gradually increasing uniformity in education, changed attitudes to authority. Instead of a teacher handing on a tradition of learning to a single pupil or a small group, writers addressed a more or less critical public, using arguments which were intelligible and acceptable to that public. Many of these writers kept abreast with ideas from the West, and some wrote for an international readership. There was lively debate between Christians (Indian as well as Western), Hindus and secularists; public debate with Christianity was also conducted in Sanskrit (Young 1981). Opponents of Hinduism cited social problems, especially caste and the condition of women, as evidence against it; many Hindus argued that these were false Hinduism (p. 12), and advocated social reform in the name of true Hinduism.

The policy of governing the people according to their own laws unintentionally changed those laws, by requiring Hindu law to be codified and standardized, and persons to be categorized as Hindus, Muslims and others so that the appropriate law could be applied to them. It also brought matters of *dharma*, which had hitherto been the concern of specialists, into the public arena, and made caste identity more public and rigid (Bayly 1999: 94, 168). Much of the education, in English and the vernacular languages, was in the hands of missionaries, despite the Company's early hostility towards them. The education which they provided was intended to create a public that would be receptive to Christian ideas, but it also created one which was critical of them.

Rammohun Roy (1772?–1833), a brahmin of Calcutta, was the first Indian of modern times to be at home in Indian and Western intellectual traditions. Rammohun held that there was one God, revealed in the design of the universe; all religious traditions taught this, and none possessed a unique revelation. True worship consisted in the contemplation of God without the aid of images or mythology, and in benevolent behaviour towards others. The various religious traditions were in agreement on these essentials of religion, differing only on inessentials (Killingley 1993). Rammohun accused both Hindus and Christians of insisting on inessentials and obscuring the universal truths which they had received.

The society which he founded, the Brahmo Samaj, though small in numbers, became an effective movement for modernization in Bengal, and inspired similar societies elsewhere, committed to monotheism and social reform (Kopf 1979). Its most influential member after Rammohun was Keshub Chunder Sen (1838–84), an enthusiastic preacher, who introduced the idea that Hindus inherited a tradition of spirituality which had made India the source of all the great religious movements of the world. Keshub turned the quest for revelation from the external world to the human heart, and met the claims of Christianity with a counter-claim for Hinduism, without actually claiming a unique revelation. These ideas were developed further by Vivekananda.

New ideas were not confined to the centres of British influence. In the Kathiawar peninsula in Gujarat a brahmin ascetic called Sahajanand (1781–1830), better known as Swaminarayan, founded a sect which is still strong in Gujarat and in Gujarati communities elsewhere. The name Narayan is one of the names of Vishnu, and reflects a belief that Swaminarayan was a manifestation of God. This sect was encouraged by British officials as a force for peace in a turbulent region. Later, another brahmin ascetic of Kathiawar who knew no English, Dayananda Sarasvati (1825–83), interpreted the Veda and *Manu* in a way that showed the influence of Victorian thought, upholding monotheism, condemning idolatry and caste, especially the hereditary authority of brahmins, and advocating scientific enquiry and commercial and military enterprise (Jordens 1978). Dayananda founded a sect, the Arya Samaj, which became a force for modernity in the Punjab. He also intended to spread Aryan culture, as he saw it, outside India, but did not put this into effect.

Some notions of Hinduism were spread in the West by the Theosophical Society, founded in New York in 1875 by the Russian Helena Blavatsky (1831–91) and the American Henry Olcott (1832–1907) to investigate ancient wisdom. An attempt to join forces with the Arya Samaj failed, but in 1882 the society established its headquarters at Adyar, near Madras, where its library remains a centre for research on Sanskrit texts. Ideas such as karma, rebirth and the subtle body (p. 34) became widely known in the USA and Britain, in versions adapted to Blavatsky's ideas of spiritual evolution. For a time Theosophy provided some Hindus, whose English education had turned them away from Hinduism, with a route into their heritage, and encouraged them to study Sanskrit texts, especially the *Bhagavad-Gita* (Sharpe 1985: 88–95).

The first effective Hindu missionary to the West was Swami Vivekananda (1863–1902), who made a dramatic appearance at the World's Parliament of Religions at Chicago in 1893. His message was a modern form of Advaita Vedanta (pp. 53f.), which he claimed was the most rational and scientific religion. To audiences in India he preached a muscular Hinduism, arguing that without the spiritual message of the *Upanishads* all efforts at social reform were doomed to failure. He received some support from Theosophists at first, but soon denounced them as outsiders who praised everything Hindu without discriminating between true and false Hinduism. In 1896 he founded the Vedanta Society of New York. This was the first Western centre of the Ramakrishna Mission (named after his guru, the mystic Ramakrishna (1836–86)), which later opened other centres in India and the West, staffed by a new order of Hindu monks. Advaita Vedanta was presented in a more academic way by S. Radhakrishnan (1888–1975), whose formidable knowledge of Western philosophy made him an ambassador of Hinduism to the intellectual classes of the West.

The changes brought by the British presence affected Hindus more than Muslims, because they were more numerous in Calcutta, Bombay and Madras, and in the English-educated class. The Indian National Congress, formed in 1885, was intended as a political forum for all Indians, but it came to be dominated by Hindus, and was distrusted by all but a few Muslims. Towards the end of the nineteenth century, as Indians were given more opportunities to participate in government, and at the same time found British promises of eventual self-government deceptive, a militantly nationalistic element developed in the Congress, using Hindu motifs in its rhetoric. This Hindu nationalism was advocated by the Marathi brahmin B. G. Tilak (1856–1920), who looked back to the Maratha king Shivaji as a champion of Hinduism. Tilak opposed legislation for social reform, on the grounds that it was foreign interference in Hinduism; he supported societies for the defence of *dharma*, and for the protection of cattle. A learned though eccentric Sanskritist, he used astronomical evidence to argue that the Veda was composed around 4000 or even 8000 BCE, making it almost as good as eternal.

Another prominent religious nationalist was the Bengali Aurobindo Ghose (1872–1950), who was educated in England but on his return in 1893 threw himself into Indian culture and politics. He became a national figure over the partition of Bengal in 1905. The province of Bengal had become over-large by the addition of Bihar to the west and Orissa to the south, and the Governor-General, Lord Curzon, solved this problem by creating a new province, East Bengal (approximately where Bangladesh is today). To Aurobindo and others, the partition was an assault on the land of Bengal, which he identified with the violent but nourishing mother goddess, Kali, whose worship is particularly popular in Bengal. Violent struggle in her defence was a sacred duty which Aurobindo equated with a Vedic sacrifice. Such appeals aroused Hindus but antagonized Muslims, who welcomed the partition because the new province had a Muslim majority. Though acquitted on a charge of seditious journalism, Aurobindo retired suddenly in 1910 to the French colony of Pondicherry, where he developed a new form of Vedanta.

Bengal was reunited in 1912, but the partition issue left a permanent scar. In turning the Congress into an independence movement, Tilak, Aurobindo and others had turned it into a Hindu movement which virtually excluded Muslims. After the First World War, Mohandas Gandhi (1869–1948) attempted to bring together an independence movement that was founded on religion but transcended religious divisions – taking advantage of Muslim indignation at the dismemberment of the Turkish empire after the war. Gandhi proclaimed that 'Truth is God', so that no one, not even an atheist, could be alienated by a struggle in the name of God. Truth, however, he understood in his own way: as shown in his autobiography, *The Story of my Experiments with Truth*, he regarded it as something never to be completely known, but to be constantly sought after through vows of abstinence, and through a non-violent approach to political and interpersonal conflict which recognizes the truth in the opponent's position while refusing to abandon the truth as one sees it. Though Gandhi found support in many non-Indian sources, such as Ruskin and Tolstoy, his ideas about truth are rooted in Hindu tradition (Chatterjee 1983; Parekh 1997). His belief that true religion transcends the boundaries between religious traditions has affinities with Rammohun, Keshub, Vivekananda and Radhakrishnan.

While Gandhi believed that God could be known by any name, his favourite name of God was Rama, the name he uttered as he died. Rama, the hero of the *Ramayana*, is worshipped by many Hindus as God (p. 53). He is also the ideal king, who reigned in perfect peace, order and prosperity during the second age of the world (p. 34). Gandhi's aim in the independence movement was not simply to end British rule, but to re-establish the reign of Rama (*Rama-rajya*). This would mean not only peace and prosperity, but an economy based on minimal consumption in self-sufficient villages, where all castes would be respected because all work was equally valued, under the authority of God, Truth, or Rama. Gandhi's political ally Jawaharlal Nehru, a secularist who championed industrialization and economic planning, found all this exasperating.

One of the features of Hinduism that emerged as nationalist symbols during the Bengal partition agitation was the *Bhagavad-Gita*: revolutionaries swore oaths on it, and recited it defiantly under the gallows. Later, Tilak, Aurobindo and Gandhi each wrote a commentary on it: Tilak in Marathi and Gandhi in Gujarati, both in prison, and Aurobindo in English in Pondicherry. Unlike the Sanskrit commentaries, each of which used the text as authority for the theology of a particular sect, the primary concern of these modern commentaries is action in the world. They all emphasize the ideal of action without desire for personal reward, a feature of the *Bhagavad-Gita* which had been highlighted earlier by the Bengali Bankim Chandra Chatterji (1838–94). While Aurobindo's shows the deepest under-standing of the *Gita*, Gandhi's, brief and published as cheaply as possible, proved the most popular; it was translated into many languages and became a handbook of the independence movement. The *Gita*'s popularity as a devotional text and as authority for the exposition of ideas increased rapidly. Since Gandhi's little book there have been dozens of commentaries, supporting different sects or individual views.

Meanwhile, Hindu political ideologies were developed which made little or no attempt to accom-modate non-Hindu communities. V. D. Savarkar (1883–1966), a Marathi brahmin and veteran of the Bengal partition agitation, wrote a book in 1924 called *Hindutva: Who is a Hindu?* Savarkar explains that Hindutva, literally 'Hindu-ness' (a Persian name with a Sanskrit suffix), is more comprehensive than Hinduism; it is a matter of race, geography and culture. Savarkar, who also translated the Italian nationalist Mazzini into Marathi, presents a nationalism of blood and soil on the European Romantic model. For him, anyone who accepts this Hindutva is a member of the Hindu nation; but those who have loyalties outside the sacred land cannot be true Hindus. So long as Muslims look to Mecca, they exclude themselves from full membership of the nation, just as Jews exclude themselves by their Zionism from full membership of European nations; the analogy, more ominous now than when he wrote, is Savarkar's own (de Bary 1958: 883f.).

2.7 Independence

It was a divided country which gained independence in August 1947: India, an old name with a new meaning, and Pakistan, a name coined in 1930, meaning 'land of the pure'. By 1961, India still had a 10.7 per cent minority of Muslims, while Pakistan had a 10.7 per cent minority of Hindus, despite over two million crossing the borders each way around the time of partition (Schwartzberg 1978: 92).

Neither Gandhi's ideal of Rama-rajya nor Savarkar's Hindutva formed the basis of the new country. India is constitutionally a secular state (the only state in the world with an explicitly Hindu constitution is Nepal). The constitution, begun in 1946 and promulgated in 1950, does not actually use the term 'secular state', but it is intended to be secular in the sense that it does not rest on or favour a particular religion. At the time of its drafting it was a political necessity that Muslims and other religious minorities should feel secure in the new polity; indeed, that the fears of Hindu dominance which had led to the demand for partition should be seen to be groundless.

The Indian constitution proclaims the equality before the law of all citizens irrespective of 'religion, race, caste, sect, place of birth'. However, this does not apply in the sensitive areas of personal law: marriage, divorce, inheritance. Despite an aspiration expressed in the constitution that there should eventually be a uniform civil code, there are separate laws for Muslims, Christians and other minorities, while the law applying to Hindus in these matters reflects the utilitarian and liberal traditions prevailing among the English-educated class which dominated the independence movement. In the 1980s Hindus voiced resentment that the tradition of non-interference in society seems to apply to the minorities but not to them (Larson 1995: 208–21, 256–61).

Another exception to the principle of equality before the law is positive action in favour of 'Scheduled Castes' (i.e. *dalits*) in the fields of education, employment, political representation, and legal protection against discrimination. For this purpose independent India, like British India, deals with hereditary groups, not individuals: what entitles a person to positive action is not the fact of being discriminated against in some legally defined way, but membership of a legally defined oppressed group, such as a 'Scheduled Caste'. Since the definition excludes non-Hindus (except Buddhists), a Christian *dalit* who suffers the same discrimination is not entitled to the same positive action (p. 47).

At the other end of the caste spectrum is the privileged position of many brahmins (though some brahmins are very poor). Brahmins provided the civil service of the typical Hindu kingdom, and this practice continued under many of the Muslim rulers, when brahmins learnt Persian and Urdu as well as Sanskrit. They found similar employment in British India, since they formed a highly educated professional class which soon took up English as a key to advancement. In India today, the proportion of brahmins in the civil service, in law, medicine, education and other professions, and in politics, far exceeds their proportion in the population as a whole, and it has even been calculated that their proportion in government employment has increased since independence (Larson 1995: 210f.).

In the twentieth century, resentment against the dominance of brahmins has been a potent factor in politics. The most successful anti-brahmin movement has been in Tamil Nadu, where a brahmin population of about 3 per cent had most of the professional jobs at the beginning of the century but has now completely lost this predominance. This movement rejects Sanskrit, and encourages speakers and writers of Tamil to avoid Sanskrit loan-words; it also protests against the dominance of North India in politics, and the promotion of Hindi, the national language; the movement associates all these with brahmin dominance. Some of its leaders have rejected Hinduism, or rejected religion altogether, notably E. V. Ramaswamy Naicker (1879–1973). More popular, however, is the rejection of forms of Hinduism associated with brahmins, Sanskrit and the north, in favour of those deities, rituals and myths which are typical of Tamil culture. Outside Tamil Nadu, many of the Marxist and other secularist thinkers of the twentieth century, who naturally opposed any ascendancy based on ritual status, were themselves brahmins, including D. D. Kosambi, E. M. S. Namboodiripad, Jawaharlal Nehru and M. N. Roy.

When the position of brahmins as intellectual leaders is challenged, the view of history in which the Aryas are the bringers of culture and order is also contested. Besides the Tamil anti-brahmin movement, this view is opposed by members of low castes. One of the first modern low-caste intellectuals, Jotirao Phooley (1827–90), gave a new twist to the story of the Aryan invasion which was already widely accepted in his time. According to him, the brahmins had invaded India and seized power from the legitimate indigenous rulers. They had invented the theory of the fourfold division of society in order to classify these rulers as *shudras*, thus denying them legitimacy (O'Hanlon 1985: 141–51). Another low-caste intellectual was B. R. Ambedkar (p. 47).

At independence the Indian National Congress, which had led the freedom movement, became the Congress Party, which provided the government of India for most of the next half-century. Increasingly, however, it owed its power to the lack of a unified opposition rather than to its own strength at the polls; it also split repeatedly. Its principle of excluding religious differences from politics was always contested, and Hindu nationalism eventually found a powerful political organization. In 1977 the Congress Party was defeated at the polls for the first time, and a disparate government was formed which included two members of the Bharatiya Jan Sangh, which represented Savarkar's ideal of Hindutva. In 1989 Congress was again defeated, and the party of Hindutva, now called the Bharatiya Janata Party (BJP), gained 108 seats. It did not take part in the government, but showed its strength by supporting a popular movement which symbolized a rejection of Congress secularism. This was a project to demolish a disused mosque, the *Babri Masjid* ('Babur's mosque'), built by the first Mughal emperor on the reputed birthplace of Rama in Ayodhya, and to replace it with a temple of Rama.

This project was full of aggressive religious symbolism. It was a token effacement of the period of Muslim power, which in the Congress reading of history had been a period of coexistence and synthesis, but in the Hindu nationalist reading was a temporary defeat of Hindutva calling for vengeance. It was also a token restoration of Rama-rajya, which in the language of the BJP meant not the reign of truth envisaged by Gandhi, but the triumph of Hindutva. Ritually consecrated bricks (recalling those used in the ancient Vedic fire-altars) were sent to Ayodhya from all over the world. Lal Advani, the BJP president, rode to Ayodhya on a truck got up as a chariot, carrying a bow, an iconographic mark of Rama. Politically, the project was an assault on the secular state, in a time of unstable governments. Advani was arrested; the government fell; the campaign resumed. Eventually, on 6 December 1992, the mosque was demolished amid violence and carnage (Larson 1995: 266–77). In 1999 the BJP was elected to power, but has distanced itself somewhat from such extremes.

In the twenty-first century, Hinduism is international; we can no longer define it as the religion of South Asia. Though South Asia remains central to it, Hinduism has sacred places in every continent (except Antarctica), and Hindu teachings are available through print and electronic media anywhere in the world. The internationalization of Hinduism has two main causes: migration in the nineteenth and twentieth centuries, and missionary activities in the twentieth.

Migration has its roots in the British period. At the end of the eighteenth century there were already Indians in Britain who had come as sailors or servants. In the late nineteenth century there were two main kinds of migration. First, professionals and students, nearly all men of the English-educated urban class, went to Britain as individuals. Second, men and women from the poorer areas were recruited in large numbers to work in Mauritius, Fiji, the Caribbean, Malaysia, South Africa and East Africa, mainly in plantations. In the twentieth century, professionals and businessmen went with their families to work in these and other countries. In the 1950s, thousands of Punjabis (Sikhs and Muslims as well as Hindus) went to the textile towns of northern England, where there was a shortage of labour. The 1961 British census showed 81,400 people born in India and 24,900 from Pakistan; there was a preponderance among them of men of working age, many of whom had left their families in India. In the 1960s, people of South Asian origin in the East African countries, many of them professionals and traders, came under pressure to emigrate; in 1972, Uganda expelled them. Some went to India, some to Britain and some elsewhere. Most of these were of Gujarati origin; others were Punjabi. By 1977 there were 307,000 Hindus in Britain, of whom 70 per cent were Gujarati and 15 per cent Punjabi (Knott 1986a: 9).

In the United States, the pattern was very different. Immigration from South Asia was rare until 1965, when a new Immigration Act gave priority to professionals whose skills were in demand. As a result, the USA now has a population of Hindus, and others from South Asia, which includes a high proportion of doctors, engineers and other professionals. This in turn has resulted in well-funded, purpose-built temples in American cities (Williams 1988: 56–62).

The worldwide Hindu diaspora varies greatly in ethnic composition and in the extent to which it has preserved Hindu traditions. Hindus in East and South Africa, especially the Gujaratis, have always been in touch with their homelands by sea. The Swaminarayan sect was promoted in Kenya, Tanganyika and Uganda by two Gujarati stationmasters on the Uganda Railway in the 1930s (Williams 1984: 175f.). Durban is a stronghold of the Arya Samaj. The Tamil Hindus of West Malaysia have similarly kept in touch with Tamil Nadu. Hindus in the Caribbean, on the other hand, poor and remote from their homelands, which spread over a vast area of north India, developed their own cultural patterns (Vertovec 1994: 274–8).

Countries with substantial Hindu populations have organizations which coordinate Hindu activities and represent the Hindu community to others. At the local level, the temple often provides a focus for activities which in the Indian situation are dispersed; as well as being a place of worship, it is a place where Hindus can wear clothes, eat food and follow social conventions which would be inappropriate or impossible elsewhere. A temple can make a Hindu community (Nye 1995). In Britain, the National Society of Hindu Temples keeps a register of temples, and publishes orders of service for rituals. An organization which seeks to bring the diverse Hindu communities of the world together is the Vishwa Hindu Parishad (World Hindu Council), founded in 1964. In India, the VHP is closely linked with militancy; abroad, it provides support and coordination, and organizes conferences which aim to unite Hindus and promote Hindutva (Dwyer 1994: 185f.).

Missionary activities, the second cause of the internationalization of Hinduism, began effectively with Vivekananda. Ramakrishna centres in the United States, Britain, France, Argentina and Switzerland continued their work with a small following of well-educated, affluent, mainly middle-aged or elderly Westerners, and more recently have attracted many Bengali Hindus. In the 1960s a different kind of mission appeared, appealing to young people interested in political protest, the search for novel experiences, and pop music. Maharishi Mahesh Yogi founded his Transcendental Meditation movement in 1957, offering a fast-track programme of meditation using a mantra (p. 51), with benefits to the individual that could be physiologically tested, as well as less verifiable benefits to society such as reduction in crime. This became especially popular when it was taken up by the Beatles in 1967. In 1971 the thirteen-year-old Guru Maharaj Ji brought another meditation programme to Britain before moving to the United States.

The most successful mission, the International Society for Krishna Consciousness (ISKCON), is also the one that shows the clearest continuity with traditional Hinduism, and the least inclination to adapt its teachings and practices to the West. This was founded in New York in 1967 by A. C. Bhaktivedanta Swami Prabhupada (1896–1977), who had undertaken to carry overseas the work of the Gaudiya (i.e. Bengali) Vaishnava Mission, founded in 1886 to promote Krishna worship in Bengal. Finding its first followers among the hippies, and fostered in Britain by George Harrison of the Beatles, it has grown into a highly disciplined worldwide movement with strong links to Bengal and to Braj, the place where Krishna lived as a cowherd. It shows its fidelity to Sanskrit textual authority, especially the *Bhagavad-Gita*, by publishing translations with commentaries and methodically printed Sanskrit texts. It attracts British Hindus, Bengalis and others, with its orderliness, its clearly articulated theology, and the uncompromising commitment of its followers (Carey 1987).

A more loosely organized movement surrounds Sathya Sai Baba (1922–), a saint rooted in the Telugu-speaking state of Andhra Pradesh, with an international following which includes many British Hindus, and an ashram in his home region which is both a flourishing pilgrimage site and the centre of an international organization. The branches of this organization vary considerably in the attention they pay to its Indian roots; some followers do not consider it a Hindu movement but a universal one.

These international movements have been made possible by modern communications, which send books, preachers, pictures, films, radio and television throughout the world. In 1987–8, Indian television broadcast the *Ramayana* in 78 episodes, soon followed by the *Maha-Bharata* in 93 episodes. These were national events; timetables of all kinds were adjusted to let people watch, and the *Ramayana* serial helped to inspire the march against the Babri Masjid (Kulke and Rothermund 1998: 312). Tapes of the serials soon went round the world. Such use of modern media brings the stories within reach of people who have no access to, or little interest in, the village storytellers and dramatic troupes that have kept the traditions alive for centuries. On the other hand, it imposes fixed versions of what have always been fluid stories, and these versions reflect modern authoritarian views (Lipner 1994: 142). Private videos, especially of weddings, tend to standardize rituals.

But modern communications also facilitate an opposite trend: the flourishing of regional sects, outside their region as well as within it. The World-Wide Web – *vishva-vyapi vitana* as it is called in Sanskrit – offers endless possibilities for variants of a tradition. The media also communicate modern theories about the political agendas that may lurk in popular narratives. *Dalits*, women, or anyone dissatisfied with a male-dominated, brahmin-dominated, authoritarian view of Hinduism, have access to physical and intellectual means for subverting it.

3 KARMA, REBIRTH AND CYCLIC TIME

One of the most widespread Hindu beliefs is that a person's destiny is formed by his or her actions, so that each action we perform will have an effect on us in the future, and each thing that happens to us is the result of something we have done in the past. This belief does not enable us to define Hinduism, since it is also held by Buddhists and Jains, while even among Hindus it takes various forms. It is often referred to as *karma* (or *karman*; these are merely two English versions of the same Sanskrit word). This word (and related words in other Indian languages) means 'action, deed' in Sanskrit, but it is used in

English to stand for the whole continuous process whereby we shape our destiny through our actions, each action having its effect, or fruit as it is often called in Indian languages.

3.1 Karma and rebirth

The process of karma does not cease at death: when we die we shall be born again in another body, to consume the fruit of our previous deeds. This other body may be a human one, but it may be the body of an animal or even a plant; it is even possible to be reborn as a god or goddess. (This is unlikely, since it requires an enormous store of merit, and gods live far longer than we do, so that vacancies rarely occur.) In the same way, the body in which we now exist is the fruit of our actions in previous births. Thus our physical condition – strong or weak, whole or disabled, beautiful or ugly; our social condition – rich or poor, brahmin or low caste; our sex; and the species we belong to – vegetable, animal, human or even divine, are all results of things we have done in the past. The *Bhagavad-Gita* compares the changes wrought by this process of rebirth to changes that are familiar in human life:

> Just as, in this body, the soul has childhood, youth and old age, in the same way it gets another body; a wise man is not confused about it . . . Just as a man takes off old clothes and puts on new ones, so the soul takes off old bodies and goes to new ones.
>
> (*Bhagavad-Gita* 2.13, 2.22)

The word translated 'soul' here means literally 'that which has a body'. 'Soul' is not a very satisfactory translation, since it has too many theological implications. What passes from body to body is often referred to as a 'self' (*atman*) or a 'living being' (*jiva*). While this, unlike the body, is essentially changeless, it carries with it what is sometimes called a 'subtle body', which includes the load of karma which determines the bodies it will inhabit. The subtle body changes, like the physical body; it can become more virtuous or wicked, wiser or stupider, and so on, as its karma changes. All these changes are of the same kind as the ones we observe within a person's lifetime, as they develop habits and skills through their activities. By repeatedly telling lies, or throwing the javelin, or whatever, you become the kind of person who does that. As one of the earliest texts that deal explicitly with karma and rebirth puts it,

> As he acts, as he behaves, so he becomes. A doer of good becomes good; a doer of evil becomes evil. He becomes good by good action, evil by evil.
>
> (*Brihad-Aranyaka Upanishad* 4.4.5)

Thus a person's destiny is shaped by their actions, and is not imposed by some higher power. Sometimes Hindus or Hindu texts mention a deity who allots destinies according to people's karma, but such a deity is merely following the system, and is not essential to it.

Most people are not aware of their previous births; that feat of memory is achieved only through highly advanced meditation. It is said that the embryo in the womb remembers them, and is so distressed by the memory that it resolves never to be reborn again. However, the traumatic experience of birth wipes out the memory, so that the baby is born without knowledge of any kind (O'Flaherty 1988: 98). Nevertheless, there are stories which narrate the passage of particular living beings through a succession of bodies; we shall see an example below. There are also warnings of the punitive rebirths which await those guilty of particular sins. *Manu* has a list of them; for instance:

A brahmin who is a thief will enter the wombs of spiders, snakes, lizards, aquatic animals, and murderous demons, a thousand times. One who seduces his teacher's wife will enter grass, bushes, creepers, and carnivorous, fang-bearing and cruel animals, a hundred times. Meat-eaters become violent animals, those who eat forbidden food become worms . . . By stealing grain he becomes a rat . . . by stealing water a duck, honey a bee . . . by stealing meat a vulture.

(In ancient India, a brahmin boy ideally spent twelve years in his teacher's house, under a vow of celibacy (p. 46). To sleep with the teacher's wife is frequently mentioned as a particularly heinous sin, because it is a betrayal of that vow, and of the pupil's duty of respectful service to the teacher. Since the teacher is a kind of father, it is also a kind of incest.)

Rebirth unites all living beings in one hierarchy, sometimes described as 'from Brahma [the ancestor of the gods] down to a tuft of grass'. This creates a moral bond between humankind and other species, which helps to explain the revulsion against meat-eating, slaughter and hunting which is frequently expressed, especially where brahmins and hermits are concerned. It also helps us to understand why there is no hard and fast line between people and gods (pp. 50, 53).

Besides rebirth, our conduct can be rewarded or punished in a heaven or hell; there are usually said to be seven hells. This belief is not inconsistent with rebirth, since the stay in a heaven or hell is not permanent, though it may be for hundreds of years. The passage in Manu from which the above examples are taken begins by saying that the various sinners spend many years in terrible hells before being reborn. Similarly, those who have won great merit go to heaven, but since their merit is finite, it can only keep them there for a finite time. After that, they return to this world to be reborn according to their previous deeds.

Karma is often associated with rebirth, but the two are not the same concept. It is possible to believe in rebirth without karma; an ancient ascetic sect called the Ajivikas did so, saying that each of us has to go through a predetermined series of bodies, which we can do nothing to change (Basham 1954: 295). On the other hand it would be difficult to believe in karma without rebirth, since it is well known that those who do good deeds are not all rewarded, and those who do evil remain unpunished till they die, while many people's happiness or suffering appears quite undeserved. Together, however, these two beliefs provide an intellectually satisfactory answer to the old question, 'What have I done to deserve this?' I may not know what I have done to deserve a particular piece of good or bad fortune, since I probably did it in a previous life; but there is no doubt that I must have done something.

3.2 Theodicy

To put it more technically, karma and rebirth answer the problem of theodicy. This word, meaning literally the justice (Greek *díkē*) of God (*theós*), was originally used in Christian theology to refer to the problem, and the various possible answers to the problem, of why God, if he is omnipotent, just and loving, allows apparently undeserved suffering. It is interesting to see how the Hindu theologian Shankara (pp. 53f.) discusses the same problem in the course of an argument that the world is created by God. Some people, he says, deny that this can be so, because we find happiness and unhappiness unevenly distributed, not only between different people but between different species. Gods are very happy, animals are miserable, and people have various degrees of happiness and suffering in between. The creator of such a world must be unfair and cruel, and yet God, according to the Veda, is supposed to be perfect. Shankara answers that the uneven distribution of happiness and suffering is due to karma.

Since the inequality in creation is in accordance with the merit and demerit of the beings that are created, God is not to blame.

(Shankara, commentary on *Vedanta-Sutra* 2.1.34)

But what of the beginning of the world? The first beings had no previous births from which to inherit good or bad fortune, so how did inequality arise? Shankara has an answer to this too.

The objection would be valid if the world had a beginning. But since the world is beginningless, there is no reason why actions and inequality should not go on and on. Each of them is both the effect and the cause of the other, like the seed and the plant.

(Shankara, commentary on *Vedanta-Sutra* 2.1.35)

The analogy of the seed and the plant (the chicken and the egg may be more familiar) implies that not only do actions cause inequality, but inequality causes actions. To put it more fully, beings perform various actions which cause them to be born in various bodies, and this causes them to perform actions, because it is impossible to be totally inactive while in a body. These actions in turn cause further embodiment, and so on.

For karma and rebirth to provide a satisfactory theodicy, the world has to be not only beginningless but endless; otherwise, some actions would remain unrewarded or unpunished. So, just as each living being passes through a beginningless cycle of action and fruit, birth and death, the world also passes through a beginningless and endless cycle of days, months and years, and even creation and dissolution. We shall see later how this happens (pp. 38f.). But we should note first that while the cycle for each living being is beginningless, it is not necessarily endless. Freedom from the bondage of karma is possible, and this freedom, or salvation, is the highest good (p. 53).

You may find it difficult to understand how a blade of grass, for instance, can have the merit or demerit that are supposed to determine its next existence. However, one's present life is not shaped only by the actions of one's immediately preceding life, and the actions of one's present life shape more than one future life. It is true that plants cannot act. Even the actions of animals are usually determined by their nature, and so do not earn merit or demerit: a lion does not earn demerit by killing and eating animals, and a deer does not earn merit by not doing so. People, on the other hand, have free will, and in the course of a lifetime each of them does many things, some good and some bad; each of these actions is rewarded or punished with an appropriate birth. Shankara explains:

Each living being has, in its former existences, accumulated many actions, some of which have pleasant results and some unpleasant. As these actions tend to produce opposite results, which cannot all be experienced at the same time, some actions, whose occasion has come, make up the present existence, while others are standing by, waiting for the right place, time and cause.

(Shankara, commentary on *Vedanta-Sutra* 4.3.14)

A story from the Puranas may make it clearer (*Vishnu Purana* 2.13). A king retired to a holy place in the forest to live as a hermit. There he practised yoga and meditated constantly on Vishnu, intending to continue in this way until he died; for, according to the *Bhagavad-Gita* (8.5), anyone who meditates on God at the time of death will reach God and not be reborn. However, one day the king rescued a motherless fawn, and became so fond of it that he neglected his meditation. When he died, his mind was still on the fawn, who watched over him like a son. Consequently he was reborn as a fawn himself, since the *Bhagavad-Gita* (8.6) goes on to say that at death you will reach whatever form of being you are thinking of at the time. Because he had reached an advanced stage of yoga, however, when he was born as a fawn he was able to remember his previous births. This knowledge made him anxious to end the cycle of rebirths, so he made his way to the holy place where he had lived as a hermit. He died there, and was reborn as a brahmin who had perfect knowledge of God, even though he was never taught anything and appeared to be uncouth and stupid.

This is a simple example involving only three lives, but it illustrates Shankara's point. The hermit-king had performed actions producing opposite results: by his yoga he was destined to have perfect knowledge, but by his infatuation with the fawn he was destined to be born as a fawn himself. These two fruits could not be experienced at the same time; and since if he had been born with perfect knowledge first he would not again have been reborn, he had to be born as a fawn first. So his infatuation with the fawn was the action whose occasion came first; and, during his life as a deer, his birth as a brahmin with perfect knowledge was on standby.

3.3 Karma and other determinants of destiny

While karma provides an intellectually satisfactory answer to the problem of theodicy, the thought that misfortune is one's own fault, the result of past deeds which one is not even aware of, still less in control of, is not psychologically satisfying. Karma is not in fact the only way in which Hindus account for good or bad fortune. It is more readily used to account for the misfortunes of others than for one's own (Leslie 1999: 31–3). So far we have been looking mainly at texts. If we look instead at the way ordinary Hindus think, we find that, rather than blaming their misfortunes on their own karma, they may appeal to other kinds of explanation (Keyes and Daniel 1983; Fuller 1992: 224–53; Ayrookuzhiel 1983: 122–4). Like anyone else, they may attribute them to the negligence or malice of others: if I fall, it may be because someone has left something to trip me up. A more distinctively Hindu explanation is the wrath of a god: the world is full of gods (p. 52), and I may have neglected to worship at a particular inconspicuous shrine, or trodden (or worse) on an invisible holy place. Another explanation is sorcery, including the evil eye: an envious look which can cause sickness or death, typically attributed to childless women who cast it on the children of others. It is also commonly said that your destiny has been written on your forehead by a god or goddess. Hindus who suffer misfortune may think of one of these reasons rather than their own karma.

Further, karma itself is not such an individual matter as has appeared so far. A child may die because of the bad karma of its parents, or a wife may be affected by the bad karma of her husband. A boatload of people may suffer disaster because of the bad karma of one of them, or they may all escape because of someone's good karma. However, an upholder of the doctrine of karma can always argue that karma is the ultimate cause. It may be your own karma that causes you to fall victim to the negligence or malice of others, or causes you unwittingly to offend a god. The god who writes your destiny on your forehead is merely giving effect to your karma. To be born to parents who are destined to lose a child may be the result of your bad karma in a previous birth, and so on. Thus whatever cause may be adduced for good or bad fortune, the ultimate cause may still be karma. Furthermore:

> Whilst the karma principle need not be the only theory which the villager turns to first of all in his search for a meaning for the misfortune he suffers, it is generally the last which he will abandon. By this I mean that he is more likely to express scepticism towards the cult of the gods or towards the idea of *tuna* [sorcery] than he is explicitly to reject the doctrine of karma.
>
> (Sharma 1978: 38)

3.4 Cyclic time

As Shankara saw in discussing the problem of theodicy, karma requires infinite time for its operation. Time is infinite, but it is not uniform; if it were, it would be impossible to measure it. As it is, time is divided into days and years by the motion of the sun, and into lunar months by the phases of the moon.

This simple observation provides a powerful reason for the Hindu belief that time is endless and beginningless. Today is always preceded by yesterday and followed by tomorrow; similarly, each year is preceded by another year and followed by another. The idea of a first day or a first year is contrary to what we observe in nature; so is a final day or year. We also observe that the rhythm of the year is accompanied by the rhythm of sowing, growth and harvesting; this practical, earthy observation underlies Hindu thinking about actions and their fruits. This is why Shankara has no difficulty in accepting that actions, and the inequality of destiny that results from them and causes them, continue through infinite time like seeds and plants.

Hindu festivals, and the calendars used for ritual purposes, are timed according to these natural cycles. Most annual festivals occur at particular points in the cycle of the moon, so the date on which they fall according to the familiar Gregorian calendar varies. For instance, Diwali, the festival of lights, can occur in October or November, but it is always the last three days of the waning of the moon. A few festivals are timed by the sun, like the Gregorian calendar: the entry of the sun into Capricorn falls regularly on 14 January. In north India it is called *Lohri*, and bonfires are lit to bring back the sun; in Tamil Nadu it is marked by the rice-boiling festival *Pongal*, which celebrates the rice harvest. There are also events that fall on a particular day in every lunar month: for instance, the eleventh day of the waxing moon and the eleventh of the waning moon are sacred to Vishnu, and the fourteenth to Shiva. The cycle of day and night also has its sacred moments: sunrise, noon and sunset. Some brahmins mark sunrise and sunset, and some noon as well, by bathing, sipping water and reciting the most frequently used verse in the Veda, known as the Gayatri mantra or Savitri mantra. Looking beyond the year, the great bathing festival called Kumbha Mela has a twelve-year cycle, following the cycle of the planet Jupiter (Lipner 1994: 296–9). Far from being uniform, time is a complex of cycles, each with its climaxes of sanctity, auspiciousness or danger.

Just as the daily cycle has two halves, day and night, the month has its 'bright half' when the moon is waxing, and its 'dark half' when it is waning. The bright half of the year is from the winter solstice to the summer solstice, when the sun rises and sets a little further north each day, and the dark half is from the summer solstice to the winter solstice, when it moves southward. To keep the cycle of lunar months in approximate phase with the year, a thirteenth month is added every two or three years. The number of days in the year is traditionally said to be 360; this, of course, is only an approximation, but it is between the number in a solar year (about 365¼ days) and the number in twelve lunar months (354).

Because gods live longer than we do, they reckon time on a longer scale. A day and night of the gods is one of our years, so some temples have annual rituals to mark the gods' going to sleep (around July) and waking (around November). Accordingly, a year of the gods is 360 of our years. Twelve thousand of these make an age of the gods (*maha-yuga*), and a thousand ages of the gods make a day of Brahma, the ancestor of the gods. At the end of this time (4,320,000,000 of our years), the world comes to an end. But time does not end there; the dissolution of the world marks the beginning of the night of Brahma, which is the same length as his day. After that Brahma wakes, and the process of creation begins again. During his night, the system of karma and rebirth is in abeyance; but when he wakes, beings continue their unequal existence according to the karma they accumulated during the previous day.

There is no need to know all the details and figures. Not all Hindus are aware of them, and the accounts in the Puranas, the *Maha-Bharata* and other texts vary (the above account is based on *Manu*). Some Puranas introduce further details to exalt a particular god: the *Shiva Purana* says that a year of Brahma is one blink of Shiva, while a Vaishnava text (the *Brahma-Vaivarta Purana*) says it is one blink of Krishna. What matters most is that cosmic time is infinite and moves in cycles, vastly longer than our years.

One further feature of cosmic time has a bearing on the topic of karma, and also on the Hindu view of history, and on *dharma* (p. 47). The *maha-yuga*, 'great age' or age of the gods, is divided into four ages called *yugas*:

Krita Yuga	4,800 years of gods	=	1,728,000 years
Treta Yuga	3,600 years of gods	=	1,296,000 years
Dvapara Yuga	2,400 years of gods	=	864,000 years
Kali Yuga	1,200 years of gods	=	432,000 years
Total	12,000 years of gods	=	4,320,000 years = 1 *maha-yuga* or age of gods

The Krita Yuga is the perfect age of the world, when people lived for four hundred years and were virtuous and happy. The other ages show a progressive decline, and we are now in the worst of the four, the Kali Yuga, when people live for a hundred years at most, and wickedness and misery abound. (The name has nothing to do with the goddess Kali.) The Kali age began in 3102 BCE, when a terrible battle was fought which forms the climax of the *Maha-Bharata*, and which brought unprecedented violence, treachery and disorder. It will not end until 428,898 CE, when Vishnu will come in the form of a white horse (or in some versions a man on a white horse) to destroy the wicked and rescue the remaining righteous. Then the perfect Krita age will begin again, followed again by decline. All historical time, therefore, is within the Kali age, in a fallen world.

That we are living in the Kali age is a result of our bad karma. Good karma could result in birth in one of the better ages; till then, one could be in one of the heavens, or some place unaffected by the cycle of ages.

3.5 Karma and cosmic time in the modern world

Karma, rebirth and cosmic time are not just found in ancient books; they are part of the worldview of Hindus today. Many Hindu death rituals are aimed at ridding the deceased of bad karma, enhancing the effect of their good karma, and ensuring a good rebirth – a further way in which an individual's karma is not their concern alone. These include recitation of texts and of names of God, gifts on behalf of the dying or dead person, offerings before and after the cremation, and the placing of the ashes in a sacred river (Firth 1997: 64, 71–92). Thousands bathe in sacred rivers, to wash away their sins or those of their ancestors. On the sixth day after a birth, some Hindus leave a red ballpoint and paper for the gods to write the child's destiny, with auspicious foodstuffs such as areca nut, rice and sugar (McDonald 1987: 61).

At a popular level, karma tends to be thought of as an inescapable fate; since most of it is inherited from a previous birth of which one has no knowledge, it is hard to feel personal responsibility for it (Sharma 1978: 34). Nineteenth-century critics of Hinduism often objected to it as a crippling fatalism, and twentieth-century *dalit* critics have denounced it as a device for justifying oppression by blaming it on the oppressed. Modern interpreters emphasize the element of free will in karma, focusing on actions in the present life rather than on past lives. Radhakrishnan, addressing a British audience, rejected the fatalistic interpretation of karma, and used an analogy to represent it as freedom:

> The cards in the game of life are given to us. We do not select them. They are traced to our past Karma, but we can call as we please, lead what suit we will, and as we play, we gain or lose. And there is freedom.
>
> (Radhakrishnan 1960: 54)

Though rebirth is not part of Christian or Jewish doctrine, it has been a familiar idea to many in the West since the nineteenth century, when it was popularised by the Theosophical Society (Knott 1986b: 24). The International Society for Krishna Consciousness (ISKCON) teaches karma and rebirth, stressing the moral responsibility that these ideas entail, and linking them to its strict vegetarianism. Prabhupada, the founder, told Americans in the 1960s that for every Kentucky Fried Chicken, Colonel Saunders would be reborn as a chicken (Daner 1976). On the other hand, Western converts to Hindu sects tend to retain the attitudes of their Christian, Jewish or atheist backgrounds, in which birth and death happen only once, and life gives no second chances. They pursue otherworldly goals as if there were no tomorrow, while South Asian Hindus often leave such things to others whose karma has given them more time and ability for them.

In the nineteenth and twentieth centuries, when the biblical view of creation was challenged by science, Hindus were able to claim that their view of time was superior because its vast scale had room for the long periods posited by geologists and palaeontologists. The scientific theory that the world began in a Big Bang, and will collapse in a Big Crunch, fits well with the day of Brahma, especially those versions of the theory in which bangs and crunches succeed one another cyclically. Hindus also claim that karma is scientific, because it explains all events in terms of cause and effect.

4 DHARMA: NORMS OF CONDUCT

We have already mentioned dharma, and seen that it is a set of norms for people's behaviour, including that of the king. It is not made by kings, though kings are particularly responsible for enforcing it. Nor is it made by the gods, since the gods themselves are subject to dharma. An older form of the word, used in the hymns of the *Rig-Veda*, means 'support, decree, arrangement, order', and dharma is often explained as something which supports society as well as ordering it. Another meaning of the word is 'natural property'. It is the dharma of fire to burn, for instance, and the dharma of water to extinguish fire. Animals also have their dharma, which is their natural behaviour: it is the dharma of the lion to kill and eat the deer, and it is the dharma of the deer to eat grass and to flee from the lion. Animals have little or no choice in their behaviour; like inanimate objects such as water and fire, they just follow their dharma. People, however, have a choice whether to follow their dharma or not, and in this context we may translate the word as 'morality' or 'law'. As we saw, because people have free will they earn merit or demerit – good or bad karma – by their actions, which animals do not. Dharma tells us which actions are meritorious and which are not, and may also tell us what kinds of rebirth or other consequence will be their reward or punishment (pp. 34f.).

In modern times the word dharma is often used to translate 'religion', and Hindus sometimes prefer to speak of 'Hindu dharma' rather than 'Hinduism'. In the context of the historical encounter of Hindus with Muslims, Christians and others, the differences that were most noticeable between these communities were differences of behaviour: how they dressed, what they ate, what patterns of marriage they followed, how they worshipped, and so on. These are differences of dharma; in Western terms they are religious differences, so the word came to be translated 'religion'. However, it does not refer to religious belief, but only to behaviour, and includes matters that may be considered outside the sphere of religion, such as the administration of justice in law-courts.

While dharma applies to every human being, it is especially the concern of the king. The king's responsibility for the behaviour of his subjects is understood in terms of karma:

> A sixth share of everyone's merit belongs to the king who protects them, and a sixth share of their demerit belongs to the king who does not protect them. Whatever Veda-study, sacrifice, gifts, or worship a man performs, the king receives a sixth share of it as his due for protecting him.
>
> (*Manu* 8.304–5)

This statement uses the analogy of the share of the produce of the land (often more than a sixth) which the king received as revenue. In the same way he receives a share of his subjects' good or bad karma, since whatever good they do is due in part to his protection, and whatever evil they do is due in part to his neglect.

Dharma is one of the three worldly aims, the other two being worldly power (*artha*, which includes wealth and political power) and pleasure (*kama*). Though these aims are often said to be those of everyone, or at least of every man, the discussions of them in ancient texts suggest that they are primarily the concerns of kings. They are listed in descending order of importance; the pursuit of pleasure is acceptable so long as it does not interfere with the pursuit of wealth and power, and these should not be sought at the expense of dharma. Beyond these three is the transcendent aim of salvation (*moksha*).

4.1 The literature of dharma

There is an extensive literature on dharma in Sanskrit. The earliest texts, composed in the late Vedic period, are the *Dharma-sutras*, which are ritual rules, mainly concerning brahmins, in the form of brief notes in prose. Later, during the period of the north Indian empires, verse manuals were composed, of which the best-known is the *Laws of Manu*, around the second or third century CE. These include ritual rules, but they also cover a much wider range of topics. There are household matters such as food and cleanliness, and matters in which the brahmin traditionally advised the king, such as inheritance, commercial law, crime and punishment. The *Maha-Bharata*, *Ramayana* and puranas also include long passages on dharma.

These texts, which are partly compilations of traditional verse maxims, were not always sufficiently explicit to be of practical use. From the seventh century, commentaries were written on them which filled in the details and sorted out the ambiguities. Commentaries could also bring a text up to date; we have already seen how a ninth-century commentator modified *Manu*'s view that Aryas should live in the north (p. 23). *Pandits* specializing in dharma also wrote digests of law for kings and their brahmin advisers. In the eighteenth century they wrote them for the British, who wished to apply Hindu law to Hindus in their law-courts.

When the dharma texts deal with criminal law they can be very severe, but on personal matters they allow considerable latitude. *Manu* (2.6) lists four sources of authority for dharma: the Veda, the tradition and conduct of those who know it, the behaviour of the good, and finally one's own satisfaction. The commentators explain that the Veda is the ultimate authority, but where it does not provide a rule one should look to the second source, and so on. The third source, the behaviour of the good, varies with different regions or even villages. In cases where it still leaves a choice, you are entitled to act as seems best to yourself. However, this does not necessarily mean that the choice you make is morally neutral; it may be a question of how virtuous you wish to be. In matters of personal behaviour, there may be a choice between a way of life which is morally acceptable, and one which is morally supreme. *Manu* gives three examples:

> Meat-eating is not wrong, nor alcohol, nor sex. They are the natural activity of beings. But abstention from them brings great rewards.
>
> (*Manu* 5.56)

Dharma is often a matter of degrees of rightness and wrongness rather than of absolute right and wrong. The doctrine of karma ensures that any penalty for less than perfect behaviour will not be permanent, while those who actively seek moral perfection have probably been prepared for it by their previous karma.

Since karma produces different kinds of people, dharma is not the same for all. The dharma that applies to Aryas, which is the main subject of the dharma books, does not apply to others; and, as we have seen, the commentators recognize regional and local customs as part of dharma. But one form of differentiation is so obvious that it is often overlooked.

4.2 Differentiation by gender

The dharma literature gives detailed instructions for the ritual and social behaviour of men, but says little about women. It is men, according to the texts, who should be initiated with the sacred thread which is the mark of an Arya (p. 44), and should then live with a teacher learning the Veda, after which they are entitled to marry. They can then perform the household rituals prescribed in the Veda, which are centred on the household fire; this can be set up and maintained only by a male householder who has been initiated with the sacred thread. The dharma of women, on the other hand, revolves around their husbands:

> Marriage is the Vedic initiation for women; serving the husband is their residence with the teacher; household duties are their worship in the fire.
>
> (*Manu* 2.67)

It is assumed that the role of a woman is that of wife and mother. Marriage, and the birth of a son, make her auspicious; if her husband dies before her, she loses this auspiciousness and spends the rest of her life as a celibate widow. A girl should be married as soon as a suitable bridegroom can be found, and can only have one husband; a widower, on the other hand, can remarry at any age.

Among hundreds of Sanskrit books on dharma, one, written in the eighteenth century, deals exclusively with the dharma of women (Leslie 1989). It details a strenuous round of daily duties for the wife, after which she should engage with her husband in equally strenuous sex – the only activity in which she is to take the initiative. It portrays women as dangerously lascivious and in need of control by men. Like many other books on dharma, it commends the wife who follows her husband in death by burning herself on his funeral pyre. The word *sati*, meaning 'true woman', is applied especially to a wife who shows this extreme form of devotion, and who thus becomes an object of worship and source of blessing. In English (sometimes in the older spelling *suttee*), the word is often applied to the practice instead of the person.

The dharma books do not tell us everything about the roles of women. Not only are these books the work of men, but they are essentially prescriptive and not descriptive, and what they prescribe is an ideal which may never have been fully practised. While they claim the authority of the Veda, they represent a different world from that found in the Vedic texts: the world of the Hindu kingdoms with their brahmin ministers. In early Vedic ritual the wife is a partner of her husband; thereafter her role becomes increasingly subordinate. The Veda also shows that women were not excluded from learning. Some of the Vedic hymns were composed by women, and we are told that the ritualist Yajnavalkya had two wives, one of whom was a theologian, while the other only knew what women know (*Brihad-Aranyaka Upanishad* 4.5.1) – implying that it was possible for a woman to study, but exceptional.

If we look outside the dharma literature, we find that women have a vigorous ritual life of their own. It is very often they who conduct most of the worship at the household shrine, and who go to the temple; these forms of worship are largely independent of the dharma rules. Another religious activity which belongs especially to women is the performance of vows (*vrat*). These are undertakings to fast, or to abstain from particular foods, on certain days of the week, month or year. Women and girls in a family or neighbourhood gather together to observe a vow, and to hear the story of its origin, which usually tells how a woman performed it when some calamity afflicted her family, and so restored welfare and happiness. A ritual role which can only be performed by young girls or married women is that of *goyni*, as she is called in Gujarati, who is ritually fed on occasions when a goddess is worshipped, and represents the goddess (Jackson and Nesbitt 1993: 68; Fuller 1992: 201f.). Women, as well as men, can act as mediums who are possessed by a goddess and speak in her name.

The dharma books restrict the social life of women:

> A girl, a young woman or an old woman should not do anything independently, even at home.
> A woman must be subject to her father in childhood, to her husband in youth, and to her sons
> when her husband is dead; she must never be independent.
>
> (*Manu* 5.147–8)

However, this restriction is not matched in practice. While widows are typically treated as poor relations, in some families they exercise authority over their sons. Further, while an unmarried daughter or a new wife has a subordinate position, those who control her are often not so much the men as the older women in the family. In North India at least, where brides are usually sought from another village, while the male descendants of a male ancestor stay in the same place, it is the women in the family who maintain a network of contacts with other villages. These contacts facilitate the traditional pattern of arranged marriage, even if the arrangement is finally ratified by men (Sharma 1981).

Finally, early marriage and the prohibition of widow remarriage apply particularly to women of the higher castes, the ones most concerned with fulfilling the prescriptions of the dharma literature. Among lower castes widows can remarry, and wives can even divorce their husbands. Differentiation of dharma by gender is thus inseparable from differentiation by caste.

4.3 Differentiation by caste

The prescriptions in the dharma books apply mainly to the males of certain castes in which boys are initiated with the sacred thread, which is a loop of string hanging over the left shoulder and down to the right hip. Initiation with the sacred thread marks a second birth, in which the teacher or guru is the father, and the Savitri mantra which the boy learns (p. 38) is the mother (*Manu* 2.170). While ordinary birth brings a boy into biological life, this second birth brings him into the life of the Veda, entitling him to learn the Veda and to perform Vedic rituals. For this reason, those who have received this initiation and wear the sacred thread are called 'twice-born', and those hereditary groups which are entitled to it are called the twice-born castes. Another term for such castes is Arya. The division of humankind into Aryas and others goes back to the Veda (p. 16), but we need not suppose that all those who are now called Arya are descendants of the Vedic people.

We have mentioned caste several times; it is now time to consider what it is. It would be wrong to expect a definitive explanation; what follows is only a summary of its characteristics. A caste is a hereditary group, separated from other such groups by endogamy and commensality. Endogamy means that marriage partners are selected within the caste and not outside it, and commensality means that members of the caste eat together and not with others. There are many exceptions to these broad statements. Alliances between kings were often sealed by a marriage, in which the partners were often of different castes. Other people can and do marry outside their caste, but it is a matter for comment. People in cities eat together regardless of caste, but when the same people visit relatives in a village they may observe commensality, especially on formal occasions such as a wedding feast. Norms exist not to prevent things happening, but to define them as abnormal.

A caste often has a distinctive occupation, whether or not all its members actually pursue it, and a distinctive diet. This means that if you belong to a meat-eating caste of leather-workers, people outside the caste will regard you as a meat-eater and a leather-worker, even if you never touch meat or leather yourself. This is an example of what is called group pollution: all members of the caste are considered polluted by the caste's occupation and diet. Group pollution can temporarily affect a family: a birth or a death pollutes the family, and every member, whether or not they were present, has to undergo a ritual of purification, often after twelve days. Anything to do with dead animals is polluting, including working in leather and eating meat. A barber is polluted because cut hair is considered dead matter. Anything that comes out of a living body is polluting, so a midwife, who is often a barber's wife, is polluted by her occupation, and a laundryman is polluted by clothes and sheets.

Each caste belongs to a particular region, though members may live elsewhere. A given village may have twenty or a dozen castes, or only one, for instance if it was given by a king to a group of brahmins. The number of castes in South Asia runs into many hundreds or even thousands, but it would be impossible to count, because it is not always certain whether a group should be called one caste or several. It may be treated by those outside it as a single caste, but its own members may recognize several endogamous groups within it. Some anthropologists call it a caste with several sub-castes, but neither of these terms has a clearly defined meaning. Further, the number of castes is always liable to change, as castes merge or split.

The castes in a given area (say, a village or group of villages) can be ranked in an order of purity, in which the highest are those from which anyone can accept food and water, while the lowest are those from whom no-one else will accept them, and with whom the others avoid contact. These last are the castes known variously as untouchables, scheduled castes, or *Harijans* ('God's people', the name given them by Gandhi); in the late twentieth century they began to call themselves *dalit*, 'crushed, oppressed'. Over 20 per cent of the total Hindu population are *dalits*; brahmins are well under 10 per cent

(Schwartzberg 1978: 106). The brahmin castes, of which there may be several in an area, usually rank highest. But purity is not the only possible criterion for ranking. In terms of material power, the highest caste is usually the one that owns most of the land, sometimes called the 'dominant caste' of the area.

The word *caste* is not Indian in origin; it comes from a Portuguese word *casta*, 'race, breed, lineage'. However, it is used as a rough equivalent of Sanskrit *jati* and of similar words in modern Indian languages. But *jati* can refer to a species, a breed of animals, a class of things, a nation of people, or some smaller group of people linked by birth, as well as to a caste. Neither word has the precise technical meaning which some anthropologists have assumed or tried to identify. Any attempt to understand caste as a single system is bound to run into contradictions (Quigley 1993: 16).

Dharma literature says less about caste than about the theory of four classes, which dates from the Vedas: brahmins, *kshatriyas* (warriors and rulers), *vaishyas* (cultivators and traders) and *shudras* (p. 17). The first three of these four *varnas*, as they are called, are Arya or twice-born, because their boys are entitled to be initiated with the sacred thread. The *shudras* are not; they are non-Arya. *Manu* defines the functions of the twice-born *varnas* in terms of the Veda, its rituals, and the gifts which often accompany them. Only brahmins are to teach the Veda, perform rituals and receive gifts, while all three twice-born *varnas* can study the Veda, have rituals performed for them, and give gifts. Besides these religious functions, *kshatriyas* are to protect the people and detach themselves from sense-objects; *vaishyas* are to protect cattle, practise agriculture, trade and lend money. The only function of *shudras* is to serve the others (*Manu* 2.88–91). In addition, the texts sometimes mention a fifth group who are outside the four *varnas*, and are extremely unclean.

While this theory is not the same as caste, it has some features in common with it. The *varnas* are (at least preferably) endogamous, and are ranked with the brahmins at the top. They often appear to be hereditary, though some texts say they are a matter of behaviour and not of birth. Among castes, some are brahmin castes, some of whose members have ritual functions, receive ritual gifts, and know the Veda, though by no means all do. The *dalit* castes correspond to the fifth group. However, between the brahmins and the fifth group it is harder to match the realities of caste with the theory of *varna*. Many castes, usually the dominant castes in their areas, claim to be *kshatriyas*, while others call them *shudras*. Similarly, many trading castes claim to be *vaishyas*, but may not be recognized as such by others. Thus the brahmin castes are the only ones whose place in the *varna* scheme is generally accepted. The dharma writers often acknowledge this fact by treating the terms *twice-born* and *arya* as synonymous with *brahmin*.

The *varna* theory, unlike caste, is neat and comprehensible: it has only four categories, or five if the *dalits* are included; they are ranked in an undisputed and unchanging order (though Buddhist texts rank the *kshatriyas* above the brahmins, and some Vedic texts suggest that this is a matter for debate); and it is widely known in South Asia. For this reason it is often used in attempts to explain caste, and some books on Hinduism refer to the *varnas* as 'the four castes'. But the features which make it comprehensible make it unlike caste, which has an indefinite number of categories which vary from place to place, and whose ranking is disputed and liable to change.

The *varna* theory provides textual authority for the division of Hindu society into functional groups. According to a myth found in the Veda (*Rig-Veda* 10.90) and repeated in the dharma books, the four *varnas* sprang from the head, arms, thighs and feet of the primeval man from whom the universe was created. To explain the great number of castes, a theory was developed that unions between men and women of different *varnas* produced offspring of various castes. Thus the offspring of a brahmin father and a *vaishya* mother is an Ambashtha, whose occupation is medicine; the offspring of a *shudra* father and a brahmin mother is a Chandala, one of the fifth group of castes (*Manu* 10.8, 10.16). Further miscegenation caused further proliferation of castes. The account is not historical, and varies between texts, but it reflects the brahmin authors' attitude to caste: they regarded it as a falling away from an original system of four *varnas*.

The *varna* theory is not only used by brahmins; it is used by other castes in their competition for rank. Whereas if purity were the only criterion, meat-eating castes would rank below vegetarians, they often rank above them, because meat-eating is appropriate to *kshatriyas*, and vegetarianism to *vaishyas*. Claims of castes to high places in the *varna* system often appeal to mythology. The Chera, Chola and Pandya kings each claimed to have provided a feast for both sides in the great battle recorded in the *Maha-Bharata* (Nilakantha Sastri 1966: 118). This implies not only a historical connection with a great event in the history of north India, but a ritual status at least equal to the descendants of the *kshatriya* Bharata. The Rajputs have a tradition that they were admitted to the status of *kshatriyas* by a great ritual of purification by fire on Mount Abu in Rajasthan in 747 CE (Kulke and Rothermund 1998: 110). All claimants to *kshatriya* rank have to contend with the myth of Parashurama, a brahmin hero who is said to have exterminated the *kshatriyas* at the end of the second age of the world.

4.4 Differentiation by stage of life

The sacred thread separates men from women, and the Aryas or twice-born from the *shudras*. But it also separates those male Aryas who engage in Vedic ritual from those who have not yet done so, and from those who have renounced it. The dharma books set out a scheme of four stages of life, known as the four *ashramas* (the word also means a community of ascetics), which applies to male Aryas. Leaving out the period from birth to initiation, the first stage starts when a boy receives the sacred thread; he then lives with his teacher learning the Veda, under strict rules of abstinence. Texts give various ages for initiation from four to twenty-four; twelve years of study are often recommended. This period of celibate studentship (*brahma-charya*) ends with a ritual bath, which makes a man ready to marry and enter the second stage, that of the householder (*griha-stha*). When his sons have sons, ensuring the continuation of his lineage, he may retire to the forest as a *vana-prastha* or hermit, with or without his wife. The fourth *ashrama* is a further stage of retirement, *sannyasa* or renunciation, in which the *sannyasi* has renounced all social ties and all ritual practices. To mark this renunciation, he abandons the sacred thread.

Hindu practice rarely follows this theoretical scheme, even among brahmins. The stage of the forest hermit is hardly ever followed, and *brahma-charya* is often reduced to a few minutes when the boy learns a mantra, mimes going in search of a teacher, and comes back to his family. In Britain, large numbers of brahmin boys are sometimes initiated together by a visiting teacher (Jackson and Nesbitt 1993: 56). The most enduring feature of the scheme is the contrast between the householder and the *sannyasi*. The householder seeks worldly prosperity for himself and his family, has sexual relations with his wife, performs household rituals, and follows the rules of purity of his caste. The *sannyasi* abjures all these concerns. However, he is not without social ties, since he may be teacher and spiritual guide to a number of families, and many *sannyasis* organize themselves into orders and monasteries.

Besides the thousands of *sannyasis*, who may be seen in procession on occasions such as Kumbha Mela, there are various other ascetics who do not fit the definitions of the dharma books. A woman, for instance, can become a *sannyasini*, adopting a similar way of life to the male *sannyasi*, free of concern with purity and pollution; or she can take on the life of a perpetual celibate student, following a strict vegetarian diet. However, only about a tenth of ascetics are women (Denton 1991: 212). In the Ramakrishna order, founded in 1897 by Swami Vivekananda, men take *sannyasa* after five years of initial training and four further years of *brahma-charya*, without passing through the householder stage. But it is more usual for men and women to devote their old age to religious practices such as worship, study, meditation and pilgrimage, without such complete and formal renunciation as is prescribed for the *sannyasi*.

4.5 Differentiation by age of the world

The difference between rule and practice is acknowledged in the dharma books themselves. One notion which enables them to do so is that of the Kali age (p. 39). The fact that most brahmins, for instance, have little knowledge of the Veda, and many of them serve temples and images, or practise agriculture, is one of the signs of the degeneracy of this age. Another is the fact that most kings do not belong to the *kshatriya varna*. The Maurya kings were *shudras*, many dynasties were of foreign origin, and the Shungas and some others were brahmins. The fact that men can be called kings merely because of their power is one of the evils of the Kali age. Another is the proliferation of castes which has muddled the primordial simplicity of the *varna* system.

4.6 Dharma in the modern world

According to the dharma books, dharma is unchanging. Different rules apply in the Kali age and in the other ages, but even this difference fulfils an eternal pattern: the rules of the Kali age apply in every Kali age. Yet interpreters of the texts have always adapted them to changing circumstances and changing views of what is right.

The nineteenth century, by bringing Hindus into contact with the English-speaking world (p. 27), exposed Hinduism to criticism, from Hindus as well as Westerners, and much of this criticism concerned the norms of Hindu society. The issues which were most discussed were the position of women, and caste. The practice called *sati* (p. 43) was condemned by many Hindus. It became illegal in 1829, though this did not prevent it from occasionally occurring. A case in 1987 aroused controversy especially because, unlike many in the past, it was a voluntary act of devotion and fortitude (Leslie 1991). Legislation permitting widow remarriage, passed in 1857, had little effect so long as men did not wish to marry widows. Opportunities for education and employment for women have done more than legislation, but problems remain.

In the area of caste, the main problems considered in the nineteenth century were the divisions between them, and the privileges of brahmins. In the twentieth century the main issue was the oppression suffered by *dalits*, and although untouchability was outlawed by the Indian constitution of 1950, oppression persists. Gandhi sought to integrate *Harijans*, as he called them, into Hindu society. His paternalistic approach was bitterly opposed by Dr B. R. Ambedkar (1891–1956), the most highly educated *dalit* of his time, who believed that Hinduism was the cause of the degraded and oppressed position of his caste and others like it. In 1956, shortly before his death, Ambedkar led a mass conversion to Buddhism, declaring that while he could not avoid the misfortune of being born an untouchable, he refused to die a Hindu (Zelliot 1996: 206). Conversion, however, whether to Buddhism, Christianity, Islam or Bahá'ism, does not protect *dalits* from exploitation and violence. On the contrary, by an oddity inherited from the British definition of scheduled castes (Dushkin 1972: 168), legal provisions for the protection and advancement of *dalits* apply only to those who are Hindus; more recently, they have been extended to Buddhists.

Dayananda Sarasvati proposed a radical solution of the caste problem, in which the multiplicity of castes would be replaced by the Vedic system of four *varnas*. Moreover, these would not be hereditary; people would be assigned to them according to their individual merits by a board of examiners. Vivekananda, Tilak and Radhakrishnan also insisted on the non-hereditary nature of *varna*, which they presented as true caste, as opposed to the false caste which prevails at present (Killingley 1991: 25–31). The non-hereditary principle is rarely carried into practice, but one movement which does so is ISKCON, where advanced devotees can be initiated as brahmins (Knott 1986b: 50).

Those who opposed innovations in ritual and social matters claimed to uphold *sanatana dharma*, 'eternal law'. This phrase had formerly been used to extol dharma in general, or particular rules, by emphasizing their antiquity and immutability; but in the late nineteenth century it took on a new meaning. It implied a claim that Hinduism, unlike other religions, upheld timeless values and could not be superseded (Halbfass 1988: 343f.). Together with the cow, *sanatana dharma* became something which all Hindus have a duty to defend. The phrase can also refer to universal Hinduism as opposed to a particular sect, or sects in general. In the Punjab, where the Arya Samaj flourishes, those who opposed it in the late nineteenth and early twentieth centuries called themselves *sanatani* Hindus. In Britain, temples which attempt to provide for all Hindus and not for particular sects are called *sanatani* temples. Another phrase is *varnashrama-dharma*, 'the norms of the four *varnas* and the four stages of life'. Traditionally this refers to two of the forms of differentiation discussed above, and implies duties at least as much as privileges; but in modern discourse it is often invoked as a justification for caste privilege and oppression.

The appeal to unchanging norms implied in the phrase *sanatana dharma* did not go unchallenged. The social reformers of the nineteenth century argued that the practices they opposed were not as ancient as they were claimed to be. M. G. Ranade (1842–1901) and R. G. Bhandarkar (1837–1925) showed that the ancient dharma texts did not sanction pre-puberty marriage of girls, but later writers had misinterpreted or even misquoted these texts to fit later practices. 'The peculiarity of our religious law is that a text is always found to justify any new custom that obtains currency' (Bhandarkar 1928: 544). In the interpretation of dharma, the most recent commentaries had been accepted as the most authoritative. In the nineteenth century this perspective was reversed, as scholars looked to the earliest texts for the most authentic views. Their search was facilitated by the availability of printed texts, and encouraged by the classical and Protestant background of many Western Sanskritists. Textual research became an ally of humanitarian ethics.

5 The gods and God

One of the questions put to Yajnavalkya when he claimed the prize of cows (p. 18) was:

> 'How many gods are there, Yajnavalkya?'
> He answered . . . 'Three hundred and three and three thousand and three.'
> 'Yes', he said, 'but just how many gods are there, Yajnavalkya?'
> 'Thirty-three.'

Yajnavalkya's first answer is a way of saying that the gods are countless. His second answer, thirty-three, is often mentioned in the Veda as the number of gods. There are more names of gods than that in the Veda, but since it is not always clear whether two names refer to different gods or the same god, thirty-three is a reasonable estimate. However, the questioner goes on asking the same question, getting a lower answer each time: 'Six'; 'Three'; 'Two'; 'One and a half'.

> 'Yes', he said, 'but just how many gods are there, Yajnavalkya?'
> 'One.'
>
> (*Brihad-Aranyaka Upanishad* 3.9)

As often in the *Upanishads*, the last answer is the one that matters; until then, Yajnavalkya is playing for time, hoping the questioner will give up before he has to part with his precious knowledge. For the casual enquirer, there are many gods, but if we persist, we find there is just one. The search for the one underlying the many is a recurrent theme of the *Upanishads*.

What we find in this text of the last millennium BCE is borne out by an anthropologist's observation:

> Ultimately, as the most casual student of Hinduism knows, all the gods and goddesses are 'one'. This is a doctrine of genuine significance, and not merely an extravagance of bookish philosophers. It is a doctrine that is reiterated frequently in the texts, but illiterate villagers are equally fluent in maintaining that although there are many deities, and although they have different and sometimes contradictory characteristics, in the end all are the same and all are one.
>
> (Babb 1975: 261)

Indian languages have different words for the many gods and the one God. A god (using the word as a countable noun (p. 9)) is *deva* in Sanskrit or *dev* in Hindi; God (an uncountable noun) has various names such as *ishvara* in Sanskrit or *bhagvan* in Hindi. Bhaktivedanta Swami, the founder of ISKCON, called the *devas* 'demigods', because they are a different kind of being from God, and to use the same word would be confusing. However, many English-speaking Hindus refer to them as 'gods'. We can mark the difference by spelling the one God with a capital G, and the many gods, or a god who is one of many, without. When a gender-free word is needed, they are usually called 'deities'.

5.1 Patterns of worship and its objects

We have already mentioned services to images as a characteristic practice of Hindus (p. 14); such services are called *puja*. *Puja* can take the form of offerings of food, water, flowers and incense sticks, either at the home shrine or in a temple, often accompanied by chanting. An image may be washed, often by placing a token drop of water in front of it, and images in temples have curtains which are drawn daily for them to wake up and go to sleep. This conflicts with the idea that the gods' day is as long as our year (p. 38); but the timetable of *puja* is for our convenience, not that of the deities. Images are a means by which deities allow worshippers to approach them, see them and show them respect. The deities do not actually need the services performed in *puja*; without them, they would not be hungry, thirsty or dirty (Fuller 1992: 68–72). (They can, however, become dangerously angry.) According to Vaishnava theologians, an image of Vishnu is a form in which he becomes embodied as an act of free grace, so that the devotee can see and serve him.

A temple may have a timetable of formal *pujas* conducted by a priest, but worshippers also come and go at other times, making private offerings with their own silent or muttered prayers. A typical posture of worship is to bow with the hands together and the fingers pointing upward, in the gesture called *anjali*. This gesture is also used in greeting people, implying deference (Fuller 1992: 3–4). Another gesture which may be made either to deities or to highly respected people (such as religious leaders, teachers or parents) is to touch their feet and then touch one's own forehead, or even to place one's head at their feet. This is a more profound form of self-abasement than bowing. Hindus are careful to guard their heads from pollution, while the feet are the part that is in constant danger of pollution from the ground. To take the dust from someone's feet and place it on your head is a way of saying that they are so far above you that your head is beneath their feet, and what is impure to them is pure to you. The feet are also a place of refuge, since someone seeking a king's or a deity's protection comes to his or her feet.

The same principle, which anthropologists sometimes call 'respect pollution', is followed when food that has been offered to a deity is distributed to worshippers, either at a temple or at a home shrine. Left-over food is normally avoided, as it has been polluted by contact with the eater. But food that has been offered to a deity, so that he or she has, ritually speaking, touched and partly eaten it, is not polluted but charged with the deity's power. Such food, when given to the worshippers after *puja*, is called *prasada*, which means 'grace'; the same word refers to the favour by which a deity uses his or her power to save a worshipper from evil. Here, too, behaviour towards respected persons is similar to behaviour towards a deity: one may receive the left-over food of one's father, or of a religious leader, as a mark of self-abasement and as a vehicle of power (Fuller 1992: 77–9). Similarly, members of the Lingayat sect ritually sip water which has symbolically washed the feet of the sect's leaders (Schouten 1991: 6).

There is thus no clear dividing line between deities and people; they are all part of the hierarchy of beings from Brahma to grass (p. 35). Not only can Hindus show respect to people in the same ways as they do to deities; they can also show disrespect to deities in the same way as to people. An anthropologist has given an example from his observation of a village in Karnataka. During a drought, the village elders wanted to know whether it would rain, so they tried a form of divination in which wet flowers are stuck on an image, after which the people ask the deity a question and watch to see if a flower falls. If it falls from the right side, it is a favourable answer; if it falls from the left it is unfavourable. In this case the deity was Basava or Nandi, the bull who is a servant of Shiva. Basava refused to answer: no flower fell. One of the elders said to him: 'Do you wish to retain your reputation or not? . . . Are you a lump of stone or a deity? . . . We will say that there is no god in the temple and that you have left the village.' Another hinted that they did not care because they could rely on the irrigation canal. The anthropologist, who was a brahmin, was allowed to sit in the shrine while the elders watched outside. He describes the atmosphere as 'not that of a group of men in awe of a great god but that of a number of reasonable men trying to coax a man lacking in good graces into right behaviour' (Srinivas 1976: 324–8).

Images are an important part of Hindu religious experience; they can be found in temples, in the open air, in homes and in places of work. To see the image, especially to receive the glance of the deity's eyes, is a form of contact with his or her grace and power (Eck 1985). As well as three-dimensional images of stone, metal, wood or plaster, *puja* may be done to brightly coloured printed pictures. Even electronic images can receive *puja*: when the divine heroes of the *Ramayana* and *Maha-Bharata* appeared on television, viewers placed garlands over their sets.

Images and pictures follow conventions of iconography which make them recognizable to the worshippers. But Hindus can also worship without any external image. They may have mental images of their favourite deities, formed through seeing actual images, and through reading and hearing descriptions in devotional poems. The sculptors and painters who make the images follow the iconographic descriptions in the *puranas* and in the rule-books of their art, which in turn are based on the mythology of the deity, so that visual, literary and mental images all reinforce each other. A particularly complex example is a Sanskrit devotional poem written around 1300 CE by a priest of the temple of the dancing Shiva in Chidambaram (p. 22). Each of its 313 verses refers to an aspect of Shiva's mythology, and to his foot upraised in the dance (Smith 1996); Shiva's raised foot is an invitation to the worshipper to seek refuge with him.

Texts themselves can make a deity present to the worshipper. A short text, usually in verse, which is used in this way or for other ritual purposes is called a *mantra*. Some mantras are Vedic verses in archaic Sanskrit which is difficult even for those who know the language; others are easily understood phrases in vernacular languages. The sacred syllable *om*, used in Vedic ritual and in highly structured meditation practices, is also used in popular forms of worship (Killingley 1986). The name or names of a deity may be recited: sometimes as a single name or a mantra containing one or more names, sometimes as a list of a thousand names (Lipner 1994: 293f.). Some simple Sanskrit mantras combine a name with the sacred syllable, such as *om shri-shivaya namah* 'prostration to glorious Shiva'; *om shri-ganeshaya namah* 'prostration to glorious Ganesha'.

Pilgrimage is an opportunity for closer contact with deities: seeing their most sacred images, visiting sites of their miraculous exploits or appearances, receiving *prasada* at great temples. The most famous of all pilgrimage centres is Varanasi, Benares or Kashi, on the Ganges (Eck 1983), but Hindus may prefer some other place because of their sectarian affiliation, or personal recommendation. However, many devotional poems remind us that God can be found without moving from home, in the worshipper's own heart. Ramprasad Sen, an eighteenth-century Bengali devotee of the goddess Kali, said:

> O my mind, why go to Kashi?
> Kali's feet are abundant salvation.
> Thirty-five million holy places rest on the Mother's feet.
> If you know your twilight prayers and follow the scriptures,
> Why go to live in Kashi?
> In the lotus of your heart, meditate on her, four-armed and loose-haired.
> Ramprasad, stay in this house,
> And you will find Kashi day and night.
>
> (Lupsa 1967: 108)

The feet of the goddess, mentioned in the second and third lines, are the place where the worshipper prostrates himself and seeks refuge. Her four arms are a common feature of the iconography of Hindu deities, indicating superhuman power, and her loose hair is a mark of wildness.

5.2 The divine feminine

Ramprasad's poem is addressed to Kali, the Mother, whose worship is particularly popular in Bengal. The nineteenth-century Bengali writer Bankim Chandra Chatterji composed a Sanskrit poem which made her into a personification of Bengal; during the partition agitation of 1905 (pp. 28f.), Aurobindo Ghose and others used this poem as a revolutionary mantra, and it was later adapted so that India rather than Bengal was the Mother. As a further stage in the politicization of the goddess, a temple of Bharat Mata, 'Mother India', has been built in Varanasi, with a map of India instead of the usual image.

Kali is one of many goddesses who are called 'Mother', and who are sometimes treated as aspects of one divine mother. She is wild and violent, and demands blood sacrifices – features which were exploited when she was used as a symbol of revolution. But she is also a nourishing mother. Such violent mother goddesses are found in many parts of India. They inflict diseases, particularly smallpox, chicken-pox and cholera, and those suffering from such diseases are thought to be possessed by the goddess. They also ensure the fertility of the land – or, in fishing villages, of the sea (Tanaka 1991: 102); and they are prayed to by childless women to ensure the birth of sons.

In mythology, goddesses are sometimes wild and destructive, but at other times are the submissive wives of male deities. The divine feminine has two aspects: the wild, demon-slaying virgin goddess, and the goddess as wife of a god (Fuller 1992: 44–8). It seems that the wild goddess of popular religion has been partially tamed in the Sanskrit tradition, and this dual aspect of the divine feminine reflects male attitudes towards women in Hindu society (Gatwood 1985). It is perhaps because of her ambivalence that the goddess has become particularly linked with Shiva, who appears in the Veda as a bringer of disease to people and cattle, but is invoked to avert disease and to cure it.

5.3 Local deities and pan-Hindu deities

The Veda says that there are thirty-three gods, and sometimes gives variations on this figure, such as Yajnavalkya's 'three hundred and three and three thousand and three' (p. 48). In later times it has often been said that there are three hundred and thirty million. This is obviously not meant to be a precise figure, but it is not an unreasonable estimate. There are hundreds of thousands of villages in South Asia, each with one or more deities. Besides these, there are sacred trees and rocks inhabited by deities, of which one village may have dozens. Each piece of land has its guardian deity who should be propitiated before cultivating the land or building on it; otherwise the work may end in disaster. And we still have not counted the deities who may exist outside South Asia, or outside our world.

Two gods in particular are exalted in mythology and worshipped in great temples: Shiva and Vishnu. For many Hindus, either Vishnu or Shiva is more than a god: one or other of them is God, the ultimate cause of the world. Those who worship Shiva as God are called Shaivas. Those who worship Vishnu, or Krishna or Rama who are commonly regarded as forms of Vishnu, are called Vaishnavas. The other gods, including Shiva for Vaishnavas, or Vishnu for Shaivas, are subordinate to God; or, following Yajnavalkya's view, they are all really one God. However, Vaishnavas and Shaivas may worship other gods on their festivals, or on particular occasions. Thus Lakshmi, goddess of wealth, is worshipped by business people at critical times, or when new account books are begun; Sarasvati, goddess of learning and the arts, by students before examinations; and Ganesha, the lord of obstacles, before any enterprise or at the beginning of many rituals, to remove obstacles and ensure success.

Shiva's mythology shows him as both protective and destructive, sexually active and ascetic. Vishnu is guardian of order, associated with kingship and Vedic ritual. These pan-Hindu gods are not necessarily the ones that every Hindu worships (Fuller 1992: 55). But numerous local gods are identified with one or other of them, without losing their individuality or local associations; goddesses are similarly identified as wives of pan-Hindu gods, usually of Shiva. The pan-Hindu goddess of wealth, Lakshmi, is the wife of Vishnu, while Shiva is the husband of Kali and many other goddesses – or rather, many other names and forms of the one goddess. Sarasvati is the wife of Brahma, the ancestor of the gods. While she is frequently worshipped, Brahma is little worshipped today, though he was in the period of the north Indian empires (Bailey 1983: 21–36).

Some other gods are kin to the two great gods. Ganesha, recognizable by his elephant's head, is the son of Shiva; so also is Skanda, Subrahmanya or Murugan, who is mainly known in Tamil

Nadu. The goddess is Vishnu's sister, while Aiyappan, worshipped in Kerala and Tamil Nadu, is the son of Shiva and Mohini, a female form which Vishnu took in order to deceive the demons (Fuller 1992: 214).

5.4 Avataras and saints

The boundary between deities and people is crossed by historical figures who come to be worshipped. Some of these are devotional poets such as the sixteenth to seventeenth-century Rajput princess Mirabai; others are teachers, such as Swaminarayan (pp. 27f.), or Chaitanya, the founder of Bengal Vaishnavism. Some are living persons, such as Sathya Sai Baba (p. 33) or the healer known as Mataji ('Mother') (Fuller 1992: 91, 177–81). Besides these people who are permanently identified with God or a particular deity, there are countless men and women who are temporarily possessed by deities, trembling and speaking in altered voices (Gold 1989; Pocock 1973; Tanaka 1991). And in a wedding, the bride and groom are treated as a god and goddess (Fuller 1992: 32f.).

Vishnu is especially associated with the concept of *avatara*. An *avatara* is a form, animal or more usually human, in which Vishnu is born in order to rescue the world from some crisis. The two best-known *avataras* are Rama and Krishna, both of whom are widely worshipped. In the Bengal Vaishnava tradition, Krishna is not an *avatara*; he himself is God, and Vishnu is one of his forms. Rama and Krishna are both remembered as kings: Rama long ago in the second age of the world, and Krishna at the beginning of the present age. But Krishna is best remembered for his playful exploits as a child brought up among cowherds, when he charmed the cowherd women with his childish pranks, and later lured them from their husbands with the music of his flute. Play (*lila*) is part of the Hindu notion of divinity: since God has no needs to fulfil, all his activity, including the creation of the world, can only be understood as play. This does not mean that God is irresponsible or amoral; Krishna's play, though sometimes capricious, is never malicious (Lipner 1994: 254–6).

5.5 Theology

Ideas of God and the gods are expressed in many forms, including allusions and riddles in the Vedas, complex devotional poetry, simple chants, and elaborate theological arguments. When Yajnavalkya said there was one god, he identified him as *Brahman*, which is not a personal name like Vishnu or Shiva. Other passages in the Upanishads identify Brahman with the universe, and with the self (*atman*) hidden in each person's heart. What Brahman means is the central question of the tradition of theology known as *Vedanta* (literally the 'end of the Veda' – that is, its ultimate purpose), whose key text is the *Vedanta-sutra* (p. 19). The *Vedanta-sutra* is so brief that it makes little sense without a commentary, and different commentators find very different meanings in it. The aim of Vedanta, as of all Hindu systems, is to show the way to salvation, freedom from karma.

The most influential commentator was Shankara (pp. 35f.), from Kerala in the far south-west, around the seventh century. Using the contrast between the one and the many which is found in the *Upanishads*, Shankara built a radical theology in which all multiplicity and individuality belong to the world of impermanence, and the true nature of Brahman is inexpressible (Mayeda 1992; Lott 1980). His theology is called *Advaita* (non-dualist) *Vedanta*, because it insists that Brahman is 'one only without a second' (*Chandogya Upanishad* 6.2.1). Shankara insists that salvation cannot be achieved by anything we do, which would only mean more karma, but only by knowledge. He sees a fundamental opposition between knowledge and action; the highest knowledge is knowledge of Brahman, which is identical with the self.

Ramanuja, a Tamil brahmin of the eleventh century, provided Vaishnava bhakti with a closely argued theology, a form of Vedanta which replaces Shankara's idea of an inexpressible ultimate with loving descriptions of the god Vishnu (Lott 1980; Lipner 1986; Carman 1974). Ramanuja holds that God, the world and our own selves are one, but only in the sense in which one's self and one's body are one: neither can exist without the other. True knowledge involves the recognition that we, like everything in the world, are part of God's body, and therefore have no other purpose than to serve him. Ramanuja's Vedanta is called *Vishishtadvaita*, 'non-dualism with distinctions', because it recognizes eternal distinctions between God, the world and our selves. Other schools of Vedanta followed, supporting particular Vaishnava or Shaiva sects. The school developed by Bengali Vaishnavism, and propagated by ISKCON, argues that the relationship between God, the world and ourselves is beyond the reach of thought. But the influence of these Vedanta theologies is mainly confined to their own sects and regions, while Advaita is known throughout the subcontinent.

5.6 Hindu worship and theology in the modern world

Hindu theology took a new direction in the nineteenth century. While debates in Sanskrit continued, the most influential arguments were conducted in English, against non-Hindus, rather than against other Hindus or Buddhists. The presuppositions of traditional debate gave way to those of contemporary Western thought. Thus Rammohun Roy used the Upanishads and Shankara's commentaries as his authority against current Hindu polytheism, image-worship and rituals, but his interpretation was coloured by Western ideas of God as the designer and governor of the world (Killingley 1993). Among the English-educated urban class, his ideas formed the foundation of a consensus on religious matters. However, his reliance on Shankara was ignored, since this class generally accepted the view of Christian critics that Advaita Vedanta saw the world as illusory and left no place for moral effort.

In the late nineteenth century, Advaita Vedanta became the basis of a new consensus. Vivekananda answered its critics by asserting that it supported social ethics and individual freedom, and was corroborated by science, particularly the theory of evolution. Later, Radhakrishnan's interpretation was influenced by liberal humanism, defining *moksha* (salvation), for instance, as 'the realisation of the purpose of each individual' (Radhakrishnan 1960: 46). He presented Hinduism as a uniquely tolerant religion which recognized all beliefs and forms of worship, both Hindu and non-Hindu, as approximations to the truth. Deities, myths, images and sacred places were for those unable to contemplate Brahman, which is beyond the limits of personality and can be known not from texts and doctrines but through philosophical reflection and mystical experience.

Radhakrishnan's view of true Hinduism suited the Westward-looking elite of mid-twentieth-century India, with their secularist politics. Today, it is harder to overlook those Hindus for whom images and sacred places are essential. Traditional practices are encouraged by militant Hinduism, and are facilitated and transformed by technology. Temples display neon signs, mantras are recited on audiotape (Bühnemann 1988: 96), and videos take the place of oral storytelling at women's fasts (Jackson and Nesbitt 1993: 70–3). The power of modern communications was demonstrated in 1995, when images of Ganesha and other deities were widely reported to have consumed offerings of milk. The news spread instantly, and the miracle was replicated in temples around the world.

International migration has affected the sacred geography of Hinduism in two ways. It has enlarged the catchment areas of traditional holy places, so that people come from all over the world to Varanasi, for instance, to bathe or to immerse the ashes of their dead. But Hindus have also established holy places in the countries where they have settled. Besides temples, whose location usually depends on the property market and the planning system, there are private houses and public places where miracles have occurred or which holy people have visited. Just as rivers in South Asia are identified with the Ganges, rivers elsewhere can be considered holy so that the ashes of the dead can be placed in them. Pramukh Swami, the head of the most internationally active branch of the Swaminarayan sect, sanctified the Beaulieu River in Hampshire for this purpose (Firth 1997: 91f.). Hinduism is constantly changing.

BIBLIOGRAPHY

Translations from Sanskrit are my own, but published translations are listed here to enable readers to read further.

Ayrookuzhiel, A. M. Abraham (1983) *The Sacred in Popular Hinduism*. Madras: Christian Literature Society.

Babb, Lawrence A. (1975) *The Divine Hierarchy: Popular Hinduism in Central India*. New York: Columbia University Press.

Bailey, Greg (1983) *The Mythology of Brahmā*. Delhi: Oxford University Press.

Ballard, Roger (ed.) (1994) *Desh Pardesh: The South Asian Presence in Britain*. London: Hurst.

Basham, Arthur Llewellyn (1954) *The Wonder that was India*. London: Sidgwick & Jackson.

Bayly, Susan (1999) *Caste, Society and Politics in India from the Eighteenth Century to the Modern Age*, New Cambridge History of India, IV, 3. Cambridge: Cambridge University Press.

Bhagavad-Gita. See Johnson 1994.

Bhandarkar, R. G. (1928) 'A note on the age of marriage and its consummation according to Hindu religious law' (first published 1891), in *The Collected Works of Sir R. G. Bhandarkar*, ed. N. B. Utgikar, vol. II. Poona: Bhandarkar Oriental Research Institute, pp. 538–83.

Biardeau, Madeleine (1989) *Hinduism: The Anthropology of a Civilization*. Delhi: Oxford University Press. (First published in French as *L'Hindouisme: Anthropologie d'une civilization*. Paris: Flammarion, 1981.)

Bühnemann, Gudrun (1988) *Pūjā: A Study in Smārta Ritual*. Vienna: Gerold & Co.

Burghart, Richard (ed.) (1987) *Hinduism in Great Britain: The Perpetuation of Religion in an Alien Cultural Milieu*. London: Tavistock.

Carey, Sean (1987) 'The Indianization of the Hare Krishna Movement in Britain', in Burghart 1987, pp. 81–99.

Carman, John B. (1974) *The Theology of Rāmānuja: An Essay in Interreligious Understanding*. New Haven: Yale University Press.

Chatterjee, Margaret (1983) *Gandhi's Religious Thought*. London: Macmillan.

Chaudhuri, Nirad C. (1979) *Hinduism: A Religion to Live By*. London: Chatto & Windus.

Daner, Francine Jeanne (1976) *The American Children of Krsna*. New York: Holt, Rinehart & Winston.

de Bary, William Theodore (ed.) (1958) *Sources of Indian Tradition*. New York: Columbia University Press.

Denton, Lynn Teskey (1991) 'Varieties of Hindu female asceticism', in Leslie 1991, pp. 211–31.

Doniger, Wendy, and Brian K. Smith (1991) *The Laws of Manu*. Harmondsworth: Penguin (cited as *Manu*).

Duff, Alexander (1839) *India and Indian Missions*. Edinburgh: J. Johnstone.

Dushkin, Lelah (1972) 'Scheduled caste politics', in Michael Mahar (ed.), *The Untouchables in Contemporary India*. Tucson: University of Arizona Press, pp. 165–226.

Dwyer, Rachel (1994) 'Caste, religion and sect in Gujarat: followers of Vallabhacharya and Swaminarayan', in Ballard 1994, pp. 165–90.

Eck, Diana (1983) *Banaras: City of Light*. London: Routledge & Kegan Paul.

Eck, Diana (1985) *Darsan: Seeing the Divine Image in India*, second edn. Chambersburg, PA: Anima.

Firth, Shirley (1997) *Dying, Death and Bereavement in a British Hindu Community*. Leuven: Peeters.

Fuller, C. J. (1984) *Servants of the Goddess: The Priests of a South Indian Temple*. Cambridge: Cambridge University Press.

Fuller, C. J. (1992) *The Camphor Flame: Popular Hinduism and Society in India*. Princeton: Princeton University Press.

Gatwood, Lynn E. (1985) *Devi and the Spouse Goddess: Women, Sexuality and Marriage in India*. Delhi: Manohar.

Gold, Ann Grodzins (1989) *Fruitful Journeys: The Ways of Rajasthani Pilgrims*. Delhi: Oxford University Press.

Halbfass, Wilhelm (1988) *India and Europe: An Essay in Understanding*. Albany: State University of New York Press.

Jackson, Robert, and Dermot Killingley (1988) *Approaches to Hinduism*, World Religions in Education. London: John Murray.

Jackson, Robert, and Eleanor Nesbitt (1993) *Hindu Children in Britain*. Stoke-on-Trent: Trentham Books.

Johnson, W. J. (1994) *The Bhagavad Gita*, World's Classics. Oxford: Oxford University Press.

Jordens, J. T. F. (1978) *Dayananda Sarasvati: His Life and Ideas*. Delhi: Oxford University Press.

Kent, Roland G. (1953) *Old Persian: Grammar Texts Lexicon*. New Haven: American Oriental Society.

Keyes, Charles F., and E. Valentine Daniel (eds) (1983) *Karma: An Anthropological Inquiry*. Berkeley: University of California Press.

Killingley, Dermot (1986) 'Om: the sacred syllable in the Veda', in Julius Lipner (ed.), *A Net Cast Wide: Investigations into Indian Thought in Memory of David Friedman*. Newcastle upon Tyne: Grevatt & Grevatt, pp. 14–33.

Killingley, Dermot (1991) 'Varna and caste in Hindu apologetic', in Dermot Killingley, Werner Menski and Shirley Firth, *Hindu Ritual and Society*. Newcastle upon Tyne: S. Y. Killingley.

Killingley, Dermot (1993) *Rammohun Roy in Hindu and Christian Tradition*. Newcastle upon Tyne: Grevatt & Grevatt.

Killingley, Dermot (1997) 'The paths of the dead and the five fires', in Peter Connolly and Sue Hamilton (eds), *Indian Insights: Buddhism, Brahmanism and Bhakti*. London: Luzac Oriental.

King, Ursula (1978) 'True and perfect religion', *Religion* 7: 127–48.

Knott, Kim (1986a) *Hinduism in Leeds*. Leeds: Department of Theology and Religious Studies, University of Leeds.

Knott, Kim (1986b) *My Sweet Lord: The Hare Krishna Movement*. Wellingborough: Aquarian Press.

Knott, Kim (1998) *Hinduism: A Very Short Introduction*. Oxford: Oxford University Press.

Kopf, David (1979) *The Brahmo Samaj and the Shaping of the Modern Indian Mind*. Princeton: Princeton University Press.

Kulke, Hermann, and Dietmar Rothermund (1998) *A History of India*, third edn. London: Routledge.

Larson, Gerald James (1995) *India's Agony over Religion*. Albany: State University of New York Press.

Leslie, Julia (1989) *The Perfect Wife: The Orthodox Hindu Woman According to the Stridharmapaddhati of Tryambakayajvan*. Delhi: Oxford University Press.

Leslie, Julia (ed.) (1991) *Roles and Rituals for Hindu Women*. London: Pinter.

Leslie, Julia (1991) 'Suttee or sati: victim or victor?', in Leslie 1991, pp. 175–91.

Leslie, Julia (1999) 'The implications of the physical body: health, suffering and *karma* in Hindu thought', in John R. Hinnells and Roy Porter (eds), *Religion, Health and Suffering*. London: Kegan Paul International, pp. 23–45.

Ling, Trevor O. (1973) *The Buddha: Buddhist Civilization in India and Ceylon*. London: Temple Smith.

Lipner, Julius (1986) *The Face of Truth: A Study of Meaning and Metaphysics in the Vedantic Theology of Ramanuja*. London: Macmillan.

Lipner, Julius (1994) *Hindus: Their Religious Beliefs and Practices*. London: Routledge.

Lott, Eric (1980) *Vedantic Approaches to God*. London: Macmillan.

Lupsa, M. (1967) *Chants à Kālī*. Pondicherry: Institut français d'indologie.

McDonald, Merryle (1987) 'Rituals of motherhood among Gujarati women in London', in Burghart 1987, pp. 50–66.

Mahadevan, T. M. P. (1956) *Outlines of Hinduism*. Bombay: Chetana.

Manu. See Doniger and Smith.

Marshall, Peter J. (ed.) (1970) *The British Discovery of Hinduism in the Eighteenth Century*. Cambridge: Cambridge University Press.

Mayeda, Sengaku (1992) *A Thousand Teachings: The Upadesasahasri of Sakara*. Albany: State University of New York Press. (First published Tokyo: University of Tokyo Press, 1979.)

Mukherjee, S. N. (1968) *Sir William Jones: A Study in Eighteenth-Century British Attitudes to India*. Cambridge: Cambridge University Press.

Nilakantha Sastri, K. A. A. (1966) *A History of South India from Prehistoric Times to the Fall of Vijayanagar*. Madras: Oxford University Press.

Nye, Mallory (1995) *A Place for Our Gods: The Construction of an Edinburgh Hindu Temple Community*. London: Curzon.

O'Connell, Joseph T. (1973) 'The word "Hindu" in Gauya Vaisnava texts', *Journal of the American Oriental Society* 93.

O'Flaherty, Wendy Doniger (1988) *Textual Sources for the Study of Hinduism*. Manchester: Manchester University Press.

O'Hanlon, Rosalind (1985) *Caste, Conflict and Ideology: Mahatma Jotirao Phule and Low-caste Protest in Nineteenth-Century Western India*. Cambridge: Cambridge University Press.

Olivelle, Patrick (1996) *Upanisads*, World's Classics. Oxford: Oxford University Press.

Parekh, Bhikhu (1997) *Gandhi*, Past Masters. Oxford: Oxford University Press.

Peterson, Indira Viswanathan (1989) *Poems to Siva: The Hymns of the Tamil Saints*. Princeton: Princeton University Press.

Pocock, David (1973) *Mind, Body and Wealth: A Study of Belief and Practice in an Indian Village*. Oxford: Blackwell.

Quigley, Declan (1993) *The Interpretation of Caste*. Oxford: Clarendon Press.

Radhakrishnan, S. (1960) *The Hindu View of Life*. London: Allen & Unwin. (First published 1927.)

Ramanujan, A. K. (1973) *Speaking of Siva*. Harmondsworth: Penguin.

Ramanujan, A. K. (1981) *Hymns for the Drowning: Poems for Visnu by Nammaḷvar*. Princeton: Princeton University Press.

Renfrew, Colin (1987) *Archaeology and Language: The Puzzle of Indo-European Origins*. London: Pimlico.

Roy, Rammohun (1906) *The English Works of Raja Rammohun Roy with an English Translation of 'Tuhfatul Muwahhidin'*, ed. Jogendra Chunder Ghose and Eshan Chunder Bose. Allahabad: Panini Office. (Reprinted New York: AMS Press, 1978.)

Sachau, E. C. (1888) *Alberuni's India: An Account of the Religious Philosophy, Literature, Geography, Chronology, Astronomy, Customs, Laws and Astrology of India about AD 1030*, 2 vols. London: Trübner.

Schouten, J. P. (1991) *Revolution of the Mystics: On the Social Aspects of Virasaivism*. Kampen, Netherlands: Kok Pharos.

Schwartzberg, Joseph E. (ed.) (1978) *A Historical Atlas of South Asia*. Chicago: University of Chicago Press.

Shankara. See Mayeda 1992; Thibaut 1904.

Sharma, Ursula (1978) 'Theodicy and the doctrine of karma', in Whitfield Foy (ed.), *Man's Religious Quest: A Reader*. London: Croom Helm, pp. 22–45. (Reprinted from *Man* 8(3) (1973).)

Sharma, Ursula (1981) 'Male bias in anthropology', *South Asia Research* 1(2): 34–8.

Sharpe, Eric J. (1985) *The Universal Gita: Western Images of the Bhagavadgita*. London: Duckworth.

Smith, Brian K. (1998) 'Questioning authority: constructions and deconstructions of Hinduism', *International Journal of Hindu Studies* 2: 313–39.

Smith, David (1996) *The Dance of Siva: Religion, Art and Poetry in South India*. Cambridge: Cambridge University Press.

Smith, Wilfred Cantwell (1978) *The Meaning and End of Religion*. London: SPCK.

Sontheimer, Günther D., and Hermann Kulke (eds) (1991) *Hinduism Reconsidered*. Delhi: Manohar.

Srinivas, M. N. (1962) *Caste in Modern India and Other Essays*. Bombay: Asia Publishing House.

Srinivas, M. N. (1976) *The Remembered Village*. Berkeley: University of California Press.

Srinivasan, Doris (1984) 'Unhinging Siva from the Indus civilization', *Journal of the Royal Asiatic Society* 1: 77–89.

Staal, Frits (1983) *Agni: The Vedic Ritual of the Fire Altar*, 2 vols. Berkeley: Asian Humanities Press.

Sweetman, Will (2001) 'Unity and plurality: Hinduism and the religions of India in European scholarship', *Religion* 31: 209–24.

Tanaka, Masakazu (1991) *Patrons, Devotees and Goddesses: Ritual and Power among the Tamil Fishermen of Sri Lanka*. Kyoto: Kyoto University Institute for Research in Humanities.

Thibaut, George (1904) *The Vedânta-Sûtras: With the Commentary by Sankarâkârya*, 2 vols, Sacred Books of the East. Oxford: Oxford University Press.

Tull, Herman W. (1989) *The Vedic Origins of Karma: Cosmos as Man in Ancient Indian Myth and Ritual*. Albany: State University of New York Press.

Upanishads. See Olivelle.

Vertovec, Steven (1994) 'Caught in an ethnic quandary: Indo-Caribbean Hindus in London', in Ballard 1994, pp. 272–90.

Vishnu Purana. See Wilson.

von Stietencron, Heinrich (1991) 'Hinduism: on the proper use of a deceptive term', in Sontheimer and Kulke 1991, pp. 11–28.

Wagle, Narendra K. (1991) 'Hindu–Muslim interactions in medieval Maharashtra', in Sontheimer and Kulke 1991, pp. 51–66.

Williams, Raymond Brady (1984) *A New Face of Hinduism: The Swaminarayan Religion*. Cambridge: Cambridge University Press.

Williams, Raymond Brady (1988) *Religions of Immigrants from India and Pakistan: New Threads in the American Tapestry*. Cambridge: Cambridge University Press.

Wilson, Horace Hayman (1961) *The Vishnu Purána: A System of Hindu Mythology and Tradition*. Calcutta: Punthi Pustak. (First published London, 1840.)

Young, Richard Fox (1981) *Resistant Hinduism: Sanskrit Sources on Anti-Christian Apologetics in Early Nineteenth-Century India*. Vienna: Gerold & Co.

Zaehner, Robert Charles (1966) *Hinduism*. Oxford: Oxford University Press.

Zelliot, Eleanor (1996) *From Untouchable to Dalit: Essays on the Ambedkar Movement*. Delhi: Manohar.

Buddhism

Kiyoshi Tsuchiya

1 TRANSCENDENTALISM

An entry of Buddhism into an anthology like this brings us back to the age-old question, 'What is religion?' Buddhism is one of the major world religions, comparable only to Christianity and Islam for its geographical expansion and historical continuity. It has seen over two thousand years of practice and has expanded from its birthplace in North India to Sri Lanka and then to Southeast Asia, to China via Central Asia and then to Korea and to Japan, to Tibet, and recently to the European West. Yet unlike Christianity and Islam, Buddhism is not monotheistic or even theistic; unlike them, since its inception out of the indigenous practices in India in the fifth century BCE it has been exhibiting its affinity with other indigenous religions such as Taoism in China, Shintoism in Japan, and Bon in Tibet. Therefore its inclusion inevitably implies the suspension of a (mono)theistic understanding of religion. At this point, what we make of 'Buddhism' is determined by what we mean by 'religion'. There has been an attempt to re-enforce the theism/atheism distinction and disregard Buddhism as a Godless non-religion. Few take this as an academically viable approach, yet fewer offer an alternative definition of religion that places Buddhism along with other religions. The problem is that a hasty answer to the question what religion is, is bound to be an inaccurate generalization. Ninian Smart suggests that we should describe religion in terms of its 'seven dimensions'. This famous approach enables us to examine a religious tradition on each dimension and describe it, rather than define it as what it is (Smart 1973). This descriptive approach allows us to discuss a religious tradition without facing the essential question. Yet even by this approach the problem concerning the definition is not entirely put away, for it still has to resort to the socio-historical definition of Buddhism, that might well be as arbitrary as the essentialist one. In my view the descriptive approach only suspends the question what religion is but does not invalidate it. Even if the essentialist approach were bound to involve a typical generalization, it at least reminds us of the question within the essence of religion and incites criticisms and further revisions. It can be a process comparable to that of a religious practice.

In this chapter I would like to define Buddhism as a form of transcendentalism, as an aspiration to reach beyond the ego accompanied by the body of practice that works towards realizing it. This definition in return allows us to speculate further as to whether monotheism is a 'particular' type of transcendentalism supported by a 'particular' understanding of the ego, whether the ritual element of religion is the prototype of transcendentalism prior to the discovery of the ego, and so on. Moreover, this definition of religion as the discovery of the ego and the aspiration of transcendence is in line with how Buddhism came into being. The Buddha was 'One Who Strives' (p. *samana*; s. *sramana*),[1] one of the wandering sages who marked the radical shift from ritual to philosophy in the history of Indian religions. Vedic ritualism reached its peak when brahmins assumed their complete control over the cosmos. At its peak, however, the ritualist stepped onto a new religious field, the 'inner' cosmos of the ego. His attention that had been directed towards the divine reached beyond it and reflected back upon himself. He thus reflects upon himself and discovers his 'self' as a new problem. This discovery marked the beginning of the philosophical period in India. From within Brahmanism a new interpretative approach to the Vedas evolved and led to the production of the Upanishads that included the famous formulation, *brahma-atma-aikya* (the identity of the cosmic principle and the individual principle). There were also those who broke away from Brahmanism. The *sramanas* such as the Buddha or Mahavira, the founder of Jainism, dropped ritual altogether and focused exclusively on this newly discovered inner 'self'. The ego is a problem to itself. It is always aware of its partiality and always assumes the whole beyond itself. Its inception and the assumption of the beyond are simultaneous. It is inherently paradoxical, and when it aspires to reach beyond itself it becomes transcendental. Buddhism can be described as a religious tradition that has been aspiring to overcome this problem and generated forms of practice for this purpose.

Obviously, this description applies not only to Buddhism but to many other religious traditions. The point is that Buddhists never claimed that transcendentalism is exclusively theirs. What is characteristic of the Buddhist tradition is that it does not specify 'what' makes transcendence possible and necessary. A monotheistic religion tends to establish itself on a clear definition of this 'what', often in terms of race, person, party, book, or a combination of them. When these definientia are upheld as unique and irreplaceable, and as foundational to the participants' practice, the 'practice' often involves jealously guarding these definitions against possible revisions. In contrast, Buddhism seems not only not to see any essential significance in these definitions but also to show an inherent resistance to them. What characterizes Buddhism is therefore not these central definitions but the ways in which these definitions have failed to establish 'Buddhist' orthodoxy or orthopraxis.

Buddhism has collected three major canons, the Pali, the Chinese and the Tibetan, with the result of encapsulating three distinct phases of its doctrinal and geographical expansion. The prototype of the Buddhist canon was laid at the first general council held immediately after the Buddha's death, where five hundred disciples collected 'the Buddha's sayings' as they remembered them. It was an oral collection, 'a communal recitation'. The period of the oral transmission is thought to have lasted at least for a few hundred years. Already in this period 'the original canon' included layers of explanations and interpretations. Even at this early stage, there seem to have been different schools of 'reciters' and

1 For Buddhist terms, p. signifies Pali words, and s. signifies Sanskrit words.

a diversity of teaching.[2] The Buddha's teaching was probably more of a pragmatic guidance than a systematic doctrine, more diverse than constant. Hence these reciters must have taken the liberty of furnishing what they thought was missing or necessary. The Pali canon, considered to have originated in the oral tradition and to be the closest to the original teaching, contains three parts called 'basket' (*pitaka*): the *Sutta-pitaka* (General Discourse), the *Vinaya-pitaka* (Moral Discipline) and the *Abhidharma-pitaka* (Interpretation). What is recorded here is thought to be the basis of the following Buddhist tradition. The Chinese and Tibetan canons include a large portion of the same content as this canon. The Pali canon is closed to Mahayana texts, indicating that it was either pre-Mahayana or, more likely, anti-Mahayana. From the first century CE Mahayanists started to produce their Sanskrit texts. They were apparently written down from the beginning, having little to do with the original oral transmission. While these Mahayana texts were ascribed to the Buddha, their content was the restatement and interpretation of the Buddha's teachings. These writings and Mahayana teachings were preserved in the Chinese canon that was the result of a strenuous effort by Chinese translators from the second to the tenth century who translated both pre-Mahayana and Mahayana texts. The Chinese added their own materials, and their canon soon grew to include thousands of volumes. The project of the Tibetan translation began in the seventh century. This canon included some Tantric texts unknown to the Chinese, reflecting the rise of Tantric Buddhism at the time of the translation. Throughout the production of these canons, the Buddhist attitude was extensive rather than selective. The inclusion of commentary and interpretation from the first canon onwards, and, in the case of Mahayana Buddhism, the inclusion of texts that were obviously pseudepigraphic, indicate that the compilers' interest in establishing their authority by 'canonizing' some texts against others was always countered by a stronger reform movement.

For the same reason, Buddhism has never been successful in establishing a central organization for controlling doctrinal and ecclesiastical matters. Some general councils were recorded in the early part of its history in order to establish the Buddha's genuine teaching. Yet, apart from the first one held immediately after the Buddha's death, these councils usually initiated new schisms and further decentralizations. Disagreement was primarily over the monastic code, but the doctrinal issues concerning their religious goal (p. *nibbana*; s. *nirvana*) also played a part. Schism must have posed a serious crisis, but on the whole Buddhists seem to have agreed to disagree in peace. There are records of serious debates and discussions, but none of heresy or persecution. With the rise and expansion of Mahayana Buddhism, the very notion of general councils and doctrinal unifications disappeared from the mind of most Buddhists.

Behind all these lies, it seems, the Buddhist acknowledgement that there are many 'Buddhas'. There were discussions by the early Buddhists as to when to expect the second Buddha, whether there were more than one Buddha in one world, and so on. These discussions show that the plural Buddha was a commonly held view among them. In their days the 'Buddha' was not a name but one of the general titles that was ascribed to those who were seen to have achieved their religious goals.[3] Religious leaders such as Gautama Siddhartha (in Sanskrit; p. Gotama Siddhattha) and Vardhamana, the founder of Jainism, were invariably called by titles such as 'Buddha'. It is in the later period that 'Buddha' became ascribed to Gautama Siddhartha alone, as well as 'Mahavira' (Great Hero) to Vardhamana

2 The *Maha-parinibbana sutta* includes a report of diverging interpretations and subsequent confusions. This passage, however, is likely to be a later insertion. *Maha-parinibbana sutta* IV. 5–12 (*Digha Nikaya* II.154).

3 The *Sutta-nipata* spares a section called 'Sabhiyasutta' to answer Sabhiya's questions to the Buddha what to do to reach one's religious goal. One of them is what is needed to be called 'a Buddha'. *Sutta-nipata* III.6.

alone.[4] Buddhism has always accepted that there are many Buddhas and various ways to enlightenment. That is, while acknowledging the central role played by the historical Buddha in the tradition, Buddhists maintain, at least in principle, that his role was accidental rather than essential.[5] Race and caste played little role in Buddhism even in civilizations where societies were structured on these distinctions.[6] Buddhism is built upon none of these foundational definitions. Consequently, Buddhist practice is not curtailed by the founder, or the canon, or the council. The effect of this is that the practice of transcendence is left open, or, left to each individual practitioner. This lack of central definition or this inherent resistance to it is in fact the root of Buddhist pragmatism.

1.1 Pragmatism

This lack of central definition is the result not of the failure to establish their tradition on a firm ground but of their persistent resistance against such an attempt. Buddhism is essentially pragmatic as to its teachings. Buddhist practice is oriented towards the experience of transcendence (to reach 'the other shore'), and their teachings are only an aid to it, some more effective than others. Dogmatization of a particular teaching would stop this doctrinal pragmatism. This pragmatism made the Buddhist teaching adaptable to various cultural and historical circumstances and contributed to the Buddhist expansion throughout Asia over a long period of time. It is important to note here that the purpose of pragmatism is transcendence. And in this sense alone transcendentalism and pragmatism are inseparable in the Buddhist practice. The well-known Parable of the Raft makes this clear.

> A man going along a high-road might see a great stretch of water, the hither bank dangerous and frightening, the farther bank secure, not frightening. But if there were no boat for crossing by or a bridge across for going from the not-beyond to the beyond, he might think: 'If I were to collect sticks, grass, branches, foliage and to tie a raft, then depending on the raft and striving with my hands and feet, I might cross over, gone beyond.' If he carried out his purpose, then, crossed over, gone beyond, it might occur to him: 'Now, this raft has been very useful to me. Depending on it and striving with my hands and feet, I have crossed over safely to the beyond. Suppose now, having put this raft on my head or lifted it on to my shoulder, I should proceed as I desire?' Now, monks, in doing this is that man doing what should be done with that raft?
>
> (*Majjihima Nikaya* I.134)

4 Gautama Siddhartha is said to have ten titles ascribed to him. They include 'Tathagata' (Thus Come), 'Arahat/Arhat' (Worthy of Respect), 'Buddha' and 'Bhagavad' (Blessed One), none of which were ascribed to him exclusively. He is also referred to as 'Sakya-muni' (Saint of the Sakya clan).

5 The *Dhammapada* mentions plural Buddhas (182ff. and 194). It is unclear here whether these 'Buddhas' are within the Buddhist tradition or without. It would be true to the spirit of early Buddhism to read it as both. The *Dhammapada* is probably the most famous and influential Pali text. The content is considered close to the original teaching of the Buddha, although the text itself might be from the later period. It presents the early Buddhist doctrine and practice in terse verses.

6 'One does not become a brahmin by his matted hair, by his clan, or by his birth; one who keeps truth and Dhamma is pure, is a brahmin.' *Dhammapada* 393. 'Do not ask his birth but ask his act.' *Sutta-nipata* 462. See also *Majjihima-nikaya* I.96 (*Sutta-nipata* 3.9).

A teaching is a way to cross a stream; it is 'for crossing over, not for retaining' (*Majjihima Nikaya* I.135). Therefore, the only valid question is the pragmatic one, that is, whether the raft is good enough to help the traveller to cross the stream. Dogmatism of any kind would intervene with this pragmatism and interrupt the crossing.

In its formative period Buddhism appears to have had a similar sentiment as the Sceptics. The Buddhist texts recorded 'six teachers of other schools', *sramanas* who, like the Buddha, renounced ordinary life and led a life of meditation and discussion outside the Vedic tradition. One of them was Sanjaya Belatthaputta, an agnostic who refrained himself from giving a decisive answer to any metaphysical question or even from pointing at other people's errors. He was the first man in the history of Indian philosophy to perform metaphysical *epoche* (Nakamura 1970: 23). Although the Buddha described his philosophy as 'eel-wiggling', this suspension of metaphysical judgement marks the starting point of the Buddha's teaching.[7] The famous parable of the elephant and the blind men is one of the earliest expositions of Buddhist agnosticism. It begins with a king gathering all the people in Savatthi (a town under his rule) who have been blind from birth and taking them to an elephant.

> To some of the blind people he showed the head of the elephant, saying, 'This, blind people, is what an elephant is like.' To some of them he showed an ear of the elephant, saying, 'This, blind people, is what an elephant is like.' To some of them he showed a tusk . . . the trunk . . . the body . . . a foot . . . the hindquarters . . . the tail . . . the tuft at the end of the tail, saying, 'This, blind people, is what an elephant is like.'

The parable thus emphasizes the paradoxical nature of blind men's 'partial' grasp of the 'whole' elephant. Asked by the king what the elephant is like, the blind men who had been shown the head of the elephant insisted that it is like a water jar, those who had seen the ear insisted that it is like a winnowing basket, and so on. The parable thus highlights their error of taking what they sensed in their limited perception for what the elephant is. The point is to depict the folly of endless dogmatic dispute that always follows that error. The last scene is this:

> Saying, 'The elephant is like this, it is not like that. The elephant's not like that, it is like this,' they struck one another with their fists.

> (*Udana* VI.4)

The parable allows two further readings beyond the futility of dogmatic dispute. The first one would be, 'Distrust these blind men and follow the one whose unimpaired vision gives you the right accounts of the elephant.' It would draw a contrast between the Enlightened One's full vision as against the blind men's limited vision of the elephant. It is assumed here that there is a 'right' vision against which the blind men's visions are 'wrong'. Buddhists, however, preferred to read this in a different way, as a warning against any form of dogmatism. The former reading is in fact a lead to another form of dogmatization. And, as seen above, there is no greater irony than for Buddhists to hold onto the teaching that teaches

---

7 See *Samannaphala Sutta* (*Digha Nikaya* I.47–86). Legend has it that two prime disciples of the Buddha were originally followers of Sanjaya Belatthaputta, and they came to the Buddha at his enlightenment, together with two hundred and fifty fellow practitioners who followed their move, leaving Sanjaya Belatthaputta to vomit blood. Nakamura reads this story as indicating that Buddhism begins with Sanjaya Belatthaputta's agnosticism yet attempts to move forward from that. Nakamura 1970: 23.

them to avoid such holding. Their reading would be, 'whatever description is partial, therefore never to be taken as the final definition'. According to this reading, no one is able to see the whole elephant. Hence the blind men are blind not because they fail to see the elephant as a whole but because they mistake their partial perception for the final truth. The blind men err not when they touch the elephant's head and fail to see the rest but when they declare that 'a water jar' is the only right description of the elephant.

There is another text that indicates that opposition to dogmatism is the central element of the Buddhist tradition. The *Sutta-nipata*, considered the oldest Buddhist text, includes a clear exposition, here in the form of an argument, of Buddhist anti-dogmatism.[8] It identifies 'desire', the dogmatic attachment to one's own particular view, as the cause of dispute. 'How can he, led by desire, caught in his likes, overcome his own view?' He cannot because 'he thinks himself to be perfect' (*Sutta-nipata* 781). As a result, he imposes his own view on others and falls into dogmatism. 'Abiding in their own views, quarrelling, scholars say: "Whoever knows this, understands the truth. Whoever rejects this, is imperfect"' (ibid. 878, 903–5). The text thus exposes the pointlessness and endlessness of their dispute in which each of these scholars invariably declares himself wise and others fools, unaware of the irony that what they say is no different (ibid. 879–81). To avoid this nonsense Buddhism maintains its pragmatism as to its teachings and insists that a teaching has only a limited applicability and that beyond that it would become not only nonsensical but also misleading.[9]

However, this is not to abandon the truth altogether. On the contrary, the same section of the *Sutta-nipata* states that 'the truth is one, there is not a second about which one wise man might dispute with another wise man' (*Sutta-nipata* 884). This is the point where Buddhism parts from simple scepticism. Clearly, this truth is not a certainty built upon dogmatic claims that the disputants tend to make. Rather, it is the wisdom to realize that all their teachings are merely relative. This realization itself is called 'the truth'. What is here emphasized is the shift of the contents of the concept 'truth' from being dogmatic to being pragmatic. Again, the Parable of the Raft maintains beyond any relativism that there is a stream and there is a way to cross it; that is, its pragmatic teaching has the clear purpose of reaching the beyond and is for this reason essentially transcendental.

Whether one acknowledges the stream and yearns to cross over to the other side is an open question. 'The beyond' remains undefined as much as the elephant as a whole is ever unknown to the blind men. 'The beyond' therefore may ultimately remain an assumption. Yet Buddhist pragmatism has no purpose or orientation other than reaching the beyond. It is 'the highest purpose' (p. *uttamattha*). So far as it is a religion, and so far as it is transcendental, Buddhism has to maintain this assumption. What is to be understood by 'the highest purpose' could vary considerably. In Mahayana Buddhism, it was nothing other than becoming a Buddha.[10] In Zen Buddhism we often encounter a blunt denial of the purpose. Even in this case Zen practitioners do not come to this denial through their doubt concerning transcendence. It is their extreme anti-dogmatism that pushes Buddhist pragmatism beyond its limit

---

8 It is the fifth part of the *Khuddaka-nikaya*, the fifth book of the Pali canon. The *Sutta-nipata*'s fourth and fifth chapters (Atthakavagga and Parayanavagga) may have antedated the rest of the text. It is in this fourth chapter that we find this argument.

9 Hence the Pure-Land Buddhists' exclusive devotion to Amitabha and the Nichiren school's exclusive reverence of the *Lotus Sutra* are exceptional. See below.

10 The non-Mahayanist goal was to become an 'arahat/arhat' (worthy of respect). 'Arahat' was one of the titles generally used for prominent practitioners. See note 4 above. Buddhists later introduced a distinction between 'Buddha' and 'Arahat', ascribing 'Buddha' to the historical Buddha alone and 'Arahat' to the rest of his disciples (*savaka/sravaka*). Mahayana Buddhism rejected this distinction and argued that every practitioner is potentially a 'Buddha'.

and leads them to an apparent disregard of transcendence. So far as their denial is accompanied by strenuous practice, their practice as a whole is an embodiment of the paradox inherent in transcendentalism rather than a denial of transcendentalism altogether.

2 THE FOUR NOBLE TRUTHS

Crossing a violent current to the far shore is a vivid symbolism that visualizes the practice of transcendence. Buddhism appears to have shared this symbolism with early Jainism (Nakamura 1970: 103). The Buddha is 'oghatinna', the one who has crossed over and gone to the far shore (*Sutta-nipata* 21: *Dhammapada* 370). Yet 'few are those who arrive at the other shore; many run up and down this shore' (*Dhammapada* 85). The current is the current of desire, 'the realm of death, difficult to cross' (ibid. 86). As a current, desire has no beginning or end. Those who are caught in it are always agitated by it, hence 'those who are caught in desires are run down in the current' (ibid. 346–7).[11] Therefore the fundamental question is 'How does one cross over the flood, cross the sea? How does one overcome suffering and become pure?' (*Sutta-nipata* 184). A religious practice is a way, or an exploration of a way, to liberation. 'He who has left behind desires of the world, overcome attachments difficult to overcome, does not drift, is not bound, does not grieve nor desire' (ibid. 948). This type of transcendentalism was widely practised in India. The current of desire was known as *samsara*, the endless chain of birth and rebirth; and liberation from *samsara* was called *moksha*, liberation.

Those who practised this were usually silent as to why they aspired to the other shore, why they aimed at transcending their desires. Desire being the source of 'three poisons' of greed, anger and ignorance is only a partial explanation, for desire here is not only a specific desire for something but primordial desire that lies behind it all. A short passage from the *Dhammapada* may shed some light on the reason for their aspiration. It mentions the 'difficulty' of being human, being mortal (*Sutta-nipata* 182). The cryptic passage does not explain why and how it is difficult. It simply points to a moment when some people realize that life drifting in the current of desire is 'difficult'. The point is that at this moment, they experience a complete overturn of pleasure and displeasure.

> Form, sound, taste, smell, and touch and ideas that are pleasing and charming so long as they last, by the world of men and gods they are deemed a pleasure; but when they cease it is deemed pain. By the noble men the cessation of the existing body is regarded as pleasure. What the world calls pleasure the noble men regard as pain; what the world calls pain, they regard as pleasure. This is the opposite of the view of the world. See how difficult it is to understand this truth.
>
> (ibid. 759–62)

They would not understand transcendentalism until they experience the 'difficulty'. However, when they experience it and feel pain and pleasure differently, they cannot but step into a path of religious practice.

The 'Four Noble Truths' is supposedly the first teaching by the Buddha on this issue. There is not enough evidence to decide whether they were truly the Buddha's first teaching or a systematization of his teaching from a later period. What is certain is that they marked the beginning of the Buddhist doctrinal tradition. The Four Noble Truths are: 'the truth of suffering, the truth of the origin of suffering, the truth of the termination of suffering, and the eight-fold way to the termination of suffering'. It

11 In 339 desire is called 'thirty-six torrents of pleasure'.

explains, (1) life is suffering; (2) suffering is caused by desire; (3) suffering can stop; (4) there is a path to the end of suffering. This progress resembles the medical practice of the day, first diagnose the disease, second find out its cause, third determine a cure, and fourth carry out the treatment.

It begins with a list of concrete examples of our unavoidable pain in life.

> This is the Noble Truth of Suffering: birth is suffering, ageing is suffering, illness is suffering, death is suffering; pain, grief, sorrow, lamentation, and despair are suffering; to be united with what one dislikes, to be separated from what one loves is suffering; not to get what one longs for is suffering; in short, the Five Groups of Grasping are suffering.
>
> (*Samyutta Nikaya* V.56)

Buddhism classifies suffering (p. *dukkha*; s. *duhkha*) into three groups. First, there is obvious pain. It includes all sorts of pain, both physical and mental. It is called 'suffering from pain'. Second, there is pain of loss. Pleasure is not long-lasting, and when taken away, it turns to pain. Therefore, pleasure is also pain. It is called 'suffering from impermanence'. Since nothing escapes impermanence, every experience of ours is suffering. This is no longer a mere description of experiential pain. It is rather a conclusion drawn from a philosophical analysis of our experience of pain. The last sentence of the quote provides us with a clue to the Buddhist speculation on the nature of suffering. 'The Five Groups of Grasping are suffering', it says. It is in fact a restatement of 'all is suffering'. The Five Groups of Grasping (p. *upadana-khandha*; s. *upadana-skandha*) are:

> The Group of Grasping 'body'
> The Group of Grasping 'sensation'
> The Group of Grasping 'perception'
> The Group of Grasping 'intention'
> The Group of Grasping 'consciousness'.
>
> (*Majjihima Nikaya* III.141)

Put together, these five 'groups' constitute the entirety of our life experience. To say 'the Five Groups of Grasping are suffering' is to say that whatever we experience is suffering.

This statement links this analysis of suffering to the other fundamental points of the Buddhist teaching, 'impermanence' (p. *anicca*; s. *anitya*) and 'non-self' (p. *anatta*; s. *anatman*). They are often put together as 'the three fundamental marks' of impermanence, suffering and non-self.[12] The Buddhist notion of impermanence is central for understanding the analysis of suffering. It is twofold, as physical change at every moment (things in one moment are physically different in another moment) and as gradual change of a living being (from birth, growth, decay to death). It simply means that nothing remains the same. Nothing is 'as it is', and everything is in constant transition. Then what about our experience of the world, and of ourselves as 'I'? The Buddhist answer is that this is a falsification. We should note that these five groups of body, sensation, perception, intention and consciousness are all 'grasped'. Thus grasping (p. s. *upadana*) leads us to assume that there exist those that are grasped and the 'I' that grasps. It is an act directly counter to the truth of impermanence. It is not only idle but also the cause of our suffering. For, in the words of a Tibetan monk, 'the very essence of life is change,

---

12 See, for example, *Dhammapada* 277–9. In Mahayana Buddhism the three marks are usually 'impermanence', 'non-self', and 'cessation' (p. *nibbana*; s. *nirvana*). When including 'suffering' it lists four, instead of three, marks.

while the essence of clinging (grasping) is to retain, to stabilize, to prevent change. This is why change appears to us as suffering' (Govinda 1961: 54). The point is that desire continually urges to grasp. By desiring, the ego grasps at its objects and grasps itself as the subject. Desire thus generates both subject and object, but in reality whatever it grasps is unreal.

The notion of impermanence was widely known in India. It also appeared in the Upanishads and the *Bhagavad-Gita*. It was Buddhism, however, that made a thorough understanding of impermanence as the utter impossibility of grasping anything. Impermanence means that everything, including ourselves, is in constant transition, therefore ungraspable. This is how Buddhism links impermanence with the doctrine of 'non-self'. In our ordinary experience we grasp things, and by grasping them we grasp ourselves as an 'I' that is grasping. If grasping is impossible, there are in truth no 'things' to be grasped and no 'I' that grasps. We should note here that the Buddhist 'non-self' (p. *anatta*; s. *anatman*) is significant both epistemologically and ethically. Ethically, realizing non-self leads to the teaching of unselfishness. The point is that this teaching is coupled with the epistemological awareness that things are ungraspable, that is, nothing can be identified as permanent and lasting substance, as it is, as *atman*. Hence, everything (everyone) is 'non-self' (*anatman*).

Thus the First Noble Truth presents the problem of suffering from different points of view. First it presents the observation of suffering drawn from our life experience, then moves on to the doctrine of 'non-ego' that is at the heart of Buddhist transcendentalism. This heterogeneity has created an interesting yet finally insoluble problem. It has been suggested that the doctrinal statement at the end was a later insertion, added to the descriptive analysis of our daily experience of suffering. It assumes a further philosophical sophistication of the later periods. It is possible, however, to think that the doctrine of non-self was there from the beginning, and that the experiential description of suffering was a lead, a 'skilful means' to explain the otherwise inaccessible doctrine. What is certain is that suffering in the First Noble Truth includes an understanding that is beyond experiential descriptions, and that understanding is related to the other fundamental doctrines of impermanence and non-self.

The Second Noble Truth returns to the experiential suffering and detects 'craving' (p. *tanha*; s. *trsna*) as the cause of suffering.

> This is the Noble Truth of the Origin of Suffering: it is craving that leads to rebirth, connected with pleasure and attachment, finding delight here and there, namely: craving for objects of senses, craving for existence, craving for non-existence.
>
> (*Samyutta Nikaya* V.56)

Craving is the cause of endless repetition of satisfaction and dissatisfaction, gain and loss, binding one to the endless chain of birth and rebirth. Of the three kinds of craving as listed at the end of the quote, the first craving for objects of senses is the cause of the Five Groups of Grasping. The second includes craving for life, growth and procreation. The third is the desire to destroy oneself in order to avoid unpleasant situations caused by other cravings. What is insightful in deeming self-mortification as another form of craving is that by this the teaching avoids the naive dichotomy of self-indulgence and self-mortification and points to the 'Middle Way' of practice. Buddhism does not accept reincarnation of an individual soul. Rather, it sees reincarnation as an endless recurrence of craving, life after life, until it is finally overcome. Becoming free from desire is all that matters, not gratifying it endlessly or avoiding it.[13]

13 Freud's analysis of human desire is surprisingly similar to the Second Noble Truth. The Buddhist understanding of craving must have been inspirational in his formulation of the 'ego-drive', 'life-drive', and 'death-

Once craving is overcome, there will be no suffering, no ego and no world. This leads to the third of the Four Noble Truths.

> This is the Noble Truth of the Cessation of Suffering; the complete extinction, destruction of this craving, abandonment, rejection, release and casting off.
>
> (*Samyutta Nikaya* V.56)

The complete extinction of craving is called *nibbana* (p.), *nirvana* (s.), meaning 'extinction'. It is the goal of the Buddhist practice, the freedom from desire and from the current of *samsara*. With this prospect of liberation, suffering is now said to be the inevitable consequence of ignorance. The Conditioned Arising (p. *paticca-samuppada*; s. *pratitya-samtpada*) explains how ignorance of the way to liberation leads to suffering. The Conditioned Arising is a system of desire, similar to the Five Groups of Graspings that explains the entirety of our experience as suffering. The twelve conditioned and conditioning links connect all aspects of our life experience, following the pattern, 'from the arising of that, this arises'.

1 As a result of ignorance, intentions;
2 as a result of intentions, consciousness;
3 as a result of consciousness, name and body;
4 as a result of name and body, the six faculties (the five senses plus mind);
5 as a result of the six faculties, contact (the engagement with the world);
6 as a result of contact, sensation;
7 as a result of feeling, craving;
8 as a result of craving, grasping;
9 as a result of clinging, becoming;
10 as a result of becoming, birth;
11 as a result of again becoming, arise
12 decay, death, grief, lamentation, suffering.

(*Majjihima Nikaya* I.38)

'Ignorance' is the ignorance of the way to liberation that inevitably leads to 'suffering'. The system shows that all human experiences, consciousness, perception, desire, individual life or rebirth, are included in it and placed between 'ignorance' and 'suffering'. Nothing is exempted from it. However, the other side of the Conditioned Arising is that the linkage is 'conditional'. When one link is broken,

drive', although he included the death-drive much later than others. Buddhist influence was evident when he explained 'Nirvana Principle' as belonging to the death-drive, as opposed to the 'Pleasure Principle' that belongs to the life-drive. As was the case with Freud, the Buddhist goal of nirvana was often confused with self-mortification, for the reason that there were passages, along with those such as the Second Noble Truth that pointed to the Middle Way, that indicated that self-mortification was indeed the goal. Consequently, the view that Buddhism was a pessimistic non-religion was common among modern Europeans. This view in turn reveals their assumption as to the essence of religion. What for some was the Divine Promise was for Freud, an atheist, an illusory projection of human desire, an opium in the otherwise unbearable world. Because of this assumption both theists and atheists regarded Buddhism as irreligious. How the Buddhist teaching of freedom from desire will intersect with the enthusiasm of illusory projection or the dejection that follows its inevitable failure is an on-going question.

every link goes too. Hence, 'from the cessation of that, this ceases'. That is, when 'ignorance' is overcome, 'suffering' ceases and so does everything in between. Nirvana is often referred to as the 'Unconditioned' (p. *asankhata*; s. *asamskrta*), indicating that it is freedom from the Conditioned Arising. It is essentially a negative term. It remains so as long as it is seen from the 'conditioned' point of view. It simply indicates the end of everything. 'When all things are cut off, the ways of language also cease' (*Sutta-nipata* 1076). However, while nirvana may not be defined by language, it is certainly an experiential truth. Therefore, Buddhist texts freely put it positively, as 'the other shore', 'an island in the flood', or as peace, truth, purity, bliss. Paradoxical though it may appear, this in itself is not unusual for transcendentalism that necessarily involves this alternation between negation and affirmation as to its final goal. The question is whether it translates this tensioned paradox into a sustainable form of practice.

The Eightfold Way in the Fourth Noble Truth is a way to realize this in practice. It is a path of self-transformation and self-liberation in all aspects of one's life, intellectual, moral and practical.

> This is the Noble Truth of the Way to the cessation of suffering, namely: right view, right intention, right speech, right conduct, right livelihood, right effort, right awareness, right meditation.
>
> (*Samyutta Nikaya* V.56)

The Eightfold Way is sometimes divided into three groups of 'morality', 'meditation' and 'wisdom': right speech, right conduct, right livelihood into 'morality' (p. *sila*; s. *sila*), right effort, right awareness, right meditation into 'meditation' (p. s. *samadhi*), right view and right intention into 'wisdom' (p. *panna*; s. *prajna*). The Eightfold Way is not the eight stages of progress but the eight simultaneous dimensions of practice.

Whatever the reason might have been, the Four Noble Truths as we have them now include both philosophical speculation and practical guidance. They begin with the experiential description of suffering and end with the practical guidance to overcome it. At the same time, they touch upon the doctrine of non-self as the basis of the whole teaching. Yet it is 'I' that suffers from the Five Groups of Grasping. And it is 'I' that overcomes suffering by practice. Here is the duality typical of the transcendental ego. It is 'speculatively' non-existent, yet 'in practice' in charge of the whole process of transcendence. To use the symbolism of the current, 'I' is always there whether it is drifting along the stream or going against the stream. Yet once it reaches the other shore, all that involved in crossing the water is no longer significant. 'At the moment of insight one abandons three things; errors to take oneself as real, doubts, and external precepts and vows' (*Sutta-nipata* 231). The *Dhammapada* uses the expression '*nirvana* of oneself' (940, 1061). It is simultaneously the speculative truth that already holds true and the practical goal that is yet to be realized by a strenuous practice. Thus the symbiosis of speculation and practical consideration in the Four Noble Truths highlights the duality inherent in the ego that aspires to overcome itself.

2.1 The sangha

From the days of the Buddha the Buddhist community was made up of those who were ordained and those who remained lay. Monks and nuns were called *bhikkhu* (p.; s. *bhiksu*) and *bhikkhuni* (p.; s. *bhiksuni*). Lay men and women were called *upasaka* and *upasika*. The ordained formed an order called *sangha* (p.; s. *samgha*). The Buddhist sangha was one of many sanghas that were rooted in the Indian spiritual tradition of wandering sages. *Bhikkhu* and *bhikkhuni*, as they were sometimes called, renounced ordinary life and everything that went with it, family, possessions, job or status, and lived on donations from the lay people. The terms *bhikkhu* and *bhikkhuni* meant 'beggar'. In the Buddhist sangha, they formed an order and facilitated their own and lay members' practice towards enlightenment. The laity carried familial and social responsibilities and practised the teaching as presented to them. *Upasaka* and *upasika* (server), as they were called, provided day-to-day support for the order such as food, medicine and accommodation. Enlightenment was recorded to be reached by both the ordained and lay practitioners.

Buddhism did not have a centralized organization, and the Buddha himself declined such an idea. Instead Buddhist monks and nuns saw themselves as belonging to 'the universal sangha', the Buddhist sangha of the past, the present and the future practitioners. For their day-to-day practice they formed regional, usually small, and autonomous sanghas called 'present sangha'. It took only four monks to form a sangha. The vision of the universal sangha, in the place of a central authority, gave them a sense of orientation in running their present sangha. In exercising their autonomy in their present sanghas, monks made their decisions in the belief that they were in support of the universal sangha.

To be formally recognized as a monk or a nun, one had to have a brief initiation rite. Five (or ten) monks had to be present at an initiation. One of the monks asked the ordinand whether he or she was qualified (whether he or she was twenty years old or older), and asked the name of his or her mentor. If no one present had objected, that person was accepted. The time and the date of initiation were recorded, for seniority in the order was the only indicator that differentiated them. His or her possession in the order was limited to an almsbowl and three robes (an underwear, an outerwear, and a coat).

The basic orientation for the Buddhist life was expressed in the precepts laid out for the laity. A lay person had five precepts to keep. They were to avoid: (1) killing ('harming living beings'); (2) stealing ('taking what is not given'); (3) unchastity ('misconduct concerning sex'); (4) lying ('false speech'); and (5) drinking ('taking intoxicant that causes heedlessness'). An apprentice had five more to avoid: (6) eating after midday; (7) entertainment such as dancing, singing, music, and the theatre; (8) ornaments such as garlands, perfumes, cosmetics and jewellery; (9) a comfortable bed; and (10) money. Monks had to keep two hundred and fifty precepts and nuns three hundred and fifty. The number of precepts vary according to different sources, but it is always the case that nuns had more precepts than monks. These precepts were detailed subsections of these ten precepts for an apprentice. Monks (and possibly nuns too) gathered at their present sanghas twice every month and recited the precepts three times. Those who broke them had to confess at this occasion. In the case of murder, sex, theft, and false declaration of enlightenment, the offender had to leave the order. For other offences, confession was enough.

Buddhism had to have a close relationship between the order and the laity in its early days. Collaboration of the ordained 'beggars' and the lay 'servers' was an economic necessity. The relative ease with which one could join and leave the order and the early records of lay members' enlightenment contributed to their closeness too. However, the Buddhist order could not resist the tendency inherent in any religious order to form a closed circle and prioritize themselves over the laity. Early Buddhist scriptures include many passages that reflected the rise of a religious elitism. In explaining the essence of his transcendentalism, the Buddha referred to the distinction between the noble and ignoble quests. 'When one pursues, while he himself is subject to decay, what is equally decaying, it is the ignoble quest; the noble quest is for him to pursue the ultimate peace or *nirvana* that is beyond decay' (*Majjihima Nikaya* I.162). The point is that the text lists as objects of the ignoble quest 'wives and children, bondsmen and bondswomen, goats and sheep, fowls and swine, elephants, cattle, horses and mares, together with gold and coins of silver' (ibid.). The story could have been meant to illustrate each individual's struggle between the noble and ignoble tendencies and to encourage one's decision to aspire for enlightenment. But it allowed another interpretation that read this distinction as between those who engage themselves in the noble quest and those in the ignoble quest, that is, the noble life of the order and the ignoble life of the laity. Here is another story. When asked why he taught some painstakingly and others not so painstakingly while he was compassionate with all living beings, the Buddha replied by pointing to the difference that a good field, a medium field and a bad field would make in sowing rice, the difference that a good pot, a coarse pot and a bad pot would make in storing water. This story clearly indicated differentiation of the order from the laity and the outsiders, although it is uncertain who wrote these passages and for what purpose. These passages in the early Buddhist texts were there to declare that the life of the monk was more desirable than that of the laity. They either encouraged the order to set up a religious elitism or merely reflected its emergence.

There were two serious consequences, one doctrinal and the other practical. First, enlightenment was institutionalized by the order. Ordination was no longer a way to renounce ordinary life but to gain a nobler lifestyle and a better understanding of the Buddha's teaching. The practice of transcendence was now described positively (as gaining enlightenment) as well as negatively (as renouncing). Second, it threatened the vital unity between the order and the laity. A reason for the Great Schism that divided the Buddhist sangha into the *Sthaviravada* and the *Mahasanghika* was the lay influence over the monastic life. The latter was more tolerant to it as its name *Mahasanghika* (Universal Assembly) indicated. These doctrinal and practical issues, that is, negative/positive descriptions of enlightenment and involvement/non-involvement of the laity, were to become the two axes on which the subsequent Buddhist history turned round. Theravada Buddhism, the only surviving school that came from Sthaviras, has retained a clear distinction between the order and the laity. Mahayana Buddhism, a spiritual if not a direct descendent of Mahasanghika, reintroduced a negative description of enlightenment as emptiness and overrode the distinction between the order and the laity.

2.2 The Abhidharma

Disagreements at the Second Council that was held a hundred years after the Buddha's death marked the first division of the Buddhist community. The Great Schism, as it was called, divided the community into two parties; the *Sthaviravada* (s.; p. *Theravada*, 'Followers of the Ancient Teaching') and the *Mahasanghikas*. The cause of the division is likely to have been a dispute over the monastic code; the reformist group that was to form the Theravada demanded a tighter code than that held by the majority. Over the next two centuries a number of sub-schools separated out from both parties. Some of these schools subsequently developed a complex speculative system known now as *Abhidharma* (s.; p. *Abhidhamma*) philosophy. The two collections of Abhidharma writings survived; the Theravadin collection in Pali, and that of the Sarvastivada (a sub-school separated from the Sthaviravada in the mid-second century BCE) that was translated and preserved in the Chinese canon. Vasbandhu's *Abhidharmakosa* in the Sarvastivada canon was the Abhidharma text most influential to Eastern Buddhism.

Abhidharma philosophy is an attempt to explain how things really are by breaking down our experience into constituent elements and analysing the causal relationship that combines these elements. These elements are called *dharmas* (s.; p. *dhamma*, 'law').[14] Abhidharma philosophers counted eighty-

---

14 Dharma is a typical multivalent term. It could mean (1) the law of things; (2) the Buddha's teaching; (3) attribute; (4) cause; (5) event. (1) 'The law of things' appears to have been the earliest meaning of dharma.

one (Theravada) or seventy-two (Sarvastivada) such dharmas, some physical, some mental, and some intentional, some logical. They are 'conditioned' dharmas, that is, they are under the causal law of conditioning and being conditioned. These dharmas, they thought, are combined and separated at every moment in accordance with their causal relationship, and a series of these combinations constitutes our experience. There are also the unconditioned dharmas that are eternal and do not partake in combination and separation of the conditioned dharmas. The Theravadins regarded nirvana alone as unconditioned while the Sarvastivadins counted three unconditioned dharmas that are all related to nirvana. The Sarvastivadins sought to explain the world and our experience, and every event that takes place there, good and evil acts and their result, karma, defilement, the end of defilement, enlightenment, the grades and contents of enlightenment, and so on, by the dharmas and their necessary combinations (Hirakawa 1977: 24–9). In breaking down our experience into these elements, Abhidharma philosophers follow the line of the doctrine of Five Groups of Grasping that analysed our experience down into the Five Groups of Grasping. The Abhidharma system reduces the ego into a bundle of dharmas and re-emphasizes constant changes of dharma-combinations. It certainly plays well with the Buddhist notion of impermanence and non-self. To understand the function of the dharmas is to realize that there is no ego and that everything is in transition. Abhidharma philosophy, often described as scholastic, is a speculative way of referring to non-self and transition, the two basic premises of Buddhism.

Dharma and transition was a contended issue. The Sarvastivadins saw dharmas as permanent, that is, existent in the past, the present and the future, yet active only in a momentary combination. For them the chain of dharma-combinations were what created the karmic continuity from the past to the future. They thought that if dharma too was momentary, as the Theravadins held it to be, there would be nothing to carry on the cause and the effect of karma. When Mahayana Buddhism presented the argument that dharma should also be empty, that is, non-existent in the past, the present and the future, it was directed primarily to the Sarvastivadins. By this argument Mahayana Buddhism reinterpreted the karmic continuity as the atemporal Conditioned Arising.

3 THE EMERGENCE OF MAHAYANA BUDDHISM

The historical origin of the branch of Buddhism that was to call itself 'Mahayana' remains obscure. It may go back as early as the first century BCE. It is uncertain whether there was a group or groups of people who initiated the movement; if there had been, then whether they were ordained or lay, whether they were aware of their revolutionary ideas. Indications are that it did not have an identifiable origin. Rather, it was the manifestation of what we might call the 'Mahayana' tendency that was always latent in Buddhism. Its radical pragmatism and broad humanism could be seen as a restatement, rather than a replacement, of the original Buddhist ideal. When it came to the front of history around the first century CE, it was equipped with a new practice and a new philosophy that supported it. Mahayana Buddhism marked a clear shift away from the historical Buddha. The purpose of practice was no longer

(2) 'The Buddha's teaching' and (5) 'event' were unique to Buddhism. The thinking behind these appears to have been: events were caused by the law of things; the Buddha's teaching is a way to explain to people the law of things and how events are caused by it. (1) 'The law of things' and (5) 'event' are primarily relevant to Abhidharma philosophy.

to follow the historical Buddha, to understand and uphold his teaching, but to re-enact his enlightenment experience.[15]

The production of its own, 'Mahayana' sutras was vital in expressing this Mahayana ethos. What characterizes Mahayana Buddhism is its literary creativity that was to produce various sets of sutras over many centuries. Whoever wrote them, the Mahayana sutras were distinctly different from the previous sutras in that they were newly written. What was presented as the Buddha's words in these sutras, in spite of the claim to their authenticity, was a literary creation. Non-Mahayanists were quick to point out that they were inauthentic, drawing on their canons that were supposed to be true records of the Buddha's words, orally transmitted for generations, then finally compiled into their canons. However, what the non-Mahayana canons presented was not the Buddha's 'exact' word, not only because they included layers of editorial revisions but also because 'the Buddha's word', even in his day, did not necessarily mean his genuine speech. The Buddha accepted as 'his' word speeches by his disciples that he thought were in accordance with his teaching. At his death, the Buddha's words, spoken by him or by his disciples under his authorization, came to an end. This is the theoretical point at which the canonization of his word began. The main concern among the followers at this point was the preservation of the Buddha's words. For this they formed the first general council. What Mahayana Buddhism did was to extend the notion of the Buddha's word a step further and to redefine it as speeches in the spirit of the Buddha's teaching. In defence of their obvious fictions the Mahayanists often resorted to their visionary encounters with the Buddha, existing no longer physically but still in spirit. The production of the Mahayana sutras thus appears to have been a deliberate reaction against the attempt of a closed canon and the orthodoxy that was emerging out of that closure. The Mahayana canons remained open to a large number of writings over many centuries. It must still be open, at least in principle, for all it takes to write a sutra is to have another visionary transmission from the Buddha. The Mahayana sutras were the product of a religious life that needed a new expression. The development of the texts and that of the new practice were inseparable to the extent that the text often included the praise of its own merit in practice, and enthusiastic devotion to the text became a part of the practice.

3.1 The Bodhisattva

A literary genre called *Jataka* (p., s.), a collections of stories of the Buddha's past lives, was the clear source of inspiration for Mahayana Buddhism. Jataka stories tell that a vast number of aeons ago the Buddha, instead of becoming an enlightened disciple of a past Buddha Dipankara, took the vow of *Bodhisattva* (s.; p. *Bodhisatta*) to practise over countless lifetimes, then to reach full enlightenment and to teach the truth of enlightenment in a time when nobody would remember it. The Buddha was then a Bodhisattva, a Buddha in the making. Mahayana Buddhism came into existence when some monks and laity called themselves Bodhisattva, meaning future Buddha, and set for themselves a religious aspiration and practice that were distinctly different from those of Abhidharma Buddhism. This step could not have been taken within speculative, scholastic Abhidharma philosophy. In the Buddha's day Buddhism did not distinguish the Buddha from an Arahat, his enlightenment from an Arahat's. As seen above, both 'Buddha' and 'Arahat' were titles that could equally be ascribed to the Buddha. By the

---

15 What kind of people prepared Mahayana Buddhism was an interesting question. It might have been born out of small groups of monks who gathered around 'new' sutras and directed their practice by 'new' ideas, or out of a non-elitistic lay movement formed by *stupa* worshippers (Williams 1989: 20–6).

time of Abhidharma, however, they were clearly distinguished. The Buddha was the one who reached full enlightenment and taught the world the way to enlightenment out of his compassion; the Arahats were those who listened to his teaching and reached his partial enlightenment. Mahayana Buddhism purposefully overrides this distinction. The Mahayana goal is no longer the Arahat's partial enlightenment but the Buddha's full enlightenment; its practice is the Bodhisattva's way. By taking this step, in the spiritual atmosphere that was closer to literary imagination than to scholastic metaphysics, the Mahayanists not only gained for themselves the aspiration for full enlightenment but also allowed themselves to partake in the Buddha's compassion manifested in the Bodhisattva's vow to lead everyone to enlightenment. For this reason they called their practice 'Mahayana' (Great Vehicle) and disparaged the practice of those who still aimed at Arahatship as 'Hinayana' (Lesser Vehicle).

The Bodhisattva's path is explained as 'the Six Perfections of Bodhisattva'. They are: generosity (*dana*), morality (*sila*), patience (*ksanti*), vigour (*virya*), meditation (*dhyana*), wisdom (*prajna*). The Six Perfections of Bodhisattva is a continuation of the Noble Eightfold Path that is grouped into wisdom, morality and meditation. What is added to these three, namely generosity, patience, and vigour, are necessary for the Bodhisattva's vow to lead all beings to enlightenment. Later four more were added to these six to make 'the Ten Stages of Bodhisattva'.

The Mahayanists thus shifted the emphasis from the goal to the path, from the final point of transcendence to its process. To assume that the goal should already be implied in the process was to assume that, to the extent that they practised the path of Bodhisattva, to the extent that they partook in the Buddha's compassion, they were already Buddha. With this shift, transcendence that had been seen as a single process became a dual process. It became both the practice to reach the transcendent goal and at the same time the compassionate practice to all sentient beings that was the result of that transcendence. Here the temporary metaphor of 'before' and 'after' is inappropriate. To use Shinran's word, here is the simultaneity of the 'going' and the 'returning' aspects of practice. The distinction of this and the other shores is no longer self-evident, for this dual process allows an overlap of the starting point and the goal of transcendence. Transcendence is no longer linear but circular. To explain this complex idea the early Mahayanist invented an ingenious narrative. Some texts tell that a Bodhisattva will, out of his immeasurable compassion, postpone his full enlightenment or turn back from it in order to lead all other beings to enlightenment. A further emphasis on the starting point of practice rather than the goal would eventually lead to the *Tathagata-garbha* (embryo or womb of enlightenment) thought in India, and then to 'the Original Enlightenment' in Chinese and Japanese Buddhism, in which every sentient being is seen to be already in, or in the process of, the full enlightenment.

THE *LOTUS SUTRA*

Mahayana Buddhism produced numerous sutras that described and propagated the Bodhisattva's way. The most influential among them were the *Lotus Sutra* and a group of sutras called the Perfection of Wisdom sutras. Both of them are thought to be from the early Mahayana period, written from the first century BCE over several centuries. The *Lotus Sutra* or *Saddharma-pundarika Sutra* (*sad* [right] *dharma* [law] *pundarika* [white lotus] *sutra*) is undoubtedly one of the most influential single sutras of all Mahayana sutras. The white lotus that appears in the title is a visual symbolism of the Buddhist ideal. As the white lotus is rooted in muddy water yet flowers unstained above it, the Buddha and his teaching, and now the Bodhisattvas and their practice, appear in this world yet bring forth an unworldly joy. A Chinese translation by Kumarajiva reads the title's 'Saddharma' not as 'right law' but as 'mysterious law', a free but spiritually accurate translation. For, as Chi-i later emphasizes, the symbolism represents the mystery that the root and the flower are clearly distinct yet at the same time they are one.

The *Lotus Sutra* became a central text of Mahayana Buddhism for its statement of 'One vehicle' (*Eka-yana*) and 'Skilful means' (*Upaya-kausalya*). 'One vehicle' means the Bodhisattva-vehicle (*Bodhisattva-yana*), which, the Mahayanist maintains, is essentially the same as the Buddha-vehicle. The notion 'One vehicle' appears in other Mahayana sutras too, but it is the *Lotus Sutra* that gives it the most emphatic presentation. It says in Book II, Chapter 2, 'there is only one way, and that alone is the Buddha's way; there is no second or third way'. The second and third ways are 'Disciple vehicle' (*Sravaka-yana*) and 'Solitary vehicle' (*Pratyeka-buddha-yana*), the two 'vehicles' of pre-Mahayana Buddhism. It thus declares that the Bodhisattva's way is the only way. Yet it does not see these two ways as fundamentally different from the Bodhisattva's way. It says that the Bodhisattva's way is cow-led while 'Disciple vehicle' and 'Solitary vehicle' are sheep-led.

Here arises the question, Why did the Buddha teach these ways that were less than the full Bodhisattva's way? The *Lotus Sutra* replies that it was because of his 'skilful means' (*Upaya-kausalya*). As the essence of the Buddha's teaching is beyond language and comprehensible only to Buddhas, the Buddha had to make it accessible to the unenlightened mass by adapting it to their need. This 'skilful means', once accepted, allows any form of adaptation. It guarantees doctrinal pragmatism and doctrinal flexibility in the Bodhisattva's way. As Williams observes, 'Any adaptation whatsoever, provided it is animated by the Bodhisattva's compassion and wisdom, and is suitable for the recipient, is a part of Buddhism' (Williams 1989: 144). And this adaptation could include teaching non-Buddhist teaching.

However, what the *Lotus Sutra* intends to present is not another 'skilful means'. It presents not the simple Bodhisattva's way that is still comparable to the other way but the essential one way, the Buddha's way, that runs through the Disciple's, Solitary, or Bodhisattva's way. These ways still fall short of fully realizing this essential one way. It was inevitable that the followers of the *Lotus Sutra* sought to find it in the *Lotus Sutra* itself. After all, the *Lotus Sutra* is the sutra that expounds that what it declares is incomprehensible and inaccessible. The *Lotus Sutra*'s powerful self-reference undoubtedly encouraged this direction. The later followers in China reinterpreted the statement 'there is only one way; there is no second or third way' as 'there is only one way, not two ways nor three ways' and indicated their view that the one way was not the Disciple's or Solitary way, nor the Disciple's, Solitary, or Bodhisattva's way. They sought for the one way that transcends them all and found, or believed to find, its full exposition only in the *Lotus Sutra*. Thus Chi-i, the third patriarch of the T'ien t'ai school in China, regarded the *Lotus Sutra* as the pinnacle of the whole of the Buddhist tradition.

There are abundant statements in the sutra of how powerful and beneficial the sutra is. If a person hears just one line from the sutra and rejoices in it for even a moment that person will surely reach full enlightenment. The sutra demands that it should not only be recited and promulgated but worshipped as if it were the Buddha himself. And the sin of maligning this sutra and its preachers is much worse than constantly maligning the Buddha (ibid.: 152). Later in Japan, Nichiren found in these passages the unquestionable justification of his political propaganda. Calling himself the practitioner of the *Lotus Sutra*, he fervently argued that the *Lotus Sutra* was the only sutra that could lead people to salvation in a period of spiritual decline. Nichiren denounced all other forms of Buddhism and demanded that the whole nation should come under the truth of the *Lotus Sutra*. Only by that could the nation and the rest of the world be transformed to the Pure Land of the Buddha. Nichiren even claimed his mastery over the nation by the authority of the *Lotus Sutra*. 'Those who propagate the Lotus of Truth are indeed the parents of all men living in Japan . . . I, Nichiren, am the master and lord of the sovereign, as well as of all the Buddhists of other schools' (quoted in ibid.: 164). His conviction was the direct result of the sutra's self-reference, and his prophecy was its enactment. The Nichiren-shu, the sect formed by his followers, practises the chanting, 'I believe in the *Lotus Sutra*', believing that it gives merit to everyone.

The *Lotus Sutra*'s narrative quality also contributed to the extent of the influence that it has had. The sutra is full of stories and parables. Explaining how 'skilful means' works, it tells a story of a doctor whose sons were poisoned. Although he prepares an effective medicine for them, some of them are so deranged by the poison as to refuse his medicine for its colour and taste. What the father does at this point is to fake his death and disappear to a foreign country, leaving in his will that the sons should take his medicine. The shock at the news brings the sons to their senses and they take the medicine. The father reappears and declares that his death was 'a skilful means' (*Lotus Sutra*, ch. 15). This is a narrative version of the Mahayana doctrine that the Buddha did not die at his death but only went back to his former state after appearing to this world in a human form as a 'skilful means'. The *Lotus Sutra* gives a reason for devising the Buddha's fake death. It is to remind the practitioners that they should not take for granted the Buddha's eternal presence. For 'although the Buddha is standing in front of them, few actually see him'.

The *Lotus Sutra*'s narrative includes that of body-burning. The twenty-second chapter tells how one Bodhisattva burned himself to death, another his arm or finger as the offering to the Buddha and his teaching. Numberless Buddhas are said to have praised them and said, 'Good, good . . . this is the real courage the one with the great will to seek for dharma can show; this is the real offering to the Buddha and to his teaching.' This account could be an apologue depicting the Bodhisattva's selflessness in its extreme form. There are, however, records of self-immolation throughout Buddhist history. Chinese pilgrims to India witnessed cases where Buddhists engaged in religious suicide. The custom was subsequently brought to China. There, finger-burning was practised well into modern times. In Japan, along with the spread of the Pure Land teaching from the latter half of the tenth century, there were cases of religious suicide by burning, drowning or fasting. The records tell that people revered and praised this practice. During the Vietnam War several Vietnamese monks revived this extreme practice and burned themselves to death as offerings to the wish for peace.

Other Mahayana sutras from the same period include narratives of sex and violence as variant forms of 'skilful means'. Mahayana Buddhism would theoretically accept any behaviour as 'skilful means' if it was conducted in the spirit of the Bodhisattva. In order to make this point, on rare occasions some sutras resort to narratives of sex and violence. In the *Upayakausalya Sutra* the Buddha, when he was a Bodhisattva, spent a night with a girl who was in love with him and was going to kill herself if her love had not been reciprocated. Also, the Buddha in his past life killed a man. This was the only way to prevent that man from killing 500 others and consequently falling to the lowest hell for a long time. We may leave open whether sex and violence could be an act of compassion. Yet we may not be quick to dismiss these accounts as just 'story' or another 'skilful means'. For, there seems to be a possible link, distorted or not, between these accounts and the behaviour of a cult leader who indulges in sex and violence for 'spiritual' reasons.

THE DHARMA-KAYA

It is important to remember that Buddhism is not hinged upon the person of the Buddha. The Buddha himself disregarded the importance of 'his' person and advised against making it the foundation of Buddhist practice. When he said 'one who sees me sees Dhamma (p.; s. *Dharma* "teaching"); one who sees Dhamma sees me', what he meant was that he was a vessel of his teaching and not the other way round (*Samyutta Nikaya* III.22.87.13). At his death he made clear to his followers that Dharma and

Vinaya (p., s. 'precepts') were to be their guide. However, for those who had immediate contact with the Buddha, his death was a devastating event. For, he was the only Buddha that lived and died among them, and that made himself accessible to them. They certainly needed a guiding figure or principle that could give them a sense of orientation. They explored the Buddha's presence through both narration and philosophical speculation. The point is that from the beginning they were free to expand what they believed the Buddha was and to present what they thought were appropriate qualities of the Buddha. Along with many, often legendary, accounts of the Buddha's life and his past lives, Buddhists developed philosophical discussions regarding the essence of the Buddha that we now call 'Buddhology'.

In its early stage Buddhology made a single distinction between the Buddha's essence and appearance, or, 'the Dharma-kaya' (Law-body) and 'the Rupa-kaya' (Form-body). The Sarvastivada school stated that the Law-body was the essence of his teaching and insight and that the Form-body was the equivalent of the historical Buddha who was born in this world. Later the same school gave an interpretation that the life of the historical Buddha was a 'play' (*lalita*) of the essential Buddha. Mahayana Buddhology began with the same distinction. Yet the original purpose of their Buddhology was to present the Dharma-kaya as the full Buddhahood that would include his personality rather than his teaching and insight. Mahayana Buddhology thus released the Buddha's personal qualities such as his enlightenment and compassion from the bounds of time and place. The Dharma-kaya in early Mahayana Buddhology was the eternal and universal enlightenment and the cosmic compassion. Throughout these speculations Mahayana Buddhology maintained that the Rupa-kaya that appeared in this world was only 'a skilful means' of the Dharma-kaya. The *Lotus Sutra* gives a vivid presentation of the eternal enlightenment.

> An inconceivable number of thousands of millions of aeons, never to be measured, is it since I first reached enlightenment. I have never ceased to teach the law. I seized many Bodhisattvas and led them to Buddha-knowledge. During these aeons I brought myriads of millions of beings to maturity.
>
> (*Lotus Sutra*, ch. 16)

The Buddha's birth, his experience of enlightenment, his teaching and his death are all 'skilful means' to lead the mass to enlightenment. The *Lotus Sutra* explains, 'I gather a congregation of my disciples and reveal myself to them . . . and then I say to them, "Monks, I am not extinct; my disappearance was a skilful means"' (ibid.). As to his cosmic compassion, it is 'like a cloud rising above the world and covering all spaces and enveloping the earth . . . like this great cloud, filled with water . . . pouring out a mass of water and refreshing this earth . . . like a cloud shedding its water without distinction' (ibid., ch. 5).

This binary Buddhology was expanded in the fourth and fifth centuries CE by the Sarvastivadins and the Yogacarins. They felt the need of a synthetic figure in the dichotomy of the Rupa-kaya and the Dharma-kaya. They introduced the *Sambhoga-kaya* (Bliss-body) that was thought to be as personal as the Rupa-kaya *and* as cosmic as the Dharma-kaya. They thus formulated the trinary Buddhology of the *Nirmana-kaya* (Manifest-body), 'the Sambhoga-kaya' (Bliss-body) and 'the Dharma-kaya' (Law-body). The Nirmana-kaya is what the Rupa-kaya used to be, a Buddha like the historical Buddha Gautama that appears in the world with physical shape. The Sambhoga-kaya is not terrestrial like the Nirmana-kaya. It is the body that has practised all the way to enlightenment and now enjoys the result in some celestial realm. As indicated above, the point is that it is both personal and cosmic.

The original purpose of Buddhology is to mediate a person and the cosmos by the figure of the Buddha and to present the Buddha as the cosmic personality, the personality as large as the cosmos itself. Now this need is met by introducing the Nirmana-kaya and the Sambhoga-kaya that represent the two aspects of the Buddha's being, that is, his life and his teaching in this world and his enlightenment that turned out to be in the other worlds. That is, there is no personality left for the Dharma-kaya. Although the Dharma-kaya had a tendency to become impersonal and abstract from the beginning of Buddhology, this trinary Buddhology certainly accelerated it. The Dharma-kaya comes to represent ideas that philosophical schools saw as most fundamental. Abhidharma philosophy called it 'reality' (*dharmata*) or 'thusness' (*tathata*); the Madhyamaka school called it 'emptiness' (*sunyata*); the Yogacarins called it 'Storehouse Consciousness' (*alayavijnana*). In the Tathagata-garbha thought it was identified with the *Tathagata-garbha* (the embryo or matrix of the Buddha) itself. Following the *Mahayana Parinirvana Sutra*, East Asian Buddhism rephrased it as 'Buddha-nature' (*Buddha-dhatu*) and placed it at the centre of their doctrinal speculations.

This development is made visible in the two corpuses of texts of the Buddha's death called *Mahaparinibbana-sutta* or *Mahaparinirvana Sutra* (large, perfect nirvana). As seen above, the Buddha's death was the point of departure of Buddhology, and these radically different accounts of the same event are a clear reflection of different stages of Buddhology. The first one, a non-Mahayana text in the Pali canon, is seen to be the standard account of the Buddha's death for its attention to factual details. The second one, a Mahayana sutra, probably from the fourth century, exhibits a powerful Buddhology supported by the Mahayana argument that the Buddha's death was only a skilful means and the Dharma-kaya was eternal and unchanging.

The origin of Mahayana Buddhology, however, may already be found in the non-Mahayana account of the Buddha's death. It is in this that the Buddha declares that the dharma is beyond his personal being. More interestingly, the text contains the account, possibly a later addition, of the Buddha's last meditation at his death. Here the Buddha practises two types of meditation, meditation with the perception of form and meditation without. He begins with the first step of meditation with form and reaches the last stage, then moves on to a mystical, formless meditation, then to the final stage of cessation of perception and sensation; then he comes back all the way to the first stage. He then starts again and strikes the very middle of the two meditative practices and dies, or, passes on to *parinirvana*, nirvana without a living body, as the Buddha's death was called. This meditative round-trip and its completion at the middle point indicate the continuity rather than the distinction of the two meditative practices. The point is that here the two types of meditation (meditation with forms and meditation without) appear to correspond to two kinds of nirvana (nirvana with a living body and nirvana without). That is, the meditative practice appears to represent the continuity rather than the division between the Buddha's *nirvana* and *parinirvana*, that is, his life and death. Read in this way, this passage already presents, if not any form of Buddhology as such, certainly a Buddhological orientation.

3.2 Emptiness (*sunyata*)

Over several centuries Mahayanists produced sutras that carried the phrase 'Perfection of Wisdom' (*Prajna-paramita*) in their titles. The oldest of them was the *Astasahasrika Prajna-paramita Sutra* (8000-line sutra) from the period between the first century BCE and the first century CE. Two short and well-known sutras, the *Vajracchedika Prajna-paramita Sutra* (*Diamond-Cutter Sutra*) and *Prajna-paramita Hrdaya Sutra* (*Heart Sutra*), were from the fourth century CE. They later compiled these sutras into the *Maha-prajna-paramita Sutra* (*Large Perfection of Wisdom Sutra*) that turned out to be by far the largest sutra in Buddhism. For some reason this compilation excluded the shortest, the *Heart Sutra*. It was explained later that this was to show that to understand the full implication of 'Perfection of Wisdom' it would take six hundred volumes of the *Large Sutra*, yet to see its essence it would only need one page of the *Heart Sutra*. These sutras argued that the Bodhisattva's practice should be accompanied by a view that every thing is 'empty' (*sunya*). Mahayana Buddhism emphasized 'emptiness' and argued that every thing lacks its inherent identity, and is therefore 'empty'. By realizing emptiness the Bodhisattva refrains from grasping anything that is in truth empty. The point is that the Bodhisattva's compassion and selfless practice and his view that everything else is essentially empty are inseparable.

This argument was not a new one brought forth by Mahayana Buddhism. On the contrary, the Mahayanist believed that they were merely reviving the core of the original teaching of the Buddha that they saw was lost in the development of the Abhidharma. It is true that early Buddhism taught detachment by pointing out that everything was transitory, therefore ungraspable. Its central teachings such as Five Groups of Grasping and Conditioned Arising were presented as the proof of the idleness of our attachment. It argued that one's 'self' was derived from one's grasping things around and that, since these things are transitory and ungraspable, one's self is equally transitory and ungraspable. It also used the word *sunya* (empty) or *sunyata* (emptiness) in presenting this argument. A passage from the *Sutta-nipata* said, 'Be always mindful, break the view caused by self-attachment, and see the world as empty' (1119). Moreover, we find a couple of sutras in the *Majjihima Nikaya* from the Pali canon that anticipated the doctrinal interpretation of emptiness. They are called the Large and Little 'emptiness' Sutras for their specific discussions on emptiness (*Majjihima Nikaya* 121, 122). The *Little Emptiness Sutra* understood emptiness as absence and introduced the practice of speculating on it. This practice was a way to realize the three aspects of absence: that it was 'empty', that it had 'no characteristics' and that it was 'not worthy of attachment'. This threefold realization was called 'the three gates to liberation'. The *Large Emptiness Sutra*, while analysing emptiness into eighteen types, touched upon the notion 'emptiness of emptiness' (*sunyata sunyata*). While pointing out that things external and things internal were equally empty, it stated that this emptiness in itself was also empty.

Thus the doctrinal basis of emptiness was laid out in the non-Mahayana sources. What Mahayana Buddhism did was to place it at the centre of their philosophy and practice. In particular, what distinguished the Mahayana from the non-Mahayana philosophy was the treatment of dharma. As seen above, *dharma* has many meanings. Among them two meanings were particularly instrumental in establishing the non-Mahayana tradition, dharma as the Buddha's teaching and as a law of things in Abhidharma philosophy. Mahayana Buddhism, by declaring that dharma was also empty, rejected the foundational understanding of dharma both as the Buddha's teaching and as the foundation of Abhidharma metaphysics. For the Mahayanists it is not foundational dharma but non-foundational emptiness that should be the basis (or non-basis) of Buddhist philosophy and practice. This is what they meant when they criticized the Sarvastivada school and said that early Buddhism had realized the emptiness of one's self but failed to see the emptiness of dharma.[16] They believed that the Buddha's teaching, when properly understood, should lead to this realization of the emptiness, which they called the Bodhisattva's wisdom.

The perfection of wisdom is only one of the Six Perfections of Bodhisattva, but is the last and the most important one. For here 'wisdom' (*prajna*) is synonymous with the realization of emptiness. The word *prajna* was apparently a common word meaning 'excluding doubt' (Williams 1989: 42). When contrasted with *jnana* (knowledge), *prajna* meant the wisdom to see all in one while *jnana* meant the

---

16 Williams (1989: 16) reminds us that there may have been a non-Mahayana sutra that argued the emptiness of dharma. *Lokanuvartana Sutra*, which was later accepted as a Mahayana sutra, could be from one of the subschools of Mahasamghikas called Purvasailas. This sutra could be written under the influence of Mahayana sutras, although Williams sees no positive evidence to assume that.

knowledge to distinguish one into many. Thus the word *prajna* gradually came to mean the intuitive realization of the whole truth. When used by Buddhism as one of their 'three learnings' of precepts, meditation and wisdom, it came to mean the thorough understanding of the central teaching that everything was in transition. Mahayana Buddhism re-emphasized this understanding and used the word as meaning the realization of emptiness of everything. The *prajna* thus became the final and most important practice of the Bodhisattva's Six Perfections.

The wisdom sutras insisted upon continuity from the Buddha's basic teaching to their doctrine and argued that their emptiness was the accurate understanding of the teaching of the Five Groups of Grasping. The *Heart Sutra* states:

> While practising the profound *prajnaparamita*, the bodhisattva Avalokitesvara saw in this way: he saw the Five Groups of Grasping to be empty in themselves. The bodhisattva Avalokitesvara said to venerable Sariputra, 'O Sariputra. Form is empty, its emptiness is form. Emptiness is no other than form, form is no other than emptiness. Form is emptiness, emptiness is form. In the same way, "sensation", "perception", "intention", and "consciousness" are emptiness. Thus, Sariputra, all dharmas are emptiness.'

In pointing to the impossibility of grasping, it puts a particular emphasis on the first group of grasping, grasping of form. 'Form is emptiness, emptiness is form'; that is, whatever we perceive is empty, whenever we grasp something we in truth grasp emptiness. It thus highlights the inherent peculiarity of our perception that whatever we perceive is essentially insubstantial (empty) yet it is always with us. Relying on this epistemology, it goes on to declare that the very basis of the Buddhist doctrines is empty.

> There is no birth and no cessation. There is no impurity and no purity . . . no ignorance, no end of ignorance; . . . no suffering, no origin of suffering, no cessation of suffering, no path to the end of suffering, no wisdom, no attainment, and no non-attainment.

The Bodhisattva thus discards what was thought to be the foundational distinctions between samsara and nirvana, between ignorance and enlightenment. He sees them all as empty. By this realization the Bodhisattva's mind becomes clear. The point this sutra makes is that this realization 'is' the final enlightenment.

> Therefore, Sariputra, since the Bodhisattvas have no attainment, they abide by means of *prajnaparamita*. Since there is no veil of mind, there is no fear. They rise above falsity and attain complete enlightenment. All the buddhas of the three times, by means of Perfection of Wisdom, fully awaken to unsurpassable, true, complete enlightenment.

By this 'unsurpassable, true, complete enlightenment' the Bodhisattva is already a Buddha.

The concept of emptiness is not a Mahayana invention, or for that matter, not even a Buddhist invention. In fact *sunyata* meant zero in Indian mathematics, which is now known to have been the first formulation of the number zero. As seen above, early Buddhism used the word in its teaching of detachment. Yet it is Mahayana Buddhism that placed emptiness at the centre of its philosophy and carried out a thorough reinterpretation of the Buddhist tradition in terms of emptiness. It regarded emptiness as epistemologically, ontologically and practically significant. It saw emptiness as the recognition of the paradox of our perception (epistemology), the negation of all that appears to exist (ontology), and the utter selflessness of the Bodhisattva who realizes it in his day-to-day practice. One obvious effect was the breakdown of the distinction between the sacred and the secular, between the noble and ignoble quests. Previously, the practice in the sacred circle had been clearly distinct from that in the secular circle. Here the practice of transcendence had been made tangible in a particular lifestyle. As suggested above, this distinction might have contributed to the split between the order and the laity. When emptiness invalidates this distinction, there can only be two choices as regards the practice of transcendence: either to see that every life was potentially transcendental as the Mahayanists maintained, or to see in emptiness the end of all transcendental practices as non-Mahayanists sometimes did.

NAGARJUNA

Along with presenting their sutras, Mahayanists also produced their own 'treatises' (*sastra*). Mahayana Buddhism was to see various schools and subschools evolving from within its scope. These schools produced their own 'treatises' to explain their philosophies. The most prominent philosophical schools in Indian Mahayana were the Madhyamaka and the Yogacara. Nagarjuna is the founder of the Madhyamaka 'Middle Way' school. It was also called 'Sunyata-vada' (Teaching of Emptiness) for their emphasis on emptiness. The school was succeeded by Buddhapalita, then Bhavaviveka, who initiated a new interpretation of Nagarjuna and formed a school called Svatantrika-Madhyamaka at the beginning of the sixth century. A century later, Candrakirti criticized Bhavaviveka's move away from Buddhapalita and founded the Prasangika-Madhyamaka school, claiming that it is the final form of what the Madhyamaka could be.

Nagarjuna lived between the middle of the first century and the second century CE in South India. His [*Mula*]*Madyamaka-karika* (Verses on [the Fundamentals of] the Middle Way) is the foundational text for the Madhyamaka school. It presents a thorough exposition of Mahayana emptiness. Although this text lacks references to the Perfection of Wisdom sutras, the Bodhisattva or even Mahayana itself, his argument is clearly an elaboration of Mahayana speculation on emptiness.

Nagarjuna's argument intends to show, as systematically as possible, that there is no finality in dharma. The philosophical tool he uses for this is the logic of Conditioned Arising. According to Nagarjuna, one already errs when one recognizes 'something' and identifies it as 'something'. For everything is conditioned, therefore nothing is 'as it is'. As it is, it is empty. In chapter 15 of his *Verses on the Fundamentals of the Middle Way*, Nagarjuna points to the logical impossibility that something that arises according to conditions should have its 'own nature' (*svabhava*). And if there is nothing that is not conditioned, there is no 'own nature'. Further, if there is no 'own nature', there is no 'other nature' (*para-bhava*) that is 'own nature' of something else. According to Nagarjuna, whatever one sees is empty, a sort of illusion (*maya*) that does not have its inherent existence.

The purpose of this argument is to remind us of the inherent paradox of our perception. Whatever one sees is illusion, that is, non-existent; yet, as an illusion, it is always with us, and so to that extent it is not non-existent. Nagarjuna resorts to the 'four-cornered negation' to show how our logical language comes to its dead end when dealing with this paradox. In chapter 22, verse 11, he says, 'One may not say that something exists, nor that it does not exist; nor that it both exists and does not exist, nor it neither exists nor does not exist.' Nagarjuna's 'middle way' does not allow a simple yes or no. His 'middle way' thus involves this epistemological, ontological and logical instability. Nagarjuna's is a thorough argument. If nothing is outside conditions and if everything is related in this way, then what is true is not a 'thing' that has to be abstracted from this relevance but relevance itself. Nagarjuna points to dichotomies such as 'short and long', 'above and below' and shows that these distinctions are all relative. Nothing is inherently short or long. Therefore, he continues, there is no ultimate distinction between the Conditioned and the Unconditioned, that is, between samsara and nirvana either. There is a passage in the Early Buddhist texts that presented the teaching of Conditioned Arising in relation to the middle way between existence and non-existence of this world (*Samyutta Nikaya* XII.2.17). By referring to this passage, however, Nagarjuna's real intention is to take the logic of Conditioned Arising a step further and to argue that nothing, not even nirvana, is unconditioned. Hence the goal of the Buddhist practice is not to attain nirvana that is erroneously thought to be beyond Conditioned Arising but to realize emptiness that every conditioned being really is. 'Nirvana and samsara', as Peter Harvey puts it, 'are not two separate realities, but the field of emptiness, seen by either spiritual ignorance or true knowledge' (Harvey 1990: 103). Emptiness is not a tangible goal of transcendental practice. Nagarjuna denies the finality of emptiness as much as that of dharma. Emptiness, he argues, is not another, superior reality. The truth is that it is also empty of itself. Following this warning, later Mahayanists often emphasized that attachment to emptiness would be far more harmful than any other form of attachment.

Nagarjuna's argument results in reformulating the distinction between conventional truth (*samvrti-satya*) and ultimate truth (*paramartha-satya*). In Abhidharma philosophy the ordinary experience of 'I' and 'the world' was said to be conventional. The point of Abhidharma philosophy was to deny the reality of this experience. It was to show that conventional 'truth' was not true and the metaphysic of dharma alone was ultimately true. According to Nagarjuna, however, dharmas are not a degree more real than the illusory 'I' and 'the world'. From this point of view, both Abhdharma's conventional and ultimate truths are merely conventional. They are equally empty. Ultimate truth is nothing but the realization of emptiness of all. Hence it is no longer possible to keep the dichotomy of conventional and ultimate truths as Abhidharma philosophy did. These two 'truths' are not contradictory but complementary views on the one and same reality, emptiness. What happens at the end of this argument is the recovery of ordinary reality. It was once discarded as conventional falsification, but it is now reinstated as conventional truth, that is, not ultimate but only conventional, nevertheless not falsehood but truth.

Non-Mahayana schools argued that Nagarjuna's philosophy would destroy the whole Buddhist tradition. Mahayana schools, however, thought that it marked a new beginning that initiated their new practice, the Bodhisattva's way.

3.3 The Yogacara

The *Samdhinirmocana Sutra* (*Unravelling Mystery*), possibly the earliest Yogacara text from around the beginning of the fourth century, says that there have been three 'Turnings of the Wheel of Dharma'. The first turning is the Buddha's teaching of the Four Noble Truths, 'the Turning of the Wheel of Dharma' (*Dharma-cakra-pravartana Sutra*) as the Buddha's first teaching was called. The second turning is the teaching that everything is empty, presented in the Perfection of Wisdom sutras and expounded by Nagarjuna and the Madhyamaka school. According to the *Unravelling Mystery Sutra*, however, these two turnings were merely skilful means; they were incomplete and resulted in disputes among those who took them to be their final teaching. The third turning, it insists, is this sutra itself that is to be the final teaching after which there will be no dispute. This account is a clear indication of how the early Yogacarins placed themselves in the doctrinal development in Mahayana Buddhism. Although its claim to the final teaching was countered by many more disputes throughout the history of Buddhism, the sutra nevertheless predicted right that the Yogacara school should become a major philosophical school after Nagarjuna and the Madhyamaka school.

Following Nagarjuna's argument of emptiness, the Yogacara school carried out a further investigation into the paradox of our perception. It came up with the answer that it was because of the way our mind functioned. Whatever we perceive, it argued, is produced by our mind just like a dream or illusion. All that appears to us is representation from within our mind. All there is, is 'representation only' (*vijnapti-matra*). However, we are oblivious of this and take these representations as reality out there. We thus create 'our world' from these illusory products of our mind and, by doing so, identify ourselves as the perceiver of that world, as the 'I'. The assumption of the 'I' and the world is an error. By tracing the origin of the representation of the 'I' and the world in our mind, Yogacara philosophy presents an ontological argument, not for the 'I' or the world, but for our mind that is the origin of all. And by deeming the assumption of the 'I' and the world as an error, it reintroduces the distinction between truth and falsehood and, more importantly, reintroduces a way to move beyond this falsehood. After Nagarjuna's complete relativization of ignorance and enlightenment, or, samsara and nirvana, that must have caused a sense of profound disorientation, this Yogacara argument offered a new orientation and incentive for the practice of transcendence. The purpose of the practice, they argued, is for our mind to rid itself of the error of taking illusion for reality and to recover its original state of purity and equanimity. The Yogacara school emphasized the practice of meditation as the way to that goal. This gave them the name 'Yogacara' (Meditation-Practice) school. Also, they were called the 'Vijnana-vada' (Consciousness-Teaching) or 'Citta-matra' (Mind-Only) according to their doctrine. The prototype of their Mind-Only theory and the emphasis upon meditation could be found in as old a text as the *Dhammapada*.[17] What the Yogacara school did was to highlight these early suggestions and form them into a systematic theory, then to give the theory an elaborate exposition. Their philosophy was to have a widespread and lasting influence throughout the Buddhist world.

The Yogacara school's foundational sutras were the above-mentioned 'Unravelling Mystery' sutra and the *Lankavatara Sutra* ('Arrival in Lanka Island') from the fifth century. The brothers Asanga (the fourth century) and Vasubandhu (the fourth to fifth century) gave the initial systematic exposition of the Yogacara philosophy. Asanga's main work was the *Mahayana-Samgraha* (*Summary of the Mahayana*). He was probably the author of the *Madhyanta-Vibhaga* (*Discrimination between the Middle and the Extremes*) too, though legend had it that it was given to him by his teacher, the Bodhisattva Maitreya. Vasubandhu was the author of the *Trimsatika-karika* (*Thirty Verses*), the *Vimsatika-karika* (*Twenty Verses*).[18]

THE *ALAYA* CONSCIOUSNESS (*ALAYA-VIJNANA*)

The *Ch'eng Wei-shih Lun* (*Completion of the Doctrine of Mind-Only*) is a collection of commentaries on Vasubandhu's *Thirty Verses*, compiled and translated into Chinese by Hsüan-tsang (596–664). It is

---

17 See, for example, 1, 2, 13 and 14.
18 Vasubandhu's other writing included the *Vimsatika-vrtti*, his own commentary on the *Vimsatika-karika* (*Twenty Verses*), the *Tri-svabhava-nirdesa* (*Exposition of Three Natures*) and his commentary on the *Madhyanta-Vibhaga* (*Discrimination between the Middle and the Extremes*). He might have been the same Vasubandhu who was the author of the *Abhidharma-kosa*, a masterly summary of Abhidharma of the Sarvastivada school and a critical commentary on this summary, the *Abhidharma-kosa–bhasya*, written from the point of view of the Sautrantika school. Some suggested that Vasubandhu might have been involved in the Sarvastivada, then changed over to the Sautrantika before converting to the Mahayana to follow his brother Asanga.

a good summary of the fully developed Yogacara philosophy. Hsüan-tsang's translation has had a sustained influence upon East Asian Buddhism. It points out the basic problem of our perception.

> These phenomena of the 'I' and the world, though within the consciousness, seem, because of (false) mental discrimination, to be manifested in the external world. That is why all sentient beings, from time without beginning, have believed in them as a real 'I' and real world. The case is like that of a man in a dream, who, under the force of this dream, in which his mind manifests what seem to be all kinds of external objects, believes that these really exist as external objects. What the ignorant thus imagine to be a 'real' *atman* and 'real' *dharmas* are all absolutely devoid of (objective) existence. They are simply established in this way in accordance with these people's own mistaken beliefs. This is why we maintain that they are false.[19]

It is our ignorance that keeps us from realizing this. By reminding us of this epistemological slumber, this philosophy reiterates the anxiety that our perception is inherently false. Everything seems, but nothing 'is'. Thus the 'I' and the world are the 'seeming I' and 'seeming world'; we cannot deny their existence as illusion, but 'despite their seeming appearance as such they do not have the nature of a real I and real world' (ibid.).

It is the deepest layer of our consciousness called '*alaya* (storehouse) consciousness' (*alaya-vijnana*), that produces these illusions. According to the Yogacara theory, all of our past deeds and events, that is, all of our karma, are stored as 'seed' in this storehouse consciousness. These 'seeds' from the past are the cause of all illusions we have now. Once perceived, these illusions in turn are stored in the *alaya* consciousness and become the cause of another illusion in the future. In modern psychology the *alaya* consciousness may be called the subconscious or the unconscious and the 'seeds' latent memories stored in it. Yet, as a school of Buddhism the Yogacara seems to attach greater importance to the function of our mind than any depth psychology would. It makes the point that all our experiences, the whole cycle of Conditioned Arising, comes out of the *alaya* consciousness. Our experience is stored in the *alaya* consciousness, evolves into our consciousness when it is ripe, then is stored again till it becomes ripe to evolve as another experience later. The *alaya* consciousness is thus burdened by the karmic continuity of illusory experience.

The Yogacara philosophy sees eight levels of consciousness. It counts the five senses (sight, hearing, smell, taste and touch) as distinct levels and, as the sixth, the thought consciousness that coordinates these sensations, that we may call 'apperception'. These six are not always activated. During sleep, for example, they are inactive. The *alaya* consciousness is the eighth. It is the basis of the rest of consciousness. As the *Completion of the Doctrine of Mind-Only* says, 'the basic consciousness is the *alaya* consciousness, because it is basic for the birth of the other kinds of consciousness, both soiled and pure' (ibid.: 313). The religious problem lies between the seventh and the eighth consciousnesses. The seventh is called the *manas* consciousness. It is here that the six levels of sensations are organized into a meaningful experience. The problem is that this *manas* consciousness is also the self-consciousness that generates the false notions of the 'I' and the world. It 'grasps', and by that generates the dichotomy of 'the grasper' and 'the grasped' (*grahaka* and *grahya*). This seventh consciousness thus 'perpetually thinks about the ego, to which it clings' (ibid.: 312). Consequently, it causes all the problems associated with the 'I'.

---

19 Translated from Chinese by Fung Yu-lan. His translation reads '*atman*' and '*dharma*' in the place of the 'I' and 'the world' (1950–2: II.304).

This *manas*, which spontaneously and perpetually links itself with the *alaya* consciousness, has a reciprocal relationship with the four fundamental sources of affliction. What are these four? They are ego-ignorance and ego-belief, together with self-conceit and self-love. Ego-ignorance means lack of understanding. It is to be ignorant of the nature of the ego, and deluded as to the principle that there is no ego. Therefore it is called ego-ignorance. Ego-belief means the clinging to the ego. It wrongly imagines certain things to be an ego when they are not so. Therefore it is called ego-belief. Self-conceit means pride. Basing itself on the belief in an ego, it causes the mind to assume a high and mighty air. Therefore it is called self-conceit. Self-love means a greedy desire for the self. Because of its belief in the ego it develops deep attachment for it. Therefore it is called self-love.

(ibid.: 312–13)

The seventh consciousness, by producing the experience of the 'I' and the world, is the cause of the whole chain of ignorance and suffering.

These four (ego-ignorance, ego-belief, self-conceit and self-love), by their constant rise, disturb and pollute the innermost mind, and cause the outer operating consciousnesses perpetually to produce defiling elements. It is because of these . . . that sentient beings are bound to the cycle of transmigration without being able to escape. That is why they are called the afflictions.

(ibid.)

The first to the seventh consciousnesses consist in our ordinary consciousness. The eighth is the deepest one that is beyond, or rather beneath, the ordinary consciousness. It is beyond the ordinary 'I' and its self-consciousness. The problem is that the seventh and eighth consciousnesses, the *manas* and the *alaya*, are similar in their functions, both lie underneath the other six consciousnesses, and both are active all the time in forming our experience. Yet the *manas* consciousness is the place of epistemological falsification and the cause of ignorance and suffering. The question is whether there is a way to subsume the self-centred *manas* consciousness into the self-less *alaya* consciousness. In answering this question, the Yogacara presents the theory of the three aspects of our perception.

THREE ASPECTS

It is by the doctrine of the three aspects that the Yogacara presents its way to liberation, to detachment from the erroneous assumption of the 'I' and the world. The three aspects are: (1) 'the constructed aspect' (*parikalpita svabhava*), (2) 'the other-dependent aspect' (*paratantra-svabhava*), and (3) 'the perfect aspect' (*parinispanna-svabhava*). The first aspect is the ordinary aspect of our perception that forms our experience of the 'I' and the world. However, the second, other-dependent aspect reveals that our perception, when based upon the 'I' and the world, is the result of 'construction' or falsification. It reveals that our perception is involved in the karmic repetition of illusion. The third, perfect aspect is realizable when we become fully aware of the mechanism of our perception and rise above the false assumption of the 'I' and the world. The *Completion of the Doctrine of Mind-Only* explains this in the order of (2), (1) and (3).

(2) The mind and its attributes, together with the manifestations evolved by it, are engendered through numerous conditioning factors, and are thus like a conjurer's tricks which, not existing

though they seem to exist, deceive the ignorant. All this is called 'the other-dependent aspect'. (1) The ignorant thereupon perversely believes in them as an ego and as dharma . . . But like 'flowers in the sky' they are non-existent both in nature and aspect. All this is called 'the constructed aspect'. (3) These things, which are thus dependent on others and are wrongly regarded as an 'I' and as the world, are all empty. The genuine nature of consciousness thus revealed by this 'emptiness' is called 'the perfect aspect'.[20]

By realizing the perfect aspect the eight levels of consciousness are all 'turned over'. It is the transformation of the whole of our perception. By this transformation our perception becomes pure and clean, that is, free of all tainted seeds. The eighth, *alaya*, consciousness then becomes the round mirror consciousness (*adarsa-jnana*), the seventh, *manas*, consciousness becomes the equanimity consciousness (*samata-jnana*), the sixth consciousness becomes the subtle observation consciousness (*pratyaveksana-jnana*), sight, hearing, smell, taste, and touch consciousnesses become the action-accomplishing consciouness (*krtya-anusthana-jnana*).

The purified mind perceives only the pure world.

These purified consciousnesses can, like any ordinary consciousness, evolve external manifestations. 'These embodiments and realms are manifested through the evolutions of taintless consciousness . . . In common with their evolving consciousness, they are entirely good and untainted, they are the accumulated result of the Truth of the Right Path, and not that of suffering.'

(ibid.: 338)

According to the Yogacara, this is the Bodhisattva's wisdom.

The undiscriminating wisdom of the Bodhisattva takes no hold upon the objective world, and accepts no kind of sophistry about its appearance. He is now said really to abide in the genuine and transcendent nature of Mind-Only, that is, he experiences the Bhutatathata (Suchness, both '*bhuta*' and '*tathata*' meaning 'as such'). His wisdom and the Bhutatathata are on the same plane, both being equally divorced from the aspects of subject and object.

(ibid.: 336)

Whether there is an illusion after the 'turn over' may still be a question. The 'turn over' may not be the end of the epistemological paradox that an illusion is non-existent, yet, as an illusion, it is not non-existent. After the turn over, however, this paradox may no longer be a problem. An illusion, when we cease to take it as something real and cling to it, is no longer misleading. It is our attachment to it that makes the paradoxical nature of illusion a serious problem. But when we accept that an illusion is just an illusion, then the question is not that important. By this detachment we can cultivate the wisdom of non-discrimination. Then, although illusion may remain illusion, it is no longer delusion.

20 Ibid.: 329, with minor changes.

3.4 The Tathagata-garbha

Chinese Buddhism listed three distinct schools of Mahayana Buddhism in India: the Madhyamaka, Yogacara and 'Tathagata-garbha' schools. It even counted the Tathagata-garbha tradition as the fourth turning of the Wheel of Dharma. The Indian and Tibetan traditions did not count the Tathagata-garbha tradition as a separate school. This was probably because there were no prominent Indian philosophers associated with the tradition who could have developed the thought to a systematized argument. Since its appearance in the middle fourth century, it nevertheless made an important contribution to Mahayana Buddhism in India and further primarily through its interaction with other schools, particularly with the Yogacara.

The basic argument of this tradition is that every sentient being has the Buddha-nature. 'Tathagata-garbha' means the Perfect One in embryo. As seen above, 'Tathagata' is one of the titles attributed to the Buddha, meaning 'the Perfect One'. The Tathagata-garbha argument is that every sentient being has within itself this 'Tathagata' quality in its embryonic form. That is, every living being, however deluded and defiled, has a chance to nurture this embryo to its full maturity. The first definition of the Tathagata-garbha is its inherence in every sentient being.

> All the living beings, though they are among the defilements and hatred, anger and ignorance, have the Buddha's wisdom, Buddha's eye, Buddha's body sitting firmly in the form of meditation.[21]

Sentient beings are ignorant of this treasure within themselves. What the Buddha does is to point it out to them and encourage them to realize its full potential. The *Tathagata-garbha Sutra* sometimes reads 'Tathagata-garbha' as matrix of the Perfect One. Every sentient being then is a womb of this inherent Buddha-nature. In either case the passage to enlightenment is seen as the growth of this embryo into the full Buddha-nature.

As seen above, a strong Mahayana argument like this shifts the emphasis from the end to the beginning of practice. In this, the question is not so much as to the goal of transcendence but its beginning. In Tathagata-garbha thought the way to realize the goal of transcendence is to remove obstacles that obscure the Buddha-nature that already exists in every sentient being. The Buddhist task is still the complete transformation of oneself from within, yet Tathagata-garbha thought insists that the beginning of this transformation is already given in the form of the Tathagata-garbha. The rest of the task is to remove the stains that obscure this inherent Buddha-nature.

The basic texts of Tathagata-garbha thought are the *Tathagata-garbha Sutra*, from the early third century, and the *Srimala-devi-simhanada Sutra* (the *Lion Roar of Queen Srimala*) composed between the middle second and the middle third centuries. The text called the *Ratnagora-vibhaga* (*Analysis of the Treasure-nature*) or the *Uttara-tantra* (*Treatise on the Supreme*) is also important for its systematic exposition of Tathagata-garbha thought. The *Mahayana Mahaparinirvana Sutra* (*Mahayana Great Perfect Peace*), a later Tathagata-garbha sutra from the fourth century, becomes particularly influential to East Asian Buddhism by redefining the Tathagata-garbha as the 'Buddha-nature' (*Buddha-dhatu*) and calling it the 'I' (*atman*). The *Arrival in Lanka Island Sutra* of the Yogacara school includes the Tathagata-garbha thought as well as the Yogacara teaching of the three aspects, the eight consciousnesses. The sutra identifies the Tathagata-garbha with the Yogacara's *alaya* consciousness, the deepest consciousness that is primarily pure and unstained. The *Ta-ch'eng ch'i-hsin lun* (*Treatise on the Awakening of Faith in*

---

21 Translated by Takakusu Junichiro, quoted by Williams 1989: 97.

the Mahayana) follows this and presents the notion of original enlightenment that is to become particularly important in East Asian Buddhism.

Tathagata-garbha thought can be seen as a phase in the development of Buddhology that originated in the Buddhist attempt to get beyond the historical Buddha. The point of introducing the *Dharma-kaya* was to see the Buddha-nature beyond the Buddha's historicity and locality. The Dharma-kaya as the omnipresent, cosmic Buddha is the result of the temporal and spatial expansion of the Buddha. Tathagata-garbha thought marks a unique step in this development. It points to the internalization, as well as the expansion, of the Buddha-nature. Hence it presents the notion of the Tathagata-garbha, the embryo Buddha in every sentient being. The *Lion Roar of Queen Srimala Sutra*, for example, insists that this internal Buddha-nature is the Dharma-kaya, only obscured by external defilements. The point is that that the internal Buddha-nature and the external Dharma-kaya have to be essentially the same. The growth of the embryo gradually removes this obscuration, and leads, at the end, to the grand fusion of the external and internal Buddha-nature.

The *Mahayana Mahaparinirvana Sutra*

The *Mahayana Mahaparinirvana Sutra* (*Mahayana Great Perfect Peace*), like other Tathagata-garbha sutras, has two points to make: the definition of the Buddha-nature, and its latency in every sentient being. As to the Buddha-nature it has to state from the outset that the Buddha-nature is not the same as defilements.

> As for what the Buddha-nature does not have, so-called good, bad, and neither good nor bad karmas and their fruits, defilements, the five skhandas and the twelve links in the chain of dependent origination [Conditioned Arising].[22]

A sentient being therefore is a strange mixture of the Buddha-nature and defilements caused by karmas. This is why explanations of the latency of the Buddha-nature are so central in Tathagata-garbha thought. The point is that the strange mixture is best described by this latency. It would be wrong to yield it to a rigid distinction of enlightenment and defilement, for the latency is a form of suspension of that distinction. It is described, for example, as water 'hidden' beneath the surface of the earth.

> If you say that sentient beings need not practise the holy paths, that is not true. Good sons! It is like a man travelling in the wilderness who approaches a well when thirsty and tired. Even though the well is dark and deep and he cannot catch sight of any water, he knows that there must be water [at the bottom]. And if with various opportune means, he gets hold of a can and a rope and draws the water up, he will see it.

> (ibid.: 72)

Here the latency is explained as obscuration. The following example uses a temporal metaphor.

> All sentient beings will have in future ages the most perfect enlightenment, i.e. the Buddha-nature. All sentient beings have at present bonds of defilements, and so do not now possess the thirty-two

---

22 Translated and quoted in Liu 1982: 68.

marks and eighty noble characteristics [of the Buddha]. All sentient beings had in past ages [deeds leading to] the elimination of defilements, and so can now perceive the Buddha-nature.

(ibid.: 70)

These explanations of the latency invariably emphasize the need of practice. Tathagata-garbha thought has to guard itself from a settlement of the latency either into enlightenment or defilement. If such a settlement is in place, there is no possibility of practice. For, if there is enlightenment alone, there is no need of practice; if defilement alone, there is no point of practice. Nagarjuna's philosophy also attempted a destabilizing of this rigid distinction between enlightenment and defilement, along with that between the noble truth and the ordinary truth, between samsara and nirvana. The point of these attempts is to translate the tension inherent in the notion of latency into a form of genuine practice. The *Mahayana Great Perfect Peace Sutra* gives an illustration of how this either/or can intervene with practice.

Suppose someone declares that he has already attained the most perfect enlightenment. When asked for the reason, [he replies,] 'It is because [the Buddha teaches that all sentient beings] have the Buddha-nature. Since whosoever is in possession of the Buddha-nature should have already attained the most perfect enlightenment, [I declare] that I have attained enlightenment now'. It should be understood that such a person is guilty of sin. Why? It is because even though [all sentient beings] have the Buddha-nature, they have not yet cultivated various beneficial means, and so still have no vision of [the Buddha-nature]. Since they still have no vision, they have not attained the most perfect enlightenment.

(ibid.: 72)

Another example presents the latency as mere oblivion. In all these examples the sutra's emphasis on the latency of the Buddha-nature is coupled with its insistence on the need for practice. The embryo is still latent, and it should not be taken as actual.

What happens if the latency fails to encourage practice? Then the argument like Tathagata-garbha thought hits an immediate dead-end and ends up providing answers to questions to which no answer should be given. The Buddha dismissed questions such as 'whether the world is finite or infinite', 'whether the Tathagata exists or does not exist after death' (*Majjihima Nikaya* I.63). The *Mahayana Great Perfect Peace Sutra* quotes these questions and deems them as leading to attachment. These questions are a thinly disguised expression of the questioner's anxiety. The real question is 'What happens when I die?' This question is self-centred and concerns the small 'I' alone. To the question whether the world is finite or infinite, 'I', for example, could reply that it should be infinite when 'I' am enlightened. When 'I' am enlightened, 'I' partake in the Buddha-nature and am no longer impermanent. However, the point is that this 'I' is no longer the previous 'I', the small self-centred 'I' for which alone these questions mattered. The truth is that enlightenment and all practice leads towards enlightenment have nothing to do with these questions. They are not only irrelevant but also obstructive of practice.

In spite of all these warnings, the *Mahayana Great Perfect Peace Sutra* does present a positive description of the Buddha-nature. For the latency is still a positive rather than a negative expression. Moreover, the sutra describes what it is like to realize the Buddha-nature beyond its latency. Here is another example of the ongoing problem of a negative and positive presentation of the Buddhist goal, nirvana. When enlightenment is seen from this, unenlightened, end, it is described only negatively, as enlightenment is not like this or like that. But when the world is seen from the enlightened point of view, it is no longer to be denied but affirmed. Hence nirvana is called the 'island in the middle of flood', the 'highest bliss', and so on. One of the most remarkable examples of positive expression, however, is found in the *Mahayana Great Perfect Peace Sutra*. In early Buddhism, to see *nitya, sukha, atma, subha* (permanence, pleasure, 'I', purity) when there is only impermanence, suffering, non-self and impurity is the prime error to be overcome. The *Mahayana Great Perfect Peace Sutra* affirms that when enlightened we experience permanence, pleasure, 'I' and purity. As seen above, there are examples, in early Buddhism and after, where enlightenment is described as 'permanent', 'pleasure' or 'pure'. Yet no other sutras affirm the 'I' as an enlightenment experience. It is simply because the 'I' is that which the Buddhist overcomes at the moment of enlightenment.

> Since the tathagata is eternal, we describe it as the 'I'. Since the *dharmakaya* of the tathagata is boundless and all pervasive, never comes into being nor passes away . . . we describe it as the 'I'. Sentient beings are actually not in possession of such an 'I' and its . . . properties. Nevertheless, since [all of them] will definitely attain the most supreme form of emptiness . . . we designate them . . . 'Buddha-nature'.
>
> (Liu 1982: 71)

Some see in this affirmation of the 'I' an influence from Hinduism that argued for the identity of *brahman* (the cosmos) and *atman* ('I') in the late Upanishads. Clearly, whether the 'I' is always 'I' that constantly and endlessly to be overcome, or is to be affirmed at the end of its self-transformation, is an essential, yet always open, question. The passage thus highlights one of the most fundamental questions of religion. The *Mahayana Great Perfect Peace Sutra*, however, explains that the reason for mentioning the 'I' is not an essential but a pragmatic one.

> When the brahmins heard that the Buddha-nature is the 'I', there immediately arose in their minds the thought of the most perfect enlightenment; and soon, they left the household life to practise the path of enlightenment. All birds of the air and animals of the land and the sea [who were also present at this discourse] also resolved to attain the supreme enlightenment, and with the arising of such thought, they soon abandoned their [animal] form. Good sons! The Buddha-nature is in fact not the 'I'. For the sake of [guiding] sentient beings, I described it as the 'I'.
>
> (ibid.: 88)

That is, calling the Buddha-nature the 'I' is a skilful means (*upaya*) to entice some Hindus to Buddhist practice. This pragmatic explanation is rather anti-climactic for such an essential question as the 'I'. Yet it remains true that the tension between the negation and affirmation of the 'I' is the force behind any religious practice.

The *Mahayana Great Perfect Peace Sutra* was to become the foundational sutra of the Nirvana School in China. The sutra's popularity in China and its influence in Chinese Buddhism were considerable. Although the school and the study of the sutra declined in the seventh century, its argument and ideas were absorbed into the spirit of Chinese Buddhism and remained deeply influential throughout its history. In Japan Dogen expressed his Zen ethos by choosing a passage from the *Mahayana Great Perfect Peace Sutra*, 'everywhere exists the Buddha-nature' and purposefully misreading it as 'all existents are the Buddha-nature'. Whether a mistake or not, Dogen's point in this reading was quite clear: the Buddha-nature is not potentiality but actuality.

THE AWAKENING OF FAITH

The *Ta-ch'eng ch'i-hsin lun* (*Treatise on the Awakening of Faith in the Mahayana*), often shortened as *Awakening of Faith*, is a compact summary of late Mahayana philosophy. It now exists only in Chinese translation. No Sanskrit text, not even a fragment, has been discovered. There is no Tibetan translation. The existent translation attributes its 'original' to Asvaghosa, a famous Indian poet from the second century. Judging from its content, however, it is certain that the text is from the fifth or sixth century. Many scholars doubt its Indian origin. In support of this they point out that the treatise seems to have left no marks on the development of Mahayana philosophy in India. They instead suggest a Chinese origin of the treatise. Even so, it is uncertain whether it was written by a Chinese monk in Chinese, or by a foreign monk, possibly an Indian or Persian, who lived in China or Central Asia, and subsequently translated it into Chinese. The Chinese records tell us that it was 'translated' into Chinese twice, in the sixth and seventh centuries. This 'translation' was to become one of the most influential texts in East Asian Buddhism.

The *Arrival in Lanka Island Sutra* combines Yogacara teaching and Tathagata-garbha thought by identifying the Tathagata-garbha with the Yogacara's *alaya* consciousness. By this procedure Yogacara epistemology absorbs Tathagata-garbha thought and gains a Buddhological expression for the purity of the *alaya* consciousness. At the same time Yogacara epistemology gives Tathagata-garbha thought a chance to manifest its full doctrinal potentials. The *Awakening of Faith* is a prominent example of this development.

The *Awakening of Faith* begins with the argument that the mind is simultaneously empty and non-empty, that is, the mind prior to perception, the *alaya* (storehouse) consciousness without content, is 'empty', but 'non-empty' in itself. The mind is 'truly empty . . . because from the beginning it has never been related to any defiled states of existence, it is free from all marks of individual distinction of things, and it has nothing to do with thoughts conceived by a deluded mind' (Hakeda 1967: 34). Yet at the same time it is 'non-empty'. The mind, devoid of illusions, 'is eternal, permanent, immutable, pure, and self-sufficient; therefore, it is called "non-empty"'. This non-empty aspect is 'the sphere that transcends thoughts and is in harmony with enlightenment alone' (ibid.: 35–6). That is, it is non-empty as the basis of enlightenment. The mind as regards defilement is essentially 'empty', yet full or 'non-empty' as regards enlightenment.

The greatest obstacle for this argument is the apparent simultaneity of enlightenment and defilement in sentient beings. The *Awakening of Faith* reinterprets this simultaneity, which is central to Tathagata-garbha thought, as the strange concurrence of the originally pure mind (the *alaya* consciousness) and the defilement it subsequently accumulates.

> What is called the Storehouse [*alaya*] Consciousness is that in which 'neither birth nor death' [enlightenment] diffuses harmoniously with 'birth and death' [defilement], and yet in which both are neither identical nor different. This Consciousness has two aspects which embrace all states of existence and create all states of existence. They are: (1) the aspect of enlightenment, and (2) the aspect of nonenlightenment.
>
> (ibid.: 36–7)

The aspect of enlightenment is the Buddha-nature inherent in every sentient being; it is, as the *Awakening of Faith* puts it, 'the original enlightenment'. But this original enlightenment is mixed up with defilement. The *alaya* consciousness thus contains both enlightenment and defilement. It is therefore 'the compound consciousness'.

However, the concurrence of enlightenment and defilement is not a definite dichotomy. Adopting Tathagatha-garbha thought, the *Awakening of Faith* argues that the original enlightenment is essential while defilement is accidental, or to use a temporal metaphor, the original enlightenment is permanent while defilement is temporary. The *Awakening of Faith* uses the symbolism of water (essence) and a wave (accident) to illustrate this.

> This is like the relationship that exists between the water of the ocean and its waves stirred by the wind. Water and wind are inseparable; but water is not mobile by nature, and if the wind stops the movement ceases. But the wet nature of water remains unchanged. Likewise, man's Mind, pure in its own nature, is stirred by the wind of ignorance. Both Mind and ignorance have no particular forms of their own and they are inseparable. Yet Mind is not mobile by nature, and if ignorance ceases, then the continuity [of defilement] ceases. But the essential nature of wisdom remains unchanged.
>
> (ibid.: 41)

The *Awakening of Faith* also reinterprets the latency of the Tathagata-garbha in presenting the argument that the original enlightenment is the same as the process of the actualization of enlightenment. As Hakeda noted, 'the process of the actualisation of enlightenment in the original reads simply "the beginning of enlightenment"'. Hakeda's translation is helpful in highlighting the fact that it has a beginning in time, that is, it is a process. In this sense it is clearly distinct from the original enlightenment that is by definition atemporal. Therefore, when the *Awakening of Faith* insists on their identity, what it does is to emphasize the close correlation between them. The original enlightenment has to have its temporal manifestation that is 'the process'; and for the process of enlightenment even to begin, it has to assume the prior, that is, 'original', enlightenment. The *Awakening of Faith* insists on the identity of the origin and the process (that is, the latency of the Tathagata-garbha) and argues that they are distinct only when contrasted with non-enlightenment. Non-enlightenment is nothing but the failure to realize the original enlightenment. Because of this failure, although the original enlightenment is eternal, the process of the actualization of enlightenment has a definite starting point.

> The original enlightenment is in contradistinction with the process of actualisation of enlightenment; yet the process of actualisation of enlightenment is none other than the original enlightenment. Grounded on the original enlightenment is nonenlightenment. And because of nonenlightenment, the process of the actualisation of enlightenment can be spoken of.[23]

The *Awakening of Faith*, in presenting this complex argument, resorts to an effective use of the mirror metaphor that it adopted from Yogacara speculation. In its words, 'the characteristics of the essence of enlightenment have four great significances that are identical with those of empty space or that are analogous to those of a bright mirror' (ibid.: 42).

> First, [the essence of enlightenment is like] a mirror which is really empty. It is free from all marks of objects of the mind and it has nothing to reveal in itself, for it does not reflect any images.
>
> (ibid.)

---

23 Ibid.: 37–8, with changes.

That is, the mind is originally empty of defilement like the mirror prior to reflecting any image. Yet since it is empty, it potentially reflects 'everything' as it is. Because it is empty the mirror is not limited in time and space, that is, it is 'original'. This is the fullness (that is, non-emptiness) of the original enlightenment.

> Second, [it is, as it were] a mirror . . . serving as the primary cause [of the actualization of enlightenment]. That is to say, it is truly nonempty . . . It is eternally abiding One Mind . . . And none of the defiled things are able to defile it, for the essence of wisdom is unaffected.
>
> (ibid.)

That is, it is non-empty as the basis of the process of the actualization of enlightenment. These two 'significations' concern the original enlightenment. The following two are about the process of the actualization of enlightenment.

> Third, [it is like] a mirror which is free from [defiled] objects [reflected in it]. This can be said because the nonempty state is genuine, pure, and bright, being free from hindrances . . . and transcending characteristics of that which is compounded.
>
> (ibid.)

'That which is compounded' refers to the latency of the Tathagata-garbha. The process of the actualization of enlightenment is the process of getting over the concurrence of enlightenment and defilement and 'actualizing' the latent Tathagata-garbha. This surely has a practical effect.

> Fourth, [it is like] a mirror . . . serving as a coordinating cause . . . it universally illuminates the mind of man and induces him to cultivate his capacity for goodness, presenting itself in accordance with his wish.[24]

The point of this mirror metaphor is that it symbolizes all 'the four significations' of enlightenment at once. As seen above, the first two of the four concern the original enlightenment, in theory and in practice respectively; and the latter two the actualization of enlightenment, again in theory and in practice. The mirror metaphor thus symbolizes the essential sameness of the original enlightenment and the process of the actualization of enlightenment, also the unity of theory and practice in both.

The mirror metaphor is to become one of the most prominent symbolisms in East Asian Buddhism. Whenever it is mentioned, it implies, with varying degrees, the discussion of the *Awakening of Faith* that reinterprets Tathagata-garbha thought in the context of Yogacara epistemology.

4 FROM INDIA TO CHINA

Buddhism gradually spread to the regions outside India, and by the second century BCE it reached the area called Central Asia, north of Tibet. Buddhism reached China through this area around the beginning of the Common Era. The region was the crossroad of three distinct civilizations, the Mediterranean, the Indian and the Chinese. These civilizations were connected by a trade route called the Silk Road that

24 Ibid.: 42–3.

ran through Central Asia. Caravans that travelled this route carried not only silk and other materials but also religions. Although much of their own worldview remains obscure, it appears certain that the inhabitants of this area practised a remarkable degree of religious syncretism. As a Persian descent, they inherited Zoroastrianism. They accepted 'foreign' religions such as shamanism from the north, Nestorian Christianity and later Islam from the west, as well as Buddhism from the south. They also nurtured Manichaeism, a particularly eclectic religious practice with elements from Zoroastrianism, Buddhism and Christianity. All of these religious traditions found their ways to China. For the Chinese, Buddhism was originally only one of those foreign religions that 'the Westerners' brought to them.

The importance of religious practice in this area at around the beginning of the Common Era is undeniable. Both Christianity and Mahayana Buddhism were in their formative period, and they, and possibly Judaism, and later Hinduism and Islam, as well as religions that did not survive, could have received a substantive influence from the syncretic practice of this region. What does this mean for the study of religion? It means that a comparative study of religions, for example between Christianity and Buddhism, may not be merely speculative, that it may have a historical justification. This is of course only an assumption. It nevertheless challenges our commonly held view that Christianity and Buddhism are religious traditions that are historically independent of each other. It forces us to reconsider notions such as 'authentic' Christianity or 'authentic' Buddhism. We can certainly highlight elements that are exclusively Christian or Buddhist and label them as 'authentically' Christian or Buddhist. We have to ask, however, whether such 'authenticity' is another name for impoverishment, whether, instead of arguing for their unique and independent status, we should find these elements' relevance to other religious traditions. We have to ask finally whether we should look beyond the confines of Christian or Buddhist authenticity and reach out towards a 'religious' authenticity.

It is through Central Asia that Buddhism reached China. The Buddhist practice in this region remained influential to Buddhism in China for several centuries. Pure-Land Buddhism and Zen, the two trends of Buddhism that were to become most prominent in East Asian Buddhism, were among a number of different schools of Buddhism initiated in this area.

The Chinese acceptance of Buddhism is one of the most remarkable events not only in the history of Buddhism but also in the history of religion. There are few examples of a powerful nation, endowed with an ancient civilization possibly as old as human history itself, adopting a religious practice that was entirely foreign to them. Another example would be the Roman conversion to Christianity, but the Chinese acceptance of Buddhism gives quite a different picture. It was surprisingly smooth, without aggressive evangelism or forced conversion, and little political manoeuvre. Also, it was without persecution. There were a couple of recorded incidents, but they were nothing comparable to the systematic persecution that Christians suffered under Roman rule. In China the Chinese took a genuine intellectual and spiritual interest in this foreign practice, learned its sutras and gradually and voluntarily adopted it.

It would be wrong to use the term 'conversion' in this case. For what they did was to reinterpret the whole tradition according to their own interests. In adopting Buddhism, the Chinese exercised their elaborate interpretative schemes and sophisticated critical judgement. Their own philosophical tradition provided tools for interpretation and criticism. As a result, Chinese Buddhism was from the beginning a distinctly Sinicized form of Buddhism.

The process of acceptance can be seen in three phases: (1) translation, (2) initial interpretation called 'Ko-yi Buddhism', and (3) systematization by T'ien t'ai and Hua yen schools and simplification by Pure-Land Buddhism and Zen.

4.1 Translation

The scheme of translation was initiated by the Buddhist scholars in Central Asia who were competent in Sanskrit and Chinese, and probably quite a few more languages. One such monk was said to be able to understand 36 languages. The pioneer translators were An Shi-kao (in the Chinese capital Luoyang between 147 and 167), who translated non-Mahayana sutras, and Lokaksema, who came to Luoyang a little later than An Shi-kao and translated Mahayana sutras for the first time. The period of systematic translation began with Kumarajiva (344–413, also from Central Asia), who translated 35 sutras and produced more than 300 volumes of translation. His translation included the *Lotus Sutra*, the *Sukhavativyuha* (*Array of Happy Land*) Sutra, the *Vimalakirti-nirdesa* (*One Free of Stains*) Sutra, and the *Diamond-Cutter Sutra*. His translation was known for fluency. Also, he introduced Nagarjuna's philosophy to China. In the next century, Paramartha (499–569) came from India via sea and translated Yogacara texts. For this he is regarded as the founder of the Chinese Yogacara school. Another hundred years later Hsüan-tsang (602–64) travelled to India via Central Asia and brought back numerous sutras and commentaries. He subsequently translated 75 sutras and produced 1,330 volumes. His translation marked the new period in the history of translation for its breadth and accuracy. His primary interest was in Yogacara philosophy. In the next century, Amoghavajra (705–74, from Central Asia) translated Tantric texts. In this the importance of monks from 'the Western Region', as they called Central Asia, was obvious. China thus received Buddhism from Central Asia, spiritually as well as topographically.

From the period of translation the Chinese showed their distinct preference for Mahayana Buddhism. As seen above, the Chinese closely followed the development of Mahayana Buddhism in their translation. One of the reasons would be that Mahayana Buddhism attached less importance to the historical Buddha. For the Chinese who were removed from the historical Buddha by time, distance and culture, this was undoubtedly a welcome feature. In this sense the history of Buddhism is the history of the declining importance of the historical Buddha since the Buddha's own denial of any importance of his historical/physical being.

4.2 Ko-yi Buddhism

The first phase of interpretation based upon the early translations (that is, before Kumarajiva) is called Ko-yi Buddhism. The name *ko-yi* (extending the idea) indicates the method of analogy employed by early Chinese Buddhists in their interpretation of Buddhism. They appropriated Taoist terminology and 'extended' it to explain Buddhist discussions. In China there was a strong socio-political religion, Confucianism, and an equally strong naturalist religion, Taoism. Traditionally these two indigenous religions formed a set of alternatives for the Chinese spirit. Between the spectrum of Confucianism and Taoism, Buddhism, a religion of renunciation and detachment, appeared closer to Taoism than to Confucianism, which was already the powerful state religion of the Han dynasty. Consequently, Buddhism at its entry to China was interpreted along the Taoist line of thinking. The collapse of the Han dynasty in 221 CE marked a strong Taoist revival. This was also the time when the Chinese paid serious attention to Buddhism.

Resorting to their *ko-yi* (analogical) method, the Chinese thought that they discovered the essential identity between Taoism and Buddhism. The key was to identify Buddhist 'emptiness' with Taoist 'nothing'. Following this identification, they decided that Buddhism was actually Taoism only expressed in a foreign language.

> From the K'un-lun mountains eastward the term 'Great Oneness' [*tao*] is used. From Kashmir westward the term *sambodhi* [perfect enlightenment] is used. When one looks longingly toward 'nothing' (*wu*) or cultivates 'emptiness', the principle involved is the same.

> If we examine closely its [Buddhist] teachings about purifying the mind and gaining release from the ties, and its emphasis upon casting aside both 'emptiness' and 'being', [we find that] it belongs to the same current as do the Taoist writings.[25]

This analogy was extended to all the key concepts of Buddhism. Thus achieving enlightenment was explained as obtaining the Tao; the *Arahat* became 'true person' (*chen-jen*); and nirvana was understood as Taoist 'non-action'.

Ko-yi Buddhism was later criticized for being inaccurate and far fetched. As the translation scheme progressed, they learned more of Buddhism and became aware of the difference between intuitive Taoism in China and systematic and argumentative Buddhism in India. However, what Ko-yi Buddhism attempted and achieved was an interesting case of comparative philosophy. A Buddhist argument that begins with emptiness is always phenomenological, while Taoist speculation on the Tao (nothing) as the origin of everything is essentially ontological. Phenomenology and ontology are expressions of essentially different orientations: while an ontologist finally aims at the grasp of the ultimate, a phenomenologist acknowledges the impossibility of such a grasp and aims at remaining in resigned detachment. As in Tathagata-garbha thought, the ontological reinterpretation of emptiness was not unknown in Indian Buddhism. In China, by identifying 'emptiness' as Taoist nothing, Ko-yi Buddhism carried out this reinterpretation in the distinctly Chinese, that is, Taoist, context. This Taoist-inspired ontological orientation was to become an essential characteristic of Chinese Buddhism, to a greater extent than we usually assume.

During the Period of Disunity (221–589), there were 'Six houses and seven schools' of Buddhism in China. The seven schools were: (1) the School of Original Non-being, (2) the Variant School of Original Non-being, (3) the School of Matter As Such, (4) the School of Non-being of Mind, (5) the School of Stored Impressions, (6) the School of Phenomenal Illusion, (7) the School of Causal Combination. The first two schools were from the period of Ko-yi Buddhism. Characteristically, they advocated the identity of the Taoist nothing and the Buddhist emptiness. Tao-an (312–85), the founder of the School of Original Non-being, was recorded as saying that 'non-being lies prior to the myriad kinds of evolution, and that emptiness is at the beginning of the multitudinous shapes' (Fung 1950–2: II.244). The Variant School of Original Non-being was recorded as arguing that 'before there were yet material things, there was then non-being; therefore being issues from non-being' (ibid.: 246). This is virtually a repetition of a passage from the *Tao Te Ching*, 'Heaven and Earth and the ten thousand things are produced from Being; Being is the product of Non-being.'[26] These arguments were clearly more Taoist than Buddhist in presenting non-being as the origin of everything rather than arguing that everything was inherently empty. As to practice, Tao-an said, with a distinct Taoist tone, that one should 'but rest his mind in original non-being'.

---

25 The first statement is by Liu Ch'iu, the second by Fan Yeh, quoted in Fung Yu-lan, *A History of Chinese Philosophy*, vol. II, p. 240. There was a more Sino-centric account, 'a theory' that the Buddha was Lao-tsu in disguise. '[The theory] claimed that Buddhism was a debased form of Taosim, designed by Lao-tzu as a curb on the violent natures and vicious habits of the "western barbarians", and as such by imposing celibacy on Buddhist monks, Lao-tzu intended the foreigners' extinction.' *Encyclopaedia Britannica*, 'Buddhism in China'.
26 *Tao Te Ching*, chapter 40.

It was Kumarajiva's translation of Nagarjuna's treatises that made clear that Buddhist emptiness was not the same as Taoist non-being. The School of Matter As Such and the School of Non-being of Mind attempted to determine what was said to be empty. The former thought that matter was empty; the latter argued that the illusory contents of the mind were empty. The School of Stored Impressions and the School of Phenomenal Illusion appear to have been the result of the introduction of Yogacara philosophy to China, each representing one of the Yogacara school's central arguments. The School of Causal Combination appears to be grappling with the notion of karma, which was foreign to the Chinese mind.

Seng-chao (384–414) might have been the first Chinese philosopher who read Nagarjuna and came to understand that the Buddhist emptiness was not like the Taoist non-being that was seen as the positive origin of everything in spite of its negative prefix. He certainly noticed that emptiness pointed to the peculiarity of our illusory perception. He left a remark, 'all things are really in one way not existent and in another way not non-existent' (Fung 1950–2: II.264). He was aware that it was this phenomenological paradox and not the Taoist ontology that was at the centre of Buddhist philosophy. He also made an insightful remark on the Wisdom (*prajna*) that is the realization of emptiness: 'though void, the Wisdom illuminates; though it illuminates, it is void' (ibid.: 268).

4.3 Sudden enlightenment

Tao-sheng (*c*.360–434), a contemporary of Seng-chao, raised an interesting question as to the nature of enlightenment experience. The question was whether enlightenment was gradual or sudden. If gradual, enlightenment is seen as achieved by travelling through several progressive stages (*bhumi*) of practice over many lives. If sudden, it is seen as the whole experience that cannot be divided into stages. In a sense this is a question inherent in Buddhism from the beginning. Enlightenment is certainly more than the accumulation of skills and good deeds, but at the same time it cannot be irrelevant with regard to daily practice. Tao-sheng emphasized that enlightenment itself was the experience of breaking-through into another reality.

> The 'accumulation of learning' can merely serve as preparatory work; as far as the final state of 'non-being' is concerned, this can only be reached in a single flash of insight. Everything done previous to this final experience may be called learning, but it cannot be regarded as enlightenment itself. Strictly speaking, in fact, there is not even such a thing as 'gradual enlightenment'.
>
> (ibid.: 277)

However, if this breakthrough were entirely irrelevant to practice, there would be no Buddhist practice and no transcendence. The truth is that 'gradual enlightenment' and 'sudden enlightenment' are the two aspects of enlightenment, continuation and concentration. The point is to steer away from falling into this alternative trap of 'either gradual or sudden'.

Tao-sheng was nevertheless right in pointing out that the Indians tended to see enlightenment as gradual while the Chinese decidedly preferred it to be sudden. The difference is that while the Indians accepted karmic rebirth and saw their practice lasting over many lives, the Chinese thought that enlightenment was realizable in this life. Indian Buddhism certainly upheld the vastly long journey of continuous learning and practice. 'The mother's milk they had drunk in the course of their long journey through *samsara* is greater than the water in the four great oceans' (Gethin 1998: 113). This journey would last for aeons. And this is how they explained the length of one aeon.

> Suppose there was a great mountain of rock, seven miles across and seven miles high, a solid mass without any cracks. At the end of every hundred years a man might brush it just once with a fine Benares cloth. That great mountain of rock would decay and come to an end sooner than ever the aeon. So long is an aeon. And of aeons of this length not just one has passed, not just a hundred, not just a thousand, not just a hundred thousand.
>
> (ibid.)

In the same line of argument, Abhidharma philosophy grouped people into 'four practices and four fruits': *srota-apanna* was the one who would realize enlightenment after a maximum of seven reincarnations to the human and heavenly realms; *sakrd-agamin* was the one who would through a rebirth to heaven, then coming back to this world for enlightenment; *anagamin* was the one who would have one rebirth in a heavenly realm for enlightenment; *arhan* was the one that realizes enlightenment in this life. However, these expositions of the continual aspect of enlightenment did not deny the other aspect that at the final moment it would be a sudden experience. In this sense, as Tao-sheng argued, 'there is not even such a thing as "gradual enlightenment"' (Fung 1950–2: II.277).

This difference between the Indian and the Chinese is thus a difference in emphases, on either the continuous or the concentrated aspects of enlightenment. Tao-sheng explained this as the difference between the intellectual temperaments of the Indians and the Chinese.

> The people of China have a facility for mirroring (i.e., intuitively comprehending) Truth, but difficulty in acquiring learning. Therefore they close themselves to the (idea of) accumulating learning, but open themselves to that of the one final ultimate. The foreigners (of India), on the other hand, have a facility for acquiring learning, but difficulty in mirroring Truth. Therefore they close themselves to (the idea of) instantaneous comprehension, but open themselves to that of gradual enlightenment. Though gradual enlightenment reaches (a certain point), it remains in the dark about the fact that Truth is to be instantaneously perceived.[27]

Tao-sheng, a Chinese, emphasizes the concentrated aspect of enlightenment, but he also acknowledged that the two aspects are inseparable.

> Though knowledge resides in the one final ultimate, it is unconnected with the hopes aroused by the accumulation of learning. The Chinese are right (in saying) that the comprehension of Truth cannot be gradual, but wrong in asserting that the way toward it involves no learning. The foreigners are right (in saying) that the understanding of Truth embraces learning, but wrong in asserting that the way toward it is gradual.

Some would detect in this Tao-sheng's Taoist influence. It may well have been the case that his learning of Taoism prior to Buddhism led him to this question. Yet the point is that the question of two aspects of enlightenment is inherent to Buddhism. It may have been his Taoist learning that made him aware of the question, but the question itself was not created by him but only highlighted by him in this cross-cultural exercise through which the Chinese came to terms with Buddhism.

---

27 Ibid.: 276–7. It is uncertain where Tao-sheng's mirror metaphor came from. The mirror metaphor as representing epistemology is found in Taoist writing as well as Buddhist Yogacara.

5 PHILOSOPHIZATION AND SIMPLIFICATION

Buddhism in China became fully established during the period of the Sui and T'ang dynasties (590–906). Doctrines such as the universal Buddha-nature (*Dharma-kaya*), the presence of the Buddha-nature in every sentient being (*Tathagata-gharba*), and sudden enlightenment contributed to this development. The basic characteristic of Chinese Buddhism that became obvious during this period was that the Chinese saw enlightenment as near to themselves. When they restated the Tathagata-garbha as the 'original' enlightenment, the Chinese virtually declared that enlightenment for them was enlightenment 'here and now'. Their effort therefore was directed not so much towards reaching enlightenment as towards philosophically describing what enlightenment is or practically embodying it in some form of daily practice. Describing enlightenment, they presented a thoroughly systematic speculation; embodying it, they developed a thoroughly simplified form of practice.

The T'ien-t'ai and Hua-yen schools of Chinese Buddhism described enlightenment in a sophisticated philosophical language. They studied and reinterpreted all the major doctrines and presented their own doctrine as a synthetic totality. Their speculative philosophy was thus simultaneously systematic and inclusive.

In contrast, Pure-Land Buddhism and Ch'an (or Zen in Japanese) represented a thorough simplification of practice. They established themselves when they identified their simple forms of practice, *Nien-fo* (*Nembutsu* in Japanese) for the Pure Land and 'sitting (meditation)' for Zen. They carried out a simplification of practice under the slogan, Pure Land's '*Nembutsu* alone', or Zen's 'sitting alone'. They are practical responses to the serious problem posed by the doctrine 'enlightenment here and now'. The doctrine allows only two practical orientations, either to reject or accept it. Rejecting enlightenment, there would be no point of practice; accepting it, there would be no need of practice. In either case practice becomes difficult. Hence, Pure-Land Buddhism rejects enlightenment here and now yet has to move towards retaining the possibility of practice, if not in this world, certainly in the next. Zen accepts enlightenment here and now and yet has to explore a way to retain practice.

5.1 T'ien-t'ai

The name T'ien-t'ai (j. *Tendai*), 'Heavenly Terrace', comes from the mountain where the third patriarch Chi-i (538–97) stayed. Chi-i was the actual founder who laid the doctrinal foundation of the school. He was one of the most prolific writers of Chinese Buddhism. His writing included the *Miao-fa lien-hua ching hsuan-i* (*Profound Meaning of the 'Lotus Sutra'*), the *Miao-fa lien-hua ching wen-chu* (*Phrases of the 'Lotus Sutra'*), and *Mo-ho Chih-kuan* (*Great Calm and Insight*). They are called 'the Three Large T'ien-t'ai texts'. Chi-i is known for his systematic and synthetic approach to doctrinal matters.

Philosophical systematization was initially practised in a particularly Chinese environment. By the time the Chinese had engaged themselves in a comprehensive study of Buddhism, the Buddhist tradition already included many different teachings of the non-Mahayana and the Mahayana teachings, and different teachings within Mahayana Buddhism. They needed a scheme to decide which of them was the most important teaching and, at the same time, to understand Buddhism as a whole that could express itself in these diverse, sometimes contradictory, teachings. What they did was to determine one sutra as containing the Buddha's final teaching, and to arrange other sutras and teachings as stepping stones towards that final teaching. A philosophical school of Chinese Buddhism such as the T'ien-t'ai or Hua-yen was equipped with a thorough study of the sutra which it regarded as final, and a chart that interpreted other sutras in such a way as to indicate that they were a necessary preparation for that final sutra. This practice was called *p'an-chiao* (classification of teaching). The T'ien-t'ai school thus chose the *Lotus Sutra* as the final sutra, and the Hua-yen school upheld the *Avatamsaka* (*Flower Garland*) *Sutra*.

Chi-i's *p'an-chiao* is called 'Five Periods and Eight Teachings'. It is the most established example of this exercise. He arranged major sutras into 'five times' and divided their teachings into eight groups according to form and content. The Five Periods are 'the Time of the *Flower Garland*', 'the Time of Deer Park', 'the Time of the Extension', 'the Time of Perfection of Wisdom' and 'the Time of the *Lotus* and *Great, Perfect Peace*'. The 'Time of the *Flower Garland*' is immediately after the Buddha's enlightenment, when he teaches the essence of his enlightenment but is unable to be understood by his disciples. This is the time of the *Flower Garland Sutra*, comparable to the sun at dawn, whose rays touch only the highest mountain peaks. The 'Time of Deer Park' is when he taught non-Mahayana teachings. This is also known as the time of 'inducement' or 'attraction' since the purpose of the teachings is to prepare the disciples for Mahayana. The sun is at the point that illuminates the lowest valleys and canyons. The 'Time of the Extension' is the time of Mahayana Buddhism in general. It is the time of sutras such as the *Vimalakirti nirdesa* (*One Free of Stains*) *Sutra* and the *Arrival in Lanka Island Sutra*, and comparable to the sun at 8 a.m. (the time of the monk's meal). The 'Time of Perfection of Wisdom' is when the doctrine of emptiness is emphasized. It is comparable to the sun at 10 a.m. The 'Time of the *Lotus* and *Great, Perfect Peace*' is the time of the sutras of these names. The *Lotus Sutra* is considered to be the final doctrine taught by the Buddha uniting the temporary teaching of the three vehicles (Sravaka, Pratyeka Buddha and Bodhisattva) into one vehicle. The *Great, Perfect Peace Sutra* is a summary of the previous teachings and a source of enlightenment. It may have been a compromise for Chi-i to include the *Great, Perfect Peace Sutra* here next to the *Lotus Sutra*. By this procedure Chi-i managed to combine the *Lotus Sutra*'s 'One Vehicle' argument with the Tathagata-garbha thought that was the central argument of Chinese Buddhism. This is the time comparable to the sun at high noon, which illuminates the entire earth without distinction (Matsunaga and Matsunaga 1974–6: I.152).

The teachings found in these sutras are divided twice into four steps, according to method and according to content. According to method, they are the 'Sudden', 'Gradual', 'Esoteric' and 'Indeterminate' doctrines. The 'Indeterminate' is inclusive of the previous three. According to content, they are the Doctrine of the Three Pitakas (non-Mahayana), the Doctrine Common to All (teaching of emptiness), the Distinct Doctrine (Mahayana Buddhism in general), and the Round Doctrine that is perfect and final. What the T'en-t'ai school presents is, needless to say, the 'Indeterminate', 'Round' doctrine that is the grand synthesis of all teaching (ibid.: 153).

Chi-i's *p'an-chiao* thus involves the recapitulation of the basic tenets of the Madhyamaka and the Yogacara schools. Chi-i's distinct style of thinking, which I would describe as 'expansive systematization', operates in this recapitulation. It is detectable, for example, in his reinterpretation of emptiness. Chi-i argues that emptiness is threefold. He claims to have discovered 'the Threefold Truth' of emptiness in the triple statement of the *Heart Sutra*, 'form is empty, its emptiness is form; emptiness is no other than form, form is no other than emptiness; form is emptiness, emptiness is form'. For Chi-i, this statement is not a simple repetition of the doctrine of emptiness but the precise presentation of three aspects of emptiness that are 'emptiness', 'illusion' and 'middle'. In this passage Chi-i identifies two opposite vectors, 'from illusion to emptiness', and 'from emptiness to illusion'. According to Chi-i, the first phrase of the passage, 'form is empty, its emptiness is form', represents the first vector 'from illusion to emptiness', and the second phrase, 'emptiness is no other than form, form is no other than emptiness', represents the second vector 'from emptiness to illusion'. The third phrase 'form is emptiness, emptiness is form' is the middle way of the two vectors, the synthetic unification of the two opposite movements.

Chi-i thus sees in emptiness both the 'going' and the 'coming-back' aspects. What he does in this formulation therefore is to distinguish the two vectors and to integrate them into 'the middle way'. According to Chi-i, these three aspects are inseparable, that is, they are 'the Threefold Truth'.

Under the influence of the *Arriving in Lanka Island Sutra*, Chi-i's discussion, like other Buddhist philosophers' discussions in China, is rooted in the Yogacara doctrine of 'Mind Only' reinterpreted as the Tathagata-garbha. His famous teaching 'three thousand realms in one thought' is a direct result of this doctrine. Chi-i mentions this teaching only once in the *Mo-ho Chih-kuan*, yet the T'ian-t'ai school later makes it into their ultimate teaching. 'One thought', according to Chi-i, embraces the 'three thousand worlds'. Chi-i provides an argument as to why it is 'three thousand'. The point is, however, that this teaching is the expression of the original enlightenment. The mind that contains in its momentary thought the totality of the macrocosm represents the original enlightenment; and the mind that sees at once everything of all the realms, of the past, the present and the future, would be the Buddha's mind, that is, fully enlightened.

Chi-i also devised the systematic scheme of meditation. He lists four kinds of meditative practice to achieve 'Calm and Insight'. This scheme is particularly important because it includes what are to become the sole practices of Pure-Land Buddhism and Zen. The four kinds of meditation are 'perpetual-sitting' meditation, 'perpetual-practice (walk)' meditation, 'half-practice, half-sitting' meditation, and 'non-practising, non-sitting' meditation. 'Perpetual sitting' is to sit for ninety days, facing a statue of the Buddha in the lotus position. It is also known as 'single practice' because involving nothing but sitting. 'Perpetual practice' is to chant the name of the Buddha Amitabha and walk around the statue of the Amitabha for ninety days. The practice is thought to lead to the visualization of the Buddhas of the ten directions. 'Half-practice, half-sitting' is the combination of the two. 'Non-practising, non-sitting' is a form of meditation practised in daily life without restrictions upon physical posture. The practitioner could be walking, sitting, eating or lying down (ibid.: 157–8). We see here that the T'ien-t'ai school is systematic and synthetic both in doctrine and in practice. It is not a coincidence that the Japanese monks who established Pure Land and Zen in Japan were originally trained in the T'ien-t'ai school. In the process of simplifying their practices, they identified one aspect of the T'ien-t'ai practice as representing the rest of the synthetic practice. They then traced it back to its Chinese origin and transplanted it onto Japanese soil.

5.2 Hua-yen

The Hua-yen school is another equally philosophical and distinctly Chinese school of Buddhism. Its basic text is the *Buddhavatamsaka-nama-mahavaipulya-sutra*, usually shortened as the *Avatamsaka* sutra (*Flower Garland*). *Avatamsaka* translates as *Hua-yen* in Chinese and *Kegon* in Japanese. Chapters of this large sutra were originally separate sutras. They were compiled into one sutra in Central Asia around the third century, with some writings added at the time of compilation. The first comprehensive Chinese translation was by Bodhibhadra in the early fifth century. The full translation came out in the late seventh century. The sutra commanded respect and devotion among the Chinese who eventually formed a distinct school in the late sixth century.

The Buddha in the *Flower Garland Sutra*, as in the Tantric sutras, is not the historical Buddha but the Buddha Vairocana, 'Great Illumination' (*vai* means broad; *rocana* comes from the root *ruc* that means light). The Vairocana in the *Flower Garland Sutra* does not teach but only approves the teachings by the great number of Bodhisattvas who follow him. The Vairocana himself is the source of the light, and the cause of enlightenment.

> The Buddha constantly emits great beams of light;
> In each light beam are innumerable Buddhas . . .
> The Buddha-body is pure and always tranquil;
> The radiance of its light extends throughout the world.
>
> (cited in Williams 1989: 122)

Some see an influence from Zoroastrianism in its use of the light metaphor in describing the Buddha Vairocana. Of whatever origin, the light metaphor certainly is central to the Hua-yen philosophy. The point is that by the light metaphor the Hua-yen philosophers in China reinterpreted the Buddha's enlightenment as his illumination of the world. Thus the enlightenment experience is redefined in the Hua-yen school as the new vision of the world. The goal of Buddhist practice, according to Hua-yen, is to have this visionary experience.

The Hua-yen school began in the sixth century in China. The third patriarch, Fa-tsang (643–712), was a prolific writer and produced a number of treatises on Hua-yen philosophy such as the *Chin Shih-tzŭ Chang* (*Essay on the Golden Lion*), the *Hua-yen Ching Yi-hai Pai-men* (*Hundred Theories in the Sea of Ideas of the 'Flower Garland' Sutra*), and the *Hua-yen Ao-chih Wang-ching Huan-yüan Kuan* (*Cultivation of the Contemplation of the Mysterious Meaning of the 'Flower Garland' Sutra*), as well as commentaries on the *Awakening of Faith* and the *Brahmajala Sutra* (a pseudographic sutra, probably composed in China yet influential in East Asian Buddhism for its exposition of the *Bodhisattva-sila*). The light metaphor dominates Hua-yen philosophy, and much of Fa-tsang's philosophical discussion deals with, directly or indirectly, the philosophical meaning of the light metaphor.

Fa-tsang begins with the standard Mahayana doctrine that everything is empty and the realization of emptiness is enlightenment. In his word, 'comprehension of the fact that from time without beginning all the illusions fundamentally have no reality, is called enlightenment' (quoted in Fung 1950–2: I.356). He also recognizes the inherent paradox of our perception.

> Form, inasmuch as it has no inherent nature of its own, is 'empty'; but inasmuch as it gives the illusion of having seeming qualities, it is 'existent'. The best thing (to say) is that illusory form, inasmuch as it lacks any inherent substance of its own, cannot be differentiated from emptiness; and that genuine emptiness, being all perfect, penetrates to what lies beyond existence. By viewing form as empty we achieve Great Wisdom.
>
> (ibid.: 342–3)

Thus enlightenment, for Fa-tsang as well as for many other Mahayana philosophers, is the realization of the emptiness of illusions. For Fa-tsang, however, enlightenment is also illumination. The point is that at this visionary moment the whole of the illusory world appears (or reappears) as a grand vision. Hence,

> All things of the senses are revealed in their true essence, and become merged into one great mass. Great functions arise, every one of which represents the Absolute . . . The myriad manifestations, despite their variety, harmonize and are not disparate. The all is one, for all things equally have the nature of non-being. The one is all, for cause and effect follow in an unbroken sequence.
>
> (ibid.: 346–7)

Thus enlightenment is nothing but the vision that reveals infinite interdependence, or, interpenetration, of 'the myriad manifestations'. Enlightenment is an experience of seeing that 'each implies the other and freely rolls up or spreads out'. This, Fa-tsang argues, is 'the perfect teaching of the One Vehicle' (ibid.: 347).

Fa-tsang explains this as the vision of free contraction and extension, both spatial and temporal. It is to see in a particle of dust the whole space, and in a moment the whole span of time. Fa-tsang provides a detailed exposition of 'roll up' and 'spread out'.

> This means that a particle of matter, though it lack any nature of its own, yet embodies everything extending within the ten directions: such is what it is to be spread out. (Likewise) what lies within the ten directions, though it lack any essence of its own, may yet, in compliance with causation, be wholly manifested within a particle of matter: such is what it is to be rolled up . . . Rolled up, all things are manifested within the single particle of matter. Spread out, the single particle of matter permeates everything. The spread-out is the rolled-up, because in the single particle is gathered the all. The rolled-up is the spread-out, because in the all is gathered the single particle. That is why (the Absolute) can freely be rolled up or spread out.
>
> (ibid.: 349)

And he sees the same contraction and extension in time. 'Since a single instant lacks any essential nature of its own, it becomes interchangeable with a great aeon, and since a great aeon also lacks any essential nature of its own, it belongs to a single instant' (ibid.: 354).

Fa-tsang explains this interpenetration as the interpenetration between 'principle' and 'thing'. Chinese philosophers knew this distinction prior to the introduction of Buddhism to China. 'Thing' could mean a thing we perceive and an event we experience and could be paraphrased as phenomenon. 'Principle' is the noumenal principle that permeates this realm of phenomenon. This is a particularly Chinese distinction. In Buddhism Seng-chao first mentioned it, then the Hua-yen school placed it at the centre of their discussion of enlightenment. The Hua-yen argument begins with dividing 'the realm (*dharmadhatu*) of noumenon' and 'the realm of phenomenon'. The realm of noumenon is the realm of enlightenment and the realm of phenomenon is our ordinary, illusory perception.

For Fa-tsang, the realm of principle is the Tathagata-garbha that is latent in our perception of things and events.

> [The realm of principle] is the substance of the dharma-nature which lies within the Tathagata-garbha, and from all time it is, through its own nature, self-complete and sufficient. It is neither stained by contact with defiling elements, nor purified by cultivation. That is why it is said to be by its own nature clear and pure. Its substance shines everywhere; there is no obscurity it does not illumine. That is why it is said to be all-perfect and brilliant.
>
> (ibid.: 341)

We should note that Fa-tsang here adopts the light metaphor in describing the Tathagata-garbha. This Tathagata-garbha is said to be the mind that not only is pure but also illuminates. It illuminates the realm of phenomenon. The goal of the Hua-yen epistemology is therefore no longer the realization of the emptiness of illusion, but it is the illumination of illusion. Here, light and illusions that it illuminates are inseparable. In the Hua-yen terminology, this vision is the realization of the 'unimpededness' between light and illusion, 'unimpededness' between the realm of noumenon and the realm of phenomenon. Further, as the fourth patriarch Cheng-kuan (?738–839) argued, since the realm of noumenon permeates the realm of phenomenon, it leads to the 'unimpededness' among phenomena. This is the final goal of Hua-yen speculation. The Hua-yen school thus lists four realms (*dharmadhatu*): the realm of phenomenon, the realm of noumenon, the realm of unimpededness between noumenon and phenomenon, the realm of unimpededness among phenomena. 'Unimpededness' is clearly derived from the light metaphor. For it describes the way the light illuminates the myriad phenomena and forms them into a grand vision.

Thus 'emptiness' reinterpreted by Fa-tsang and the Hua-yen school is no longer 'empty'. If the Hua-yen scheme leads to enlightenment that is the illumination of illusion, its goal is no longer to eliminate illusion but only to illuminate it. Here, as in Chi-i's system, illusion is an integral part of the vision. As Fung Yu-lan suggests, Fa-tsang and the Hua-yen school in this respect follow the general trend of Chinese thought (ibid.: 359). It simply aims at transforming our ordinary perception into the vision of the whole world as it is.

We find in Fa-tsang's tenfold explanation of this vision many examples of a vivid symbolism which is worth mentioning here. 'Indra's net' was taken from the *Avatamsaka Sutra*. It is said to be the net decorated with jewels at each loop so that each jewel reflects not only every other jewel but also all the reflections of other jewels on it. When his students failed to understand the meaning of this, Fa-tsang was said to try another example.

> He took ten mirrors, arranging them, one each, at the eight compass points and above and below, in such a way that they are a little over ten feet apart from each other, all facing one another. He then placed a Buddha figure in the centre and illuminated with a torch so that its image was reflected from one to another . . . In this way each mirror not only reflected the image of the mirrors, but also all the images reflected in each of those other mirrors.
>
> (ibid.: 353)

Here the mirror metaphor and the light metaphor are merged into one, marking the final point of Chinese Buddhism in its philosophical recapitulation of the enlightenment experience.

5.3 Pure-Land Buddhism

Pure-Land Buddhism teaches the way to be reborn to the Buddha Amitabha's 'Pure Land'. This rebirth is thought to be granted solely by Amitabha's grace. Hence the school emphasizes the devotion to Amitabha rather than one's conscious practice. Behind this is a pessimism called 'the latter-day Dharma' and the recognition that proper Buddhist practice is no longer possible in such a degenerate period. Only when reborn in the Pure Land would one become able to practise properly and reach enlightenment. Thus the goal for the Pure-Land practitioner is no longer enlightenment in this life but rebirth in the Pure Land where practice leading to enlightenment is guaranteed.

The Buddha-Lands are invariably called 'Pure Lands'. These Buddhas are the *Sambogha-kaya* (Bliss-body), that is celestial as against the terrestrial *Rupa-kaya* (Form-body), yet still personal as against the cosmic *Dharma-kaya* (Law-body). Each 'Bliss-body' is said to be presiding over his own world, and many 'Buddha-Lands' are called *sukhavati* (happy land). 'Pure Land' appears to have been the Chinese interpretation of happy land. Pure-Land Buddhism chose the Buddha Amitabha's land, because it was believed to be the best of all. The Larger Array of the *Happy Land Sutra* tells how, many aeons ago, the Bodhisattva Dharmakara resolved that he would produce his Buddha-Land that would combine the best of all, then made forty-eight vows that he would become a Buddha only when he could produce such a Pure Land. According to the Pure-Land doctrine, Dharmakara has become the Buddha Amitabha and now presides over his Pure Land. Since he is believed to have achieved final enlightenment, all of his vows are regarded as fulfilled. His forty-eight vows were in the form: 'If in my land, after I have attained Buddhahood, this vow would fail, then may I not attain final enlightenment.' The belief in Amitabha's vow is thus the basis of Pure-Land Buddhism. Accordingly, Pure-Land practice is directed to the devotion of Amitabha. Unlike other forms of Buddhism its goal is not enlightenment; its emphasis is on the saving grace of Amitabha rather than on one's own practice.

Three sutras are regarded as foundational to Pure-Land Buddhism. The Larger and Smaller *Array of the Happy Land*, and the *Amitaur-dhyana Sutra* (*Meditation on Amitaus*).[28] The *Array of the Happy Land Sutras* could be from the first century CE or earlier. The *Larger Array of the Happy Land Sutra* includes Amitabha's forty-eight vows. The *Meditation on Amitaus Sutra* was probably composed in Central Asia or China. It is about the visualization of Amitabha and his Pure Land. The *Smaller Array of the Happy Land Sutra* is sometimes regarded as the concluding texts of the three sutras, but not necessarily chronologically, for its depiction of the Pure Land and its inhabitant.

Pure-Land Buddhism was originally an interesting combination of a meditative and a devotional practice, both of which might have been adopted from foreign traditions. 'Amitabha' means infinite light, and his land is said to be in the western region of the universe. This light metaphor, as scholars pointed out, might have been influenced by Zoroastrian sun worship. The metaphor epitomizes the practice of the visualization of Amitabha and his Pure Land. 'The Pure Land' was originally an expression of a visionary experience, similar to that found in the Hya-yen school. Certainly the *Meditation* sutra seems to expound the meditative visualization of the Pure Land. Also, Vasubandhu (the influential Yogacara philosopher) in his commentary on the *Larger Array of the Happy Land Sutra* described the condition of the unenlightened as the 'realm of pollution' and of the enlightened as the 'realm of purification'. He then equates the perfections of the 'realm of purification' with the description of the Pure Land found in the *Larger* Sukhavati-vyuha (*Array of the Happy Land*) *Sutra* (Matsunaga and Matsunaga 1974–6: II.43). Here the Pure Land is primarily a meditative vision one receives at the moment of his enlightenment. There is also a devotional element in Pure-Land Buddhism. Scholars have noted the similarity between its devotional faith in the Amitabha and the Messiah worship practised in the Mediterranean world. The Pure Land schools in East Asia emphasized this devotional element and simplified their doctrine and practice in this direction.

In China, T'an-luan (476–542) formulated the distinction between practice by 'one's own power' and that by 'the other power'. The latter is not a practice in the traditional sense of the word, for it only involves the wish to be reborn in the Pure Land and the faith in Amitabha's vows that promises it. Its goal is no longer self-transformation by practice but the transition from this life to the life in the Pure Land by the saving grace of Amitabha. T'an-luan insisted that devotion to Amitabha was superior to traditional Buddhist practice since the former was 'easy' and accessible to everyone while the latter was 'difficult' and impracticable. He identified *Nien-fo* (j. *Nembutsu*), the chant 'Devotion to Amitabha', as a viable practice that was an expression of one's devotion to Amitabha. This was based upon the eighteenth vow of Amitabha. 'If, upon the attainment of Buddhahood, all beings in the ten quarters who aspire in sincerity and faith to be born in my land, recite my name up to ten times and fail to be born there, then may I not attain the Supreme Enlightenment.'

Tao-ch'o (562–645) followed T'an-luan's argument and distinguished the Gate of the Holy Path and the Gate of the Pure Land. This is a sort of Pure-Land *p'an-chiao*, deeming all the previous forms of practice as belonging to the Gate of the Holy Path. According to this *p'an-chiao*, the Gate of the Pure Land is better than the Gate of the Holy Path because the 'Easy Path', as he called the practice of the

---

28 Amitabha (Infinite Light) is sometimes called Amitayus (Infinite Life).

Gate of the Pure Land, is practicable by those who were ill-equipped to practise anything else. Behind this argument was the pessimistic view of his time that he thought was 'the latter-day Dharma'. 'The latter-day Dharma' is the degenerate age that was believed to begin one and a half thousand years after the Buddha's death that should mark the decline in Buddhism and morality as predicted by the *Lotus Sutra*. Tao-ch'o argued that in such a time no one was able to follow the Holy Path by his own power, hence he must rely on the Pure Land path that is 'easy'. That is, in the latter-day Dharma, one's own power must be replaced by 'the other power' that is nothing but the power of Amitabha. He also attempted to mediate the meditative and devotional approaches by resorting to Buddhology. Amitabha for him was both the *Dharma-kaya* and the *Sambhoga-kaya*; the *Dharma-kaya* as the infinite light that is approachable through meditative practice and concentration, and the *Sambhoga-kaya* as a saviour approachable through faith. Amitabha's *Sambhoga-kaya*, according to him, was a *upaya* for those who are incapable of practice that would lead to enlightenment in this life.

Shan-tao (613–81) too emphasized faith in the Amitabha's vow and insisted that it had to be 'sincere, deep, and accompanied by an overriding desire for rebirth in Amitabha's Pure Land' (quoted in Williams 1989: 261). He also emphasized the contrast between the Pure Land and the 'impure land' of the degenerate age.

5.4 Pure-Land Buddhism in Japan

Since its formal introduction to the Japanese court in the middle of the sixth century, Buddhism contributed to the state ritual that was believed to ensure the protection and peace of the nation. It was not until the middle of the tenth century that the Japanese noticed the importance of the philosophical/ethical side of Buddhism. The Tendai (the Japanese for T'ien-t'ai) school became prominent during this period. The Japanese became convinced of their misfortune to live in the day of *Mappo* (the latter-day Dharma) when in the middle of the eleventh century the power of the centralized government was weakened by a series of political and social upheavals. They discovered Pure Land 'elements' within the syncretic Tendai practice as a way to find peace in a time of unrest. The promise of the Pure Land by Amida (the Japanese for Amitabha) gave the troubled soul consolation and hope. The Pure Land elements were found most notably in Genshin's *Ojo Yoshu* (*Summary of Rebirth*), as well as various literary works of the period such as the *Tale of Genji* (*Genji Monogatari*) by Lady Murasaki and poems by Saigyo. In architecture, the building and garden of Byodoin assimilated the Pure Land on earth. Also, paintings of Amida's visit visually depicted the hope for rebirth to the Pure Land. 'Raigo' (visitation and reception), as these paintings are called, is Amida's visitation to man at the moment of his death.[29]

A century later Pure-Land Buddhism saw a further doctrinal clarification and practical simplification by Hōnen (1133–1212) and his disciple Shinran (1173–1262), who became the founders of, respectively, the Jodo and Jodo Shin sects in Japan. Simplification in Pure-Land Buddhism culminated in two slogans: doctrinally, 'nothing but' the trust in Amida's vow; practically, 'nothing but' Nembutsu. This process of simplification was driven by the growing awareness of an individual's helplessness in

---

29 Raigo is the fulfilment of Amida's nineteenth vow that says, 'If, upon the attainment of Buddhahood, I will appear at the moment of death to all beings of the ten directions committed to enlightenment and the practice of good deeds, who seek to be born in my land and fail to be born there, then may I not attain supreme enlightenment.'

the period of Mappo. This pessimism propelled Pure-Land Buddhists 'to reject the Impure Land' and 'to yearn after the Pure Land'. Nothing other than Amida's compassion expressed in the Original Vow could facilitate the transition from the 'Impure' to the 'Pure' Land. Their deep pessimism was thus countered by their hope for this transition. Often their firm trust in Amida's promise was a way to translate the misfortune of having to live in the degenerate age into the joy of hope. Hōnen said, 'joy . . . as high as the heavens above and as deep as the earth beneath . . . always . . . returning thanks for the great blessedness of having in this life come in contact with the Original Vow of the Amida Buddha' (quoted in Williams 1989: 266).

Shinran completed the simplification of doctrine and practice by stressing the 'other' power (j. *tariki*) that was Amida's power. His point was quite simple: nothing but Amida's grace should matter. Accordingly, for him Nembutsu was no longer a form of practice but only an expression of one's devotion to Amida. When there was a dispute among Hōnen's disciples as to whether Nembutsu up to seventy thousand times a day was a respectable practice, Shinran made clear his view that 'One Nembutsu', meaning single-minded devotion to Amida, was a superior form of practice. Nembutsu for him was nothing more than a by-practice of this devotion.

> The indestructible true mind is called true faith and true faith is certainly provided with the Name [the name 'Amida' in the Nembutsu]. However, the Name is not necessarily provided with the faith supported by the power of the Vow.[30]

'One Nembutsu' is thus the simplest form of practice in Pure-Land Buddhism. It is clear that Shinran was ready to drop Nembutsu along with all other forms of practice in order to guard against 'empty Nembutsu' that lacked its devotional content.[31]

Shinran's 'the other power' doctrine changes the meaning of 'ease' of the 'easy path' that Pure-Land Buddhism was meant to be. Originally it was said to be easy because it did not require any other practices that they thought became impracticable under the latter-day Dharma. Simply, one could not do anything better than to have faith in Amida's promise. This is only a negative meaning of 'ease'. For Shinran, however, 'the other power alone' is not a negative but a positive statement. Shinran argues that these practices are not only impracticable but also, and more seriously, misleading. All these practices, according to Shinran, are done by 'self-power' (j. *jiriki*), therefore intervene with absolute trust in Amida. For, any deliberate act involves ego and an egocentric view such as 'I practise', 'I meditate', 'I fast', or 'I believe'. Hence practice done by self-power generates self-reliance and positively hinders one's faith in Amida's grace. Shinran thus rejects all wilful practices and emphasizes 'faith' as against these practices, even as against faith as a choice. Shinran's practice is indeed 'easy', for it is just to have trust in Amida's promise. Yet it is a difficult way, for it is to do nothing else. Doctrinal simplification in Pure-Land Buddhism thus reaches Shinran's 'pure faith', free from the contamination of the egocentric self and the stain of 'self-power'.

Shinran firmly believes that when one drops all effort, one receives faith in Amida's promise as an unconditional gift. Only it has to be preceded by the realization that no effort has any effect. For Shinran, faith itself also is a gift from Amida. Shinran regards all that matters in Pure-Land Buddhism, sincerity, faith, hope for the Pure Land, as a product of the merit accumulated by Amida in his practice

---

30 *Kyogyo Shinsho*, quoted in Matsunaga and Matsunaga 1974–6: II.99.

31 From the same doctrinal basis, Ippen (1239–89) initiated a school of Pure-Land Buddhism called 'Ji shu'. He taught to 'throw away' everything. His practice included dancing as well as chanting.

as a Bodhisattva. Amida, out of compassion, transfers them to unenlightened sentient beings and offers them the sure promise of rebirth in his Pure Land. In his words:

> As all sentient beings hear his [Amida's] Name, joyful faith is awakened in them leading to one thought, for [Amida's] sincere mind is 'transferred' to them. When they seek to be born in that land, they will instantaneously attain it and reside in the irreversible state.[32]

This gift has nothing to do with any form of practice. Hence it has nothing to do with good or evil. The difficult question about the relevance or irrelevance of this gift and morality was first raised by Hōnen.

> While believing that even a man guilty of the ten evil deeds and the five deadly sins may be born into the Pure Land, let us, as far as we are concerned, not commit even the smallest sins. If this is true of the wicked, how much more of the good.[33]

Hōnen's way is a compromise. While stressing the gratuitous nature of Amida's promise, he also tries to maintain a code of conduct. Hence he states, 'if this [the promise of the Pure Land] is true of the wicked, how much more of the good'. Shinran immediately detects a hint of self-reliance in this compromise. He refuses to compromise and restates Hōnen's conclusion as this.

> If even a good man can be born in the Pure Land, more so an evil man.[34]

'A good man' is Shinran's irony. For Shinran, a good man is the one who conceitedly practises by self-power. In contrast, an evil man is the one who has to give up all hopes of practice and cling to Amida's promise alone. Shinran is well aware of the danger of this statement that appears to endorse wilful wrongdoings. For Shinran, however, 'wrongdoings' are never wilful but simply inevitable. This statement comes from his awareness of his own 'wrongdoings', that is his inability to carry out proper practices. Since an attempt to get over these inevitable 'wrongdoings' is bound to lead to egocentricity, all he can do is to rely upon Amida's grace and to keep his hope alive.

For Shinran, Amida's grace and his devotion to Amida are one set. To use his words, 'the outgoing aspect' (from a practitioner to Amida) and 'the returning aspect' (from Amida to a practitioner) are ultimately one. After all, they are the two sides of Amida's compassion. This radical identity is unthinkable. As he puts it, 'non-reason is reason'. The point is that on the basis of this 'non-reason' Shinran, towards the end of his life, presents the notion of spontaneous practice.

> For rebirth in the Pure Land cleverness is not necessary – just complete and unceasing absorption in gratitude to Amida. Only then does the Nembutsu come forth effortlessly. This is what is meant by naturalness. Naturalness, therefore, is that state in which there is no self-contrivance, just as the grace and strength of Amida.
>
> (quoted in Williams 1989: 273)

---

32 From the *Array of the Happy Land Sutra*. Matsunaga and Matsunaga 1974–6: II.100.
33 *Hōnen Shonin Denki*, quoted in Matsunaga and Matsunaga 1974–6: II.69.
34 *Tannisho*, 3.

Thus Shinran's goal turns out to be a spontaneous devotion to Amida. And that restores 'harmony and tolerance' in his mind.

> When faith is firmly established, attainment is achieved through Amida's means, our own contrivance is not involved. The more we realise our limitations, then the more we look up to the power of the Vow, and as a consequence of Naturalness a mind of harmony and tolerance will arise.
>
> (quoted in Matsunaga and Matsunaga 1974–6: II.105)

This ideal of Pure-Land Buddhism is the practitioner who practises spontaneous Nembutsu in the mind of harmony and tolerance. Shinran clearly sees as achievable the devotion and practice that are cleansed of every hint of egocentricity. The spontaneous practitioner, although he is still in the Impure Land, would see himself already in the Pure Land. Pure-Land Buddhism began with the recognition of impurity of this world and the image of the Pure Land. Its goal was the transition from this Impure Land to Amida's Pure Land. Shinran, however, by identifying the outgoing and returning aspects, indicates the possible identity of the Impure and the Pure Lands, that is, initiates a form of transcendentalism within Pure-Land Buddhism.

5.5 Zen

What is called Zen in Japanese (*dhyana* in Sanskrit; *jhana* in Pali; *Ch'an* in Chinese) originated in Yoga, the well-known meditative practice of India. The Buddha practised meditation. Meditation ever since has been an essential part of Buddhist practice. Zen Buddhism in China and Japan is a type of Buddhism that places the utmost emphasis on this practice. The doctrinal history of Buddhism, from early Buddhism's Conditioned Arising, Mahayana Buddhism's emptiness, empty mind, and Tathagata-garbha thought, to Chinese Buddhism's original enlightenment and sudden enlightenment, finally to 'enlightenment here and now', is itself Zen Buddhism's philosophical lineage. Zen is an attempt to put this last doctrine into practice. However, Zen always places enlightenment outside such a lineage. This is the only viable way to think of enlightenment, according to Zen, for enlightenment is by definition beyond the limitation of time and space. It thus maintains that enlightenment is above a history of whatever kind, be it the history of doctrine, the history of Buddhism as a whole, or the personal history of an individual practitioner. Enlightenment is transmitted 'from mind to mind'; and the transmission is intuitive 'without the use of words' or any other form of mediation. Ultimately, this atemporal and aspatial transmission is that from an enlightened to another enlightened, that is, from a Buddha to another Buddha.[35]

As to a definition of what Zen Buddhism is and is about, it is futile to look for one in Zen Buddhism itself. As it places itself beyond such a definition, Zen only explains itself in paradoxical statements. These statements are found in several collections of Zen masters' sayings, and they are unanimous in stressing the idleness of such a definition. Their paradoxical sayings are nonetheless helpful in seeing to what Zen aspires. For, while they refuse to present any positive definition, they are clear and precise about what Zen is not meant to be. One such paradoxical statement is 'spiritual cultivation cannot be

---

35 Zen Buddhism points to a phrase in the *Lankavatara Sutra* for the justification of this stance. The sutra says 'Not a word', indicating that truth is beyond word.

cultivated' (Fung 1950–2: II.393). Conscious effort, according to Zen, only enhances the grip of ego. In the words of Shen-hsiu (c.600–706):

> Cultivating and abiding in emptiness, [one] is bound by that emptiness; cultivating and abiding in meditation, [one] is bound by that meditation; cultivating and abiding in quiescence, [one] is bound by that quiescence; cultivating and abiding in silence, [one] is bound by that silence.
>
> (Shen-hsiu, quoted in ibid.: 395)

This is a reminder of Nagarjuna's warning against the attachment to emptiness. If there is a form of practice that does not fall into this trap, it can only be described paradoxically, for example, as 'cultivation through non-cultivation' (ibid.: 392).

Thus the purpose of spiritual cultivation is nothing but to discover that the ordinary mind does not need cultivation, that it is in itself already enlightened. The following conversation between a master and a disciple illustrates this distinctly Zen attitude towards practice.

> Teacher asked Nan-ch'üan: 'What is the way?' Ch'üan replied: 'The ordinary mind is the way.' The Teacher then asked whether it could be something aimed for. 'By delineating it, you turn your back on it,' was the reply. The Teacher went on: 'But if you do not delineate it, how do you know it is the way? The way is not classifiable as either knowledge or non-knowledge,' Ch'üan replied. 'Knowledge is illusory understanding; non-knowledge is blind lack of understanding. If you really comprehend the indubitable way, it is like a vast emptiness.'
>
> (ibid.: 397)

The way, this 'vast emptiness', is beyond our grasp. What is characteristic in Zen is that this realization leads to the (re)discovery of the ordinary mind. If it is all that is in Buddhism, indeed 'there is nothing much in the Buddhist teaching' (ibid.: 402). Enlightenment then is nothing more than the realization that the ordinary mind should simply remain ordinary.

> If you comprehend it [enlightenment], where is that which you did not comprehend before? What you were deluded about before is what you are now enlightened about, and what you are now enlightened about is what you were deluded about before.
>
> (Ch'in-yüan (1067–1120), quoted in ibid.: 399)

Zen Buddhism thus re-emphasizes the standard Mahayana doctrine that there is no difference between enlightenment and delusion, hence there would be no difference before and after enlightenment. As seen above the return to the ordinary is a particularly Zen orientation. Enlightenment is just to recover the ordinary mind and to realize that 'the mountain is the mountain, the river is the river', and return to the ordinary life. This ordinary life, however, is free of attachment. In Hsi-yün's words, 'to eat all day yet not swallow a grain of rice, to walk all day yet not tread an inch of ground, this is to be the man who is at ease in himself' (ibid.: 404).

If there is any orientation in Zen Buddhism, it is the return to the banality of everyday life. The point is that this return may involve no practice at all. Thus the question concerning the need or not of a particular practice has always been at the centre of Zen. On this issue, Shen-hsiu, the founder of the Northern School of Chinese Zen, wrote a hymn:

The body is like the *Bodhi*-tree,
And the mind like a clear mirror.
Carefully we cleanse them hour by hour
Lest dust should fall upon them.[36]

He upheld the doctrine of gradual enlightenment, and thus emphasized the importance of practice. According to Shen-hsiu, although enlightenment is already achieved by the mind that is like a clear mirror, it is essential to keep it clean. Thus, his practice still 'aims at' the stage in which there is no dust. Hui-neng (638–713), one of Shen-hsiu's younger colleagues and the founder of the Southern School of Chinese Zen, rebutted Shen-hsiu's argument. He parodied Shen-hsiu's hymn and wrote:

Originally there was no *Bodhi*-tree,
Nor was there any mirror.
Since originally there was nothing,
Whereon can the dust fall?
(ibid.: section 8)

While Shen-hsiu tries to retain its traditional practice of meditation, Hui-neng refuses to acknowledge anything intended or intentional. Hui-neng can legitimately argue that enlightenment is beyond definition or description. 'Enlightenment here and now' is just there, and it requires no more word or practice. What is certain is that 'enlightenment here and now' is ultimately the end of Buddhism itself.

Dogen (1200–53), the founder of the Soto school in Japan, also found himself caught in the dilemma between 'enlightenment here and now' and the need of practice. The answer he finally found for himself was quite simple: enlightenment and practice should be inseparable. His point is that the dichotomy of enlightenment practice is erroneous in the first place. If one ceases to see practice as a 'way' to gain enlightenment or enlightenment as the reward of practice, there will be no need of separating enlightenment and practice. According to Dogen, practice and enlightenment are originally one and inseparable. In Dogen's words:

The fish swims in water without ever mastering the water, the bird flies in the air without ever mastering the air . . . and if the bird is placed outside of air it will surely die, as the fish will surely die placed outside water. One must realize that water is life and air is life . . . Considering this fact, if there should be birds and fish who try to fly or swim only after they have mastered the air and water, then they will never find a path nor a place in either the air or water. When one realizes this in accord with his own actions, then that is Genjo Koan [manifestation and achievement of truth].[37]

That is, the fish is 'already' swimming; the bird is 'already' flying. One is already enlightened and practising.

Dogen described his enlightenment experience as the 'dropping off' of body and mind. He realized it when he heard his master's roar, 'Why do you sleep? You must drop off the body and the mind!' (ibid.: 238–9). At that event, the master could have said 'cast out the dust of the mind' in Chinese and

---

36 *Liu-tzu T'an-ching* (*Platform Sutra* of the Sixth Patriarch), section 6.
37 'Genjo Koan' in *Shobogenzo*, in Matsunaga and Matsunaga 1974–6, II.238–9.

Dogen might have misunderstood it, wilfully or not, as 'the dropping off of body and mind'. In any case the master was said to approve of Dogen's (mis)understanding. What Dogen had in mind was the essential paradox of Zen practice. His breakthrough came when he realized that there was a form of practice that was effortless and spontaneous when one liberated oneself from the body and mind. Zen practice is inevitably the exercise of the body and mind, yet its purpose is to be free from them. It is to cultivate spontaneity by the practice that constantly denies the very spontaneity. Dogen is well aware that there would be no logical solution to this. Dogen, however, insists that one could get beyond this paradox. He sees in his 'dropping off of body and mind' the forgetfulness of all the purposes and intentions. In this recovery of the original spontaneity, Dogen clearly sees that the dichotomy of enlightenment and practice is merely secondary to it.

6 TRANSCENDENTALISM AGAIN

Theravada Buddhism settled in Sri Lanka from the third century BCE and spread to Southeast Asia excluding Vietnam. Theravada Buddhism today is based upon the practice established by the fourth and fifth centuries CE and is considered as retaining elements of early Buddhism. In India, Mahayana Buddhism marked the period of Tantric Buddhism from the fifth century. Tantric Buddhism was an attempt at translating the doctrine of enlightenment here and now into ritualistic practices such as chanting (*mantra*) and vision (*mandala*). Although deemed as only a 'means' (*upaya*), these rituals were nonetheless considered as the instance of enlightenment. Tantric Buddhism considered itself as the completion of Mahayana Buddhism. Tibet accepted this Buddhism in the early seventh century and developed a distinct tradition that is now found in Tibet, Nepal, Bhutan and Mongolia. In East Asia, Buddhism in the forms of Pure Land and Zen became dominant, although philosophical discussions presented by schools such as T'ien-t'ai and Hua-yen remained influential. In these areas Buddhism is or once was an established tradition. Buddhism found in these 'Buddhist' countries is mature and stable. Buddhism has ceased to be prevalent in India and China, but its influence is clearly detectable in Hinduism and Neo-Confucianism that were to become the dominant philosophy/religion in India and China respectively.

The new frontier where Buddhism poses a serious challenge is the West. Its challenge is serious, not because the number of Buddhist temples and practitioners in the West has been steadily increasing in the past decades, but because the West, from the middle of the nineteenth century, has been taking a serious interest in Buddhism, as well as other Eastern religions, and because this 'Orientalism' involves an in-depth encounter of Christianity with Buddhism. This Christian encounter with Buddhism appears similar to the Chinese encounter with Buddhism that was primarily intellectual and spiritual, inherently critical and comparative, and productive of numerous translations and commentaries. The strength and maturity that the Christian tradition exhibits in this practice is similar to that of the Chinese at its encounter with Buddhism. At the same time, the Christian–Buddhist encounter is a unique event and opens up a new comparative perspective. The broadest description of this comparison would be that they are different in that Christian practice is within a monotheistic framework and the Buddhist one is without.

We saw in the beginning that Buddhist transcendentalism had no anchoring point. Its trajectory, therefore, has to come back to the starting point. Buddhist transcendentalism is circular. This circularity can be seen most clearly in the Buddhist emphasis on ordinary practice. The earliest case was the Buddha's advice to Malunkyaputta not to seek for a metaphysical solution but to concentrate on his own practice. Mahayana Buddhism was a reaction against an attempted closure of transcendental practice. This same circularity appears in Pure-Land and Zen Buddhism. Pure-Land Buddhism is unique in the Buddhist tradition for upholding the linear transition from this land to the pure land of Amida and in stressing devotion rather than practice. As we saw above, however, this linear, devotional transcendentalism suddenly becomes circular by the hand of Shinran, who, probably unwittingly, pushed Pure Land transcendentalism beyond its limit. In contrast, Zen Buddhism, in its emphasis on the daily practice, purposefully overrides the distinction between enlightenment and practice. Zen thus openly endorses the circularity of its transcendentalism. It is the Christian–Buddhist encounter that reminds us of this circularity in Buddhism. More importantly, it is this encounter that presents to us the question whether this circular transcendence is transcendence at all, whether a journey that is bound to come back to the starting point is a journey at all, whether in the end of this journey the ego just rediscovers its same old self.

The question whether Buddhist transcendence is just a grand self-deception is a valid question. If there is anything to be gained in this circular transcendentalism, it is a possible sanctification of ordinary practice. Both Shinran and Dogen posit the moment when practice becomes spontaneous. That is, if there is any goal in their practice, it is the 'effortlessness' of practice. To repeat the same point, the question whether their transcendentalism that changes nothing is transcendental at all is a valid question.

The Christian–Buddhist encounter poses another, equally serious question. Because of its circular transcendence, Buddhist practice does not suffer from the separation between theoria and praxis. Buddhist theory simply points out that the ego is impossible and thus supports the practice of overcoming the ego. Here theoria and praxis have the same orientation. Buddhism is therefore simultaneously philosophy and religion. Although with some exceptions, the very distinction between philosophy and religion appears essentially alien to Buddhism. Zen Buddhism often propagates its anti-intellectualism; yet, as seen above, Zen itself is meant to be an embodiment of the philosophical tradition of Buddhism. Christianity, on the other hand, is not simultaneously philosophy and religion. In fact, the distinction between reason and faith is constitutive of the Christian tradition. It may be for the simple reason that the linear transcendence from the ego to God refuses any theoretical understanding. Here reason and faith are essentially separate, and, consequently, an exploration for a form of mediation is in itself a task, presumably non-ending. Here the split between theoria and praxis prevents one from regulating one's daily practice according to a philosophically convincing worldview. The question is whether the goal that is by definition beyond reason is an acceptable goal, whether a praxis that aims beyond theoria is an anomaly as a religious practice.

Thus the Christian–Buddhist encounter reveals two questions, one inherent in Buddhism and the other equally inherent in Christianity. These are the questions that are so fundamental that they would remain forgotten without a reminder. The Christian–Buddhist encounter is one such reminder.

▌ BIBLIOGRAPHY

Canons

The Jataka or Stories of the Buddha's Former Births. E. B. Cowell, R. Chalmers and W. H. D. Rouse
  (1895–1907). London: Pali Text Society.
Majjihima Nikaya: Middle Length Sayings. I. B. Horner (1954–9). London: Pali Text Society.
The *Udana.* P. Masefield (1994). London: Pali Text Society.
The Group of Discourses (Suttanipata). K. R. Norman (1992). London: Pali Text Society.
Word of the Doctrine (Dhammapada). K. R. Norman (1997). London: Pali Text Society.

Samyutta Nikaya: The Book of the Kindred Sayings. C. A. F. Rhys Davids and F. L. Woodward (1917–30). London: Pali Text Society.

Digha Nikaya: Dialogues of the Buddha. C. A. F. and T. W. Rhys Davids (1899–1921). London: Pali Text Society.

Anguttaranikaya. F. L. Woodward and E. M. Hare (1932–6). London: Pali Text Society.

Most of the Pali Canon has been translated into English by the Pali Text Society.

The Chinese canon, together with the Japanese texts included in *Taisho Shinshu Daizokyo*, is being translated into English by the Numata Center for Buddhist Translation and Research, 22 volumes to date.

Other English translations from the Pali and other canons are found in a number of publications and websites.

Anacker, S. (1986) *Seven Works of Vasbandhu, the Buddhist Psychological Doctor.* Delhi: Motilal.

Bando, S., and H. Stewart (1996) *Tannisho: Passages Deploring Deviations of Faith.* Berkeley: Numata Center for Buddhist Translation and Research.

Bharati, A. (1993) *Tantric Traditions.* Delhi: Hindustan Publishing.

Bloom, A. (1965) *Shinran's Gospel of Pure Grace.* Tucson: University of Arizona Press.

Bowker, J. (1975) *Problems of Suffering in the Religions of the World.* Cambridge: Cambridge University Press.

Chang, G. C. C. (1971) *The Buddhist Teaching of Totality.* Pennsylvania: Pennsylvania State University Press.

Ch'en, K. (1964) *Buddhism in China: A Historical Survey.* Princeton: Princeton University Press.

Cleary, T. (1983) *Entry Into the Inconceivable: An Introduction to Hua-Yen Buddhism.* Honolulu: University of Hawaii Press.

Cleary, T. (1984–7) *The Flower Ornament Scripture.* Boston: Shambhala.

Cleary, T. (1986) *Shobogenzo: Zen Essays by Dogen.* Honolulu: University of Hawaii Press.

Conze, E, (1958) *Buddhist Wisdom Books.* London: Allen & Unwin.

Conze, E. (1959) *Buddhist Scriptures.* London: Penguin.

Conze, E. (ed.) (1964) *Buddhist Texts through the Ages.* New York: Harper & Row.

Cook, F. H. (1977) *Hua-Yen Buddhism: The Jewel Net of Indra.* Pennsylvania: Pennsylvania State University Press.

Donner, N., and D. Stevenson (1993) *The Great Calming and Contemplation: A Study and Annotated Translation of the First Chapter of Chi-i's Mo-ho Chih-kuan.* Honolulu: University of Hawaii Press.

Dumoulin, H. (1988–90) *Zen Buddhism: A History.* New York: Macmillan.

Fung, Y. (1950–2) *A History of Chinese Philosophy.* Princeton: Princeton University Press.

Garfield, J. L. (trans. with commentary) (1995) *The Fundamental Wisdom of the Middle Way: Nagarjuna's Mulamadhyamakakarika.* Oxford: Oxford University Press.

Gethin, R. (1998) *The Foundation of Buddhism.* Oxford, Oxford University Press.

Gombrich, R. (1988) *Theravada Buddhism: A Social History from Ancient Benares to Modern Colombo.* London: Routledge.

Govinda, A. (1961) *The Psychological Attitude of Early Buddhist Philosophy.* London: Rider.

Gregory, P. N. (1987) *Sudden and Gradual: Approaches to Enlightenment in Chinese Thought.* Honolulu: University of Hawaii Press.

Hakeda, Y. (1967) *The Awakening of Faith: Attributed to Asvashosha.* New York: Columbia University Press.

Harvey, P. (1990) *An Introduction to Buddhism: Teachings, History and Practices.* Cambridge: Cambridge University Press.

Hawkins, B. K. (1999) *Buddhism*. London: Routledge.

Hirakawa, A. (1977) *Bukkyo Tsushi*. Tokyo: Shunjusha.

Hirakawa, A. (1990) *A History of Indian Buddhism*. Honolulu: University of Hawaii Press.

Kalupahana, D. (1992) *A History of Buddhist Philosophy*. Honolulu: University of Hawaii Press.

King, S. (1991) *Buddha Nature*. New York: State University of New York Press.

LaFleur, W. (ed.) (1985) *Dogen Studies*. Honolulu: University of Hawaii Press.

Lindtner, C. (1982) *Nagarjuniana: Studies in the Writings and Philosophy of Nagarjuna*. Copenhagen: Akademisk Forlag.

Liu, M. (1982) 'The doctrine of the Buddha-Nature in the Mahayana Mahaparinirvana Sutra', *Journal of the International Association of Buddhist Studies* 5(2), Lausanne: University of Lausanne.

Lopez, D. (ed.) (1995) *Buddhism in Practice*. Princeton: Princeton University Press.

Matsunaga, D. and A. (1974–6) *Foundation of Japanese Buddhism*. Los Angeles and Tokyo: Buddhist Book International.

Murti, T. R. V. (1955) *The Central Philosophy of Buddhism: A Study of the Madhyamika System*. London: Allen & Unwin.

Nagao, G. (1989) *The Foundational Standpoint of Madhyamika Philosophy*. Albany: State University of New York Press.

Nagao, G. (1991) *Madhyamika and Yogacara: A Study of Mahayana Philosophies*. Albany: State University of New York Press.

Nakamura, H. (1970) *Genshi Bukkyo: Sono Shiso to Seikatsu*. Tokyo: Nihon Hoso Shuppankai.

Pye, M. (1978) *Skilful Means: A Concept in Mahayana Buddhism*. London: Duckworth.

Ruegg, D. S. (1981) *The Literature of the Madhyamaka School of Philosophy in India*. Wiesbaden: Harrassowitz.

Schumann, H. W. (1973) *Buddhism: An Outline of its Teachings and Schools*. London: Rider.

Skilton, A. (1996) *A Concise History of Buddhism*. Birmingham: Windhorse.

Smart, N. (1973) *The Phenomenon of Religion*. London: Macmillan.

Streng, F. (1967) *Emptiness: A Study in Religious Meaning*. Nashville: Abingdon.

Takakusu, J., and K. Watanabe (eds) (1924–34) *Taisho Shinshu Daizokyo*, vol. 12: *Mahaparinirvana sutra*. Tokyo: Taisho Shinsu Daizokyo Publishing Society.

Takeuchi, Y. (ed.) (1993–5) *Buddhist Spirituality*, vol. 1: *Indian, Southeast Asian, Tibetan, Early Chinese*; vol. 2: *Later China, Korea, Japan and the Modern World*. New York: Crossroad.

Wayman, Alex (1973) *The Buddhist Tantras: Light in Indo-Tibetan Esoterism*. London: Routledge & Kegan Paul.

Wilhelm, R. and H. G. Ostwald (trans.) (1985) *Tao Te Ching: The Book of Meaning and Life*. London: Penguin.

Williams, P. (1989) *Mahayana Buddhism: The Doctrinal Foundations*. London: Routledge.

Yampolsky, P. B. (trans.) (1967) *Platform Sutra of the Sixth Patriarch*. New York: Columbia University Press.

Judaism

Alastair Hunter

CHAPTER 3

1 UNTRUTHS, HALF-TRUTHS AND SHEER NONSENSE: BALANCING THE ACCOUNT

1.1 Judaism's Credo

> Hear, O Israel, the LORD is our God, the LORD is one. You shall love the LORD your God with all your heart and with all your soul and with all your strength.
>
> (Deuteronomy 6.4–5)

If one thing can be said to characterize Jewish faith as distinct from practice it is that ringing declaration from the heart of the Torah. Here the fundamental belief of Judaism is voiced, in a dramatic affirmation which encapsulates the first two commandments; and here also the response demanded of the faithful Jew is made clear. This 'creed', known as the Shema from its opening word in Hebrew, contains much that repays further study, not least the fact that the only verb of action it contains is 'to love'.

This may seem surprising at first glance, since it runs counter to what is often assumed and stated about the nature of Judaism. The propaganda (that is hardly too strong a word to use) of centuries of Christian influence has created a series of stereotypes about its rivals (especially Judaism and Islam) which portray them in harsh and unattractive terms, contrasting *law* with *grace*; *ritual practice* with *loving concern*. Yet when we actually look at the declaration which forms the core of Jewish belief, the word we find used to present the human side of the relation is 'love' (Hebrew *'ahab*). And let us be clear about one thing: the Hebrew verb used in this passage is as wide-ranging in its meanings as is the English.[1] It indicates passion as well as commitment, both enthusiasm and loyalty, and it is used of God's concern for humankind just as definitely as it is of love between human beings (about one fifth of its occurrences in Tanakh[2]). For example,

> It was because the Lord loved you and kept the oath that he swore to your ancestors, that the Lord has brought you out with a mighty hand and redeemed you from the house of slavery, from the hand of Pharaoh king of Egypt.
>
> (Deuteronomy 7.8; cf. Isaiah 63.9; Jeremiah 31.3)

and, in a memorable passage,

> When Israel was a child, I loved him,
> and out of Egypt I called my son.
> I led them with cords of human kindness,
>   with bands of love.
> I was to them like those
>   who lift infants to their cheeks.
>   I bent down to them and fed them.
>   (Hosea 11.1, 4)

There is a clear reciprocity of emotion implicit in the Shema: it is *because* God first loved Israel that every Jew is commanded to respond in love and with wholehearted commitment and enthusiasm: *all* your heart (the devotion of the mind and will), *all* your soul (the commitment of one's whole being), *all* your strength (an unusual word,[3] whose normal meaning is 'very' – perhaps best interpreted as the utmost application of one's energies to the service of God).

The principle of *response* is a key to understanding how the (to an outsider) seemingly burdensome laws and rituals of Judaism can become a source of celebration – nicely symbolized in *Simchat Torah*,

---

1 The clearest evidence of this can be found by consulting the relevant entry in Clines, *Dictionary of Classical Hebrew*, vol. 1.
2 As an alternative to expressions like 'Hebrew Bible' (which is not quite accurate, because part of Daniel and Esther is in Aramaic) and 'Hebrew Scriptures' (which can be misleading because of assumptions made on the basis of Christian usage), it is common to find the term *tanakh* used to describe the three sections of the canon. Tanakh is an invented Hebrew word formed by taking the initial letters of the three sections of the canon as an acronym. Thus: *T orah – N evi'im – K etuvim; T – N – K; TaNaKh*. The vowels have no particular significance – they simply permit us to pronounce the word. The 'extra' letter *h* at the end is a consequence of the way that Hebrew is pronounced, and indicates that the *k* should be sounded roughly like the *ch* in the Scottish word *loch*.
3 It is only used in this sense in one other place – 2 Kings 23.25, which is effectively a quotation of Deuteronomy 6.5.

the joyful celebration at the end of the year's readings of Torah which rounds off the sequence of autumn festivals of Rosh Hashanah, Yom Kippur and Sukkot. The canard, originating with Paul, that Jewish observance is designed to *earn* salvation makes this incomprehensible. But the prologue to the Ten Commandments in Deuteronomy 4.32–40 makes it perfectly clear that Judaism enacts a response to God's free and gracious acts of redemption – and that (in the words of 5.3: 'Not with our ancestors did the Lord make this covenant, but with us, who are all of us here alive today') what God did *then* applies to us *here and now*. Though it is usually printed in prose form, I have set this passage out as blank verse in order to convey something of the dramatic effect which is present in the Hebrew but tends to be lost in translation:

1 (32a)   Ask now about former ages,
                        long before your own,
                   ever since the day that God created human beings on the earth;
                        ask from one end of heaven to the other:
2 (32b–34)   Has anything so great as this ever happened or has its like ever been heard of?
                   Has any people ever heard the voice of a god speaking out of a fire
                        as you have heard and lived?
                   Has any god ever attempted to go and take a nation for himself from the midst of
                        another nation
                   by trials, by signs and wonders,
                   by war, by a mighty hand and an outstretched arm,
                   and by terrifying displays of power,
                   as the Lord your God did for you in Egypt
                   before your very eyes?
3 (35–6)   To you it was shown so that you would acknowledge
                        that the Lord is God;
                   there is no other besides him.
                   From heaven he made you hear his voice
                        to discipline you.
                   On earth he showed you his great fire,
                        while you heard his words coming out of the fire
4 (37–8)   Because he loved your ancestors,
                   he chose their descendants after them.
                        He brought you out of Egypt
                            with his own presence,
                            by his great power,
                        driving out before you
                            nations greater
                            and mightier than yourselves,
                        to bring you in, giving you their land
                            for a possession,
                            as it still is today.
5 (39–40)   So acknowledge today and take to heart
                   that the Lord is God in heaven above and on the earth beneath
                        there is no other.
                   Keep his statutes and his commandment, which I am commanding you today

for your own well-being
and that of your descendants after you,
so that you may long remain in the land
that the Lord your God is giving you
for all time.[4]

While this is not the place to engage upon an analysis of these verses, the drama, the recurring motifs, and the sense of past and present bound up together with the drama of God's redemption make for a powerful poem. Perhaps it may seem strange to begin an account of Judaism with a poem – but there is a truth in this approach which more straightforwardly descriptive explanations miss.

1.2 Reliable and unreliable sources of knowledge

In the previous section we noted that certain prejudices and stereotypes are endemic in views of Judaism from outside. What we shall do now is to examine briefly the principal sources from which many people obtain their information about the Jews and their religion. These are three in number: the New Testament, European (largely Christian) educational traditions, and popular opinion.

It is important to recognize at the outset that each of these three sources is both anti-Jewish and anti-Semitic: terms which themselves would benefit from some further definition. The former refers to a (possibly legitimate) antagonism towards Jews by Christians who saw them as their rivals in the attempt to win converts from interested groups in the Roman Empire.[5] While Rabbinic Judaism as it finally shaped itself eschewed proselytizing, and indeed actively discourages would-be converts, it was not so in the first two centuries of the common era (CE). Many gentiles attached themselves to synagogues in the Diaspora, and these 'God-fearers', as they were termed, were on the road towards conversion to Judaism. Since the first Christian groups were themselves associated with synagogues, it is not surprising that by as early as the fifth decade of the first century, when Paul and his associates began to evangelize among the gentiles, the two religions were competing for converts in the same circles. Christian criticisms of the Jews were to some extent motivated by this competition; and from the other side, Jewish rhetoric was not infrequently directed at Christians.

The term 'anti-Semitic', however, signifies a wholly reprehensible incitement to hatred of the Jews by a process of demonizing and dehumanizing them. It was this process, first hinted at in the New Testament,[6] and virulently endemic throughout the nearly two millennia of Christian dominance, which had its most vicious (though by no means its only) genocidal outcome in the Holocaust, known also by its Hebrew term 'Shoah'. These are matters to which, sadly, it will be necessary to revert as we progress into the modern era.

---

4 For another poetic version, see Everett Fox's translation in *The Five Books of Moses* (New York: Schocken Books, 1997).
5 It is clear from Rabbinic sources that this antagonism was heartily reciprocated. Ancient Jewish sources have many bitter things to say about both Jesus and his followers. This is a fact. Whether either side was justified in holding such opinions is a different matter.
6 There is some debate as to whether there is anti-Semitism as such in the New Testament. Undoubtedly by the second century fiercely anti-Semitic polemics were being issued by leaders in the Church. It may be, however, that within the New Testament itself the rhetoric is still at the level of mutual mud-slinging. The jury is out.

THE NEW TESTAMENT

> Matthew 23.23:
> Woe to you, scribes and Pharisees, hypocrites! For you tithe mint, dill and cumin, and have neglected the weightier matters of the law, justice and mercy and faith.

> John 5.16 (after Jesus heals a man on the Sabbath):
> And this was why the Jews persecuted Jesus, because he did this on the Sabbath.

> Revelation 3.9:
> Behold, I will make those of the synagogue of Satan who say that they are Jews and are not, but lie – behold, I will make them come and bow down before your feet. (Cf. John 8.31, 44.)

The New Testament consists of four Gospels, ostensibly narratives of the life of Jesus; a work in the form of a historical narrative (the book of Acts) which describes events and personalities from the early years of the development of the Christian Church; various letters (of which a number are attributable to Paul); and an apocalyptic work (the book of Revelation) which includes a series of visions about the end of the world.

Given that the New Testament is devoted to the cause of Christianity, it is not surprising that it should be less than friendly to Judaism. What is alarming, notwithstanding, is the extreme nature of the abuse which is heaped on the Jews – a few examples are provided above. No doubt this can be in part explained as simply one example among many of the level of rhetorical abuse which the ancients typically hurled at each other. What makes the phenomenon as found in the New Testament especially dangerous, though, is the status of that book as the foundation document for the Christian churches. Because the churches have regarded the New Testament as being above reproach, and have taken its statements as having divine authority, the rhetoric levelled at the Jews in its pages has been taken as literal truth and the historically inaccurate descriptions it contains have been presented as if they were facts about Judaism. This is not the place to enter upon a detailed critique of these misconceptions; suffice it to say at this stage that they include the explicit charge that the Jews are the children of the devil, and the accusation of deicide. This kind of material, used by people who had reason to wish the Jews ill, makes the New Testament deeply problematical as a source of 'knowledge' about the Jews.

EUROPEAN EDUCATIONAL TRADITIONS

> The Jews are guilty collectively of the crime of deicide, since their fathers condoned the execution of Jesus.

> The Jews are incorrigibly sinful since they have wilfully rejected the very Messiah for whom they waited, and who was clearly indicated by their own prophets.

> The Jews have regularly conspired to undermine Christian states by taking control of various key instruments of power, such as banking, trade and intellectual resources.

It is a truism that history is always written by the victors. The history of the Church, for example, is littered with the corpses (both literal and metaphorical) of Christian groups which came to be regarded as 'heretical' by what became the 'orthodox' Church. But of course the definition of what is heretical and what is orthodox very much depends upon the beliefs of those who have the power to attribute the labels. Similarly, the triumph, under Constantine and his successors, of Christianity meant that the Jews now faced not simply a rival, but a dangerous and powerful enemy. Early Christian writings, and a number of the Church Fathers, display a range of adversarial approaches to Jews and Judaism. Some represent theological disagreement (for example, the *Epistle of Barnabas*), others, like Justin Martyr, Tertullian and Origen, write in a more thoroughly condemnatory mode.[7] The Jews' supposedly self-inflicted punishment, brought about by their rejection of Jesus as Messiah, is regularly referred to. The most extreme of the early group is St John Chrysostom, whose *Eight Sermons Against Judaizers* contains some very robust language. The argument that all of these were addressed more to the risk of Christians finding Judaism attractive than to direct attacks on Jews is somewhat disingenuous, in that they provide the basis for continuing – and increasingly vitriolic – attacks in the medieval period. Jews experienced the loss of civil rights, actual and potential discrimination, and periodic pogroms during which local communities were incited to violence against their Jewish neighbours, often for no other reason than to suit the vested interests of a local mandarin. The history of the Jews of York and their massacre in 1190 provides an instructive example of the way that theological rhetoric had become violent polemic. In part the York massacre was motivated by the widespread belief, whose earliest manifestation is the case of St [*sic*] William of Norwich, that Jews sacrificed children for Passover purposes. Those who had economic or political reasons for repression could readily motivate popular opinion to extremities of violence. The discrimination against the Jews which marked (and marred) so much of the history of Christendom led in the long term to a habitual and unthinking anti-Semitism so unremarkable that it became part of the familiar culture of everyday life. There was no shame and no discredit in the expression of what would now be regarded as offensively anti-Semitic remarks. Martin Luther's *The Jews and Their Lives* is just one particularly distressing example of this appalling trend. Thus the so-called emancipation of the Jews, when it came, was founded on very dubious assumptions: the freedom of the Jews was in general not granted as a means of denying the prejudice of Christendom, but as a gracious act by a Christendom which had discarded none of its prejudices. The malignant character of such an emancipation became only too clear when the Nazis established the Third Reich.

Some of these prejudices were given spurious authority in the forged *Protocols of the Elders of Zion*,[8] a malign and malicious libel which (despite having been discredited soon after its appearance) had a pernicious influence on early twentieth-century attitudes to the Jews. Sadly, this mischievous document still has currency in neo-Nazi circles (witness the number of websites devoted to it) and forms part of the extremist denunciation of Israel in some Arab rhetoric.

POPULAR OPINION

> As soon as Jews move into the neighbourhood they take control of property and make sure their own kind join them.
> You can easily tell a Jew from his or her appearance.
> Jews as a nation are rude and argumentative.

While popular opinion is academically the least respectable source of information, it is nonetheless the route by means of which most of us gain most of our knowledge. Popular opinion is regularly fed and

---

7 Justin, *Dialogue with Tryphon*; Tertullian, *Against the Jews*; Origen, *Against Celsus* (Book II).
8 See further pp. 166–7 below.

renewed by prejudices from religious and educational traditions, by the fears and misconceptions of individuals confronting what they perceive to be strange, and by the deliberate machinations of demagogues.

Notions such as that of a plot by Jewish industrial capitalists to take over the Western economy have no substance in reality, but are still widely believed. The canard that you can tell a Jew physically by means of certain caricatured facial features still surfaces in anti-Semitic cartoons and resonates in the popular mind. No doubt this kind of shorthand is true of all social groups ('mean' Scots, 'thick' Irish, and so on), and it is often dismissed as 'just a joke'. But jokes can turn nasty, and the attribution of 'national' characteristics modulates from a reason for harmless laughter to an occasion for murderous mockery. For all these reasons it is vital to counter popular views of Jewishness (as of any other ethnic group) if we are to attain a fair and balanced knowledge of Judaism, and a society in which justice is even-handed.

1.3 'Judaism is not a Christian heresy'

Many criticisms of Judaism seem to assume that what is wrong with the faith of the Jews is that it is not enough like Christianity. When the point is made as bluntly as that, we might readily agree that it is hardly an adequate critique of a religion to accuse it of not being sufficiently like another faith. Yet this persists even among people who have long since abandoned any formal affiliation to the Christian Church – as is demonstrated by the depressing regularity with which such students affirm in examination answers and essays in religious studies that Judaism's 'failings' relate to its lack of certain 'Christian' qualities. Jewish 'rejection of the Messiah' is perhaps the most common of these criticisms – a tribute, perhaps, to centuries of Christian propaganda (Jews have, of course, *not* rejected the Messiah; Judaism believes that the Messiah has yet to come). The other commonplace is the crude characterization of Judaism as a religion of law in contrast with Christianity's affirmation of grace (see my comments above, pp. 116f.) – a cliché which presumably derives in the end from Paul, though most of those who continue to perpetrate it have never read a word of that apostle's teaching.

The fact that we speak glibly of the 'Judaeo-Christian tradition' (conveniently forgetting just how marginalized the 'Judaeo' part is) and assume a shared history and shared scriptures means that it is particularly difficult to acknowledge Judaism's validity as a religion independent of Christianity from within a Christian cultural context. I shall have more to say about the common history of the two in the next section; here I shall consider the theological and scriptural problems raised by this 'common heritage'.

BELIEF IN MESSIAH

The conviction that Jesus is the Messiah is central to Christianity. It is widely supposed that Judaism expects the coming of Messiah. Why then do the Jews not simply accept Jesus (who was undoubtedly a Jew) as the Messiah?

The fundamental problem here is that, on any understanding of the nature of Messiah as described in Tanakh or in the many messianic writings of the two centuries prior to the time of Jesus, the Christian claim is simply unfounded. Jesus did not usher in the messianic age of peace, he did not lead Israel to victory over its enemies, the rule of God has not been established on earth. Therefore Jesus, far from being Messiah, was just one more of the many pretenders to that office who came and went (mostly violently) in the troubled years before the first revolt against the Romans in 66 CE. The two most famous messianic pretenders in Jewish history are probably Bar Kochba (leader of the second Jewish war against the Romans, 132–5 CE), who established a short-lived kingdom in Judaea, and Sabbatai Sevi (1626–76), whose movement in 1665–6 gained considerable support among European Jews, but ended disastrously with his arrest in Istanbul and his conversion to Islam (to the dismay of his followers).

For most Jews today, the concept of the Messiah is somewhat distanced from everyday religious belief and practice. It registers to some extent as an ethical desire to see the reign of God established on earth, and in this form the idea of a messianic age tends to be substituted for that of a personal Messiah. In the realm of religious politics there are links between some forms of Zionism and the belief that the establishment and defence of the modern state of Israel is in accordance with, or a preparation for, God's Messiah. There are, of course, fringe groups, such as Jews for Jesus, which go so far as to re-appropriate Jesus as the Jewish Messiah; they, however, can hardly be described as part of the main body of modern Judaism. More is said on this subject in section 4 of this chapter.

SHARED 'OLD TESTAMENT'

When we want to talk about 'the Old Testament' it is clear that there is right at the start a problem of definition: which version to choose? Even different Christian traditions use different versions – thus the Catholic tradition regards the Apocrypha as canonical, but the Reformed tradition rejects them, and the Orthodox tradition accepts a different set of apocryphal books! The Jewish Bible has the same books as the Reformed churches, but in a very different order (see the box below). Thus, even allowing for the different language used, there are difficulties in the way of laying claim to 'the same scriptures'. Translation is also a material point of difference, for while one or two more recent English versions produced by the churches have consulted Jews, there is an inevitable theological *tendenz* which may often be subconscious. Use of the Jewish Publication Society translation of Tanakh is advised as a counterbalance.

▌ BOOKS IN TANAKH

Torah	Jeremiah	Ketuvim
Genesis	Ezekiel	Major texts:
Exodus	(B) The minor prophets:	Psalms
Leviticus	Hosea	Proverbs
Numbers	Joel	Job
Deuteronomy	Amos	Megillot:
	Obadiah	Song of Songs
Nevi'im	Jonah	Ruth
Former prophets:	Micah	Lamentations
Joshua	Nahum	Ecclesiastes
Judges	Habakkuk	Esther
1 and 2 Samuel	Zephaniah	Others:
1 and 2 Kings	Haggai	Daniel
Latter prophets:	Zechariah	Ezra
(A) The major prophets:	Malachi	Nehemiah
Isaiah		1 and 2 Chronicles

But for the purposes of our study of Judaism there is a much more difficult question: is 'Old Testament' a valid title at all? Think about what it means. 'Old' implies the existence of 'New' – specifically, the 'New Testament'. Conversely, the association of the New Testament with the Old suggests that one has been superseded by the other. Now it is patently obvious that the Jews do not recognize the standing or authority of the New Testament, and this leaves us with a serious lack of shared viewpoint between what Christians call the Old Testament and what Judaism refers to as the (Jewish) Bible. And 'Testament' refers to a very specific theological belief – namely that the 'testament' or 'covenant' between God and Israel, first made with Abraham, then successively with David, Moses and the generation of Ezra, is in continuity with the Church's relationship to God.

The different order of books in the Jewish Bible is not an accident. For Judaism the first five books – the books of Moses, sometimes called the Pentateuch and known in Hebrew as the *Torah* – are of primary significance. Next comes the section known as the Prophets (Hebrew *Nevi'im*), which covers what Christian readers think of as the historical books (Samuel and Kings) as well as the canonical prophets. Finally, and of least authority, are the rest of the books – the Writings (Hebrew *Ketuvim*). Furthermore, rabbinic methods of interpretation of Scripture are very different from those of the Christian tradition. I will have more to say about these matters later; for the moment I want simply to observe that what seemed at first glance to be a point in common is in fact a point of separation.

SHARED BELIEF IN THE SAME GOD

Here is a real stumbling block. Christians regularly and quite unthinkingly assume this to be an unproblematic issue. The God of Abraham, Isaac and Jacob, the Living God (as Pascal famously put it) is the same God who is 'the Father of our Lord and Saviour Jesus Christ'. But think about this for a moment and from a Jewish perspective. Remember that the central belief of Judaism is 'The LORD is our God; the LORD is One' and the commandments include the divine declaration, 'I am the LORD your God; you shall have no other Gods before me.' What must such a faith make of the Christian doctrine of the Trinity: God the Father, God the Son, God the Holy Spirit, three in one and one in three? Does this not cut at the very roots of the uniqueness and oneness of the Deity? The same God? Really?

THE COVENANT

The Bible records a number of covenants between God and Israel, sometimes with the people as a whole, sometimes with specific individuals. Significant for Christian theology is the passage in Jeremiah 31.31–4 which speaks of a new covenant. The Latin word 'testament' translates the Hebrew word for 'covenant'. Hence the Christian 'New Testament' has arguably a locus in the Jewish Bible. But once again, from the standpoint of a Jew, this is a very odd argument. Jeremiah's oracle is addressed to the Israelites – or, more specifically, to the remaining residents of Jerusalem – and speaks of a promise to that people. How can this covenant then refer to a gentile group usurping the Jewish people's religion some six centuries later?

THE CLAIM TO BE ISRAEL

The use of the name 'Israel' to describe both the Jews and the Christian Church implies a continuity and a shared experience which is in fact quite spurious. The Church as 'Israel' supersedes and supplants the Jews as 'Israel'. While both uses of the term are in some sense metaphorical, the metaphor is at least geographically and historically appropriate in the latter case. It hardly helps to label one 'Israel' and the other 'New Israel' – that brings us right back to the problem with 'Old' and 'New' Testament and 'New Covenant'.

In each of the above examples, and in others not discussed, we find that Christian perceptions of 'Jewish' concepts are so far from the mark from a Jewish perspective as to render them quite alien to the spirit of Judaism. Judaism, we must insist, is not a form of Christianity. Indeed, insofar as Christianity departs from the strictly monotheistic position of Judaism, and adds a second set of scriptures to the Hebrew Bible, it could be argued that it is Christianity which is the heretical offshoot of Judaism.

2 THE ROOTS OF JUDAISM

There are three sorts of answer to the question of the origins or roots of Judaism. First there is the popular or 'naive' approach, which sees Abraham as the father of the Jews and therefore the source of Judaism. From this perspective the call of Abraham to move with his family from Haran into the unknown territory of Canaan marks a fundamental beginning, the momentous event which gave birth first to the patriarchal family specially covenanted to God, and in due course to the covenant people (through the baptism of fear in Egypt and the Red Sea).

Theologically, however, there is much to be said for the primacy of two later events: the giving of the Mosaic law at Sinai, and the establishment of the Torah-based 'Great Synagogue'[9] in the time of Ezra. These have a good claim to give Judaism (as it has developed over the last two millennia) its characteristic features: a faith in which each individual, respecting the gracious activity of God in offering redemption, responds by living in accordance with the law given through Moses as interpreted and defined by the Rabbinic oral tradition which began with Ezra. In one of the *tractates* (or chapters) of the Mishnah, that known as *The Ethics of the Fathers* or *Pirké Avot*, a seemingly historical summary is given which suggests an answer to our question. The *Ethics* begins:

> Moses received the Torah from Sinai and transmitted it to Joshua; Joshua to the Elders; the Elders to the Prophets; and the Prophets to the men of the Great Assembly.

Two points are important here. First, the founding figure is defined to be Moses; and second, the event which marks the beginning of Rabbinic Judaism is Moses' reception of the Torah. It would be fair to

---

9 The Great Synagogue (*kneset haggedolah*) is believed to have functioned from its initiation by Ezra (see Nehemiah 8) and to have continued until around 200 BCE, when it is supposed to have been replaced by two institutions led by the *zugot* (pairs of scholarly leaders) – the Sanhedrin and the Bet Din. In Chapter 1 of the Mishnah tractate *Avot*, five pairs are named, beginning with Yose ben Yoezer and Yose ben Yochanan, and ending with Hillel and Shammai. The first named in each pair is traditionally attributed the title *nasi'* (leader) of the Sanhedrin, the second *'ab* (father) of the Bet Din. This arrangement came to an end with the establishment of the rabbinic dynasty of Hillel, from early in the first century CE (though precise dates cannot be determined).

say that this point of origin is generally accepted by the majority of Jews. It identifies both the essential Scripture of Judaism and its ideal interpreter.

However, we should at least acknowledge the findings of historical study, which are rather sceptical about the existence of any Rabbinic institutions in the period prior to the Maccabees and their royal successors, the Hasmoneans[10] (164–63 BCE). From this perspective the Great Synagogue appears to be a fictional extrapolation from Nehemiah 8, and the Bet Din a reading back into the past of later Rabbinic tradition. There remains the Sanhedrin, whose existence is amply testified for the first century CE. It is difficult to determine precisely what arrangements may have existed earlier, but it seems likely that from around 300 BCE there would have been a 'council of elders' (*Gerousia*) which may have been replaced by an incipient Sanhedrin under High Priestly control during the early Hasmonean period. This would fit nicely with the Hasmonean appropriation of the office of High Priest. The Pharisees (who are in effect the precursors of the Rabbis) may have had some part in the affairs of the Sanhedrin, but they only came into their own with the destruction of the Temple in 70 CE and the new, non-sacrifice-based Judaism for which they provided both the political and the religious stimulus.

2.1 The historical beginnings of Rabbinic Judaism

Whichever of the three answers about 'roots' we may prefer, there is no doubt that the period from 70 to 200 CE[11] was one of major importance for the definition and development of Judaism. It is in this period that the title 'Rabbi' begins to be used; this is when debates about the exact content of the Jewish canon and the precise detail of the sacred text take place;[12] and the earliest codification of the oral law, or *halakhah*, which issued ultimately in the Mishnah of Rabbi Judah (*c*.200 CE) is formed at this time.

Rabbinic Judaism, then, emerges from a situation of seeming defeat and despair (a fact enshrined in the Jewish fast of the ninth day of the month of Av when various calamities, including the two destructions of the Temple in 587 BCE and 70 CE, are commemorated). The zealot-inspired revolt against Rome had ended with the last resistance at the hill fortress of Masada finally crushed in 73 CE (the huge earth ramp which the Romans built to gain access can still be seen). A faith which had for centuries depended upon the celebration of priestly sacrificial rites at the sacred altar of God was suddenly cut off from its city and temple. A people for whom the great pilgrim festivals had formed

10 They are the same family. The successful revolt against the Syrians was mounted by the family of Mattathaias, whose son Judas was nicknamed 'Maccabaeus' (that is, 'the hammer'). Their ancestral name was Hasmon, and this was adopted with the establishment of the ruling dynasty under Jonathan and his successors.

11 Without making too much of it, we should note that these dates might seem surprising in the light of the familiar assumption that Christianity 'replaced' or 'superseded' Judaism. Given that the New Testament was largely complete by around 150 CE, half a century *before* Mishnah (and several centuries earlier than the Talmud), we must reject once and for all any simplistic picture of a fully developed 'Judaism' in the time of Jesus. It would be far closer to the truth to recognize that both Judaism and Christianity emerged out of the highly diverse cultural and religious context of first-century Palestine, and developed thereafter in their different ways over the succeeding centuries.

12 Though the famous 'Council of Jamnia' which is supposed to have settled the canon *c*.90 CE is almost certainly legendary, it is clear that discussions about which books should be recognized as canonical took place in the Sanhedrin which met there from about 80 to 130 CE. As for the text, evidence from the Dead Sea Scrolls suggests that by the first century the early proliferation of text types has been replaced by a more or less uniform Hebrew tradition.

the high point of the religious year were no longer able to make the pilgrimage to Jerusalem. In short, Rabbinic Judaism, while maintaining a theoretical hope of the restoration of the Temple, is in fact a religion without a temple, without a sacrificial system, and with no *realistic* hope of ever restoring these older religious forms. No doubt there are eccentrics who have plans to rebuild the Temple in Jerusalem (having first shifted the Muslim sanctuaries a couple of miles to the east!); but many of them have little idea what they would do with it were it to be built, and few could imagine the reinstatement of sacrifice. For it was one of the triumphs of the Pharisees and their successors the Rabbis that they found a theological answer to the conundrum: How can Jews worship without a temple? After the destruction of the Temple the focus shifted to the Torah, its extension into the oral law, and a cohort of interpreters – the Rabbis – who successfully defined what Judaism was to become. There is an important sense in which Judaism is a child of the first Jewish revolt against the Romans.

2.2 The religious principles of Rabbinic Judaism

THE DUAL LAW

The fundamental religious starting point is the doctrine of the double law – the written and the oral. These are not to be understood as separate phenomena or revelations, but a single unity, the second inherent in the first and serving to interpret and explicate what is written in Torah.

This belief is dramatized in *Avot* chapter 1, which begins with an account of the descent of the Law from Moses, via Joshua, the elders, the prophets and the men of the Great Synagogue, to a sequence of teachers beginning with Simeon the Just and ending with Rabbi Judah. The sequence thus covers (in principle) some fourteen centuries from 1200 BCE to 200 CE, from the publication of the Torah of Moses to the publication of the Mishnah of Rabbi Judah. Moreover, it ensures that there was (again in principle) no break in continuity: the Law in its fullness was given to Moses and has safely reached its destination in the founding text of Rabbinic Judaism.

Of course, that simple description is not the whole story. The halakhah which forms the substance of Mishnah is rather different from the Torah which is contained in the books of Moses. The sequence gives an impression of a single coherent tradition, but this is historically and theologically questionable: it contains notable time lapses, for example, and it makes no reference to any other tradition – as if the Rabbinic view were the only one which had ever existed. But the importance of *Avot* 1 lies not in its historical accuracy, but in the religious beliefs which it enshrines or implies. Such as, that halakhah is nothing but the proper explication of Torah, implicit in the law as given to Moses, but requiring the succession of teachers to spell it out. Such as, that it is the responsibility of each teacher not just to receive the ancient tradition but to contribute to it his [sic] own further insights. Such as, that what is of prime importance is the actual practice of one's religion as spelled out in the detailed oral law (*Abot* 1.17 'Simeon [Gamaliel's] son said: All my days I have grown up among the Sages and I have found nothing better for a man than silence; and not the expounding [of the Law] is the chief thing but the doing [of it]; and he that multiplies words occasions sin.' Danby's version). Since this traditional presentation sees a straight line through from Moses to Rabbinic Judaism, it follows that the latter is therefore the proper – indeed the only – successor to the temple worship of the past. The Rabbis are in consequence the direct heirs to Moses, and what they say is only 'in other words' the Torah of Moses.

THE STUDY OF TORAH AND HALAKHAH

The highest calling of the observant Jew is the study of Torah, and its halakhic interpretation. The Rabbis teach that ideally such study ought to be a person's sole business twenty-four hours a day; short of that impossible ideal, the principle of an educated, literate community with extensive written religious resources has proved to be a significant defining feature of Judaism. It is no coincidence that the pursuit of the knowledge of God's law in all its intricacy has frequently gone hand in hand with a thirst for knowledge and understanding of all kinds; Judaism valued literacy and intellectual curiosity *for religious reasons* long before the Enlightenment and the rise of the Western notion of academic study. This is not to suggest that all knowledge was equally valued, or that complete freedom of expression was in place. The fate of Spinoza, rejected by his own synagogue, is testimony to the restrictions, in Judaism as in most religions, which orthodoxy imposes upon the free spirit.

This sense of the importance of learning spills over into both the language and the practice of the Rabbinate. The *summa* of halakhic tradition is, of course, the Talmud (see below), and the term of respect for those who devote themselves to its study is *talmid hakham*. The shared etymology is the verb *lamad*, meaning 'to learn'. The Talmud is the learning or lore of the oral law; a *talmid hakham* is best translated as 'a disciple of the wise'. And the work of a Rabbi is at heart that of scholarly interpretation. After many years of training at a Yeshiva, where he (in Reform Judaism, women also) is expected to gain extensive knowledge of the Talmud both in breadth and in depth, the Rabbi's duties with the congregation are precisely those of the informed scholar who interprets for the people the meaning of Torah and halakhah. The recent trend towards a pastoral role similar to that of priests and ministers is an interesting cultural development which is in fact a denial of this fundamental calling. And it is important also to remember that even scholarship is not meant to be the *sole* preserve of the Rabbinate: from the beginning Judaism expected (and continues to expect) that *all* its adherents at least aspire to be *talmide hakhamim*.

THE DUTIES OF OBSERVANCE

Knowledge goes together with action, theory with praxis (to adopt the jargon of the liberation movement). Thus to be a Jew in the traditions of the Pharisees and the Rabbis is to be dutiful in practice just as much as it is to be faithful in belief. This is the point at which the greatest degree of incomprehension attends the outsider's gaze. Why on earth impose upon yourself all these burdensome rules? What is the point of the rituals of purity? What possible benefit can be derived from dietary laws, whatever logic they might have had in the quite different physical and ecological environment of ancient Israel?

There are perhaps four specifics which attract most comment: Sabbath observance; the rules regarding what may be eaten, and in what circumstances; the purity laws; and the obligation to tithe. And, as we previously noted, there are both theological and historical (or rather, anthropological) explanations which may be offered. I shall deal with the latter first, with the caveat that these are (a) merely hypotheses and (b) quite inadequate to our understanding as to why Jews *continue* to adhere to these observances. For that, the theologically based discussion is far more significant, and so in each case the theological position is presented last.

Sabbath observance is arguably one of the clearly definitive contributions of Judaism to the world. The seven-day week which we take for granted is indisputably drawn from Jewish practice, whether or not the secular world continues to pay any heed to its religious *raison d'être*. Neither does it matter that Christendom subsituted the 'Lord's Day' (Sunday) for the Sabbath (Saturday) – the *principle* is unchanged. Scholars have proposed that the description Sabbath in Tanakh may owe something to a Mesopotamian tradition in which the term *shapattu* was used to refer to the fifteenth day of the month (the full moon), and the seventh, fourteenth, twenty-first and twenty-eighth days were considered days of possible ill-omen when a person should abstain from pleasure and undertake no important work.[13] These have the effect of dividing the lunar month into four parts; and while they cannot be identified with weeks properly speaking (since the lunar month varies from 28 to 30 days), the creative move to a regular seven-day cycle could have borrowed from this tradition. This is given additional credence when we realize that the theologically creative developments in the post-exilic period (when Sabbath and other observances were more strictly imposed) are attributable to the Babylonian Jewish returnees. Theologically, however, the observance of Sabbath is first of all directly enjoined by God, and, second, commemorates both the climax of creation (Exodus 20.11; cf. Genesis 2.2–3) and the redemption from slavery in Egypt (Deuteronomy 5.13). It is the occasion for celebration (abstaining from everyday work is intended to leave the worshipper free to enjoy God) and, far from being a burden, ought to be a solace. Some of this comes across in the following song, taken from the Sabbath liturgy:

> Were our mouths filled with song like the sea,
>> Our tongues with the sound of joy like its endless waves;
> Were our lips broad with praise like the very skies,
>> Our eyes shining with light like sun and moon;
> Were our arms stretched forth like the wings of heaven's eagles,
>> Our feet as light and swift as birds –
> All these would barely suffice to thank You,
>> Lord, our parents' God and ours,
> Even for a thousandth part of Your goodness to us.
>> You redeemed us from Egypt,
>>> brought us forth from bondage
>> You fed us in hungry times,
>>> sustained us in plenty;
>> You saved us from the sword,
>>> protected us from plague,
>> Uplifting us from all our most persistent ills.
> Thus far have Your mercies been our help,
>> Your kindness never failing.
> Do not abandon us, Lord God,
>> ever.[14]

Some traditions go further, celebrating Sabbath as a quasi-divine female figure endowed with blessings. Thus the following,[15] from the Zohar 2.135a–b:

---

13 See, for example, U. Cassuto, *A Commentary on the Book of Exodus* (Jerusalem: Magnes Press, 1967), p. 224.

14 From the Sabbath Liturgy, in Arthur Green (ed.), *Jewish Spirituality from the Bible through the Middle Ages* (London: SCM Press, 1989), after p. 165.

15 Ibid., after p. 307.

> The Secret of Sabbath:
> She is Sabbath!
> United in the secret of One
> to draw down upon her the secret of One.
> The prayer for the entrance of Sabbath:
> The holy Throne of God is united in the secret of One,
> prepared for the High Holy King to rest upon Her.
> When Sabbath enters She is alone,
> separated from the Other Side,
> all judgements removed from Her.
> Basking in the oneness of holy light,
> She is crowned over and over to face the Holy King.
> All powers of wrath and masters of judgement flee from Her.
> There is no power in all the worlds aside from Her.
> Her face shines with a light from beyond;
> She is crowned below by the holy people,
> and all of them are crowned with new souls.
> Then the beginning of prayer
> to bless Her with joy and beaming faces . . .

Seen in such light, the 'restrictions' of Sabbath observance become instead the simple preparatory duties to enable a far greater and more spiritual blessing.

Food laws are covered by the general Hebrew expression *kashrut*, from which comes the more familiar English term 'kosher'. *Kashrut* means literally 'fitness', and refers to whether a particular food is approved for use under the halakhot (plural of halakhah) dealing with diet. The rules vary: some foods are always held to be impure (Hebrew *terefah*; Yiddish *treyf*), such as pork, shellfish or anything containing blood; some are impure in certain circumstances, such as milk mixed with meat, or yeast at pesach (Passover). Since the decision as to whether a particular product might or might not be kosher is highly technical, the Rabbinate in many countries has a system of approval by means of which food products can be marked so that the customer can recognize at a glance what is permissible.

All very well, no doubt; but why? This is perhaps the most puzzling of Jewish particularities. We can, of course, readily recognize our own cultural boundaries as regards eating. The British feel queasy confronted by snails or frogs, delicacies in France. Horse-meat is fine for pets, but not (we think) for humans, though other Europeans disagree. In some parts of the world dogs are eaten, and a variety of bugs and insects – not popular items on even the most avant-garde menus in London! But we are not really talking (except indirectly) about cultural prohibitions. No doubt the thought of pork and shellfish *becomes* revolting to practising Jews in the same way that dog might be to Europeans, but the *prior* existence of a religious prohibition is only relevant to the former. Some have attempted to find anthropological explanations. It is widely affirmed that wild boars in the Middle East carry many diseases, and so it was in fact very wise of God (on health grounds) to ban pork. Such 'explanations' are patently risible: the absence of the requisite bacteriological knowledge renders the thesis void, and it does not even begin to touch the much wider range of forbidden food. Mary Douglas, particularly in her ground-breaking study *Purity and Danger*, but also in futher studies of Leviticus and Numbers,[16]

---

16 Mary Douglas, *Purity and Danger* (London: Routledge, 1991 (1966)); *Leviticus as Literature* (Oxford: Oxford University Press, 2001 (1999)).

has argued that such taboos may have a basis in early attempts at the definition of *categories* of life. Shellfish look like insects, but live in the sea, where (properly speaking) only scaled fish ought to be found. Links between types of hooves and forms of mastication and digestions might explain other rules. The famous ban on mixing meat and milk seems less easy to explain. It is based on a single half-verse injunction, 'You shall not boil a kid in its mother's milk' (Exodus 23.19 = 34.26 = Deuteronomy 14.21; the Hebrew is identical in each instance), which seems highly specific. Some have argued (though the evidence is uncertain) that this reflects a ban on a Canaanite practice, but the wider extension of the rule reflects nicely the way that halakhic interpretation works, taking a perhaps cryptic phrase from Torah and deriving from it some underlying principle which may then be applied in general.

Fascinating though such speculation may be, it is largely irrelevant to the question of observance, which relates ultimately to the principle we have already noted: obedience in response to grace. The whole of Torah is God's will for Jews; however interesting the 'why' may be, the proper response is 'do it'. This is God's will and we are – thankfully – not required to understand God's motives before we carry out God's wishes. Perhaps some light may be shed from the perspective of purity (which we shall turn to shortly), in the sense that proper and improper foods belong to the broader realm of the need to keep oneself pure for the sake of holiness. Hence the strange resonance of the word *treyf*, which originally in Hebrew meant 'torn in pieces' and referred to a domestic animal which had been found mauled by an unknown wild beast. In such circumstances the animal had to be deemed unclean, and so the simple expression 'mauled' was transferred to its consequence 'unclean'. Subsequently it has acquired a further metaphoric meaning and can be applied to the gentile world in general; thus Isaac Bashevis Singer, 'In our home, the "world" itself was *treyf*'.[17]

Purity rituals have their proper place in that liminal realm where the human and the divine intersect. Ritual impurity is an almost tangible quality which is unavoidable in certain circumstances, and requires ritual cleansing to be removed. It is emphatically *not* a matter of ethics or wrongdoing – Judaism does not teach that a person can erase their moral debts by performing a superficial rite.

Most religions have scope for some sense of the holiness of God and the incompatibility of that sanctity with the merely human. The rituals surrounding the celebration of the Eucharist in many Christian traditions, for example, are designed to separate the wine and bread involved from 'all common use and purpose'; and the reason for this is not dissimilar to the sense of the sacred which persuades a Jew that the sacred Torah scroll is a holy thing not to be treated casually.

Anthropologically, then, there is nothing surprising about the concept within Judaism of sacred space and sacred things which are marked out as part of the mysterious presence of God among humans. The Ark in which the Torah scroll is kept in the synagogue is a reminder of the innermost holy place which was at the heart of the Temple. It was there that God chose to be present, and so only once a year, and under controlled circumstances, could the High Priest enter that area. The scriptures themselves were defined by the Rabbis as 'defiling the hands' (discussions concerning the canonicity of disputed texts asked whether or not they *defiled the hands*). This strange expression meant that they partook of such holiness that anyone who handled them was in danger of carrying the divine quality improperly into the secular realm, and so had to wash their hands thereafter.

The means of purification (apart from hand-washing) is the *mikveh*, or ritual bath – an essential part of every Orthodox Jewish community. Its main uses now are in relation to the formal impurity which women acquire during menstruation or childbirth – the bath restores purity at the end of the

---

17 Quoted in Lewis Glinert, *The Joys of Hebrew* (Oxford: Oxford University Press, 1992), p. 247.

period of separation. It is also a feature of conversion, though it is important not to associate it with the Christian rite of baptism, whose purpose is quite different. The *mikveh* restores the individual to purity, or, in the case of a convert, confers on him or her that status for the first time. Baptism symbolizes the removal of *moral and religious sin*, and symbolizes a death in Jesus. These are utterly different matters. The *mikveh* is also customarily used as part of the preparation for Yom Kippur, and after contact with the dead.

Tithing was first instituted to provide for the priestly and the Levitical cadres in ancient Israel, because their religious duties debarred them from owning land. It was originally a proportion of the produce of the land (ancient Israel was almost certainly not a cash economy), and was given in part to priests and Levites locally, and in part taken to Jerusalem. After the destruction of the Temple problems arose. The priestly families survived (as the surname *Cohen* testifies), but with the disappearance of their primary duties there was dispute as to whether they or the Levites should receive tithes. Indeed, as the Rabbinic era progressed and more emphasis was placed on scholarship, a tendency arose of paying tithes to priests or Levites who were also *talmide hakhamim* (scholars) and indeed to the latter even if they did not belong to the priestly or Levitical groups.

The relevance of tithing outside the land of Israel is disputed. Since its origins lie in an offering from the produce of the Promised Land, it could be argued that this is a halakhah which need not be observed in the Diaspora. Nevertheless, there is evidence from ancient times that it *was* observed in Egypt. In modern Judaism the principal form of giving is now understood as *tsedaqah* (charity) – though the word itself in biblical Hebrew refers to justice. Thus the rather formal system of tithing in respect of religious officials has given way to that of the provision of financial support for the poor and the needy in the name of justice.

Finally, although the Hebrew word for 'tithe' (*ma'aser*) means 'one tenth', the precise proportion is not pedantically determined. Giving is done freely and according to one's ability, not as a legalistic response to a mathematical formula.

2.3 The Mishnah and Tosefta

It is well known that the Christian Church has a second collection of canonical texts alongside the Old Testament. The *New Testament* contains accounts of Jesus' life, a history of the early Church, letters from Paul and others to various Christian communities, and an apocalyptic work describing the end of the world. In the course of time, the New Testament came to have great authority for the Church – in many ways greater than that of the Old Testament.

A similar, but in important ways distinctive, process can be seen in the development of Judaism during the first and second centuries CE. Since the basis of Jewish life is obedience to the will of God as expressed in Torah, it is of great importance that individuals and the community as a whole should know what are the practical implications of the Torah for day-to-day life. In earlier times 'being Jewish' seems to have been mainly defined by the observance of the great pilgrim festivals described in Tanakh, and the celebration of the various rituals and sacrifices associated with the Temple in Jerusalem. But as circumstances changed, and as the community became scattered, the need to address what it meant to be Jewish grew more urgent. Eventually, with the destruction of the Temple by the Romans in 70 CE, a radically new approach was called for if the Jewish community was to survive with its faith intact.

ROLE OF THE PHARISEES

The *Pharisees* and, later, the *Rabbis*, are the key to this change. Sometime after the era of Ezra and Nehemiah a group known as the Pharisees began to develop a system of interpretation of Torah which served as a guide to practical living. We do not now know exactly when the Pharisees originated; the surviving historical evidence (principally from the Jewish historian *Josephus*, who wrote towards the end of the first century CE) indicates that they were an identifiable group by the late second century BCE. Josephus (who, like Paul, claims himself to have been a Pharisee) gives us a short portrait of the group, and indicates that they were in opposition to the ruling group, the *Sadducees*:

> Now, for the Pharisees, they live meanly, and despise delicacies in diet; and they follow the conduct of reason; and what that prescribes to them as good for them, they do; and they think they ought earnestly to strive to observe reason's dictates for practice. They also pay a respect to such as are in years; nor are they so bold as to contradict them in anything which they have introduced; and, when they determine that all things are done by fate, they do not take away the freedom from men of acting as they think fit; since their notion is, that it hath pleased God to make a temperament, whereby what he wills is done, but so that the will of men can act virtuously or viciously. They also believe that souls have an immortal vigour in them, and that under the earth there will be rewards or punishments, accordingly as they have lived virtuously or viciously in this life; and the latter are to be detained in an everlasting prison, but that the former shall have the power to revive and live again; on account of which doctrines, they are able greatly to persuade the body of the people; and whatsoever they do about divine worship, prayers, and sacrifices, they perform them according to their direction; insomuch that the cities gave great attestations to them on account of their entire virtuous conduct, both in the actions of their lives and their discourses also.
>
> The doctrine of the Sadducees is this: That souls die with the bodies; nor do they regard the observation of any thing besides what the law enjoins them; for they think it an instance of virtue to dispute with those teachers of philosophy whom they frequent; but this doctrine is received but by a few, yet by those still of the greatest dignity; but they are able to do nothing of themselves; for when they become magistrates, as they are unwillingly and by force sometimes obliged to be, they addict themselves to the notions of the Pharisees, because the multitude would not otherwise bear them.
>
> (*Antiquities* XVIII.1.3–4, in *The Works of Flavius Josephus*, translated by William Whiston (1880))

The New Testament also makes frequent reference to the Pharisees, much of it critical. Unlike Josephus, the former seems to lump Pharisees and Sadducees together in its general disapproval of the whole Jewish establishment. Despite this misrepresentation of the two groups, even the New Testament makes it clear at a number of points that the Pharisees were an honourable and respected group in first-century Judaea. Consider, for example, the following passages:

> The scribes and the Pharisees sit on Moses' seat; therefore, do whatever they teach you and follow it. (Matthew 23.2)

> The story of Nicodemus clearly indicates that the supposed stand-off between Jesus and the Pharisees was not the whole story. Nicodemus later appears in the scene where Joseph of Arimathea takes Jesus's body for burial, and assists him. (John 3.1–15; 19.38–42)

The Book of Acts includes the story of how Gamaliel, a leading Rabbi of the dynasty of Hillel, persuades the council (presumably the Sanhedrin) to allow the followers of Jesus to make their case freely and be judged by God rather than human opinion. (Acts 5.33–9)

Paul claims himself to be a Pharisee, albeit in a context where he is determined to create argument between the Pharisees and the Sadducees during his hearing in the Sanhedrin. (Acts 23.6–11)

The main bone of contention between the two groups lies in their different approaches to Scripture. The Sadducees believed that it should be interpreted quite literally. Thus the commandments in Torah are not to be reinterpreted for new circumstances. They are intended for the proper running of the cult and temple in Jerusalem alone. In direct contrast, the Pharisees developed the process of interpretation called *halakhah* which made it possible to apply the regulations of Torah in circumstances quite different from those in which they were originally given.

> The word *halakhah* comes from a Hebrew verb which means 'to walk'. Literally, then, *halakhah* means something like 'the way', although it now stands for the oral law developed by the Pharisees and the Rabbis.

By means of the halakhah the Pharisees sought to bring the 613[18] commandments of Torah up to date for their own day. With time, a number of rules of interpretation emerged which permit a quite flexible reading of the Torah – these are summarized below, in Section 3. It was not, however, until much later in the Rabbinic period that the oral laws were formalized. In the Pharisaic period (from about 200 BCE until 70 CE) halakhah developed as a growing body of opinions about specific situations. These opinions were often anonymous, but sometimes were associated with particular named individuals. It is a characteristic feature of Pharisaic and Rabbinic tradition that subsequent views did not displace earlier opinions. Rather, a chain of tradition would develop, in which the different views of different authorities were recorded. Examples of such 'chains of tradition' are given below.

▌ EXAMPLE OF A 'CHAIN' OF OPINION IN MISHNAH PESAHIM 3.3

The discussion concerns the preparation and baking of dough for Passover:

'Rabban Gamaliel says, "Three women knead dough together and [then] bake in the oven one after another in sequence."'

'And sages say, "Three women work with the dough. One kneads, while the next rolls out, and the third bakes."'

'Rabbi Aqiba says, "All women, all wood, and all ovens are not to be taken as equivalent."'

---

18 Traditionally the total number of commandments in Torah is taken to be 613. The numerical value of the Hebrew word *torah* is 611, and this is the number of commandments given through Moses; the other two being the first two statements of the Decalogue, given directly by God at Sinai. The Talmud divides them into 365 negative precepts (corresponding to the number of days in the year) and 248 positive (the number of parts of the human body) (Talmud *Makkoth* 23b).

▋ EXAMPLE OF A 'CHAIN' OF OPINION IN MISHNAH SOTAH 9.10–15
(only v. 15 is quoted here)

The discussion concerns the decline of religious virtues through the generations:

When Ben Azzai died, diligent students came to an end.

When R. Meir died, makers of parables came to an end.

When Ben Zoma died, exegetes came to an end.

When R. Joshua died, goodness went away from the world.

When Rabban Simeon b. Gamaliel died, the locust came, and troubles multiplied.

When R. Eleazar b. Azariah died, wealth went away from the sages.

When R. Aqiba died, the glory of the Torah came to an end.

When R. Hanina b. Dosa died, wonderworkers came to an end.

When R. Yose Qatnuta died, pietists went away.

When Rabban Yohanan b. Zakkai died, the splendour of wisdom came to an end.

When Rabban Gamaliel the Elder died, the glory of the Torah came to an end, and cleanness and separateness perished.

When R. Ishmael b. Phabi died, the splendour of the priesthood came to an end.

When Rabbi died, modesty and fear of sin came to an end.

(Jacob Neusner, *The Mishnah: A New Translation* (Yale University Press, 1988))

In all probability the number of Pharisees, even in the early first century, was quite small, though ancient opinions differ. Josephus speaks of there being 6,000 – but he writes from a pro-Pharisaic position, and from a period in the late first century when Rabbinic Judaism was for the first time the dominant form of the religion. Elsewhere in the Mishnah it is recorded that all the Pharisees met in a house in Jerusalem – suggesting many fewer than Josephus's figure![19]

The traditions speak of an intense rivalry between the 'schools' of two famous Pharisees – Shammai and Hillel – who apparently flourished around the end of the first century BCE and the beginning of the first century CE. There is also evidence of the existence of groups who followed the Pharisaic line, but adopted very strict and exclusive regulations for their life. These 'Associates' (*chaverim*) practised the strictest kind of ritual purity, imposed upon themselves extremes of tithing, and would only eat with those whom they knew to be as observant as themselves. Others were more liberal in their approach to observance, and in general it may safely be said that a whole spectrum of practice and opinion, from complete exclusivity at one end, to full integration in wider society at the other, was to be found in first-century Pharisaism.

This great diversity is one of the main reasons why no single authoritative definition of 'correct practice' emerged. Instead, varieties of opinion were preserved, at first as part of a growing oral tradition. As the volume of *halakhot* grew, however, written collections of these important traditions began to appear. We do not now possess the earliest of these, though some of the materials found at Qumran and other Dead Sea sites are similar to the Rabbinic writings which were eventually codified (for examples, see Geza Vermes, *The Complete Dead Sea Scrolls in English*, Penguin Books 1997, in particular section A 'The Rules' and section F 'Bible Interpretation'). It is generally believed that the community

19 Josephus, *Antiquities* 17.2.4; Mishnah *Shabbath* 1.4.

which produced these texts and traditions was similar to the Pharisees in beliefs and practices, but had taken the extreme step of forming themselves into a totally isolated sect in the interests of preserving their purity.

The Sanhedrin at Javneh and Usha

The Sanhedrin was the Jewish ruling assembly in Jerusalem until 70 CE. It appears to have been dominated by priestly and Sadducean interests, though Pharisees were also members of it. With the destruction of the Temple, both priests and Sadducees lost their influence, and the new establishment at Javneh was predominantly a Pharisaic enterprise. When the leaders of the Pharisaic movement set up their academy and Sanhedrin at Javneh after the failure of the Jewish revolt of 70–3 CE, it rapidly became important to clarify the halakhot defining the life of the community.

A number of traditions preserved in Mishnah and in other places give us information about the leadership at Javneh and the issues they discussed or decided upon. It was by no means plain sailing. There were heated disagreements – leading on one occasion to the deposing of the then leader, Gamaliel II. Not everyone in the surviving Jewish community accepted the authority of the Rabbis (the title first given to scholarly Pharisaic leaders in the latter part of the first century). Rabbinic writings contain scathing descriptions of the so-called 'people of the land' ('ammei ha-'aretz) who knew little or nothing of Torah and avoided the obligations of tithing and of food and purity rules wherever they could. But gradually the tide turned in favour of the teachings and interpretations of the Rabbis. It seems very probable, though we have no direct evidence of this, that the first codifications of halakhah began to appear in the period.

The process which began at Javneh was, however, abruptly brought to an end with the second Jewish revolt under Bar Kochba in 132 CE. Its defeat led to the transformation of Jerusalem into a Roman city, and to Judaea becoming a Roman colony, Palestine. Jews were largely excluded, and the Rabbinic centre at Javneh disappeared. However, not all Jews had taken part in the revolt, which may well have been confined to Jerusalem and south-east Judaea, and a new academy was soon established at Usha in Galilee. Here the 'dynasty' of Rabbinic leaders was reinstated, and the process of formation of halakhic Judaism resumed.

▌ DYNASTY OF HILLEL

PRE-JAVNEH	JAVNEH	USHA
Hillel	Yohanan ben Zakkai (70–85)	Simeon III (140–75)
Simeon I	[NB: Not of the dynasty of	Judah I (175–217)
Gamaliel I (c.30–c.50)	Hillel]	[Also known as 'Rabbi' and
Simeon ben Gamaliel (55–70)	Gamaliel II (85–?)	'Ha-Nasi']

Publication of the Mishnah

Eventually, under the leadership of Rabbi Judah Ha-Nasi ('the Prince') – known to Rabbinic tradition simply as 'Rabbi' – the now extensive body of halakhot was codified. Round about 200 CE the Mishnah was published. It was divided into six sections (sedarim), and each section into individual books or 'tractates' (*massekhtot*). The Mishnah was an attempt to put into authoritative form how Jews who belonged to the community of Rabbinic Judaism should live. It is not in the main either a theological or an ethical work, though one tractate – *Avot* – does deal with ethical issues.[20] The purpose of Mishnah is to provide for the proper fulfilment of obedience to Torah in practical situations, not to offer opinions on the nature of faith. In the main, ethical matters are assumed to be the responsibility of the individual, and do not require specific regulations. This quasi-legal character of Mishnah makes it very different from the New Testament, which is much more concerned with right belief and ethical practice than with the details of observance.

One of the strange things about Mishnah is that it includes extensive legislation relating to the Temple and its associated rites and rituals. This is curious because, by 200 CE, Rabbinic Judaism had apparently given up any hope of a restored Temple, and was firmly committed to the halakhic approach to observance. This is supported by the fact that, as we shall see, Talmud, which comments on Mishnah, has nothing to say about these Temple tractates. It has been proposed that the Temple material was in fact developed during the Javneh period, when hopes still existed of a restored Temple in Jerusalem. If this is so, the presence of these tractates in the final form of Mishnah is indirect evidence that at least some of the mishnaic traditions may have been in written form during the Javneh period, and so impossible to exclude from Rabbi Judah's codification.

■ MISHNAH – DIVISIONS AND TRACTATES

1st Division *Agriculture (zeraim)*	*2nd Division* *Appointed times (moed)*	*3rd Division* *Women (nashim)*
Berakhot	Shabbat	Yebamot
Peah	Erubin	Ketubot
Demai	Pesahim	Nedarim
Kilayim	Sheqalim	Nazir
Shebiit	Yoma	Sotah
Terumot	Sukkah	Gittin
Maaserot	Besah	Qiddushin
Maaser Sheni	Rosh Hashshanah	
Hallah	Taanit	
Orlah	Megillah	
Bikkurim	Moed Qatan	
	Hagigah	
4th Division *Damages (nezikin)*	*5th Division* *Holy things (kodashim)*	*6th Division* *Purities (tohorot)*
Baba Qamma	Zebahim	Kelim
Baba Mesia	Menahot	Ohalot

20 Many scholars consider *Avot* to be a later addition to Mishnah. Its position in Mishnah differs in different texts, and it has no talmudic commentary. Further, its first two chapters serve to authorize the tradition within which Mishnah was produced, suggesting that *Avot* may have originated as a secondary work designed to support Mishnah and increase its authority.

4th Division	5th Division	6th Division
Damages (nezikin)	*Holy things (kodashim)*	*Purities (tohorot)*
Baba Batra	Hullin	Negaim
Sanhedrin	Bekhorot	Parah
Makkot	Arakhin	Tohorot
Shabuot	Temurah	Miqvaot
Eduyyot	Keritot	Niddah
Abodah Zarah	Meilah	Makhshirin
Abot	Tamid	Zabim
Horayot	Middot	Tebul-Yom
	Qinnim	Tadayim
		Uqsin

Whatever Judah and his colleagues may have hoped with the publication of Mishnah, in the event this proved to be not the end but only the beginning of the process which was to lead to the great defining document of Rabbinic Judaism, the Talmud. In the next section we shall describe the character of the Talmud and say something about its development.

TOSEFTA

Alongside Mishnah, but probably a little later in date, there is a collection called the Tosefta. The name itself means 'addition' or 'supplement', and it appears to be either a supplement or a rival to Mishnah. It is organized in a similar fashion, but contains a number of halakhot which contradict those in Rabbi Judah's compilation.

The existence of Tosefta is both a boon to scholars and a political enigma. The former because it provides parallels to the material in Mishnah which can aid the process of historical analysis (a task to which Jacob Neusner and his colleagues have devoted much energy). The latter in that its existence seems to hint at a struggle for power and authority which belies the seeming supremacy of the Hillelite dynasty. Some have seen in Tosefta a direct challenge to Rabbi's attempt to create, as it were, a final authoritative form of Judaism.

Since it was not the subject of further commentary by the Talmudic scholars, Tosefta has a further contribution to offer, namely a source of opinions which may have been later censored as Judaism moved towards its broad consensus within the general terms made possible by Talmud. This is, of course, a *very* broad consensus – though medieval and early modern manuals of conduct, and the development of culturally settled religious traditions, would greatly reduce the available options – but none the less open to challenge both in detail and in principle. The nineteenth-century emergence of Reform Judaism is testimony to that fact.

2.4 Some parallels with Christianity

There are intriguing parallels to be drawn between Christian and Jewish developments in respect of the idea of 'fulfilment of Torah'. For Judaism, the fulfilment of Torah is to be found in the halakhah, that great compilation of oral case-law which found its home eventually in the Babylonian Talmud, but whose foundation document is the Mishnah. For Christianity the law and the prophets are summed up in the person of Jesus, the Word incarnate, and the revelation of this new teaching is contained in the books of the New Testament. Halakhah serves to guide the Jew in his or her longing to live in accordance with and in obedience to the will of the God who has already shown *hesed* (faithful love) to the people of Israel; it is thus an essentially inward-looking process, specifically designed for limited application: Rabbinic Judaism is not a proselytizing religion, and argues that God has a separate covenant and law for the gentiles – the Noachic covenant.[21] The God/man in Christianity, on the other hand, bridges the gulf between God and humankind, and offers a means of reconciliation through which *hesed* can be received by people who were formerly lost in their sinful state. Hellenistic Christianity is thus in essence an evangelistic faith: that is, its news is news for the whole world. Whether these differences were always inherent in the two different approaches to the idea of 'fulfilment', or whether they were historically conditioned, is hard to decide. Certainly there was an element of proselytism in Jewish circles prior to 70 CE (in Rome, for example, and perhaps in Alexandria), and the journeys of Paul as recorded in the book of Acts imply the existence in most Diaspora towns of 'God-fearers' more or less closely attached to the synagogues. After the fall of Jerusalem and the destruction of the Temple, however, Rabbinic Judaism (perhaps wisely) concentrated much more on the establishment of a secure community based on the revived Sanhedrin in Yavneh and the development of a dynasty of Rabbinic leaders claiming descent from the great Hillel. The second revolt, around 132 CE, pretty well settled the matter: Judaism was a way of life for Jews, and was increasingly on the defensive as Christianity became more and more aggressively missionary. It may be that Diaspora communities remained outward-looking for a somewhat longer period; but the very existence of a Christianity which actively 'poached' gentile God-fearers, and the spread of Rabbinic views as to the proper nature of Judaism after the end of the Temple and its system of sacrifice, combined to reinforce the respective tendencies of the two faiths. It may even be that Matthew's notorious Pharisees who 'traverse sea and land to make a single proselyte' could be better understood as apologists to fellow Jews of the Rabbinic 'line'.

3 THE MEDIEVAL FLOWERING OF JUDAISM

If we define the Middle Ages as the period from 500 to 1500 CE, we discover that a truly amazing quantity and quality of Jewish religious and intellectual development belongs to that era. What we also discover is that this flowering is most striking in regions under Islamic rule. The reasons for this are not entirely clear, but it may be suggested that Islam's position was from the beginning and in principle tolerant of what it defined as the 'religions of the book', while Christianity was both exclusive in principle and specifically antagonistic towards the Jews. Other, perhaps subsidiary explanations may be put forward. Islam's theology was closer to that of Judaism, and had no particular grudge to bear regarding the death of Jesus. Also, the sheer rapidity of the early Arab conquests meant that its considerably expanded territories could not quickly be culturally and religiously assimilated. Hence the tolerance of existing religious sensitivities enabled a working relationship to develop. This is not to deny

---

21 In Judaism there is no requirement that the whole of humankind become Jewish. Rather, non-Jews will be judged by how they conform to the laws given by God to Noah (Genesis 9.1–17), which the Talmud (*Sanhedrin* 56a–b) defines as: establishing courts of justice, and refraining from idolatry, blasphemy, incest, murder, robbery, and eating flesh cut from a living creature.

that, in the longer term, non-Muslims experienced some discrimination, increasingly so as the Muslim population came to predominate. But compared with the ferocity of periodic Christian blood-letting among Jews, life in the Islamic empires was comparatively free.

Undoubtedly, too, the great intellectual explosion in the Islamic world benefited Jewish scholarship. The hidden influences of the Greek thinkers who were mediated by Islamic scholars, and the need to define and interpret Jewish beliefs and writings in the context of a confident and burgeoning Muslim society of philosophers and mystics, provided an atmosphere in which debate could take place both within Judaism and between religions. The emergence of commentaries (*midrashim*) on Scripture, philosophical and theological treatises, linguistic studies and mystical writings in this period is testimony to its creative forces.

3.1 The Talmuds

HISTORY AND CHARACTER

Supreme among these various developments is the gradual emergence of the Talmud. The publication of Rabbi Judah's Mishnah, whatever he may have intended, produced in turn a vast secondary commentary (the *gemara*) representing the interpretations offered by the generations of scholars who followed him. The scholars whose halakhot are collected in Mishnah are known collectively as the Tannaim, from a Hebrew word meaning to recite or repeat, and in Aramaic, to teach: it was they who preserved and added to the oral tradition, teaching it and repeating it. But the sheer volume of tradition must have made it increasingly difficult to handle the material orally, and so the post-Mishnaic period saw the development of written commentaries produced by the Rabbinic academies of Palestine and Babylonia. These scholars came to be known as the Amoraim (Hebrew 'to speak'), whose original task was to translate the Hebrew of the traditions into the Aramaic which the people understood (a responsibility which also produced the *targumim* – interpretations of the scriptures in Aramaic). However, they subsequently were understood more generally as interpreters of Mishnah – the authors of the additional material which gradually accumulated in the two centuries after Rabbi Judah.

The fascination of Talmud lies in its openness and its vast extent. Unlike the very specific scriptures of the Christian and Muslim faiths, Talmud (whose centrality to Judaism cannot be challenged) is a collection of opinions not one of which in itself may be taken to be an authoritative decision. Nevertheless, the authority for everything a Jew does under God is undoubtedly to be found in Rabbinic study of the Talmud. It is thus an authority which is not authoritative, and is not held to be itself Scripture; rather it is the compendium of the oral law which makes it possible for a Jew to be obedient to Torah: and it is Torah, together with the Prophets and the Writings, which alone deserves the title Sacred Scripture. The daunting extent of the Talmud is part of the process, for no human volume of such size could even potentially be entirely consistent and coherent. In effect, where both Islam and Christianity place their interpretations and traditions (the *hadith* and the writings of the Church Fathers) in a supplementary category, Judaism makes these central *in principle*.

The character of the Talmud is inseparable from the process which led to its formation. Its sprawling, idiosyncratic accumulation of anecdote, personal history and legal opinion testifies to long centuries of free response, often by a kind of word-association, in which rival (though not antagonistic) academies developed their ever more sophisticated understanding of both the theory and the practice of Judaism. And theory is an important word: much of what went on was of the nature of an abstract pursuit of the implications and consequences of a given halakhah in all conceivable (however unlikely) circumstances. There is almost a playfulness (if one dare use such an expression) about this, a sense that what was happening arose from a community which was free from other burdens and so able to pursue the pleasures of the mind (always, of course, in the service of Torah and with the awareness of the ultimate reference of everything to God).

There are two editions of the Talmud. The earlier, completed around 400 CE, is the Jerusalem (*Yerushalmi*) Talmud. It is somewhat shorter in extent, and less authoritative than the Babylonian (*Bavli*) Talmud, which dates from the early sixth century (though, as we shall see, its editing probably continued for some time thereafter). The two differ considerably both in the content of their commentary where they deal with the same Mishnah tractates, and in the fact that there are some tractates commented upon by one and not the other, and some on which neither comment (see the box below).

▌ BABYLONIAN (B) AND PALESTINIAN (J) TALMUDIC COMMENTARY ON THE TRACTATES OF MISHNAH

1st Division Agriculture (zeraim)		2nd Division Appointed times (moed)		3rd Division Women (nashim)	
Berakhot	b, j	Shabbat	b, j	Yebamot	b, j
Peah	j	Erubin	b, j	Ketubot	b, j
Demai	j	Pesahim	b, j	Nedarim	b, j
Kilayim	j	Sheqalim	j	Nazir	b, j
Shebiit	j	Yoma	b, j	Sotah	b, j
Terumot	j	Sukkah	b, j	Gittin	b, j
Maaserot	j	Besah	b, j	Qiddushin	b, j
Maaser Sheni	j	Rosh Hashshanah	b, j		
Hallah	j	Taanit	b, j		
Orlah	j	Megillah	b, j		
Bikkurim	j	Moed Qatan	b, j		
		Hagigah	b, j		

4th Division Damages (nezikin)		5th Division Holy things (kodashim)		6th Division Purities (tohorot)	
Baba Qamma	b, j	Zebahim	b	Kelim	
Baba Mesia	b, j	Menahot	b	Ohalot	
Baba Batra	b, j	Hullin	b	Negaim	
Sanhedrin	b, j	Bekhorot	b	Parah	
Makkot		Arakhin	b	Tohorot	
Shabuot	b, j	Temurah	b	Miqvaot	
Eduyyot	b, j	Keritot	b	Niddah	b, j
Abodah Zarah	b, j	Meilah	b	Makhshirin	
Abot		Tamid	b	Zabim	
Horayot	b, j	Middot	b	Tebul-Yom	
		Qinnim		Tadayim	
				Uqsin	

The existence of two Talmuds is to some degree a reflection of the differing historical fortunes of the Jews in the Roman Empire and beyond its boundaries. The Jews of Palestine and Galilee gradually found themselves in an increasingly Christian world, and although the succession of Rabbinic leaders continued into the beginning of the fifth century, the major centres of Judaism had shifted to Babylonia. There were Jews in Babylonia from the sixth century BCE, and the community there had in general good relations with the ruling powers. The region never came under the control of Rome, and so, until the Arab Muslim conquests of the seventh century, the Rabbinic schools in Babylonia flourished where their counterparts in Palestine found themselves restricted. Even after the Muslim conquests (as we have already seen) Judaism was relatively free to continue its independent development. Thus the processes which produced the Talmud were not cut short in Babylon, and editing continued beyond the received date for its completion. The scholars who arranged and edited the Babylonian Talmud in the sixth and seventh centuries are known as the *Savoraim* ('thinkers'). They in turn were succeeded by the *Geonim*, a term of respect from a Hebrew word meaning 'proud' which was accorded to the heads of the two leading Babylonian academies at Sura and Pumbedita – positions which continued until the eleventh century. The Geonim held both spiritual and intellectual leadership in Judaism of the time, and were responsible for the promulgation and teaching of Talmud, which in this period became established as the definitive guide for the Jewish people.

■ THE DEVELOPMENT OF HALAKHAH – A SUMMARY

General terms of respect

Pharisee – used *c.*160 BCE–70 CE
Rabbi – used after 70 CE
Talmid Hakham or Hakhamim ('Disciple of the wise')

Terms relating to historic periods

Tannaim – the scholars whose teaching is collected in Mishnah (70–200 CE)
Amoraim – title used for the scholars whose teaching is collected in Talmud (200–500 CE)
Savoraim – the scholars who edited and revised the Babylonian Talmud (500–700 CE)
Geonim – heads of the Babylonian academies who taught Talmud (700–1100 CE)
(*All dates are approximate*)

One of the fascinating aspects of the long process of development of the 'definitive' Talmud is that it began as an oral tradition in the pre-Christian age, saw its first published form well into the Christian period, and reached its final definition about a century into the Islamic era. Inevitably, in a volume which is looking at a variety of religious traditions, the question arises of the extent (if any) to which mutual influences may be detected. Undoubtedly the Qur'an knows something of both Jewish and Christian scriptures, and it is tempting to speculate as to possible influences of the Rabbinic 'chain of authority' mode upon the *hadith* traditions of Islam. The New Testament is openly indebted to the Greek Old Testament, and provides evidence of awareness of some Rabbinic and Pharisaic traditions.[22]

22 See, for example, Phillip Sigal, *The Halakah of Jesus of Nazareth According to the Gospel of Matthew* (Lanham, MD: University of America Press, 1986).

On the other hand, it has long been argued that some of the directions taken by Judaism in the late first and early second centuries were in response to the encroachments of an increasingly aggressive Christianity. And at the latter end of our period some have seen the threat posed by Muslim teachings and legal opinions as a particular spur to the final work on the Talmud, given that the two faiths occupy in many ways similar intellectual territory and practical observance. While there can be no final answer to such questions, they remind us of the closely interdependent nature of the religions of the book, and make their mutually bloodstained relationships all the more poignant.

MODE OF DISCOURSE

The commentary in Talmud is frequently directed towards the explanation of ambiguous points in Mishnah, or the discussion of things which are not explicitly covered there. Its sheer size, and the character of its commentary, mean that it cannot be treated as a source of 'literal' statements of an absolute kind. Rabbinic training involves an intimate familiarity with the vast extent of Talmud, and the ability to debate and interpret current issues on the basis of that familiarity. Questions are settled not by recourse to a single definitive quotation but by the expression of an opinion which carries weight because of the Rabbi's training and personal character. Such opinions, however, are not 'final': in Rabbinic Judaism, no-one has the last word! Philip Birnbaum[23] illustrates this point nicely:

> Harry A. Wolfson, who has been recognised as one of the most influential minds of our time, depicts the method of talmudic study in the following terms: Confronted with a statement on any subject, the talmudic student will proceed to raise a series of questions before he satisfies himself of having understood its full meaning. If the statement is not clear enough, he will ask: 'What does the author intend to say here?' If it is too obvious, he will again ask: 'It is too plain, why expressly say it?' If it is a statement of fact or of a concrete instance, he will then ask: 'What underlying principle does it involve?' If it is a broad generalization, he will want to know exactly how much it is to include. Statements apparently contradictory to each other will be reconciled by the discovery of some subtle distinction, and statements apparently irrelevant to each other will be subtly analyzed into their ultimate elements and shown to contain some common underlying principle.

The following modern discussion (Unterman 1981: 40f.) shows how the most controversial issues can be discussed on the basis of talmudic teachings, but not necessarily resolved.

> . . . whilst the *Talmud* makes any number of statements about prophecy and revelation, and even lists which biblical books or parts of books were written by which prophets, it pictures Moses as not being able to understand the Judaism of the second century.

> > When Moses ascended on high he found the Holy One, blessed be He, sitting and binding crowns on the letters. He said to Him: Master of the universe who necessitates this from You? He replied: There is someone who will appear at the end of a number of generations, and Akiva ben Joseph is his name, who will exegetically derive mountains upon mountains of laws from each and every stroke.

23 P. Birnbaum, *Encyclopedia of Jewish Concepts* (New York: Hebrew Publishing Company, 1975), p. 640.

He said to Him: Master of the universe show him to me.

He replied: Turn backwards.

He [Moses] went and sat at the end of the eighth row and he did not know what they were saying. He felt weak. When a particular point was reached the pupils said to him [i.e. R. Akiva]: Rabbi, from where do you know this? He said to them: It is a law of Moses from Sinai. His [i.e. Moses'] mind was put at rest.

[TB *Menachot*, 29b]

It is certainly possible to interpret this story as saying that Judaism undergoes religious development and that the talmudic rabbis recognized that it had grown and changed by the mishnaic period into a form unrecognizable to its biblical progenitors. This story has to be set side by side with other teachings . . . which claim that not only did Moses receive the Pentateuch from God, but that he also received the *Mishnah*, the talmudic discussions, the *aggadah*, and even what a mature student will expound before his teacher in future times, at Sinai.

[see TJ *Peah* 2.4]

Finally, here is an example from within the Babylonian Talmud itself (*Pesahim* 114a) which illustrates how the Amoraim struggled to clarify the teachings of the Tannaim. In Mishnah[24] *Pesahim* 10.2, in the course of giving directions for the Passover meal, a difference of opinion is recorded:

When they have mixed the first cup of wine – the House of Shammai say, 'He says a blessing over the day, and afterward he says a blessing over the wine.' And the House of Hillel say, 'He says a blessing over the wine, and afterward he says a blessing over the day.'

How (if at all) can this conflict be resolved? What we encounter in Talmud is a *process* which is itself as interesting as the resolution of the problem, a mixture of legal and theological principles with references to other Rabbinic authorities. And even though an 'answer' is provided, the diligent Talmudist might well be able to modify that conclusion by a careful examination of other, possibly at first sight unrelated, passages of Talmud. To parody the song, 'It ain't what you say, it's the way that you say it' which matters more. What follows is an attempt to summarize the key elements of the argument. First, the Talmudic comment,[25] which I have divided into sections for convenience of reference:

[1] Our Rabbis taught: [These are] the matters which are disputed by Beth Shammai and Beth Hillel in respect to the meal: Beth Shammai maintain: He recites a blessing for the day [first] and then recites a blessing over the wine, because the day is responsible for the presence of the wine; moreover, the day has already become sanctified while the wine has not yet come. But Beth Hillel maintain: He recites a blessing over the wine and then recites a blessing for the day, because the wine enables the *kiddush* to be recited. [2] Another reason: the blessing for wine is constant, while the blessing for the day is not constant, [and of] that which is constant and that which is not constant, that which is constant comes first. [3] Now the law is as the ruling of Beth Hillel. Why state [another reason]? – [This:] for should you argue: there we have two [reasons], whereas here there is [only] one. [I answer that] here also there are two, [for of] that which is constant and that

24 Mishnah translation by J. Neusner (Yale University Press, 1988).

25 *The Talmud* (London: Soncino Press, 1960).

which is not constant, that which is constant comes first. [4] 'Now the law is as the ruling of Beth Hillel': that is obvious, since there issued a *Bath Kol*? – if you wish I can answer that this was before the *Bath Kol*. Alternatively, it was after the *Bath Kol*, and this is [in accordance with] R. Joshua who maintained: We disregard a *Bath Kol*.

[1] There are two arguments in support of Shammai's position: (a) since it is the festival day which introduces the need for wine, the day has priority, and (b) when a day dawns it is automatically sanctified, therefore should be first in blessing. Hillel, by contrast, has only one argument in his favour: *Kiddush* cannot be said without wine, so the wine must be blessed first.

[2] Perhaps sensitive to the traditional rivalry between the schools, Talmud then offers another argument in support of Hillel's position: since wine always requires to be blessed, but not the day, and that which is constant takes priority, it follows that the wine should be blessed first.

[3] These points are then appraised. It is observed that generally *halakhah* goes with Hillel rather than Shammai (according to the *Bath Kol* – i.e. the Voice of God heard from heaven); so why adduce the additional argument in [2]? Answer: to counter the possible objection that, despite this divine authority, the fact that Shammai has two reasons to Hillel's one could sway the argument.

[4] The passage concludes with a discussion of the status of the *Bath Kol*. The Rabbis were generally speaking uneasy with claims to divine authority which circumvented reasonable argument and the rational appeal to Torah; hence the postscript here which claims that, for different reasons, the *Bath Kol* appeal cannot settle the matter. Either (a) the ruling was given *before* the *Bath Kol* was heard, in which case it did not apply, or (b) we are elsewhere instructed by R. Joshua that 'we should disregard a *Bath Kol*'. This last refers to a famous story, recorded elsewhere in the Talmud (*Baba Mesia* 59b), which describes an encounter between Rabbi Eliezer and Rabbi Joshua. The former was attempting, without success, to convince his colleagues of the rightness of his opinion, and appealed first to a series of miraculous events and finally to heaven itself to support him. The sceptical Rabbis, unimpressed by miracles, are finally confronted by a *Bath Kol*:

> [R. Eliezer] said to them: 'If the *halachah* agrees with me, let it be proved from Heaven!' Whereupon a Heavenly Voice cried out: 'Why do ye dispute with R. Eliezer, seeing that in all matters the *halachah* agrees with him!' But R. Joshua arose and exclaimed: '*It is not in heaven.*' [Deuteronomy 30.12] What did he mean by this? – Said R. Jeremiah: That the Torah had already been given at Mount Sinai; we pay no attention to a Heavenly Voice, because Thou hast long since written in the Torah at Mount Sinai, *After the majority must one incline*. [Exodus 23.2]
>
> R. Nathan met Elijah and asked him: What did the Holy One, Blessed be He, do in that hour? – He laughed [with joy], he replied, saying, 'My sons have defeated Me, My sons have defeated Me.'

Incidentally, this example of intertextuality, where the Talmud quotes itself, is indicative of the kind of editing and revising which went on in the last two centuries of the production of the work.

3.2 The commentaries and grammars

EARLY PERIOD

From the earliest times commentaries on the major biblical texts have been produced. The first we know of are the *targums*, or 'translations' of Tanakh into Aramaic. These were originally designed to provide an explanation of the scriptures for those attending the synagogue who did not understand Hebrew. But they are more than simple translations, for they include additional stories, passages of interpretation and explanation, and attempts to explain difficulties. Unlike the Septuagint, which was authorized to serve the needs of the Egyptian Diaspora, and set out to be a faithful translation, the targums were never intended as a substitute for the Hebrew Tanakh. They were employed alongside the reading of the Hebrew text in communities where the biblical language remained in force as the language of the synagogue service.

In addition to the targums we have early commentaries (the Hebrew word is *midrash*): the *Mekhilta* (on Exodus), the *Sifra* (on Leviticus) and the *Sifré* (on Numbers and Deuteronomy). From a later period comes a collection known as Midrash Rabbah (the 'great commentary') which deals with the whole of the Torah and the five scrolls (Canticles, Ruth, Lamentations, Ecclesiastes and Esther). Largely anonymous, they can only be very approximately dated; essentially they represent a gradual midrashic process parallel to that of halakhah, and belonging broadly to the eras of the Tannaim and the Amoraim.

CLASSIC COMMENTARIES

The great period of commentaries, however, was the eleventh to the thirteenth centuries, when a series of major works appeared against which all future endeavours in this field would be judged. The undoubted leader is Rashi (1040–1105), whose commentary is widely used to this day. A native of northern France, his commentary deals both with traditional Rabbinic interpretations and with explanation of the plain meaning of the text. It is in the latter that he is most original, contributing significant philological readings. Rashi also produced a commentary on the Talmud which is still included in printed editions of it. The two most distinguished of his successors are Ibn Ezra (1089–1164) and Nachmanides (Ramban) (1194–1270). Ibn Ezra, a native of Spain, moved to Rome in 1240 and subsequently became an itinerant scholar. He may have produced commentaries on most of the Bible, but it is his Torah commentary which is most important. Ibn Ezra's work is more complex than that of Rashi, and he is prepared to challenge many traditional interpretations, even those of the Talmudic sages. Major features are his use of etymology and grammar, and his practice of drawing upon his own life experience for illustrations. The last of the trio, Nachmanides (also Spanish, though he migrated to Israel in 1267), commented only on Torah. He approaches the text in a more holistic fashion, attending to the sequence of passages rather than the minutiae of individual verses, and seeking the deeper meaning of the law. He refers to both Rashi and Ibn Ezra, and analyses the aggadic and halakhic interpretations of the earlier sages.

■ HOW THE RABBIS GOT THEIR NICKNAMES

Many Rabbis are known by nicknames constructed from the first letters of the individual's title and name. Thus:

Rashi = *R*abbi *Sh*lomo *I*tzchaki
Rambam = *R*abbi *M*oses *b*en *M*aimun (Maimonides)
Ramban = *R*abbi *M*oshe *b*en *N*achman (Nachmanides)

GRAMMARS

Many of the commentaries made important use of grammatical information in the process of elucidating the text. The formal study of grammar was also carried out in this period, the greatest and most influential of the grammarians being David Kimchi (1160–1235), the scion of a Rabbinic family from Narbonne. Building on earlier work, he produced a grammar, the *Mikhlol*, and a lexicon, the *Sefer ha-Shorashim*, which had a profound influence on Christian Hebraists of the Renaissance.

MIDRASH

This rather general term is broadly equivalent to the expression *exegesis* used in biblical studies. Thus, in itself it does not imply any specific mode of enquiry, but rather both the *process* and its *outcome*. Jacob Neusner (1987: 8f.) sets out three uses of the word: first, referring to the types of scriptural exegesis carried out in Judaism; second, a word for a collection of exegeses of scripture (for example, a midrash of the Book of Joshua); and third, a specific composition in which a particular thought relating to some verse of Scripture is set out. The actual content of these midrashim varies according to the process used. Aggadah, for instance, bears on narrative or folkloristic additions to or explanations of Scripture, while halakhah deals with legal rulings and interpretations. The methodology of midrash is summarized in the next two subsections which deal with the rules of interpretation and the distinction between *peshat* and *derash*.

RULES OF INTERPRETATION

In the modern period the practice of commentary in Western Europe has been largely turned towards historical and factual explanation, focused largely on what the Rabbis would term the 'plain meaning' of the text. The literal meaning of the text became the most important focus for comment, partly in reaction against the more allegorical and symbolic forms of interpretation which had predominated in the Church prior to the Enlightenment. Rabbinic exegesis is quite different in character, though it conforms strictly to its own set of rules and conventions; what follows is a summary of the principal conventions.

The rules of Rabbinic exegesis fall into two categories: first, the thirteen *middot*, rules for deriving oral law from written Torah attributed to Rabbi Ishmael, expanding upon a set of seven attributed to

Hillel; second, the techniques of *peshat* and *derash* which enabled Rabbinic scholars to handle the detailed interpretation of Scripture.

The thirteen middot[26]

1 Inference is drawn from a minor premise to a major one, or from a major premise to a minor one.

   For example, something forbidden on an ordinary festival is the more firmly forbidden on Yom Kippur; on the other hand, if an action is permitted on Yom Kippur, it is the more permissible on an ordinary festival.

2 If words or phrases occurring in two passages are similar, it can be concluded that what is expressed in one applies also to the other.

   In Exodus 21.2 the phrase 'Hebrew slave' is ambiguous – it may mean either a gentile slave owned by a Jew, or a Jewish slave. Deuteronomy 15.12, which reports the same law, makes it clear that the second case is intended, since Deuteronomy refers explicitly to the slave as 'your Hebrew brother'.

3 A general principle which is exemplified in specific biblical laws is applicable to all related laws.

   Thus Exodus 21.26–7 states that where certain specific injuries are inflicted upon a slave by his or her owner, the slave is to be set free. The Rabbis concluded that *any* injury inflicted upon a slave leads to freedom.

4 When a general statement is followed by specific instances, only these apply.

   Though Leviticus 18.6 states that no-one should marry a relative, it is followed by a detailed list. Only the specified relationships are forbidden.

5 Conversely, when a specific case is followed by a generalization, the general rule applies (e.g. Exodus 22.9).

   The verse deals with disputed ownership of a lost item which has been recovered. It begins with a list of specific items (ox, donkey, sheep, clothing), but adds at the end 'or any other loss'.

6 Given the sequence 'generalization–specification–generalization' it is the specific which governs the interpretation.

7 When it is for the sake of clarity that a generalization is followed by a specific example, or vice versa, rules 4 and 5 do not apply.

8 When a generalization is laid down, and afterwards specified in a new statement, the specification is there to guide our interpretation of the general principle.

   In Deuteronomy 22.1 anyone who finds lost property is to return it to its owner. In the next verse the specific 'garment' is mentioned. The point is that 'lost property' is to be understood as applying only to objects likely to have an owner, or bearing some mark of possession.

9 If a general law is enunciated, followed by a specific case similar to the general, the purpose is to indicate a lesser punishment in that case.

   Exodus 35.2–3 prescribes the death penalty for work done on the Sabbath. There follows an injunction against lighting a fire on the Sabbath – this would incur a lesser penalty.

10 Where a specific case is enunciated which is in a material respect different from the general case, the specific rule applies.

11 When a general law is stated, followed by a specification relating to a new matter, none of the terms of the general law apply unless Scripture explicitly states that they do.

26 The discussion of the thirteen rules in this section is based on the entry 'Rules of Interpretation' in Philip Birnbaum's invaluable *Encyclopedia of Jewish Concepts* (New York: Hebrew Publishing Company, 1975).

12 A dubious word or passage should be explained from its context or from a subsequent expression.

13 If two biblical passages contradict each other, a third passage is required to reconcile them.

Peshat *and* Derash

Peshat denotes an approach to the interpretation of Scripture which has two aspects: (1) discovering, through historical means, the original or contextual meaning of the text; and (2) the use of largely philological methods. *Derash* has as its principal motivation the discovery of the actuality of God's will for the people 'here and now'. It is an intensely practical process of interpretation which ignores the historical meaning, and employs linguistic rules which are in the main independent of both context and the rules of biblical language. These are often designed to maintain an appropriate theological position in regard to interpretation. It seems that, although these terms are now distinguished from each other, this distinction was not original. From being largely synonymous in earlier usage, it appears to have been as a result of Rashi's approach to commentary that they were given their precise and distinctive references.

A number of features of the Rabbinic treatment of the text have a bearing on these distinctions, since what is meant by philological methods differs considerably from scientific philology as understood in the Academy. Essentially, *derash* treats the Bible as a single monolithic unit – all its language is equally applicable in every place, so that the clarification of a puzzling passage can be carried out on the basis of comparisons which take no account of historical or literary context. Thus the grammatical forms and syntactical structure of biblical Hebrew are more or less ignored, and each and every detail is explored for significance – for example, repetitions or duplications have separate meanings on each occurrence. An example of this peculiar to Judaism is the process of *gematria*, where the letters of a word are given their numerical values.

Derash also engages in reinterpretation where anthropomorphic or anthropopathic language is used of God; it employs allegorical methods where a verse appears to be trivial or redundant; and it resorts to non-literal interpretation to resolve contradictions. On the other hand, it will make use of excessively literal readings where seemingly superfluous or unimportant words occur (e.g. 'this' or 'these').

3.3 Philosophy and ethics

MAIMONIDES AND HIS CONTEMPORARIES

Both Christianity and Islam place great emphasis on faith, as defined by adherence to fundamental statements of belief. This is not the case for Jews. Faith, for a Jew, is seen in trusting God rather than in making statements about what God is like; being a Jew is being part of a people rather than being able to subscribe to statements of faith. Obviously from biblical times onwards, being a Jew has been very much tied up with God and how one responds to God in the practical situations of life. But there is little interest in trying to produce articles of faith. In the Middle Ages Maimonides (1135–1204) formulated his thirteen principles, and these are still recited in the morning service, but they are the exception rather than the rule. Maimonides came from Cordoba in Spain, but moved later to Egypt when an extremist Islamic group came into power in Spain. He was very much influenced by Aristotle, and as a result his philosophical position belongs within a tradition shared also with Islam and Christianity in which great theological questions were debated from a fundamentally classical standpoint. Maimonides completed his *Guide for the Perplexed* in 1190; and it has earned its place as one of the great philosophical works of its time, and certainly of the profoundest importance for the future development of Judaism.

Although it won almost immediate acclaim, not everyone accepted that his project was a legitimate one. Maimonides, influenced by Aristotelianism, sought to combine the rational philosophy of the Greeks with the traditional faith of the Jews. He tried to give a rational basis to the *mitzvot* (commandments and laws) by suggesting that, first, they encouraged social stability, second, they worked for the moral development of the individual, and third, they instilled correct religious ideas which could lead a person to God. Attractive as this might seem to those of a humanistic bent, the process could be seen as undermining the unqualified authority of God, whose commandments do not require a *human* rationale. At this point, therefore, Maimonides was challenged even by those who otherwise supported him.

Although Judaism is not normally thought of as a credal religion, Maimonides' series of thirteen articles which he identified as being of the essence of Jewish belief have often been taken as a kind of creed for Judaism. They are belief in

1 the existence of a Creator and Providence;
2 the unity of the Creator;
3 the non-physical nature of the Creator;
4 the eternal existence of the Creator;
5 the sole right of the Creator to be worshipped;
6 the words of the prophets;
7 the character of Moses as the greatest of all prophets;
8 the revelation of the Law to Moses at Mount Sinai;
9 the immutability of the revealed Law;
10 the omniscience of God;
11 the reality of retribution in this world and in the hereafter;
12 the coming of the Messiah;
13 the resurrection of the dead.

It is important to stress that these principles have been deduced by human ingenuity, they are not principles from God. Therefore they are fallible, for only God has complete authority.

It is interesting to reflect on the extent to which matters dealt with by Maimonides are held in common with the other religions of the book. It would be hard to find disagreement as regards the first six. Numbers 7, 8 and 9 belong fairly specifically to the Jewish perspective, and of the remaining four, it would be the belief in the coming Messiah which would find significant disagreement.

In several respects Maimonides' emphases were in conflict with traditional Judaism. His resistance, for instance, to the literal understanding of any kind of physical description of God (such as is found in the Tanakh itself) led him to condemn such views as heretical. This rejection of anthropomorphism and a high-minded demand for philosophical sophistication left him open to the charge of alienating simple pious Jews. Of more significance was opposition to some of the implications of his philosophical basis for traditional teaching. Thus Maimonides was willing to reinterpret Rabbinic and biblical teachings in conformity with reason; worse still, he attempted to put the *mitzvot* on a rational footing.

Maimonides was part of a flourishing Jewish philosophical tradition within the Islamic world which included such figures as Saadia (852–942), a native of Fayyum in Egypt who later became Gaon of the Rabbinic academy at Sura, Solomon ibn Gabirol (*c*.1021–55) and Judah HaLevi (*c*.1075–1141), both

Spanish. His critics included Gersonides (Levi ben Gerson of Bagnols in Provence, 1288–1334) and Crescas of Barcelona (1340–1410). These represent only a selection of this lively tradition, which continued in Spain even after the Christian conquest of that country.

ETHICS AND BEHAVIOUR

Religions like Christianity which make salvation dependent on a personal decision by the individual to commit themselves to a particular belief and a particular way of life often have difficulty with those, like Judaism, whose emphasis lies elsewhere. Since the individual is not regarded in Judaism as being 'radically evil' – that is, inevitably corrupt by virtue of the mere fact of having been born – there is correspondingly no requirement for a radical change of nature. We are as the Almighty made us, and the individual is called to obedience on the basis of what he or she is.

Sin and wrongdoing are thus faults and failings for which we bear responsibility, and for which we must therefore take the consequences. They do not signify or symbolize a deep and unbridgeable chasm between the human and the divine. The divine is of course infinitely other and cannot be approached by human beings; but this is a consequence of the inherent nature of the two, and has nothing to do with sin or a supposed fall from grace.

These observations have some bearing on the question of ethics in Judaism. It is often claimed that Christianity has its own very special ethic, characterized by the teachings of Jesus in the Gospels. In particular the Sermon on the Mount (Matthew 5–7) is held to encapsulate the essence of Christian ethics. How true this claim is may be open to question: many of the supposedly 'Christian' virtues are also found in other religious and non-religious systems, and there may in the final analysis be very little that could be said to be uniquely 'Christian'. Be that as it may, the belief that Christianity is an 'ethical' religion tends to colour its perception of other faiths, and can lead to the posing of quite inappropriate questions. It could be argued, for instance, that it is strictly meaningless to seek an account of Hindu ethics, given the doctrine of karma and the belief that each life is the working out of the consequences of the previous one. To ease the circumstances of the individual who holds such beliefs might in fact run counter to his or her best interests – though a severely deterministic account of the matter would be able to resolve the paradox. But then, does the term 'ethics' have any meaning whatsoever in a strictly deterministic view of life?

Judaism does not teach that there is any special virtue in being ethical.[27] This is a basic requirement of the human condition, and has no application to religious questions. This can be summed up in the two-covenant theory. There is a general covenant which provides for the whole of humanity (the Noachic Covenant) and which was given after the Flood. This provides the basis for all human life. Its specific terms are set out above (note 21). Then there is the Covenant with Abraham and Moses which is applicable only to the Jews, and which lays on them a whole series of obligations which must be carried out in consequence of one's birth as a Jew. These commandments are to be carried out not because they are ethically correct by some abstract ethical norm, but because God has commanded them. The actions which are entailed are good because they are commanded by God; they are emphatically *not* commanded because they are ethically right. The key to understanding this is found in two terms: love and obedience. The Shema, it will be recalled, announces the one God and then demands

27 Which is not, of course, to suggest any hint of antinomianism or of *unethical* behaviour; it is simply that there is no specifically Jewish ethic, unless we interpret the obedience to Torah and halakhah as an ethical matter.

the response of love. God chose the Jews, not because they were great in worldly terms, but because he loved them. God took them out of Egypt, out of slavery, and gave them a good land in which to live. And in return, the love of a Jew towards God is shown in the faithful observance of the Torah, the keeping of the commandments as interpreted by the oral law.

In order to enable the proper performance of the increasingly complex system of obligations which the halakhot inspired, various attempts were made to codify and simplify them for general use. The most successful of these was the *Shulchan Aruch* (the name means 'prepared table') written by Rabbi Joseph Karo (1488–1575). His intention was to produce a summation of Rabbinic opinions which would serve as a practical guide for the observance of traditional Judaism. The need for such a guide is apparent: the sheer size of the Talmud, its inaccessibility to ordinary Jews, and the volume of secondary Rabbinic writing, make it impossible for any but the most skilled to find their way around the primary sources. Karo's technique involved comparing the opinions of three major predecessors and adopting any view which was held by at least two of them, except where the majority of ancient authorities opposed them. Karo's three authorities were Maimonides, Isaac ben Jacob Alfasi (1013–1103), who wrote a practical summary of the Talmud entitled *Halakhoth*, and Asher ben Yechiel (1250–1327). In addition, Karo based the form of his guide on that produced by Asher's son, Jacob ben Asher (1280–1340). Rabbi Jacob's guide, known as the *Sefer ha-Turim*, or simply, *Tur*, was divided into four parts:

Orach Chayyim	'The Way of Life', dealing with Jewish religious practice at home and in the synagogue.
Yoreh De'ah	'The Teacher of Knowledge', covering things allowed and forbidden, including dietary laws.
Even ha-Ezer	'The Stone of Help', which treats the subject of marriage, divorce, and family matters.
Choshen ha-Mishpat	'The Breastplate of Judgement', concerning various aspects of civil law.

The *Shulchan Aruch* was first printed in Venice in 1565. Thanks in part to the medium of print, and to its inherent value, the book was quickly recognized as a major contribution. A series of critical glosses prepared by Rabbi Moses Isserles (1525–72) helped to put right certain defects, and the combined volume continues to the present day to be the principal guide to the practice of Judaism.

3.4 Zohar and kabbalah

ORIGINS

The word *kabbalah* originally meant simply 'tradition', but is now synonymous with a particular Jewish mystical tradition which seems to have its roots in a form of gnosticism. Early Rabbinic tradition grew to be very suspicious of all forms of mysticism (hence the Rabbinic ban on study of Ezekiel 1 and the Genesis creation accounts except under controlled circumstances[28]). Despite this unease, the great

---

28 See Mishnah *Hagigah* 2.1, 'They do not expound upon the laws of prohibited relationships before three persons, the works of creation [Genesis 1] before two, or the Chariot [Ezekiel 1] before one, unless he was a

Rabbi Akiva is associated with the mystical tradition, and a legend[29] tells of how he and three other sages entered paradise. Despite Akiva's advice to them, all of the others died or were mentally disturbed; only Akiva returned unscathed. In general the mystics sought both esoteric knowledge of the Godhead and personal ecstatic fulfilment (see the warning quoted in note 28: 'Whoever reflects upon four things would have been better off had he not been born: what is above, what is below, what is before, and what is beyond'), but it was only in the second millennium that formal doctrines began to develop which came to constitute kabbalistic mysticism as a specifically Jewish phenomenon.

The kabbalistic movement developed on the basis of influential texts such as the *Bahir* ('Book of Clarity'), edited in Provence in the twelfth century, and the *Zohar* (the 'Book of Splendour'). The latter become in effect the bible of kabbalism, and great antiquity is claimed for it, though it first appeared in Spain around 1280 where it is associated with the kabbalist Moses de Leon. Though he himself claimed it descended from R. Simeon ben Yochai, one of the great Tannaitic sages of the second century, this attribution has long been discredited and the work is seen as that of de Leon himself and his successors.

TEACHINGS OF THE ZOHAR

The starting point is the absolute and inaccessible origin of everything, the hidden Godhead, entitled *Ein Sof* (which means literally 'without end') – the endless, eternal One. Of course, if that were all that could be said, there would be no way for humans to make any progress. But just as Philo's[30] absolute God, *ho ōn* ('He who is') was mediated through the Logos ('the Word'), thus providing limited accessibility in the direction of an equally remote being, so the Zohar spoke of 'emanations' (*sefirot*) – a phraseology which is strongly reminiscent of gnosticism. These are: (1) the Crown; (2) Wisdom; (3) Intelligence; (4) Greatness, or Love; (5) Power, or Judgement; (6) Beauty, or Compassion; (7) Lasting Endurance; (8) Majesty; (9) Righteous One, or Foundation of the World; (10) Kingdom, or Diadem.[31] The *sefirot* are sometimes presented as the branches of a tree linking earth and heaven (reminiscent, perhaps, of the Norse tree Yggdrasil), sometimes as the organs of the primal man, *Adam Kadmon*. These emanations help to shape and control reality, and a grasp of them will enable a person better to engage in the constant struggle between good and evil in which humankind, through Torah observance, has a key role to play. The concept of the primal man was to take on greater significance in Lurianic kabbalism.

sage and understands of his own knowledge. Whoever reflects upon four things would have been better off had he not been born: what is above, what is below, what is before, and what is beyond.' (Neusner's translation.)

29 Talmud *Hagigah* 14b.
30 Philo of Alexandria was a Jewish philosopher who flourished from the end of the first century BCE to the beginning of the first century CE. His work included many treatises devoted to demonstrating the validity of Jewish faith in the light of Stoic and Platonic philosophy.
31 This is basically the list given in *Encyclopedia Judaica* X.570f.

THE LURIANIC KABBALAH

The Kabbalah became influential through its centre at Safed, in northern Galilee, where a community of mystics, Jews expelled from Spain, was established at the beginning of the sixteenth century. Its leader Moses Cordovero (1522–70) undertook the work of systematizing the Kabbalah – the Zohar is essentially a midrashic type of work with no attempt at analytical or philosophical order. However, it was his successor, Isaac Luria (1534–72), who proved the major figure in the development of kabbalism. Luria came to Safed from Egypt in 1569, and was taught by Cordovero; however, he quickly became a leading teacher in his own right, and gathered around him a circle of disciples who would preserve and record Luria's oral teaching.

Building on the Zohar, Luria offers an explanatory system for the existence of life and of human beings and their relationship to the divine which goes far beyond the earlier teaching. The central doctrine of the Lurianic Kabbalah is that of *tzimtzum* – the withdrawal of *Ein Sof* into himself, thus creating a vacancy within which the process of creation can begin. The creative process then commences with the projection of the divine light into empty space. In this system, Adam Kadmon is the highest embodiment of that light, and thus in some respects represents the ideal human, or rather, the highest ideal to which humans may aspire (again, there are similarities with Philo's teaching that it is in the realm of the Logos that the most spiritually advanced of human beings encounter the least that may be deemed to partake of God).

The divine light was held in vessels (*kelim*) belonging to the ten sefirot. However, vessels belonging to the lower sefirot were unable to hold the light, and shattered. The resulting sparks were imprisoned in the broken pieces, thus necessitating a work of repair (*tikkun*). It is this task which is the duty of humankind, and is understood in Judaism as being the performance of the *mitzvot* with the right intention as regards the Kabbalah. When every individual has completed this work the messianic age will begin, since primeval harmony will have been restored. It is interesting that at this point the goal of kabbalism meets the stated beliefs of the Rabbis – that Messiah will only come when the commandments have been fulfilled.

Lurianic kabbalism was to a degree discredited by the events surrounding Sabbatai Sevi and was taken up in a modified form by the Chasidic movement (see the section on Messianism, below). In modern times a new interest in the Kabbalah has emerged, in keeping with many other 'New Age' movements.

4 MESSIANISM

It is often assumed that Judaism is a messianic faith, and that Jews eagerly await the coming of the Messiah. While Maimonides included a belief in the coming of the Messiah as the twelfth of his thirteen articles (see pp. 149–50 above) it is more accurate to say that this is a rather minor note in the symphony of Jewish faith. The more characteristic attitude since the Mishnah has been a recognition that no doubt, in God's good time, Messiah will appear, but since there is nothing humans can do about the matter, it is as well to say nothing. Here is an example of the typically dry humour with which the subject is often treated:

> Many Jews have long been skeptical of predictions announcing the imminent arrival of the
> Messiah. The first century sage Rabban Yochanan ben Zakkai once said: 'If you should happen
> to be holding a sapling in your hand when they tell you that the Messiah has arrived, first plant

the sapling and then go out and greet the Messiah.' An old Jewish story tells of a Russian Jew who was paid a ruble a month by the community council to stand at the outskirts of town so that he could be the first person to greet the Messiah upon his arrival. When a friend said to him, 'But the pay is so low,' the man replied: 'True, but the job is permanent.'[32]

To say this is not to deny that important messianic movements have appeared regularly in the history of Judaism, from the first century to the twentieth. But none of these has ever found a place in the mainstream of Jewish life and faith, and when it has appeared it has often been with devastating consequences. We will look more closely at two particular cases, one from the seventeenth century and one contemporary; but first, the following health warning might be timely:

> A sober reading of Jewish history . . . indicates that while the messianic idea has long elevated Jewish life, and prompted Jews to work for *tikkun olam* (perfection of the world[33]), whenever Jews have thought the Messiah's arrival to be imminent, the results have been catastrophic. In 1984, a Jewish religious underground was arrested in Israel. Among its other activities, the group had plotted to blow up the Muslim Dome of the Rock in Jerusalem, so that the Temple Mount could be cleared and the Temple rebuilt. Though such an action might well have provoked an international Islamic jihad (holy war) against Israel, some members of this underground group apparently welcomed such a possibility, feeling that a worldwide invasion of Israel would force God to bring the Messiah immediately. It is precisely when the belief in the Messiah's coming starts to shape political decisions that the messianic idea ceases to be inspiring and becomes dangerous.[34]

4.1 Sabbatai Sevi

Several messianic movements are recorded in the first and second centuries CE (including the one which became Christianity), but since the debacle of the second revolt, under Bar Kochba, Rabbinic Judaism has discouraged speculation in this field. That this is generally wise guidance may perhaps be seen from the exemplary case of the seventeenth-century messianic movement of Sabbatai Sevi.[35] Not least of the interest of this movement is its roots in Lurianic kabbalism – for, as we shall see, that same tradition gave rise to a more lasting and creative development in the form of Hasidism. Given the contemporary fascination with all things esoteric, and the way that modern Hasidism uses Kabbalah in an almost New Age fashion, it is intriguing – and perhaps diagnostic – to find that a *messianic* application should prove to have catastrophic consequences.

Prior to Sevi's appearance, developments within Lurianic kabbalism had led to an emphasis on messianic expectations, linking a spiritual view of the 'restored world' with popular folk traditions concerning the Messiah. Thus the essentially political concept of the Messiah became meshed with the

---

32 Quoted from Joseph Telushkin, *Jewish Literacy* (New York: William Morrow, 1991), p.545.
33 See also 'The Lurianic Kabbalah', p. 154 above.
34 Telushkin, *Jewish Literacy*, pp. 546f.
35 The most comprehensive account of this movement is G. Scholem's monumental *Sabbatai Sevi* (1973); a briefer and more accessible treatment is contained in his essay, 'The crypto-Jewish sect of the Dönmeh (Sabbatians) in Turkey', in *The Messianic Idea in Judaism* (1971): 142–7.

more esoteric and mystical realm. It seems likely that the Lurianic school did not contemplate the appearance of a messianic pretender who would attempt to bring about the *tikkun olam*, but rather understood the matter to be entirely in God's hands, relating essentially to inner renewal.

Sabbatai Sevi (1626–76) was a kabbalist in the Lurianic tradition who had from time to time made claims of a messianic kind. These had been generally ignored until Sevi moved to Jerusalem, where in 1665 he was endorsed by a prophetic figure, Nathan of Gaza (1644–80), who announced that the year of messianic redemption would be 1666. From its initial success in the east, the Sabbatian movement spread rapidly throughout the European Diaspora, finding particular support in Amsterdam. A particularly interesting feature of the movement is that it was by no means restricted to uneducated circles. The fulfilment of the messianic task was to take place in Constantinople, where Sevi's followers expected him to remove the Sultan's crown and initiate the new age. Accordingly, many of them travelled with him to that city.

However, Sevi was (not surprisingly) arrested by the Sultan in Adrianople and given a choice: martyrdom if he maintained his messianic claims, or conversion to Islam. He chose apostasy, and thus (seemingly) put an end to his own messianic claims. But at this point an interesting phenomenon intervened – a classic example of cognitive dissonance,[36] where disappointed believers cope by denying the facts which seem to contradict their faith. This can be done either by a blank refusal of the truth of the new facts (as with Creationists, who simply aver the truth of the biblical creation narratives over against the scientific work of the last two hundred years) or by reinterpreting them in a non-intuitive way. It was this latter approach which led to the survival of a hidden form of messianic Judaism for something like a century and a half; for the apostasy of the Messiah was interpreted as a necessary event in God's plan, not a betrayal by a weak human being. Moreover, texts like Isaiah 53 were used to set this humiliation in the context of Hebrew prophecy – thus the Sabbatian movement echoes the earlier response of Christianity to a similarly disheartening event: the death of the Messiah.

4.2 Jewish Christians, Jews for Jesus and Messianic Judaism

The term 'Jewish Christian' has both an ancient and a modern reference. In accounts of the early days of Christianity it designates those whose acceptance of the messiahship of Jesus did not prevent them continuing to uphold the traditions of their Jewish birthright. This group became isolated from both Christianity and Rabbinic Judaism, and eventually disappeared.

In modern times the term has been revived to describe Jews who have converted to Christianity but who insist upon retaining their claim to be Jewish. Since the doctrines (and perhaps more importantly the practices) of Christianity are significantly at odds with what would normally be understood as Judaism (see 1.3, this chapter), the claim to be both Jewish and Christian, however sincere, poses problems for many more traditional Jews. Most who apply this description to themselves are content to let it be a personal matter, and do not see their belief as imposing on them a special *mission* to Jews.

However, a variation of this phenomenon is the 'Jews for Jesus' organization (http://www.jfjonline.org) which, with various Jewish messianic sects, actively promotes the messiahship of Jesus of Nazareth (whom they make a point of referring to by the Hebrew form of his name, Yeshua) as a Jewish dogma. To some extent such groups are contemporary modifications of long-standing Christian missionary enterprises,

---

36 See on this subject R. P. Carroll, *When Prophecy Failed* (London: SCM Press, 1979), and L. Festiger, *When Prophecy Fails* (Minneapolis: University of Minnesota Press, 1956).

and are regarded (understandably) with some suspicion by Orthodox and Reform Jews alike. Insofar as the phenomenon is a device by means of which proselytizing can be more effectively pursued (often supported by lavish funding from evangelical Christian groups in the United States), its credentials must be sharply questioned. The information in the following box, taken from the organization's website, suggests that mainstream fears are not unfounded.

▮ JEWS FOR JESUS

What we do

We communicate creatively! Jewish people tend to dismiss evangelistic methods and materials that are couched in Christian presuppositions and lingo, because they reinforce the assumption that Jesus is for 'them' not 'us.' In order to get beyond that assumption, we have to be innovative in the following areas:

Literature: We write and illustrate hand-lettered pamphlets with plenty of humor in an informal, conversational tone. (We take God seriously but we try not to take ourselves too seriously.) We call these gospel tracts 'broadsides' and our staff hand-delivers more than eight million of these 'invitations to interact with the gospel' each year. (We have animated a few of our broadsides here. For instance, *I Thought I Was an Olympic Superstar and Jesus Made Me Kosher*.) We also publish quite a few evangelistic books, including testimonies of Jewish people who believe in Jesus (such as *Jewish Doctors Meet the Great Physician*), as well as books on prophecy (such as *Future Hope*). We also publish *ISSUES*, an eight-page evangelistic publication for Jewish seekers.

Witnessing Campaigns: Campaigns are super-concentrated times of short-term outreach. We intensify an aspect of our regular missionary work – street witnessing – by sending our own staff and plenty of volunteers on sorties (tract passing expeditions) four times a day for two hours at a time. We usually conduct these campaigns during the summer months in New York City, Toronto, Paris, London, Moscow and various other cities throughout the former Soviet Union.

If you would like us to reach out to your Jewish friends, but feel they are not ready to receive a call, try our letter of witness program. We'll send your Jewish friend the testimony of a Jewish believer in Jesus via letter, along with a copy of our bimonthly publication, *ISSUES*. We will offer your Jewish friend a free subscription to *ISSUES*, as well as other literature geared for Jewish seekers if he or she is interested. You can submit your Jewish friend's name and address online using this form.

The Messianic Jewish Alliance of America (http://www.mjaa.org/about4.html) has a less overtly evangelistic website – but Cohn-Sherbok (2000: xii) reports that at least some traditional Jews regard messianic Jews as 'evangelical Christians deceiving innocent Jewish people away from their ancestral heritage'. However, it is instructive to read the organization's statement of belief, which seems to be evangelical Christian, with a few Hebrew terms employed to give it a Jewish appearance, and the rival organization Jews for Judaism (http://www.jewsforjudaism.org/j4j-2000/index.html) is in no doubt about the real agenda of the MJAA.

▌ MESSIANIC JEWISH ALLIANCE OF AMERICA

What does the MJAA believe?

We believe in one G–d as declared in the Sh'ma (Deuteronomy 6:4), who is Echad (a compound unity) and eternally existent in three persons: G–d, the Father, G–d, the Son, and G–d, the Holy Spirit (Ruach HaKodesh – Isaiah 48:16–17, Genesis 1:1, Exodus 3:6, Ephesians 4:4–6).

We believe in Messiah Yeshua's deity (Isaiah 9:6, John 1:1, 4), His virgin birth (Isaiah 7:14), His sinless life, His atoning death (Isaiah 53, Psalm 22), His bodily resurrection, His ascension, and His future return in power and glory.

We believe that the Bible, consisting of the Tanach (Old Covenant Scriptures) and the B'rit Chadasha (New Covenant Scriptures), is the inspired, infallible, and authoritative Word of G–d (Psalm 119:89, Proverbs 30:5–6, 2 Timothy 3:16–17).

We believe in G–d's eternal covenant with Abraham, Isaac, and Jacob. We, therefore, stand with and support the Jewish people and the State of Israel and hold fast to the Biblical heritage of our forefathers.

While some of these movements and organizations may seem to the outsider to be rather esoteric, there is no doubt that they pose considerable problems for Judaism today – for if Orthodox and Reform synagogues are unable to make common cause (pp. 165f.), it will be all the more difficult to resist the inroads of forms of messianic Judaism which cut at the very roots of both belief and tradition.

▌ 5 TOWARDS MODERNITY: HASIDISM AND THE HASKALAH

The Hasidic movement represents a modern (i.e eighteenth-century) renewal of European Judaism in the direction of a pious mysticism rooted in the older Kabbalah. It remains influential to this day, most notably in the Lubavicher sect. The Haskalah is the Jewish Enlightenment (the word means literally 'culture' or 'enlightenment') which began in Germany in the eigthteenth century. In some ways they may be characterized as twin poles of modernity, reflecting respectively the *emotional* and the *rational* reworking of what had been primarily a religion of observance and tradition. Of course, these two strands had never been absent, as the Kabbalah on the one hand, and the writings of Philo of Alexandria[37] and Maimonides on the other exemplify.

37 See note 30.

5.1 The Hasidic movement

Against the background of the Sabbatian disaster a new movement emerged in Poland. Its founding figure is Israel ben Eliezer (1700–60), known as the Baal Shem Tov, or Besht.[38] Self-taught, he worked as an itinerant faith-healer of mystical experience, and came to be seen as an alternative to the traditional talmudic authority of the Rabbinic leadership. He wrote nothing down, and what has been preserved by his disciples is imperfect. Buber (1974: 12) records one prayer of his, 'Lord, it is known and manifest to you how much rests in me of understanding and power, and there is no man to whom I could reveal it,' which perhaps indicates something of the Besht's confidence in his calling. Many of the teachings attributed to him sound curiously familiar in the modern world of New Age and nature religions. There is a key difference, however, in that Hasidic teachings are directed towards the worship of the one God of Judaism. Thus the Besht's belief in the equality of all before God and the possibility of communion with God in the countryside should not be too quickly identified with modern romanticism. Buber sums up the Besht's teaching thus (1974: 14):

> All outward teaching is only an ascent to the inward; the final aim of the individual is to become himself a teaching. In reality, the upper world is not an outward but an inward one; it is 'the world of thought'.
>
> If, then, the life of man is open to the absolute in every situation and in each activity, man should also live his life in devotion. Each morning is a new summons. 'He arises in eagerness from his sleep, for he is sanctified and has become another man and is worthy to create, and imitates God by forming his world.' . . . When a man prays in the fire of his being, God Himself speaks the innermost word in his breast. This is the event; the external word is only its garment.

ISRAEL BEN ELIEZER – THE BESHT: A SUMMARY OF HIS TEACHINGS

1   Emphasis on the subjective side of religion.
2   We serve God with all our actions, not just *mitzvot*.
3   The key idea is devotion.
4   Religion is egalitarian – the least may display the greatest evidence of the divine spark.
5   The importance of the *Tsaddik* – the man close to God, who channels divine energy and is a kind of intermediary.

His main disciple was Rabbi Dov Baer, the Maggid of Mezeritch. Though himself already a recognized scholar, he was influenced by the subjective side of the Besht's teachings. He was able, on the basis of his own knowledge of the Kabbalah, to give form and structure to the movement. His young disciples became in turn the leaders of Hasidism, and the title *Tsaddik* came to be applied to the leadership.

In time the Tsaddikim came to have great influence, being both charismatic leaders and holders of power in their communities. The Tsaddik 'is looked upon by his disciples and adherents as the living incarnation of the Torah'.[39] This was seen by some as an abuse, and in particular the role of intermediary between God and individual human beings was regarded with considerable suspicion. More mundanely,

38 See p. 147, 'How the Rabbis got their nicknames'.
39 Birnbaum, *Encyclopedia of Jewish Concepts*, p. 520.

the use of alcohol and the practice of song and dance in worship were frowned upon. However, Hasidism today has been more or less normalized as a regular form of Judaism.

In modern Judaism, Hasidism may best be described as a charismatic, intellectual and traditionally observant movement which combines an adherence to distinctive outward forms (ringlets, beards, styles of dress) with a set of teachings and beliefs which (as we have already seen) share something with the movements of the New Age. This not surprisingly creates tensions – those within the movement who find themselves drawn to the intellectual traditions of the Enlightenment may well encounter frustration, and the strictness of its observance makes for a somewhat limited range of social encounters outside Hasidism. Perhaps the best studies of these phenomena are to be found in the novels of Chaim Potok.[40]

CHABAD-LUBAVITCH: A MODERN HASIDIC GROUP

The following provides a summary of the most famous of the modern Hasidic groups – Chabad-Lubavitch (http://www.chabad.org/) – based on information on its website.

Chabad-Lubavitch is a philosophy, a movement, and an organization. It considers itself to be the most dynamic force in Jewish life today.

Philosophy. The word 'Chabad' is a Hebrew acronym for the three intellectual faculties of *chachmah* (wisdom), *binah* (comprehension) and *da'at* (knowledge). The movement's system of Jewish religious philosophy, the deepest dimension of G–d's Torah, teaches understanding and recognition of the Creator, the role and purpose of Creation, and the importance and unique mission of each Creature. This philosophy guides a person to refine and govern his and her every act and feeling through wisdom, comprehension and knowledge

The word *Lubavitch* is the name of the town in White Russia where the movement was based for more than a century. Appropriately, the word Lubavitch in Russian means the 'city of brotherly love'. The name Lubavitch conveys the essence of the responsibility and love engendered by the Chabad philosophy toward every single Jew.

Movement. Following its inception 250 years ago, the Chabad-Lubavitch movement swept through Russia and spread in surrounding countries as well. It provided scholars with answers that eluded them and simple farmers with a love that had been denied them. Eventually the philosophy of Chabad-Lubavitch and its adherents reached almost every corner of the world and affected almost every facet of Jewish life.

Leadership. The movement is guided by the teachings of its seven leaders (*Rebbes*), beginning with Rabbi Schneur Zalman of Liadi, of righteous memory (1745–1812). These leaders expounded upon the most refined and delicate aspects of Jewish mysticism, creating a corpus of study thousands of books strong. They personified the age-old, biblical qualities of piety and leadership.

40 *The Chosen* (1967), *The Promise* (1969), *My Name is Asher Lev* (1972), etc.

And they concerned themselves not only with Chabad-Lubavitch, but with the totality of Jewish life, spiritual and physical. No person or detail was too small or insignificant for their love and dedication. In our generation, the Lubavitcher Rebbe, Rabbi Menachem Mendel Schneerson of righteous memory (1902–94), known simply as *the Rebbe*, guided post-Holocaust Jewry to safety from the ravages of that devastation.

Organization. The origins of today's Chabad-Lubavitch organization can be traced to the early 1940s when the sixth Lubavitcher Rebbe, Rabbi Yosef Yitzchak Schneersohn of righteous memory (1880–1950), appointed his son-in-law and later successor, Rabbi Menachem Mendel, to head the newly founded educational and social service arms of the movement. Motivated by his profound love for every Jew and spurred by his boundless optimism and self-sacrifice, the Rebbe set into motion a dazzling array of programmes, services and institutions to serve every Jew. Today 4,000 full-time emissary families apply 250-year-old principles and philosophy to direct more than 2,700 institutions (and a workforce that numbers in the tens of thousands) dedicated to the welfare of the Jewish people worldwide.

5.2 The Haskalah

Building on the work of seventeenth-century thinkers like Newton, Descartes and Locke, the European Enlightenment redefined the approach to knowledge in the eigthteenth century, placing rationalist, sceptical and empirical scientific ways of handling information and argument at the heart of the scholarly enterprise. Just as this movement posed a real threat to traditional Christian religion at the hands of men like Voltaire and Hume, so the Jewish communities of Western Europe were drawn into a similar process. Though the main progress of the Haskalah took place in the late eighteenth and early nineteenth centuries, it is important to recognize the contribution made at a much earlier point by a key seventeenth-century scholar from Amsterdam – Baruch Spinoza.

SPINOZA – THE PRECURSOR (1632–77)

Note that Spinoza was dead before the Besht – Baal Shem Tov (1700–60) – was born. This is important for the different Jewish experience in different parts of Europe, in that just as the Enlightenment was largely a Western European experience, so the Jewish communities of East and West reacted differently, and at different times, to the crisis of modernity. To some extent there is a correlation with the different Jewish cultural traditions known as *Sephardic* (Spain, Portugal) and *Ashkenazi* (Franco-German, Central and Eastern Europe).[41] Many of the intellectual giants of medieval Judaism lived in Spain or Portugal under Muslim rule, and were scattered through Western Europe when the new Christian regimes began to expel, persecute and forcibly convert the Jews. Many settled in the Netherlands, and Spinoza was himself of the Sephardic tradition. His philosophy was influenced by Descartes, scientific thought, and secular and Christian thinking.

41 British Jews in the main belong to the Ashkenazi tradition, a fact reflected in their Hebrew pronunciation.

Baruch (or Benedict – the Latin form of the name, which means the same thing: *blessed*) Spinoza's most influential publications were *Tractatus Theologico-Politicus* (1670) and *Ethics*, the second being published posthumously in 1677.[42] While we might not today find Spinoza's thought shocking, he was in his day held in such opprobrium by his fellow Jews that he was expelled from the synagogue for his heterodox beliefs.

Essentially, he sought to take a purely rational approach to questions of belief, rejecting naive ideas of revelation and inspiration. He was one of the forerunners of nineteenth-century biblical criticism, exploring an equally rational approach to the Bible which led him to formulate many of the key questions which would later be taken up by Simon, Wellhausen and other nineteenth-century biblical scholars. Spinoza, like Mendelssohn later, does not (unlike Philo and Maimonides) claim to be simply reinterpreting what is already in Scripture. He is conscious of innovation, of not being bound to the tradition – in this they both differ from Kabbalah and Hasidism.

MOSES MENDELSSOHN (1729–96) AND THE HASKALAH

The Haskalah proper began in the late eighteenth century in Germany and spread to Central and Eastern Europe in the nineteenth century. It arose among Jews of a liberal and modern cast of mind who, influenced by the increasingly secular tone of contemporary scholarship, aimed at bringing the best of modern European culture and secular knowledge into the mainstream of Jewish intellectual and religious life.

The principal challenges were to traditional religion and to the exclusively talmudic nature of Jewish education. Its proponents sought to broaden education into the humanities, introducing a variety of secular subjects into the curriculum. One of the first hurdles was the status of Hebrew: since the only legitimate study was deemed to be that of the Talmud, newer subjects were approached in the initial stages via the medium of German written in Hebrew characters. Thus Moses Mendelssohn translated the Bible into German, written in Hebrew letters, and provided a Hebrew commentary (called the *Biur*).

Mendelssohn is rightly credited with being the founder of the Jewish Enlightenment. A friend of Kant and Lessing, with their encouragement he ventured into the field of philosophy, publishing essays in German. However, his most influential writings deal with Judaism, which he discussed in terms of the rationalist principles which Spinoza had earlier deployed. In essence, Mendelssohn believed that reason always took pride of place over revelation. This did not imply a denial of the traditional belief in God as a perfect, wise and just being; rather it entailed the principled conviction that such beliefs did not depend upon miracles and revelation: reason alone is sufficient to discover the reality of God. Perhaps his most influential work was *Jerusalem* (1773); the following is a characteristic statement of his position:

> It is true that *I recognize no eternal truths other than those that are not merely comprehensible to human reason but can also be demonstrated and verified by human powers* . . . I consider this an essential point of the Jewish religion and believe that this doctrine constitutes a characteristic difference between it and the Christian one. To say it briefly: I believe that Judaism knows of no revealed religion in the sense in which Christians understand this term.

---

42 Spinoza intended to publish the *Ethics*, but withdrew it when it became apparent that the work, which had circulated in manuscript, was likely to meet with a hostile reception.

Miracles and extraordinary signs are, according to Judaism, no proofs for or against eternal truths of reason . . . For miracles can only verify testimonies, support authorities, and confirm the credibility of witnesses and those who transmit tradition. But no testimonies and authorities can upset any established truth of reason, or place a doubtful one beyond doubt and suspicion.

(Mendelssohn 1983: 89–90, 99 (author's emphasis))

The threat faced by Jews in Western Europe was that of complete assimilation. What Mendelssohn and others sought as an alternative to the impossible strictures of tradition was a middle road which would ensure the survival of Judaism without unnecessary compromise of religious truth.[43] The religious outcome was the threefold division of Judaism into Reform, Orthodox and Conservative synagogues (see below); sadly the intellectual outcome was an assimilation which was ultimately unsuccessful in the face of the Russian pogroms of the late nineteenth century and the resurgence of virulent anti-Semitism in the form of the Holocaust in the twentieth.

5.3 Reform, Orthodox and Conservative Judaism

Perhaps the key question in the efforts of leading German Jews to bring about religious reform was the status of *tradition*. All parties recognized that Judaism was a religion of many traditions which had developed gradually over many centuries, and which some now felt posed an intolerable burden. Some of these were legal, to do with right behaviour and practice; but many were habitual, forming a highly restrictive set of dress styles, educational restrictions, linguistic usage and codes of personal appearance which seemed to the reformers to have neither religious purpose nor rational defence. Some (like the forms of dress affected by priests and ministers of Christian churches) were little more than the ossified fashions of another age or another place. Setting out to modify or modernize these was a shared objective; where the different reformers disagreed was in how far the process of modernization might be taken.

REFORM JUDAISM

The first of the new movements to emerge was Reform Judaism, which began with the introduction of reforms of liturgy and service by Israel Jacobson in 1810. Further liturgical developments took place with the 1819 prayer book for the Hamburg temple (revised in 1841), and the gradual modification of doctrine. Hopes of a return to Zion, of the rebuilding of the Temple, and of the reinstitution of sacrifice were abandoned, and the Reform prayer book moved to an understanding of the Messiah as relating to the whole of humanity under the influence of two key radical figures, Samuel Holdheim (1808–60) and Abraham Geiger (1810–74).

The first British Reform congregation was the West London Synagogue (1840), and the movement has gathered momentum, particularly in the USA, where the Union of American Hebrew Congregations has around 800 affiliated synagogues. In North America the movement is defined by three declarations

---

43 In Eastern Europe the Haskalah was tantamount to Westernization, and was strongly resisted. Its opponents were the traditionalists, the Hasidim, and the Mitnaggedim (originally opponents of the Hasidic movement, but later united with them in opposition to modernization).

of belief and practice: the Pittsburgh Platform of 1885, the Columbus Platform of 1937, and the Centenary Perspective of 1976. These can readily be consulted at the Reform Judaism website (http://rj.org/rj.shtml), where the following brief statements of general principle are set out. The key features of the movement are summarized in the following.

Reform Judaism respects the autonomy of the individual; understands itself to be a people created 'in the image of God', dedicated to *tikkun olam* – the improvement of the world; it is heir to a body of *evolving* traditions; accepts and encourages pluralism; accepts the obligation to study the traditions.

▌ REFORM JUDAISM: CHARACTERISTICS

Family: Children of Jewish father and non-Jewish mother are recognized as Jewish. Both Bar and Bat Mitzvah are recognized. Some Rabbis will officiate at mixed marriages.

Synagogue: Female Rabbis are recognized, prayers are in the vernacular, men and women sit together, and women may lead worship.

Beliefs: No resurrection, survival of the soul, so cremation is permitted. Religion is voluntary – acceptance by the individual. There is only partial observance of *kashrut* (the dietary laws). There is no requirement for purity rules for women. Open to interreligious dialogue and worship.

ORTHODOX JUDAISM

Despite its name, Orthodox Judaism in fact emerged as a distinct movement in response to the emergence of Reform – in fact the description 'orthodox' was first used as a term of abuse by Reformers. In part this was a simple defensive move, reaffirming the old traditions and banning anything new. But in Germany a more constructive orthodoxy emerged, under the leadership of R. Samson Raphael Hirsch (1803–88). While restating the infallible biblical and talmudic revelation, he nonetheless recognized and advocated the need for Jews to gain a secular education and to be active participants in the life of the wider community.

He applied an old Rabbinic slogan, *Torah im derekh eretz* ('Torah together with the way of the land', Mishnah *Avot* 2.2), which originally meant that Torah should be accompanied by a secular occupation. This he widened to mean that Judaism (*Torah*) should live at peace with the culture and society of the time and place where Jews lived. Probably a majority of those who now regard themselves as Orthodox follow a broadly Hirschian approach, expecting their Rabbis to have a university education and to preach in the vernacular, and in varying degrees flexible about observance while holding to its priority in principle. Within the traditions thus designated, however, there are also Ultra-Orthodox groups which adhere strictly both in practice and in principle to the halakhic rules, and who might well view the less strictly observant with some disapproval.

Orthodox Judaism as a whole regards Reform with deep suspicion, and often with antagonism – to the extent that intermarriage between the communities can be difficult, since the genuine Jewishness of members of Reform congregations is called in question both through their liberal attitude to *kashrut* and through their recognition of children of Jewish fathers and non-Jewish mothers (as being Jewish).

■ ORTHODOX JUDAISM: CHARACTERISTICS

Family: Only children of Jewish mothers are recognized as Jewish. The main emphasis is on male children, though to some extent Bat Mitzvah is also recognized. Rather traditional views of the roles of men and women in the home.

Synagogue: Only male Rabbis recognized. Prayers are wholly in Hebrew, and men and women sit separately, and women never lead worship.

Belief: Cremation is not permitted. Religion is by birth; individual choice is of less importance. There is rigorous observance of *kashrut*. Purity rules for women are adhered to. It is open to inter-religious dialogue, but not shared worship.

CONSERVATIVE JUDAISM

The third main branch of modern Judaism emerged as a kind of middle way. It is rooted in the thinking of Nachman Krochmal (1785–1840), who influenced the 'Science of Judaism' movement. One of his followers, Zacharias Frankel, a founder of the Historical School of Jewish studies, argued that Reform Judaism had gone too far. In his view a proper historical and intellectual critique of both Bible and Rabbinic teaching would lead to a purification rather than an abandonment of the traditions.

The Jewish Theological Seminary Association was founded in 1886/7, but only gained an effective religious focus with the appointment in 1902 of Solomon Schechter as its president. The United Synagogue of America, founded by him in 1913, is now the largest grouping of Jewish congregations in the USA.

While discontinuing the use of the *mikveh* for women and allowing mixed seating and vernacular prayers in synagogue, Conservatism remains on the whole suspicious of biblical criticism and traditionalist in mood. Changes may be made, but with reluctance (such as permission to drive to synagogue on the Sabbath).

6 ANTI-SEMITISM AND THE HOLOCAUST

6.1 Anti-Semitism

Anti-Semitism is that form of racism which is directed against the Jews. It does not refer to anti-Arab sentiment or to discrimination against Islam. These phenomena of course exist, but the English term 'anti-Semitism' is not properly used to describe them.

It is therefore quite in order to speak of Arab or Muslim anti-Semitism – that is, bigoted prejudice against Jews on the part of Arabs or Muslims. That this exists is undoubted: one of the current sources of copies of the long-discredited malicious hoax *The Protocols of the Elders of Zion* is often quoted as an authority among anti-Semitic Muslims. A brief survey of the character and history of this document in provided below – it would not be appropriate to reproduce its contents, since these are both inflammatory and false.

THE PROTOCOLS OF THE ELDERS OF ZION AND ANTI-SEMITISM

A quick trawl of the Internet reveals something like 1,500 sites discussing this document. Many are designed to discredit it, but some still treat it as a reliable authority providing evidence of a supposed, but quite fictitious, Jewish world conspiracy. The *Protocols* are an undoubted forgery, originated by a German anti-Semite, Hermann Goedsche, in 1868. Using an earlier satirical attack by Maurice Joly on Napoleon III, Goedsche constructed his fiction of a Jewish conspiracy. The text was translated into Russian, and later revised by the Russian secret police (the Okhrana), eventually being made public in 1905 by the priest Sergius Nilus. English translations reached Western Europe in 1920, and the whole thing was exposed as a forgery in the *London Times* in 1921. Despite this, the *Protocols* continued to circulate and be given credence, and formed an important part of the Nazi justification of their genocide against the Jews. (See further: http://www.nizkor.org.)

It is not the purpose of the preceding remarks to suggest that anti-Semitism is now a predominantly Middle-Eastern matter. The concern is to make it clear that the word itself has a very particular meaning and should not be improperly extended for political reasons. Indeed, it is fair to say that until the nineteenth century the condition of the Jews in Muslim countries was generally much better than in Christian lands.

In this section we will concentrate on the contemporary phenomenon of anti-Semitism. Undoubtedly it has long antecedents, going back in the view of some to the New Testament itself. Certainly by the medieval period in Europe active discrimination against Jews and the incitement of mob violence against Jewish communities were common. These were given both theological and racial justification which meant, effectively, that being a Jew was a crime against both God and the state. While neither pretext is now justified by either the church or the state, the need to be well informed about the threat of anti-Semitism remains – despite the lessons of the 1930s and 1940s, we seem collectively to be no nearer to the achievement of a genuinely tolerant society. That other forms of racism also flourish in modern European society simply makes the point more convincingly.

The 'theory' of anti-Semitism (as distinct from the older European religious hatred of the Jews) was based on the distinction between Semitic and 'Aryan' language groups first recognized in the eighteenth century. (The latter term has now been replaced with 'Indo-European'.) In itself a perfectly legitimate linguistic account, it unfortunately gave rise to an associated and quite unfounded theory of corresponding 'races'. There are, of course, no scientific grounds whatever for dividing humankind into separate 'races'. The genetic character of *all* human beings is identical to such an extent that interbreeding is always possible, and differences *within* ethnic groups are as great as those *between* them. There is, in short, only one human race, to which we all belong.

This spurious science, however, gave birth to the pernicious idea that separate 'Semitic' and 'Aryan' races could be identified corresponding to the languages. In due course supposed 'racial characteristics' were described, and these came to be identified with modern communities. 'Aryan characteristics' were taken to represent the elite of humankind, and associated with Germans. Conversely, 'Semitic characteristics' were held to represent the worst of human types, and were associated with the Jews. That all of this is a completely unfounded farrago with no scientific basis whatsoever did not, unfortunately, prevent its rapid dissemination. In nineteenth-century Germany it held a particular attraction: since it was directed against the Jews as a people rather than Judaism as a religion, it gave a population which was coming to resent Jewish assimilation into German society a weapon which remained effective even in the face of conversion to Christianity. The economic and political success of emancipated Jews roused envy which combined with older forms of religious anti-Semitism to form a potent brew. When the economic depression of the 1930s struck, the ground was prepared for popular acceptance of the lethal doctrines of the Nazis. The conspiracy of world Jewry as presented in the *Protocols*, the desire for a scapegoat which commonly accompanies economic failure, and the racial theories of nineteenth-century anti-Semitism combined to write the death sentence for six million Jews.

▮ THE KEY FEATURES OF ANTI-SEMITISM

1 The false theory of distinct human races.
2 The mistaken assumption that different language groups imply the existence of different racial groups.
3 The arbitrary assignment of physical characteristics to the hypothetical racial groups.
4 The further unfounded claim that 'Aryans' are superior and 'Semites' inferior.
5 The lie that there is a Jewish conspiracy to 'take over' Christian society.

▮ THE MAIN RESULTS OF ANTI-SEMITISM

1 The legitimation of personal prejudice.
2 The toleration of actively anti-Jewish organizations.
3 The dissemination of abusive literature.
4 Physical attacks on Jewish property and religious places.
5 Actual violence against individual Jews.

6.2 The Holocaust

A holocaust is literally a sacrifice which is 'completely consumed' (Greek *holo* – complete; *caust* – consumed) by the fire of the altar. Nothing is left to be used by either the priest or the people. In lay language it refers to acts of terrible destruction, particularly by fire. Since 1945 the word has acquired a special meaning, referring to the attempt by the Nazis to eliminate the whole of the Jewish population of the territories under their control.

In recent years the word has begun to be used to describe a wide variety of tragic events, some not dissimilar to the Nazis' pogrom (for example, the killing by Pol Pot's regime in Cambodia of millions of innocent people, the massacres in Rwanda, and at the beginning of the century the genocide against the Armenians), but many quite different in character. For this reason the Hebrew term *Shoah* (which literally means 'whirlwind') has become current in English in an attempt to make clear the distinctiveness of what happened under the Nazis.

The uniqueness of the Holocaust

Why does this matter? What is special about the deaths of Jews (apart from the sheer unimaginable dimensions of the slaughter)? Why do we have to reserve a special word to describe it?

First, despite the long history of anti-Semitism in Europe, and the occurrence of numerous violent outbursts against Jewish communities, there had never been before the Nazis a deliberate intention to commit literal genocide – to murder the whole of the Jewish people. This alone makes its special character indisputable and of sombre significance for future generations.

Second, the ruthless efficiency with which the Nazi machine operated serves as a reminder that we now possess the means to kill great numbers of people without those carrying out the executions being required to have any physical dealings with their victims. The division of responsibility among a great many different functionaries makes it psychologically (though not morally) plausible for people to claim that they 'did not know' or were 'only obeying orders'.

Third, the fact that the Holocaust was the climactic outcome of the deliberate anti-Semitism built into the Christian definition of European civilization means that it cannot be pushed aside as a Nazi aberration. Without the active or passive complicity of the majority of Christian Europeans the Holocaust would have been impossible, for where local populations actively opposed the Third Reich's plans, Jewish communities had a much greater chance of survival. The murder of six million Jews was in general Christian Europe's responsibility, despite the existence of honourable exceptions, and the formal end of the Nazi regime has not eradicated that guilt. Thus the uniqueness of the Holocaust is at least in part a consequence of the special nature of anti-Semitism in Europe, and in those regions to which it has been exported.

Fourth, the Holocaust has one highly unusual (and sinister) claim to uniqueness in the phenomenon of denial. There is a sizeable industry devoted to the quite ridiculous assertion that the Holocaust never happened and was invented by the Jews and their allies as a propaganda weapon. In other circumstances this would be laughable – but the menace of continuing anti-Semitism makes this a far from trivial matter. Few historical events are better documented, from evidence of Hitler's decision to employ the 'final solution' (*die Endlösung*) down to the massive pictorial, documentary and personal testimonials from both sides to the true dimensions of what actually happened.

For these reasons we cannot leave the Holocaust to be quietly forgotten with the passage of time. Not because vengeance should be sought from the guilty, but because the special nature of the Holocaust carries implications for what we do today, and serves to warn us against the sin of apathy.

THE NARRATIVE OF THE HOLOCAUST

The Nazi myth of a pure Aryan civilization with its concomitant need to eradicate flawed or unacceptable elements of the population was a major plank in their programme for the restoration of Germany in the 1930s. The economic and political success of a rejuvenated Reich was perceived to be dependent on the establishment of a pure race and the removal of those who were held responsible for Germany's problems.

Although homosexuals and people suffering from mental handicap were also singled out for eradication, the Jews (and to a lesser extent the Romanies) were unequivocally identified as the major threat to the Aryan 'master-race'. The election of the National Socialist Party to power and Hitler's appointment to the office of Chancellor in 1933 marked the beginning of a period of persecution which only ended with the final defeat of the German armies in 1945. The passing of the Nuremberg Laws in 1935 stripped the Jews of all rights and left them unprotected by law. In effect, from that time on merely to be a Jew in Nazi-held territory was to be deemed to be outside the law, guilty of the crime of Jewishness, punishable by death. The nine months from May 1941 saw a series of crucial events and decisions which marked the final end of any hope for the survival of millions of Central and East European Jews – for details, see below.[44]

The Nazi 'final solution' was made possible by means of a network of trains, effective communications, detailed lists, pedantic efficiency, a huge bureaucratic machine, and a total commitment to genocide. Even in the last months of the war, enormous energy and expense was devoted to the *endlösung*.

▎ THE FINAL SOLUTION (*ENDLÖSUNG*)[45]

20 May 1941
Goering bans all emigration of Jews from occupied territories because of the 'doubtless imminent final solution'.

31 July 1941
Goering instructs Heydrich 'to carry out all the necessary preparations with regard to organizational and financial matters for bringing about a complete solution of the Jewish question in the German sphere of influence in Europe'.

28 October 1941
Adolf Eichman: 'In view of the approaching final solution of the European Jewry problem, one has to prevent the immigration of Jews into the unoccupied area of France.'

16 December 1941
Hans Frank (Nazi administrator in Poland): 'The Jews must be done away with in one way or another . . . We must annihilate the Jews wherever we find them and wherever it is possible in order to maintain here the integral structure of the Reich.'

20 January 1942
The Wannsee Conference.

30 January 1942
Hitler's broadcast, in which he declared: '. . . the war will not end, as the Jews imagine it will, namely with the uprooting of the Aryans, but the result of this war will be the complete annihilation of the Jews'.

---

44 One of these – the Wannsee Conference – was memorably treated in a drama, *The Conspiracy*, shown on BBC TV in January 2002; an excellent book on the subject (not related to the drama) was published about the same time – see Mark Roseman (2002).
45 See Gilbert 1985: 285.

CONSEQUENCES OF THE SHOAH

The horrors of the Holocaust pose questions concerning both Jewish and Christian concepts of justice and the nature of God which cannot be avoided. What kind of just and loving God could permit such a horror as the Shoah? How can the death camps be reconciled with belief in the chosenness of Israel? What does the Christian claim to be the new Israel mean when this 'new Israel' is implicated in the genocide of the 'old' Israel?

Whether we believe that God is dead, having perished at Treblinka, or that the answer to the question 'Where was God in Auschwitz?' is to pose another question, 'Where was man?', it cannot be denied that traditional rather cosy theologies have been radically called in question by the Shoah. The suffering of the Jews, for long a scandal to those who proclaim the love of God as manifest in Jesus, can no longer be quietly ignored by Christian theologians. And the popular assumption that obedience to the Torah issues in worldly prosperity (or, in biblical terms, that success in the Promised Land follows hard on the heels of faithful adherence to the one God) can no longer be affirmed.

Both Jewish and Christian thinkers and theologians have struggled with these issues. Some of the results are listed in the suggested further reading in the bibliography; but there are no authorities here. Each of us has to come to some personal accommodation with the horrifying truth without benefit of an orthodox doctrine or a simple answer. It is part of the fascination of the Shoah that it will not let us go once we have first looked into its depths.

The cry 'Never again!' has a special power for Jews. It reminds them that one of the fundamental reasons for the existence of the State of Israel today is the need to ensure that 'never again' will the Jews as a people be bereft of hope as – at times – they were under the Nazis. The refusal (on tactical diplomatic grounds) by the British Government to allow refugee ships to put in at the harbours of Palestine during the Second World War caused the needless deaths of many who had fled the Third Reich, and who had nowhere else to go. Thus the achievement of an independent Jewish state in 1948 has a significance which goes far beyond the demands of nationalism. It symbolizes the determination of those who survived the Holocaust never again to succumb without effective resistance to the enemies of Judaism.

Outside Israel also, the lessons of the Shoah have been learned. Jewish communities are everywhere alert to the resurgence of anti-Semitism, and no longer accept discriminatory or offensive treatment or remarks without complaint. They have learned the hard way that toleration of the bigot encourages further bigotry; a lesson which society as a whole has perhaps still to absorb. One of the lessons of the Holocaust for all of us, whether Jew or gentile, is that to allow prejudice and bigotry to go unchecked is a recipe, not for peace, but for aggression. Just as the playground bully must be challenged, so must the racist.

Perhaps the most exciting, certainly the most encouraging, consequence of the Holocaust has been the growth of a great variety of discussions between Jews and Christians. Dialogue has in very many situations taken the place of suspicion. This is especially important in that many of the initiatives have come from the Jews themselves, the very people who might reasonably have been expected to wish to have nothing to do with those whose religious traditions had done so much to make the Shoah possible.

Yet this is still a very delicate rapprochement. Antagonisms are still rife on both sides, and, under-standably, many Jews would reject out of hand the idea of conversation with Christians. It would require a separate chapter to discuss properly the issues involved in dialogue; let it suffice to say for now that an opportunity exists for open conversation – without guilt – between the adherents of two faiths which have, for the best part of two millennia, been sworn enemies.

However, there is a dark side to the question of dialogue; for we must ask whether any similar possibility can operate within the extreme tensions existing today between Israel and Palestine. This is not strictly speaking a Jewish–Muslim affair (there are Christian Palestinians, and Muslim and Christian Israelis); but so long as no kind of peace exists between these two political entities there can be no real dialogue.

7 ZIONISM AND THE LAND OF ISRAEL

7.1 Zionism

'Zion', of course, is a biblical name for the holy city of Jerusalem. Originally the name of one of the hills on which it stands, it has come to signify the whole city, and indeed the whole land of Israel. 'Zionism', then, is simply the belief that the Jews should have a homeland in Israel. That simple fact, however, is clouded by a massive amount of prejudice, misunderstanding and misinformation. Consider, for example, the following statements:

Zionism is a fundamentalist Jewish movement.

Zionism and Palestinian rights are incompatible.

All Zionists are politically right-wing.

Zionism was introduced by religious enthusiasts.

The aim of Zionism is to create an exclusively Jewish state in Israel.

The statements above are all false. Yet they are in one form or another frequently stated as though they were incontrovertibly true. Political factions have used the word 'Zionist' as a term of abuse, and both left-wing and Arab critics of Israel have increasingly come to use the word as though it defined a hostile conspiracy by Jews worldwide to oppress Palestinians in particular and Arabs in general. This 'conspiracy theory' is no new phenomenon. It harks back to the rhetoric of the Nazis, who used such forged documents as the *Protocols of the Elders of Zion* as part of their propaganda against the Jews. It is therefore of the greatest importance to have some knowledge of the facts of Zionism in order to counter such pernicious misinformation.

The term was coined in 1893 by Nathan Birnbaum, but was given currency by the advocacy of Theodore Herzl, who wrote in support of the establishment of a Jewish homeland, and convened the First Zionist Congress in Basel in 1897. He remained its president until his death in 1904, and worked tirelessly to gain international support for the aims of the Congress. It is interesting to note that, although the central aim was to achieve a Jewish state in Israel, other suggestions – including Argentina and Uganda – were also put forward, but with little support.

The central assumption of Zionism is that the Jews, despite having been dispersed throughout the world, remain an identifiable people with a distinctive religion, and do not desire assimilation into their host cultures. It should perhaps be made clear that this does not mean that Jews in the Diaspora are 'bad citizens', or lack commitment to the laws and conventions of those countries in which they are settled. The possibility of dual citizenship and multiple loyalties is now widely recognized, with the increasing mobility of individuals and communities in the modern world. In many ways the Jews have pioneered in this field.

Despite the popularity of Zionism among the generality of Jews, Herzl's programme met with significant opposition from two quarters. Many Orthodox Jews were unhappy with what seemed to be a political programme designed to achieve an outcome which ought really to be left to God. On this view, the return to Israel (*aliyah*) would accompany the coming of Messiah, an event entirely of God's doing. To attempt to pre-empt this, for whatever human reasons, was therefore to attempt to interfere with the divine will, and would end in disaster. The second category of opposition was that of Liberal Jews who believed that the future of their people lay in a wholehearted commitment to the principle of emancipation, if not assimilation, within the Diaspora. We have seen already, from our study of the Holocaust, how ill-fated was this belief. A modified form of this political opposition came from Jewish socialist movements which thought that Jews ought to work for change in their own countries.

From late in the nineteenth century a policy of purchasing land in Palestine was followed, in the hope of an eventual return. The kibbutz movement which began in 1918 established agricultural collectives, some religious, some socialist, which still form an important part of the economy and culture of Israel. But the first real advance in the campaign for a state was the Balfour Declaration of 1917, issued by the then British Foreign Secretary. Its terms were as follows:

> The British Government favours 'the establishment in Palestine of a national home for the Jewish people, and will use their best endeavours to facilitate the achievement of this object, it being clearly understood that nothing shall be done which may prejudice the civil and religious rights of existing non-Jewish communities in Palestine, or the rights and political status by Jews in any other country'.

This declaration was incorporated into the mandate granted by the League of Nations to Britain to govern Palestine after the First World War. However, in 1939 the British reneged on this commitment and proposed to establish an Arab-dominated state.

Faced with a determined military campaign by Jewish nationalists after 1945, the British handed the question of Palestine to the United Nations, which voted to partition the territory into a Jewish and an Arab state. The British withdrew in 1948, and the State of Israel was proclaimed by David Ben Gurion on 14 May 1948.

While it may seem that the aims of Zionism had thereby been realized, this was of course only the start of a long and bitter struggle. Here is a list of the conflicts which have involved Israel since its foundation:

1948   Israel invaded by Egypt, Syria, Lebanon, Jordan and Iraq.

1956   Israel invades Sinai. Eventual withdrawal, but Israel left in possession of the sea port of Eilat.

1967   The Six Day War. After a military build-up by Egypt and her allies, Israel makes a pre-emptive strike. The most notable achievement of this campaign was the capture of East Jerusalem and the opening of the Western or Wailing Wall to Jews.

1973   Yom Kippur War. Following a surprise attack by the Egyptians on the Day of Atonement the Israeli Army defeated its attackers.

In 1979 a peace treaty was signed with Egypt; but considerable tension remains. Both the West Bank and the Gaza Strip continue to be the focus of Palestinian unrest (partly deriving from the ineffectiveness of Arafat's Palestinian Authority and partly from Israeli economic discrimination), and the achievement of a lasting peace between the various peoples in the region remains a distant hope.

1987   First *intifada* – rising of West Bank and Gaza Arabs against Israeli occupation.

1993–5   Discussions leading to the Oslo agreement.

Unfortunately the assassination of Rabin and the election of a Likud government under Binyamin Netanyahu led to the stalling of further talks. Ehud Barak's Labour government of 1999–2000 was widely perceived to have failed to make any inroads, and after his notorious 'walkabout' on the Temple Mount Ariel Sharon came to power promising a military solution. The second *intifada* began in September 2000.

It is this delicate and tense situation which has prompted bitter propaganda and harsh actions on both sides. Whatever may be the merits of the different cases, four factors in particular make it hard to reach a lasting settlement: the explicit refusal of several of Israel's neighbours to recognize its right to exist (though the proposals tabled under the auspices of Saudi Arabia in March 2002 would seem to remove that fear); the Palestinian resentment of right-wing Jewish settlements in the midst of what is internationally agreed to be Palestinian territory; the perennial Jewish insecurity about security, well-founded – it must be admitted – on the basis of terrifyingly regular suicide bombings; and finally the future of Jerusalem.

It is necessary to bear these problems in mind when Zionism is being discussed. Any community which perceives itself to be under threat of violence will defend itself. Those who believe in the right of Israel to exist as a state whose ethos is Jewish and in which Jews will be able to live in safety, free to follow their religion, are hardly asking too much.

Zionists are essentially those who defend these rights. They can be found in all forms of Judaism – Orthodox, Reform and Liberal – and on different points of the political spectrum. There is nothing in Zionism which excludes the rights of non-Jews in Israel. The Balfour Declaration (see p. 172) which was agreed in negotiation with leading Zionists such as Chaim Weizmann, who became the first President of Israel in 1948, makes this quite clear. Indeed, the abuse of the term which is exemplified by the list of lies with which this section began, is nothing less than yet another form of the anti-Semitism which still (despite the Holocaust) bedevils European attitudes to the Jews.

7.2 Eretz Yisrael

The extent of the tourist industry alone shows the continuing fascination that the land of Israel holds for millions of people. It is doubtful if any other place on earth has as many sacred sites per acre, and the rival claims of Jews, Christians and Muslims to its religious guardianship alone would keep the Israeli Ministry of Religious Affairs in constant session.

The phrase *Eretz Yisrael* is Hebrew for 'the land of Israel'. This reflects the fact that the name 'Israel' by itself refers not to a geographical territory but to a people. It is indeed quite common to speak of modern Israel as simply *Ha'aretz* ('the Land'). Thus to use the word 'Israel' is already to beg the question. If it is not a land – if it refers primarily to a people – what are we dealing with when we conjure up an entity which we call 'the land of Israel'? This is a not-unimportant point, for it raises explicitly the question of the significance of the creation of a modern 'state' called 'Israel'.

To some, it is the political territory which provides a secure home for the Jews as a people. It is governed in this view as a state like any other, and need take on no special religious significance. At another extreme, the Ultra-Orthodox reject the legitimacy of 'Israel' in its post-1948 form; though having said that, their continuing to live there creates something of a paradox.

Between these extremes there are a range of more or less religious interpretations of the importance of Israel. The promise of the land is of course a fundamental part of the blessing given to Abraham and his descendants. Thus any normative understanding of what constitutes Judaism must include a place for the land. This means that the possession of territory in what we know as Israel cannot be a neutral geo-political fact. It is resonant with religious meaning.

In a different way, this holds also for Christians. They do not believe that the literal promise of a land is to be carried forward into Christian expectations. But the importance of pilgrimage to the 'holy places' has given the land of Israel a secondary role in pious Christian thinking which comes very close to seeing it as an indispensable part of belief.

With all these conflicts of interest – not to mention the disputes over land rights which can flare into violent conflict between Arab and Jewish Israelis – it is hardly surprising that *Eretz Yisrael* remains a problematic concept. It is worth asking, therefore, what exactly 'Israel' consists of – and recognizing that it very much depends which map one is consulting. Whether it is the (probably exaggerated and possibly fictitious) map of the 'empire' of David and Solomon, or the kingdom called 'Israel' which flourished between Galilee and Shechem in the eighth century BCE, or the post-exilic province of Judah which was little more than the hinterland of Jerusalem, or the Hasmonean kingdom of Alexander Jannaeus with its conquests in Samaria and Idumea, or the Arab province which was for thirteen centuries (not counting the Crusader interlude) under Muslim rule, there is little chance that any two cartographers will agree as to the proper boundaries.

When this delicate exercise in drawing maps has been successfully completed, perhaps there will (at last) be peace in the Middle East.

BIBLIOGRAPHY

General

Clines, David J. A. (1993) *The Dictionary of Classical Hebrew*, vol. 1. Sheffield: Sheffield Academic Press.
De Lange, Nicholas (2000) *An Introduction to Judaism*. Cambridge: Cambridge University Press.
Goldberg, David J., and John D. Rayner (1989) *The Jewish People*. Harmondsworth: Penguin.
Jacobs, Louis (1996) *The Jewish Religion: A Companion*. Oxford: Oxford University Press.
Neusner, Jacob (1990) *Torah Through the Ages*. London: SCM Press.
Shmueli, E. (1990) *Seven Jewish Cultures*. Cambridge: Cambridge University Press.
Unterman, Alan (1981) *Jews: Their Religious Beliefs and Practices*. Brighton: Sussex Academic Press.

Belief

Ariel, David (1995) *What Do Jews Believe?* London: Random House.
Cohen, Shaye J. D. (1999) *The Beginnings of Jewishness*. Berkeley: University of California Press.
Jacobs, Louis (1984) *A Guide to Jewish Belief*. West Orange, NJ: Behrman House.
Wittenberg, Jonathan (1996) *The Three Pillars of Judaism*. London: SCM Press.

Liturgy and practice

Elbogen, Ismar (1993) *Jewish Liturgy: A Comprehensive History*. Philadelphia, PA: Jewish Publication Society.

Jacobs, Louis (1987) *A Guide to Jewish Practice*. West Orange, NJ: Behrman House.

Reif, Stefan C. (1993) *Judaism and Hebrew Prayer*. Cambridge: Cambridge University Press.

Midrash, Mishnah and Talmud

Bialik, H. N., and Y. H. Raunitsky (1992) *The Book of Legends: Legends from the Talmud and Midrash*. New York: Schocken.

Halivni, David (1986) *Midrash, Mishnah and Gemara*. Cambridge, MA: Harvard University Press.

Holtz, Barry W. (ed.) (1984) *Back to the Sources: Reading the Classic Jewish Texts*. New York: Summit.

Neusner, J. (1987) *What is Midrash?* Philadelphia: Fortress.

Neusner, J. (1991) *The Talmud: A Close Encounter*. Philadelphia: Fortress.

Neusner, J. (1992) *The Mishnah: Introduction and Reader*. Valley Forge: Trinity Press International.

Steinsaltz, Adin (1976) *The Essential Talmud*. New York: Basic Books.

Philosophy (including Philo)

Fackenheim, Emil L. (1996) *Jewish Philosophers and Jewish Philosophy*. Bloomington: Indiana University Press.

Kraemer, J. L. (1991) *Perspectives on Maimonides*. Oxford: Published for the Littman Library by Oxford University Press.

Sandmel, S. (1978) *Philo of Alexandria: An Introduction*. Oxford: Oxford University Press.

Schumacher, E. F. (1978) *A Guide for the Perplexed [Maimonides]*. London: Cape.

Mysticism and Messianism

Buber, M. (1974) *The Tales of Rabbi Nachman*. London: Condor.

Cohn-Sherbok, Dan (2000) *Messianic Judaism*. London and New York: Cassell.

Idel, Moshe (1987) *Kabbalah: New Perspectives*. New Haven: Yale University Press.

Idel, Moshe (1998) *Messianic Mystics*. New Haven: Yale University Press.

Jacobs, Louis (1972) *Hasidic Prayer*. London: Routledge & Kegan Paul.

Neusner, Jacob, W. S. Green and E. Frerichs (eds) (1987) *Judaisms and their Messiahs at the Turn of the Christian Era*. Cambridge: Cambridge University Press.

Scholem, Gershom (1954) *Major Trends in Jewish Mysticism*. New York: Schocken.

Scholem, Gershom (1971) *The Messianic Idea in Judaism*. New York: Schocken.

Scholem, Gershom (1973) *Sabbatai Sevi: The Mystical Messiah*, Bollingen 93. Princeton: Princeton University Press.

Haskalah (the Jewish Enlightenment) and varieties of modern Judaism

Lipman, V. D., and S. Lipman (eds) (1985) *The Century of Moses Montefiore*. Oxford: Published for the Littman Library by Oxford University Press.

Mendelssohn, Moses (1983) *Jerusalem or On Religious Power and Judaism* (1783), trans. Allan Arkush; Introduction and Commentary by Alexander Altmann. Hanover: University Press of New England.

Nadler, Steven M. (1999) *Spinoza: A Life*. Cambridge: Cambridge University Press.

Neusner, J. (1995) *Judaism in Modern Times*. Oxford: Blackwell.

Sorkin, David J. (1996) *Moses Mendelssohn and the Religious Enlightenment*. Berkeley: University of California Press.

Judaism and Christianity

Böckenförd, E. W., and E. Shils (eds) (1991) *Jews and Christians in a Pluralistic World*. London: Weidenfeld & Nicolson.

Hilton, M., and Gordian Marshall (1989) *The Gospels and Rabbinic Judaism*. London: SCM Press.

Vermes, G. (1973) *Jesus the Jew*. London: Collins.

Anti-Semitism

Keith, Graham (1997) *Hated Without a Cause? A Survey of Anti-Semitism*. Carlisle: Paternoster.

Maccoby, Hyam (1996) *A Pariah People: The Anthropology of Antisemitism*. London: Constable.

Poliakov, L. (1974) *The History of Anti-Semitism*. London: Routledge & Kegan Paul.

Rubin, Miri (1998) *Gentile Tales: The Narrative Assault on Late Medieval Jews*. New Haven: Yale University Press.

Holocaust

Berkovits, Eliezer (1973) *Faith after the Holocaust*. New York: Ktav.

Cohen, Arthur A. (1981) *The Tremendum: A Theological Interpretation of the Holocaust*. New York: Crossroad.

Fackenheim, Emil (1997) *To Mend the World: Foundations of Post-Holocaust Jewish Thought*. Bloomington: Indiana University Press.

Finkelstein, Norman G. (2000) *The Holocaust Industry*. London and New York: Verso.

Frank, Anne (1997) *The Diary of a Young Girl*. Definitive Edition. London: Viking.

Gilbert, Martin (1985) *The Holocaust*. Glasgow: Collins.

Levi, Primo (1987) *If This is a Man; The Truce*. London: Abacus.

Lipstadt, Deborah (1994) *Denying the Holocaust*. London: Penguin.

Roseman, Mark (2002) *The Villa, The Lake, The Meeting: Wannsee and the Final Solution*. London: Allen Lane.

Rubenstein, Richard L. (1966) *After Auschwitz: Radical Theology and Contemporary Judaism*. Indianapolis: Bobbs-Merrill.

Wiesel, Elie (1985) *The Night Trilogy* (1972). New York: Hill & Wang.

Zionism and Israel

Cohn-Sherbok, D. (1992) *Israel: The History of an Idea*. London: SPCK.

Coughlin, Con (1997) *A Golden Basin Full of Scorpions: The Quest for Modern Jerusalem*. London: Little, Brown & Co.

Goldberg, Michael (1997) *Why Should Jews Survive?* Oxford: Oxford University Press.

Wasserstein, Bernard (2001) *Divided Jerusalem: The Struggle for the Holy City*. London: Profile Books.

Wheatcroft, Geoffrey (1996) *The Controversy of Zion, or How Zionism Tried to Resolve the Jewish Question*. London: Sinclair-Stevenson.

Christianity

Alison Jasper

Throughout the world Christian traditions still exert a considerable influence on cultural practices and social attitudes, and although there is decreasing church attendance in some parts of the globe, in other areas communities identifying themselves as Christian are more than holding their own. I aim, not simply to trace a general historical narrative of the Christian churches, but to describe something of the multiplicity of their concerns – both traditional and contemporary – throughout the world.

1 KEY TEXTS

Introduction

When we think about the key or foundational texts of the Christian religion, we probably think, first and foremost, of the Bible. This brings together Hebrew scriptures (the 'Old Testament') with texts that originated specifically in the earliest years of the Christian churches and refer to the accounts and teachings of Jesus and his first followers (the 'New Testament'). This collection would appear to be foundational for most Christians in the sense that it is perceived as a historical witness to the life, death and resurrection of Jesus Christ, who is regarded as the founder and continuing leader of the Christian Church. It also locates the man Jesus of Nazareth and his first followers firmly within an existing religious context, implicitly claiming that he fulfils and exceeds the earlier foundational Hebrew texts; most notably the five books of the sacred Law (Torah), the origins and history of God's people, and the teachings of the prophets.

However, this present review of Christianity is located in a set of specific historical, philosophical and cultural circumstances. These circumstances are characterized, for example, by a greater familiarity with the concerns of Western European Christianity but also by a concern with feminist and post-colonial critique as well as with the wider-ranging projects of postmodernity. And so, in relation to the question of key texts – including the Bible – this treatment of Christianity will inevitably reflect the geographical, social, economic and political locations of its author. Hopefully it will also seek to recognize the challenges of other voices, asking, for example:

- Who chooses 'foundational' Christian texts? Why *this* Bible? What is at issue here cannot simply be reduced to questions of subject matter or spiritual and theological value. If Christianity is genuinely to be regarded as a 'world religion', then arguably these values themselves need to be contextualized in terms of different Christian cultures, differentiated by various types of location. Issues of power are unavoidable: racism, sexism, white Eurocentricity and economic privilege play into the selection process.
- What is the nature of a theological text? In the past, the truth or authority of any text in the Western world was thought, simply enough, to be guaranteed by external authority; a newspaper report of the spread of foot-and-mouth disease describes and represents an actual epidemic affecting real producers and retailers in Britain in 2001. Similarly, the argument would go, the biblical text describes and represents the actual actions of a transcendent God in the world. However, this model of how we understand texts has been challenged, for example, by suggesting that written and spoken language does not refer in a simple way to actual things or objects but that we build up patterns or structures of language which may relate to some outside reality but in a much more complicated way.[1] This has had some serious consequences for the way in which we decide which should be key theological texts within the Christian tradition. If their status cannot be guaranteed by the external warranty of God's will, how can the choice be made?

1.1 Key texts: the formation of the biblical canon

Within the Christian tradition as a whole there have been many texts of importance and antiquity. For example, among those Indian Christians who attribute the origins of their religion to the arrival of Thomas, one of Jesus' original twelve disciples, on the Malabar coast in the second half of the first century CE,[2] there are lyrical sagas such as the *Margam Kali Paau*, the *Rabban Pattu* and the *Thomma Parvam*, telling about 'the Coming of the Way of the Son of God'. But for most Christians, the Bible is different. Not only is it foundational in the sense that it is proximate to the historical events and focuses on the figure of Jesus, but it is widely regarded as the key, and in some cases the only presently

---

1 In more recent times, this discussion has been particularly associated with the work of linguists Ferdinand de Saussure (1857–1913) and Roman Jakobson (1895–1982).
2 See Hastings 1999: 148.

available, vehicle of divine revelation. In other words, the Bible is foundational in so far as it provides Christians with a context in which they may truly encounter Jesus and hear God speak, and this is the 'foundation' or centre of their personal or communal religious experience.

The Christian Bible, in more or less the form in which it is known today, has held an undisputed position in the Christian churches since at least the fourth century. In view of this, it is interesting to note that even the early record of its development as an identifiable text up until that point remains very much in the realm of historical contingency. There has been little attempt to develop a strong tradition or single story about the origins of the New Testament itself as a text,[3] although it is certainly true that the study of the origins of the two Testaments has occupied an enormous amount of energy, paper and print since the beginnings of the modern critical historical approach to biblical interpretation in the Western world during the eighteenth and nineteenth centuries. But there is nothing really equivalent, for example, to the traditions about the origin of the Qur'an within Islam[4] or the Books of the Law within Judaism[5] or indeed to the Christian traditions about the birth of Jesus; the baby in the stable, the Word made flesh.[6] Nor, in the earliest days, is such great weight placed on the original texts themselves, that they could not be translated into other languages; the authorities clearly did not regard the original *koinē* Greek of most Christian texts, or the Hebrew of the ancient Jewish scriptures, as sacred languages. For example, Jerome, a leading Latin scholar, was actually commissioned by Pope Damasus to produce a Latin translation of the whole Bible from the Hebrew and Greek, for the Western churches in 382 CE. And this early translation was certainly not the first.

Equally, there is no attempt to disguise the fact that the Christian Bible took a while to achieve its now familiar shape and content. The English word 'Bible' is derived, ultimately, from a Greek word meaning 'the books', and this word reflects the almost haphazard origins of the New Testament as a collection of individual works; scrolls stored together, perhaps at first in wooden chests. The first attempt to fix a definitive 'New Testament' seems to have been a second-century collection formed by the 'heretical' Christian called Marcion (d. *c*.160 CE) which included texts more or less equivalent to modern versions of Luke's Gospel and to some of Paul's letters. Marcion wanted to omit altogether the older Hebrew scriptures of Christianity's Jewish heritage. However, his rejection of the themes of judgement, prominent in the Hebrew scriptures, in favour of that of love he saw as the primary message of the Gospel, was ultimately condemned. All the same, it seems clear that the issue of which books should be chosen and which rejected was a matter of fairly open discussion within at least a section of Christian opinion at this early period.

No matter, then, that the Bible is regarded by most present-day Christians as key or foundational in the sense that it represents the earliest account of the life and work of Jesus, fulfilling the ancient Hebrew scriptures, and forming a vehicle of divine revelation. It still owes its form and shape, to some extent, to the choices made within the earliest Christian centuries. And of course it should not be forgotten that one consequence of making choices is that something is inevitably excluded or lost. Some

3 It could be said, however, that there was a common understanding in the Church of the medieval West that God dictated the words of Scripture to the authors, and this idea is sometimes depicted in contemporary illustrations of the evangelists at work.

4 Islamic tradition teaches that the words of the Qur'an were dictated by the Archangel Gabriel to the Prophet. The Text of the Qur'an, the 'blueprint' so to speak, is in heaven.

5 There is, of course, a specific story describing how God gives the law to Moses for the benefit of the people of Israel which is told at length in the Old Testament book of Exodus, chapters 20–40.

6 See Matthew 1.18–2.23 and Luke 1.5–2.52. See John 1.1–18.

texts read and used by early communities of self-identified Christians did not make it into the 'canonical' New Testament that eventually took shape. For example, we now know that there were a number of gnostic 'Gospels', Coptic translations from the Greek, concerned with the figure of Jesus and his disciples, dated to the period between the third and fifth centuries CE. Examples were rediscovered in 1945 at Nag Hammadi[7] in Upper Egypt among a collection of papyrus codices. And there are other rejected texts of whose existence Christian teachers and scholars have been aware for much longer, including the extraordinary second-century work the *Acts of Paul*, in which a feisty, virginal female figure called Thecla follows Paul and then undertakes her own autonomous Christian mission with fiery devotion. Neither the gnostic Gospels nor the *Acts of Paul* reflected the kind of theology that was ultimately declared orthodox by the early ecumenical councils of the Christian Church. And the later dating of some of the texts makes it possible that they were left out because they were more obviously later works of imagination and reflection rather than personal recollection of Jesus and his immediate followers. Nevertheless, the choice of the Church's ecumenical councils – dominated by powerful, educated men – failed to ratify some key texts that were popular with other sectors of the Christian community.

The first clear indication that we have of a fixed 'New Testament' or a list of works related specifically to the experiences of the early Christian Church and officially sanctioned by it comes in 367 CE when, in a letter, Bishop Athanasius of Alexandria lists the 27 books that, in most modern Christian churches, constitute the New Testament. By the early fifth century there are signs that the listing was widely accepted as authoritative in Western churches centred on Rome as well as in Eastern churches centred on Constantinople to the East. Since that time, Western Christian theological thinking, and most particularly that located within the traditions of Protestant Christianity, has intensified the principle of the centrality and ultimate authority of the Bible, Old and New Testaments – a principle often referred to as *sola scriptura*.[8] Protestant Reformers from John Calvin[9] to Karl Barth[10] have argued that the authority of the Christian Church and its teaching and preaching must ultimately be derived from its conformity to Scripture.[11]

1.2 Theological 'canon'?

In the development of wider theological and spiritual traditions within Christianity, there has been a process of 'canon formation' analogous to the process of drawing up a biblical canon, although less

---

7 The Nag Hammadi Corpus: A collection of papyrus codices was found in Nag Hammadi in Upper Egypt in 1945. The papyri, Coptic translations from the Greek, are mostly dated to the period between the third and fifth centuries, although some may have an even earlier origin. There are over forty works, of which the majority are of gnostic Christian origin and represent a primary source of knowledge about gnosticism. They were previously unknown. The MSS are now all in the Coptic Library in Cairo, Egypt.

8 See McGrath 1998: 179–81.

9 See the words of Calvin quoted in McGrath 1998: 179, 'we hold that the Word of God alone lies beyond the sphere of our judgement and that father and councils are of authority only in so far as they agree with the rule of the Word'.

10 Karl Barth, *Church Dogmatics* I/1: 283–4, quoted in Watson 2000: 58.

11 This does not mean that all Protestant theologians advocate uncritical acceptance of the literal truth of all biblical texts. They generally keep faith with a long-established tradition from the earliest days of the Christian Church that the Bible is a text which may be read on a number of different levels.

formalized. In view of these critical issues, the following choice of key figures or texts must be seen to be highly particular. Most figures or texts have been chosen because their key influence or value has been continually attested within the Western Christian tradition; Augustine, Aquinas and the Reformer Martin Luther would come under this heading. But there are other figures and texts whose 'canonical' centrality would be debated; Julian of Norwich, Hildegard von Bingen and Rosemary Radford Ruether would come under this heading. The latter choices figure both as critique of the tradition and as potentially valuable contributions to a more diverse and inclusive view of Christianity, although it might well be argued that, in such a limited space, no collection could be universally representative.

THE NICENE/CONSTANTINOPOLITAN CREED (325 CE)

Properly speaking, the Nicene Creed was a short statement issued after the Council of Nicaea – a meeting of church leaders from both Eastern and Western churches (hence 'ecumenical'), called by the first 'Christian' Emperor, Constantine, in 325 CE and directed specifically against the ideas of an influential priest living and working in Alexandria called Arius. It concluded with four anathemas denouncing Arianism, that is the teachings put forward by Arius. Both this short form of the creed and the longer form, familiar today from many church liturgies, are statements of belief. This creed or statement of belief includes the term *homoousios* (of one essence). Arius had caused a crisis by starting to say that Christ was neither absolutely God – because he says 'the Father is greater than I'- nor absolutely man – because he was 'the Word of God'. Using the term *homoousios* avoided the suggestion that the Son was somehow less than the Father. Using the concept of *ousia* – translated as essence – implied that one essence could be shared by the two distinct persons of the Father and the Son. Needless to say, the definition did not satisfy everyone. In the first place, it was suspect because it did not rule out the idea that the Father and the Son were indistinguishable.[12] And, of course, it also employed a concept derived not from Scripture but from Greek philosophy. Ultimately, however, the term *homoousios* came to be widely accepted. The longer version, sometimes known as the Nicene/ Constantinopolitan Creed (325 CE) to distinguish it from the shorter version, was approved at a council of the churches in Constantinople in 381 CE and at the Council of Chalcedon in 451 CE, becoming a statement of Western orthodox teaching about the Christian idea of the Trinity.

The theologians of Nicaea were trying to respond to questions about the nature of God. A modern theologian, Ian Markham (1996: 261), suggests that the creed 'captures the moment when the Church committed itself to the doctrine of Trinity. God is a dynamic unity. Within the godhead there is relationship. You cannot have love in isolation, and as God is love there must be relations in God.' In the Western church this is named or expressed in the notion of the procession or spiration of the Holy Spirit out of the loving relationship between Father and Son.

Some modern feminist theologians have found the doctrine of the Trinity disturbingly masculine, leaving little scope for any notion of the feminine within the nature of God. However, it is clear that, in the earliest Christian context, the teaching helped to distinguish the unique view of the Christian community and set it apart from other worldviews in a definitive sense. Their trinitarian view of God set them apart from polytheists, who believed in many gods and goddesses, and from the Roman state religion, which until the time of Constantine had accorded the Emperor the status of divinity. Christians still regarded themselves as monotheists – believers in one single transcendent God. But, increasingly,

---

12 This had been the position associated with a third-century theologian called Sabellius.

they also wanted to distinguish themselves from the most closely related group of monotheists – the Jews. And this was a more difficult matter. The experiences of Jesus' followers had led them to propose that he was more than a man, perhaps the Messiah or the Son of Man as these titles were understood within contemporary forms of Judaism. But by the time of Nicaea, most Christian theologians had come to view Jesus in terms that went a long way beyond Jewish titles; Jesus was God. Nicaea offered the best solution to that conundrum.

AUGUSTINE (354–430)

Augustine was the son of a Christian mother and a pagan father who lived all but five years of his life in north Africa. In his adolescence and early adulthood, he abandoned the Catholic Church of his mother only to return to it much later, as he says in his *Confessions*, set on the road to conversion by a passion for true wisdom instilled in him by reading the philosophy of the non-Christian Latin writer Cicero.

Some theorists of religion have seen the question of evil and the justification of God's power in the face of evil as an important factor in the development of religious ideas; that is to say, religion, its rituals and even its ritualized forms of discussion in churches and universities is part of the way in which we cope with the forms of evil we experience. Augustine is associated, within the Christian Church of the Western world, with arguments related to a proper or an 'orthodox' view of Christian theology, but he is also a very important contributor to the discussion concerning the nature of evil. Augustine put forward a number of explanations for sin or evil in the world that he related to the goodness of God. Although he had been, for a short period of time, a Manichaean – an adherent of a radically dualistic philosophical sect – he ultimately rejected this dualism, this opposition of good and evil and the idea that there was constant battle going on between these evenly matched powers. God's purposes, he decided, were always good and ultimately effective. It was just that we were very often blind to the larger picture or to the more comprehensive planning of the divine.

Nevertheless, his view of sexual desire, for example, retains some elements of dualistic thinking in so far as it is dependent upon a view of sexual desire as an absence of self-control in extremely negative terms. Augustine believed that children were born as a result of *concupiscentia*. This term for sinful human desire implies an overwhelming weakness of will or loss of self-control. Augustine came to see sexual desire as a particularly good illustration of the idea, presumably because he himself had experienced its power in his youth. It was sinful desire because he believed that human beings were made in the image of God only in so far as they were rational creatures. Deliberately to put aside rational control was, for him, like turning away from everything of ultimate value and significance in human nature and obliterating the image of God. Moreover, Augustine thought that this tendency towards *concupiscentia* was inherited – hence the term 'original' sin used to describe his ideas of the origins of human sin. He argued that human beings all inherited their tendency towards sin from the first human couple at the very beginning. Every conception was the occasion for passing on the taint of this sin – like venereal disease, as one commentator puts it! (Armstrong 1993: 107).

A large proportion of Augustine's writings have a polemical sense since he spent much of his life defining and defending what he saw as 'orthodoxy'. The most familiar of his other texts are undoubtedly the *Confessions*, a unique and often moving account of his own life and conversion to Christianity, and the *City of God*, which is arranged in twenty-two books and appears to have taken thirteen years to write. It was inspired by the events of 410, in which year the barbarian Alaric took Rome, marking a definitive step in the dissolution of the Roman empire. At a time of extreme uncertainty and anxiety, Augustine set about writing a Christian philosophy of history.

HILDEGARD OF BINGEN (1098–1179)

Hildegard of Bingen was born in the Alzey area, south-west of Mainz, and dedicated to God at the Benedictine monastery at Disibodenburg by her parents at the tender age of 7 or 8, but she willingly made her profession as a teenager. In Hildegard's case, it was probably her visionary experience that guaranteed her reputation for sanctity and gave her, somewhat later on in life, both authority and freedom in the Church. But it should be said that she was, by any standards, a woman of energy, talent and wisdom. She wrote, and illustrated theological works, inspired by her visions. She founded and ran a monastery, composed music, wrote a treatise on medicine, corresponded with kings and queens and even occasionally preached to congregations of religious men. But, significantly, finding herself in a position to influence influential men, she continued, circumspectly, to refer to herself as 'a poor little woman'.

The third of her three major theological works, *De Operatione Dei*, contains a commentary on the Prologue of John's Gospel, which is a passage about God's creative Word entering into the world in the form of a human being. In this work as a whole, then, Hildegard sees the human form – the micro-cosmic entity of the human body and soul – as a representation of the macrocosmic entity of the universe including heaven and hell. The human form is the paradigm or model of divine incarnation to be seen in all the rich and fantastic detail of the created universe as well as in the particulars of the life of Jesus of Nazareth.

Although her work, originally written in Latin, survived through the centuries, it is only very recently indeed that it has been translated and published for more general readers. And one of the reasons why her work has become popular in recent years – apart from the fact that I have already noted that she is a woman who was clearly able to find some way of working creatively within a strong patriarchal culture – is undoubtedly the sense in which her work is seen to imply some greater value and significance for the created world in its beauty and variety. That God would become human was part of the original plan in her view and not simply the result of human sinfulness.

We should be careful not to run away with the idea that Hildegard was a revolutionary or proto-feminist theologian, however. The pattern of a thoroughly Augustinian view of human sin and sexuality is still detectable within what she writes. However, as a woman, it is arguable that her experience and understanding led her in theological directions that have not been considered definitive within Western Christianity and therefore her contribution – especially as it has been taken up more recently – may be related less to a definition of the Christian community than to a critique of existing definitions.

THOMAS AQUINAS (1225–74)

In the Western world, St Thomas is among the best-known theologians of what is called the Middle Ages. Although he was born in Italy he spent most of his working life in Paris and other northern universities. His work was strongly influenced by the classical Greek philosopher and scientist Aristotle, whose work was introduced to him by his teacher Albertus Magnus, particularly through the work of the Islamic philosophers Avicenna (980–1037) and Averroes (1126–98) which became available in Latin translations at the beginning of the thirteenth century.

He is often credited with the attempt to bring together, or in some sense reconcile, reason and faith – without confusing them – by claiming that rational knowledge of God is possible, even if conclusive proof is not. His most well-known work, begun towards the end of his life and never completed, was the *Summa Theologica* (from 1265 onwards), and in this work he attempted to show how it could be argued that God existed, on the basis of rational arguments. He set out five lines or ways of argument in support of the existence of God, and underlying all of them is the fundamental idea that the ordering of the world itself contains the most convincing evidence of God's wisdom and existence. These five lines of argument have a similar structure, based upon the idea that everything within our experience has a cause. Ultimately, he identifies God with the origin of all movement, existence and value. His arguments for the existence of God are frequently considered within the field of a traditional philosophy of religion under the heading of 'cosmological arguments'.

In terms of religious theory, Aquinas's work, like that of Augustine and the texts of conciliar creeds, could perhaps also be related to that ideological element of religion which establishes and supports the coherence of a particular worldview and helps to fill out and make clearer its symbols (Geertz 1985: 67).

JULIAN OF NORWICH (C.1342–AFTER 1413)

Like the work of Hildegard of Bingen, Julian's *Revelations of Divine Love* has survived the passage of the years and indeed gained the status of a minor classic within the Western Christian Church partly, perhaps, because Julian laid claim to a particular spiritual experience of divine visions that undoubtedly countered the disadvantage of being female.

Julian was probably so-called after the Church of St Julian in the East Anglian city of Norwich, England, to which it is believed she was attached as an anchoress. During the Middle Ages, it was a fairly common practice for men or women to be 'enclosed' in a small set of rooms or a cell attached to a church. They were solemnly installed using the liturgy for a funeral. Subsequently, 'dead to the world', they spent their life in prayer – or sometimes they performed counselling and teaching work – but they rarely left these rooms again until they died. Their upkeep was sometimes provided for by wealthy and important people who required the anchorite or anchoress to pray for them. Since Julian's fame rested largely on the accounts of her visions and her mystical reflections on these, it is difficult to determine the course of events in her life; to be sure, for example, whether her visions occurred before her entry into the anchorage or afterwards. She was not, as was Hildegard, drawn into many external activities and relationships outside.

However, from her writings we learn that Julian had prayed for a long time for three things: for an understanding of Christ's suffering; for the experience of being genuinely close to death; and for the three 'wounds' of true contrition, loving compassion and the longing for the will of God. When she was thirty, she suddenly became extremely ill, and on 8 May 1373, when her family and friends believed she was dying, she had a series of sixteen visions of the suffering and death of Christ, of God's love and care as well as experiences she took to be caused by the devil. She wrote a short account of her visions on her recovery, in English, and then spent the next fifteen to twenty years meditating and thinking about the meaning of these visions. Eventually she wrote a longer text, once again in English, the language of ordinary people rather than the language of the 'sacred' Vulgate text of the Bible.

Initially, very much like Hildegard, she was inhibited by her gender and her lack of formal education which, as a woman, would not have been available to her on the same terms as to a man: 'But God forbid that you should say or assume that I am a teacher, for that is not and never was my intention; for I am a woman, ignorant, weak and frail. But I know very well that what I am saying I have received by the revelation of him who is the sovereign teacher . . . This revelation was made to a simple, unlettered creature' (cited in Jantzen 2000: xii).

Julian's meditations are complex and dense, and require what Grace Jantzen calls 'a great deal of theological chewing' (ibid.: 90). But one key theme of her work is that the meaning of Christ's life and death are summed up in and as love. This is related to another aspect of her teaching which has sparked off a great deal of interest in her work more recently: the idea of the motherhood of God which makes its appearance only in the later, longer text. Here Julian links the motherhood of God more traditionally with the motherhood of the Church but more interestingly with the suffering of Christ. Just as a mother, Christ suffers to bring us to birth. In her reflections on the Trinity, Julian associates divine motherhood with God the Son and the characteristics of wisdom and knowledge. The motherhood of Christ is shown in the sense that it is he who has given us life in the first place, as divine wisdom creates the world at the behest of the Father.

MARTIN LUTHER (1483–1546)

In the words of Andrew Pettegree, it was ironic that Luther should turn out to be the catalyst for such dramatic change in the Christian Church in Western Europe and a founding father of the Protestant Reformation because he was in many ways a 'Catholic success story' (Hastings 1999: 243). Coming from fairly humble origins as the son of a local mine owner, he was educated in cathedral schools and, once he joined the Augustinian monastery at Erfurt, encouraged to pursue his studies. He very quickly made his mark as a lecturer in moral philosophy at Wittenberg University and as an effective preacher. He became a doctor of theology and professor of Scripture at Wittenberg in his twenties and by the age of 36 he had been made vicar of his order with the charge of eleven Augustinian monasteries.

However, though his was a success story in the public sense, he continued to suffer from feelings of deep depression, and these undoubtedly affected the direction his theology took, especially in relation to the Christian ideas of judgement and salvation. He felt overwhelmed and oppressed by the idea of God's judgement – how could he possibly match up to the standard required? How could he be saved given that he felt himself to be so sinful? The answer came, for him, through reading the New Testament and, in particular, Paul's letter to the Romans where, at 1.17, he read that 'The just shall live by faith.' He came to the conclusion that this meant his salvation, his release from the consequences of sin, was the result of God's free gift. In other words, his freedom was not dependent upon what he did or did not do but upon God's generosity, of which the guarantee was the death and resurrection of Jesus.

At the same time as he was working out this spiritual crisis in his own life, he became involved in a wider movement of protest that was beginning to take shape against some of the practices of the contemporary medieval Church. The particular crisis that propelled him into the limelight concerned the sale of indulgences, an essentially devotional practice that was, nevertheless, wide open to abuse. Given his own sensitivity to the view that spiritual benefits – in the case of indulgences some lessening of punishment or period of purification in the afterlife – could be gained by any human actions, the suggestion that such benefits could be bought for money would have seemed utterly abhorrent to him. In addition, in this case, the whole business was connected quite openly to a financial transaction between the Pope and Albrecht of Brandenburg, the bishop of Magdeburg, a transaction underwritten by the Fuggers of Augsburg, Germany's principal banking house. In response to the vigorous preaching of Albrecht's agent, Luther published his ninety-five theses against indulgences – basically a challenge to debate – in October 1517. Due to the, by now well-established, technology of printing, Luther's theses were distributed widely throughout Europe over the coming months, during which time Luther prepared himself for the inevitably negative reaction from the church authorities.

Luther seemed to grow in confidence the more he was challenged. In April 1521 at Worms he had his final show-down with the representatives of the Pope (Leo X) and refused to recant in the face of their charge of heresy. Condemned by the Pope but supported by ordinary people and local princes, who had their own agendas for disliking church or foreign papal influence in their affairs, he encouraged his followers to abandon many traditional practices and teachings, including that of transubstantiation (the belief that the wine and bread of the Eucharist[13] become the blood and body of Christ during the consecration of the elements during the Mass), special reverence for Mary and other saints, and daily Mass. He spoke in increasingly bitter terms of the church hierarchy, eventually dismissing the Pope entirely as an agent of the Antichrist. In 1524, he finally abandoned his religious orders and married a former Cistercian nun, Catherine of Bora.

He was an effective and prolific writer. His most influential writings, apart from his German translation of the Bible, were probably the three tracts published in 1520, *The Babylonian Captivity of the Church*; *On the Freedom of a Christian Man*; and *To the Christian Nobility of the German Nation*. In this last publication he laid down his call for the reform of both the Christian life and the organization of the Church in terms that, to him, reflected more closely the lives and ideals of the first Christians.

However, it should be noted that his ideas of church reform did not include any equally thorough-going challenge to social order. Although he spoke reverently of marriage as part of God's plan for humankind, for example, his view of marriage relegated wives to the domestic sphere and did not preclude boxing their ears for minor faults. And his refusal to support the German peasantry in the Peasants' War of 1525 – when many of them rose in revolt against their landlords spurred on by Luther's teachings of the equality of Christians before God – is of course well known. Clearly their understanding of the terms of equality before God ultimately differed from his.

JOHN CALVIN (1509–64)

After the death of Luther, the movement we now call Protestantism, which owed its beginnings to him and which had initially spread far and wide within Europe, began to show signs of decline. On the one hand, there were increasingly acrimonious disputes between Protestant leaders, while on the other hand, the Catholic Church finally began to respond to the demands for church reform that had made so many Christians ready to accept the revolutionary ideas of Luther and his followers in the first place. This movement for reform in the Catholic Church was ultimately launched formally at the great reforming Council of Trent in 1545.

Jean or John Calvin was born in France and became involved with French Protestantism at a period in French history during which its Catholic kings had become increasingly hostile towards it. He left France because of persecution and wrote, in exile, the first draft of his *Institutes of the Christian Religion*, a description of his own particular evangelical faith and church order. He eventually settled in the Swiss city of Geneva in 1541. His *Institutes* inspired the interest and admiration of a number of leading Protestant figures. Its idea of church order was characterized by regular preaching and catechetical instruction for all the people, combined with close regulation of the business and moral life of the community. In Geneva, Calvin instituted the consistory, a group of leading laymen and ministers which met regularly to enact this moral supervision. These ideas were not in themselves revolutionary at the time, but the rigour with which they were put into practice, together with Calvin's own reputation as

---

13 Eucharist is taken from the Greek word for thanksgiving and refers, of course, to one of the central rites or sacraments of the Christian Church, the celebration and re-enactment of Jesus' last meal with his disciples which, through Jesus' words and actions recorded in the Gospels, becomes a prefiguration of his death and resurrection. See, for example, Luke 22.14–20.

a theologian and preacher, meant that Geneva came to represent something of an ideal in Protestant Europe. In Scotland, John Knox called it 'the most perfect school of Christ that ever was on the earth since the days of the Apostles' (cited in Hastings 1999: 259). Calvinism produced an extremely vigorous and dynamic reform of church order characterized by great moral energy.

Among Calvin's teachings, the doctrine of Predestination has been given much attention. This doctrine, which can be found in the writing of a number of Christian theologians as far back as Augustine, teaches that, after Adam's Fall, God did not will the salvation of all men but that Christ died only for the elect, an elect chosen without reference to merit on their part. A number of these theologians, including Calvin himself, believed equally that the damned were not damned by any fault. Calvin does give some space to this doctrine in the *Institutes*, but he tends to draw the conclusion that it belongs to the awesome and mysterious idea that all our fates depend upon the will of God alone. It appears in the section of the *Institutes* after that dedicated to God's grace. Much of the bad press Calvinism has received is due to the related idea that even if the work and behaviour of the community cannot ensure salvation, it is necessary to maintain the community of the elect. There is then a strong incentive to moral perfection and an equally strong inclination towards self-righteousness and 'Puritanism'. It seems that for many of Calvin's followers, the emphasis of the terms of God's grace was put in different places.

FRIEDRICH D. E. SCHLEIERMACHER (1768–1834)

Schleiermacher is sometimes called 'the father of modern hermeneutics'. He saw that a study of how language works was important, although he did not himself develop a fully-fledged theory of linguistics. He also recognized that understanding presupposes language and subtends human communication.

Schleiermacher was a preacher within the Reformed, Protestant tradition, a theologian and also a translator of classical Greek and Latin texts. But although he was, of course, concerned with what is called biblical interpretation or exegesis, he was also interested in the broader issues of understanding texts in a philosophical sense. In general terms he was a respected figure in Germany during the nineteenth century. However, though he considered himself very much a man of religion, the things he said made some Christian commentators suspicious of him. In fact, his most famous book, *Religion: Speeches to its Cultured Despisers*, first published in German in 1799, was an attempt to win educated people back to religion, from which he felt they had begun to drift away.

However, in works like his *Academy Addresses*, he argued that what he called 'the art of understanding' needed proper theorizing and that theologians as interpreters of Scripture should expect to conform to the principles of this theory and not expect special privileges because they were reading Scripture. In other words, he began to suggest the idea that the Bible was a book and, in many respects, a book like any other. To know that the Bible was a sacred book the reader had first to read and understand it. She couldn't expect, either, to find it crystal clear without the same sort of effort required for reading any other text. Neither could she assume, before she started trying to understand the text, that its authority came from some external authorizing force 'out there', although this might be her final conclusion. In addition, just as with any other text, he argued that readers should not take passages out of context. Individual passages of Scripture should be read within the context of the whole of the Bible, for example. And again, just as with any other text, he argued that a reader should not read just one interpreter but use all the sources for help that she could find. In the broadest possible terms then, we could say that Schleiermacher argued that the personal or subjective dimension of understanding – which he rated as highly significant – must always be accompanied by an objective dimension including a proper regard to, for example, the grammatical conventions and context of any text, including Holy Scripture.

KARL BARTH (1886–1968)

Karl Barth was born in Switzerland, the son of a Protestant professor of theology in Berne. After finishing his studies at university, Barth became, initially, a pastor but, immediately after the First World War, published his first major work, a commentary on Paul's letter to the Romans in which he first voiced his radical questioning of current theological ideas, which had a particularly strong impact in the post-war years characterized by pessimism and discontent. Already, the scriptural focus of his work, and the sense in which Barth looked back to the Reformation theologians with their insistence on the supremacy and transcendence of God and the worthlessness of human reason, was clearly evident.

On the basis of this first successful publication, Barth moved into the academic sphere full-time as a professor at Göttingen and later in Münster and then Bonn. When Hitler came to power in 1933, Barth immediately gave his support to the 'Confessing Church', a group of German evangelical Christians which opposed the 'German-Christian' Church Movement sponsored by the Nazi party. He was largely responsible for drawing up the Barmen Declaration of 1934, a formulation of the Confessing Church's theology. Although, at first, Barth had maintained that Nazism was simply a matter of secular politics, ultimately he came to feel that neutrality was impossible, and he refused to take an oath of allegiance to Hitler. As a result he lost his job, and so in 1935 he left Germany and returned to Switzerland to work at the university in Basle.

Barth began his *Church Dogmatics* in 1927, but it took him twenty years to complete this work of systematic theology which, Francis Watson claims, is first to last an attempt to study 'the agreement of church proclamation [i.e. contemporary Christian discourse with its focal point in the act of preaching] with the revelation which is attested in Holy Scripture' (Watson 2000: 58). In strong contrast with the liberal Protestantism of his background, which looked for some accommodation with the increasingly secular and scientific culture of early twentieth-century Europe, Barth argued in defiance of Schleiermacher, for example, that the Bible is the Word of God, its authority, truthfulness and trustworthiness guaranteed by the divine speech act that is Jesus (ibid.: 61).

JÜRGEN MOLTMANN (1926–)

From 1967 to 1994, Jürgen Moltmann was professor of systematic theology at Tübingen in Germany. However, during Moltmann's lifetime the world has become a smaller place, and although he was perhaps most influenced by the theology of Barth in his early career, he has developed a much greater openness to movements and ideas outside his Protestant base over the last fifty or so years. He has been involved in Christian–Marxist dialogue as well as with the peace movement and the Greens. He has shown considerable interest in Roman Catholic theology, Orthodox theology and the liberation theologies of the Third World. Moltmann's major works can be divided up into two 'series' of books. The early trilogy comprises *Theology of Hope* (1964), *The Crucified God* (1972) and *The Church in the Power of the Spirit* (1975). Five further volumes written from 1980 make up the second series, which he regards as an open-ended form of contribution to theological discussion; a form of dialogue which does not necessarily exclude or discount insights from other disciplines or other understandings of reality but judges them in relation to his vision of the Church's mission to and for the whole world.

The key theme of Moltmann's early work takes up a central idea from the work of the German Idealist philosopher Hegel (1770–1831). Put very simply indeed, Hegel saw, in the movement of human history, a process of conflict and confrontation and adjustment whereby we come to recognize how we are part of an all-encompassing 'Spirit' or 'Absolute' that is slowly coming to consciousness of itself. The processes of sometimes bitter conflict, confrontation and then readjustment that Hegel identified in this great coming to consciousness seemed suggestive to Moltmann in relation to how we can understand the extremely challenging narrative of the death and resurrection of Jesus. There was, he thought, something so absolutely contradictory in the opposites of Jesus' life and death and yet out of this opposition, where death and suffering meet life and resurrection, comes a new understanding and resolution. Moltmann's theological scheme is strongly trinitarian, and in these terms, the clash of opposites results in a form of resolution which is represented within his work by the Holy Spirit moving out into the world to make God's promise to the world ever more evident.

ROSEMARY RADFORD RUETHER (1936–)

Rosemary Radford Ruether, a writer and thinker coming out of a Roman Catholic tradition, offers a feminist critique of Christian Church and theology. Ruether discloses the fundamentally dualistic and hierarchical worldview that Christianity has absorbed, particularly from its roots within the Graeco-Roman world, and from later apocalyptic writings within Judaism that break with a cyclical understanding of history and with other earlier Jewish traditions that are more holistic in their view of human beings and human communities as belonging to and being part of nature.

Within the context of Greek thought such a movement to escape from mortality is caught up within a more thorough-going dualism, expressed, as Ruether sees it, in destructively sexist terms:

> In *Timaeus* Plato says that when the incarnate soul loses its struggle against the passions and appetites, it is incarnated into a woman and then into 'some brute which resembled him in the evil nature which he had acquired'. The hierarchy of spirit to physical nature as male to female is made explicit. The chain of being, God–spirits–male–female–non-human–nature–matter, is at the same time the chain of command. The direction of salvation follows the trajectory of alienation of mind from its own physical support system, objectified as 'body' and 'matter'.
>
> (Ruether 1983: 79)

The combination of these notions within Christianity resulted, so Ruether claims, in a multiple sense of alienation. Thus, the subjective self is alienated from the objective world because the world is seen as, in itself, lacking a benign sense of order or as simply the context of human suffering as we wait for final redemption. The realm of nature is alienated from the spirit, which is no longer located within either the rhythms of seasonal change or the occasional cataclysmic interruption. Moreover, within a patriarchal culture, such ideas are viewed androcentrically – from the perspective of the male, identified as 'human' in a normative, ideal sense. This precipitated a further alienation: of the masculine from what was regarded or identified symbolically as feminine. Thus God becomes masculine, creates out of nothing, transcends nature and dominates history by ultimately terminating it altogether.

The roots of Ruether's transformed theology which seeks to foster the full humanity of women are diverse. She draws on the prophetic–liberating principle of the Bible, denouncing systems of domination and individualism, and on various religious groups which have from time to time promoted an egalitarian and counter-cultural vision – for example gnostics, Montanists and the Quakers. Apart from the categories of orthodox Christian theology, she takes inspiration from some pagan goddess religions. She considers the insights of liberalism, Marxism and Romanticism. From the conversation between such different points of view, she constructs a Christianity that denounces all systems of domination, and develops a sense of the mutuality of all people whatever their class, colour or gender. In addition she places considerable emphasis on humankind in its ecological context.

Her first ground-breaking book was entitled *Sexism and God-Talk*, published in 1983, in which she argued that in spite of the Church's sexism, Christ himself could still be expressed through a theology of spirit in multiple forms and did not simply have to be limited to the masculine nature of Jesus of Nazareth. In more recent work she has continued to maintain her critique of the Christian Churches as sexist but to suggest a form of exodus church she calls 'Women-Church':

> As Women-Church we claim the authentic mission of Christ, the true mission of church, the real agenda of our Mother–Father God who comes to restore and not to destroy our humanity who comes to ransom the captives and to reclaim the earth as our Promised Land. We are not in exile, but the church is in exodus with us. God's Shekinah, Holy Wisdom, the Mother-face of God has fled from the high thrones of patriarchy and has gone into exodus with us.
>
> (*Women-Church: Theology and Practice of Feminist Liturgical Communities*, San Francisco, 1985: 72)

2 THE CHURCH AND THE WORLD: A VARIETY OF APPROACHES

Introduction

Over the centuries the Christian Church has viewed its relationship with the world in a number of different ways. For example:

- The Church and state are one organic whole, in which civil authorities accept the teaching and values of the Church and have the responsibility of regulating or even enforcing them.
- The Church is a spiritual guardian in a 'fallen' world, keeping our eyes on eternal values and standards beyond this mortal life.
- The Church is 'in exile', a persecuted community which holds the line against a hostile world or represents the Body of Christ in all its vulnerability in the world.
- The Church is a 'prophetic', sometimes socially reformist and spirit-filled community speaking for the poor and marginalized, including the non-human world, and against quietism or the corruptions of wealth and power.
- The Church is a missionary community, preaching the Gospel or good news of salvation to the whole world.

These alternatives do not provide an exhaustive view of the Churches' relationship with the world and a number of these views may coexist to some extent within the various Christian communities.

2.1 The early Christian Church

Under the searching light of a modern feminist hermeneutics – the kind of biblical interpretation initiated by scholars like Elizabeth Schüssler Fiorenza in the 1970s and 1980s – the earliest Christian Church emerges as a spirit-filled community of the prophetic and socially revolutionary kind. For example, in the New Testament book of Acts, we read that, meeting together after his death, the followers of Jesus are miraculously filled with spiritual power. They go out into the streets of Jerusalem, filled with pilgrims from far and wide, and speak words taken from the Hebrew scriptures that everyone hears in their own language.[14] The words lend themselves to revolutionary conclusions. They suggest that God's Holy Spirit and its characteristic powers and effects are available to all, irrespective of gender, age or social and economic status. The reality of the situation – whether or not women did actually exercise a socially unconventional spirit-filled ministry in the early Church – is still contested. There is little direct evidence of any formal women's ministry. However, indirect evidence can be found to support the idea. In a letter to the Christian Church in Corinth, the Apostle Paul appears to have become involved with a dispute over whether or not women should cover their heads during worship (1 Corinthians 11.3–16). The dispute concerns notions of female modesty. Paul's efforts to discourage women from uncovering their heads suggests that, fundamentally, he shares notions of female modesty with the Corinthians. But what is notable is that Paul expresses no criticism of women praying and prophesying publicly, exercising some kind of public ministry and leadership of the community.

Fiorenza argues that, within the earliest Church, Peter's vision of the spirit-filled ministry of all God's children, irrespective of gender, may actually have been realized to some extent. But there is also evidence to suggest that if the vision was expressed in the earliest Church, it soon came under pressure and that there was greater conformity to social norms as time passed. And indeed, in the New Testament book of 1 Timothy[15] it sometimes seems as if the author wants to identify godliness with social conformity. For example, the author suggests that slaves should submit to their masters and not be disrespectful or disobedient because their membership of the Church implied some challenge to the conventional barriers between slave and master.[16] He appears extremely concerned that members of the Church retain the respect of those outside the Christian community by not flouting social conventions. However, if the author of 1 Timothy seems to identify aspects of the unconventional with the power of evil, it may well have been in part because such unconventional behaviour was likely to focus undesirable attention on the Church from outside.

2.2 The Church and the world: from Constantine onwards

The Church of 1 Timothy is clearly a Church under pressure. Its concern for a quiet life may well be a reflection of actual social conflict. A generalized persecution began very soon after the inauguration of the community of Jesus' followers. Christian resistance to the official religion of Rome – Christians would pray for the Emperor but not offer sacrifices to him – caused resentment from the earliest years,

---

14 See Acts 2.17–18. Peter's words are a quotation from Joel 2.28–9.
15 Scholars generally agree that 1 Timothy was the work of an author writing sometime later than the apostle Paul but adopting the mantle of his authority by using his name. It can probably be dated at some time in the first half of the second century CE.
16 See 1 Timothy 6.1–2. See also 3.7; 5.14.

and the refusal to participate in sacrifices and offerings to the gods, including the Emperor, was blamed for misfortunes of every kind. The Apostle Paul was executed by the Roman government, and the Emperor Nero began persecuting and torturing Christians in Rome in 64 CE. There was continuing sporadic violence and official hostility towards Christianity for over two hundred years before Constantine. During this time many within the Church saw themselves as a community of saints and martyrs, and the witness of the Christians who suffered helped to build a sense of solidarity within the early Church as a community of resistance. Of course, not every Christian took the view that resistance was the way forward, and the controversy over the break-away Christians called the Donatists in the fourth century was caused by their refusal to accept the membership within the Church of those who had escaped martyrdom under persecution by, according to one view of the matter, compromising their faith. Significantly, however, the persecution of the Christians appears to have been unsuccessful in the long term in its aim to wipe out the Christian sects. Even opponents were frequently impressed by the way in which so many members of Christian groups faced torture and death in the strength of their faith rather than by compromising their beliefs.

The world outside the church community is therefore defined in the early centuries by its godless values and, sometimes, by its active hostility to God either as the sphere of the devil inspiring mischief within the community or as the source of persecution from without. At the same time, the Church is the spirit-filled community charged to preach repentance to all, and to perform baptism in the name of Christ and maintain its beliefs and practices intact. These pressures together sometimes produced a sense of the liminality of the church community, shaking time-honoured securities and rocking the boat of social and theological conventions, rubbing up, sometimes very uncomfortably, against a caution and wariness that appeared sometimes almost to equate social conformity with God's will.

So it is clear that, from the earliest years of its existence, the Church's relationship with its cultural and historical context was fraught with complexity. While many Christians thought of themselves as set apart from the world outside the Church, and no longer accountable to the political and social powers and authorities of the day, there was really no way in which they could entirely dissociate themselves from that world. One of the most significant interactions that occurred between the Church and its cultural and historical context in the first centuries was, of course, its relationship with the Roman Empire, within whose borders it came into existence.

2.3 Constantine: first Christian emperor

In 284 CE a soldier from Illyricum (Dalmatia) had forcibly taken power in the Roman Empire, becoming the Emperor Diocletian. In the middle decades of the third century the Empire had been in crisis, with barbarian invasions almost toppling it from power. Diocletian undertook some massive reorganizing of the Empire to try and stabilize its political, economic and military situation and, among other things, divided its government between East and West. He took responsibility for governing the East himself, settling in Byzantium, and set Constantius Chlorus up as Emperor in the West, centred on Rome.

Towards the end of his reign, during which time Christianity in the Empire continued to grow in numbers, Diocletian became anxious about its infiltration into the civil service and the high command of the army – especially through the influence of the wives of these high-flying careerists! – where he looked especially for absolute support of his unquestioned and divine authority. Encouraged by his deputy Galerius he instigated a brutal persecution, compelling Christians to sacrifice to the gods of the Empire and seizing and burning their books and scriptures when they refused to hand them over.

Many were martyred and the Church was torn between those who were prepared to compromise with the Emperor's demands in order to save lives and those who were not prepared to do so under any circumstances.

When Diocletian died in 305, the persecutions died down fairly quickly in the West but were kept going and indeed intensified in the East by Galerius, who succeeded him. However, the year after Diocletian's death, Constantius Chlorus, Emperor in the West, also died, and his son Constantine – destined to become the first Imperial sponsor of Christianity – was acclaimed as successor by the legion in what is today the city of York in England, where he was at the time of his father's death. In spite of military support, Constantine's succession to his father's position was not a foregone conclusion and he had first to defeat his rival Maxentius. Constantine, whose mother seems to have had Christian sympathies and who may have had Christians among his advisers, finally faced Maxentius – who had by that time taken control of Italy and North Africa – at the battle of Milvian Bridge in 312. Constantine chose this moment to invoke the aid of the God of the Christians, putting a Greek monogram of the first letters of the name of Christ XP (CHR) on his standard. Though the odds were against him, Constantine won the battle, and thus began his momentous association with the religion of Christianity.

In 311, Galerius had given up the persecution of Christians in the East because it was obviously not working and, after *his* death, Constantine was able to persuade Galerius' pagan successor, Licinius, to operate a policy of toleration for all religions. However, Constantine was dissatisfied with Diocletian's division between East and West and he made the final move to reunite his Empire by removing Licinius in 324 CE. Although the Emperor Constantine was not actually baptized as a Christian until just before his death in 337 CE,[17] he continued to be guided by his Christian advisers. Constantine believed that he had important responsibilities as a Christian emperor. The theory behind this imperial role was developed by the Christian historian Eusebius of Caesarea (*c.*260–*c.*340), who brought together elements of divine kingship from the Greek-speaking world with Christian ideology and a particular imagery. And this became the model for the Emperor in Eastern Christianity over the succeeding thousand years. He – or, interestingly enough in one or two cases when there was an empress in her own right, she – was seen as the living icon of Christ, God's vicegerent on earth. As God regulates the cosmic order so the Emperor/Empress was thought to regulate the social order in an analogous sense. The Emperor or Empress was crowned in the image of heavenly kingship, and his or her responsibility was to guide humans on earth following the pattern of his or her prototype, Christ.

In other words, Constantine believed that, modelled on such an icon or image of Christ, he had the obligation and the authority to regulate what went on in the Church so that Christians worshipped God appropriately across his empire. The consequences of fulfilling this work, bringing everyone within the Empire into conformity with this vision of God's will for the world, were political and social order. Correspondingly, failure to do this would result in divine anger or disfavour and might even affect salvation in the next world. In other words, Constantine viewed peace and harmony in the Christian Church within the Empire as a high priority. In addition, he increasingly saw Christianity as the legitimate religion of his empire and the existence of other religions or cults – towards which he had been fairly tolerant in the early days of his reign – in the light of a potential danger to his realm. By the time he inaugurated his new capital city, Constantinople, a transformed Byzantium on the Bosphorus, in 330 CE, ceremonies were being conducted by Christian clergy alone without the assistance of pagan priests.

---

17 Such a delay before baptism was a relatively common practice before about 400 CE, since the nature of the penances and discipline required after the confession of post-baptismal sin were so severe.

This view of the Emperor's role in the divine scheme of things explains why Constantine became involved, for example, in the Council of Nicaea in 325 CE, called to adjudicate between 'correct' and 'heretical' views on dogmatic matters, even though he was not himself either a theologian or a priest. In terms of the Eastern Church, there was no conflict between the Church as an institution and the Church as the community of the Spirit; they were one organic body. Although the Emperor was effectively more powerful than the Eastern Patriarch, the head of the Church, he saw himself as accountable to God for his empire's religious health. The issues and outcome of the Council of Nicaea we have covered to some extent already in looking at the original short credal text as a response to the ideas of Arius about the natures of God the Father and God the Son, leading to a clear statement of Christian trinitarianism. This then became the basis for the so-called Nicene–Constantinopolitan Creed used ultimately in both Eastern and Western Churches. This Council of Nicaea was the largest assembly of bishops called until that time and represented both the Eastern Church with its senior patriarch in Byzantium/Constantinople and his colleagues from Alexandria, Antioch and Jerusalem as well as representatives from Rome and the Western Church, hence the reference to the Council as 'ecumenical'.

2.4 East and West: the first Christian centuries

One consequence of Constantine's decision to adopt Christianity across the whole of the Christian Empire in its earliest days, was that from being something that might get you killed, it suddenly became a matter of some considerable advantage to be a Christian. In an age of patronage, advancement and opportunity were strongly related to the influence and support of wealthy patrons. Where these patrons were Christians, it was simply natural to 'join the winning team'! And, just as persecution had put considerable pressure on the Christian Church before the advent of Constantine, so the sudden reversal of policy towards it exerted a new kind of pressure. How to maintain genuine religious conviction and how to avoid the hijacking of the Church's properly theological concerns by the power and influence of individual patrons, including the Emperor, was clearly seen by some as problematic, once the persecution ended.

One response to this, in line with the various types of relationships between the Church and the world, was the monastic movement. At the very point at which the actual martyrdom of Christians at the hand of pagans had become a thing of the past, individuals and small communities sprang up representing an asceticism that expressed, in this new context, a challenge to normative or conformist traditions, pushing the boat out a little, going against the grain, and in this way forcing the whole Church community to think about its identity once more.

The origins of the monastic movement are often attributed to the Egyptian saints, first Antony towards the end of the third century and then Pachomius in the early years of the fourth, who felt drawn to a life of prayer and asceticism – holy poverty. However, Kallistos Ware notes that they were probably not, in fact, the very first to make this way of life publicly their vocation, and he refers, for example, to the 'convent' of virgins, a structured women's community, into whose care Antony was able to put his sister when, after the death of his parents in his twenties, he made his decision to take up the life of the hermit, living in the isolation of the desert.[18] Of course, in a sense, this development can be seen clearly to have been of a piece with the ascetic traditions within Christianity from the beginning when the Gospel of Matthew records Jesus' words in the Sermon on the Mount about worldly

18 See Ware 1990: 123–61.

anxiety.[19] It seems, however, that Pachomius was among the first to set up formal monastic communities, starting with one in 313 at Tabennesis in Upper Egypt, close to the Nile. Antony, in contrast, remained essentially a hermit, the prototype of what was called in the Eastern Church the *geron* or charismatic elder, someone with spiritual wisdom capable of guiding others.

In the Eastern Church, though monasteries where men and women lived in communities following a particular order were certainly established, hermits and holy men living apart from society were perhaps more common than in the Western Church. And, more a difference of emphasis perhaps than real substance, the duties of religious women and men in the Eastern Church was always thought to be, first and foremost, prayer, holiness and spiritual guidance – rather than scholarship and good works. Perhaps it could be said the monasteries and hermits of the Eastern Church represented a divine presence in the world to a greater extent than a spiritual alternative to the world. In both East and West, however, the 'martyrdom of blood' seen under persecution was replaced by a call to asceticism which in some sense might be said to challenge the process of assimilation to the values of the world beyond the Church, as yet one more pressure on the developing identity of the various Christian communities.

IN THE WEST

From this point onwards, however, the differences between the Eastern and the Western Churches become ever more significant. In the West, Eusebius' vision of church and state as one organic whole had dissolved by the end of the fifth century. The former Western Roman Empire eventually disintegrated under waves of invaders from the north. A landmark in the Western Church during this period was Augustine's work, *On the City of God* (*De Civitate Dei*), written after the fall of Rome to the barbarian forces of Alaric the Visigoth in 410 CE. Part of Augustine's motivation for writing the work was to challenge the idea that this catastrophe – from the point of view of the ruling elite of Rome and many of its citizens – was the result of abandoning the traditions of pre-Christian religion and ritual which had continued to exist, although in decline, side by side with the imperial sponsorship of Christianity. But the picture he drew of two cities, strongly contrasting Christianity and the world, fostered a view of the relationship between worldly rulers and spiritual powers very different from that drawn up by Eusebius for Constantine in the previous century.

Many of those who invaded the Western Empire from the north were not Christians, although some followed the traditions of Arius, whose teaching had been condemned as heretical by the ecumenical Council of Nicaea in 325 CE. However, Christians in the West continued, on the whole, to maintain their faith, regarding the Popes in Rome as the leaders of the universal Church and, in spite of the loss of their imperial sponsorship, continuing to adhere to teachings drawn up originally by the ecumenical councils of East and West from Nicaea (325) to Chalcedon (451). And, in fact, this period saw many existing Christian communities develop as strong missionary bases[20] for the conversion of Western Europe.

Some scholars argue[21] that the barbarian invasions that brought an end to the Empire in the West also largely destroyed the infrastructure of secular education and learning in that sector of the Empire.

19 Matthew 6.25–34.
20 An example of this might be the Anglo-Saxon Christian communities that sponsored the English missionary saints Boniface and Lioba in Germany during the eighth century. See, for example, McLaughlin 1990: 99–122.
21 See McManners 1990: 130.

Learning survived in the hands of the Church, but there it served the needs of the clergy rather than the laity. Partly as a result, it is suggested, the Church in the West became centred on a monarchical view of the Papacy, the highest Church authority in Rome, which made authoritative decisions while the laity became an increasingly ill-educated and passive element in the organization of the Church. However, in 800 a Frankish[22] prince, Charlemagne, was crowned by the Pope in Rome taking the title of 'Holy Roman Emperor'. Harking back, of course, to the role adopted by Constantine, the new Christian Emperor evidently saw himself as allied with the Papacy in the Western world and repudiated any influence on Western affairs of either state or church that the Eastern Emperor might have wanted to take upon himself. But, very much like Constantine, Charlemagne also saw himself as responsible both for the temporal realm and for the maintenance of order within that realm including the proper worship of God. To this end he secured new territory through wars and enforced Christianity on all within those territories. He also took upon himself the task of reforming and standardizing monastic rule within all monasteries and took a lively interest in the advancement of learning.

IN THE EAST

In the East, Eusebius' vision of the Emperor as head of state and church also came under pressure, although in different ways. For one thing, the Eastern Church was split after 451 CE (the Council of Chalcedon) by an intense disagreement between 'heretical' monophysites (believing only in the divine nature of Christ),[23] and the 'orthodox' duophysites (believing in both the divine and human nature of Christ). And then, just as had been the case in the West a few centuries earlier, the Eastern Empire became subject to non-Christian invading forces by the end of the seventh century. Large areas of the Near-Eastern territories of the Eastern Empire had been conquered, and in these places Orthodox – and, in North Africa, Coptic – Christianity had become a minority religion, tolerated at best within a Muslim empire. By the ninth century, its influence in the West was increasingly constrained by the alliance between the Papacy and Charlemagne and his successors in the West and Muslims in the East. However, in contrast to the West, the Eastern empire maintained its traditions of secular learning much longer, so that its laity were probably better educated and thus more critically engaged. Perhaps in consequence, the Church in the East continued to determine its position on doctrinal matters by holding councils of bishops and patriarchs from its various dioceses rather than simply allowing either Emperor or Patriarch to make decisions themselves or within an inner cabal. For Christians in the East, these councils were, like the Eucharist, an expression of God's continued presence in the Church on earth.

Clergy too were organized differently in East and West, partly, no doubt, as a reflection of these historical and ideological differences. In the East, although bishops were required to be monks, from the sixth or seventh century priests were very largely married men who worked like other men, whether as farmers or manual labourers or schoolteachers. This meant that they were less sharply distinguished from the lay people they served. In the Western Church from the eleventh century onwards priests were required to be unmarried, making the significance of the lives of ordinary people within the Church seem ever more marginal to its central concerns.

22 The Franks were originally Germanic tribes, converted to Christianity at the end of the fifth century.
23 This group included the Coptic Orthodox Church, the Ethiopian Orthodox Church and Syrian Orthodox Church of the Malabar in South India, although some would say the monophysitism of the Indian church was not so marked.

RELATIONSHIPS BETWEEN WEST AND EAST

Constantine's Empire, which embodied the concept of an organic unity between Christian church and state across East and West, was not long-lived in practical terms, although it continued to provide a powerful model for the relationship between the spiritual and secular and this was taken up, of course, by Charlemagne and his successors in the West. However, the period between the eighth and the fifteenth centuries also saw a steady deterioration in relationships between Christians in East and West in the context of increasingly complex relationships between church and state.

During the eighth century, for example, the Eastern Emperor Leo III took up the cause of those who opposed the Orthodox practice of venerating icons (pictures of saints or religious figures thought to focus the worshipper's attention during prayer and meditation and often associated with miraculous events and healings). Icons were destroyed and many of those who wanted to keep them were cruelly persecuted. The head of the Western Church at the time, Pope Gregory III, became involved in the controversy, taking sides against the Emperor and condemning him. Feelings ran very high in this matter of the 'iconoclast controversy' and resentments rumbled on for years.

In the eleventh century (1054), papal legates, bearing messages from the Pope to the head of the Eastern Church in Constantinople, were turned away. The Patriarch had grown suspicious of Western efforts to extend the influence of the Papacy in the East and he decided to make his feelings plain by refusing to receive the messengers. In return, the Pope, the head of the Western Church, outraged the Patriarch and his supporters by excommunicating him from the Church, thereby assuming ultimate authority over Eastern as well as Western Christians.

Finally, East and West fell out most dramatically over the Crusades. In 1095, the Eastern Emperor Alexios asked the Papacy to appeal for military help to repel the Turks who were making incursions into his territory. A Papal appeal to Western Christians to come forward and defend the Christian faith against the Muslim invaders elicited a strong response. The forces mustered in this way recaptured a good deal of territory lost to the Muslims and went on to remove Jerusalem from Muslim control. But many of the 'Crusaders' subsequently refused to recognize the original Byzantine ownership of territory they had won from the Muslims or to hand it back to the Emperor, thereby subverting the original reasons for Alexios' appeal to the Pope. The Second and third Crusades increased distrust and hostility between Greek-speaking and Latin-speaking Christians, and this eventually came to a head in 1204 when Western crusaders sacked Constantinople and divided the Eastern Empire up between various Western powers. Far from defending the Orthodox Church's constituent rights and authority, the Papacy set about replacing the ecclesiastical hierarchy of the Greek-speaking Orthodox Church with Latin-speaking Catholics. Eventually the Eastern Empire, very much weakened by the attack of 1204, collapsed after the sack of Constantinople by another Turkish invasion in 1453. The Papacy in the West clearly saw itself as superior to the Eastern patriarchs with their conciliar structures. It grew in political influence and worldly power, coming to see its role as more authoritative than strictly prophetic.

THE CHURCH IN THE EAST UNDER PERSECUTION ONCE AGAIN

In the East, Muslim Turks allowed the Orthodox Church to continue functioning in a minimal sense within its empire, but Christians were placed in a position of inferiority, heavily taxed, forbidden to evangelize or show visible signs of their faith. Once again, Christians in the Eastern world faced persecution and, once again, many accepted martyrdom while some became Crypto-Christians, conforming outwardly to Islam but practising Christianity in secret. Just at the point where, in the

Western world, opportunities for education were increasing literacy and lay demands for reform and renewal in the Church, educational opportunities were being lost in the East. The Turkish invasion destroyed the infrastructure of Christian education in the empire to which the Church had made a substantial contribution. Faced with continuing hostility and persecution, the leadership of the Eastern Orthodox Church became increasingly defensive, choosing very largely to conform with the limitations laid down for it by the Turks, neither offering a strong critique of the political realities of their situation nor being part of the political structures. Dynamic leadership of the Orthodox Church passed, to some extent at this time, to the Orthodox Church of Russia, which saw itself as the heir to the Byzantine Empire and the Eastern Church's traditions of mystical theology, hesychastic asceticism[24] and its distinctive liturgy or forms of worship.

2.5 The Christian Church in the Western world: the Protestant Reformation

In the early medieval world of Western Europe,[25] the Church's authority, uncoupled from imperial support or control, was thought to be concerned with ultimate spiritual realities rather than material ones. But by the end of the medieval period, the Papacy had become a highly sophisticated political figure in Western European politics, with wealth and military influence. So, the Catholic Church, centred on Rome, was deeply implicated in values and concerns of the world in which it operated. The most powerful clergy and the Western European princes came from similar families and backgrounds. They had similar ambitions. The Church-as-Papacy had begun to – as it were – take on the old imperial role, wielding spiritual and political power together across Western Europe. And in this sense, the Church in the West at the end of the Middle Ages was in good shape.[26] However, it was at this point that the Christian Church in the West underwent a major renegotiation of its relationship with the secular Western world, and the reasons for this are various. For example, at this time there is a detectable expansion of lay literacy as university education and 'clerical' work ceased to be a monopoly of the clergy. In some parts of Europe, clergy found work in the employment of pious confraternities of laymen[27] who sometimes expected more of their clerical employees than did the Church. There is also evidence of increasing dissatisfaction with what is seen as corruption in high places[28] and of ignorance among ordinary clergy. In a number of ways, lay people were beginning to demand something different. In one sense, what people seemed to want was a more 'perfect' Church understood as separated or apart from 'the world', or something that more nearly resembled the perceived simplicity and egalitarianism of the New Testament Church. And in some respects, both the Protestant Reformation, and the Catholic Church's Council of Trent (1545–63) which led to the beginning of what is often referred to as the Counter-Reformation, represent movements within late medieval Western Europe for renewal and reform in this direction. The Reformers began to make a

---

24 *Hesychia*, inner stillness or silence of the heart, is achieved by constantly repeated prayers, for example the Jesus prayer: 'Lord Jesus Christ, Son of God, have mercy on me.' Hesychasts sometimes also practise a breathing technique to help attain a vision of divine light and so union with God.

25 This period could be said to have begun as early as the cessation of the Western Empire in the fifth century under pressure from northern 'barbarians'.

26 By this time, the Roman Catholic Church was Europe's biggest landowner and provider of hospitals and schools.

27 The German city of Hamburg had 99 in 1517.

28 The famous incident in 1517, in which Martin Luther nailed up his ninety-five theses against indulgences on the door of the Schlosskirche at Wittenberg, represents one example of such dissatisfaction with clerical behaviour.

clearer distinction between the Church centred upon the Papacy in Rome and the Church understood as a spirit-filled community, often with a prophetic vision – less hierarchy, simplicity of life, clear religious mission. This opened the way to further religious dissent, following on, of course, to persecution and war[29] as some countries in Europe lined themselves up against the Papacy and those who supported its monopoly of religious power and leadership.

NON-CONFORMITY

By the early years of the seventeenth century, the Reformation was well established in many European countries. In some it had the status of an 'established church', that is to say one ratified and supported by the state. The Reformist spirit once unleashed, however, the impetus was hard to slow, and there were already a number of Christian communities which adopted the approach of 'non-conformity', that is, precisely, a refusal to conform to the doctrines, polity or discipline of any 'established church'. The term 'non-conformity' was first used in the seventeenth century in the established Church of England to describe those within the church who wanted to believe its doctrines but did not want to accept its discipline and practice especially in matters of ceremony. But the term came to describe all dissenters from established churches, particularly those with Protestant sympathies. And so a conflict was clearly set up between a view which sees state and church together as representative of God's rule on earth in both spiritual and material realms, and a more 'prophetic' view of the Church as an extra-ordinary community, at odds with worldly power and authority, offering a deeper truth, a clearer insight, a critique of delusion and folly. There follows some examples.

The Quakers

One example of a non-conformist group is the Society of Friends,[30] commonly known as the Quakers, founded by George Fox (1624–91), an Englishman from Leicestershire. In 1643 Fox gave up all ties to friends and families and proclaimed that truth and freedom are to be found in the Inner Light of the living Christ which all may experience without the need for intermediaries, such as priests and clergy for example. In this way he lodged a protest against those Protestants who had – to his mind – slipped back into the old way of thinking that they had initially criticized. He restated the original Protestant belief that the human soul could encounter its Creator directly and offered a prophetic vision of the freedom and equality of all believers. He argued that the Church of England, for example, which was officially 'Protestant', was deeply embedded in the hierarchical structures of the world. The Friends believed that the Anglican[31] clergy, for whose education and maintenance they were expected to pay and to whom they were then expected to pay respect, prevented people from recognizing their essential freedom and equality before God as indeed did their prescribed forms of service. They stopped going to church, refused to pay tithes, to swear by any 'authority' other than their own word, to remove hats to anyone as a mark of respect or to speak to anyone with the 'respectful' 'You' form of address, preferring the, at the time, more familiar 'Thou' and 'Thee'. Returning to the texts of the New Testament and a vision of the first 'spirit-filled community', they supported the vocation of women to preach the Gospel

29 However, the Thirty Years War, 1618–48, was the last occasion on which a general European war was fought for essentially religious reasons.
30 Originally 'Friends of the Truth'.
31 I.e. relating to the Church of England.

in public. Fox's solution to the problem of how such a 'spirit-filled' community can have structure without reabsorbing the undesirable values of the world beyond, was to set up a system of meetings aside from worship. While worship was entirely determined by what the Quakers saw as the direction of the Spirit, meetings for management of the community were fundamentally democratic structures that imposed on everyone in the community the duty of care and responsibility for everyone else. No ministers were appointed. Not surprisingly, Fox and his followers experienced severe persecution and there were deaths and executions before the Act of Toleration was passed in Britain in 1689.

Non-conformity in America and the United States

Another example of the wider phenomenon of 'non-conformity' can be seen in the United States of America where, in the new Republic formed towards the end of the eighteenth century, old ways of looking at the relationship between church and society were very much under review. Many of the first North American colonies had been founded as part of a great outpouring of religious excitement associated with the Protestant Reformation in Western Europe, but the Constitution of the Republic enshrined, from the start, a freedom of conscience with regard to religion. Although the Christian religion continued to be seen by very many people as vital to anchor morality and give ultimate meaning, Americans clearly did not want 'established' churches or undemocratically elected religious authorities. As a result, the history of the Christian churches in America and the United States is one of sometimes quite extraordinary 'non-conformity'. For example, Mother Leaf Anderson's (1887–1927) mission, as part of the New Orleans Spiritual Church movement in the first half of the twentieth century, can be seen as one outcome of a movement of religious revival, sometimes called the Second Awakening, in which Christian communities could be said to have moved away definitively from establishment and regulation. Anderson's church as spirit-filled community also expresses a 'prophetic' mission in the context of the Southern states. Against the legacy of slavery, only very recently abolished, Anderson's woman-led mission among African Americans challenged both racism and sexism. Anderson set up eleven Eternal Life Spiritual Churches before settling in New Orleans as her headquarters. In the spiritualist church, adherents prophesy, heal, pray, see spirits and interpret selections from the Bible, or are taught to do these things. Anderson's church, and the spiritualist movement altogether, present a challenge to the term 'Christian'. God, in Anderson's spiritualist traditions, is a radically transcendent non-patriarchal being. Anderson plays down the importance of Jesus the man, seeing him as merely the earthly body of a spirit. Her spiritual tradition was eclectic, reflecting many cultural influences and drawing on Protestantism, occultism, voodoo, Italian American folk-religion and possibly even Native American traditions. Anderson nevertheless takes her place within a spiritual tradition which has clear connections to more mainstream forms of Christianity which recognize the Church as the spirit-filled community to some extent at odds with human institutions, including other churches.

Scottish Presbyterianism

Presbyterianism, in general, refers to a form of church organization most characteristic of Christian churches influenced by the Protestant Reformer John Calvin. Presbyterian churches are governed through a series of what are effectively courts, with successively larger areas of jurisdiction. The Kirk-Session of minister and church elders governs a particular local congregation. The Presbytery, consisting of ministers and representative elders from a group of churches, governs the churches in that area. Synods contain representatives from several presbyteries within a larger area and the final court is the General Assembly. These are bodies to which representatives are elected.

The doctrine of Presbyterian churches is traditionally Calvinist and, for Calvin, the marks of the true Church are that the Word of God should be preached there – preaching is of central significance

– and that the sacraments should be rightly administered. However, Calvin was also concerned with the administration and discipline of the Church, and another mark of the Church as it emerges in his writing is a public exercise of discipline through its constitutive 'courts'. For the Calvinist, in an ideal situation, there would be no conflict between the Church and the state authorities, since the Presbyterian Church would have a monopoly of religious worship and the state would support the Church by administering civil penalties to reinforce its moral teaching. Civil magistrates, in other words, would be God's lieutenants. Calvin made another significant distinction as between the visible and the invisible Church. The invisible Church consists simply of the elect known only to God. The visible Church on the other hand is the community of believers on earth including good and evil, elect and damned. This latter community, he believed, should be regulated in moral behaviour through the consistory courts of the Church, supported by civil government.

The Presbyterian Church, then, appears on one level to reflect the model of a church and state as a single unit. However, within some contexts it also takes on the character of 'non-conformity'. The only fully Presbyterian state-church was in Scotland, where the reformed Church of Scotland was established on Presbyterian lines by John Knox (1517–72) – a great admirer of Calvin – under King James VI of Scotland. The Church of Scotland had a confession of faith known as the Scottish Confession from as early as 1560, although this was later subsumed under the terms of the Westminster Confession, ratified by the General Assembly in Edinburgh in 1647. Presbyterian attitudes in Scotland towards the government of the state took the fundamentally Calvinist view that the civil authority should support the Church. So, not surprisingly, when James VI[32] attempted to bring about greater conformity between the two Protestant churches of England and Scotland, by imposing the forms and practices of the established church in England, there was great offence and protest.[33] In 1637, the English Archbishop Laud's efforts to impose the Book of Common Prayer in Scotland caused a riot in Edinburgh. A National Covenant drafted in 1638 pledged all who signed to resist 'all those contrary errors and corruptions according to our vocations' and led to an armed confrontation with the forces of the King, Charles I. However, Charles I lost support of his Parliament – many of whom were English Presbyterians – and under the Puritan leader Cromwell (an Independent not a Presbyterian) there were moves to eradicate episcopacy, the hierarchical system of clergy as priests and bishops, in England. Under the Protectorship of Oliver Cromwell, there was a move to reform the English church, making it more like the Scottish church. Although, ultimately, England reverted to Anglicanism after the restoration of Charles II, attempts to reform the English church during the protectorate led to the drawing up and ratification of the Westminster Confession in London by 1648. This was a statement of Calvinist teaching which remains a key document within modern-day Presbyterianism as a worldwide phenomenon.

32 James VI of Scotland inherited the throne of Elizabeth I of England, becoming also James I of England.

33 James VI tried to impose a hierarchical system of bishops on Presbyterian Scotland. This was made worse when the English Archbishop Laud also tried to make the use of the Book of Common Prayer obligatory in Scotland. The Prayer Book was considered far too close to the forms of Roman Catholic worship and prayer for Scottish Presbyterians. For example, they objected to the Prayer Book liturgy which was based on certain seasons and holy days of the Christian year. They wanted simply to recognize the Sabbath with its biblical warrant.

2.6 The Christian Church: communities of resistance and renewal

VATICAN II (1962–5)

During the eighteenth and nineteenth centuries, the Roman Catholic Church in Western Europe was somewhat on the defensive. Overshadowed to an extent by the cultural forces of Protestantism, and still somewhat unsure how to respond to the secularizing tendencies of Enlightenment thinking, it opted to maintain its sense of continuity with the past. The First Vatican Council (1869–70) stressed the constancy of the Roman Catholic Church and effectively confirmed the thirteenth-century works of Thomas Aquinas as the standard for Roman Catholic theology in the nineteenth century. By the end of the Second World War, however, there were clear signs of more robust theological engagement with the modern world.

The Second Vatican Council was called by Pope John XXIII, in response, as he saw it, to the inspiration of the Holy Spirit, and the Council began its sessions in 1962. Pope John XXIII died in 1963, but his successor Paul VI carried the work on to its conclusion in 1965. The Council had taken four years to organize, consulted several thousands of theologians and invited many observers from non-Catholic churches. It generally expressed new openness to 'the world'. Against the background of one-sidedly supernaturalist theology stressing the presence of God's grace within the Church, the Second Vatican Council took a more immanentist view, emphasizing the sense in which Roman Catholic Christians could detect the presence of grace in the signs of the times and in the world. This led to a new attitude towards other Christian churches and some movement towards ecumenism,[34] repentance for anti-Semitism, and some acknowledgement of other faith traditions. In relation to the world in which the Roman Catholic Church existed, there was a view of humanity as a whole as the context of God's gracious activity.[35] The trend towards seeing grace at work in the world and the desire expressed for modernizing and making the Church more relevant was also reflected in the decision to move away from forms of service held in Latin, and towards the vernacular. In addition there was a perceptible shift in the Church's concern towards rethinking the role of the laity, issues of justice and peace and social and political issues in so-called 'Third World' countries.

Interestingly, the Protestant theologian Karl Barth, who was invited to the Council but was too ill to attend, later expressed the belief that the theologians of the Council erred too far in the direction of accommodating to the world and, for him, ran the risk of being subjugated by the world. He felt dialogue with the world was taking precedence over proclamation to the world. In general terms, the Roman Catholic hierarchy and some aspects of the laity[36] have seemed to concur with his reservations, although perhaps less for theological than political reasons. Certainly in reaction to the development of liberation theology in the South American continent, the Roman Catholic hierarchy appear sometimes to have reacted with suspicion and even hostility.

34 In this context, ecumenism refers to attempts within the modern Christian churches to move closer together through a process of meeting with and listening to each other.

35 See the Papal pastoral constitution *Gaudium et Spes*.

36 For example, Opus Dei, an ultra-conservative Roman Catholic organization incorporating both clergy and lay people, some in positions of considerable influence.

LIBERATION THEOLOGY

The development of liberation theology in South America was undoubtedly related to the theological impetus of Vatican II but comes into recognizable form after the second Conference of Latin American Bishops (CELAM) held at Medellín in Colombia in 1968 at the request of Pope Paul VI. One of the most significant contributors to the movement was Gustavo Gutiérrez, who published in Spanish in 1971 *A Theology of Liberation*. Gutiérrez and others of a like mind were influenced by aspects of Marxist social analysis. This connection with Marxism, a philosophy committed to materialism and atheism, has been the ostensible reason for some of the Roman Catholic Church's suspicion of the movement. However, it seems likely that increased lay involvement in 'base communities'[37] was at least as threatening to the hierarchy of the Roman Catholic Church.

Living in a continent in which there were huge and increasing discrepancies between the wealthy and the poor, and some of the most oppressive and dictatorial political regimes in the world, liberation theologians concluded that the Church should put itself on the side of the poor and oppressed in any situation and identified the violence implicit in social and political structures just as much as in actual physical brutality. In this respect they were inevitably courting official disapproval, since the hierarchy of the Roman Catholic Church at that point was undoubtedly more strongly identified with the wealthy and powerful than with the poor and oppressed. Liberation relating to the whole person and not simply to dematerialized spiritual needs is regarded by liberation theologians as an essential aspect of salvation, and the Christian story is reread as a highly political confrontation with oppressive social structures. It is an essentially practical teaching seeing right belief (orthodoxy) as coming out of right action.

Black theology in South Africa can also be viewed as a form of liberation theology developing out of circumstances comparable to those in South America and in response particularly to the experiences of South Africa under the system of apartheid.[38] The Church, identifying with the powerless, is seen to represent a challenge to the structures of 'worldly powers'. Since 1994 when Nelson Mandela was elected as President of the first non-racial democratic government in South Africa, the churches have continued to play their part in a critical, prophetic sense. But they have also begun to see their work in terms of helping the civil authorities restore and maintain forms of peaceful and just government. For example, Desmond Tutu, Anglican Archbishop of Cape Town, chaired the government commission on Truth and Reconciliation (1995) which he helped to set up in order to review past injustices under the apartheid system and mediate between victims and perpetrators of violence.

Women-Church is a global community taking inspiration from some aspects of liberation and feminist theology. Church here is defined through creative ritual, mutual support and a developing form of spirituality. It emerged as a definitive concept in the United States in 1983, coming out of an organization called the Women's Ordination Conference. It sees grass-roots 'base communities' of women as representing a movement of the Spirit both inside and beyond the institutional churches. It is a way of bringing together under one title all groups of women involved in an exploration of spirituality emerging from Christian faith experience. It has no permanent leadership and no real centralized form of organization and names loosely interconnected and usually spontaneous initiatives. The Women's Alliance for Theology, Ethics and Ritual in Maryland provides resources and maintains

---

37 Base communities consisted of groups of families with lay (non-clergy) leadership in worship and teaching.
38 A policy of 'separate development' as between black and white people enforced within South Africa prior to the election of Nelson Mandela.

a directory of organizations which wish to be listed under this movement, but the list does not constitute the extent of Women-Church.

Some groups see this as a context in which women can grow towards full liberation before reintegrating with mainstream churches. Some think of it as an 'exodus' church or a church in exile or as a Spirit church within the tradition – a sort of parallel tradition rooted in women's wisdom and vision of justice for all. Characteristically 'base communities' are ecumenical and not essentially exclusive of men except in so far as women are thought to need space apart. Elisabeth Schüssler Fiorenza talks about Ecclesia, in *In Memory of Her* (1983) for example, as a whole community of women – like the people of God as this term is used in the Christian Old Testament – who share a vision as well as talking, telling stories, listening and table-fellowship.

3 WESTERN CHRISTIANITY AND THE CHALLENGES OF THE MODERN WORLD

Introduction

From the era of the ecumenical councils onwards, Christianity had claimed to provide the authoritative, overarching structure of meaning. In self-identified 'Christian' communities from East to West and within the remit of their missions worldwide, Christianity told the sacred story in which all things found their significance. However, within the modern world this claim has been increasingly challenged.

3.1 From Aristotle to the Big Bang!

Historically, science, or the pursuit of knowledge about the world, existed in harmony with the Christian religion in the West. Christianity encouraged people to investigate the world they lived in, believing that this is a way to learn about God's creation. This remains the position of many scientists who would continue to call themselves Christians today. But the potential for challenge has been there from a relatively early date in Christian history. For example, in the thirteenth century, the works of the Greek philosopher Aristotle (384–322 BCE) were translated from the original Greek into Latin, and interpretation of this by Muslim scholars was read by Thomas Aquinas. Aquinas then helped make Aristotle's ideas about knowledge/science more widely available. This was undoubtedly highly significant, and, in many ways, modern scientific method based upon the collection of empirical evidence still reflects the insights of the Greek philosopher. But Aristotle was not a Christian of course. Discovering Aristotle's works of science forced Christians to recognize that there was important knowledge to be gained from outside the Christian canon.

Over the years there have also been a number of rather more heated disputes between scientists and Christian communities that have championed traditional structures of meaning as definitive. Galileo Galilei (1564–1642) famously provoked a crisis within the Roman Catholic Church of Western Europe when he tried to defend the heliocentric[39] viewpoint of the earlier scientist Nicholas Copernicus (1473–1543). In spite of the weight of informed opinion behind him, the Roman Catholic Church

---

39 Galileo argued against the accepted viewpoint of his day, that the Sun and not the Earth was at the centre of the planetary system.

found him guilty of heresy. Although there was precedent for recognizing that the Bible had to be interpreted in the light of available knowledge in any particular context – a principle of accommodation restated by Foscarini, a Roman Catholic contemporary of Galileo – the Roman Catholic Church at the time decided to take the more literal approach to the Bible with which heliocentric ideas inevitably clashed. This was partly, no doubt, to do with the fact that, at the time, the Roman Catholic Church was trying to defend itself against criticism from Protestant Reformers. The Reformers advocated revolutionary change in order to recover the simple authentic Christianity of the earliest Church, which, they argued, the Roman Catholic Church had buried beneath wealth, worldly power and hierarchical structures. The Roman Catholic Church responded by pinning its colours to an idea of enduring, unchanging tradition. Against this background, allowing a radically new interpretation of the Bible (in the light of new information available) looked too much like change. Galileo's position was rejected as self-evidently false teaching simply because it was new and had not been offered before.

Today the increasingly sophisticated narrative or story told by modern science, by its very power to explain and manipulate forces we previously regarded as mysterious, represents an increasingly serious challenge to the Christian churches' claim to know how human meaning and significance is authenticated. As with Galileo's argument with the Roman Catholic Church, disputes are frequently focused on questions of biblical interpretation. This is hardly surprising of course since, for most Christians, the Bible is a chief if not the chief source of this authoritative, religious knowledge. For example, both the idea that our universe is the result of a vast cosmic explosion more than 15 billion years ago – the so-called Big Bang theory – and the idea that we, as a species, are the result of a long process of evolutionary development – a form of Charles Darwin's (1809–82) theory of evolution by natural selection – appear to contest a literal understanding of the creation stories in Genesis 1–3. Christian responses range from an apparently blind 'creationism' that claims the literal truth of the creation stories in Genesis 1–3, to the view that Christianity is not, in any case, necessarily concerned with supernatural beings or ultimate causes. A more 'mainstream' response to the challenges set up by developments in cosmology might be associated with the work of the British scholar John Polkinghorne (1930–), a theoretical physicist and an ordained priest in the Anglican Church. Fundamentally, following the long line of 'cosmological'-type arguments, Polkinghorne works with the 'scientifically given' and argues that the intricacy and complexity of the natural world together with the sheer unlikeliness of something so delicately balanced simply 'happening'[40] are strong arguments for the purposeful and created nature of the cosmos.

A number of Western Christians have, over the years, also taken up the challenge set for traditional Christian teaching about the meaning and purpose of human life by Charles Darwin's theory of evolution by natural selection. The theory provided an explanation for the nature and existence of humankind without reference to God or Genesis. In response, the French Roman Catholic priest and scientist Pierre Teilhard de Chardin (1881–1955) proposed a cosmic Christian vision: the universe itself is an evolutionary process which is constantly moving in the direction of greater complexity and higher states of consciousness towards a final goal summed up in the supremely personal universal Christ. His position is thus: (1) I believe that the universe is in evolution; (2) I believe that evolution proceeds towards the spiritual; (3) I believe that the spiritual is fully realized in a form of personality; (4) I believe that the supremely personal is the universal Christ. His work has been criticized for its lack of scientific rigour and some see it as overly optimistic, but it represents a genuine attempt to find

---

40 This argument is sometimes given the title the 'anthropic principle' since it still sees the formation of this planet and the evolution of humankind as an end or goal of creation.

points of connection between scientific and religious thinking. Interestingly the Roman Catholic Church did not give him permission to publish his work because it appeared unorthodox. It was not published until after his death. Tom Torrance (b. 1913), a Scottish Presbyterian theologian, is another Christian who took up Darwin's challenge. He argued that both Christian theologians and scientists like Darwin and his scientific heirs are responding to a 'given reality'. In other words he is a theological realist believing that theology is not reflection on human experience but on the *reality* of God's self-revelation in the world. Scientists and theologians respond in different ways to this reality. Torrance sees validity in 'natural theology'. That is to say, he believes that science can reveal evidence of God's work in the world apart from the special revelation of Jesus Christ.

Tom Torrance was therefore open to the sciences, believing that evolutionary ideas were certainly compatible with Christian theology even if they could not be reconciled with a literal understanding of the biblical story of creation in Genesis. And many Christians publicly concede that Scripture does not have to be interpreted literally. In saying this, however, they are not necessarily giving up all characteristic metaphysical notions about the existence of God. And so the argument with science is joined once more with a number of thoughtful scholars presenting Theology and Natural Science as two exclusive theories competing for hearts and minds on the level of underlying explanation in two different respects; science answering the question 'How?' and Christian theology based upon traditional biblical interpretation answering the question 'Why?' But this is far from a definitive end to the argument! Perhaps the strongest challenge from science in general terms lies in the argument from simplicity; the idea that demonstrable laws of nature provide clearer, simpler and more elegant explanations of events than speculative hypotheses about supernatural beings.

Traditional Christian insistence on an idea of God as creator of the world and on Christ as incarnate (God as human in the world) works in favour of positive evaluation of the human material condition and the value of human wholeness. The scriptural vision of Jesus as someone who healed the sick of body and mind also works to support a positive view of medicine, as a vocation, and of advances in medical science (as also advances in ecology and veterinary science). However, the traditional Christian evaluation of spiritual values as in some sense higher or more important than material values, and a more general suspicion of embodiment and physical appetite detectable particularly in the writings of Augustine but also in those of other church fathers and teachers, also figure in the evaluation of medicine. This is evident in some Christian discussions of modern fertility treatments, abortion, the treatment of AIDS and the development and manufacture of forms of contraception and protection against sexually transmitted infections. Some Christian churches take a highly public stand on these issues. For example, the Papal encyclical, *Gaudium et Spes*, states that life must be protected with the utmost care from the moment of conception and that abortion and infanticide are 'abominable crimes'. In these cases then there is the potential for medical science to work together with Christianity but also for Christians and medical scientists, once again, to be at odds.

SCIENCE AND THE CHRISTIAN RELIGION – DONNA HARAWAY: A CRITICAL POSTSCRIPT

Donna Haraway is an American biologist who sees in the work of some modern biotechnologists, the uncritical use of the Jewish and Christian story of God and his chosen people ('salvation history'). In other words she argues that many scientists and those who sponsor and market new forms of biotechnology, as well as many ordinary citizens in the Western world who profit from their work, assume without question the primacy of 'humankind' – sometimes 'mankind' – over all other living organisms. They have internalized the religious story of 'salvation history' as essentially a story about human (sometimes 'man's') progress. She sees the evidence for this in advertisements for products and proposals for projects that are put forward in this growing field. Haraway argues that by emphasizing the primacy of the 'chosen people', that is humankind and not other forms of life, in their 'journey' towards a 'promised land' that is a vision of a certain form of human perfection, the exploitation and destruction of our biosphere is somehow explained away or even justified. This is illustrated, for example, in a picture by Lynn Randolph which appears on the front cover of Haraway's book.[41] The picture is called 'The Laboratory or the Passion of OncoMouse'. OncoMouse™ is the trademark of a particular patented transgenic animal; a mouse which is guaranteed to develop a particular form of cancer in a matter of months and which is used by scientists trying to develop treatments for human cancer. It stands in critical counterpoint to the 'manufacturers'' (Dupont) advertisement. In the picture by Randolph, the hybrid nature of the mouse is symbolized by its human arms, legs and breasts while, interestingly, the helpless suffering of the product is symbolized by its crown of thorns, making reference to the sacrificial nature of Christ's death – for the sake of humankind – in much traditional Christian theology. Haraway's approach looks critically at fundamental values and attitudes represented within Christianity and challenges its anthropocentricity as unjustified and dangerous.

Christian responses to this criticism again may range from referring to a preconceived notion of authority, derived from the Bible or church tradition, to a recognition that Haraway's criticisms have a point. That is to say some Christians do recognize the need for Christian theological reflection on the nature of God's relation to the whole created world. Sallie McFague, for example, argues that we need new metaphors or models for God. Conceiving of God as Lover and Healer, for example, as she outlines these metaphors, makes God's work in creation naturally refer to the value of the whole of creation and not just 'man'.

3.2 The challenge of Enlightenment philosophy

In the countries of Western Europe the development, during the seventeenth and eighteenth centuries, of an increasing faith in human reason, the values of scientific rationality and the importance of social justice is generally referred to as the Enlightenment. This philosophical and intellectual movement has had an extraordinarily long-lasting impact on Western thought. It eventually forced a philosophical revolution, whose effects are still felt today, whereby the hypothesis of a transcendent, divine being can be seen to be a seductive but ultimately paralysing story or perhaps a projection. A hermeneutic of suspicion demands that any claims about this God need supporting evidence. Three important figures who applied a suspicious hermeneutic to the traditional religion of Western Europe during the nineteenth and twentieth centuries and who continue to influence our ways of thinking in the Western world and beyond are Friedrich Nietzsche, Karl Marx and Sigmund Freud.

THE 'DEATH OF GOD': FRIEDRICH NIETZSCHE (1844–1900)

The death of God, as taught by traditional Western Christianity, is the death of Jesus that brings about 'atonement'. That is to say Jesus' cruel death on a cross is believed to heal the break with God, cancel the debt owed to God by humankind and satisfy the claims of eternal justice in the relationship between

---

41 *Modest_Witness@Second_Millennium.FemaleMan©_Meets_OncoMouse™*.

God and humankind caused by human sin. In the work of the modern theologian Jürgen Moltmann – written after the implications of the Holocaust and destruction of two world wars had begun to sink in – only the death of Jesus on the cross is sufficient to do justice to the negativity and innocent suffering of our world. It is the prerequisite and pledge of God's promise for new creation. However, alongside these, perhaps, more conventional Christian views, the 'death of God' describes a philosophical challenge to the idea of God. It has been particularly associated with the German thinker Friedrich Nietzsche. Nietzsche, like so many of his contemporaries, was impressed by the ideas published by Charles Darwin. For Nietzsche an important question raised by Darwin's theory was that if human beings have evolved this far, might they not still be evolving? Where would this lead? It certainly did not tie in very closely with the spirit of biblical Christianity which stressed the significance of human life in its present form, quite distinct from other animals. Nietzsche thought that Darwin's theories brought the whole idea of 'human nature' into question. He suggested human beings of his time simply represented a bridge between the ape and the *Übermensch* (superman). Ultimately he rejected the claims of Christianity to have access to a transcendent world and he pilloried with some passion the tendency of Christianity to stress a higher, non-worldly form of existence as the foundation for all our higher values. This, he argued, was simply a way in which human beings expressed their profound dissatisfaction with the world in which they lived and which basically sapped their strength and resolve to act and to live to the fullest extent. To the way of sin and salvation he attributed to the Judaeo-Christian tradition, he preferred an earlier view of life as tragic, associated in his mind with the writings of the early Greek poets and playwrights. He believed that suffering and death were to be faced with as much dignity as possible in the acknowledgement of their inevitability. Most famously, perhaps, he claimed that 'God is dead' and that we (modern European humankind) have killed him. In this way he seems to have acknowledged the very profound trauma involved in fully accepting the inevitable 'death' of an ancient and powerful idea. But he was a passionate philosopher, attempting always to release the energy of life lived to its full potential from what he saw as false and disempowering claims about another life or future heavenly rewards. His characteristically nihilistic approach to all the accepted values of nineteenth-century Western Europe drives his uncompromising attacks on all forms of hypocrisy and self-deception.

A particular kind of Christian response to Nietzsche's 'death of God' idea can be seen in work of 'atheology'. For example, in 1967, the American atheologian Tom Altizer invited theology 'openly and fully to confront the death of God' (1967: 15). For Altizer, '[h]aving come to the realization that Christian theology cannot survive apart from a dialogue with the world, it is increasingly being recognised that dialogue is a mutual encounter: faith cannot speak to the world unless it is prepared to be affected by that world with which it speaks' (ibid.: 17). Altizer argued that faith could not be 'given and autonomous' (ibid.). This would be 'nonincarnate' and he sees such faith as a retreat from reality. Altizer follows Nietzsche's view that traditional Christian views of God which formulate ideas of God as a being in the realm of the transcendent spiritual also obstruct the passion and fullness of this human life by essentially devaluing it or even emptying it of value except in so far as it relates to some other realm. Altizer sees in Nietzsche's 'nihilism' a form of mysticism, that is to say a form of acknowledging and accepting the absolute mystery of human life rather than endlessly trying to tie it down or naturalize it or reduce it to manageable or falsely optimistic dimensions. So, for Altizer, the term 'death of God' refers not so much to the idea that people are no longer interested in God, or that secularism has killed him off, as to the idea that traditional ideas of God must die, must be dissolved, if sense, meaning, significance and joy are to be found afresh.

KARL MARX (1818–83)

The political and economic theorist Karl Marx was particularly influenced by the work of two philosophers, Georg W. F. Hegel and Ludwig Feuerbach. Marx adapted Hegel's 'dialectical' way of understanding history and political conflict, arguing that there had always been class conflict between the 'haves' and the 'have-nots' from the time of slavery or feudalism to his own day where capitalist industrialists (the *bourgeoisie*), exploited industrial workers (the *proleteriat*). And, following Hegel again, he believed that a system that is internally inconsistent – as he thought the capitalist system was – will ultimately collapse. He predicted that from this political conflict a classless society would emerge in which no-one would be exploited or suffer the deprivations of poverty. From Feuerbach, Marx took his passion for the material world in which real people lived and suffered. Feuerbach had shocked the world of German Idealist philosophy in the middle of the nineteenth century with his criticism of Christianity and his view that the world was not simply constituted by ideas but by the physical realities of life. Feuerbach's down-to-earth materialism was well expressed in his famous conclusion: 'You are what you eat.' Marx, like Feuerbach, believed that human beings were defined by the way in which they coped with living in a physical world, in other words their ability to produce and consume food and other material goods.

Marx and Engels, who together published *On Religion* in 1844, argued that 'Man makes religion, religion does not make man. In other words religion is the self-consciousness and self-feeling of man who has either not yet found himself or has already lost himself again'[42] . . . and most famously of all, 'Religion is the sigh of the oppressed creature, the heart of a heartless world, just as it is the spirit of a spiritless situation. It is the opium of the people.'[43] Marx – whose ideas of 'religion' were, of course, drawn from the Judaeo-Christian tradition of Western Europe – argued that it was an ideology that masked reality and encouraged some people (the *proleteriat*) to submit to oppression and alienation in order to serve the needs and interests of the powerful (the *bourgeoisie*). In other words it was a form of social control.

However, it is notable that for many of the liberation theologians, for example, Marx's analysis of the causes of poverty and economic oppression around the world has been a useful tool in the cause of freedom. While it has changed and moulded theology, it has not destroyed it.

SIGMUND FREUD (1856–1939)

Traditional Christian teaching about human nature largely stems from two key theological ideas: creation and salvation. Human beings were created by God but chose to turn away from God, preferring to sin. God taking pity on their misery became human in the person of Jesus and by his death on a cross, achieved the reconciliation of all or some sinners to God. The psychoanalyst, Sigmund Freud, wrote the essay, 'The Future of An Illusion', in 1927 to challenge this Christian drama and relocate responsibility for the happiness or unhappiness of our lives in the inner logic of developing human identities. Solomon and Higgins suggest that in this essay he 'outraged the world by giving just the sort of explanation least wanted, that human conduct by its very nature is based on vile, murderous, incestuous motives. So much for the enlightened thesis that human beings are basically good. Sexual

42 Quoted in Bocock and Thompson 1985: 11.
43 Bocock and Thompson 1985: 11.

desire was everywhere, and everywhere repressed. Unhappiness was inevitable and civilization itself was its cause' (1996: 254).

In brief, then, Freud describes developments within human society, such as the development of a religion, as analogous to the development of individual human subjects. In the development of the child, the father quickly comes to represent what is longed for and what is also feared. He has power over the young child and its mother. The child wishes, and comes to believe, that his father has power over all that causes him to be anxious. For this reason his power is also to be feared. This pattern is projected in religious notions of God. In other words, the psychic force of religious ideas is derived from individual perceptions of childhood helplessness and fear which can be truly terrifying. By the same token human drives, including towards instinctual pleasures, are constrained because this is forbidden by the Father/God on pain of dire punishments in this world or the next. Thus civilization of one form is maintained. But – Freud argues – it is maintained by an illusion. An illusion is not the same thing as an error, however. It is derived from human *wishes*, and this makes it very difficult to dislodge or disprove. Freud is concerned that, after a very long trial period, the illusion of religion has become a delusion, 'incompatible with everything we have laboriously discovered about the reality of the world' (cited in Gay 1995: 705). It simply hasn't 'delivered the goods'. The majority of humankind has not been made happy, or comforted or reconciled to life and does not lead an especially moral existence under the sway of religions. Put somewhat simplistically, Freud suggested, in the larger context of his work, that the child normally progresses beyond the stage at which the father is given unquestioning love and obedience. So should humankind. The illusions of religion are analogous to the early stages of human development in which the father is in place as guarantor of safety provided obedience is absolute. Freud believed that humanity in the nineteenth and twentieth centuries had begun to develop beyond this stage, and urgently needed education according to a 'reality principle', our God λογος (ibid.: 720), which he defined as that of scientific rationality. This would help humanity to get beyond the illusion that obedience to God could make everything all right, and also recognized that the loss of many pleasures and gratifications was a price that had to be paid for any benefits of civilization.

While not wishing at all to underestimate the significance of those nineteenth and twentieth-century thinkers – Marx and Freud among them – who have seen religion (usually meaning Christianity) as a projection of one sort or another, the theologian Hans Küng responds robustly: 'But does that conclusively prove that God is *only* a projection, that God is only a consolation conditioned by interests or only an "infantile illusion" as Sigmund Freud was later to argue, along the same lines? "Only" or "nothing but" sentences must be treated with suspicion. They suggest a certainty for which there is no foundation' (1995: 13).

3.3 Challenges of secularism, pluralism and postmodernism

SECULARISM

In the modern Western world of changing technology and scientific development certain forms of the sacred story, for example those that emphasize a heavenly reward in the afterlife, no longer seem so appealing as a focus for spiritual and moral effort. The word 'secular' means, in origin, that which belongs to its own time. The concept has a long history, but the first use of the term is associated with G. J. Holyoake in about 1850. Holyoake spent six months in prison for blasphemy – for putting forward 'the doctrine that morality should be based on regard to the well-being of mankind in the present life, to the exclusion of all considerations drawn from belief in God or a future state' (Edwards 1969: 15). A theory or hypothesis of 'secularization' in the Christian churches became popular in the 1960s and 1970s. It was particularly associated with the name of Bryan Wilson (1966). Wilson concluded that ideas about science, self and society first put forward in the nineteenth century and gradually disseminated throughout Europe were ultimately responsible for the detectable decline in church membership and the marginalization of the Church as an institution in mid-twentieth-century Britain. The theory of secularization is said to go back at least as far as the Protestant Reformation. It was also related to the way in which developments in science and medicine had reduced many of life's uncertainties and, it was suggested, made religion (still largely assumed to be Christianity) unnecessary. However, more recently the theory has been criticized. In the first place, critics suggest, it rests on an inaccurate reflection of the historical situation. In other words, it is difficult to trace a simple linear pattern. Looked at carefully, it is possible to see that there are periods of religious enthusiasm in Europe and periods where religion appears to play a less important role throughout the whole of the two thousand years of Christian history. Second, secularization as a theory appears to be Eurocentric. Looking at Christianity as a global phenomenon challenges the hypothesis. For example, there was an upsurge of evangelical and fundamentalist Protestantism in parts of South America during the 1980s. Moreover, if religion is not restricted to Christianity, we might point to the rise of Islamic fundamentalism and the role played by religion in Bosnia and the Middle East. These examples certainly seem to challenge the idea that religion as a whole has lost its power to attach and motivate. Moreover, some critics of the secularization idea have suggested that declining membership in European churches may have more to do with social than 'intellectual' factors. In other words, greater leisure options, changing patterns of work and greater mobility have undoubtedly led to changes in patterns of church worship, but this is not the only possible indicator of religious interest or involvement (Gill 1993).

Moreover, from the perspective of Christian believers, concern with this world *may* be profoundly religious. For example, in the *Letters and Papers From Prison*, written while awaiting execution by the Nazis for his part in a plot to assassinate Hitler, the German theologian and pastor Dietrich Bonhoeffer (1906–45) calls on Christians to face the fact that God as a 'working hypothesis' is no longer necessary for science, politics, morality or even for religion. Christians, he argued, must 'grow up' and take responsibility for themselves. They could not assume that God was a 'given' factor (a sort of *Deus ex machina*). But this was not really a concession to 'the godlessness of the world' but a call for faithfulness 'to the cross' which actually exposes this godlessness. In other words, for Bonhoeffer, being faithful meant, precisely, living life with a view to the things of God; for example, living in loving community with others. It meant giving up concerns that seemed to him to be 'worldly', like striving for heavenly rewards or eternal life beyond the grave.

PLURALISM

Changes associated with the development of technologies of communication and travel have made increasingly unavoidable much greater contact with different cultures in the modern world. This exposure has had a challenging effect in traditionally Christian communities for a number of reasons. First of all there has been a view that Christianity supplied the ideologies and norms that hold society together. Since Christianity is regarded as the source of moral norms, challenge to its traditional teaching can be seen as a threat to the whole fabric of the community or even the country. For example, in a recent public controversy in Scotland over whether teachers should be allowed to represent a homosexual lifestyle to their pupils as a legitimate alternative to heterosexual marriage, many Christian people felt the status of Scotland as a properly moral community was being threatened by this challenge. To them the controversy took on dimensions much greater than a challenge to the specific sexual norms of particular branches of the Christian Church in Scotland. Second, exposure to different moral and religious perspectives can be threatening to many Christians who believe Christianity to be in a category of its own and not simply one more example of 'a religion'. In other words, for many Christians, full 'saving' knowledge of God must be the goal of human existence and this can come only through the worship of Christ within a recognized Christian church tradition. The specific Christian church of which they have experience represents the ultimate guardian of saving knowledge.

In response to the challenge of pluralism and exposure to radical difference, the German Protestant theologian Karl Barth took the conservative view that Christ was still the only way to salvation. But, at the same time, his views allowed scope for a more compassionate vision of the divine, since he also supported the idea of universal salvation. In an ultimate sense and according to God's own saving will, he believed that all people would eventually be brought to faith in Christ. Karl Rahner (1904–84), a Roman Catholic theologian, argued that non-Christian religious traditions might have access to the saving grace of God in Christ within their own traditions. In other words, he held to the principle that salvation may only be had through Christ but allows other religious traditions to include elements of the truth. Of course, there are difficulties with both these approaches. Not the least of these is that they are both located within a very particular context yet the kind of claims that are being made are universal in character. Both theologians wrote and worked as members, albeit within different traditions of Christianity, of an elite group of white, male, European academics and clergy. Their experience and training was hardly designed to give them insight into the context of those outside their own religious and cultural traditions, and the categories with which they worked – for example their concern with 'salvation' – are essentially Christian. It appears to remain the responsibility of non-Christians to learn these new terms rather than of Christians to immerse themselves in different religious traditions. In *God and the Universe of Faiths* (1973) John Hick argued that we should move away from a Christ-centred approach towards a God-centred approach. In this 'Copernican' revolution, Hick wanted to put God at the centre rather than Christianity. He took the view that God is available through all traditions. This approach certainly takes a radical approach to the Christocentricity characteristic even of many modern Christian theologians and writers, but, of course, not all religious traditions are concerned with 'God'; certainly not 'God' as defined in Western Europe.

POSTMODERNISM

Postmodernism is perhaps most usefully described by the French philosopher Jean-François Lyotard (b. 1924) as the rejection of all universal theories and ideas, including forms of political totalitarianism[44] and religious metanarratives or overarching stories in terms of which all events can be interpreted or judged. One example of such a religious metanarrative might be the idea of 'salvation history' – the idea of God working his purpose out in the events of history leading to the eventual salvation of his own people. Postmodern writers from a variety of different perspectives challenge any idea of singular

---

44 As a young man, Jean-François Lyotard was much taken with forms of Marxism which he later rejected. Perhaps the most important work by Lyotard is *The Postmodern Condition: A Report on Knowledge* (1979), in which he targets knowledge, science and technology in advanced capitalist societies.

or ultimate 'truth'. They would tend to argue that our knowing takes place within contexts or structures in which the relationships between different individuals and ideas are specified.

Arguably the primary aim of a postmodernist critique of Christianity is not to replace it with a bleak and barren relativism (truth is whatever the next person says it is) but, rather, to challenge the tendency of human institutions to naturalize and rationalize the grossest of monopolies, that is to make forms of oppression and evil appear necessary and good because those who undertake them have privileged access to the truth. For example, the Inquisition was established in Castile by Queen Isabella in 1480 initially to wipe out 'secret Jews' (Jews who pretended to conform to Christianity but secretly practised their own religion). It was premised upon the idea that the Castilian Catholic hierarchy had access to ultimate truths and that conformity to these truths justified any amount of cruelty and destruction. Some modern Christians might see a similarly destructive pattern in the enforcement of various heterosexual norms within many Christian communities.

In *Theology and Contemporary Critical Theory* written in 1996, the British theologian Graham Ward suggests that postmodernist and modern critical theory do not have to be seen as essentially opposed to Christian theology. He argues that, in fact, postmodernist forms of analysis reveal the extent to which so-called 'discourses of truth' since the Enlightenment – those which seem to have divested the Christian religion of its mystery – can themselves be shown to be alternative 'metanarratives', and this opens the way to what Ward calls a 're-enchantment' of the world in terms of an ongoing questioning.

3.4 The challenge of evil: the Holocaust

The term 'Holocaust' is taken from the Latin Bible's word for 'whole burnt offering'. Today it is the word used in the English language for the systematic discrimination against and expropriation, deportation and annihilation of European Jews by Nazi Germany between 1933 and 1945. Katharina Von Kellenbach describes it as the 'legally sanctioned, bureaucratically administered and industrially organized mass murder of approximately six million women, men and children' (Von Kellenbach 1996: 145). The Holocaust challenges Christianity in two ways. First of all, it forces Christians to recognize the legacy of Christian anti-Semitism which undoubtedly helped to bring about the Holocaust in the first place. Second, it focuses attention on the Christian notion of God as good in the face of the overwhelming suffering inflicted, in this case, on Jews and some other proscribed groups.

ANTI-JUDAISM

Christian anti-Semitism or anti-Judaism goes back a very long way in the history of Christianity: 'Anti-Judaism can be defined as the tendentious denigration of Judaism for the purpose of elevating, through contrast, another religion or an ethnic group. Because of the linkage of nascent Christianity to the Hebrew Bible and Judaism, explanation for the split between the two religions became a necessary component of Christian theology' (Heschel 1996: 12). In other words, from the start, Christianity has encouraged the negative stereotyping of Jews for its own purposes. Jews have been characterized as 'Christ-killers', references to 'the Jews' in the New Testament being quoted in support of a general hostility towards and scapegoating of a group of people whose separate cultural practices have tended to make them stand out as different in mainstream Christian culture. Examples of 'elevating through contrast' include, for example, interpretation of the letters of Paul focusing upon a distinction between religious law (Torah) and faith in God's grace (expressed through the incarnation of Christ).

Traditionally, Christians have argued that faith in Christ sweeps away the necessity of the Jewish law, often regarded as 'external' and legalistic. In other words, an internalized faith in Christ is contrasted with and elevated above obedience to external law. Arguably this polarized distinction does little justice to the positions of either Paul or Rabbinic Judaism.

The Western Church's attitude towards 'usury' or claiming interest on money borrowed also comes under the heading of 'elevating through contrast'. In the past there was a Christian prohibition of 'usury'. Christians argued on the basis of an Aristotelian/Thomist idea of money as 'barren', that money was simply a means of exchange for goods to be consumed and that it was therefore only proper to return the sum borrowed. But Jews were explicitly exempted from this prohibition by the Roman Catholic Church at the Fourth Lateran Council in 1215. They were nevertheless despised for the practice by Christians, some of whom continued to make use of the service offered. The rise of capitalism in Europe saw this prohibition of usury gradually abolished but not the hostility and stereotyping it had fostered.

A more modern example of 'elevating through contrast' can be found in the work of some Christian commentators who contrast Jesus' sympathy for women with a view of Judaism and Jewish religious teachers that portrays them as uniformly dismissive in their dealings with women. Ross Kraemer argues – on the basis of analysis of New Testament and Jewish texts – that there were other Rabbis, contemporary with Jesus, who were prepared to talk with and discuss religious issues with women (1999: 35–49). Equally, she argues that the view of Jesus as someone who was especially sympathetic and interested in the condition of women has been very much exaggerated in the interests of Christian apologetics.

Modern theologians have begun to recognize the extent of Christian anti-Semitism, but they have not always found it easy to deal with the challenge. For example, Karl Barth accepts the special role and 'election' of the Jews as the chosen people of God. But he cannot accept the Jewish view of what Peter Ochs calls 'Israel's "no" to Christ' (1997: 615). For Barth, the law is fulfilled in Christ. So, although Barth advocates solidarity between Jews and Christians, his attitude towards Judaism in its difference from Christianity is ambivalent. Some would regard Barth's approach as still, basically, anti-Semitic and would claim that what is essential is the acknowledgement of the ineradicable differences that exist between Christianity and Judaism.

More recently, some radical theologians like Rosemary Radford Ruether (1974) have argued that anti-Judaism is part and parcel of New Testament teaching which therefore needs major revision. Others suggest that the key to the situation lies in Christianity abandoning the idea of itself as a form of ideology promoting stability and coherence across Western culture and dealing in ultimate truths. Instead it should perhaps see itself as a minority community with, perhaps, a religious vocation *comparable* to that of Judaism. Theologian Paul van Buren, for example, describes Christianity and Rabbinic Judaism as two 'Ways' of walking after the God of Israel that emerged in first-century Palestine.[45] For van Buren, Christ, his birth, death and resurrection, represent the gathering of a gentile church into the worship of Israel's God. He argues that neither one Way nor the other truly separates faith in God from good works as the fruits of God's Spirit.

45 See, especially, *Theology of the Jewish–Christian Reality*, parts 1–3, by Paul van Buren (1980–8).

The problem of evil

The Holocaust also figures as a particularly horrifying instance of a more general problem about divine power, responsibility and existence. This problem has, traditionally, been formulated as a 'trilemma', most famously set out by the third-century non-Christian philosopher Sextus Empiricus: 'those who firmly maintain that god exists will be forced into impiety; for if they say that he takes care of everything, they will be saying that god is the cause of evils, while if they say that he takes care of some things only or even of nothing they will be forced to say that he is either malevolent or weak, and manifestly these are impious conclusions' (1996: 175). Sextus Empiricus is often regarded as a 'Sceptic'. The Sceptics' recipe for an untroubled soul and general tranquillity in a world full of suffering,[46] was to avoid definitive beliefs in religious and philosophical matters. Sceptics like Sextus Empiricus also pursued a method of ruthlessly questioning everything in order to achieve this end. In the early Christian centuries, the trilemma was more liable to lead people towards dualism than atheism, which was a relatively unusual belief at that time. For example, dualistic gnostics, like the second-century Christian heretic Marcion, resolved the trilemma by claiming that this world with all its evils was the creation of a lesser deity, the God of the Hebrew scriptures, and not the God revealed in Christ.

Other more 'orthodox' attempts by Christians in the earliest centuries to resist the challenge of evil and suffering included the view that evil entered into a perfect world with the Fall – the consequence of a perverted use of human free will[47] – or that they were the means of perfecting humankind – a form of person- or soul-making.[48]

However, in the modern Western world the challenge of evil to the God of love has become acute, partly, perhaps, because of important changes in the way in which the West looks at the world. Since the Renaissance period, Western culture has begun – slowly – to re-evaluate worldly happiness and pleasure as goods rather than things of which to be suspicious. The Enlightenment philosophers and their heirs have also weakened the explanatory force of the story of the Fall which implied that no human being suffered 'innocently'. Moreover, modern medicine increasingly suggests sickness, injury, handicap (and even mortality) are extraordinary rather than the common lot of us all. So, arguably, theodicy – the efforts of Christian theologians to account for evil and suffering – has only become a *necessity* in the modern Western world. In *Evil and the God of Love* (1966) John Hick suggests that there is no single Christian tradition of theodicy but a multiplicity of voices. Philosophers, poets and Holocaust survivors, however, frequently speak of the evil represented in the Nazi genocide as inexpressible; a mystery utterly beyond explanation or justification in any terms. It is simply something to remember and never forget.

3.5 The challenge of feminism

In Western Europe and North America, during the eighteenth and nineteenth centuries, many women and men were inspired by the ideas that led to the French and American Revolutions. Some people recognized that the ideals of freedom and equality that had fired up revolutionaries against the aristocratic first estate in France and against colonial powers in America could also be applied to

---

46 *Ataraxia* – a concept that may have come, originally, from contact with India.
47 This was the position of Augustine, for example.
48 The Church Father Irenaeus favoured a form of this argument.

the situation of slaves or to women in general; both were groups of people who laboured for the economic advantage or domestic comfort of those who exploited them. Those who wanted to make the ideals of freedom and equality a reality for women set great store at this period on education and the right to participate within democratic political systems. Many men, of course, remained sceptical about women's aspirations in these respects. They saw women as essentially different from men. Women were commonly regarded as mysterious and attractive – important even – but also as weaker and ultimately dependent on men for protection and guidance. The education of a girl was thus a very different thing from that of a boy. And politics was a matter for men and not women.

In America, the campaign for women's rights had its origins in the anti-slavery and temperance campaigns. The exclusion of women delegates, including Elizabeth Cady Stanton, from the World Anti-Slavery Convention held in London in 1840 resulted in the Seneca Falls Convention of 1848 with its Declaration of Sentiments applying the principles of the American Declaration of Independence to women. Susan B. Anthony and Elizabeth Cady Stanton founded the National Woman's Suffrage Association, addressing similar issues to their British counterparts; for example, the status of married women, divorce law reform and, of course, suffrage for women.

The middle of the twentieth century sees the end of what is often called 'first wave' feminism. Up to that period, women had typically worked towards equality or parity with men. The goal was to do away with discrimination on basis of gender and solutions could be found in education and the law.

'Second wave' feminism opened up a new discussion, focusing on the differences between men and women and the way in which the difference represented by women – in terms of their sexuality, their experience or the way in which a woman's unique role in reproduction was given value or significance – had previously been either devalued or ignored altogether. The second wave of feminism describes how, historically, the masculine has been regarded as 'normative'. This is a way of analysing the situation of women and other groups of 'non-normative' humans like the poor, non-whites and homosexuals. In other words, in the past, the world was seen from the perspective of the (white, affluent, heterosexual) male, and the experience or viewpoint of people outside this group was seen as diverging from the 'norm'; irrelevant or even, in some cases, as perverse and evil. A 'second wave' feminist analysis also helps us to see why women have sometimes been 'successful' in a male world and why some are very critical of feminist ideas. In a world in which the male is the norm, women can succeed by accommodating to this idea in one way or another without seriously challenging it. For example, women can succeed in the male world of manual and clerical labour, business or the professions by giving up the traditional female role of wife and mother and traditional feminine attitudes and becoming more like single men in the workplace. Or they can combine the two approaches, functioning on two fronts both as career worker and as carer and domestic manager. Women who succeed in these two categories are less likely to be critical of the system within which they operate because they have made considerable sacrifices to conform to the normativity of male-centred work practices, values and goals.

In 1968, Mary Daly published her first feminist book, *The Church and the Second Sex*, a sweeping feminist critique of the patriarchal Church expressed with a passion but, at that time, also with a great optimism that change was possible. What she saw as being wrong with Christianity as a patriarchal religion was its symbol system, which she thought made the common-or-garden, day-to-day oppression of women appear part of the order of God's creation and thus quite proper. As she puts it: 'If God in "his" heaven is a father ruling "his" people then it is in the "nature" of things and according to divine plan and the order of the universe that society be male-dominated' (1973: 13). Daly's work is explosive, expressive of a great passion and compassion for women in a misogynistic world. But there is such a strong sense of advocacy for women in what she writes that it sometimes appears to drown out any more 'nuanced' approach to the history of Christian thought. Daly now considers herself to be 'postchristian', no longer restricted by the Roman Catholic traditions of her early upbringing.

Rosemary Radford Ruether is another feminist writer and thinker coming, like Daly, out of a Roman Catholic tradition. She offers a different critique of Christian church and theology which she believes results in a multiple sense of alienation. The subjective self is alienated from the objective world because the world is seen as, in itself, simply the context of human suffering as we wait for final redemption. The realm of nature is alienated from the spirit, which is no longer located within the rhythms of seasonal change. Moreover, within a patriarchal culture, such ideas are viewed androcentrically, that is, from the perspective of the male. This precipitates a further alienation: of the masculine from what was regarded or identified symbolically as feminine. Thus God becomes masculine, creates out of nothing, transcends nature and dominates history by ultimately terminating it altogether.

The roots of Ruether's transformed theology which seeks to foster the full humanity of women are diverse. She draws on the prophetic-liberating principle of the Bible, denouncing systems of domination and individualism, and on various religious groups which have, from time to time, promoted an egalitarian and counter-cultural vision – for example gnostics, Montanists and the Quakers. Apart from the categories of orthodox Christian theology, she takes inspiration from some pagan goddess religions. She considers the insights of liberalism, Marxism and Romanticism. From the conversation between such different points of view, she constructs a Christianity that denounces all systems of domination, and develops a sense of the mutuality of all people whatever their class, colour or gender. In addition she places considerable emphasis on humankind in its ecological context.

A further feminist theologian out of the Roman Catholic tradition, Elisabeth Schüssler Fiorenza, develops another approach. She sees feminist scholarship as, in the way it works, revolutionary, requiring a whole new perspective. Fiorenza's technique is to read the biblical texts with her eyes open to the possible participation of women – to engage in a process of radical suspicion of traditional hermeneutics, that is the formal interpretative methodology or way in which understanding the scriptures takes place. She recognizes that women may well have been controlled and frequently silenced in the early Church, but she is aware, too, of how the biblical texts themselves and those who have commented and preached on them have often sought to make women yet more silent and compliant.

Feminist theory as applied to Christian theology has made many Western Christian communities very uncomfortable as it challenges forms of patriarchal authority that undoubtedly underpin both Christian theological ideas and the organization of Christian institutions, and it challenges these at the most intimate and unavoidable level of family life. The most radical of feminist critics have even seen this as reason enough to leave the Western Christian churches altogether. However, a number of feminist theologians and biblical scholars continue to keep faith with the Christian texts and traditions, arguing that they still contain resources for human – and non-human – liberation and well-being.

4 THE CHURCH BEYOND EUROPE

Introduction

'Christianity' has frequently been presented as if it was a universal concept which bears, across history, the character of Western European Christianity at any particular time. Of course, such a view has been vigorously contested by scholars of religion like Adrian Hastings, and by an increasing body of work concerned with 'postcolonialism' or the politics of subordinating the subjectivity of the colonized to that of the colonizers in the ongoing drama of Western political and cultural expansion. Christianity revealed through a postcolonial critique appears, more often than not, as a cultural imposition. Arguably, some Christian missionaries have always been aware of the tension between following Jesus' instructions to '[g]o therefore and make disciples of all nations, baptizing them in the name of the Father and of the Son and of the Holy Spirit' (Matthew 28.19–20) and the intrinsic value of other cultures or the respect due to all people as children of God. However, the tension has often been dispelled by the assumption that, Christianity being the truth, the ends justified any means and that any form of behaviour was allowed in the cause of converting people to Christianity and 'saving' them. This conviction has undoubtedly allowed some Western Christians to indulge in wholesale exploitation and destruction of cultures they regarded as alien, primitive, 'uncivilized' and therefore 'un-Christian'.

4.1 India: the Church of St Thomas

However, there have always been Christian communities whose origins owe relatively little to the missionary activities of Western Europeans. The early Christian community of the Thomist Church in India, for example, seems to have retained a very distinctive identity from the beginning. For example, it appears to have included a cross-section of Indian society but not, in any material sense, to have challenged its traditional caste system.[49] In so far as there are outside influences on the Thomist Church these appear to come from the Syrian Christian Churches of Chaldea and Persia, from where, at a later date, its patriarchs and leaders were recruited. In the far south of India the Church of St Thomas, worshipping in the Syriac language, may well have been established sometime in the first Christian century. Traditions of this church sometimes say that St Thomas – the twin; one of Jesus' disciples – came to south India in the 50s of the first century, across the sea. Or sometimes they say that he came overland from the north.

The oldest literary account of the Apostle's mission is the *Acts of Thomas*, a Syriac document which was certainly being read in the fourth century CE and which may even be older. The *Acts of Thomas* relates the story of how, following the risen Jesus' commandment in the upper room to go out and make disciples, Jesus' disciples divided the world up and cast lots to decide which of them should go where. Thomas was assigned to India. The tradition has it that Thomas was, by trade, a builder and carpenter, and that he travelled to India, ostensibly to fulfil a building contract for an Indian king, Gundaphorus, who wanted him to construct a new palace. When Thomas reached India, so the story goes, he was so disturbed by the poverty and the luxury he saw that he gave away all the funds he had been given to build the palace and told the king that he was building a palace in heaven by teaching about the God who healed the sick and drove out demons. He was thrown into prison, but the same night, the king's brother died and on entering heaven saw the palace Thomas was building for his brother. When he was given leave to communicate this news to his brother, King Gundaphorus was converted and became a follower. There are also various traditions in the *Acts* and elsewhere in lyrical sagas that tell of Thomas's martyrdom in India. Historical references, however, are very inconclusive, except that it does appear there really was a King Gundaphorus in India in the first half of the first century.

From the fifteenth century, however, the Thomist Church of India did come under increasing pressure from European (*Farangi*) and especially Portuguese expansion in the form of trade initiatives

---

49 Put somewhat schematically, this is the view that everyone is born into a *jati* or birth caste group and a *varna* or occupational class and that they must follow the path or duty (*dharma*) required by their birth. Outside these groupings there are the outcasts or 'untouchables' who do menial work.

supported by Portuguese military forces and accompanied by missionaries of the Western Church centred in Rome. There were certainly some missionaries who adapted themselves to the cultures of India and tried hard to work with the people they hoped to convert to their own brand of Christianity. However, this Western Christian expansion into India in the fifteenth to seventeenth centuries eventually found itself in confrontation with the Thomist Church. At first relations were good. The Portuguese gave the Thomist communities protection from powerful local rajas or princes, and from hostile Islamic forces along the Malabar coastline of the Indian Ocean, parallel to which most of the Thomist Christians lived. In return the Thomist Christians used their influence to gain the Portuguese a profitable share in the spice trade. However, conflicts arose. The Portuguese were undoubtedly disturbed by the Thomist Christians. For one thing, there was some doubt as to their orthodoxy or 'correctness'. The doubt related to the teaching of the ecumenical councils about the nature of Christ.[50] Their scriptures were suspect too, because they were in Syriac and not in Latin. Thomist Christians would not venerate images of Christ and the saints because this was one way in which they expressed their separation from many popular forms of Hinduism, within which images play an important part. Also their priests had secular jobs and many were married.

The Thomist Christians were clearly equally disturbed by the Portuguese. Apart from disagreements about Christian doctrine and practice, Thomist Christians were horrified by the *Farangi* violations of purity/pollution norms; for example their practice of eating beef. They were also distressed by their general arrogance, cruelty and intolerance. Both sides found the cultural differences hard to bridge and, no doubt as a reaction to these differences, the Thomist Church was at one point even subjected to horrors of the Inquisition. The Portuguese attempted to bring about changes in the Thomist Church. For example, they effected a blockade to prevent contact with any Syriac patriarchs and then imposed bishops and archbishops of the Western Church. In 1653, the Thomist Church declared that it would not tolerate any further interference and, cut off from the Syriac churches, decided to install their own religious leader or 'High Metran' from among their own clergy; the first truly native Indian archbishop.

In 1663, the Dutch conquered the area and ended Portuguese rule in that part of India. However, the Portuguese and their Western missionaries had undoubtedly, by this point, made considerable inroads into the Thomist Church. A candidate for High Metran sponsored by the Papacy remained alongside that chosen by the Thomist Church itself, and there has been, from 1662, when a number of Thomist Christians realigned themselves with the Roman Church, a dual tradition within the Christian communities of Malabar. The Thomist Church continues to exist today, still expressing its own distinctive traditions but undoubtedly altered significantly in the process of resisting pressure from the Portuguese colonial incomers.

50 The councils had agreed that Christ was a single person equally human and divine. But some Christians preferred the 'heretical' view that there were two separate persons in Christ: one human and one divine. These people believed that Jesus' mother was mother to the human person but not the divine person. In other words she was not *Theotokos* or the mother/bearer of God. This particular belief, often referred to as 'Nestorianism', takes its name from Nestorius, who died in about 451 CE and who was declared a heretic because of his opposition to the term *Theotokos*, used of the Virgin Mary.

4.2 Africa: the Ethiopian Church

Another example of a Christian church which, in origin, owed very little to the missionary activity of Western colonial powers can be found in Africa. Before the seventh century, Christianity had been well established in the northern coastal areas of Africa. The Christian monastic movement with all that implies for later Western European culture, for example, which had begun in Egypt, continued, after the disagreements between duo- and monophysite Christians, to be an important centre of Coptic Christianity. Alexandria was one of the major centres of Christian worship and scholarship for nearly seven centuries before it was captured in 641 CE by Muslim forces sweeping along the North African coast. Coptic Christianity in the Nile valley and further south in Nubia continued to flourish for a while after the collapse of other African Christian communities under pressure from Islam. But, by 1500, Christianity had virtually disappeared from this entire area. However, one Christian community did survive in Ethiopia, the mountain kingdom of Aksum. In the fourth century two young Christian merchants from Syria had visited Aksum, whose culture and language could be characterized as Semitic and in which there may well have been a Jewish presence at the time. The two merchants gained influence and spread the Christian message in the court of its king, Ezana, and Bishop Athanasius in Egypt was persuaded to consecrate a bishop for the new church they established there. From the earliest days this church in Ethiopia laid emphasis on the Jewish heritage of Christianity, seeing itself as the heir of Judah with a foundational myth of how its kings were descended from the son of King Solomon and Sheba, Menelik I. Another foundational story reflects the good relations with surrounding Muslim powers that this church enjoyed for some centuries. The story tells of how the persecuted companions of the Prophet Muhammad, fleeing from Mecca, found refuge in Ethiopia.

However, in the sixteenth century, the Ethiopian Christians felt so threatened by their Muslim neighbours that they sought military assistance from Christian Portugal to resist the hostility of a Muslim general known as Gran ('the left-handed'). The Portuguese responded to this request for help, bringing their Christian missionaries with them. The missionaries, as in India, sought to increase the influence of the Western Church, and in so doing introduced dissension and disputes over doctrine that had not previously existed in the Ethiopian Church. In 1632, King Fasiladas of Ethiopia responded by dissolving the union that had been formed with the Roman Church and expelled the Jesuits, an influential order of Western missionaries. Ethiopian Christianity is an indigenous African form of the Christian faith largely distinct from Hellenic or Roman models. For example it integrated African concepts of kingship into Christianity and it was also able to incorporate traditional African ideas of the spirit world into its worldview without the sort of conflict seen in contacts between later Western Christian missionaries and Africans. Even in terms of marriage customs, Ethiopian Christianity found ways of integrating Christian and traditional values. Although the Christian tradition brought to Ethiopia in the fourth century had frowned on polygamy, polygamy was an integral, well-established and, in terms of the existing culture, useful practice. It was the basis on which alliances were formed and deals concluded. So, to avoid incurring the penalties or divine displeasure of participating in the eucharistic rites of the Christian Church in a state of technical sinfulness, the eucharistic rite was largely relegated to the very young and very old, that is, those not actively involved in polygamous relationships.

4.3 The epic tale of Christian missionaries

EARLY CHRISTIAN MISSIONS: CASE HISTORY OF IRELAND

Christianity has been a missionary religion from the earliest times. The missionary expansion of Christianity begins to take place, traditionally, during the lifetime of Jesus himself, to be carried on by the first generation of Christians after his death and resurrection. The work of preaching the Gospel to non-Jews in and beyond the confines of Judaism is referred to in the Gospel accounts of the life of Jesus although the New Testament gives the Apostle Paul the leading role in this missionary outreach to the non-Jews, or gentiles, within the Hellenistic cultures of the Roman Empire. Later on we learn how Christian missionaries travelled east into Persia and south into Africa and India carrying Christianity beyond the Empire. Within the Empire we know of the expansion of Christianity, in spite of persecution at first, but ultimately sponsored by the Emperor himself.

Even if missionaries to Ireland – at and beyond the very farthest western reach of the Empire – do not appear to have arrived in the wake of its armies, Western imperial expansion played a part, of course, in the arrival of Christianity in that place. This expansion facilitated travel and communication from the earliest centres of Christianity, and after 325, of course, influential Christians began to make a powerful play for its normativity throughout the Empire. Christianity appears to have reached Ireland via mainland Britain, where it arrived with missionaries from Rome or Gaul some time from the second to third centuries. The Christian evangelizing of Ireland is traditionally attributed to Patrick (c.385–c.462), who is thought to have been the son of a Roman official born in Britain or Gaul. In Ireland, Christianity eventually replaced the rich and varied traditions of druidism, but this undoubtedly left its mark on the character of later Irish Christianity.

Within the pre-Christian druidic culture of Ireland it appears, from such sources as are available,[51] that the knowledge of history and laws and religious practice was preserved orally. When, in Christian times, the Irish monks began writing about the mythic/historical past of Ireland they began, of course, a process of excision and selective interpretation of the earlier, oral traditions. But there was certainly also some assimilation of older non-Christian traditions into the Celtic Church. One figure who seems to have gone through the process of assimilation into the literate Christian culture of early Irish Christianity is the figure of Brigit. Brigit was, by pre-Christian tradition, the daughter of a powerful tribal god, the Dagda. Her name, meaning 'the Powerful One' or 'Queen', indicates her significance and power and links her with a north-British tribal goddess called Brigantia, with whom she may perhaps be identified. She appears sometimes in a threefold form or as a 'triple goddess', seemingly a device to express her varying powers. In Ireland, Brigit is concerned with childbirth and fertility as well as with wisdom and poetry. As a Christian saint, Brigit's prominence in Ireland is, then, perhaps hardly surprising. Biographies of the Christian Brigit (also known as Brigid or Bride) began to appear after her death in 524 CE, suggesting perhaps that as a historical figure, the woman who is attributed with founding the first women's religious order in Kildare made a considerable impact on church and community. Accounts of her life, however, undoubtedly draw on the mythic memory of the goddess. The saint, of whose life very few details are known reliably, figures as the daughter of a druid who performs miracles such as hanging her cloak on a sunbeam or possessing a cow who produces a lake of milk to feed the hungry.

51 Sources include some Latin and Greek accounts by writers interested in the barbarian peoples of Europe as well as the accounts of Irish Christian monks.

CHRISTIAN MISSIONS: CASE HISTORY OF THE AMERICAS

The explorer Christopher Columbus's 'discovery' of America in 1492 coincided with a period of Spanish history when strong rulers – Columbus's sponsors, Isabella and Ferdinand of Castile, and their heirs, Charles V and Philip II – were in a position to take advantage of the material benefits that accrued from his and subsequent explorations. However, Isabella in particular was also extremely pious. It was during her reign, and with her encouragement, that the Church in Spain had established the Holy Inquisition, initially to root out Jews and, increasingly, any other kind of 'non-conformer'. It was during her reign that Granada, the last Iberian Muslim kingdom, was annexed. In the early Middle Ages Christians, Jews and Muslims had found a way of coexisting relatively peacefully in this part of the world, but Isabella and Ferdinand not only brought this to an end in the Iberian peninsula but also sponsored the export of a characteristically rigid form of 'conviction Catholicism' to the Americas. Their tightly interwoven religious, political and military aspirations were given a boost in 1493 when Pope Alexander VI (a Spaniard) issued a Papal Bull giving to rulers of Spain responsibility for evangelization of all the new land seized by the Spanish in the Americas. In this case, then, the motivation of the colonizing power explicitly included the desire to impose a strong degree of religious and cultural uniformity on the colonized peoples.

It should be said that the religious motives of the rulers of Spain and of some high-placed Catholic clergy – if not to the taste of modern Christians – appear to have been genuine and serious. Isabella forbade the enslavement of those she counted as her new pagan subjects while encouraging their evangelization. However, the Conquistadors who undertook the various invasions of the Caribbean islands and the continent of southern America seem to have been of a different kind of character; generally adventurers with little to lose and gold on their minds. As a result a large proportion of the native population of the area were forced into slavery (the *encomienda* system) and very many died as a result of brutal treatment and European-imported illnesses. For example, smallpox decimated the Aztecs in Mexico and contributed very significantly to their defeat by Hernán Cortés, who compounded the damage by the wholesale destruction of indigenous cultures – families, economy, religion, buildings – in that location.

Some of the native population took to the new religion imposed on them by their conquerors and began the process of assimilation. One often-quoted example of this relates to the vision of the Virgin Mary granted to a native Mexican, Juan Diego, in 1531 which led – against initial Spanish resistance – to the establishment of a shrine to Our Lady of Guadalupe on a site close to a pagan shrine to Tonantzin, 'Mother of the Gods'.

Many Western Catholic clergy made little protest against the exploitation and brutal marginalization of Native Americans and their cultures. Increasingly the Spanish administrators on the ground viewed the Americas as a province of Spain, and the clergy thought less and less of their work as a mission to the pagan population and more as the regulation of a normative religious culture. However, there were some who did protest at what they saw as unjust and un-Christian. One such priest was Bartolomé de Las Casas (1484–1566). Born in Spain, he went to America in 1502 and was ordained there as a priest. He was part of an expedition whose object was to conquer the island of Cuba where he obtained his own *encomienda*. Las Casas was so appalled at the conditions of his enslaved workers, however, that he set them free and, aged 31, returned to Spain to write and to campaign in defence of Native American rights. His approach was (and remains) controversial. With some support from other churchmen he succeeded in getting the crown of Spain to order the emancipation of all slaves (1542) and to curb the worst excesses against Native Americans by reforming the *encomienda* system. But the changes imposed from Spain were resented throughout the Americas. Las Casas continued to be strongly critical of both the colonial powers in Spain and the brutality of the colonists. And there were limits to what he could do and say since his approach depended on upholding the ultimate moral authority of the Spanish crown over the colonists.

His best-known works are probably *Historia de las Indias* and *Apologética Historia Sumaria*, both written in the 1550s. In terms of his defence of Native American culture, history and rationality, he went as far as to offer justification of the practice of human sacrifice within Aztec culture – frequently referred to then as now as an example of inhuman cruelty – as understandable in terms of a natural expression of the duty of humankind to God. He had a profound understanding and respect for Native American cultures and disagreed vehemently with the more questionable methods of some missionaries which included mass baptisms.

CHRISTIAN MISSIONS: CASE HISTORY OF WESTERN MISSIONARIES IN AFRICA

The slave trade with Africa continued until well into the nineteenth century, so for a long time much of the contact between Western Christians and Africa was related to this profitable if pernicious colonial practice. However, protest against slavery, particularly by religious groups such as the Society of Friends (the Quakers), was growing throughout the eighteenth century and really hit its stride at the height of evangelical revivalism in the late eighteenth century. Charismatic preachers and speakers, such as the Wesley brothers and George Whitefield, addressed the issue of African slavery alongside the moral dangers and metaphorical slavery of alcoholism in prayer meetings and preaching across Britain and in the United States. The evangelical movement incorporated a strong sense of the gospel's moral message, according to which it condemned the brutality and cruelty of slavery. However, it also continued to support the Christian evangelism of non-Christian peoples and nations although deploring the state-sponsored mission such as the Spanish and Portuguese had favoured in earlier centuries, or those missions 'piggy-backing' on trade ventures such as were operated by chaplains with Dutch trading companies. As a result, many voluntary missionary societies were established at this time, sending Christian ministers abroad as, for example, a group of twelve Baptist ministers led by William Carey and sent to India in June 1793, supported by the Baptist Society for the Propagating of the Gospel. Christianity was still seen overwhelmingly as something beneficial for all, under the benevolent rule of Western and crucially Christian colonial powers in Africa.

However, although benevolent in some senses – missionaries like the Scottish David Livingstone, for example, made it their business to publicize, to home as to colonial governments, the effects of the slave trade on Africa – it is clear that missionaries were frequently guilty of confusing Christianity with the Christianity of the colonial power. They routinely insisted, for example, on the centrality of literacy and reading, which were not, generally, of great significance in African tribal society. They frequently excluded women from positions of church influence without acknowledging the important role traditionally held by African women in spiritual aspects of life. They often saw it as part of their remit to dismantle the characteristic patterns of African societies. Adrian Hastings, for example, refers to the missionary of the LMS (London Missionary Society, established 1795) John Mackenzie, who talked enthusiastically of 'weakening the communistic relations of members of a tribe among one another and letting in the fresh, stimulating breath of healthy individualistic competition' (Hastings 1999: 210).

More recently, however, it is clear that Christianity has taken root in Africa with increasing 'Africanization'. In 1939, the Roman Catholic Diocese of Masaka in Uganda became the first Catholic diocese in Africa to be staffed entirely by African clergy with an African bishop. Nevertheless, suspicion still remains between mission-founded Christian churches in Africa – sometimes coloured by the values and interests of the colonial era as well as by Western-oriented theological traditions – and independently founded Christian communities with much higher levels of assimilation to pre-Christian African traditional values.

4.4 The Church in North America

The sixteenth and seventeenth centuries were a period in European history, of course, of great religious upheaval and change. It was also an age of discovery and expansion, and at this time many people from European Christian traditions began to look to the American colonies as a sort of 'Promised land', some seeing themselves, very consciously, as the new people of Israel, called by God to settle a new country as their biblical counterparts, in the Old Testament book of Exodus, had followed Moses out of slavery in Egypt into a new land of Canaan.[52] Colonial expansion in North America brought many different forms of Western Christianity to the continent. The European colonists included French and Spanish – and later, Irish – Catholics; English Anglicans initially loyal to the British monarchy and distinguished by their fondness for the Prayer Book; English and Dutch Puritans from a more Reformist Protestant background; French Huguenots (Calvin originated from this group); and German Pietists (Christians of Protestant origin but who had an emphasis on personal piety and missionary outreach) among others. They also brought their attitudes of suspicion and separatism with them. Religious diversity continued to trouble many settlers, as did the radical 'otherness' represented by the presence of both Native Americans and slaves of African origin with their totally distinctive religious and cultural traditions.

In the first half of the eighteenth century, North America saw what is sometimes called the first 'Great Awakening'. The term refers to a generalized reawakening of Christian vision which also marks, in a way, the beginnings of a characteristically American Christianity departing in important ways from the religion of the colonial powers. Important figures in this first 'Great Awakening' included the Englishmen George Whitefield (1714–70) and his colleague and companion John Wesley (1703–91), the founder of the Methodist Church. Whitefield was a notable and inspiring preacher who, like Wesley, made a number of visits to North America. Although, in some ways, Whitefield was a more rigid and certainly a more Calvinist theologian than Wesley, both laid great emphasis on the importance of conviction and popularized a form of itinerant preaching. Interestingly, too, John Wesley strongly favoured the abolition of slavery, and Wesley's support for abolitionism illustrates another unique tension within American Christianity as a whole. In other words, from this point onwards there is a constant uneasy argument within the Christian communities as to the justification of slavery. Many in the South, who saw the possession of slaves as an integral part of their social and economic stability, wanted to claim that slavery was a Christian institution of trust and dependence. Opposition to this view continued, however, fuelled by an emphasis within Protestant revivalism on moral rectitude and social justice. Meantime, the slaves themselves, largely adopting the Protestant framework of the slave-owning classes, began to adapt it in important ways to express their own particular and communal experience of oppression and longing for freedom.

On the wider political and military front there were a series of major and violent struggles in America between the colonial powers of Britain and France during the course of the eighteenth century. That struggle was eventually resolved in favour of Britain. However, finally released from the considerable burdens on their lives and liberty that these struggles had imposed, the colonists turned their anger on

---

52 See Albanese 1999: ch. 5: 'Restoring an Ancient Future: The Protestant Churches and the Mission Mind'.

the colonial power of Britain itself. Frustrated by what they viewed as arbitrary and irrelevant administration from an increasingly foreign-seeming government, they finally broke from Britain to form an independent republic (Declaration of Independence 1776), the United States of America. George Whitefield's eloquent impassioned preaching and his freedom from the traditional institutional constraints of the Anglican Church had focused a growing dissatisfaction with this strongly colonial church and its clergy. In effect it added to the ever-increasing sense of alienation from distant British colonial powers and the values they represented. The first Great Awakening, then, refers to a process of widespread change and development towards a form of evangelical Protestantism which was to become widely characteristic of American Christianity within the late colonial period and on into the first century of the new Republic. And the establishment of the new Republic was, of course, highly significant for American Christianity as a whole since it was at this point that religious freedom of conscience was clearly established, being actually written into the new Constitution.

However, although religious freedom was established by the Constitution of the United States, there was a sense that the claims of religion still needed to be restated – in some way short of 'Establishment' – after the upheaval of the war for independence (1775–81). And within scarcely a couple of generations of the first, a second 'Great Awakening' occurred as if in response to that expectation. Some of those who participated in the second 'Great Awakening' were theological revivalists, returning to and gaining inspiration from the theology of the first European Protestant Reformers. Timothy Dwight (1752–1817), president of Yale College, and Lyman Beecher (1775–1863) in New England belonged to this group. However, revivalism took a rather different form with many others. One famous demonstration of the direction a popular revivalism was taking at this time occurred at the Cane Ridge revival meeting of August 1801, where commentators make mention of participants running, jerking, singing and joining in barking 'exercises'. In general terms people within the new Republic appeared to have been receptive to forms of evangelical Protestantism which were increasingly diverse, under the pressures of a popular democratic impetus. If Christianity was the religious tradition of the colonial powers, it was well on the way to being reformed within a series of vibrant new American cultural traditions.

The popularity of different forms of Revivalism seems to have favoured the growth in the eighteenth century of Methodist and Baptist churches so that by the early 1840s Baptists and Methodists constituted about two-thirds of the Protestant Christians in the United States. However, in the 'unregulated' condition of American Christianity as a whole, there was also a tremendous growth in the variety and vitality of Christian groups outside these two churches. In fact not all the developing religious communities of the time could even be included, comfortably, under the description of 'Christianity', and there remained some like the Mormons, founded by Joseph Smith – a young man confused by what he saw as Christian sectarianism leading up to 1820 – and the Transcendentalists – believing that nature and this world are broad avenues into the spiritual realm – who were considered by many Christians to be well outside any form of evangelical alliance. Nevertheless, a sense of underlying Christian evangelical solidarity remained characteristic of the largest proportion of religious communities at this time.

In the nineteenth and twentieth centuries there was some faltering and falling away from Christian belief altogether, under the same pressures to which Western Europe was subject at this time. In particular, the publication of Darwin's theories and the development of new methods of 'higher criticism' – which suggested the Bible was not essentially different from other books and could be analysed in a similar way to any other book of literature, poetry or philosophy – shook the religious foundations for some Americans. The effectiveness of these challenges in the United States indicates that, however independent politically, elements within the new Republic continued to identify fairly closely with the values and cultural traditions of the former colonial powers. But, at the same time, evangelical Christianity in America received a tremendous boost from, for example, the popular revivalist preaching of Dwight L. Moody (1837–99), who put his faith in a simple but effective presentation of the three *R*s: Ruin by sin, Redemption by Christ and Regeneration by the Holy Ghost.

In her book *America: Religions and Religion* (1999) Catherine Albanese sees the religious scene in the United States at the end of the second millennium as characterized by an irreversible pluralism which produces both expansive and contractive movements; a sometimes unsettling diversity even within that subsection of the total religious culture which can be described as Christian and which encompasses everything from the traditional hierarchicalism of Roman Catholicism to the practice of snake-handling and drinking strychnine (Matthew 16.18). As case studies in these movements she focuses on two particular examples: the New Age movement and conservative Protestantism (Albanese 1999: ch. 11). Albanese presents the New Age movement as a contemporary development of a generalized, popular, metaphysical religion, having its roots in Mesmerism, Swedenborgianism and Spiritualism, which she characterizes by their concern with breaking down rigid distinctions between the spiritual and the material. For example, Mesmerism explained how one person could 'mesmerize' another in terms of a sort of spiritual fluid that could be transferred from one person to another. Similarly, Swedenborg spoke of divine fluid entering the human world and described trance journeys to heavenly palaces which had very much the character of positive earthly experiences. Spiritualists have generally believed that spirits and humans could communicate because, essentially, they were made of the same basic substance in different forms. Similarly, in a New Age concern with ecology and the environment, Albanese sees a movement to break down the rigid distinctions of spiritual and material; if the material world in which we live cannot absolutely be distinguished from what is enduring and spiritual, we cannot simply dismiss it. This then is an expansive movement, taking terms and ideas from diverse sources including Asian and Eastern religions as well as quantum physics. But equally, Albanese suggests, in its ultimate aim to bring about healing in the lives and bodies of living things, including the planet, there is an enduring view of a world in need of restoration that comes from the deeply rooted Christian traditions of the American people.

In Albanese's study, a form of conservative Protestant Christianity represents the opposite movement of 'contraction'. Protestant Christianity is clearly very healthy in the present-day United States and remains the dominant religion, so this is not a matter of contracting numbers. The contraction refers to the sense in which some communities of conservative and fundamentalist Christians have been developing more rigid boundaries around their communities, in contradistinction to the informality and inclusiveness of the New Age phenomenon or even the 'broad church' mentality of the earlier evangelical commonality between different American Protestant churches. Contraction in this context represents a more demanding form of personal or communal identity in terms of cultural conformity. For example, Albanese documents the phenomenal rise in attendance at rallies organized by the group known as the Promise Keepers during the 1990s. These rallies, reminiscent perhaps of the revivalism so popular in America in the eighteenth and nineteenth centuries, saw thousands of, largely white, men make public commitment or promises, among which were a commitment to the leadership of husbands and fathers within the home and to Christian mission and evangelism in the country. Albanese suggests that expansive and contractive movements balance each other out, but notes some potential for extremism in a context in which there is no religious common ground such as has been served historically by the broadly evangelical Protestantism of American Christianity.

Christianity has accompanied the colonizing Western Europeans in their expansive movements across the American continents. These colonizing Europeans have undoubtedly done terrible and irreparable damage to the cultures and religious traditions of many other peoples, often on the understanding or under the pretext of Christian evangelism and mission. Sometimes, they have been conscious of the tensions created by the nature of Christianity as a missionary religion concerned with love and justice. Sometimes, colonized communities have been able to withstand the worst excesses of the colonizers as they made their moves on the territories of the heart and mind by taking and reshaping the traditions of the incomers within older, more resistant spaces and visions.

BIBLIOGRAPHY

Albanese, C. (1999) *America: Religions and Religion*. California: Wadsworth.

Altizer, T. (1967) *The Gospel of Christian Atheism*. London: Collins.

Armstrong, K. (1993) *The End of Silence: Women and Priesthood*. London: Fourth Estate.

Armstrong, K. (1994) *A History of God*. London: Random House.

Bainton, R. (2000) *Christianity*. New York and Boston: Houghton Mifflin (Mariner Books). (First published 1964.)

Beckerlegge, G. (ed.) (1998) *The World Religions Reader*. London and New York: Routledge.

Bocock, R., and K. Thompson (eds) (1985) *Religion and Ideology*. Manchester: Manchester University Press.

Chopp, R. S., and S. Greeve Davaney (eds) (1997) *Horizons in Feminist Theology*. Minneapolis: Fortress.

Clack, B., and B. Clack (1998) *The Philosophy of Religion: A Critical Introduction*. Cambridge, Oxford and Malden, MA: Polity Press with Blackwell.

Daly, M. (1968) *The Church and the Second Sex*. London: Geoffrey Chapman.

Daly, M. (1973) *Beyond God the Father*. London: Women's Press, 1985.

Detweiler, R., and D. Jasper (eds) (2000) *Religion and Literature: A Reader*. Louisville: Westminster/John Knox Press.

Edwards, D. (1969) *Religion and Change*. London: Hodder & Stoughton.

Empiricus, S. (1996) *Sextus Empiricus's Outlines of Pyrrhonism*, trans. Benson Mates. New York and Oxford: Oxford University Press.

Ford, D. (ed.) (1997) *The Modern Theologians: An Introduction to Christian Theology in the Twentieth Century*. Oxford: Blackwell.

Gay, P. (ed.) (1995) *The Freud Reader*. London: Vintage.

Geertz, C. (1985) 'Ideology as a cultural system', in R. Bocock and K. Thompson (eds), *Religion and Ideology: A Reader*. Manchester: Manchester University Press.

Gill, R. (1993) *The Myth of the Empty Church*. London: SPCK.

Hastings, A. (ed.) (1999) *A World History of Christianity*. London: Cassell.

Heschel, S. (1996), in *Dictionary of Feminist Theologies*, ed. L. M. Russell and J. Clarkson. Louisville: Westminster/John Knox Press.

Hick, J. (1966) *Evil and the God of Love*. London: Macmillan.

Hick, J. (1973) *God and the Universe of Faiths*. London: Macmillan.

Jantzen, G. (2000) *Julian of Norwich: Mystic and Theologian* (1987). London: SPCK.

Jasper, D., and S. Prickett (eds) (1999) *The Bible and Literature: A Reader*. Oxford: Blackwell.

Kraemer, R. (1999) 'Jewish women and women's Judaism(s) at the beginning of Christianity', in R. Kraemer and M. D'Angelo (eds), *Women and Christian Origins*. Oxford: Oxford University Press.

Küng, H. (1995) *Christianity: The Religious Situation of Our Time*. London: SCM Press.

Larrimorre, M. (2001) *The Problem of Evil*. Oxford: Blackwell.

Loades, A. (ed.) (1990) *Feminist Theology: A Reader*. London: SPCK.

Lyotard, J.-F. (1979) *The Postmodern Condition: A Report on Knowledge*. Manchester: Manchester University Press.

McGrath, A. E. (1994) *Christian Theology: An Introduction*. Oxford: Blackwell.

McGrath, A.E. (1998) *Historical Theology: An Introduction to the History of Christian Thought*. Oxford: Blackwell.

McGrath, A. E. (1999) *Science and Religion: An Introduction*. Oxford: Blackwell.

McLaughlin, E. (1990) 'Women, power and the pursuit of holiness in medieval Christianity', in A. Loades (ed.), *Feminist Theology: A Reader*. London: SPCK.

McManners, J. (ed.) (1990) *The Oxford Illustrated History of Christianity*. Oxford and New York: Oxford University Press.

Markham, I. (1996) *A World Religions Reader*. Malden, MA, and Oxford: Blackwell.

Ochs, P. (1997) 'Judaism and Christian Theology', in D. Ford (ed.) (1997) *The Modern Theologians: An Introduction to Christian Theology in the Twentieth Century*. Oxford: Blackwell.

Riches, J. (1993) *A Century of New Testament Study*. Cambridge: Lutterworth.

Rogerson, J. (1999) *An Introduction to the Bible*. London: Penguin.

Rogerson, J. (ed.) (2001) *The Oxford Illustrated History of the Bible*. Oxford: Oxford University Press.

Ruether, R. R. (1974) *Faith and Fratricide: The Theological Roots of Anti-Semitism*. New York: Seabury Press.

Ruether, R. R. (1983) *Sexism and God-Talk*. London: SCM Press.

Smart, N. (1989) *The World's Religions: Oral Traditions and Modern Transformations*. Cambridge: Cambridge University Press.

Solomon, R., and K. Higgins (1996) *A Short History of Philosophy*. Oxford: Oxford University Press.

Von Kellenbach, K. (1996) in *Dictionary of Feminist Theologies*, ed. L. M. Russell and J. Clarkson. Louisville, KY: Westminster/John Knox Press.

Ward, G. (1996) *Theology and Contemporary Critical Theory*. London: Macmillan.

Ward, K. (2000) *Christianity: A Short Introduction*. Oxford and Boston: Oneworld.

Ware, K. (1990) 'Eastern Christendom', in J. McManners (ed.), *The Oxford Illustrated History of Christianity*. Oxford and New York: Oxford University Press.

Watson, F. (2000) 'The Bible', in J. Webster (ed.), *The Cambridge Companion to Karl Barth*. Cambridge: Cambridge University Press.

Weaver, M. J., J. Bivins and D. Brakke (1997) *Introduction to Christianity*. London: Wadsworth.

Webster, J. (ed.) (2000) *The Cambridge Companion to Karl Barth*. Cambridge: Cambridge University Press.

Wilson, B. (1966) *Religion in Secular Society*. London: Watts.

Islam

Lloyd Ridgeon

INTRODUCTION

A question that appears in several chapters of this book concerns the possibility of transcending prejudice and preconception to present a fair and objective depiction of any given religious tradition. Many would argue that this is impossible as all humans are ultimately trapped in their own unique subjectivity, and therefore it is completely unrealistic to assume that even the adherents of any religious tradition can portray 'reality' in the same way. So if there is no single, essential Islam, in what way is it possible to make any meaningful statements about Islam? Are we ultimately limited to gross generalizations, the kind that has been criticized by Edward Said?

> 'Islam' as it is used today seems to mean one simple thing but in fact is part fiction, part ideological label, part minimal designation of a religion called Islam. In no really significant way is there a direct correspondence between the 'Islam' in common Western usage and the enormously varied life that goes on within the world of Islam, with its more than 800,000,000 people, its millions of square miles of territory principally in Africa and Asia, its dozens of societies, states, histories, geographies, cultures.
>
> (1981: l)

In *Orientalism* (1978), Said argues that Western scholarship on the Orient (and therefore Islam) has produced an essentialist and negative portrayal of Islam in order to legitimize political and imperial goals, and he implied that the legacy of this scholarship is still present today. Given the difficulty in overcoming subjectivity and the dangers of orientalism, how does one approach Islam? One method that has received much attention was offered by the historian Marshall Hodgson. His portrayal of Islam was based on regarding Islamic doctrinal beliefs as 'a core . . . surrounded by a series of ever widening concentric circles of cultural practice of ever diminishing religious relevance and legitimacy' (cited in Binder 1988: 107). Therefore it is necessary (despite Said) to essentialize Islam to a certain degree if it is at all possible to speak of Islam as a world religion. However, in contrast to Hodgson, it is useful to speak of a core of *practice*, rather than doctrine, as a useful defining characteristic of Islam. This is because it is practice of the five pillars (namely, stating the *shahada* (or testament of faith), prayer, fasting, paying the alms tax and pilgrimage) that provides a sense of identity for Muslims which nurtures and promotes an Islamic community. In essence the five pillars lead Muslims to contemplate and envisage a perfect world order, and it is this interpretation of the meaning of rituals that has resulted in divergent doctrinal positions. Performance of the rituals (orthopraxy), then, characterizes Islam rather than doctrine (orthodoxy), if it is agreed that in Islam there is no equivalent of a Christian Church to sanction doctrine, although the reality has been different on occasions (see Calder 1996: 996).

The depiction of Islam presented in this chapter is divided into sections reflecting the five pillars (and a sixth, *jihad*, which has sometimes been called the sixth pillar). In each section one of the pillars is examined in conjunction with a discussion of relevant doctrinal issues. Thus it is hoped that this chapter provides a basic introduction to Islamic faith and practice. The first section examines the *shahada*, which is linked to an examination of Islamic doctrines concerning God and a discussion of the prophet Muhammad. The next section focuses upon prayer, which leads into an analysis of Sufism. The third section investigates the fast which is inextricably connected to the Qur'an and various doctrinal positions adopted by major Islamic thinkers regarding Islam's sacred text. In the fourth section the focus turns to the alms tax, which I have linked to Islamic law. The fifth pillar, the *hajj*, is the most elaborate and distinctive of Islamic rituals, and as the *hajj* is specifically Islamic it is only appropriate to examine what Muslims have said about the 'other', and therefore the fifth section investigates Islam and pluralism. Finally *jihad* is considered from a political perspective, with an investigation of the Sunni and Shiite concepts of power, and finally the perspectives of several contemporary Islamic thinkers are considered.

The need to understand the various manifestations of Islam is urgent given the contemporary political climate. Rightly or wrongly, the coverage of Islam by the British media in 2001 did not present a very positive image of Islam. First, there were demonstrations/riots in northern English cities which subsequently led to the accusation that Muslims (among others) were leading 'parallel lives', divorced from the 'mainstream' British community. And of course there were the events of 11 September 2001 and the subsequent conflict in Afghanistan that were allocated copious media coverage. The demonstrations/riots should have come as no surprise to anyone familiar with the conclusions of the report published by the Runnymede Trust, entitled *Islamophobia: A Challenge for Us All*, which warned of the 'corrosive effect of Islamophobia on interpersonal, community and international relations' (1997: 61). The findings were largely ignored by the then home secretary, Jack Straw, yet some leading figures in British society have responded to Islam in a positive manner. Prince Charles's interest in Islam is well known, especially after 1994 when he expressed a desire to be regarded as 'defender of faiths'. Moreover, the British Prime Minister Tony Blair had an interest in Islam even before the events of 2001, as he is said to have read the Qur'an three times on his holiday to Portugal in 1999 (*The Times*, 10.3.00). It remains to be seen whether or not these interests and concerns are applied in international and domestic spheres.

1 THE TESTAMENT OF FAITH (*SHAHADA*)

'I testify that there is no god but God, and Muhammad is the messenger of God.'

Becoming a Muslim is easy, for as most Muslims will confirm, all it requires is a voluntary and public declaration of the *shahada*, cited above, three times. However simple it may appear, the *shahada* has contained a myriad of meanings for generations of Muslims; indeed, each believer has a unique conception of its two subjects, that is, God and Muhammad. By examining the interpretations of the two sentences within the *shahada* it will become apparent that Islam is not a monolithic entity. Indeed, an investigation into how Muslims have meditated upon the concept of the divine will inevitably yield diverse results, as will speculation on Muhammad the man, and the myths surrounding his life.

1.1 'There is no god but God . . .'

The unity of God is a fundamental theme running throughout the Qur'an, which Muslims believe was revealed to Muhammad (2.162; 6.19; 16.22; 23.91–2). The opposite of belief in the unity of God is *shirk*, or association of other gods with God. Other deities that were worshipped by the Arabs of Muhammad's time in the seventh century are mentioned (53.19–20), and Jews and Christians are also criticized for associating others with God. *Shirk* is the worst sin in Islam, something which God does not forgive (4.48, 116), and associators are prohibited from entering paradise (5.72). This sin is not merely a matter of worshipping other 'deities', but *shirk* includes more mundane idols, such as material comforts that distract people from God. God, or Allah, is described in the Qur'an with many attributes, and most commonly he[1] is called the Compassionate and the Merciful, yet he is also described by names that convey the majesty of the divine, such as the Slayer and the Abaser. Some of these names are included in the so-called 'ninety-nine names' of God, which Muslims use as the basis for contemplating the divine. Many books were written discussing these names, perhaps the most famous being that of the medieval theologian Ghazali (d. 1111), which has been translated into English as *The Ninety-Nine Beautiful Names of God* (Ghazali 1992).

The Qur'an refers to God's names several times: 'God's are the fairest names' (7.180) and 'Praise the name of your Lord Most High' (87.1). Muslims are advised to enumerate the ninety-nine names of God in a *hadith* (a saying attributed to Muhammad) that states the reward for such devotional acts will be entrance to paradise (cited in Ghazali 1992: 49). The pleasures of heaven may have been sufficient motivation for some Muslims to worship God by reciting his names, yet for others the names held the key that unlocked the mysteries of the divine nature. This section highlights how four Islamic groups have focused upon certain of God's names to explain their theological and devotional positions. These four are the Mu'tazilites, Islamic philosophers, Sufis and 'orthodox' Muslims as represented by al-Ash'ari (d. 935).

First, it is useful to consider God's names *Al-Wahid* (the Unique), and *Al-'Adl* (the Just), which were the source of inspiration for a group of Muslims called Mu'tazilites, a very broad school of Muslims that has been described as the 'first articulate theological movement in Islam' (Fakhry 1997: 16). They emerged from the dispute concerning whether or not a sinner could still be a believer. Wasil ibn Ata

---

1 The Qur'an employs the male personal pronoun for God, and therefore I will continue to do so when referring to God.

(d. 748), considered the founder of the movement, claimed that the sinner was neither a believer nor an unbeliever, a position that stood in contrast to the more extreme view propagated by another school, the Kharajites, that it was legitimate to exclude sinners from their community, even resorting to executing them. At the opposite end of the spectrum were the Qadarites, who argued that God pre-ordained or compelled sinners in their actions, and therefore the sin was not the sinner's fault and s/he should not be excluded from the community. The Mu'tazilites adopted a pragmatic approach between those of the Kharajites and Qadarites, and recognized that God, as the Just, and not man, would reward or punish sinners or believers.

Mu'tazilite speculation on God's name 'the Just' raised the profound theological question of whether or not God does what is best for humans. If God is good and just, does he offer guidance for all of his creatures, including those who live outside the Islamic empire and have not heard the Qur'an? Moreover, God as the Just provoked some Mu'tazilites to ask whether God's laws are good because he sent them down, or because the laws were good in themselves. If it could be established by human reason that the laws were good in themselves, then there would be little use for divine Scripture, a notion that was anathema to the more 'orthodox' theologians.

Another complex issue addressed by the Mu'tazilites concerned whether or not God's attributes were eternal (the implication being that if they were indeed eternal, then they could be considered deities along with God, which would open the door to *shirk*). Related to this discussion was the issue of whether a just and omniscient God is compatible with belief in an eternal Qur'an (85.21), which was considered God's eternal speech. It was pointed out by the Mu'tazilites that the 'eternal' Qur'an narrates episodes in the lives of Moses and Pharaoh; Moses is a prophet and obeys God's commands, whereas Pharaoh is a sinner because he disobeys Moses and God. Now, if the Qur'an is eternal, this leads to the conclusion that God knew that Pharaoh would sin. This negates the idea that man, or Pharaoh, has free will or the chance to do good, and this being the case, how is it possible for God to have the name 'the Just', not allowing Pharaoh a sporting chance of obeying the divine laws?

Such arguments prompted the Mu'tazilites to the conclusion that the Qur'an was created. A created Qur'an avoided any possibility of portraying God's attributes as eternal, since he alone was *al-Wahid* (the unique). The doctrine of the created Qur'an became a major issue in the ninth century, when the Caliph of the Abbasid Empire centred in Baghdad adopted it as official doctrine. An inquisition (*mihna*) took place between 827 and 849, and those 'orthodox' jurists who denied the created Qur'an were imprisoned and tortured, and some were executed. Those who resisted included Ibn Hanbal (780–855), who rejected this doctrine and also the Mu'tazilite allegorical understanding of certain anthropomorphic Qur'anic verses about God. For example in 38.75 the Qur'an describes God with hands, and Mu'tazilites claimed that such hands refer to God's helping grace. Ibn Hanbal denied the permissibility of such non-literal readings of the Qur'an, and 'orthodox' theologians pointed to the Qur'an 42.11, that 'nothing is like Him', as an indication that finite human reasoning could not attain to the infinite reality of God. The position of Ibn Hanbal with regard to the seemingly contradictory nature of some of God's names is contained in the phrase 'without asking how', a statement that 'resulted in an intellectual cul-de-sac in which acceptance triumphed over analysis and incomprehension over reason' (Netton 1994: 4). 'Orthodoxy', as expressed by the tenth-century theologian al-Ash'ari, declared that God's attributes or names are neither he nor other than he. These disputes still have a certain resonance in the contemporary age, as conflict arose among the Muslim groups in Britain during the 1970s and 1980s concerning how to interpret the anthropomorphic verses (Geaves 2000: 56).

Although aspects of Mu'tazilite reasoning took them beyond the pale of elements of Islamic 'orthodoxy' as represented by al-Ash'ari, it was the Islamic philosophers who pushed the God of 'ortho-doxy' (who creates in time, guides his people through prophets, and is very much a 'hands-on' God) out of the universe to become transcendent and remote from creation. Such a deity was of course not considered anthropomorphically, and like the Mu'tazilites, the philosophers attempted to portray God using the *via negativa* (that is, saying that God is neither this, nor that), with the result that nothing much could be said at all about the nature of God. As a result the philosophers such as al-Farabi (870–950) tended to employ those names of God, including 'the First', that helped to convey the meaning of their discussions of God as Necessary Being, the cause of all creatures and contingent being.

The celebrated Islamic philosophers, such as al-Kindi (d. *c.*868), al-Farabi and Ibn Sina (Avicenna, d. 1037), were very much inspired by Hellenist and Neoplatonic cosmology and philosophy. The cosmology of the Islamic philosophers posited the Earth as the centre of the universe, which was encompassed by the seven heavens, like layers of an onion. Surrounding the seven heavens were two further layers, outside of which lay the ultimate realm of existence, that of God, or pure existence, about which nothing can be said. To describe existence in a positive manner involves all kinds of problems, such as calling God an eternal speaker (as described above).

Some philosophers regarded the universe as eternal rather than taking the more orthodox view that God created the world. This was due to the Neoplatonic idea that the origin of the universe lay in an emanation from the One (or God) who is constantly emanating. Not to create (or emanate something similar to itself) would be a deficiency in the One, since a perfect thing is mature and all mature things reproduce. The One emanates an intellect, from which appears another intellect and heaven, and this process of emanation continues until the heavens and intellects (i.e. the material and spiritual dimensions of the universe) are completed. Physical matter (or Earth) is reached with the last and most impure emanation. Philosophers such as Avicenna provoked the wrath of the 'orthodoxy' represented in some of the writings of Ghazali, who accused the philosophers of heresy on three counts. These were belief in the eternity of the world, God's knowledge of universals but not of particulars, and the denial of bodily resurrection (Fakhry 1997: 68–72).

For many Muslims the abstract ideas of the philosophers did not do justice to the full range of religious experience. Certainly, describing God in terms of existence, and the use of negation were among important methods to understand God, but the Islamic community also found it necessary to clothe God to make him accessible to the ordinary believer. Indeed, the Qur'an frequently speaks of God being intimately close to the believers, and it offers examples, such as sending down *sakina*, or peace, upon the hearts of Muslims (48.17, 26).

In contrast to the philosophers who adopted the *via negativa*, and thus removed God to a somewhat transcendent realm, the Sufis, or Islamic mystics, brought him back to the centre of the universe, in fact, to the heart of their own very being. A name that the Sufis frequently used for God was the Light, which is a Qur'anic term (24.35). One influential school of Sufi thought explained that any existent entity in the world reveals something about God, as all entities share in having 'being', the one thing that pervades and unites all entities with God. These ideas will be discussed in detail in section 2 of this chapter.

One of the major figures of the formative period of Islam was al-Ash'ari (d. 935), and as Watt has commented, 'up to his time there seemed to have been nothing but the wrangling of sects, whereas with him there came into being a rationalistic form of Sunnite theology which has persisted ever since' (1998: 303). The Sunnis became the dominant theological group in Islam, and although there are various interpretations of this theology (since there is no real orthodoxy in Islam), it is useful to discuss al-Ash'ari's form of what became known as Sunni Islam and examine how he attempted to settle the disagreement concerning God as just and free.

The so-called creed of al-Ash'ari attests that Muslims are those who have faith in God, the angels, the sacred books, the messengers, Muhammad's prophecy, the resurrection, God's reward and punishment of humans, and the existence of heaven and hell. He held that the Qur'an was uncreated and was

God's very speech, thus it was eternal like his other attributes, but somehow different from his essence. On the problem of human free will against divine pre-determination, al-Ash'ari argued that everything in existence is brought about by God, and the atoms of existence are adjusted by God at each moment. If this re-adjustment is small then humans perceive continuity in the world, whereas large changes are explained by humans as 'miracles'. Since God is the maker of all change, such an 'atomistic' view of existence does not allow for human free will, and this implies that God creates all human acts, good and evil. And this leads to questions of theodicy, mentioned above with regard to Moses and Pharaoh. Al-Ash'ari argued that although God is the creator of all acts, humans acquire these acts by participation in them. The responsibility of human acquisition of these acts is difficult to determine, as Gibb has stated: 'In so far as this is more than a merely verbal accommodation, it would seem to imply that on a psychological level man continues to act as if he were free, and thus, though in reality acting of necessity, "acquires" the responsibility for acts and their attribution to himself' (1983: 187). In this way, al-Ash'ari believed that he preserved the Qur'anic assertion of 52.21 that 'every man will be retributed for what he has acquired', while at the same time guarding the divine as the sole creator of all acts, and 'this has remained ever since the official doctrine of Sunni Islam' (ibid.).

1.2 '. . . and Muhammad is his messenger.'

> I ask Thee, O our Lord, to employ us in his usages, to cause us to die in his community, to number us in his band, under his banner, and to make us his companions, to supply us from his reservoir, to give us to drink from his cup, and to give us the boon of his love.
>
> (Padwick 1961: 140)

The above prayer indicates the intense love that Muslims have for their prophet, Muhammad. So far, little attention has been paid to the second element of the *shahada*, which affirms that Muhammad is God's messenger, yet it should not be neglected as peripheral to the message of Islam. Many Muslims consider the first half of the *shahada* to be universal for theistic religious traditions, but the second half provides Islam with its particular colouring. Many of the laws contained in the Qur'an are rather general in scope and do not always cover day-to-day situations, and therefore it is the role of Muhammad, his sayings and actions, that are utilized by Muslims to establish the basis for all activity that is not explained explicitly in the Qur'an. The following discussion contains three main elements: an investigation of Muhammad's life, the criticisms that have been levelled against him by non-Muslims, and the difference between Muhammad the man as portrayed in the Qur'an and the mythical Muhammad that evolved in the Islamic tradition.

Muhammad was born in 570 CE in Arabia, into the Quraysh, one of Mecca's leading clans, and since he was orphaned while still a child, he was raised by various members of his family. At the age of 25, he married a wealthy widow named Khadija, and engaged in managing her commercial interests. Islamic tradition holds that at the age of 40, he received the first of a series of revelations that came at intervals for the rest of his life. When he made public these revelations, Muhammad was derided by many Meccans, but he continued to preach the message of God that was severely critical of the pagan beliefs and selfish lifestyle of the new urban merchant classes of Mecca. The revelations stressed faith in monotheism, the bodily and spiritual resurrection, the day of judgement, and it rejected female infanticide, and encouraged protection of the weak, needy, orphans and widows. In all, this threatened the interests of the Meccan elite who subsequently imposed a trade boycott upon

Muhammad and the small group of Muslims who were also on occasions subject to physical attack. The Meccan rejection of the revelations Muhammad believed he had received must have been incredulous for him, as the message was one based on reason. It was a perfectly rational argument to believe in God (as the Qur'an points to the creation and nature as evidence of God's existence, and to history as proof of his continuing determination of events). If it is accepted that God exists, then by necessity a good God will guide his creation, which of course requires messengers (angels), prophets who receive the message, and holy books in which the message is contained. The essence of Islam then is belief or faith in God, the angels, Muhammad, the holy books, and God's determination of events.

Yet Muhammad was rejected by the Meccan elite, was persuaded of the need to leave Mecca, and was invited to settle in the city of Yathrib, later known as Medina. He and his followers migrated there in 622, and this migration, or *hegira*, is the year from which the Islamic calendar commences. In Medina, the Islamic community was still very weak, for having uprooted their homes and trades, the Muslims had no stable economic foundation. Moreover, Muhammad faced criticism from some Jewish tribes in Medina and also from Meccans who were determined to snuff out Muhammad and his movement, following a series of raids performed by some Muslims on their trade caravans that ran back and forth between Arabia and Syria. A series of skirmishes and battles between the Meccans and their allies against Muhammad resulted in the consolidation of the Islamic community in Medina. Gradually more Meccans sided with Muhammad, who also attracted support from various tribes around Medina. By 630 the Meccans surrendered to him, and by the time of Muhammad's death, much of Arabia had either accepted Islam or else enjoyed treaties with the Islamic community.

Islam and Muhammad have not enjoyed particularly sympathetic coverage from nineteenth and early twentieth-century orientalists, who have often cast aspersions against Muhammad's moral conduct. A typical example is their attempt to discredit Islamic belief in the Qur'an being a genuine revelation of God. Several sayings of Muhammad (known as *hadith*) refer to him experiencing what these orientalists refer to as 'fits' and 'epilepsy' when he received revelations (Archer 1924: 14–23). Moreover, it has been argued that what Muhammad considered to be revelations were little more than 'hallucinations', and these 'fits' were in the main merely a device for securing sanction for his 'revelations'. The views of such orientalists are as difficult to substantiate as they are to disprove, and therefore add little to our knowledge of Islam. Indeed, they are damaging if the aim is to understand why Muslims have such a strong attachment to Muhammad. Criticisms of Muhammad have come not just from some Christians and sceptics of the modern secular world, but also from some individuals of Muhammad's own age. The Qur'an contains verses that indicate Muhammad was accused by the Meccans of composing the revelations himself (69.44–5), of being a poet (69.43–4), and being possessed by the *jinn*, or fiery demons (68.2). These criticisms were answered in the Qur'an, which challenged Muhammad's adversaries to produce a better chapter than those found in the Qur'an (11.13). Moreover, the Qur'an offers parallels between Muhammad's life and the experiences of the biblical prophets in order to suggest that Muhammad is indeed a messenger of God. For example, the Qur'an describes Joseph's rejection of the deities that people themselves invent and name (12.38–40), and Muhammad recites the Qur'an that criticizes the gods that the Meccans have invented and named (53.24). Reference is also made in the Qur'an to the followers of an unnamed prophet (Saul and David?) who were driven from their homes but remained reluctant to fight on the battlefield (2.247–8), and the Qur'an describes some of Muhammad's followers in the same way (2.215–17). There are also many parallels between Moses and Muhammad. Moses had to flee from Egypt, and Muhammad was forced to escape from Mecca. There were members in the communities of both that had heard the message but chose to disbelieve (2.92 and 4.46), and both prophets were given the *furqan*, or criterion of right and wrong (2.52 and 3.3). In fact the difficulties Muhammad faced were the very same that all prophets come up against, such as being opposed (25.31) and being accused of lying (6.34).

Orientalists also criticized the morality of Muhammad's marital life, for he was married to nine women by the end of his life, whereas Islamic law permits only four wives at any one time (4.3). The Qur'an confirms that Muhammad had been granted a special dispensation (33.50), and Islamic scholars were later to point out that several of these marriages were to elderly women who had lost their husbands fighting in the Islamic cause and had no-one to offer them any form of protection, and others were marriages of political alliance.

Another criticism that has been levelled at Muhammad and Islam is the supposed military and aggressive nature of Muhammad's community. It is necessary to bear in mind that in his attempt to establish an Islamic community, Muhammad was frequently operating from a position of weakness since he was opposed by the majority of Meccans and several Jewish tribes. On many occasions he and his community were struggling for survival. Yet by the end of his life, it seems that Muhammad believed that Islam was a 'universal' religion, although there have been differences of opinion about whether he understood this would be achieved by the pen or the sword. The Qur'an confirms that Islam is not an 'otherworldly' religion, and that each person is charged with a duty to protect the rights of the community. This duty, however, has been the centre of conflict because there have been individuals who have not wished to be members of the Islamic community.

It has been argued that Muhammad's own understanding of himself was determined by the Qur'an, which stresses his humanity (18.110; 41.6; 93.5; 17.90–4) and rejects his possession of miraculous powers or abilities (Welch 1979). His humanity is evident in verses that instruct him to ask God to forgive his sins (47.19–21), and which state that he erred (93.6–8). There is also a direct criticism of Muhammad when he preferred to ignore a blind man in order to speak with a rich man (80.1–11). Muhammad's task as a warner who cannot perform miracles or foretell the future is stated explicitly in 7.188; the only miracle is the Qur'an itself. Moreover, Muhammad did not have absolute authority over his community, as he was obedient to God and followed the laws of the Qur'an, which told him to consult the members of the community (3.159).

Despite the Qur'an's constant affirmation of Muhammad's humanity, Muslims came to revere the Messenger of God to such an extent that it is now quite an 'orthodox' belief that on judgement day he will be given permission to intercede and beg mercy for his community. This seems to contradict the Qur'anic verses that state reward in heaven and punishment in hell are a result of the individual's own effort expended here on earth. This elevation of Muhammad was the natural outcome of his pre-eminent leadership of the community. As the Qur'an states, Muhammad is the 'best model' for the believers (33.21) and it is necessary to 'obey God, and obey the messenger' (4.59). Contemplating the perfection of humanity in Muhammad was (and is) one method to understand God; after all, Muhammad was reported to have said: 'He who has seen me has seen God.' In addition, his favourite wife A'isha remarked that Muhammad's character was the Qur'an, which is the word of God. Indeed, the connection between Muhammad and God was drawn even closer by the medieval period when many Islamic philosophers and Sufis spoke of a 'pre-existent' Muhammad as a kind of Logos. That is to say, they spoke about the Muhammadan Light, or the Muhammadan Reality as the first thing created by God from which all other things derive their being. Moreover, many Muslims have an unshakeable faith in the reality of Muhammad's miracles, basing their beliefs on very vague references in the Qur'an. Evidence of Muhammad's splitting of the moon, according to such Muslims, is found in 54.1, and his 'Night Ascent' (when he was taken from his bed in Arabia to Jerusalem, and from there through the heavens until he eventually witnessed and conversed with God before returning to his bed in Arabia in the same night) was referred to in 17.1. Regarding the Night Ascent, one contemporary, academic Muslim has stated:

> The spiritual experiences of the Prophet were later woven by tradition, especially when an 'ortho-doxy' began to take shape, into the doctrine of a single, physical, locomotive experience of the 'Ascension' of Muhammad to Heaven, and still later were supplied all the graphic details. . .
>
> (Rahman 1966: 14)

Moreover, the veneration of Muhammad reaches an extent that many Muslims consider him imma-culate, or sinless ('isma), finding evidence for this in the Qur'anic verse which speaks of Muhammad having his breast expanded, and a burden (perhaps his impure creaturely nature) lifted from him (94.1–2). According to some Muslims, all the prophets are protected from committing any sin in order to preserve God's word from any error or corruption in the process of transmission to God's creatures.

In evaluating Muhammad's importance in Islam, one need only pay attention to his sayings (hadith) which are considered by most Muslims only second to the Qur'an in terms of being a guide for believers. Volumes of hadith were compiled and became a significant factor in defining the character of the emerging Islamic community. Indeed, the early books of hadith indicate that the distinction between the word of God (the Qur'an), and the word of Muhammad (hadith) was somewhat blurred. This was partly due to the existence of the so-called sacred sayings (hadith qudsi). Hadith qudsi are non-Qur'anic sayings reported by Muhammad that begin with 'God said that . . .'. Islamic theologians concluded that such sayings contained the meanings that God desired to convey, but the wording was specifically Muhammad's. One conclusion that has been drawn from this blurring of the distinc-tions between divine speech and Muhammad's speech is that the early Islamic community contained the roots of deep spirituality, and that Muslims were aware of 'the inner relatedness of all things including man and God' (Graham 1977: 110). It is interesting to speculate on a link between the spiritual tradi-tion of God's word coming in a non-Qur'anic form through Muhammad, and the development in mystical Sufi thought of the concept of divine inspiration (ilham). According to the Sufis, it is through inspiration that God's connection with his creation is maintained after revelation (wahi) ceases with the sealing, or end of prophecy with Muhammad. (The Sufi worldview is provided on pp. 241ff.).

Whether as a mortal prophet who did not perform miracles, or as an immaculate individual who enjoyed the closest of proximity to God, Muhammad is venerated by Muslims all over the world. An insult against the prophet is an insult against Islam. The controversy that erupted in 1989 over Salman Rushdie's book, *The Satanic Verses*, in which the Prophet was allegedly slandered, made this conspicuously clear. Yet Rushdie was not the first person to suffer from the wrath of indignant Muslims who have felt that their Prophet was insulted. Schimmel notes that Ibn Taymiyya, who was one of Islam's most 'puritanical' theologians, was accused of a lack of respect for Muhammad when he protested at the veneration of his footprint (Schimmel 1985: 65).

2 PRAYER (*SALAT*)

> Have you not seen that everyone in the heavens and the earth glorifies God, and the birds spreading their wings? Each one knows its *salat* and its glorification.
>
> (24.41)

Whereas the first pillar may lead the individual to contemplate the nature of God through speculative discourse, the second pillar, prayer, is a means to proximity with the divine. That is to say, prayer may draw the believer into what s/he believes to be an intimate, experiential relationship with God. The Qur'an has much to say about prayer; indeed, there are many kinds of prayer.

1. *Salat* is the ritual prayer that is commonly known in the non-Islamic world through images of Muslims prostrating themselves in unison towards the *Ka'ba* in Mecca. Yet *salat* is multi-dimensional, and the Qur'an mentions three kinds of *salat*. The first is the *salat* that God performs for the benefit of the individual, in order that he or she may come from darkness to light (33.43). The second is the *salat* that all creatures perform, whether they realize or not. God has knowledge of all things, indeed everything that the creatures do is because he has willed it, as expressed in 24.41 (cited at the beginning of this section). The third *salat* is that mentioned in 11.113: 'And perform the *salat* at the two ends of the day, and the watches of the night. Surely good deeds will wipe out the evil deeds; that is a reminder for those who remember.' It is different from the second *salat* in that the individual makes what s/he considers to be a conscious choice in its performance. The Qur'anic prescription for *salat* appears to be three times each day; however, Islamic tradition established the performance of *salat* five times daily. The words of the *salat* are chosen from the verses of the Qur'an, but the opening section of the Qur'an, the *fatiha*, is recited with every ritual *salat*.

In Islamic countries, Muslims are reminded of the time for *salat* by calls from loudspeakers attached to the minarets of mosques. The times of *salat* are specific and are also printed every day in national newspapers. In the Sunni tradition, the times begin with the *fajr* prayers at dawn. The second is the *zuhr* prayer at midday. The *asr* is the late afternoon prayer, the *maghreb* is the prayer at sunset, and the final prayer of the day is the *isha*, which is performed after twilight.

The prayers are performed facing the *Ka'ba* in Mecca (see pp. 265ff.). The Islamic community, like the Jewish, had directed their prayers to Jerusalem, but this practice was proscribed and the Qur'an commanded Muslims to face the *Ka'ba* (2.144), the direction of which is indicated in mosques by a niche, or a *qibla*. This feature of Islamic practice was probably instituted to give the nascent community an identity distinct from that of the Jews and Christians in Arabia of Muhammad's time. Today, the visual image of rows of Muslims performing their prayers together in a mosque is one of the most stereotypical, yet still powerful, inspirational and evocative images that the Western media broadcasts when focusing upon Islam. Indeed, the communal nature, especially of the congregational prayers on Friday, is sanctioned in the Qur'an (62.9). Again, this serves to differentiate the Muslim from the Christian day of worship on Sunday and from the Jewish day of rest on Saturday. The Friday prayers include a *khutba*, or sermon, performed by an *imam*, or prayer leader from the *mihrab* (an elevated structure in the mosque), in which there is usually a commentary upon topical affairs concerning the Islamic community.

Any discussion of prayer in Islam must include reference to the ablutions that Muslims must perform before performing the *salat*. Since the *salat* is considered to be an occasion when the believer speaks to God, it is little surprise that s/he must ensure the utmost condition of purity; after all, when Moses approached the sanctity of Mount Tuwa, and spoke to God, he was commanded to doff his sandals (20.12). The ablutions that Muslims perform (which are carried out with water, and if this is not available, with earth) have their basis in the Qur'an, which in 5.6 mentions four regions of the body that the believers should wash. These are their faces, their hands up to the elbow, their heads, and their feet up to the ankles. Although there are other forms of ablutions, it is not possible to discuss them here, for the present discussion of purity in Islam leads into an analysis of Sufism, the mystical dimension of Islam. Therefore, it is useful here to mention very briefly the interpretation of ablutions given by Ghazali, for his understanding of purity may have been inspired by the Qur'anic fourfold classification. Ghazali has been acclaimed the greatest Muslim after Muhammad (Watt 1962: 114), thus his 'spiritualization' of ablutions should be taken seriously. The first and highest form of purity is that of the innermost heart, and this is achieved by concentrating solely upon God. Second is the purity of the manifest heart from unworthy attributes, such as jealousy, pride, hypocrisy and greed. Third, Ghazali discusses the purity of bodily organs and limbs from sins, such as telling lies, and eating prohibited foods. The last form of purity is the cleanliness of the body and one's clothes, that is, the purity that is found in the literal understanding of 5.6 of the Qur'an (Ghazali 1983: 139–40).

2. Whereas the *salat* is an obligatory component of Islamic ritual, the *du'a'* is a private supplication, in the manner of a particular request. It does not necessarily have to glorify God, and the origin of this private supplication is found in the Qur'an: 'Supplicate me and I will respond to you' (40.60), and the Qur'an contains examples of how other prophets supplicated God (3.191, 93–4; 14.35–41).

3. Supererogatory prayers are those that glorify God but which are additional to the *salat*. They are mentioned in the Qur'an in 17.79, for the believer is encouraged to perform these prayers during the latter part of the night. 73.1–7 commands Muhammad to remain on vigil for more than half the night and to recite the verses of the Qur'an in a loud voice. In addition, the *hadith* mention supererogatory prayers, such as the following, which has God say that he acts through the believer:

> My servant never ceases drawing near to me through supererogatory works until I love him. Then, when I love him, I am his hearing through which he hears, his sight through which he sees, his hand through which he grasps, and his foot through which he walks.

The Sufis performed these supererogatory prayers five times daily (in addition to the five prescribed ritual prayers), in the morning, the mid-morning, early afternoon, between sunset and evening, and late at night.

4. Another form of prayer mentioned frequently in the Qur'an is the *dhikr*, which literally means remembrance; for example, 'O you who believe! Remember God with much remembrance' (33.41), 'And remember your Lord within yourself humbly and with awe, and under your breath by morning and evening' (7.205). *Dhikr* became an extremely important Islamic devotional practice.

5. Aside from the above prayers, many Islamic communities have their own particular prayers, some of which may be performed privately or in a group. For example, Shiites (see section 6.3) are fond of the Komayl prayer which is held on Thursday evenings, as well as prayers that are specific to certain months of the Islamic calendar, such as the litany recited during the month of Sha'ban.

If the *shahada* is a way to understand God, then prayer is the method by which the Muslim may believe that s/he feels or experiences the presence of God. In this respect prayer may be considered the most spiritual element in Islam, and many *hadith* and much of the Islamic tradition confirm this view. For example, there is a *hadith* that states that what the 'Night Ascent' was to Muhammad, prayer is to the believer. In other words, through prayer, the Muslim can enjoy direct communication with God. The remainder of this section will focus upon Islamic spirituality or mysticism, otherwise known as Sufism.

2.1 Sufism

'[The Sufis are] . . . the biggest society of sensible men there has ever been on earth.'
(Ted Hughes, cited in Geaves 2000: 66)

Sufism is a manifestation of Islamic belief and practice that has been interpreted in a variety of fashions, ranging from that which considers it to be the perfect expression of Islam to the view that regards it as a deviation from the 'pristine' version of Islam. Sufis themselves claim that the movement is derived from the example of Muhammad, although some mystics, typified by Abu Hafs Umar Suhrawardi (d. 1234), argued that the pre-Islamic prophets were Sufis (Sarraf 1991: 92). Contemporary Muslims such as Rahman view Sufism as a reflective, pietistic movement that commenced after the death of Muhammad (2000: 82). The word Sufism was used from the eighth century for a group of ascetics and mystics in the region of Iraq. It has been suggested that this was a period that witnessed the codification of Islamic law into four schools for the Sunnis, when Shiism began to take a definite form, and when the *hadith* literature was collected in authoritative volumes. In other words, each group in Islamic society was defining itself as a distinct entity, and those who stressed the esoteric dimension of Islam became known as Sufis (Danner 1972). Although there is no consensus concerning the origin of the term Sufism, it is generally accepted that it is derived from the Arabic *suf*, meaning wool. Therein lies a connection with those who adopted an ascetic lifestyle, such as Christian mystics of the Middle East who are known to have worn woollen garments. Yet at this time there was still great diversity among ascetics and mystics, some of whom did not describe themselves as Sufis.

By the eighth and ninth centuries, some mystics began to speculate on the possibility of witnessing God during their earthly existence. This contradicted those religious scholars of an exoteric ilk who maintained that it was possible to witness God only after death. Yet the mystics legitimized their claims with reference to two Qur'anic verses: 'Upon that day faces shall be radiant [i.e. through seeing God]' (75.22–3) and 'Glory be to him [God], who carried his servant [Muhammad] by night from the Holy Mosque to the Farthest Mosque' (17.1). This last verse is taken by the Sufis to refer to Muhammad's Night Ascent, which provided an example for generations of Sufis of the possibility of experiencing God – despite the sealing of prophecy that came with Muhammad's messengership. The Night Ascent is the archetypal journey to God, and the first detailed descriptions of such an ascent for individual Sufis are attributed to Bayazid Bastami (d. 874). It is worthy to note that Bastami is accredited with the ecstatic utterance 'Glory be to me, how great is my majesty.' For the more 'orthodox' theologians, such an exclamation smacked of self-deification (and bears a striking resemblance to the 'Glory be to him' ascent verse of the Qur'an).

Sufism began to flourish as a mass movement in the medieval period, as it was organized into groups that resembled Christian monastic orders. By the twelfth and thirteenth centuries these orders were distinctive due to the emphasis they placed on both obedience to the master, or leader of the order, and also to their particular practices by which the aspirant was supposed to draw closer to God. Despite the diversity of Sufi orders in the medieval period there were characteristics that revealed a degree of homogeneity between them. The practical link common among Sufi orders was the *dhikr*, and the theoretical element that was frequently discussed by Sufi masters concerned the nature of existence.

For many Sufis, the *dhikr* came to be a mantra, repeated hundreds or thousands of times. A typical *dhikr* was (and still is) the testament of Islam; others include the various names of God. Some Sufis prefer a verbal *dhikr*, others a silent *dhikr*, uttered under the breath, and it developed into a breathing exercise by which, according to Sufis, it is possible to determine the spiritual levels of the *dhikr*-reciter.

Individual Sufi masters engage in training aspirant Sufis, and the former understand the phenomena that their disciples witness (such as coloured lights, or stars, the moon and sun) when they recite the *dhikr*.

In essence, the *dhikr* is a practice that enables the aspirant to concentrate entirely upon God. Aziz Nasafi, a thirteenth-century Persian Sufi, described four levels of *dhikr* that reflect this idea. The first level is when the *dhikr* is verbal and the reciter's mind may wander away from God to other affairs of the world, such as business in the bazaar. The second level is when the reciter performs the *dhikr* verbally and also in the heart. At this level, the reciter is aware of his shortcomings and disobedience to God. The third level is both verbal and in the heart, and the reciter can perform worldly tasks in a formal manner, for his heart is still focused upon God, and so he is aware of his obedience to God. The final level occurs when the *dhikr* becomes dominant over the heart. This is the moment that God takes control, and the Sufi is unaware of him/herself. This last level is a point that introduces an interrelated discussion of the reality of existence, be it that of the individual or that of God, and of whether or not witnessing God is a result of God's reward for the Sufi's devotion.

It is possible to distinguish two main views with regard to the Sufi interpretation of the reality of existence. One of these is that expounded by Yahya Shihab al-Din Suhrawardi (d. 1191), who was influenced to a great degree by the works of the Islamic philosophers. Suhrawardi included a hierarchy of emanations from the Godhead in his mystical worldview, and understood the human task as a return to the Godhead back past the celestial emanations. Other Sufis, including Aziz Nasafi, preferred to describe existence as belonging to God alone, in which case the phenomena of the universe are regarded as either God's *manifest* dimension or else a reflection of God's existence. Nasafi's understanding of existence skirts the borders of pure monism, but he is always quick to assert the complete transcendence of the ultimate, *non-manifest* dimension of God that can only be theoretically posited, and cannot be grasped even by mystical insight. God can be known, but only to a limited degree. Describing God in such a manner was dangerous during several eras of history in parts of the Islamic world, because it offended those Muslims who held there was an utter distinction between man and God, and rejected any notion of mystical connection, let alone ontological unity. The 'traditionally' minded religious scholars therefore regarded the statements by Sufis such as Hallaj, who exclaimed, 'I am the Truth [i.e. God]', as blasphemous. More detailed theological discussions developed from the eleventh century onwards, perhaps as the Sufi response to the growth and influence of Islamic theology and philosophy. Yet, such speculative metaphysical discussions were peripheral to the practice of Sufism. It was held that by engaging in prayer, the *dhikr*, and other Sufi practices, metaphysical 'truths' would gradually be unveiled to the Sufi.

The Sufi masters stated that even if the Sufi engaged in ascetic practice and religious effort, there could be no guarantee that metaphysical truths would be revealed. However, a spiritual hierarchy or framework was established by which aspirants could understand the level of their progress on their ascent towards God. At any particular moment, the Sufi existed within a 'station' (*maqam*), and s/he entered this station on the basis of his or her own intellectual and practical effort. Indeed Sufis such as Ansari (d. 1089) described an elaborate system of stations (his list contained one hundred). Within each station, the Sufis considered it possible for God to bestow a 'state' or a mystical experience that would reflect the knowledge of that station. Thus the states experienced by Sufis in the station of 'trust in God' were different from those in the station of 'fear of God'. Yet reaching to a higher station became increasingly arduous, as did maintaining one's spiritual level. Thus the prophets and the so-called saints of Islam (Friends of God) abided in the most difficult levels of all.

The connection between the Sufi understanding of these stations and states and ritual Islamic practice such as prayer and purity seems to have its origin in the Qur'an: 'And during the latter part of the night, pray as an additional observance. For your Lord may raise you to a praiseworthy station' (17.79). And of course in order to perform prayers Muslims have to be ritually pure, so they perform ablutions.

Related to mystical states are two concepts which cannot be ignored in any discussion about Sufism, and which shed some light upon how Sufis understood the relationship between the believer and God. These two concepts are annihilation (*fana*) and subsistence (*baqa*), both of which are Qur'anic terms: 'Everything in [the earth] is annihilated, but the Face of your Lord, full of majesty and nobility, subsists' (55.26). By analysing these two concepts, the Sufis probed the nature of humanity. Just as Plato discussed man by using a metaphor of a charioteer with two horses (one urging to the sensual, the other to the spiritual or rational), so too the Sufis held that man is driven by his physical make-up to desire worldly things, whereas his intellectual or spiritual faculties urge him to higher matters. Such a division was highlighted in the Qur'an which states that man was made of clay (20.57), but that he became animated when God 'blew of his spirit' into Adam (15.29), the archetypal human being. In general, the aim of the Sufis in their practices is to make the spirit dominant over the body, and in this way they speak of annihilating or dominating everything that separates them from God. Thus, when the Sufi experiences a mystical state, the creaturely nature is annihilated, and what remains (or what subsists) is the spirit that originates from God. Herein lies the mystery of Islamic mysticism. Does the spirit pertain to the believer, God, or both? Celebrated Sufis such as Ibn Arabi (d. 1240) pointed out that the Qur'anic verses state that God blew *of* his spirit into Adam, rather than blowing his spirit into him. So although it appears there is some degree of identity between the two, a distinction is always preserved between them. For this reason, Ibn Arabi coined the famous phrase *helnot he*, meaning that in some respects humans are similar to God but in others they are not.

Throughout its history Sufism has been subjected to much criticism, and the following provides a summary of the most important arguments of its opponents.

1. Many Sufis discussed existence in terms of all things possessing an interior (or spiritual) meaning and exterior (or phenomenal) meaning. The interior meaning of prophecy is 'Friendship of God' (*walayat*), which is explained as the intimate relationship the individual shares with God, whereas prophecy pertains to the exoteric dimension of rituals and commands. So although prophecy came to an end with Muhammad, God's connection with the believer is maintained by the Friends of God (the Sufis). Discovering interior meanings through mystical experience sometimes resulted in interpretations about existence, Islamic law and ritual about which the more 'orthodox' jurists disapproved. Indeed some Sufis were accused of abandoning the holy law (*shariah*) and followed their own opinions without basing their judgement on Islamic tradition. One example of this concerns the consumption of wine (alcohol being forbidden according to Islamic law), and this was an accusation levelled in particular against a Sufi order named the Bektashi that had many members in Anatolia. Such criticisms may have been influenced by images of wine-drinking that appear frequently in Sufi poetry, yet properly understood, partaking of wine is a metaphor for the intoxicating love that God pours for the Sufis. In addition to concerns about the corrupting influence of wine were the fears concerning the Sufi practice of dancing to music (*sama'*). Beloved by many Sufis from the twelfth century onwards (and probably earlier), the *sama'* was believed to induce 'states', yet some religious scholars condemned the *sama'* as they thought it stimulated man's baser instincts. Indeed, it is known that during the *sama'*, some Sufis tore open their clothes and danced breast to breast with one another. Of course this has led to accusations of pederasty and the practice of gazing at beautiful young boys. Again, one has to understand the symbolism and meaning that Sufis found in the world of phenomena. For such mystics, it was quite legitimate to witness something of God in the character traits and physical attributes of those around

them, including young males. This did not mean that they engaged in homosexual activities; rather, most Sufi texts speak of chastity, or else of engaging in sexual relations with one's wife for the ultimate purpose of spiritual enlightenment.

One group of Sufis who achieved notoriety were the Qalandar, who are mentioned in manuscripts as early as the eleventh century but seem to have been widespread some two hundred years later. Their distinctive practices included a gypsy-like lifestyle (wandering throughout the Islamic world, from India through to North Africa), shaving their heads, eyebrows and chins (all contrary to the tradition of Muhammad), and donning green cloth or animal skins, all of which must have sent shockwaves through any city or village where they settled temporarily. In addition, they were accused of wine-drinking, of using hashish and of ignoring the rituals of the holy law, such as the five daily prayers and the communal obligations that Islam sets upon the individual. However, the Qalandars themselves argued that they were constantly with God and that their spiritual life with him took precedence over any obligation towards their fellow human beings. Even today, the Qalandars (also known as Malangs) survive in parts of Pakistan and India. They consider themselves as God's brides, keep themselves chaste and dress in female apparel on certain festivals (Ewing 1984). In essence, the Qalandar movement was primarily antinomian, perhaps with the aim of startling the Islamic community out of a preconceived, stagnant worldview.

2. A second criticism concerns the 'unveilings' that Sufis believed they had experienced which were interpreted by mystics (such as Nasafi and especially those of the school of Ibn Arabi) in a manner that held the scent of monism or pantheism. Despite the claim by such mystics that their worldview accepts neither absolute unity between man and God nor total separation, other Muslims have rejected the Islamic validity of Ibn Arabi's Sufism. 'Ibn Arabi was thoroughly monistic. This monism at the metaphysical level is undoubtedly pantheistic. To say that everything is a manifestation of God in its own measure is a form of polytheism' (Rahman 2000: 85). At the height of their ecstatic mystical experiences some Sufis uttered 'monistic' words or phrases that other Muslims considered blasphemous. One of the most famous cases is that of Hallaj, of 'I am the Truth [i.e. God]' fame, who was executed in 922, subsequent to certain political shenanigans. Hallaj's exclamation was problematic both for theologians who sought to distance God from his creation, and also for some Sufis who believed the secrecy of God's intimacy with man should be preserved among the Sufi elite. This explains the comment of Ghazali (himself a Sufi of great reputation) that 'the killing of him who utters something of this kind [i.e. "I am the Truth"] is better in the religion of God than the resurrection of ten others' (Ernst 1985: 14).

3. The ontological worldview of Ibn Arabi's existential school has been criticized because monism can result in relativism. If everything and everyone is a manifestation of God, then there is nothing profane in the world, and even Satan is performing God's will. So 'the monistic-pantheist mentality produced a . . . type of fatalism that could not fail to numb the moral faculties' (Rahman 2000: 89). This danger is connected with the idea of Islam being a social polity in which all members are supposed to play an active role. It has been claimed by some Muslims that ecstatic Sufism has resulted in its adherents withdrawing from society, epitomized in the following saying of Abdul Quddus of Gongoh, which was cited by Muhammad Iqbal, an Indian reformist of the early twentieth century: 'Muhammad of Arabia ascended the highest Heaven and returned. I swear by God that if I had reached that point, I should never have returned' (Iqbal 1934: 118).

4. Another reason for opposition to the Sufis can be explained by the political significance of a Sufi claiming to have knowledge of God. The religious scholars regarded themselves as guardians and

interpreters of Islamic law, and therefore they occupied a very influential place in society, frequently enjoying privileged access to the Caliph or Sultan. Since some Sufis claimed intimacy with God, it was believed by their followers that they would be in a better position to tell the community about God's will, rather than the religious scholars. Major Sufi figures such as Hallaj were frequently caught in the battles waged by intriguing politicians, and his execution had probably as much to do with the political manoeuvring within the royal court as it did with his ecstatic statements. Another major Sufi who was condemned to death by secular authorities was Yahya Suhrawardi (d. 1191) because his 'illuminationist political doctrine' sought to 'illustrate and legitimize his own idea of divine inspiration, with its manifest signs, as the basis for authority to rule' (Ziai 1992: 344). Yet there was no uniform Sufi view with regard to relations with political leaders. Some Sufis, such as Aziz Nasafi, advised followers to avoid all relations with men of position and titles, whereas other Sufi shaykhs, such as Ahrar (d. 1490), are known to have fostered good ties with political rulers in Central Asia, hoping to make them better Muslims.

The extent to which it has been possible for Sufism to enter the political sphere is perhaps best illustrated with reference to the Naqshbandi order, which was influential in the Ottoman empire and in Moghul India. The Naqshbandis have been characterized by a sober form of Sufism, in contrast to the ecstatic form with its distracting rites (Mardin 1991: 123), and this was of great assistance to the central authorities who desired to exercise control of peripheral areas through the implementation of a sober form of Sunnism. Naqshbandi influence has remained strong in modern Turkey as it was rumoured in the 1980s that the brother of the Turkish prime minister was a Naqshbandi as were five ministers (Mardin 1991: 134; Ayata 1991: 224). Indeed the Naqshbandis have even been labelled 'fundamentalist' because of their political-religious agenda (Mardin 1993).

5. Mention must also be made of Sufis who criticized charlatans adopting the trimmings of Sufism in order to deceive people and gain some kind of benefit. By the ninth century Sufis were associated with ascetics who attempted to flee the concerns of worldly life; however, this meant that such individuals occasionally had to rely on the charity of the faithful, and naturally the system was open to abuse. Indeed, a group known as the Banu Sasan became infamous as tricksters in conning people into giving alms. Sufis themselves, such as Hujwiri (d. 1063), recognized that 'true spiritualism is as rare as the philosopher's stone' (Hujwiri 1976: 7) and that 'today Sufism is a name without a reality, but formerly it was a reality without a name' (ibid.: 44). In the modern period accusations of charlatans abusing Sufi ideals have continued, including those from respected academics and politicians, such as Taha Hussein, Egypt's minister of education in 1950, Dean of the Faculty of Arts 1936–9 at the Egyptian University, and Nobel Literature Prize nominee.

Despite all of these criticisms, many believers claim that Sufism has enriched Islam in many ways, and there is a consensus among scholars that Sufism injected into Islam a much-needed measure of spirituality. This is in contrast to the religious works and arguments of the theologians and philosophers that are frequently characterized as dry and ossified, and which held little appeal for the majority of believers. Sufism inspired Muslims to speculate on God's immanent presence, and it permitted them to believe in the possibility of participating in direct experience of the divine. Islam for the mystics was not a matter of 'bland' ritual repetition; ritual there was, but each moment was pregnant with potential and possibility.

During the medieval period, many Sufis propagated the idea that 'everything is he [God]', that is, all existence, all humans, are manifestations of the divine. Given this, the conclusion that all beliefs are genuine representations of at least one level of truth is not too far removed. Viewed negatively, as reflected in the views of Rahman, such a belief can lead to relativism. Yet a more positive interpretation is that Sufism resulted in the integration of individuals into society. It provided a flexible framework that actively endorsed pluralism but at the same time regulated diversity within the religious tradition by advocating adherence to the five pillars at the manifest level. By the medieval period Sufism had evolved into a mass movement, and had become significant in the cohesion of society. This was particularly the case in periods of insecurity, such as in Central Asia and the Middle East before and after the devastating Mongol invasions of the thirteenth century. It has been claimed that the individuals of large cities such as Balkh were followers of Sufi shaykhs (Hujwiri 1976: 5). Moreover, the mystical influence extended beyond the orders, for there existed Sufi-inspired social institutions that were regulated by a Sufi code of ethics. This was the case of the *zur-khaneh* (literally, house of strength) in the Persian world, which was a gymnasium for males that served both as a semi-military bastion in times of threat, and also as a focus for charitable, chivalrous activity. At the regular gatherings of the *zur-khaneh*, the members engaged in physical exercises that were sometimes accompanied with the chanting of the didactic and ethical verses of Sufi poets. As an institution that inspired varying levels of social cohesion, identity and security, we should mention the influence that Sufism had upon the establishment of both particular wards within cities and the trade guilds. Thus Sufism extended into realms of theological speculation, ethics, politics, economics and art.

There can be little doubt that the impact of Western powers on Islamic lands since the beginning of the nineteenth century and the influence of increasingly secular thought has brought changes to Islam and Sufism. Within Islamic circles, thinkers have responded to these new circumstances, and although they have not rejected Sufism outright, they have desired certain reforms in the Islamic mystical tradition. For example, Muhammad Abduh (d. 1905), who was the leading religious scholar in Egypt at the turn of the nineteenth century, accepted Sufism so long as it discarded its superstitions. Ahmad Khan (1817–98) in India was much influenced by Western sciences and reason, and he called for Sufi interpretations that focused upon ethical teachings, and rejected the miraculous powers attributed to the various Sufi masters. (These miraculous powers included beliefs in the efficacy of curing the sick by writing prayers on pieces of paper that were then washed in water, which was then drunk by the patient as a cure.) Such an 'irrational' version of Sufism was described and rejected by many leading twentieth-century intellectuals, including Rashid Rida (1865–1935) in Egypt and Ahmad Kasravi (d. 1946) in Iran. Perhaps the most dramatic step was taken by Kemal Ataturk, who was the leader of the newly established Turkish republic. In 1925 the Sufi orders were outlawed in Turkey, their properties were appropriated by the government and public Sufi activity was banned.

Yet despite the criticisms by intellectual-rationalists (who regard Sufism as little more than a collection of superstitious beliefs), and also by politicians (whose attempts to undermine Sufism may be attributable in part to the fear of the masses who can be mobilized by the orders), Sufism remains a thriving force in many areas of the world. It has been estimated that more than one-third of the adult male population of modern Egypt are active Sufis (Gerholm 1997: 136). Mystical Islam also remains strong in virtually all areas of the Islamic world. Indeed, the pervasive nature of Sufism is reflected in the politics of many states: one of the most important examples of mystical influence is found in the worldview of Ayatollah Khomeini, which was partly based on the works of Ibn Arabi. It has even taken root in the West, and orders are flourishing in both Britain and the United States. One indication of this is the vast amount of Sufi literature that is now available, and in recent years, English translations of the thirteenth-century Persian mystical poet Rumi sell more than any other poet (*Christian Science Monitor* 25.11.97). Some interpretations of Sufism in the West have held an attraction for the educated classes, typified by the writings of Idris Shah and Doris Lessing. This kind of Sufism has been labelled 'Universal Sufism' because it minimizes the specific Islamic elements and concentrates on more universal spiritual values. However, the more 'traditional' form of Sufism in Britain is strong among the Barelvi Muslims (of Pakistani origin), and it has been claimed that 'Sufism in its variant manifestations is the dominant form of Islam as practised by most Muslims throughout the world' (Geaves 2000: 1).

3 FASTING (*SAWM*)

Fasting which is prescribed in 2.183–7 is in continuity with, and markedly different from, the previous semitic religions: both Judaism and Christianity have their own form of fasting; however, only the Islamic fast occurs in *Ramadan*, the month when the Qur'an was revealed to Muhammad. Islamic tradition heightened the sacred nature of this month, as Muhammad is reported to have said,

> The month of *Ramadan*, the month of blessings has come to you, wherein God turns towards you and sends down to you His special mercy, forgives your faults, accepts prayers, appreciates your competition for the greatest good and boasts to the angels about you. So show to God your righteousness; for verily, the most pitiable and unfortunate one is he who is deprived of God's mercy in this month.
>
> (Bakhtiar 1995: 50)

The descent of the Qur'an is associated by Muslims with the 'Night of Power', which according to 97.1–5 is 'a night better than a thousand months' because the angels and the Spirit come down to accomplish all commands. The exact date of the Night of Power is unknown, although it is thought to have occurred on an odd date during Ramadan, and therefore Muslims spend much of their time in retreat (*i'tikaf*) in mosques during this period, engaged in acts of worship. This practice is suggested in 2.187, and is also believed to have been the tradition of Muhammad himself. There are several elements to *i'tikaf*. First, the whole of the Qur'an is recited; each night a section is read, so that by the end of Ramadan, the Qur'an is completed in thirty sections. Second, in addition to the usual cycles of prayer, Muslims perform a special, non-compulsory prayer called the *Tarawih* and believers may also recite the *dhikr* more frequently. At the end of the month of Ramadan, Muslims commence the holiday, the *Ayd al-Fitr*, during which friends are visited, foods prepared, and the poor-due, or a charity offering, is given to the needy.

Fasting during Ramadan is a religious obligation, and it is a practice that is within the capacity of most physically healthy people. Yet there are exemptions for individuals who find difficulties in observing the fast, or else are incapable of committing themselves to it. That fasting includes aspects of a communal nature, such as spending time together in mosques, assists some individuals in observing its requirements. Yet, the Islamic fast does not necessitate a completely ascetic way of life, since after daylight hours believers are allowed to partake of food and drink, and engage in sexual relations with their spouses. Despite this, the famous Pakistani theologian Mawdudi (d. 1978) describes the fast during Ramadan as a period of 'sustained intensity' (1982: 186). This contrasts with the other prescribed acts of worship, for the pilgrimage to Mecca need only be performed once in a lifetime, the alms tax is paid once a year, and the *salat* takes a few minutes each day. Fasting during Ramadan may add up to a total of 360 hours, and this is no easy undertaking, and is a sure sign of faith. Mawdudi states that because it is a difficult religious command, many people might be tempted to break the fast in private, and for this reason, despite the communal activities that Muslims engage in during Ramadan, it is essentially a private affair between the individual and God. Since it may be broken in private, strict observance is a matter that can only be known by the individual and God, unlike performance of the pilgrimage, engaging in ritual prayer (especially the communal Friday prayers) and paying the alms tax, which are all witnessed by other members of the Islamic community. Given its arduous nature, it is hardly surprising that there are many *hadith* that affirm the reward that the faster will enjoy. Ghazali stated that fasting 'is distinguished from the other pillars of Islam by its special and peculiar position in relation to God, since He said through the mouth of His messenger "Every good deed will be rewarded from ten to seven hundred fold except prescribed fasting which is endured for My sake and which I shall reward"' (Bakhtiar 1995: 12).

Despite certain communal and ascetic dimensions of the fast, Muslim scholars have indicated that the purpose of engaging in this particular act of worship is to strengthen one's own piety and spirituality. Ghazali refers to this spiritual proximity in a short treatise entitled *The Mysteries of Prescribed Fasting* (Bakhtiar 1995: 12–27). The fast is of three kinds: one for the general public, another for the select few, and a third for the elite among the select few. The fasting of the general public is nothing more than refraining from satisfying the stomach and sexual appetite. The select few understand the fast as remaining vigilant and keeping the ears, eyes, tongue, hands and feet from doing wrong. Ghazali cites a *hadith* that states: 'Five things break the prescribed fast: the telling of lies, back biting, tale-bearing, perjury, and the casting of coveting and lustful eyes' (ibid.: 22). The elite among the select few, however, progress a stage further and view the fast as a fast of the heart which is broken by contemplating anything other than God. Such intense spirituality was taken by some Muslims beyond the parameters of Ramadan, typified by Abd al-Qadir Gilani (a contemporary of Ghazali) who exclaimed that religious fasting is limited by time, while spiritual fasting is forever and lasts throughout one's temporal and eternal life (ibid.: 169). Since the fast is intimately connected with the Qur'an, it is appropriate that the remainder of this section should examine this 'sacred text'.

3.1 The Qur'an

Indeed, it is a noble Qur'an, in a treasured book touched only by the purified.

(56.77–9)

Muslims believe that the Qur'an (which means 'recitation') is the word of God that was recited by the angel Gabriel to Muhammad, containing 114 chapters (*suras*), 6,236 verses (*ayas*) and 77,934 words. In recent years the claim that the Qur'an we possess today is the same as that Muhammad believed he had received has been questioned by a handful of non-Muslim, Western scholars. (The earliest extant manuscripts of the Qur'an are not complete, and are dated no earlier than 690, some sixty years after Muhammad's death.) The works of John Wansbrough have provoked much discussion in Western academic circles, and it is clear why many Muslims refute his argument that 'the Muslim scripture is not only composite, but also . . . that the period required for its achievement [i.e. its "canonization"] was rather more than a single generation [after Muhammad's death]' (1977: 44). Such research has been criticized for several reasons, one of them (acknowledged by Wansbrough himself) and perhaps the most frequently employed being that the Qur'an, as recitation, was received by an oral culture and preserved in the minds of believers until it was written down.

Academic speculation aside, the Qur'an has been (and remains for Muslims) a link between the believer and the divine, and is the reference point of all meaning. Faith in the sacred nature of God's word leads some Muslims to preserve the Qur'an from the touch of impure hands; moreover, many believers kiss the book before and after reading it, and out of respect allocate it the highest shelf in their bookcase. The Qur'an occupies the central role in the life of the Muslim; aside from being the basis of law (covering matters ranging from inheritance, marriage and divorce) it also provides a worldview that advocates its idea of virtuous living and harmonious human relations. All Muslims are encouraged to learn the Qur'an in Arabic, and to this end those Muslims living in the West in the modern age have established classes where their children learn the Qur'an in Arabic by rote. One of the most celebrated cases of a child-*hafiz* (a child who has memorized the Qur'an) in recent times is that of an Iranian, Seyyed Muhammad Tabataba'i, who, at the age of five, astounded Saudi Arabian officials during the 1997 Hajj pilgrimage with his knowledge of the Qur'an. Subsequently, Tabataba'i was taken to Europe to display his mastery of the Qur'an (*Echo of Islam*, 1997). Memorizing the Qur'an has been encouraged by groups that hold diverse Islamic interpretations, for many legalists and philosophers have been among the ranks of the *hafiz*, as have the Sufis. The sixteenth-century Persian mystic Jami expressed this poetically: 'A Sufi who does not know the Qur'an by heart is like a lemon without a scent' (Schimmel 1983: 131). It has provided the inspiration for much spiritual activity (as already noted during the month of Ramadan), and is the source of Islamic liturgy. Indeed, it is necessary for Muslims to learn some sections of the Qur'an in order for the *salat* to be performed properly. The *fatiha* of the Qur'an is always included in the *salat*, which is incomplete without the perfect recitation of other verses of the Qur'an. One recent work gives an indication of the reverence that a middle-class family had for the Qur'an in Iran some thirty years ago when the Shah was attempting to create a more secular society:

> At every important moment of life people had recourse to the Koran; a verse was pinned onto a new-born baby's clothing, during the marriage ceremony people absorbed themselves in reading the Koran at one point and the young bride had her photograph taken with the Book in her hand; you passed under the Koran three times . . . before going on a journey; you consulted it through a religious authority before taking any important decision; it was used to ward off bad luck, in case of illness for example, and naturally there were recitals from it for the dead. Daily life was placed under its protection; the pediments of houses were often decorated with ceramic or wrought iron verses.
>
> (Adelkhah 1999: 106)

And the observation of C. Padwick still rings true for many Muslims: '[The Qur'an] lives on among its people, [it is the] stuff of their daily lives, taking for them the place of a sacrament. For to them these are not mere letters or words. They are the twigs of the burning bush aflame with God' (1961: 119). The Qur'an provides many expressions which have become familiar even in English. These include *insha' Allah* (or 'God willing' which is used for actions of intent in the future), *masha' Allah* (or 'what God willed' which is used to convey surprise at a fortuitous outcome) and *al-hamd Allah* (or 'praise be to God'). One has to agree with Schimmel, who noted that the sound of the Qur'an 'defines the space in which the Muslim lives' (1994: 150). If the sound of the Qur'an assists in the focus of Islamic identity, then so too does visual contemplation of the written Qur'anic word. Several styles of calligraphy developed in the course of Islamic history, and producing exquisitely handwritten copies of the Qur'an has been considered a major act of piety and art. Indeed some Muslims find the written word of the Qur'an present everywhere in the world of phenomena, as Renard states: 'God is the calligrapher who writes with the pen of the human heart. Every beautiful face is like a flawlessly executed copy of the Qur'an' (1996: 127).

Yet the Qur'an is not easy to comprehend, as Islamic scholars have indicated:

> The reader may find . . . [the Qur'an] . . . so foreign to his notion of what a book should be that he may become so confused as to feel that the Qur'an is a piece of disorganised, incoherent and unsystematic writing, comprising nothing but a disjointed conglomeration of comments of various lengths put together arbitrarily. Hostile critics use this as a basis for their criticism, while those more favourably inclined resort to far-fetched explanations, or else conclude that the

Qur'an consists of unrelated pieces, thus making it amenable to all kinds of interpretation, even interpretations quite opposed to the intent of God Who revealed the Book.

(Mawdudi 1988: 8)

And European critics such as the Scottish essayist Thomas Carlyle (1795–1881) have also voiced their opinion about problems they have faced when reading the Qur'an:

I must say, it is as toilsome reading as I ever undertook. A wearisome confused jumble, crude, incondite; endless iterations, long windedness, entanglement; most crude, incondite; – insupportable stupidity, in short! Nothing but a sense of duty could carry any European through the Koran.

(1840, reprint 1869: 233)

3.2 The Qur'an as a text

One Muslim scholar, al-Qurtubi (d. 1258), listed several reasons why the Qur'an should be considered a miraculous book.

1 its language excels all other Arabic language
2 its style excels all other Arabic style
3 its comprehensiveness cannot be matched
4 its narrations about the unknown can only result from revelation
5 its lack of contradiction with the sound natural sciences
6 its fulfilment of all that it promises, both good tidings and threat
7 the knowledge it comprises (both legal and concerning the creation)
8 its fulfilment of human needs
9 its effect on the hearts of men.

(Von Denffer 1985: 149)

Many of these arguments do not stand up to the kind of literary criticism that has developed in the West (see, for example, A. Jasper, 1.8, D. Jasper, 3). This is especially the case with the first two points, which depend entirely upon one's context and preferences, for, of course, tastes in literary style change over the course of time. The third point, moreover, may be true for some believers who view the comprehensiveness of the Qur'an in *general* terms, rather than particular. The argument depends on what is meant by 'comprehensiveness', for the Qur'anic injunctions about 'mundane' topics such as inheritance, divorce, etc., are more particular than those found in the Gospels. However, the Hebrew Bible provides more extensive laws than those found in the Qur'an concerning dietary laws. The fourth point, narrations about the unseen and the unknown, is also problematic, such as the Qur'anic 'prophecy' of Islam's victory over other religions (9.33). Does this mean the immediate victory of Islam over its neighbours in the years following Muhammad's death? Does it mean the Ottoman conquest over Constantinople and the Balkans? And what should modern Muslims make of this verse in the light of the nineteenth and twentieth centuries? Is it justifiable to say that Islam is victorious, in the present day, over other religions? Some may say that it is. But the important point to make is that these points raised by a medieval Islamic scholar are not watertight in the modern age. Some Muslims may believe several points remain valid, but they certainly require different explanations as to why they are so.

However, it is clear that the Qur'an remains a source of immense inspiration and is the very basis of contemporary Islamic life for those Muslims who are aware of the implications of modern literary criticism. Such Muslims find a modern meaning to the concept of *i'jaz*, or the miraculous nature of the Qur'an, a topic to which we shall return in due course.

The non-Muslim has difficulty in appreciating the value of the Qur'an (even as a non-sacred text) for several reasons. The first is the linguistic barrier, for *Arabic recitation* of the Qur'an, regardless of its 'sacred' nature, contains sounds and literary structures that will be missed by non-Arabic speakers. Second, the non-Muslim from the West is usually more familiar with texts that have a linear structure, in other words, a distinct beginning, middle and end. The Qur'an, for the 'un-initiated', does not have a linear structure, and neither does it present a systematic portrayal of Muhammad's life, and it is only after much study that its shape appears. The appreciation of the Qur'an's structure has commenced in the West; for example, one scholar suggests that the Qur'an reflects an apocalyptic worldview, and given the imminence of this apocalypse, the fundaments of belief (which are belief in God, God's judgement of man, and the resurrection) are repeated regularly so that believers would not be surprised or confused when reminded of them continually; as Marshall Hodgson remarks, 'Almost every element which goes to make up its message is somehow present in any given passage' (cited in Brown 1991: 89). And Norman Calder, an eminent Islamicist, witnessed the Qur'an's internal cohesion: 'Contained between a prayer and a prayer, drawing together past time (narrative), time present (law), and time future (apocalypse), rhythmic in its themes, and in its language, with patterns of recurrence and patterns of development, and an overall flow towards a pre-ordained end, the intimate giving of its closure and parting – few books are so obviously unified, so obviously demand to be experienced as a whole' (1997: 54). Third, non-Muslims unlike believers do not bring with them the baggage of 1,400 years of history that includes commentaries and interpretations of the Qur'an, legends and stories about the life of Muhammad and his companions, and their own personal experiences and expectations of Islam. Such baggage may assist Muslims to comprehend vague and obscure passages, and thus strengthen their belief in the Qur'an's sacred nature, but at the same time it may also lead them to understand any section of the Qur'an in a manner that differs from a literal reading of that section. The following addresses these three issues in more detail.

1. First is the issue of the Qur'an in Arabic. As God's very speech revealed in Arabic (a point stressed several times in the Qur'an) it is held that in some way, *Arabic* recitation of the Qur'an provides a greater degree of proximity between the Muslim and God than non-Arabic recitation. Some Muslims hold that a translated Qur'an diminishes the sacred nature of the book, and the permissibility of rendering the Qur'an into a non-Arabic tongue has been a contentious issue. It was not until the medieval period that it was translated into Persian, and only in 1822 into Urdu. The Qur'anic stress of the 'Arabic' revelation caused some scholars to speculate that there was a period in which it is possible to speak of the 'Arabization' of Islam (see p. 269). Although this view has been rejected by most scholars, it is indeed the case that Arabs today take great pride that the Qur'an was revealed in Arabic, and perhaps is an important component of contemporary Arab nationalism within an Islamic worldview, as well as being one of the components that provides Muslims with a sense of unity.

2. The second issue, namely whether or not the Qur'an possesses a coherent structure, is a weightier matter by far. 'Standard' Islamic belief (if one can speak of such a thing) states that the order of the *suras* had been established by God, since there is a *hadith* which says: 'Gabriel used to repeat the recitation of the Qur'an with the Prophet once a year, but he repeated it twice with him in the year he [the Prophet] died' (Bukhari, *Sahih*, 6.520). This suggests to Muslims that the original structure of the

Qur'an was divine and perfect. However, Muslims faced the prospect of losing this 'perfect' Qur'an following the death of many companions of Muhammad who had memorized the Qur'an. Therefore, during the Caliphate of the third caliph, Uthman (d. 656), it was decided to write down the revelations for fear of losing or forgetting them. To this end, those companions who had their own *ayas* or *suras* of the Qur'an (which may have been scribbled down on parchment or palm leaves) were brought together to compile the revelations in the form of a book. Some Western scholars believe that it is at this stage of the process of assembling the Qur'an into book form that the *ayas* of one period of revelation may have become mixed with those from another period. This, of course, would have had an impact on the style, cohesion and coherence of the book. One issue of debate concerning the structure of the Qur'an concerns the order of the *suras*, and the following is a summary of some of these:

a   After the *fatiha*, the *suras* appear to be ordered on the basis of their length, thus the longest *sura*, al-Baqara, comes after the *fatiha*, and this is followed by the second longest *sura*, al-'Imran. However, the order of the *suras* based on decreasing length breaks down very quickly (the longest ten *suras* in order are 2, 4, 3, 7, 6, 5, 9, 11, 16, 10). It has been suggested that this trend of decreasing length of *suras*, matched also by a transition from long *ayas* to short *ayas* within the *suras*, is a literary device that points the reader to the end or closure of a section (Calder 1997: 53).

b   After 29 *suras*, following the expression 'in the name of God', there appears an individual letter of the Arabic alphabet, or else a group of several letters. Some scholars have argued that these letters are not part of the revelation of the Qur'an itself, rather, they were added when the command was issued by Uthman to compile an authoritative Qur'an, which meant comparing and contrasting the various versions possessed by several of Muhammad's companions. The letters, it is argued, are abbreviations of the names of these companions. However, other scholars believe that these letters were part of the original Qur'an, for *sura* 26 starts with the following: '*Tah, Sin, Mim*. Those are the signs of the Manifest Book.' One of the interesting points to note is that the 29 *suras* which have the 'mysterious letters' seemed to be grouped together. Thus *suras* 2 and 3 start with ALM, as do 29, 30, 31 and 32, and 40–46 begin with HM.

c   It has been argued that other factors that have influenced the order of some of the *suras* include the date of revelation, main topics of the *sura*, and the introduction of the *sura*. For example, *suras* 57–66 are kept together despite their varying length because, it is claimed, they were revealed at the same period in Medina. *Suras* 10–15 describe the prophets, and 91, 92, 93 and 95 begin with an oath.

The above discussion has highlighted that there are many unresolved questions related to the order of the *suras*, the mysterious letters, and the structure of the Qur'an. The *suras* may have been so ordered on the basis of several of the above conditions. Commenting on the structure of the Qur'an, Shah Waliullah, the eigthteenth-century Indian theologian, observed that it resembles a collection of epistles by a king, which often have the same themes but which nonetheless differ from one another because they were composed at different times and for different situations (Robinson 1996: 270). For example, the story of Moses' rod transforming into a serpent occurs in 7.117 – a late Meccan *sura* – in 20.20 – an early Meccan *sura* – and in 26.32 – a middle Meccan *sura*.

One valid question that may be asked regarding the order of the *suras* concerns just why Muslims and non-Muslims have spent so much time investigating this topic. The answer is that it is essential to know which *ayas* are abrogating *ayas* and which are abrogated (in other words, which *ayas* were revealed to replace previous *ayas*). Only in this way is it possible to comprehend the 'perfect religion' of Islam, or the final and complete Holy Law that God sent to humanity. On this basis Muslims reject any claim that abrogation is a way to explain that God 'changed his mind' or that Muhammad was making up the verses in response to new contexts. (See for example *aya* 16.101, 'And if We replace an *aya* by another – and God knows best what He reveals – they [the non-believers] say: "You [Muhammad] are only a forger."'

Since the *ayas* were revealed at different stages of Muhammad's prophetic life it is not surprising to discover some that appear contrary to others: some *ayas* praise the People of the Book (Jews and Christians) and others portray them in a negative light. One of the most commonly cited examples of *ayas* that indicate a change in position are those that concern the consumption of intoxicating drink. Wine is considered in a positive manner in *sura* 16.67: 'And from the fruits of palms and vines, you get wine and fair provision. Surely, there is in that a sign to a people who understand.' This *aya* is tempered by 2.219: 'They ask you about wine and gambling, say: "In both there is great sin and some benefit for people. But the sin is greater than benefit."' And then, an increasing negativity towards wine is revealed in 4.43, which exclaims: 'O believers, do not approach prayer while you are drunk.' This *aya* does not proscribe consuming intoxicating drinks at all times; however, 5.90 goes a stage further: 'O believers, wine, gambling, idols and divining arrows are an abomination of the Devil's doing; so avoid them that perchance you may prosper.'

To repeat, Muslim scholars were at pains to determine the chronology of revelation to arrive at the final form of the Holy Law. The concern to discover abrogating *ayas* contributed no doubt to the development of Islamic sciences, since the occasion of revelation (*asbab al-nuzul*) could be determined, it was argued, by referring to the *hadith*, and through linguistic and contextual analysis of the Qur'an. However, those scholars who assiduously cling to the concept of abrogation deny the universal spirit of the Qur'an, as perceived by F. Rahman (see p. 282), and miss its apocalyptic style in presenting the whole in every part: 'It does not matter in what order you read the Koran: it is all there all the time; and it is supposed to be all there all the time in your mind or at the back of your mind, memorized and available for appropriate quotation and collage into your conversation or writing, or your action' (Brown 1991: 90).

3.   It is He who sent down upon you the book in which are clear *ayas* that are the essence of the book, and others ambiguous. As for those in whose hearts are swerving, they follow the ambiguous part, desiring dissension, and desiring its interpretation, and none knows its interpretation save only God.

(3.7)

The Qur'an admits that some of its *ayas* are unclear or ambiguous, and it is the nature of humans that religious texts (especially the 'ambiguous') be interpreted to reflect new contexts. Interpretation of the Qur'an, however, has been carried out by 'orthodox' believers according to a hierarchical structure of rules. First, 'ambiguous' *ayas* of the Qur'an should be understood or explained with reference to other Qur'anic *ayas*. This necessarily means that anyone who undertakes such a study should know the occasion of revelation of each *aya*, and therefore be able to establish whether any particular *aya* has been abrogated. Second, Muslim interpretation rested on the *hadith* literature from Muhammad, then the sayings of his companions, then those that followed them, and finally from material and knowledge derived from Jews and Christians.

Yet there were differences among Muslims in Qur'anic interpretation, notably between the Sunnis and Shiites. One of the most well-known examples is found in *aya* 3.7, which for Sunnis reads: 'None knows its [the Qur'an's] interpretation save only God. And those firmly rooted in knowledge, they say: "We believe in it; all is from our Lord."' However, Shiites claim that there are no punctuation marks in the earliest manuscripts of the Qur'an, and therefore the following is a permissible reading of the *aya* in question: 'None knows its interpretation, save only God and those firmly rooted in knowledge; they say, "We believe in it; all is from our Lord."' Those firmly rooted in knowledge according to the Shiites are their leaders, or *Imams* (see pp. 275ff.).

Beyond differing interpretations of the Qur'an based on grammar, there have been interpretations found through the discovery of new meanings in the text. In this respect the Sufis should be mentioned. Mystics including Ayn al-Quzat Hamadani (d. 1131), one of Iran's most celebrated Sufis, were fond of citing the following *hadith*: 'Indeed there is an outer meaning and an inner meaning for the Qur'an, and its inner meaning has another inner meaning up to seven inner meanings' (Ayn al-Quzat 1962: 3). And modern Islamic interpretations of the Qur'an vary from those who adopt a literalist position on certain *ayas*, to those such as the contemporary Iranian thinker Abd al-Karim Soroush who discusses *aya* 3.7 cited above, and claims that every verse of the Qur'an has been suspected of being ambiguous at one time or another (Soroush 1998: 249).

3.3 Limits of interpretation

Related to the idea of interpretation of the Qur'an is the issue of what Muslims can say about their own belief, and how Islamic concepts and motifs can be utilized to express beliefs, experiences and ideas. The most controversial case in recent years is, of course, Salman Rushdie's *Satanic Verses*. The book works on several levels: it is a critique of a British society that has been characterized as 'Islamophobic', and it also asks significant theological questions of Islam (and indeed of many other religious traditions). The issue that concerns us here centres on the issue of the Satanic Verses, that is, the episode reported in Islamic history when Muhammad believed he had received revelations legitimizing the intercession of Arab deities between the non-Muslims and God. The Qur'an later stated that these were not in fact 'revelations' but whisperings from Satan. Rushdie utilizes this episode (and barely disguises its origin) to make a legitimate point: how does anyone know that the divine has been experienced? More specifically for Islam it begs the question of the authenticity of the Qur'an being God's word, and the role of Muhammad in the revelatory process.

Islamic theologians have decidedly rejected any active involvement by Muhammad in the process, and any attempt to explain revelation has been extremely difficult, even in the modern period. Thus Fazlur Rahman's following remarks caused public demonstrations in Pakistan:

> The Qur'an is thus pure Divine Word, but of course, it is equally intimately related to the inmost personality of the Prophet Muhammad whose relationship to it cannot be mechanically conceived like that of a record. The Divine Word flowed through the Prophet's heart.
>
> (Rahman 1966: 33)

The articulation of wrath by those who consider certain interpretations of religion to be blasphemous is a major obstacle for the development of artistic and original responses, Islamic in nature and inspired by the Qur'an, to the problems that Muslims experience in the modern age. Religious wrath has its source in voices that reject Western cultural hegemony, and are intolerant of interpretations of Islam other than their own. Typical of such voices was that of Sayyid Qutb, the leader of the Muslim Brotherhood in Egypt who was executed in 1966, and who advocated the use of violence against those who did not accept his brand of Islam (even though they professed allegiance to other interpretations of Islam). This type of worldview regards 'Holy Scripture' as sacred, immutable and perfect, and therefore not to be made the subject of any parody or criticism. Muslims who encourage imaginative interpretations of Scripture in response to the requirements of the contemporary age are frowned upon by those of Sayyid Qutb's ilk. It is not, perhaps, an exaggeration to say that a cloud of fear hangs over some regions of the Middle East, such as Egypt, where certain 'Islamic' groups engage in acts of terror against literary and academic individuals who have attempted to make the Qur'an comprehensible and relevant in the modern age. Indeed, even official Islam in Egypt, in the form of al-Azhar, the leading Islamic University that is supported by the Egyptian government, has played a major role in weeding out literary works that it considers blasphemous. It may be useful to cite just two examples of how the 'extremist' interpretation of Islam has gagged some representatives of the literary establishment.

In July 1999 al-Azhar was responsible for banning ninety-four books from the bookshop of the American University of Cairo. One of those censored was Khalil Gibran's famous work *The Prophet*, which is said to be the most widely read book of the twentieth century (Fisk 1999: 13). The ban on *The Prophet* had nothing to do with the content between the covers. The problem lay with the cover itself, which depicted a sketch by Gibran of a youthful man that al-Azhar believed was a picture of Muhammad. (The portrayal of Muhammad contravenes Islamic tradition, which is based on two Qur'anic *ayas* (5.92; 59.24).)

Another literary work that has been surrounded in controversy in Egypt is *Children of Gebelawi* (*Awlad al-Haratina*), written by the 1988 Nobel Prize winner for literature, Najib Mahfouz. *Children of Gebelawi* was serialized in an Egyptian newspaper in 1959, but it was heavily criticized by the authorities in al-Azhar, and subsequently has never been published in book form in Egypt. Mahfouz's intellectual leanings are reflected in the major themes of the book: socialism, science and social justice. It is both these themes and also the form of *Children of Gebelawi* that provoked the uproar. Mahfouz divided his book into 114 chapters (the same as the number of *suras* in the Qur'an), and proceeded to describe how the attempts of humanity to save itself from tyranny have failed. Gebelawi (or God) is described as the owner of a big house, and is portrayed as sick, old and incompetent. Subsequent chapters focus on his sons (prophets) that some Muslims would consider pejorative. For example, Jabal (Moses) is presented as a magician, Rifa'a (Jesus) is described as effeminate, and Qasim (Muhammad) is characterized as a womanizer and a madman. Finally, Mahfouz brings the chain of prophets/reformers to an end with Arafa, an individual who personifies science and knowledge. Arafa indirectly kills Gebelawi (God), and suggests that science is the religion of our time.

Aside from al-Azhar's criticisms, Mahfouz was condemned by the Egyptian populist preacher Shaykh Kishk, and a *fatwa* was issued against him by Shaykh Abd al-Rahman, who said, 'If such an edict [*fatwa*] had been published years ago, Rushdie would never have dared to publish his blasphemies' (Netton 1996: 81). (Rahman himself was implicated in the bomb explosion at the World Trade Centre in New York in 1993 in which six people were killed and over a thousand injured.) In 1994, Mahfouz was attacked and stabbed in the neck as he was walking in a Cairo street. The fury of the Islamic 'extremists' was based on Mahfouz's depiction of God as weak, and eventually dying, the disrespect shown to the prophets, and the portrayal of a new prophet after Muhammad, who according to Islamic tradition is the seal and last prophet.

It is always problematic to make generalizations about 'extremists' within any religious tradition. Such 'extremists' certainly do not represent the majority of the Egyptian population, and al-Azhar, despite its draconian measures against Gibran and Mahfouz, has not made an official call for the execution of any modern literary individual (even Salman Rushdie). The articulation of religious wrath, however, is not unique to the modern age, for it is possible to cite other examples of religious rage and intolerance of 'otherness' in Islamic history, such as the *Mihna* (see p. 233) and the execution of Sufis who claimed a relationship to God that was too close for the more 'orthodox' religious establishment. In addition, religious wrath appears in all religious traditions, and it is certainly not an essential characteristic of Islam. If Islam is to be judged on the basis of the Qur'anic text alone, then the comments of Fazlur Rahman provide a balanced and fair assessment of its literal message. He sees 'a unitary and purposive will creative of order in the universe: the qualities of power or majesty, of watchfulness or justice and of wisdom attributed to God in the Qur'an with unmistakable emphasis are, in fact, immediate inferences from the creative orderliness of the cosmos' (1966: 34).

Moreover, it is a relatively easy task to find a compassionate voice when sifting through Islamic history, a typical example being Islam's relatively generous and peaceful treatment of non-Muslims when Europe was persecuting various Christian sects and Jews in the medieval period. In addition, each generation of Muslim scholars and theologians has thrown up imaginative interpretations of the Qur'an, and in every age there has been an abundance of Sufi literature that on the whole is inclusive and pluralist in nature. The comments of Ayn al-Quzat Hamadani provide a useful example: 'Do you think that the glorious Qur'an is a [specific] address to [just] one group, or a hundred, or even a hundred thousand groups? Each *aya*, even each letter is an address to one person, but the intention is for another person, or another wise man' (1962: 8).

Indeed, Islam's tolerant voice has even permitted parody, such as the famous work of the blind Syrian poet al-Ma'arri (d. 1057). His *Epistle of Forgiveness* utilizes the same literary devices as the Qur'an (such as opening with oaths, short rhyming sentences), and employs strikingly similar images to the Qur'an that describe the natural world that is common to the Middle East, and warnings of impending doom. Nicholson (1930: 318) believes that al-Ma'arri wrote verses in response to the Qur'anic challenge for someone to compose *suras* like those found in the Qur'an. When this challenge was not taken up (in other words, when a new religion did not appear), Muslims began to argue that this failure was an indication of the special nature of the Qur'an. Islamic scholars employed the word *i'jaz* (literally, incapacitation) to describe the inability of humans to produce anything like the Qur'an. Early Muslim thinkers held that *i'jaz* was due to the Qur'an's sublime style and beauty of expression, and others argued that it was actually the result of God preventing humans from imitating it. Moreover, Muslims were convinced that *i'jaz* proved the miracle of Muhammad's messengership. Although there is historical evidence of a few attempts to produce *suras* similar to those in the Qur'an – such as those by Muhammad's contemporaries Zayd ibn Amr and Musaylima (Peters 1994a: 125, 158) – it is probably the case that subsequent attempts were regarded as a challenge to those in authority, including the Caliph and religious scholars, and so these attempts were suppressed. (One of the most recent examples of suppression of post-Qur'anic 'sacred' texts occurred between 1847 and 1850 in Iran when Ali Muhammad Shirazi, also known as the 'Bab', produced a 'divine' text called the *Bayan*. In 1850 he was executed following an alliance between the secular and spiritual authorities.) A modern Egyptian scholar of Islam, Nasr Hamid Abu Zaid, has also indicated that opening up new discussions on *i'jaz* remains dangerous. Yet his own works suggest that the effectiveness and continuing relevance of the Qur'an constitutes *i'jaz*, which in this way becomes subjective rather than normative:

> The Qur'anic language captured the imagination of the Muslims and the Arabs from the very moment of its revelation, and . . . it affected almost every field of knowledge: theology, philosophy, mysticism, linguistics, literature, literary criticism, and the visual and other arts. The linguistic structure employed in the exposition of God represents only an example (a very representative one however) that illustrates the very specific nature of the Qur'anic *parole* in its relation to the Arabic *langue*. It seems that *parole* in this specific case dominates *langue* by transforming the original signs of its system to act as semiotic signs within its own system. In other words, the Qur'anic language comes to dominate the Arabic language by transferring its linguistic signs to the sphere of semiotics, where they refer only to one absolute reality which is God . . . The

function of such a transformation is to evade the seen reality in order to establish the unseen Divine Reality of God; that is why everything in the whole of seen reality, from the top to the bottom, is, according to the Qur'an, nothing but a 'sign' which refers to God.

(Abu Zaid 1998: 209–10)

Abu Zaid's argument, of course, can be applied to other sacred texts of other religious traditions (e.g. pre-modern Judaism and Christianity). It can also be applied to texts which have assumed 'sacred' dimensions, but which are not 'religious' in the conventional sense of the word. Such an interpretation still leaves the writer open to the criticism and threat of others who understand *i'jaz* in a more 'normative' fashion.

In the case of al-Ma'arri, it has been suggested that he held 'revelation' to be a product of the human mind (Nicholson 1930: 317), yet it seems he was not faced by the articulation of anger experienced by Abu Zaid (who was hounded out of Egypt and into Europe). Nicholson adds appropriately, 'we may wonder that the accusation of heresy brought against him was never pushed home and had no serious consequence' (ibid.: 320). In other words, the articulation of wrath may be sounded only when the beliefs and lifestyles of individuals become threatened, and this does not seem to have been the case in the community in which al-Ma'arri lived. Indeed, he must have felt secure enough to compose the following:

Hanifs [Muslims] are stumbling, Christians all astray,
Jews wildered, Magians far on error's way.
We mortals are composed of two great schools –
Enlightened knaves or else religious fools.
(Nicholson 1930: 318)

In the secular West, space is allocated for both 'traditional' expressions of religious devotion and more 'imaginative' forms of religion and cultural sentiment. One wonders to what extent this will be permitted for Islam in the East and in the West in the twenty-first century. Much will depend on how Muslims perceive religious institutions, and to what degree they desire to follow the norms and regulations that such institutions establish. It will be interesting to see what effect the Western scepticism of institutions has upon Muslims living in the West, and also whether the challenges of modernity, advances in education levels and increasing degrees of information technology inspire Muslims to meditate on the Qur'an and emerge with new interpretations of Islam that are compatible with their heritage and the modern age.

4 THE ALMS TAX (*ZAKAT*)

Those who spend their wealth in the way of God are like a grain [of wheat] that grows seven ears, each carrying a hundred grains. God multiplies further to whom he will.

(2.266)

Like fasting, *zakat* (or paying the alms tax) has a religious pedigree according to the Qur'an, as it is associated with prophets prior to Muhammad (Jesus and Isma'il in 19.30, 54; Isaac and Jacob in 21.73; and Moses in 7.156). In its lexical origin, *zakat* is not an Arabic word, most probably it is derived from the Syriac or Aramaic word *zakutha*, meaning purity. However, the Qur'anic term *zakat* came to signify a form of obligatory charity or alms tax that was seen as a means of purifying the believer's wealth. *Aya* 92.18 speaks of the person who offers his wealth in self-purifcation, and further connections between paying the *zakat* and purification are suggested in those Qur'anic *ayas* where *zakat* is mentioned directly after ritual prayer (which is invalid without the purifying ablutions). *Aya* 2.42 is typical of at least ten others: 'Perform the prayer, give the alms-tax and bow down with those who bow down.' In addition to *zakat*, the Qur'an speaks of another form of charity, namely *sadaqa*, which also appears to function as a tool for purification. *Aya* 9.104 exhorts: 'Take of their wealth a free-will offering (*sadaqa*) to purify them.' Purity then is the link between prayer and *zakat* as Murata and Chittick have indicated: 'Just as ablutions purify the body and *salat* purifies the soul, so *zakat* purifies possessions and makes them pleasing to God' (1994: 16). Another way that Muslims have considered *zakat* is exemplified in the works of Mawdudi. He states that the *zakat* should be understood as a sacrifice of one's wealth, and this prepares the believer for the ultimate sacrifice which is to lay down one's life in the way of God (1982: 215).

It is also stressed in the Qur'an that the manner of giving charity is vitally important. *Aya* 2.276 advises believers to make charity offerings in secret, giving to the poor, and this will atone for sins. Moreover, when one makes a donation, there should be no niggardliness (47.38), nor should it be considered a fine (9.98). And believers should not be arrogant about their donations (2.269). The alms-tax is frequently contrasted with usury, which is prohibited (30.37). In fact, alms is compared in the Qur'an to a loan given by the individual to God, for which the believer is promised a great reward (5.12; 30.39).

Aside from its function of purifying believers' wealth, the payment of *zakat* may have contributed in no small way to the economic welfare of the Muslim community in Mecca. It has been argued, however, that during the Meccan period when Muslims were few in number, *zakat* was an unnecessary form of private charity (Schacht 1934). This view is hard to reconcile with the fact that Muhammad's Meccan adversaries imposed a trade boycott on the Muslims, and several felt it necessary to emigrate for a while to Abyssinia. It is generally agreed that payment of the *zakat* became obligatory during the Medinan period. At this time the need for charity increased because the conflict in which the nascent Muslim community found itself necessitated finance for fighting, and also resulted in higher numbers of Muslims who were orphaned, or widowed, sick or injured, and needed looking after (2.278).

In addition to its function as a tool of purification and as financial assistance, *zakat* also contained a degree of political significance that should not be overlooked. The payment of *zakat* by various Arabian tribes during the Medinan period was an explicit acknowledgement that Islam had been accepted.

It appears that the exact amount of *zakat* was not fixed during Muhammad's lifetime, but was established by the first Caliph, Abu Bakr. The Sunni law-schools settled the amount of tax on various products, such as 10 per cent on fruits and crops, and 2.5 per cent on gold and silver and merchandise. As with the other Islamic injunctions, the *zakat* is practical in that the poor are not obliged to pay. If a believer's income does not reach a certain ceiling, then he is exempt from payment. Of course, the more spiritually minded in the Islamic community gave much more than the usual 2.5 per cent. A Sufi anecdote, told by Hujwiri, illustrates the point, for he reported that Abu Bakr gave away all that he possessed, and on being asked by Muhammad what he had left behind for his family, answered, 'God and his messenger' (Hujwiri 1976: 315).

The *zakat* was collected in the Islamic world until the colonial period in the nineteenth and twentieth centuries, and with the subsequent establishment of independent states in regions where attachment to Islam is strong, there have been diverse understandings of the role of *zakat* in the contemporary world. Given that *zakat* is a means to eradicate economic hardship and inequality, it is not surprising that some Muslims found parallels between the aims of *zakat* and those of socialism. Perhaps the most famous of such individuals was Gamal abd al-Nasser, the President of Egypt from 1956 to 1970, who declared the compatibility of Islam and socialism. Some Islamicists have rejected socialism because of its connection with atheistic communism, but have held that *zakat* and Islamic taxation can be reintroduced to finance an Islamic state. Such was the view of Ayatollah Khomeini during his period in exile before coming to power in Iran in 1978. However, it was all too soon discovered that Islamic taxes were not adequate to satisfy the financial demands on the modern state, and the Islamic Republic of Iran was obliged to collect forms of direct and indirect taxes, which it had previously considered illegitimate (Schirazi 1998: 238).

The *zakat* rate in the premodern period of Islamic history clearly is not sufficient to meet the level of taxation set by modern states in the developed world. Some 'Islamic' states have introduced *zakat* in a manner that differs markedly from the *zakat* of the classical Islamic era. For example, Pakistan and Saudi Arabia levy the *zakat* on companies whereas traditionally it had been a tax on individuals. In addition, these states have also redefined the categories that should be included within the *zakat*. Malaysia also maintains the *zakat*, and adheres more closely to the manuals of classical Sunni law that do not mention certain trades, including industrial workers, bureaucrats, businessmen, shopkeepers, growers of rubber, coconuts, and other tropical crops.

Since *zakat* is a pillar of Islam that emphasizes the social character of Islam, it is appropriate that the remainder of this section examines the role of Islamic law, and how it has been formulated, since it is this law that by and large regulates the social interactions of Muslims.

4.1 Islamic law

The foundation of Islam is the Qur'an, yet it does not always provide believers with details on how they should behave in certain circumstances. While Muhammad was alive the issues upon which the Qur'an provided only limited guidance were not problematic because the believers accepted Muhammad's advice on the Qur'anic *ayas* in question. This guidance was offered in an *ad hoc* fashion as problems arose (Coulson 1964: 22). Such an 'unsystematic' development of Islamic law continued after Muhammad's death, as the first four caliphs, in conjunction with other leading members of the community, instructed Muslims in areas that the Qur'an had left general, by referring to the example set by Muhammad. If no example was brought forward, then believers could continue the existing practice of the locality. Yet Muhammad's example was not always followed. For example, he did not name a successor, whereas the first caliph, Abu Bakr, did, and the second caliph, Umar, appointed a committee on his deathbed to choose his successor. The points here are, first, that there were several kinds of customary practice (*sunnas*) that believers could emulate: the prophetic *sunna*, the *sunna* of Muhammad's companions, and the *sunna* of the location; and, second, that during the formative period of Islam there was a far greater degree of flexibility in how Muslims came to decisions when compared with some of the rigid systems that emerged in the following centuries.

As the early Islamic empire expanded, the law had to adapt to changing circumstances. For example, problems developed when those companions who had known Muhammad were scattered in various cities, and inevitably differences arose concerning their understanding or recollection of the prophetic *sunna* (that is, how Muhammad acted or what he said). Under these circumstances Muslims resorted to the prevailing custom of the location to settle issues of contention, and this resulted in discrepancies of practice within the Islamic empire. Moreover, the growth of the empire meant that finding solutions to the problems raised by an ever-expanding number of Muslims was becoming increasingly difficult.

Therefore, during the Umayyad period, when the empire stretched across Central Asia, the Hejaz and North Africa, it was left to the provincial governors to appoint religious judges, and this contributed to the emergence of local schools of law (*madhhab*) in Basra and Kufa (located in what is now Iraq), Medina and Damascus.

Of these schools of law that were established during the eighth century one of the largest was called the Hanafi school, named after Abu Hanifa (d. 767), who was a native of Kufa, and this school has been described as the 'most liberal and flexible of the four Sunni schools' (Robinson 1999: 151). Abu Hanifa considered the Qur'an as the basis of Islamic law, and he believed that laws could be found through *qiyas*, or analogical reasoning. *Qiyas* involves the discovery of the common basis between a documented case and a new situation; in effect, it meant that the jurist replied on his own opinion (*ra'y*) to identify what would be considered 'Islamic'. Moreover, the concept of *istihsan* (or approving something preferable) was an important tool in the Hanafi *madhhab*, and this enabled jurists to go beyond the letter of the law, which was just what the second caliph, Umar, had done when he refused to enforce the amputation of thieves' limbs during a period of famine (Robinson 1999: 152). Aside from *qiyas* and *istihsan*, the Hanafis also relied upon consensus (*ijma'*), which is described below.

The practice of *qiyas* and *ra'y* inevitably resulted in diverse opinions, and therefore some degree of conformity was seen by many Muslims as desirable for the community. This was achieved through *ijma'*, which is the agreements reached by the so-called 'successors' (those who followed Muhammad and his immediate companions) and later generations of jurists on the basis of the teachings of the Qur'an and the prophetic *sunna*. Yet *ijma'* has been considered a more dynamic tool for the Muslim community in solving any problems or disputes because 'it determined what the Sunna of the Prophet had been and indeed what the right interpretation of the Qur'an was. In the final analysis, therefore, both the Qur'an and the Sunna were authenticated through Ijma'' (Rahman 1966: 74).

The Maliki school of Sunni law was named after Malik b. Anas (d. 796). He favoured the *ijma'* of the Medinan jurists, but allowed for a fairly liberal attitude towards Islamic law by permitting the principle of *istislah* (or public welfare). *Istislah* admitted new laws that had no textual basis in the Qur'an, so long as they promoted the interest of Islam. The reason for the emergence of this school has been described as a 'reaction against the earlier more speculative approaches to law' (Robinson 1999: 153). Of great significance when discussing Malik is the treatise attributed to him named *al-Muwatta*, in which the aim is to establish law based upon the prophetic *sunna* by citing the sayings of Muhammad.

A third school of Sunni law is the Shafi'i *madhhab*. Created by Muhammad al-Shafi'i (d. 820), this school attempted to unify the various *madhhabs* of his time by establishing a hierarchical structure of references for jurists to facilitate their law-finding. Most important, of course, was the Qur'an, and second to this was the *hadith*. This point was not universally accepted by the schools that had accepted the prophetic *sunna* 'as it was lived in the practical tradition' (Rahman 1966: 60). In other words, al-Shafi'i rejected the practical and local *sunna* because it included elements which were pre-Islamic and were the cause of disunity in the community. He believed this disunity could be eliminated by establishing the *sunna* upon the *hadith*. (Investigation into the *hadith* literature became a science in itself within the Islamic world, and this will be mentioned in the following section.) A third source of law-finding in the Shafi'i school was *ijma'*, and al-Shafi'i gave it a new twist by defining it as the consensus of the whole community, not just that of the legal scholars, or of a local community. Finally, al-Shafi'i accepted *qiyas* as the jurist's fourth tool in the law-finding process. Although the Hanafis and Malikis accepted the importance of the *hadith*, they were able to bypass it to a certain degree through their adherence to the principle of *ijma'*, which functioned as the interpreter of the *hadith*.

The fourth Sunni law school is that of the Hanbalis, named after Ahmad Ibn Hanbal (d. 855). A great admirer of al-Shafi'i, Ibn Hanbal stressed the pre-eminence of the Qur'an and *sunna* (the latter being understood through the *hadith* literature). The difference between the Shafi'i *madhhab* and the Hanbali *madhhab* is that there has been a tendency for the latter to apply a rigorously literal interpretation of the Qur'an and sound *hadith* in the law-finding process. Despite this it is worthy to note that there have been famous Hanbali Sufis (such as Abdullah Ansari (d. 1089) and Abd al-Qadir Gilani (d. 1166)), who as a group are renowned for passing beyond the letter to the inner meanings of things. Moreover, the Hanbalis rejected the *ijma'* tradition of the Hanafis, and this resulted in the production of independent, personal enquiry (*ijtihad*) by individual jurists, and some of these achieved great fame, such as Ibn Taymiyya (d. 1328).

Most Shiites follow the Ja'fari school of law, which finds law on the basis of the Qur'an, the *hadith* of Muhammad (which were transmitted by Ali) and the sayings of the Imams. The Ja'fari school permits *ijtihad* (whereas the door of *ijtihad* was by and large considered closed by the medieval period in the Sunni *madhhabs*), and *ijma'* is not acceptable for Shiites. Instead Shiites are obliged to follow the opinions (which are fallible) of senior religious clerics (*marja' taqlid*) – literally source of emulation – and it is not permissible to follow the decisions of a deceased *marja*. In this way, Shiite law can be dynamic and respond to changing social circumstances.

THE *HADITH*

Very early in the history of Islam, Muslims recognized the significance of *hadith*, and about one hundred years after Muhammad's death, collections of them appeared. Although these now exist as manuscript copies, the earliest is probably that attributed to Munabbih, who died in 719–20. In the early collections, two types of *hadith* were included without there being any distinction made between them. The first kind is the *hadith*, and the second is the *hadith qudsi* (divine saying). Whereas the *hadith* report the speech or action of Muhammad, the *hadith qudsi* report through Muhammad what God said. Sometimes there is little difference between the two, for example there is a *hadith qudsi* that states: 'If my servant desires to meet me, I desire to meet him', and this is mirrored by a *hadith*: 'Whoever desires to meet God, God desires to meet him.'

The *hadith qudsi* function as a kind of middle ground between the *hadith* (prophetic word) and the Qur'an (divine word), that is, they are a form of non-Qur'anic revelation. The significance of the *hadith qudsi* is that for the formative Islamic community after Muhammad's death the distinction between divine word and prophetic word was blurred. Thus, despite the Qur'anic insistence on both Muhammad's human nature and the Qur'an's divine origin, the early Islamic community was able to 'recognise and accept Muhammad's own *active, intimate, human* involvement in the revelatory process'[2] (Graham 1977: 29). According to Graham, these sayings 'were popularly ascribed by the first generation of Muslims to the Prophet without excessive concern as to whether he was speaking in inspired 'prophetic' manner as the mouthpiece of God or was simply speaking as an ordinary man who had been chosen by God for an extra-ordinary task' (ibid.: 89). This discussion on the *hadith qudsi* suggests that from a very early period of Islamic history Muslims regarded Muhammad as more than just a human being, and the dynamics of contemplating the nature of revelation led, by the time of al-Shafi'i, to the notion 'that the Prophet's legal decisions were divinely inspired' (Coulson 1964: 56).

Once al-Shafi'i had established the *hadith* literature as second only to the Qur'an in the hierarchy of sources for law-finding, it was already recognized that many of the so-called sayings of Muhammad

2 The italics are Graham's.

had been fabricated for political and doctrinal reasons. Therefore, scholars developed ways to discover the authenticity of any given *hadith*. Ibn Hanbal travelled much in what is now Arabia and Iraq in search of individuals who had memorized or made collections of *hadiths*. It is said that he examined 750,000 *hadith* reported on the authority of the companions of Muhammad, and of these he selected 30,000 as genuine. The 'genuine' *hadiths* were those that included an *isnad* (that is a chain of transmission), along with the actual saying of Muhammad. So, a 'genuine' *hadith* would contain an *isnad* like: 'A told me that B said he heard C say that D had reported that he had heard from Muhammad.' Scholars of *hadith* investigated the reliability of those individuals within such chains of transmission, and if it were proved that certain individuals were liars, or if it were shown that it was historically impossible for A to have met B, then the *hadith* was not accepted. This system was not devoid of problems, because many of the earliest texts (such as Munabbih's) cite *hadiths* without *isnad*. This does not indicate the unreliability of such *hadith*, but rather the acceptance by the author who recorded the *hadith* of the character of the individual (most probably a companion of Muhammad) who reported the *hadith* in question. Of course there is no guarantee that a sound *hadith* (in terms of *isnad*) had not been fabricated by unscrupulous individuals.

In the ninth century, two comprehensive collections of *hadiths* were produced that are regarded as the authoritative versions up to the present day. These are the collections of Bukhari (d. 870) and Muslim (d. 874). Bukhari examined a total of 600,000 *hadith* from which he believed 7,275 were sound (*sahih*), thus the name *Sahih*, of his compilation. The collections of Bukhari and Muslim classified the *hadith* by subject matter (rather than Ibn Hanbal's method of arranging *hadith* according to the name of the companion who heard Muhammad's words), and this simplified the task of the jurist in law-finding.

PUNISHMENT

Although the Qur'an does not provide detailed regulations on all aspects of life, it was recognized by those formulating the law that there were six acts, or rather crimes, for which the penalties are clearly specified in the Qur'an and *sunna*. These six (known as the *hadd* – pl. *hudud*) are theft (amputation of the hand), fornication (100 lashes, as stated in the Qur'an 24.2), adultery (stoning to death), false accusations of unchastity (80 lashes), wine-drinking (40 to 80 lashes) and banditry (ranging from amputation of an arm to exile). In the modern age, many have commented on the severity of such punishments, and these judgements have been countered by some Muslims in their beliefs that, first, the *hudud* serve as a deterrent and, second, it is very difficult to implement them, since it is not easy to prove the guilt of an offender. In the case of adultery, guilt can be proved by self-confession or with the evidence of four eye-witnesses. Moreover, scholars have indicated that the jurists were reluctant to implement the *hudud*, and devised all kinds of ruses to avoid adhering to the letter of the law. Husayn Ahmad Amin, a contemporary 'liberal' Muslim writer from Egypt, gives the example of how jurists escaped from applying the laws for amputation by stipulating thirty-eight conditions to exclude many acts from the category of theft. These included stealing books for the purpose of learning, poverty, stealing public money (since the thief had a share in the wealth in any case), and stealing during periods of excessive heat or cold (Abu-Zahra 1998: 95).

Many of the so-called 'liberal' Muslims argue in a similar fashion to Amin, that the social context of the modern age is very different from that of Muhammad and the companions, the period from which the early scholars drew legal norms. In the words of Abdallahi Ahmad al-Na'im (a Sudanese-born legal scholar): 'By the same token that *shari'a* [Islamic law] as a practical legal system could not have disregarded the conception of human rights prevailing at the time it purported to apply in the seventh century, modern Islamic law cannot disregard the present conception of human rights if it is to be applied today' (1998: 227). The reasoning behind this 'liberal' interpretation has been summarized by the Egyptian jurist Muhammad al-Ashmawi:

> Of some 6,000 Qur'anic verses, only 200 have a legal aspect, that is approximately one thirtieth of the Qur'an, including the verses which were abrogated by subsequent ones. This shows that the principal object of the Qur'an is moral in nature: it is concerned to inscribe the fault in the soul of the believer, to elevate his conscience and morality in order that it might be its own proper shari'a in the sense of the way leading to God. Also, even when a Qur'anic law is applicable, this should be in the context of faith and justice, beyond any judicial partiality or deviation. On the other hand, judicial norms being by nature local and temporary, God more often left expressly to humans the work of regulating the details and the freedom to review them with a view to possibly substituting others in function of the needs of each country and epoch.
>
> (Al-Ashmawi 1998: 51)

Yet the 'liberal' Islamic position is countered by the reality that the *hudud* have been, and continue to be, implemented by various 'Islamic' states in the modern period. For example, in 1995 192 people were executed under Islamic law in Saudi Arabia (*The Guardian*, 24.10.99: 27). Yet some of those who have been called 'fundamentalists', such as Mawdudi, are more circumspect about the implementation of the *hudud*. According to Mawdudi's rather idealistic portrayal of society, these punishments can only be carried out in a perfect Islamic state. When the perfect Islamic state is created, all Muslims will adhere to the shariah, and therefore there will be no crime to necessitate the implementation of the *hudud*. Despite his arguments, shariah law has been introduced in Pakistan from the 1980s onwards, yet 'the *hadd* punishments did not deter robbery, rape, murder, theft, or drug abuse. If anything they encouraged the brutalisation of society. Pictures of public whippings sustained Western misapprehensions and misconceptions concerning Islam' (Talbot 1998: 277).

THE CONSERVATIVE CHARACTER OF LAW-FINDING?

Fiqh, or jurisprudence for Sunni Muslims, is based on the sources of law, or *usul*: the Qur'an, *hadith*, *ijma'*, *qiyas*, and hermeneutic disciplines (including historical, linguistic, rhetorical and logical sources). Once the four *madhhabs* had been established, any jurist who wished to find a law had to do so with reference to the sources, and this was the system that became known as *taqlid*, or imitation. *Ijtihad*, or systematic free-thinking, was denied by the Sunni schools of law (although a few Hanbali jurists such as Ibn Taymiyya (d. 1328) rejected a strict adherence to *taqlid*, and practised *ijtihad*). Any jurist who stepped outside the realm of *taqlid* committed innovation (*bid'a*), a term that has extremely negative connotations in the Islamic world. Thus, it has been said that the door of *ijtihad*, or independent reasoning, was closed with the creation of the four schools of law. Although it might be assumed that such a situation could produce highly conservative and inflexible legal opinions, it has been argued that this has not necessarily been the case. Each generation, after the deaths of the four founders, produced legal works that summarized or expanded the achievements of the preceding generations, and this in turn provided the basis for their own contemporary expansion. In this process, jurists were conforming to the principle of *taqlid*, yet it did not follow that such law-finding was stultifying or resulted in the petrifaction of the community (Calder 1997: 64). Indeed, jurists of the Hanafi school, for example, explored the concepts of hypothetical cases of law and through cunning contrivances (*hilal*) exploited the letter of the law to produce unexpected results. For example, it was argued by one scholar that if the people had their goods taken by 'outlaws', while claiming it was collection of *zakat*, the people were still obliged to repeat the distribution of *zakat*. However, this view was rejected by a later jurist who claimed that this illegitimate collection could be rendered valid (and therefore not have to distribute the *zakat* again) if the people formulate the intention of giving these 'outlaws' the *zakat*. This is because the 'outlaws' are in fact debtors to the Muslims, since the wealth really belongs to the Muslims, and if they returned this wealth they would have less than the people. Therefore the 'outlaws' should be included among the ranks of the poor who are legitimate recipients of the *zakat*! (Calder 1996: 989–90). Islamic jurists, therefore, should not be regarded as dry and formalistic. Many of them were also Sufis, and it has been through this combination of the legal and the mystical that 'Muslims . . . have, historically, found self-realization as Muslims' (ibid.: 997).

Despite this, Islamic jurists have been criticized, partly because of their penchant for abstract and theoretical situations that produced works that 'had no bearing on the practical life of the Muslims' (ibid.: 995). This habit was criticized by Muslims of the modern era, and the following remarks of Ayatollah Khomeini are quite revealing:

> Present Islam to the people in its true form, so that our youth do not picture the *akhunds* [clerics] as sitting in some corner in Najaf or Qum [holy cities for Shiites], studying the questions of menstruation or parturition instead of concerning themselves with politics.
>
> (1981: 38)

With the onset of modernity, the Muslim world has had to respond to a world that has changed radically, and legal scholars have been challenged to assess the permissibility of performing many acts that the Qur'an and *sunna* do not deal with explicitly. As a result there has been a desire among Muslim reformists to examine legal structures. *Talfiq* (adopting the legal ruling of any of the four *madhhabs* that is most appropriate for the circumstances) had been advocated by Shah Waliyullah, one of the leading jurists in eighteenth-century India, and by Muhammad Abduh in late-nineteenth-century Egypt. Moreover, Abduh argued for the necessity of applying *ijtihad*, as have the majority of the Islamic reformists of the modern period. Despite the influence of the West and its secular law (indeed perhaps because of this influence!) Islamic law has been adopted by many modern states in the Middle East as the basis of their constitution (for example, Pakistan, Egypt and Iran).

5 PILGRIMAGE (*HAJJ*)

Of all the five pillars of Islam, it is the *hajj* (which Muslims are obliged to perform at least once in their lifetime if they are able) that contains the most specific and formalized rituals, and much has been written about their origins, symbolism and meaning. The *hajj* rites are not always comprehensible to Muslims, as Ghazali in the twelfth century commented, they do not satisfy reason or human senses, but must be accepted as obedient acts of service to God. However, Muslims (and for that matter many non-Muslims) would reject the kind of statements made by one Western academic that 'some of the rituals seem almost childish' (Robinson 1999: 144). The following suggests that the rites are far from 'almost childish' and although they may be enigmatic, the rituals have enriched the lives of many different kinds of Muslims.

5.1 The *hajj* rites

Before setting off, the pilgrim must ensure that his family is provided for, and all debts are paid. In effect, he is on a journey to 'God's house' the *Ka'ba*, situated in Mecca. Since it is generally accepted by Muslims that humans meet God on the Day of Judgement, visiting God's house, and, by extension, God, the pilgrim considers himself 'dead' to the world. To use a common phrase of the anthropologist Victor Turner, the pilgrim enters a *liminal* stage on starting out for the *hajj* (1974: 177–8) because he has symbolically died from the world, but remains within it, in a sense of heightened spirituality at the expectation of meeting the divine. On entering the sacred site past a boundary marker (*miqat*), the pilgrim dons a seamless, white cloth known as the *ihram*. Again, this is symbolic of a death-shroud Muslims use in which the dead are buried, but it also functions to level the distinctions between the various Muslims, reinforcing the Qur'anic ideal of equality among believers. The pilgrim also announces his intention to perform the *hajj* by proclaiming the *talbiya*: 'Here we are O Lord, here we are . . .' He then heads for the *Ka'ba*, which is little more than an empty chamber, built of stone, 15 metres high, 12 metres long, and 10.5 metres wide, and is draped in a black covering. As Ali Shariati (a twentieth-century Islamic reformist from Iran) asks in his treatise on the *hajj*:

> Why is it [the *Ka'ba*] so simple lacking colour and ornamentation? It is because God Almighty has no 'shape', no colour and none is similar to Him. No pattern or visualisation of God that man imagines can represent Him. Being omnipotent and omnipresent, God is 'absolute' . . . Having six sides, the appropriate structure is a cube! It encompasses all directions and simultaneously their sum symbolises no direction!
>
> (1977: 23)

The pilgrim approaches the *Ka'ba*, and either touches or points to the 'black stone' which is encased in silver and embedded in the east corner of the *Ka'ba*. Regarded by some as a meteorite, the black stone symbolizes God's right hand, thus touching or pointing to it re-enacts the covenant between God and man, that is, man's acknowledgement of God's Lordship. (This covenant is referred to in *aya* 7.171.) Other Iranian Muslims have described a more intimate reality for the black stone, which Muslims attempt to kiss on completing the circumambulation of the *Ka'ba*. For example, the thirteenth-century Sufi Rumi stated: 'The pilgrim kisses the black stone from his innermost heart because he feels the lips of the beloved [God] in it' (1957: no. 617). The pilgrim circumambulates the *Ka'ba* seven times in an anticlockwise direction.

On completing seven circuits around the *Ka'ba*, the pilgrim proceeds to the 'station of Abraham', located opposite the east corner of the *Ka'ba*. The station of Abraham is a stone in which there are footprints, and Muslims believe that it was from this point that Abraham stood and laid the cornerstone of the *Ka'ba*. Indeed, the Qur'an states that Abraham and Isma'il raised its foundations (2.126). (The Qur'an also states that the *Ka'ba* was the 'first house' founded for mankind (3.96), which, for Muslims, implies that it was built by Adam.) At the station of Abraham, the pilgrim prays, and perhaps re-enacts and internalizes the major events in the life of Abraham, who smashed idols (21.58), rebuilt the *Ka'ba*, thereby calling all others to Islam and God, and was prepared to sacrifice his own son (37.104). Recalling these events, the pilgrim manifests his unity of intention with other Muslims, but at the same time affirms his own individuality, since by this point, the Muslim will have smashed his own personal idols and will be prepared to make his own private sacrifices to God. The prayers at the station of Abraham complete the rites of circumambulation (*tawwaf*).

Next the pilgrim reaches a well known as Zamzam, and drinks three draughts of its water, and then he performs a ritual of *sa'i*, which takes place between the hills of Safa and Marwa. The distance between these two hills is about a quarter of a mile, and the pilgrim runs and walks seven times on the path connecting the two. This symbolizes the actions of Hagar, who bore Isma'il to Abraham, and Islamic tradition holds that Abraham left Hagar and Isma'il at the *Ka'ba* (or site of the *Ka'ba*), and returned alone to Syria. In her desperation to protect Isma'il, Hagar searched frantically for water, running several times between the hills of Safa and Marwa. Once the *sa'i* is completed, that is, after starting at Safa, and passing back and forth, ending at Marwa, the pilgrim has his head shaved, removes the *ihram*, and puts on his everyday clothes. This is the end of a lesser pilgrimage known as the *umra*, which can be performed at any time during the year.

The *hajj* proper, however, has a specific time for its performance, namely from the seventh to the thirteenth of the Islamic month of *Dhul-Hijja*. On the eighth the pilgrim performs the rituals for the *umra*, and then proceeds to Mina, three miles east of Mecca, where prayers are offered. On the ninth, the pilgrim journeys to the plain of Arafat, a further nine miles away, repeating the *talbiya* and other prayers of forgiveness. From midday until sunset, the pilgrim stands on the plain of Arafat, a rite known as *wuquf*, and begs God for forgiveness, and then a sermon is given with congregational prayers. At sunset the pilgrim proceeds to Muzdalifa, reciting the *talbiya* and prayers of forgiveness, and the night is spent there in prayer. On the tenth, the pilgrim collects small pebbles and returns to Mina where there are three stone pillars, and he casts seven pebbles at a pillar known as *jabal al-aqaba*, which is an action symbolic of stoning Satan. Now the pilgrim can sacrifice a sheep, goat or camel, and have his head shaved, and return to the *Ka'ba* for an additional circumambulation and *sa'i*, before returning to Mina. The stoning of the pillars according to some traditions was first performed by Abraham, who was tempted by Satan to ignore God's command to sacrifice his son. And these traditions hold that the sacrifice during the *hajj* recalls Abraham's preparedness to sacrifice Isma'il, although, of course, God allowed him to substitute a ram for his son.[3] On the eleventh the pilgrim casts seven pebbles at each of the three stone pillars, and spends the rest of the time in remembrance of God and prayer. He repeats this on the twelfth, and again on the thirteenth before returning to the *Ka'ba* and performing the circumambulation, prayers at the station of Abraham, and drinking the water of Zamzam.

SIGNIFICANCE OF THE RITUALS

Modern, Western scholars have been intrigued by the *hajj*, especially the origins of the rites. Opinions on this have ranged from those who identify Jewish prototypes behind the rituals to others who see them as modifications of 'pagan' Arab practices. For Muslims, however, the origins of the *hajj* lie entirely with God, who sent Gabriel to teach Abraham the rituals. The Abrahamic connection does not suggest to Muslims that the rites are Jewish, because Abraham is considered an Islamic prophet (see below). The search for the origins of the *hajj*, however, is not so important if our aim is to appreciate the significance that the performance the *hajj* has upon the believer. This significance has been touched upon by Victor Turner, in his discussion of *communitas*, the spontaneous communal bond that results from social levelling and the shared experience of liminality[4] (1969: 96). The *communitas* of the *hajj*

---

3 On the sacrifice and the identity of the son see Firestone 1990: 105–59.

4 A liminal state (from the Latin *limen*, or threshold) is one in which the subject slips through the usual classi-fications that define people, such as class, status, law, custom, etc. In such a state, the subject passes from the 'structures' of society to 'anti-structure'. See Turner 1969: 94–130.

is best illustrated in the experience of Malcolm X, who made the *hajj* in 1964 as a follower of the Nation of Islam, a society of black Americans that considered Elijah Muhammad (d. 1975) God's last prophet, and advocated segregation from the white community. His experience of eating from the same plate, sleeping on the same rug, praying to the same God resulted in a sense of brotherhood and spirit of unity that resulted in Malcolm X shedding his allegiance to the Nation of Islam and devoting his life to 'true' Islam (Malcolm X 1966: 419). Another interpretation of the *hajj* experience (similar to Turner's *communitas*) was presented by Ali Shariati, who describes what happens on donning the *ihram*:

> Everyone 'melts' himself and assumes a new form as a 'mankind'. The egos and individual traits are buried. The group becomes a 'people' or an '*Umma*'. All the I's have died in Miqat;[5] what has evolved is 'We'. By the time you leave Mina you should have integrated into the *Umma*. This is what Abraham did. You are also supposed to act like Abraham: 'Surely Abraham was a nation (*Umma*) obedient to God, a man of pure faith and no idolator' [Qur'an, 16.120]. At last, one is all, and all is one! Everyone is equal. The society of polytheism is converted into one of monotheism, or *Tawhid*. This is the Umma or the society which is onto the right path. It should be a society which is perfect, active and led by Islamic leadership (*Imamat*).
>
> (1977: 11)

For Shariati, then, the efficacy of the *hajj* is one that transforms both individual and society, but not in any magical fashion, for the transformation is a spiritual realization. But the efficacy of the pilgrimage can be considered with reference to a *hadith* which suggests to some Muslims that performance of the *hajj* is a sacramental or magical ritual: 'The pilgrim [of the *hajj*] intercedes for four hundred of his relatives and is as sinless as on the day his mother gave birth to him' (cited in Peters 1994b: i). What is noteworthy in the *hadith* is that there are benefits to both individual and society. From a personally efficacious perspective, the *hajji*, i.e. the person who has performed the *hajj*, is awarded a great deal of respect by his neighbours on his return from Mecca, perhaps because the *hajj* originally entailed such hardships (including the burden of ensuring that one's family is provided for, and also the arduous nature of the journey).

In contrast to the idea of the efficacy of the *hajj* ritual is the view of W. Graham (1983), who denies both its sacramental or magical effect and the existence of symbolic drama, and instead believes that what is at the heart of the *hajj* is an 'overwhelming sense of coming before God to "worship and serve" with sincerity and simplicity' (ibid.: 70). Graham also argues that the *hajj* should also be regarded as a 'reformational' rite, by which he means the rituals are 'systematically set over against those of previous and contemporaneous religious traditions, especially paganism on the one hand and Judaic and Christian tradition on the other . . . ["worship and serve" rites as opposed to efficacious rites were a] self-conscious effort to distinguish its [Islam's] faith and practice' (ibid.: 66). It is probable that there are Muslims for whom 'worship and serve' may be an axiomatic attitude when performing the *hajj*, but as shown above, there are Muslims who regard the *hajj* as efficacious. Graham is also incorrect in denying the symbolic significance of the prophet Abraham, as al-Azraqi (d. 834) describes how Gabriel taught Abraham *all* the *hajj* rituals, and moreover, Islamic tradition holds that Abraham stood in despair on the plain of Arafat because God had commanded him to sacrifice his son (Denny 1994: 133).

---

5 Miqat is the place where the *hajj* is traditionally begun. It is eight miles south of Medina, and is where Muhammad commenced his Farewell Pilgrimage.

The prophet Abraham is the pivotal symbol in the *hajj*, and any discussion of him inevitably leads to a discussion of pluralism, since he is recognized as a major figure in religious traditions outside of Islam. Therefore, the remainder of this section provides a guide to issues related to pluralism, and in particular to the 'People of the Book'.

5.2 Pluralism

> Truly, *those who believe*, and those who are Jews, the Christians and the Sabi'un,[6] whoever believes in God and the last day and does right, for them is their reward near their Lord, they will have no fear, neither will they grieve.
>
> (2.62)

There has been a tendency in recent years to build bridges between the various religious traditions, and the above *aya* has often been cited by non-Muslim Westerners to demonstrate that Islam is inherently favourable to religious pluralism. Yet an investigation into the way the above *aya* has been understood by Muslims illustrates that a literal understanding of anything is impossible, as literal understandings are bound up with one's expectations, prejudices and previous knowledge. One of the significant points about 2.62, cited above, is that for some people it calls into question the necessity for people to convert to Islam and believe in the prophethood of Muhammad if other faiths have 'their reward near their Lord'. However, section 1.2 of this chapter has shown that the Islamic concept of belief or faith includes faith in God, His angels, books, messengers, and the Last Day. Therefore 'those who believe' or those who have faith could not be Christians or Jews because they had no faith in Muhammad. This helps us to understand why *traditionally* some Muslims were reluctant to include non-Muslims among those who would be saved (see McAuliffe 1991: 93–128). Some Muslims understood the Jews, Chrsitians and Sabi'un mentioned in 2.62 as those who would eventually accept Muhammad as prophet, and therefore become Muslims and be included among 'those who believe'. However, the situation has changed with the onset of modernity, as the European powers posed new challenges and threats to Islamic territories, and the globalization of the world has forced Muslims to reinterpret such verses as *aya* 2.62 in a more positive light by glossing over the thorny problem of belief in Muhammad and limiting their interpretation to belief in God alone (ibid.). To state the obvious, this shows that Islam is not *inherently* hostile to other religious traditions; to repeat the famous phrase of Aziz al-Azmeh: 'There are as many Islams as there are situations that sustain it' (1993: 1). In the present age, Islamic relations with and understandings of other religious and non-religious traditions are diverse. One extreme is the outright rejection by Osama bin Laden of what he considers to be the 'excesses' of the West, the pogroms by Muslims against Bahais in Iran during the twentieth century and the refusal to recognize any religion as valid after the sealing of prophecy with Muhammad (33.40). At the other end of the spectrum is the ecumenical position of the South African Muslim Farid Esack (1999: 28), who asks challenging questions such as the permissibility of women leading congregational prayers, and a Hindu conducting a wedding ceremony in a mosque (1997: 260). Esack does not answer the question, but the general tenor of his work leaves the reader with little doubt where his sympathies lie.

---

6 The Sabi'un are commonly believed by Muslims to be a community of star-worshippers.

However, the middle ground is probably where most Islamic values and standards lie, and it is here that an investigation into Islamic attitudes to pluralism must begin. Some positive, pluralist interpretations may be taken from those *ayas* that reflect the Qur'anic understanding of history depicting God sending many other prophets to all communities in the world (35.24; 40.78). Moreover, Islamic tradition holds that the number of prophets was 140,000. Most of the prophets mentioned come from the Semitic tradition: the most frequently cited include Abraham, Moses and Jesus.

Yet Muslims consider Islam as a more compassionate and universal religion than Judaism and Christianity, which some Muslims believe are both 'exclusivist' religions; the former being designated for a certain people with an attachment to a particular geographical area, while the doctrine of the latter (salvation through Christ) seems to deny the validity of other religions. Many Muslims claim that Islam is inclusive, but whether this means recognizing other religions on an equal footing, or whether non-Islamic traditions are considered in a somewhat patronizing fashion as having a lesser degree of 'truth', is still a matter of debate. The Qur'an's discussion of religious diversity and pluralism has been interpreted in a variety of ways with most of the focus being centred on Judaism and Christianity simply because the Qur'an has much to say on these two traditions. Therefore, the following sections will focus on Islam's relationship with these two other religions of Semitic origin.

JUDAISM, CHRISTIANITY AND ISLAM

Islamic links with Judaism are many, ranging from similarity in rituals to belief in the same prophets. It has been noted by Western scholars such as Wensinck (1982) that those *ayas* of the Qur'an which explain certain laws pertaining to ritual occur in the Medinan period when Muhammad was in close proximity with Jewish tribes, and when he was hoping that they would accept him as a prophet. However, the *ayas* of the Qur'an reflect an increasing hostility towards the Jews after the refusal of Jewish tribes to accept Muhammad as prophet. In 3.64–6, the Qur'an criticizes the exclusivity of the Jews and claims that Abraham should be considered an Islamic prophet. After all, how could Abraham be a Jew when the Torah was sent down by God after he had died? Also, during the Medinan period, the Qur'an in *aya* 2.149 instructed Muhammad and his followers not to bow down in worship to God facing Jerusalem, but instead towards Mecca, more particularly to the *Ka'ba*. In addition, greater emphasis is placed upon the Arab nature of the revelation, perhaps to make it distinct from the revelations given to the Jews (43.1–3). This has been seen as the 'nationalization' or 'Arabification' of Islam by some, and has been rejected by others (Rahman 1980: 133). The frequent mention of the Arabic revelation supports the Qur'anic argument that God sends messengers to all communities, including the Arabs. The Arab connection with Judaism appears with Abraham and his son, who in 2.126 are the builders of the *Ka'ba*, and in 2.127 pray that their posterity be Muslim. The Qur'anic attitude then to the Jews and Judaism is mixed, and in practice Muslims have adopted a wide variety of responses to Judaism on the basis of what they want to find in the Qur'an. However, it is perhaps worth repeating the conclusions of other scholars that Islamic treatment of the Jews (at least until modern times) was far more humane and tolerant than that offered by the Christian West (Lewis 1984; Cohen 1994).

The Qur'anic attitude towards Christianity is much more sympathetic than that towards the Jews, although it would be mistaken to assume the Qur'anic understanding of Christianity is one of wholehearted commendation. The Qur'anic portrayal of Christianity has puzzled scholars for many years. Some have chosen to emphasize the tolerant *ayas*, and adopt an ecumenical position, such as Parrinder, who states: 'Christians and Muslims, when they were true to the spirit of their founders, were close to each other' (1965: 165). Such a view glosses over Muhammad's opposition to his Jewish enemies (of whom 600 were beheaded after the Battle of the Ditch in 627), and the negative statements about Christianity contained in the Qur'an. Furthermore, McAuliffe has noted that criticisms of Christianity by far outnumber praise for it (1991: 4), and that until modern times Islamic interpretations of those *ayas* positive to Christianity reserved 'to but a very limited number the application of divine approval and award' (ibid.: 286). Yet these positive *ayas* portray 'neither the historical nor the living community of people who call themselves Christians' (ibid.: 287). Rather, they depict Christians in the fashion that the Qur'an would have them be. Such an idealized Christianity portrays Jesus as a prophet and precursor to Muhammad, the disciples as precursors to Muhammad's followers at Medina, and Christians as believers who are willing to accept Muhammad as a prophet and the Qur'an as divine revelation. When the ideal did not materialize, the Qur'anic revelations about Christianity became increasingly hostile (Marshall 2001: 24–5).

The following outlines some of the main issues that the Qur'an deals with in relation to Christianity.

1 Jesus is recognized as a remarkable prophet since he is called the 'breath of God' (5.110) and the 'word of God' (3.44). He was born of a virgin and performed miracles such as bestowing life upon the dead and healing the sick. However, the Qur'an denies Jesus' crucifixion, for it is stated that someone else who resembled Jesus was executed in his place (4.157). The Qur'an is not explicitly clear about whether or not Jesus died (4.158–9; 19.33), but according to Islamic tradition he was taken up to the heavens while still alive and he will return again to earth as a sign of the end of time (43.60). Jesus received revelations from God, and the Christians who obey these are regarded with respect by the Qur'an.

2 Priests and monks are praised because they are not arrogant (5.82). However, praise is tempered by criticism of Christianity. For example, the practice of monasticism is not prescribed by God, according to *aya* 57.26. Monasticism is reprehensible to Islam because the Qur'an emphasizes the communal nature of religion, whereas the Islamic view of monasticism is that it removes individuals from society. Moreover, the establishment of the Church, or a religious hierarchy, is condemned because it can lead to *shirk*, as some of the People of the Book 'take their monks as Lords apart from God' (9.31). Indeed, some monks 'consume the goods of the people in vanity and bar [the people] from God's way' (9.34). Another criticism of Christians is the alteration of the scriptures, and 2.75, which states 'a group of them did hear the word of God, then after they understood it, knowingly altered it', is taken by Islamic tradition to refer to Christians. Aside from altering the scriptures, Christians are accused of forgetting part of it (5.14).

3 The Christian concept of the Trinity is also rejected by the Qur'an because it is nothing more than *shirk* (5.72). However, the Qur'anic portrayal of the Trinity is one that modern Christians would not recognize, for according to the Qur'an, Christians regard God as 'the third of three' (5.73), the two other members being Jesus and Mary (5.116).

The 'faults' that the Qur'an found in Christianity and Judaism did not mean that Muslims found it necessary to eradicate these religions; rather, Jews and Christians were permitted to practise their beliefs within the Islamic community. After paying a poll-tax (*jizya*) they were offered protected status and were known as *dhimmis*. Of course it was hoped that they would voluntarily embrace Islam, but the Qur'anic verse 'there is no compulsion in religion' (2.258) persuaded many Muslims that the safety of non-believers was commanded by God. Islam's relationship with Judaism and Christianity has spawned many interpretations. It is a relationship that is linked intimately with the question of power, that is, how Muslims conceive of power, who holds it, and the extent to which it may be exercised. These are the questions that are addressed in the next section.

6 *JIHAD*: ISLAM AND THE STATE

Stated simply: the ultimate objective of Islam is to abolish the lordship of man over man and bring him under the rule of the One God. To stake everything you have – including your lives – to achieve this purpose is called Jihad. The Prayer, Fasting, Almsgiving and Pilgrimage, all prepare you for Jihad . . . [they] provide preparation and training for the assumption of just power.

(Mawdudi 1982: 285–91)

The quotation above from Mawdudi suggests why *jihad* is sometimes called Islam's sixth pillar. Such an all-encompassing understanding of *jihad* can be read into *aya* 22.78:

And perform the *jihad* as you ought. He has chosen you and did not impose on you any hardship in religion – the faith of Abraham. He called you Muslims before and in this [Qur'an], that the messenger might be a witness against you and that you might be witnesses against mankind. So perform the prayer, and pay the alms, and hold fast to God.

Mawdudi's aim, like many of the Islamic reformers of the twentieth century, was to liberate Islamic lands from Western, secular domination, and to create an Islamic state through *jihad*. For Mawdudi this meant basing the executive, legislative and judicial structures of government upon his understanding of the Qur'an. His Islamic government, by his own admission, conflicted with the Western democratic model of checks and balances between political structures, and so, for example, the executive is not necessarily constrained by the opinions of the legislature (1993: 41). Other Muslims have not politicized *jihad* in the same manner as Mawdudi; while they accept the command to strive in God's cause, by *jihad* they understand the performance of the five pillars without a concomitant commitment to a political *jihad*. Indeed, many reformers of the nineteenth and twentieth centuries were at pains to connect Western-style democracy with the Islamic tradition of consultation (*shura*). Other interpretations of *jihad* have stressed a 'spiritual' rather than a 'temporal' mode of *jihad*. The former is emphasized by the Sufis, and many were fond of citing a famous *hadith* that speaks of two forms of *jihad*. On returning from battle against the enemies of Islam, Muhammad is reported to have said: 'We have returned from the Lesser *Jihad* to the Greater *Jihad*.' On being asked, 'What is the Greater *Jihad*?' he replied, 'It is the struggle against the self.' Aside from the political and spiritual dimensions of *jihad*, Muslims have witnessed other forms, such as that described by the Pakistani 'modernist' Fazlur Rahman, who argues that Muslims should engage continuously in an intellectual *jihad* (otherwise known as *ijtihad*), and thus improve the conditions of the Islamic community (1982: 7–8). It is clear that *jihad*, like all other Islamic concepts, has been interpreted in a variety of ways, and in the following sections an attempt is made to highlight the political aspects related to *jihad*, in other words, the various ways that Muslims have understood *jihad* in relation to power and the political state. This will be done by focusing upon *jihad* in Muhammad's own lifetime, then within Sunni Islam, and finally in the Shiite tradition.

6.1 Islam and the state: Muhammad's example

It has been claimed that the Meccan period of Muhammad's revelation did not entail a specific claim to establish an Islamic state (Watt 1964). The revelations of this first period of Muhammad's prophetic career concern the nature of God (his power and goodness), monotheism, the return to God for

Judgement, man's response to God (worship and gratitude) and criticism of certain Meccan practices. Due to the opposition that Muhammad faced from the Meccans, he was forced to seek protection outside of Mecca, and the opportunity to consolidate his community came when he was asked to act as an arbitrator between the feuding tribes of the city of Medina. Thus Muhammad and many of the believers performed the *hegira* to this new city, and once settled in Medina, they gradually consolidated their position. In Medina the so-called 'Medinan Constitution' was made, an agreement between Muhammad and the Muslims on the one hand, and the rest of the inhabitants of Medina on the other, and this is the foundation of the Islamic community (*ummah*). The word *ummah*, used in the document, is also found in the Qur'an (2.143–4) to denote a religious community based upon a revealed scripture (Jews and the Torah, Christians and the Gospel, and Muslims and the Qur'an). Article 25 of the constitution appears to endorse a confederation of religious *ummahs*: 'The Jews of the Banu Awf are a community along with the believers. To the Jews their religion and to the Muslims their religion. This applies both to their clients and themselves, except those who have behaved unjustly or acted treacherously. He brings evil only on himself and his household.' In the constitution, Muhammad's followers are called 'believers', and Muhammad is considered the chief of this clan of believers. However, there were eight other clans in Medina that were not Muslims, which may suggest to some that the Medinan Constitution was a political agreement rather than a religious one. However, the seeds of the all-encompassing religious-political state can be read into the constitution, for it also commands, 'wherever there is anything about which you differ, it is to be referred to God and Muhammad' (and this advice is mirrored in *aya* 4.59). The recommendation to 'obey Muhammad and *those of you who are in authority*' (4.59) is of particular significance because it implies Muhammad cannot have exercised unbridled authority in the community of believers. Indeed, this is confirmed in 3.159, for Muhammad is ordered to 'consult with them in the conduct of affairs'. This is the idea of *shura*, mentioned earlier.

Although the early period of Medinan revelations and the Constitution of Medina suggest a political–religious divide, towards the end of Muhammad's life it appears that Muslims believed that these two spheres were united. This is suggested by the changing nature of references to *jihad* within the Qur'an. *Jihad* initially included the command to defend the community even if this meant taking up arms. Some Muslims were reluctant to engage in this self-defence, but circumstances compelled them to engage in military action. For example, 2.190 commands: 'And fight in the way of God with those that fight you, but aggress not: God loves not the aggressors.'

As the Islamic community became stronger in Medina the need to engage in *jihad* lessened, especially after Mecca was captured. However, some Muslims understood some *ayas* of the Qur'an to imply that Islam was a universal religion. For example, 5.3 speaks of Islam as a 'perfected religion'. One of the most contentious *ayas* for non-believers is 9.33, which states: 'It is He who sent His messenger with the guidance and the religion of the truth, in order to make it triumph over religion, all of it, even if the Associators should resent it.' This *aya* can be interpreted in a variety of ways. It may refer to an acceptance by the individual of the truth of religion in the believer's heart, or alternatively it may have a more all-encompassing meaning, involving minute regulations of all social relationships. Some Muslims hold that it was directed at other religions, since the same *sura* (9.29) contains the following:

> Fight those among the People of the Book who do not believe in God and the Last Day, who do
> not forbid what God and His messenger have forbidden, and do not profess the true religion, till
> they pay the poll-tax out of hand and submissively.

Here it is necessary to mention the poll-tax, or *jizya*, which was a tax that permitted non-Muslims to become members of the Islamic community in a political sense, in exchange for the security offered within the boundaries of the Islamic community. Non-Muslims, on paying this tax, were permitted to practise their own religion, although certain stipulations were to be enforced. These non-Muslims were known as *dhimmis*.

At Muhammad's death, it is clear that he had established an *ummah* which was both spiritual (in terms of defining what the members should believe about God, the Day of Judgement, etc.) and it was also secular in terms of how members of the community should behave towards one another. These terms 'spiritual' and 'secular' are in fact somewhat artificial for those Muslims who regard the community as sacred and governed by God's laws, for even the mundane has a divine dimension.

6.2 The Islamic state after Muhammad: the Sunni tradition

On Muhammad's death, the majority of his companions elected his friend Abu Bakr to be the Caliph, or deputy of the prophet. The institution of the Caliphate continued after his death and it can be assumed that the guidance of the community was based upon the Qur'an, the prophetic *sunna* and the local *sunna*. Yet from a very early period of Islamic history, there were challenges to and discussions on the legitimacy of the Caliphate and the boundaries of its authority. For example, there was the Shiite refusal to recognize the Sunni Caliphate (see below) and Kharijite groups that maintained that the sinner (even the Caliph if he disobeyed God's laws) should be excluded from the community. In addition, after the first four Caliphs, it had become clear to many Muslims that the person of the Caliph was not always the best person to speak on Islamic law. This was tacitly admitted when the Caliph Abd al-Malik (684–8) wrote to a respected religious leader, Hasan al-Basri (642–728), requesting advice on specific theological issues. Thus, the Caliph had become subject to certain religious restraints, and soon the limitations were becoming all too conspicuous, as there existed several independent dynasties (such as the Spanish Umayyads (756–1031), and the Fatimids in Egypt (909–1171)) that did not recognize the legitimacy of the Abbasid Caliph in Baghdad.

Under these circumstances the role of the Caliphate was scrutinized, and one scholar engaged in this task was al-Mawardi (991–1031), who stipulated several conditions that an individual must possess to become Caliph. These included the correct physical, intellectual and spiritual qualities, descent from the Quraysh (Muhammad's clan), and designation from the previous Caliph or leaders of the community. But al-Mawardi also stated that the Caliph could be deposed if he held unorthodox views, or had physical disabilities which made it impossible for him to perform his duties, or if executive power were seized in parts of the empire by local rulers (al-Mawardi 1996: 12).

In the generation after al-Mawardi, Ghazali went a stage further in defining the role of Caliph. His views reflected the necessities of the age when the Abbasid Empire was ruled in practice by local sultans, or military rulers, rather than the Caliph. For Ghazali, the Caliph was no longer regarded as conferring authority, but rather as someone who legitimized rights that had been acquired by force. He stated:

> We consider that the function of the caliphate is contractually assumed by that person of the Abbasid house who is charged with it, and that the functions of government in the various lands is carried out by means of sultans who owe allegiance to the caliphate. Government in these days is a consequence solely of military power, and whosoever he may be to whom the possessor of military power gives his allegiance, that person is the caliph.
>
> (cited in Enayat 1982: 11)

Some two hundred years after Ghazali, Ibn Taymiyya recognized the further weakening position of the Caliphate when he stated that any Muslim ruler, whether pious or not, was better than no Muslim leader at all, a standpoint that was a reaction perhaps to the Mongol invasion of the Middle East that initially deposed Islam as 'state' religion. Ibn Taymiyya wrote:

> It is obvious that the [affairs of the] people cannot be found in a sound state except with rulers, and even if somebody from among the unjust kings becomes ruler, this would be better than there being none. As it is said: 'Sixty years with an unjust ruler, this would be better than there being none.' And it is related of [the fourth Caliph] Ali that he said: 'The people have no option but to have rulership, whether pious or sinful.' People said, 'We understand the pious but why bother with the sinful?' He said: 'Because thanks to it, the highways are kept secure, canonical penalties are applied, holy war is fought against the enemy, and the spoils are collected.'
>
> (ibid.: 12)

Ibn Khaldun (d. 1406) further eroded the foundations of the Caliphate by stating that it was not the only legitimate form of government. Although it was the most desirable institution, historical circumstances resulted in the fragmentation of the *ummah* into individual units, and Ibn Khaldun considered that such units could adopt a form of Islamic government. Thus, although the Islamic world may not be united at any given time, the small units were obliged to Islamicize their politics in order to legitimize their existence. 'If royal authority would sincerely exercise its superiority over men for the sake of God and so as to cause those men to worship God and to wage war against his enemies, there would not be anything reprehensible in it' (cited in Binder 1988: 134).

In the modern age, it was with Ahmad Khan (1817–98) that the institution of the Caliphate was completely undermined. Living in the nineteenth century when the British ruled India, his main aim was to show the British that the Islamic community and Muslims could be loyal under the British crown. In this way Ahmad Khan hoped that the British would respect Muslims, who would then regain the prestige that they had enjoyed under the Moghul Empire. The Indian 'Mutiny' of 1857 caused many British to believe that an integral principle of Islamic doctrine was the unacceptability of non-Islamic rule over Muslims. Ahmad Khan rejected this and stated:

> when a Muslim enjoys protection and security under the rule of a nation not of his own faith, it is in the highest degree infamous if, from a professedly religious motive, he commits any outrage upon the person or property of those by whom he is governed.
>
> (Khan 1993: 232)

He provided a Qur'anic basis for this belief with reference to the prophet Joseph, who in *sura* 12 served a non-believing ruler. In other words, the Caliphate was unnecessary for Indian Muslims, and they should be obedient to the British crown rather than pay allegiance to the Caliph (which had passed into the hands of the Ottoman Turks).

In the twentieth century, Abd al-Raziq (a religious scholar in al-Azhar university in Cairo) made a similar point to that of Ibn Khaldun in a book entitled *Islam and the Sources of Political Authority*, published in 1925. In summarizing this work, Abd al-Raziq himself commented that

> the main point of the book, for which I have been condemned is that Islam did not determine a specific regime, nor did it impose on Muslims a particular system according to the requirements of which they must be governed; rather it has allowed us absolute freedom to organise the state

in accordance with the intellectual, social and economic conditions in which we are found, taking into consideration our social development and the requirements of the times.

(cited in Binder 1988: 131)

Abd al-Raziq believed that Muhammad should be regarded as a prophet in the purely religious sense, for he was neither a king, nor did he attempt to establish a state or government. Therefore if Muhammad was not a political leader, then the political authority of the Caliphate was completely illegitimate. Moreover, Abd al-Raziq attempted to show that the Caliphate had been based on force, and not upon *ijma'*. Had the Caliphate been based on the *ijma'* of the community, then it would have held a degree of religious legitimacy since *ijma'* itself is based on divine law. Abd al-Raziq went so far as to state that there are no specific references to the Caliphate or the establishment of it in the Qur'an or *hadith*. In effect, Abd al-Raziq's work did not separate Islam into spiritual and temporal spheres (*din wa dawlat*), but claimed that Islam was purely spiritual and had nothing whatsoever to do with politics. His views must be seen in their context, for in 1924 the Caliphate had been abolished by Ataturk (the founder of the modern Turkish republic), and several individuals had the institution of the Caliphate within their sight, including members of the House of Saud in Arabia, and also King Fuad in Egypt. Some scholars have seen Abd al-Raziq's criticisms of the Caliphate as an attempt to keep the potentially powerful position of the Caliphate out of such hands. However, his views were condemned by the majority of religious clerics in al-Azhar.

The conclusion that one can draw from this brief survey of Sunni political thought is that it is very difficult to talk about 'Islamic political theory'. In each age there have emerged intellectuals who have advocated a certain response that they believed was suitable for their community in a particular historical situation. The contemporary situation is no different, indicated by the diversity of states in the modern period (following the abolition of the Caliphate) that rule over territories in which the majority of the population is Sunni. They have ranged from monarchy (Saudi Arabia) and parliamentary Islamic democracy (Pakistan) to military dictatorship (again Pakistan) and pseudo-, secular democracy (Turkey and Egypt). It must also be kept in mind that Islam can be utilized for coercion and force in those areas where the concept of 'nation' is weak, and where the state apparatus wishes to maintain control (Iraq and Saudi Arabia).

6.3 The Islamic state after Muhammad: the Shiite tradition

To understand the Shiite interpretation of *jihad* and the state, it is necessary to return to events that occurred at Muhammad's death. There is good reason to be cautious about narratives of these events because they were recorded some time after the events by partisans of different sects. The Sunnis, as described above, believe that Abu Bakr was the first and legitimate successor to Muhammad; however, the Shiites claim that this deputyship was the rightful claim of Ali, Muhammad's cousin and son-in-law. Ali, as a youth of nine years, was the first male to publicly recognize Muhammad as the Prophet of God, and many *hadith* refer to the close relationship between the Prophet and Ali. For example, Muhammad is reported to have said: 'I am the city of knowledge and Ali is the gate.' One of the claims that Shiites make with regard to Ali's legitimate right to leadership of the Islamic *ummah* concerns the events during Muhammad's so-called 'Farewell Pilgrimage' to Mecca, which he made in the last year of his life. At a place named Ghadir Khumm, Muhammad implied that Ali would be his successor, stating: 'Of whomsoever I am lord, then Ali is also his lord. O God! Be the supporter of whoever supports 'Ali and the enemy of whoever opposes him.'

Yet Ali was passed over in favour of Abu Bakr, and it was only after the subsequent Caliphates of Umar and Uthman, that he finally became the leader of the Islamic *ummah*. Even then Ali's leadership was challenged, both by the family which subsequently held the Caliphate from 661 to 750 (the Umayyads), and also by a group who became known as Kharijites. Shiites claim that on Ali's death, the leadership (or Imamate) passed on to his son who became the new leader, or Imam. By most accounts, the new Imam, Hasan (d. 669), was unwilling to take up the challenge of leadership, but his brother Husayn revolted against the Umayyads. However, Husayn and most of his family were brutally murdered at Kerbala (in modern Iraq), and this 'martyrdom' subsequently became the ultimate expression of Shiite Islam, that is, to fight to the death for justice, for God's laws and for one's rights.

The Shiites were not a monolithic group at all, for there emerged several Shiite positions during its formative period, such as the Zaydis and the Isma'ilis. However, the major Shiite denomination in the modern period is the 'Twelver Shiite', so-called because it holds there were twelve Imams. The twelfth Imam is regarded as the 'Mahdi', or the rightly guided one who will return to earth just before the end of time to institute a period of justice, avenging all wrongs committed against true Shiites. The Mahdi is also known as the 'Hidden Imam', because he is not dead, but has entered into a period of 'occultation'; although he appears absent, he is still present in the world, and it is the duty for each Shiite to make a spiritual effort to understand his will.

Shiism has always provided a fertile ground for dissent against the ruling authority of the day. Thus, the Umayyad dynasty was overthrown in 750 by the Abbasids, a movement which was largely Shiite in origin but quickly turned Sunni on assuming power. This meant that the Shiite Imams were kept under strict surveillance by the Abbasid authorities, and it has been suggested that the twelfth Imam entered into 'occultation' for political reasons in an attempt to provide a greater degree of safety for the supporters of Shiism. The Shiite movement certainly won some powerful adherents; indeed, the Caliph al-Ma'mun appointed the eighth Imam, Reza, as his successor in 816 (however, Reza died before al-Ma'mun). Even after the occultation of the twelfth Imam, the religious-political challenge of Shiism remained a threat to the 'orthodox' authorities since several individuals claimed either to be the Mahdi returned, or else to have descended from one of the Imams, and thus to possess esoteric knowledge and power.

According to Shiites the possession of esoteric knowledge and power are among the distinguishing features of the Imams. It is claimed that this knowledge (including the 'real' meaning of the Qur'an) and the Imamate are referred to in *aya* 14.24: 'Have you not seen how God has coined a simile? A good word is like a good tree; its roots are firm, and its branches are in heaven.' The sixth Imam, Ja'far, is reported to have explained this *aya* by stating that Muhammad is the roots of the tree, Ali is its trunk, the Imams are the branches, and their knowledge is the fruit. Ja'far's commentary refers to another important quality of the Imams of the Twelver Shiite tradition, which is their descent from Ali. Another characteristic, arising from the Imams' esoteric knowledge, is that they are immaculate, or sinless.

These qualities of the Imams meant that, in Shiite eyes, they were the true leaders of the community. Only the Imam had perfect knowledge that enabled him to comprehend what amounted to just or tyrannical action, and therefore only the Imam was qualified to declare what constituted a legitimate *jihad*. The other functions of the Imam included dividing the booty acquired through *jihad*, leading the Friday prayers, implementing judicial decisions, receiving the *zakat* alms, and the *khums* (an annual tax of 20 per cent on profits). However, once the twelfth Imam entered into his state of occultation, his followers were left with no-one to perform these functions. The pragmatic solution was found by allowing the Shiite religious clerics to perform most of these tasks. The major exception was leading the *jihad*, which in effect meant that Twelver Shiites claimed that temporal power was the prerogative of the twelfth Imam alone, and that any individual who snatched the reins of power was usurping the rights of the Imam. From the time of the occultation until the modern age there have been various degrees of tension between secular rulers of Shiite lands and the Shiite clerics. On occasions the relationship worked harmoniously, especially when the rulers were just, or when they paid adequate respect to the clerics.

A major development in Twelver Shiite thought occurred during the modern period once Ayatollah Khomeini (d. 1989) began to advocate the doctrine commonly known as *velayat-i faqih*, or guardianship of the jurist. Khomeini did not accept the politically quiescent Shiite 'tradition' and argued that it was the right and the duty of the qualified religious cleric to promote and establish the just Islamic society. In Khomeini's own words:

> Not to have an Islamic government means leaving our boundaries unguarded. Can we afford to sit nonchalantly on our hands while our enemies do whatever they want? . . . Or is it that government is necessary, and that the function of government that existed from the beginning of Islam down to the time of the Twelfth Imam (upon whom be peace) is still enjoined upon us by God after the occultation even though He has appointed no particular individual to that function?
>
> (Khomeini 1981: 61–2)

> The authority that the Prophet and the Imam had in establishing a government, executing laws, and administering affairs exists also for the *faqih* [jurist]. But the *fuqaha* [pl. of *faqih*] do not have absolute authority in the sense of having authority over all other *fuqaha* of their own time being able to appoint or dismiss them.
>
> (ibid.: 64)

The extent to which Khomeini viewed the boundaries of Islamic government became manifest in 1988, when he commented:

> I say openly that the government can stop any religious law if it feels that it is correct to do so . . . the ruler can close or destroy the mosques whenever he sees fit . . . the government can prohibit anything having to do with worship or otherwise if [these things] would be against the interests of the government.
>
> (cited in Jansen 1988: 18)

Here, Khomeini utilizes the concept of *maslahat*, or expediency for public welfare, which is traditionally associated with the Sunni *madhhab* of al-Shafi'i. Some scholars have understood this as a deviation from the 'traditional' form of Shiite Islam, yet for Khomeini, the need for the government to defend Islam takes priority over everything, even over the pillars of Islam.

Up to this point, the focus on Shiism has been on the Twelver variety; however, there are other forms of Shiite belief which have contributed to the expansion of Islamic faith and civilization. Such Shiite groups include the Sevener Shiites, otherwise known as the Isma'ilis. This group holds that the Imamate passed onto the sixth Imam's eldest son, Isma'il, rather than to Musa al-Kazim (whose line leads to the twelfth Imam). The Isma'ilis split into several sects, and one of the most notable of these was the Fatimid Isma'ilis in Egypt. The Isma'ilis survive today in many parts of the world, and one group recognizes the Agha Khan as its leader. Another denomination of Shiites were the Zaydis, who upheld a claim to the Imamate from any just descendant of Ali and Fatima (Muhammad's daughter). Such a doctrine proved attractive because it opened up revolt against tyrannical rulers to a wider range of individuals. In 1980 it was estimated that the world population of Shiites was about 73 million (Momen 1985: 282), although this figure has increased dramatically since then, given the rapid increase in the

Iranian birth rate. According to the 1980 estimate, the Shiites comprised approximately 10 per cent of the Muslim population, located mainly in Iran, Iraq and Lebanon.

6.4 Modern Islam

The impact of the West upon Islamic regions began to be felt in earnest from the beginning of the nineteenth century when Napoleon invaded Egypt in an attempt to cut off British trade routes from India. But Western influence and interference reached a pinnacle in the early part of the twentieth century when Britain and France obtained a series of mandates or protectorates in the Middle East after the First World War. This meant that most of North Africa, the Middle East and India was controlled by European powers. Western hegemony in social, economic and political spheres of life was incomprehensible for many Muslims, for it was the first time in Islamic history that the majority of Muslims did not possess control of their own affairs (except for a brief period in the thirteenth century when the Mongols invaded the Middle East). Muslims asked themselves how they could regain the strength and prestige that they enjoyed under the great dynasties, such as the Moghul dynasty of India (1526–1858), or the Safavid dynasty of Iran (1501–1738). The question remains pertinent today, and several contemporary Islamic worldviews have been offered as responses to both the West and modernization. To simplify things somewhat, a classification of three groups is made in the following: 'fundamentalists', modernists, and traditionalists, although it must also be remembered that the boundaries between the groups have been and remain somewhat fluid, as individuals of different groups share some characterisitics.

ISLAMIC 'FUNDAMENTALISTS'

For a period towards the end of the twentieth century 'Islamic fundamentalism' became something of a 'buzz' word that was used by the media and politicians to label various Islamic groups. Today it is widely recognized that 'fundamentalism' is a problematic term, and attempts by scholars to identify just what 'fundamentalism' is have revealed its elusiveness. Yet even in 1995, the Secretary General of NATO made the following public statement:

> Muslim fundamentalism is at least as dangerous as communism once was. Please do not underestimate this risk . . . at the conclusion of this age it is a serious threat, because it represents terrorism, religious fanaticism and exploitation of social and economic justice.
>
> (cited in *Islamophobia*, 1997: 9)

The following highlights some of suggestions raised and problems encountered by scholars in their attempts to compartmentalize the phenomenon of 'Islamic fundamentalism'.

1. 'Affirmation of the scriptural foundations of Islam is fairly uniform across fundamentalist movements,' argues Arjomand (1995: 182); yet the same is also true of a modernist such as Rahman (see below), or 'secular Muslims' who also base their worldviews on a particular scriptural foundation.

2. It has been argued that 'fundamentalists' adopt a much more literal understanding of the Scripture. Yet this claim is also flawed, for 'fundamentalists' are often characterized by their desire to implement

the so-called *hudud* punishments, even though the exact specifications are not detailed in the Qur'an. (Another weakness of this argument can be demonstrated with reference to the views of Mawdudi, who rejected the practice of amputating the hands of thieves in his ideal Islamic state.)

3. Scholars have also characterized 'fundamentalist' groups as having a detailed political agenda that encompasses the smallest of details in the lives of individuals (Sidahmed and Ehteshami 1996: 3). In the words of Ayatollah Khomeini:

> [Islam] has rules for every person, even before birth, before his marriage, until his marriage, pregnancy, birth, until upbringing of the child, the education of the adult, until puberty, youth, until old age, until death, into the grave, and beyond the grave. [The Islamic rules] do not come to an end simply [because the person] is put into the grave . . . That is just the beginning.
>
> (cited in Dabashi 1993: 477)

Such a view contrasts with Western ideas of modernity, typified by the sociologist Anthony Giddens, who holds that the modern individual chooses his or her own lifestyle in which there are several segmental choices to be made. Of course, an Islamic life in Iran under the guidance of Khomeini included choices within Islamic parameters, but modernity holds nothing sacred. Interestingly, the kind of Islamic boundaries advocated by Khomeini have been questioned recently within Iran. 'Even prohibitions must be regulated,' stated President Khatami in 1997 (cited in Adelkhah 1999: 162).

4. One way to comprehend 'fundamentalism' is to focus upon what it rejects (Arjomand 1995). Specific examples are offered by Appleby, who claims that 'fundamentalists' in general oppose pluralism, relativism and radical individualism (1997: 4). To varying degrees this does indeed seem to be the case, and the differences among 'fundamentalist' groups to their opposition to the 'other' is influenced by political conditioning.

Analysing the reasons for 'fundamentalism' in Islamic regions is fraught with difficulty because there are specific causes within each country. However, it is possible to make several generalizations. First, 'fundamentalism' is one of the responses to Western cultural, political and economic domination, the dangers of which were articulated most famously by Edward Said in his 1978 book *Orientalism*. Said defined orientalism as 'a style of thought based upon an ontological and epistemological distinction made between "the Orient" and (most of the time) "the Occident" (1978: 2). It was claimed by Said that many politicians and academics in the West had essentialized Muslims and Islam into unchanging categories, and many of these assumptions were little more than generalizations with little foundation. Said cited Lord Cromer, the British governor of Egypt between 1882 and 1907, who argued that 'the Oriental generally acts, speaks and thinks in a manner exactly opposite to the European' (ibid.: 39). The European is a 'close reasoner' and a 'natural logician' whereas the Oriental is 'singularly deficient in the logical faculty'. Such prejudiced views were held by some into the second half of the twentieth century. Another danger of orientalism is that the dominated cultures may themselves adopt and interiorize the political, economic and social structures that the hegemonic powers wish to impose. The following example, an episode that occurred in 1962, from Nelson Mandela's autobiography, epitomizes the snares that orientalism sets for 'orientals':

> As I was boarding the plane I saw that the pilot was black. I had never seen a black pilot before, and the instant I did I had to quell my panic. How could a black man fly a plane? But a moment

later I caught myself. I had fallen into the apartheid mind-set, thinking Africans were inferior and that flying was a white man's job.

(1995: 348)

Said's *Orientalism* was instrumental in academics becoming more sensitive to the religious and cultural 'other', and increasing the care given to the methodology of research. One can only wonder why it took so long for Western academics and institutions to accept the kind of criticisms contained in Said's work when some of the main themes had already been articulated by 'orientals' themselves. One such example came from the pen of the Iranian scholar Jalal Al-e Ahmad, whose *Gharbzadegi* (Weststruckness), written in 1962, is a landmark in the modern intellectual quest for cultural authenticity. The attitude of orientalists in the West has kindled the ire of many groups and individuals in the Third World (including nationalists, socialists, and various liberation movements), and among Muslims seeking to preserve their identity in the modern world that constantly erodes tradition. So 'fundamentalists' react against Western political and economic colonialism/imperialism, and they resent the agendas set by the West upon Islamic countries that assume Western standards are normative for the whole world.

Second, it is possible to regard fundamentalism as a resistance movement to modernization (a process not necessarily linked to the West) that brings with it social dislocation and economic transformations. Cultural patterns are affected and many individuals seek comfort from change in traditional patterns of behaviour found in their Islamic heritage. This heritage was down-played by the secular regimes of the Middle East that existed after World War II and were either military or nationalist. With few exceptions, these countries were considered weak vis-à-vis the West, and had not met the expectations of their citizens.

Third, many of the regimes in the Middle East suffered the effects of unequal development during the second half of the twentieth century. That is, economic development was not matched by corresponding advancement in political participation, resulting in an educated class with no means to express their political sentiments, except through marginalized religious groups. Moreover, occasional economic downturns provided opportunities for a 'return to Islam', exploited by the 'fundamentalists'.

Reactions to the West and modernization are not specific to Islam, as other religions and cultures have also resisted the changes that these two forces bring. However, Ernest Gellner argued that the reason for the emergence and persistence of Islamic 'fundamentalism' is related not only to the West and modernization, but also to factors specific to Islam (which make Islamic 'fundamentalism' distinct from other varieties). Gellner finds the root cause in the dialectic between 'High Islam' and 'Folk Islam'. The former is the Islam of the urban scholars, middle classes and tradesmen, who all prefer an orderly, sober Islam where religious study is promoted and God is transcendent. The latter is the Islam of the urban poor, country people and tribes, where an ecstatic, mystical form of Islam predominates and God is immanent or reached through an intermediary, such as a Sufi shaykh. Gellner recognizes that the boundaries between High Islam and Folk Islam have frequently been blurred, but he claims that they have on occasions allied with one another against the ruler of the time. During such periods of revolt it is High Islam that guides the rebellion of the masses in the name of a purification of Islam and establishing justice, and the masses by and large accept the agenda of High Islam for prestige, a chance to gain wealth and to claim freedom from despotism. On the success of the rebellion the masses generally revert back to Folk Islam, until the next occasion for rebellion arises. This cyclical movement portrayed by Gellner came to an end, it is claimed, in the modern period because the social bases of Folk Islam were eroded. More people were educated well, which resulted in a movement away from the more ecstatic, mystical form of Islam, and urbanization and centralization have shifted the balance towards High Islam. Moreover, this High Islam has weakened Folk Islam by blaming it for the weakness of Islamic regions compared with the West. And it is resilient against secularization because it appeals to a native tradition, or a 'return' to Islam, removing the pain of people having to deny their own heritage. Gellner concludes his explanation of Islamic 'fundamentalism' in the following way:

> the world of Islam demonstrates that it is possible to run a modern, or at any rate modernizing, economy, reasonably permeated by the appropriate technological, educational, organizational principles, *and* combine it with a strong, pervasive, powerfully internalised Muslim conviction and identification. A puritan and scripturalist world religion does not seem necessarily doomed to erosion by modern conditions. It may on the contrary be favoured by them.
>
> (1992: 22)

Gellner's ideas, interesting though they are, require further comment. It must be stated that Gellner over-emphasizes the extent of Islamic 'fundamentalism'. While it is true that several Islamic states such as Iran, Pakistan and Egypt adopted the shariah as the basis of their constitution, this does not make them 'fundamentalist', as the shariah can be interpreted in a variety of ways. Indeed, even in Egypt, where the shariah is the basis of law, it has been estimated that more than a third of the adult male population are sympathetic to Folk Islam. One can also point to other nations where Islam is the faith of the majority, but where 'fundamentalism' plays a minor role (despite recent, short-term waves in the opposite direction), such as Turkey and Indonesia. Another fact that Gellner fails to mention is the adoption of Islam by undemocratic states in an attempt to popularize their rule by pitting Islam against the West and Israel (a notable case being Saddam Hussein in Iraq). By adopting Islam in a populist way against the West and Israel, such states are then able to interpret Islam in a 'fundamentalist' fashion to control society.

ISLAMIC MODERNISTS

Once the difference between the technology, science and material improvements in Western lands and the comparative weakness of Islamic regions became apparent in the nineteenth century, it was held by many Muslims that the only way to 'catch up' was to replace corrupt and despotic rulers with a liberal form of democracy that existed in Britain and France. Hence, a series of Islamic modernists whom we may call Islamic liberals (typified by Muhammad Abduh) produced a body of apologetic literature that claimed that 'real' Islam was no different from the democratic norms of Western Europe. Such literature has been analysed by Hourani, who concluded that 'in this line of thought, *maslaha* gradually turns into utility, *shura* into parliamentary democracy, *ijma*' into public opinion; Islam itself becomes identical with civilization and activity' (1962: 144). Such associations between Islamic concepts that appeared in early Islamic history and the practices of modern Europe have been criticized by Aziz Al-Azmeh. 'History is ensnared: it is supposed to contain modernity. Modernity is also ensnared by assuming its correspondence with that supposed past' (1993: 109). (It is ironic that the 'fundamentalists' (who are Al-Azmeh's main target) present a political system that does not pander to Western democratic norms, as in the structures delineated by Mawdudi.) Al-Azmeh's attempt at historical accuracy leads him to the following conclusions:

> This part of history – the Koran and the early period of Islam, that is the golden age of impeccable conduct – achieved currency as though it were clearly defined. But this supposed distinctness was nothing other than the result of its protection from historical inquiry: the Rightly Guided Caliphs ruled by the sword, by consultation of the aristocracy and by appointment to positions, and the

> Koran contains references to a theory of despotic government and a call for consultative govern-
> ment, without conveying precise meanings; it is impossible to derive a theory or even a prescription
> of the necessity of government, let alone institutions from early Muslim history.
>
> (1993: 109)

Another form of Islamic modernism is advocated by those individuals who are also concerned with historical accuracy but whose predominant focus is with the universal message of the Qur'an and the application of analogical reasoning to derive appropriate conclusions for the modern situation. Thus 'consultation of the aristocracy' (as understood by Al-Azmeh) does not necessarily have to remain static for centuries, for it can be transformed into a more pluralistic framework. This is the type of argument offered by Fazlur Rahman, a Pakistani scholar who occupied a chair at the University of Chicago for many years, and passed away in 1988. One of his main arguments was that it is necessary for Muslims to undertake a systematic historical analysis of each *aya* of the Qur'an. This would provide Muslims with an overall historical view of revelation, showing the universal message of the Qur'an, rather than the interpretations of specific *ayas*, the 'atomistic approach' offered by the 'so-called fundamentalists' (to use his term). Until the present time, argued Rahman, Muslims have engaged in a systematic historical analysis of the Qur'an, but only in order to discover which *aya* abrogated which, leading to the trend of particularization rather than universalization. Rahman's intention was to show that at the time of revelation the Qur'an was progressive and liberating, and it is this universal, general spirit of the Qur'an that must be applied by Muslims in the modern age. Rahman has paid attention to the position of women in Islam, for many scholars have asserted that a literal interpretation of specific Qur'anic *ayas* denies women the same rights as men regarding inheritance (4.11) and equality of testimony in legal disputes (2.282). It is argued by Rahman that the Qur'an in fact improves the lot of women compared with the pre-Islamic period, since female infanticide is forbidden, and women are at least guaranteed some rights of inheritance and awarded legal recognition, whereas in the pre-Islamic period this was not the case. Therefore in the present age women should claim more rights than those a literal reading of the Qur'an offers.

Another scholar who has been termed a 'modernist' (Nasr 1994: 302) is Muhammad Arkoun, who was born in Algeria in 1928. Having occupied a chair at the Sorbonne for many years, he is one of the most respected scholars of Islam in the West. Arkoun encourages Muslims to adopt appropriate hermeneutics to understand Islam, and his academic standpoint rejects the rationalists' tendencies as represented by the Mu'tazilites, Islamic philosophers, and Rahman's eternal, universal truth in the form of the spirit of the Qur'an. Arkoun cannot accept any emphasis on original substance or an unchanging essence, which in turn becomes the principle that is defended by a powerful elite at the expense of the views of others who advocate 'unthinkable' ideas. In other words, Arkoun is arguing for an open interpretation of Islam, not a reified version that cannot be lived. What is required is a new study of Islam which will examine the historicity of the Qur'an, the shariah and indeed all Islamic texts and movements. One commentator on Arkoun has paraphrased his worldview in the following manner.

> If, then, Muslims seek the truth about themselves, they must re-examine not simply the 'truths'
> of revelation but all the particular ways in which those 'truths' have been felt, understood,
> elaborated, justified, fashioned into orthodoxy, and experienced in context, over time and within
> geographical space . . . Such an enterprise would require the methods of modern anthropology,
> psychology, sociology, semiotics, linguistics, economics, philosophy, and perhaps other disciplines.
>
> (Lee 1997: 148)

Arkoun has adopted interdisciplinary methodologies, and he also employs the technical terminology of diverse academic fields. These factors, combined with long and complicated sentences, make his works a difficult read for students of Islamic-related studies. However, jargon and complex sentences cannot disguise the challenge that Arkoun has thrown down to Muslims, and many of them find his views unpalatable. The following passage by Arkoun should suggest why this is so:

> Modern knowledge . . . is based on the concept of social-historical space continuously constructed and deconstructed by the activities of the social actors. Each group fights to impose its hegemony over the others not only through political power (control of the state) but also through a cultural system presented as the universal one. Seen from this perspective, the Qur'an is the expression of the historical process which led the small group of believers to power. This process is social, political, cultural and psychological. Through it, the Qur'an, presented as the revelation and received as such by the individual and the collective memory, is continuously reproduced, rewritten, reread, and re-expressed in a changing, social-historical space.
>
> (cited in Kurzman 1998: 220)

Within the classification of Islamic modernists, Nasr (1994) includes the nationalists and socialists. Much of the nationalism within Islamic regions during the early half of the twentieth century was inspired by various secular Western models. The nationalism that was sponsored by the state in Turkey and Iran from the 1920s until the revival of Islam in the latter half of the century was predominantly hostile to Islam. However, there were other forms of nationalism that had their *raison d'être* in Islam itself, the case of Pakistan, created in 1947 from the Indian subcontinent, being the obvious example. Nationalism was also strong in the Arab world, and in the middle of the century there were advocates of pan-Arabism (which also included some form of attachment to Islam), including Egypt, Syria, Iraq, Libya and Yemen. (Indeed the short-lived United Arab Republic between Egypt, Syria and North Yemen was formed in 1958.)

Also included by Nasr among the category of modernists are Islamic socialists and Marxists, and under this rubric we may mention the socialism of President Nasser of Egypt, and that of the Ba'ath party of Syria and Iraq during the 1960s and 1970s. This form of socialism, by and large, has been discredited and rejected by the peoples of these regions.

ISLAMIC TRADITIONALISTS

Islamic 'traditionalists' have been defined as those Muslims who accept the heritage of Islam as an integral part of their worldview which includes the 'Sacred Book, the traditions of its Blessed Prophet, sacred law, theology, philosophy, mystical paths and a specific manner of looking at the world of nature and of creating art' (Nasr 1994: 93). For Nasr, traditionalism is different from the Islamic interpretation of the modernists, since he views many in the latter group as being inspired by Western philosophies (although he accepts that modernists such as Arkoun and Rahman have some positive elements in their works). Islamic traditionalism is also different from Islamic 'fundamentalism' because the 'fundamentalists' tend to reject much of the Islamic tradition in their attempts to recapture the 'pristine' version of Islam that they believe existed in the time of Muhammad and the first four 'rightly-guided' caliphs. It is difficult to estimate the proportion of traditionalists vis-à-vis the other Islamic interpretations; however, it is likely that this group outnumbers the modernists and the 'fundamentalists'. To a certain degree, both Islamic modernism and 'fundamentalism' emerged in the contemporary age as a reaction to modernism and the West. Islamic traditionalism also responded to the new challenge, but in its own way. Since time and space is now short, one example will have to suffice. In post-mutiny India, one group of traditionalists, who became known as the Deobandis, reaffirmed their own identity by ignoring the British-Western ways and developed a response to the modern age from within the Islamic tradition. The Deobandis established a seminary and school just outside Delhi in the aftermath of the 'Mutiny' of 1857, aiming to prepare Indian Muslims to become teachers, prayer leaders, guardians of shrines, doctors, writers and publishers. The seminary united two streams of Islamic thought: traditional theology and the sober dimension of Sufism. Confrontation with the British (i.e. physical violence) was not encouraged because change would come slowly through reforming the community, by individual spiritual and religious effort. Psychological resistance was encouraged. Guidance for the Muslim community was issued in the form of *fatawi* (judicial opinions), which meant that the leaders of the school had to exercise *ijtihad*, within the bounds of the Hanafi school. The emphasis on the *fatawi* demonstrates the desire to reform the Muslim community and also to circumvent the British law-courts. Muslims were encouraged to bring any disputes to the school rather than submit them to the British, and in this way preserve Islamic law and culture. With the emigration of many Muslims from India and Pakistan to Britain, the Deobandis have established themselves in Britain. Their experiences in British India may have assisted some Muslims to come to terms with a new life in a non-Muslim environment. The Deobandis are fighting to capture the leadership of the Islamic community in both Britain and Pakistan, for it has to battle against the more 'fundamentalist' *Jama'at-i Islami* (a party founded by Mawdudi), and the Barelwis (traditionalists who emphasize the spiritual dimension of Islam).

Whatever way Muslims decide to view their heritage, modernity poses new challenges to Islam. Gellner's views that 'fundamentalism' is the most appropriate form of Islam for the modern age stand in contrast to those of Ninian Smart, who commented:

> I believe that contemporary Islamism, though not without the modernizing tendencies, will be short lived, and Islam will rediscover Islamic modernism from the beginning of the twentieth century, together with a redeveloped Sufism, which finds it easier to cope with modern science.
>
> (1998: 86)

The extent to which Islam remains a factor in 'Islamic' societies remains to be seen as globalization and increasing levels of information technology make neighbours of Christians, Hindus, agnostics and atheists. It is highly unlikely that Islam will disappear from the politics and culture of traditionally 'Islamic' regions, even if it is only a source of opposition for the marginalized and threatened in the modern world. Islam functions as a source of identity in addition to providing spiritual meaning to its adherents. Whether 'fundamentalism' will be a lasting phenomenon is unclear; it has existed in varying strengths from the beginning of the modern period. But it is interesting that in this period in Islamic regions intellectuals have picked up and developed Western political thought, and such ideas as liberalism, nationalism, socialism have had to coexist (and sometimes compete) with those of the 'fundamentalists'. The present debate in many Islamic countries is centred on the civil society, and this, of course, with an emphasis on the individual, is a direct challenge to 'fundamentalist' interpretations. Concerning international relations, not all Muslims view the future as an inevitable 'clash of civilizations' (as predicted by Huntington) between the West and Islam. These points were recognized explicitly by the Iranian President, Muhammad Khatami, who in his address to the United Nations in 1998, stated:

> Today the Iranian nation draws on its past to contemplate a better tomorrow while defying reactionary tendencies and, backed by principles and ideas rooted in its religious, national,

historical and revolutionary heritage, and benefiting from positive achievements of contemporary civilization, marches, through trial and error, towards a promising future.

The Islamic Revolution of the Iranian people was a revolt of reason against coercion and suppression. Certainly a revolution which resorted to logic in the phase of destruction is much better disposed to resort to dialogue and reason in the phase of construction. Hence, it calls for a dialogue among civilizations and cultures instead of a clash between them.

(Khatami 1998)

BIBLIOGRAPHY

Abrahamov, B. (1998) *Islamic Theology*. Edinburgh: Edinburgh University Press.

Abu Zahra, N. (1998) 'Islamic history, Islamic identity and the reform of Islamic law', in J. Cooper, R. Nettler and M. Mahmoud (eds), *Islam and Modernity*. London: I. B. Tauris.

Abu Zaid, N. H. (1998) 'Divine attributes in the Qur'an', in J. Cooper, R. Nettler and M. Mahmoud (eds), *Islam and Modernity*. London: I. B.Tauris.

Adelkhah, F. (1999) *Being Modern in Iran*. London: Hurst.

Al-Azmeh, A. (1993) *Islams and Modernities*. London: Verso.

Al-e Ahmad, J. (1997) *Gharbzadegi*. Costa Mesa, CA: Mazda.

Appleby, R. S. (1997) *Spokesmen for the Despised*. Chicago: University of Chicago Press.

Arberry, A. (1983) *The Qur'an Interpreted*. Oxford: Oxford University Press.

Archer, J. (1924) *Mystical Elements in Mohammed*. New Haven: Yale University Press.

Arjomand, S. A. (1995) 'Unity and diversity in Islamic fundamentalism', in M. E. Marty and R. Scott Appleby (eds), *Fundamentalisms Comprehended*. Chicago: University of Chicago Press.

Ashmawi, M. (1998) 'Shari'a: the codification of Islamic law', in C. Kurzman (ed.), *Liberal Islam*. Oxford: Oxford University Press.

Ayata, S. (1991) 'Traditional Sufi orders on the periphery', in R. Tapper (ed.), *Islam in Modern Turkey*. London: Macmillan.

Ayn al-Quzat Hamadani (1962) *Tamhidat*, ed. A. Usayran. Tehran: Danishgah-i Tehran.

Bakhtiar, L. (1995) *Ramadan: Motivating Believers to Action*. Chicago: Kazi.

Binder, L. (1988) *Islamic Liberalism*. Chicago: University of Chicago Press.

Bowie, F. (2000) *The Anthropology of Religion*. London: Blackwell.

Brown, N. O. (1991) *Apocalypse – And/Or – Metamorphosis*. Berkeley: University of California Press.

Calder, N. (1996) 'Law', in S. H. Nasr and O. Leaman (eds), *History of Islamic Philosophy*, Part II. London: Routledge.

Calder, N. (1997) 'History and nostalgia: reflections on John Wansbrough's *The Sectarian Milieu*', *Method and Theory in the Study of Religion*. Berlin and New York: Mouton de Gruyter.

Carlyle, T. (1869) *Sartor Resartus and Lectures on Heroes*. London: Chapman & Hall.

Chittick, W. (2000) *Sufism: A Short Introduction*. Oxford: Oneworld.

Cohen, M. (1994) *Under Crescent and Cross*. Princeton: Princeton University Press.

Cohn-Sherbok, D. (1997) *Islam in a World of Diverse Faiths*. London: Macmillan.

Coulson, N. (1964) *A History of Islamic Law*. Edinburgh: Edinburgh University Press.

Dabashi, H. (1993) *Theology of Discontent*. New York: New York University Press.

Danner, V. (1972) 'The necessity for the rise of the term Sufi', *Studies in Comparative Religion* 6(2) (Spring): 71–7.

Dashti, A. (1994) *Twenty-Three Years*. Costa Mesa, CA: Mazda.

Denny, F. M. (1994) *An Introduction to Islam*, 2nd edn. New Jersey: Prentice Hall.

Enayat, H. (1982) *Modern Islamic Political Thought*. London: Macmillan.

Ernst, C. (1985) *Words of Ecstasy in Sufism*. Albany: State University of New York Press.

Ernst, C. (1997) *The Shambhala Guide to Sufism*. Boston: Shambhala.

Esack, F. (1997) *Qur'an, Liberation and Pluralism*. Oxford: Oneworld.

Esack, F. (1999) *On Being a Muslim*. Oxford: Oneworld.

Ewing, C. (1984) 'Malangs in the Punjab', in B. Metcalf (ed.), *Moral Conduct and Authority*. Berkeley: University of California Press.

Fakhry, M. (1994) *The Qur'an*. Reading: Garnet.

Fakhry, M. (1997) *A Short Introduction to Islamic Philosophy, Theology and Mysticism*. Oxford: Oneworld.

Firestone, R. (1990) *Journeys in Holy Lands: The Evolution of the Abraham–Ishmael Legends in Islamic Exegesis*. Albany: State University of New York Press.

Fisk, R. (1999) 'The Prophet falls foul of Egyptian thought police', *The Independent*, 28 July.

Geaves, R. (2000) *The Sufis of Britain*. Cardiff: Cardiff Academic Press.

Gellner, E. (1992) *Postmodernism, Reason and Religion*. London: Routledge.

Gerholm, T. (1997) 'The Islamization of contemporary Egypt', in E. E. Rosander and D. Westerlund (eds), *African Islam and Islam in Africa*. London: Hurst.

Ghazali (1983), *Kimiya-yi sa'adat*, ed. Husayn Khadiwjam. Tehran: Markaz-i intisharat-i 'ilmi wa farhangi.

Ghazali (1992) *The Ninety-Nine Beautiful Names of God*. Cambridge: Islamic Texts.

Gibb, H. A. R. (1983) 'Islam', in R. C. Zaehner (ed.), *The Concise Encyclopedia of Living Faiths*. London: Hutchinson.

Graham, W. (1977) *Divine Word and Prophetic Word in Early Islam*. The Hague and London: Mouton.

Graham, W. (1983) 'Islam in the Mirror of Ritual', in R. Hovanissian and S. Vryonis (eds), *Islam's Understanding of Itself*. Malibu: Undena.

Hourani, A. (1962) *Arabic Thought in the Liberal Age*. Cambridge: Cambridge University Press.

Hujwiri (1976) *Kashf al-Mahjub of Al Hujwiri*, trans. R. Nicholson. London: Luzac.

Hussein, T. (1995) *An Egyptian Childhood*, trans. E. H. Paxton. Cairo: American University in Cairo Press.

Ibn al-'Arabi (1980) *The Bezels of Wisdom*, trans. R. Austin. New York: Paulist Press.

Iqbal, M. (1934) *The Reconstruction of Religious Thought in Islam*. London: Oxford University Press.

Jansen, G. (1988) 'Khomeini's heretical delusions of grandeur', *Middle East International* 317. London.

Kedourie, E. (1992) *Politics in the Middle East*. Oxford: Oxford University Press.

Khan, A. (1993) *Political Profile of Sir Sayyid Ahmad Khan*, ed. H. Malik. Delhi: Adam.

Khatami, M. (1998) Statement to the United Nations General Assembly: http://www.un.int/iran/statement/ga/ga53001.html

Khomeini (1981) *Islam and Revolution*, trans. and annotated H. Algar. London: Kegan Paul International.

Kurzman, C. (ed.) (1998) *Liberal Islam*. Oxford: Oxford University Press.

Lawrence, B. (1998) *Shattering the Myth*. Princeton: Princeton University Press.

Lee, R. (1997) *Overcoming Tradition and Modernity*. Oxford: Westview Press.

Lewis, B. (1984) *The Jews of Islam*. London: Routledge & Kegan Paul.

McAuliffe, J. Dammen (1991) *Qur'anic Christians*. Cambridge: Cambridge University Press.

Malcolm X (1966) *The Autobiography of Malcolm X*. London: Hutchinson.

Mandela, N. (1995) *Long Walk to Freedom*. London: Abacus.

Mardin, S. (1991) 'The Naqsibendi Order in Turkish history', in R. Tapper (ed.), *Islam in Modern Turkey*. London: I. B. Tauris.

Mardin, S. (1993) 'The Naqshibendi Order of Turkey', in M. E. Marty and R. S. Appelby (eds), *Fundamentalisms and the State*. Chicago: University of Chicago Press.

Marshall, D. (2001) 'Christianity in the Qur'an', in L. Ridgeon (ed.), *Islamic Interpretations of Christianity*. Richmond: Curzon Press.

Martin, R. C., and M. R. Woodward (1997) *Defenders of Reason in Islam*. Oxford: Oneworld.

Al-Mawardi (1996) *The Laws of Islamic Governance*, trans. A. Yate. London: Ta-Ha.

Mawdudi, A. A. (1982) *Let Us Be Muslims*. Leicester: Islamic Foundation.

Mawdudi, A. A. (1988) *Towards Understanding the Qur'an*. Leicester: Islamic Foundation.

Mawdudi, A. A. (1993) *Political Theory of Islam*. Lahore: Islamic Publications.

Momen, M. (1985) *An Introduction to Shi'i Islam*. New Haven: Yale University Press.

Murata, S., and W. C. Chittick (1994) *The Vision of Islam*. London: I. B. Tauris.

al-Na'im, A. A. (1998) 'Shari'a and basic human rights concerns', in Kurzman 1998.

Najjar, F. M. (1998) 'Islamic fundamentalism and the intellectuals', *British Journal of Middle Eastern Studies* 25(1) (May).

Nasr, S. H. (1994) *Traditional Islam in the Modern World*. London: Kegan Paul International.

Netton, I. R. (1994) *Allah Transcendent*. London: Curzon Press.

Netton, I. R. (1996) *Text and Trauma*. London: Curzon Press.

Nicholson, R. A. (1930) *A Literary History of the Arabs*. Cambridge: Cambridge University Press.

Padwick, C. (1961) *Muslim Devotions*. London: SPCK.

Parrinder, G. (1965) *Jesus in the Qur'an*. London: Faber.

Peters, F. (1994a) *Muhammad and the Origins of Islam*. Albany: State University of New York Press.

Peters, F. (1994b) *The Hajj: The Muslim Pilgrimage to Mecca and Holy Places*. Princeton: Princeton University Press.

Pickthall, M. (1930) *The Meaning of the Glorious Qur'an*. New York: Dorset Press.

Rahman, F. (1966) *Islam*. Chicago: University of Chicago Press.

Rahman, F. (1980) *Major Themes of the Qur'an*. Minneapolis: Bibliotheca Islamica.

Rahman, F. (1982) *Islam and Modernity*. Chicago: University of Chicago Press.

Rahman, F. (2000) *Revival and Reform in Islam*. Oxford: Oneworld.

Renard, J. (1996) *Seven Doors to Islam*. Berkeley: University of California Press.

Ridgeon, L. (1998) *'Aziz Nasafi*. Richmond: Curzon Press.

Ridgeon, L. (1999) *Crescents on the Cross*. Glasgow: Trinity St Mungo Press.

Robinson, N. (1996) *Discovering the Qur'an*. London: SCM Press.

Robinson, N. (1999) *Islam: A Concise Introduction*. Richmond: Curzon Press.

Rumi (1957) *Diwan-e Kabir*, ed. Furuzanfar. Tehran: Amir Kabir.

Runnymede Trust (1997) *Islamophobia: A Challenge for Us All*. London: Runnymede Trust.

Ruthven, M. (1984) *Islam in the World*. London: Penguin.

Said, E. (1978) *Orientalism*. London: Penguin.

Said, E. (1981) *Covering Islam*. London: Routledge & Kegan Paul.

Sarraf, M. (1991) *Rasa'il-i Javanmardan*. Tehran and Paris: Institut Français de Recherche en Iran.

Schacht, J. (1934) 'Zakat', in *Encyclopedia of Islam*. London: Luzac.

Schimmel, A. (1983) 'Sufism and the Islamic tradition', in S. Katz (ed.), *Mysticism and Religious Tradition*. Oxford: Oxford University Press.

Schimmel, A. (1985) *And Muhammad is His Messenger*. Chapel Hill: University of North Carolina Press.

Schimmel, A. (1994) *Deciphering the Signs of God*. Albany: State University of New York Press.

Schirazi, A. (1998) *The Constitution of Iran*. London: I. B. Tauris.

Shaban, M. (1994) *Islamic History*, vol. 1. Cambridge: Cambridge University Press.

Shariati, A. (1977) *Hajj*. Bedford, OH: Free Islamic Literature.

Sidahmed, A. S., and A. Ehteshami (eds) (1996) *Islamic Fundamentalism*. Oxford: Westview Press.

Smart, N. (1998) 'Tradition, retrospective perception, nationalism and modernism', in P. Heelas (ed.), *Religion, Modernity and Postmodernity*. Oxford: Blackwell.

Soroush, A. K. (1998) 'The evolution and devolution of religious knowledge', in Kurzman 1998.

Talbot, I. (1998) *Pakistan: A Modern History*. London: Hurst.

Trimingham, J. S. (1973) *The Sufi Orders in Islam*. Oxford: Oxford University Press.

Turner, V. (1969) *The Ritual Process*. London: Routledge & Kegan Paul.

Turner, V. (1974) *Dramas, Fields, and Metaphors*. London: Cornell University Press.

Von Denffer, A. (1985) *'Ulum al-Qur'an*. Leicester: Islamic Foundation.

Wansbrough, J. (1977) *Qur'anic Studies*. Cambridge: Cambridge University Press.

Wansbrough, J. (1978) *The Sectarian Milieu*. Oxford: Oxford University Press.

Watt, W. M. (1962) *Islamic Philosophy and Theology*. Edinburgh: Edinburgh University Press.

Watt, W. (1964) *Muhammad: Prophet and Statesman*. Oxford: Oxford University Press.

Watt, W. (1998) *The Formative Period of Islamic Thought*. Oxford: Oneworld.

Welch, A. T. (1979) 'Muhammad's understanding of himself', in R. G. Hovannisian and S. Vryonis (eds), *Islam's Understanding of Itself*. Malibu, CA: Undena.

Wensinck, A. J. (1982) *Muhammad and the Jews of Medina*. Berlin: W. Behm.

Ziai, H. (1992) 'The source and nature of authority', in C. Butterworth (ed.), *The Political Aspects of Islamic Philosophy*. Harvard College of Middle Eastern Studies.

Zubaidi, A. M. (1983) 'The impact of the Qur'an and *hadith* on medieval Arabic literature', in A. F. L. Beeston (ed.), *The Cambridge History of Arabic Literature*. Cambridge: Cambridge University Press.

From modernism to postmodernism

David Jasper

The Enlightenment has always aimed at liberating men from fear and establishing their sovereignty. Yet the fully enlightened earth radiates disaster triumphant.

(Adorno and Horkheimer 1944)

1 THE ORIGINS OF MODERNISM

1.1 God and the Enlightenment

The term 'Enlightenment' is a translation of the German *Aufklärung* which is specifically related to the movement of thought in eighteenth-century Germany associated with Reimarus, Lessing and Herder and the celebration of reason. Rejecting dogmatic Christianity, such thought was guided by the belief in fundamental human goodness, by humanitarian ideals and by scientific procedures. Religiously, Enlightenment thought tended towards a Deism which has been described as:

the conviction . . . that there is natural religion and that this precedes all religions of revelation . . . in it [the Deists] saw contained the objective conditions of the good pleasure which God can take in men. They therefore declared that it was sufficient, and that to follow the precepts of natural religion, which together and individually had moral character, qualified a man for eternal salvation.[1]

In fact, however, such thinking had a profound effect upon German Protestantism with far-reaching consequences for critical thought in the nineteenth century, not least in its disintegrative effect upon the authority of the Bible and in particular the Gospels.

But the roots of the Enlightenment lie further back than the eighteenth century, in the progress of physics and mathematics in the previous hundred years and in the mathematical structure of reason in Descartes, Spinoza and Hobbes. Above all, perhaps, modern philosophy is born, with Descartes' *Meditations on First Philosophy* (1641) an almost autobiographical journey from doubt and despair to certainty. In the Second Meditation he asks:

what of thinking? I find here that thought is an attribute that belongs to me; it alone cannot be separated from me. I am, I exist, that is certain. But how often? Just when I think; for it might possibly be the case if I ceased entirely to think, that I should likewise cease altogether to exist. I do not now admit anything which is not necessarily true: to speak accurately I am not more than a thing which thinks, that is to say a mind or a soul, or an understanding, or a reason, which are terms whose significance was formerly unknown to me. I am, however, a real thing and really exist; but what thing? I have answered: a thing which thinks.

(Descartes 1996: 36)

At a stroke, the centre of all things had shifted from God to the mind of the self and its certainty of its own existence apart from matter and from all other minds. At the heart of the philosophy was the subject, and autobiographical reflection was to shift from the *Confessions* of St Augustine, for whom all was centred upon God, to the *Confessions* of Rousseau in the second half of the eighteenth century, which centre upon man 'in all the truth of nature' and a self focused upon its often morbid sensibility in despite of morality and social convention.

Deeply inspired by Rousseau, the philosopher Immanuel Kant develops the notion of freedom as autonomy in his 1784 essay 'An Answer to the Question: "What is Enlightenment?"', which begins with the affirmation that 'Enlightenment is man's emergence from his self-incurred immaturity' (Kant 1991: 54). Overcoming laziness and cowardice, Kant encourages us to have courage to use our own understanding and to make the laws which we must obey. The freedom to change, and to allow for future change, is essential, Kant portraying the focal point of enlightenment as 'matters of religion'.

But should not a society of clergymen, for example an ecclesiastical synod or a venerable presbytery (as the Dutch call it), be entitled to commit itself by oath to a certain unalterable set of doctrines, in order to secure for all time a constant guardianship over each of its members, and through them over all people? I reply that this is quite impossible. A contract of this kind, concluded with a view to preventing all further enlightenment of mankind for ever, is absolutely null and void, even if it is ratified by the supreme power.

(ibid.: 57)

1 G. Gawlick, quoted in Reventlow 1984: 289.

Even in matters of religion, in the proper exercise of freedom, man is 'more than a machine', Kant limiting science, or rather reformulating without ever rejecting it. Yet if, for Kant, the Enlightenment is driven by the Horatian motto *Sapere Aude*, 'Think for yourself', yet it was the Enlightenment which established mathematical method and science as being at the very heart of philosophy and culture. Above all, at the turn of the eighteenth century, Isaac Newton (1642–1727) set about explaining the material world by a few fundamental laws of unprecedented precision and clarity, establishing scientific paradigms which remained unshaken until the beginning of the twentieth century, and still exercise immense authority in many forms of thinking. The new order was summed up in Alexander Pope's celebrated 'Epitaph':

> Nature and Nature's Laws lay hid in Night:
> God said, Let Newton be! And all was light!

Although Newton's writings include works of biblical criticism (notably on Daniel and Revelation) and he remained a churchman, yet he privately denied the Trinity on the ground that such belief was inaccessible to reason. Concerned above all with *order* and the formulation of general laws on the basis of observation and experiment, Newton sought to transform idle conjecture and confusion into logical and coherent systems, that is, no less than a perfect copy of the divine harmony of nature. This pursuit of a clear picture of the workings of the human mind would effect a release from the chaos of earlier, unregenerate ages which were darkened by idleness or perversity. To move into the light of reason alone effects human happiness and freedom under the laws of rationality.

It was, however, the figure of Kant who unpicked this sublime vision, ushering in the anxious world of Romantics, particularly in Germany and England, and above all in his late work *Religion Within the Limits of Reason Alone* (1793).

1.2 Kant and Romanticism

Brought up within the spirit of pietism, with its emphasis on revelation and rebirth, and issuing in a practical love for fellow human-beings, Kant was a deeply religious man. Not until he was seventy, however, did he write his principal theological work, *Religion Within the Limits of Reason Alone*. Three years earlier, in the *Critique of Judgement*, Kant had acknowledged that the mechanical and teleological principles are both essential in explaining nature, yet stand in conflict with one another.[2] Science demands the mechanical principle, yet, on the other hand, Kant affirmed that 'Absolutely no human reason . . . can hope to understand the production of even a blade of grass by mere mechanical sources.' Kant readily acknowledged the threat which a modern scientific worldview poses for morality and religion, yet as a child of the eighteenth-century German Enlightenment (the *Aufklärung*) he emphasized an individualism which affirmed human moral autonomy and freedom. Thus, in *Religion*, religion is, to all intents and purposes, reduced to morality and moral experience of the divine. His thought remained very much in tune with his famous essay of 1784, 'An answer to the question: "What is Enlightenment?"', in which he examines the Horatian motto *Sapere Aude* – 'Think for yourself' (Kant 1991: 54–60).

Religion Within the Limits of Reason Alone begins with an examination of the radical evil within human nature and Kant's acknowledgement of the fall from an initial 'good estate', a belief to be found

---

2 See Greene 1960: xlv.

in religion and poetry throughout the world. At the very outset he dismisses the superficial and 'modern' belief in progress towards the good as inherent in human nature: Kant remarks crisply:

> If this belief . . . is meant to apply to *moral* goodness and badness (not simply to the process of civilisation) it has certainly not been deduced from experience; the history of all times cries too loudly against it. The belief, we may presume, is a well-intentioned assumption of the moralists, from Seneca to Rousseau, designed to encourage the sedulous cultivation of that seed of goodness which perhaps lies in us – if, indeed, we can count on any such natural basis of goodness in man.
>
> (Kant 1960: 15–16)

In Kant, radical evil lies in the power of human beings to misuse their freedom. The term he uses is the 'moral predisposition' to contradict the inherent freedom to self-determination; in a manner reminiscent of St Paul in the Epistle to the Romans 7.15 ('I do not understand my own actions. For I do not do what I want, but I do the very thing I hate.' RSV), Kant speaks of a conflict of 'incentives' and suggests that:

> The distinction between a good man and one who is evil cannot lie in the difference between the incentives which they adopt into their maxim (not in the content of the maxim), but rather must depend upon *subordination* (the form of the maxim), *i.e which of the two incentives he makes the condition of the other.*
>
> (ibid.: 31)

After Kant, German and English Romanticism at the turn of the nineteenth century is burdened with the conflict between aspiration and a sense of guilt and failure. In his posthumously published *Confessions of an Inquiring Spirit* (1840), Samuel Taylor Coleridge admitted to be one 'who is neither fair nor saintly, but who – groaning under a deep sense of infirmity and manifold imperfection – feels the want, the necessity, of religious support' (Coleridge 1840: 3). Beneath all their Promethean ambitions the great Romantics suffered an unbearable insecurity, and their sense of loss and failure was, at heart, religious. As a young man, Coleridge admitted that Kant's writings, including *Religion Within the Limits of Reason Alone*, 'took possession of me as with a giant's hand' (Coleridge 1817: 153), and yet the reduction of religion to within the limits of morality and the 'Ideas' (*Ideen*) of metaphysics – God, Freedom, Immortality – to regulative principles of which the human mind could have no constitutional knowledge, were irresolvable burdens to Coleridge's religious mind and sensibility.

The dilemma already points forward to the later nineteenth century, which came to be suspended, as Matthew Arnold was to put it,

> Wandering between two worlds, one dead,
> The other powerless to be born,
> With nowhere yet to rest my head,
> Like these, on earth I wait forlorn.
>
> (Arnold 1855)

Some, like Shelley, resolved the crisis through the route of atheism, abandoning religion and finding truth entirely within poetry and the imagination. In 'A Defence of Poetry' (1821), Shelley emphasized exclusively 'the poetry in the doctrines of Jesus Christ' and regards Christianity 'in its abstract purity' as 'the esoteric expression of the esoteric doctrines of the poetry and wisdom of antiquity' (1821: 122–3). Others, heirs of neo-classical Deism, looked to nature and its inner impulses which the individual experiences through feelings and the imagination. A pre-eminent example of this is to be found in William Wordsworth's 'Tintern Abbey' (1798):

> For I have learned
> To look on nature, not as in the hour
> Of thoughtless youth; but hearing oftentimes
> The still, sad music of humanity,
> Nor harsh, nor grating, though of ample power
> To chasten and subdue.

Even more in Germany, the philosophy of nature in Herder, Hölderlin, Schelling and Novalis informed the Romantic spirit – in Herder's words, 'Siehe die ganze Natur, bettrachte die grosse Analogie der Schöpfung. Alles fühlt sich und seines Gleichen, Leben wallet ze Leben' ('See the whole of nature, behold the great analogy of creation. Everything feels itself and its like, life reverberates to life') (cited in Taylor 1989: 369).

Yet for the great Romantic poets and thinkers in England and Germany, the interaction between the challenge to religion, the anxiety about the self and its failure (the word 'existential' was first used in 1837) and the force of nature, all subjected to the criticism of the Enlightenment, 'met in the need for a modern mythology' (Shaffer 1975: 32). Impelled massively by Kant, the Romantics were deeply religious souls from whom the old Christian certainties were slipping away and for whom, in Elinor Shaffer's words, 'in order to salvage Christianity, historical criticism had to be made constructive as well as destructive; the result was a new form of history'. This 'mythologized history' was the inheritance of the nineteenth century.

1.3 Modernity and the twentieth century

Thus far, the roots of modernity have been sought in the history of European ideas which finds its focus in Enlightenment reason, in Kant (and after him Hegel) and Romanticism. The move is defensible as we begin to look ahead to deconstruction and the postmodern, the lineage also being traced, for example, by Mark C. Taylor in his collection *Deconstruction in Context: Literature and Philosophy* (1986), which begins with Kant and Hegel and reminds us that Jacques Derrida, too, begins his seminal work *Of Grammatology* with an expression of debt to Hegel as 'the thinker of irreducible difference . . . the last philosopher of the book and the first thinker of writing' (Derrida 1976: 26). It is important to remember, also, that the great proponents of the postmodern – beginning with Heidegger, but also Derrida, Lyotard, Foucault – are all children of the Enlightenment as well as heirs of Kant.

Yet the term 'modernism' also has a more specific, more limited sense within the art and literature of the twentieth century, encompassing such movements and ideas as Dadaism, Imagism, Existentialism, Expressionism, the Absurd, Vorticism. Yet these also have their roots in the matter of discussion so far. The novelist and critic Malcolm Bradbury has written:

> What Modernism and Postmodernism share in common is a single adversary which is, to put it crudely, realism or naïve mimesis. Both are forms of post-Realism. They likewise share in common a practice based on avant-garde and movement tactics and a sense of modern culture as a field of anxious stylistic formation.
>
> (cited in Butler 1994: 1)

This anxiety, and the preoccupation with form, goes back to the early nineteenth century with its confusions and instabilities as to the identity of the self and therefore 'being' itself, expressed in new forms of historicism and a renewed send of 'myth', as ancient religious and ontological stabilities faded. Thus Nietzsche and Heidegger (as we shall see later) stress 'Being as an event' (Vattimo 1988: 3), and modernity's central characteristic is the shift from ontology to epistemology.

Altogether Hegel, most specifically in the *Phenomenology of Spirit* (1807), undergirds what Gianni Vattimo has called 'the logic of development inherent in modernity', suggesting a model of self-identity which inspired, among others, Karl Marx, and providing a coherent (if ultimately sterile) foundation at least for British theology until William Temple. Yet the characteristic condition of the nineteenth century was the anxious spirit. The pursuit of history, and for many above all the historical Jesus, was a quest for roots and stability, while such souls as Matthew Arnold followed Coleridge in their faltering before the impossible demands of Kant's 'categorical imperative', yet without the resources of Coleridge's vast intellect and subtle spirit. The moral demands of 'religion within the limits of reason alone' were simply too great for the lonely, isolated individual who has been either betrayed or abandoned by God. In his poem of 1867, entitled 'Dover Beach', Matthew Arnold imaged the 'sea of faith' withdrawing with the ebbtide, his verse becoming the title of a television series and full-length study of the history of Christian decline by the theologian Don Cupitt in 1984.

> Ah, love, let us be true
> To another another! For the world, which seems
> To lie before us like a land of dreams,
> So various, so beautiful, so new,
> Hath really neither joy, nor love, nor light,
> Nor certitude, nor peace, nor help for pain.
>
> (Arnold 1867)

Here, almost forty years before the publication of Joseph Conrad's novella, we seem to be close to the heart of darkness, even in the expansionist world of mid-nineteenth-century British imperialism. In *Literature and Dogma* (1873), Arnold seems not so very far from the spirit of Shelley in his reading of the Bible, resorting to a defence of Scripture as poetic and literary as opposed to the 'scientific' terms of the theologians, and 'God' as 'a term of poetry and eloquence', or simply 'the stream of tendency by which all things seek to fulfil the law of their being' (Arnold 1873: 22, 39). Religion, for Arnold, is sustained within the rather vague idea of poetry, but the old world seemed to be slipping away in the anxious minds of the Victorian 'honest doubters'.[3] It was not an easy or welcome transition, its sadness caught by the novelist Anthony Trollope as he describes the 'clergyman who subscribes for Colenso'[4] in the series of articles in *Clergymen of the Church of England* (1865–6):

> With hands outstretched towards the old places, with sorrowing hearts, – with hearts which still love the old teachings which the mind will no longer accept, – we, too, cut our ropes, and go out in our little boats, and search for a land that will be new to us, though how far new, – new in how many things, we do not know. Who would not stay behind if it were possible to him?
>
> (Trollope 1866: 128–9)

3 The classic study remains Willey 1956.
4 Bishop Colenso of Natal (1814–83) challenged much traditional doctrine of the Church, and questioned the authorship and historical accuracy of the Pentateuch, the first five books of the Bible, traditionally thought to have been written by Moses.

Matthew Arnold in 'Dover Beach' epitomizes the anxious Victorian, struggling in the aftermath of Kant, and one form of what Owen Chadwick has called *The Secularisation of the European Mind in the Nineteenth Century* (1975), the three great prophets of which we shall examine in section 2 of this chapter. Some churchmen in England continued to struggle to stem the tide as it ebbed on the sea of faith, notably in the publication of *Lux Mundi* in 1889, a collection of essays edited by Charles Gore, the future bishop of Oxford, which attempted 'to put the Catholic faith into its right relation to modern intellectual and moral problems'. Later in the twentieth century, the Modern Churchmen's Union continued to try and relate Anglican thought to contemporary ideas and discoveries. But such 'Modernism' within the Anglican and other churches failed to relate to the wider movements in art and ideas. Indeed, the most widely disseminated definition of the 'modern' lay within the single word – secularization. In Vattimo's words:

> Secularisation, as the modern is a term which describes not only what happens in a certain era and what nature it assumes, but also the 'value' that dominates and guides consciousness in the era in question, primarily as faith in progress – which is both a secularised faith and a faith in secularisation.[5]

But neither Vattimo nor the great student of the modern Hans Blumenberg are satisfied with this as a description of the varieties of 'modernism' which emerged in the early years of the twentieth century, in literature of the imagist poets and the stream-of-consciousness novelists, in Kandinsky and the artistic move towards abstraction, in Schoenberg's explorations into (a)tonality in music, and the radical aesthetics of Picasso's *Les Demoiselles d'Avignon* (1907). Vattimo, looking back to Nietzsche, defines modernity as 'that era in which being modern becomes a value, or rather, it becomes *the* fundamental value to which all other values refer'.[6] Blumenberg, in his magisterial work *The Legitimacy of the Modern Age* (1966), replaces the idea of progress in the modern age as the secularization of Christian eschatology (Löwith 1949) with what he calls the 'reoccupation' of theology in new positions vacated by the withdrawal of the traditional sea of faith, a hint which may begin to explain the inexhaustible religious concerns of the great prophets of postmodernity, who will be examined in sections 3 and 4 of this chapter (Blumenberg 1983: 65).

2 MODERN PROPHETS AND THE DEATH OF GOD

2.1 Karl Marx

Charles Taylor has argued that 'Marx's theory of alienation and his perspective on liberation are based not only on Enlightenment humanism but also on Romantic expressivism, and hence ultimately on the idea of nature as a source' (Taylor 1989: 388–9). The grandson of a rabbi and the son of a deist immersed in Enlightenment reason, Karl Marx was, early in his intellectual life, a student of Hegel, and his developed materialism owes much to Hegelian dialectics which, in a sense, he turns on their head. In the first of his *Theses on Feuerbach* (written, 1845), he criticizes the theoretical and abstract materialism of Feuerbach, and underlying his version of the progress of ideas is an anti-intellectualism,

5 Vattimo 1988: 99–100. See also Lübbe 1965.
6 Vattimo 1988: 231.

quite opposed to Hegelian idealism, which he sums up (with Friedrich Engels) in *The Communist Manifesto* (1848): 'What else does the history of ideas prove than that intellectual production changes its character in proportion as material production is changed?' (Marx 1888: 68).

Marx's break with the bourgeois institutions of the nineteenth century, including religion, has been seen as a new kind of religion, a kind of mirror image of Christianity itself.[7] His adage that religion is the 'opium of the people', written in 1843 (and later amended by Lenin to 'opium *for* the people'), should not be taken out of context: 'Religion is the sign of the oppressed creature, the heart of a heartless world, the soul of a soulless environment. It is the opium of the people.' Its almost wistful tone is to be heard through his reading of history as an ethicist seeking to overcome the alienation (*Entfremdung*) inherent in the oppositions – natural/unnatural, social/solitary – in society.

A profound though not a systematic thinker, Marx pursued the deep and meaningful purposes in history and the destiny of humankind with a determination not unlike Calvinist predestination, yet without abandoning the responsibility of each individual. Within this flow, religion, and all religion not just Christianity, is to be rejected as it has always been steeped in the spirit of division in society. Against this is to be set the spirit of the proletariat revolution and the result will be that: 'In place of the old bourgeois society, with its classes and class antagonisms, we shall have an association in which the free development of each is the condition for the free development of all' (Marx 1888: 70).

Learning from, and moving beyond, Hegel and Feuerbach, Marx is an atheist and irreligious, but his concern was to establish not so much the untruth of religion, but rather its negative role in the progress of society. Communism itself was not necessarily atheistic in its beginnings. Wilhelm Weitling, an early German communist, sprang from Anabaptist stock, and wrote the children's poem:

> I am a Communist small.
> Because my Lord's *no call*
> for money, then I ought
> in faith to ask for nought.
> I am a Communist child.
> Strong in my faith so mild,
> because my God I know
> to the Workers' League I go.[8]

For Marx, however, religion was merely a by-product of historical processes within society, and if Christianity and Communism hold much in common in their ideas and origins, the beliefs and practices of the Christian history of the West both dissolve in the triumphant economic progress of society.

Moving out of philosophical and into economic theory, Marx and Engels were both profoundly affected by radical theologians in their formative years – in Marx's case it was the radical Bonn thinker Bruno Bauer, and in Engels's his reading of Strauss's *Das Leben Jesu*. Bauer's reduction of the Gospel story to the imaginative workings of a single mind was merely a staging post in the development of his utopian vision. Marx was more than a moralist, he was a prophet who envisioned a new '*human* society, or socialised humanity', and he dismisses not only theology but philosophy as well for: 'The philosophers have only *interpreted* the world, in various ways; the point, however, is to *change* it' (Marx 1888: 286).

---

7 For a denial of this reading, see Chadwick 1975: 66–7.
8 Werner Post, *Kritik der Religion bei Karl Marx* (1971), quoted in Chadwick 1975: 77.

His vision is, thus, never a static one, and this accounts for much of the complexity, even the incoherence, of his thought. In Marx's dialectic materialism organic life and its development contains a contradiction, for only thus can it live and progress. He remained, at heart, a Romantic. Engels expresses the point most succinctly in his *Anti-Dühring* (the original title of his work was *Herr Eugen Dührings Unwälzung der Wissenschaft* (1878)):

> Life is therefore also a contradiction, which is present in things and processes themselves, and which constantly asserts and solves itself; and as soon as the contradiction ceases, life too comes to an end, and death steps in. We likewise saw that also in the sphere of thought we could not avoid contradictions, and that for example the contradiction between *man's inherently unlimited faculty of knowledge* and its actual realisation in men who are limited by their external conditions and limited also in their intellectual faculties finds its solution in what is, for us at least, and from a practical standpoint, *an endless succession of generations, in infinite progress* . . .
>
> (1956: 200)[9]

It is not difficult to see how the thought of Marx and Engels translated into one of the most powerful and, ultimately, tragic political and social ideologies of the twentieth century. As socialists, their vision of the good society was inherently anarchistic inasmuch as its central concern was never with the organism of society itself, but the individual happiness of the lives within it. Marx's prophetic voice was taken up by followers like Lenin after the spread of Marxist ideas among the Russian intelligentsia in the 1890s, and translated into a political ideology that, in many ways, ran absolutely counter to the founding vision. Marx, unlike Lenin, was never a politician at heart (Conquest 1972: 13–33). Yet Karl Marx remains crucial in that shift of understanding which took place in the nineteenth century after Kant, Romanticism and Hegel, and which created the characteristics of the 'modern' mind and its focus, religious or otherwise, away from the traditional European perspectives on God, faith and the self. As Charles Taylor expressed it, Marx, together with Fichte, Hegel and others, defined modern thought in their insistence on autonomy in the generation of forms and ideas: 'the aspiration is ultimately to a total liberation' (Taylor 1989: 364).

2.2 Friedrich Nietzsche

Friedrich Nietzsche (1844–1900), even more than Marx, spoke with a prophetic voice, a philosopher who was at heart a poet, and a deeply religious soul who spits out two millennia of the 'slave morality' of Christianity in a bid for freedom beyond the limits of philosophy and history. In the *Genealogy of Morals* (1887), Nietzsche dismisses the New Testament as a repository of 'petty sectarianism, a rococo of the spirit, abounding in curious scrollwork and intricate geometries and breathing the air of the conventicle', but expresses the highest regard for the Old Testament, in which he finds 'great men, a heroic landscape, and one of the rarest things on earth, the naiveté of a strong heart' (1956: 281–2). Nietzsche is, above all others, the prophet of postmodernity, and not only, as we shall see, in his proclamation of the death of God and his affirming of 'eternal recurrence', but in his style and practice as a writer – aphoristic, ironic, intensely personal – like Kierkegaard, by self-referentiality putting referentiality itself into question and 'forging new possibilities of connection between self and the world'

---

9 Emphasis added.

(Magnus et al. 1993: 188). In Nietzsche's work, as in Derrida's later (Habermas 1987: 185–210), the distinctions between philosophy, literature and even theology are levelled. His first publication, *The Birth of Tragedy* (1872), which established his exploration of the limits of language in its critique of rationalism and modern culture, was met with academic hostility. He was, at the time, professor of classical philosophy at Basel University.

Like Marx and Kierkegaard, Nietzsche is a product both of the Enlightenment and of Romanticism, but tragically aware of his distance from them. He took the strongest issue with the Idealism of Kant, and specifically its distinction between 'noumena' and 'phenomena' (things-as-they-appear), insisting, in *Human, All Too Human* (1878–80), that everything has *become* what it is, an insistence which later emerged in the maxim, 'become what you are'. Kant's distinction is fundamental also to the thought of Arthur Schopenhauer, who nevertheless is a profound influence on Nietzsche, although he was finally to reject him. Schopenhauer's atheism and pessimistic determinism leave us with little option but to endure life as best we can. Such was Nietzsche's lot, though he never ceased to struggle against this dark philosophy. But it was, above all, Hegel who foreshadowed Nietzsche, though on the surface the two thinkers could hardly be more dissimilar. Massively systematic and absolutely the philosopher, Hegel wove into his system his own interpretation of Christianity, and yet anticipates Nietzsche's explicit proclamations in subtle and ambiguous ways. As the contemporary 'death-of-God' theologian Thomas Altizer[10] has suggested:

> Now even if there is no direct exposition of the 'death of God' in [Hegel's] *Science of Logic*, every movement of this exposition is an abstract embodiment of that 'death'. Not only does a metaphysical transcendence here disappear, but every trace of a truly and finally transcendent God has vanished, and that vanishing is the realisation of a pure and total immanence. This is a purely abstract form of that total immanence that Nietzsche will enact in this proclamation of Eternal Recurrence.
>
> (1993: 21)

In *The Gay Science* (1882), Nietzsche proclaims the death of God, through the lips of a madman, a typical rhetorical gesture. For searching with his lantern for the God who is not to be found, the madman goes about unheeded, like a prophet whose time has not yet come. No-one listens to him, and, for them, the event which he proclaims 'is still distant from them' – yet they themselves are the murderers, and their churches the tombs of God. For Nietzsche, European consciousness has not yet caught up with the consequences of its own deeds. But his own post-Christian 'gospel' centres upon the ancient notion of eternal recurrence, which is an insistent reminder that each consciousness must always *be* in the eternal present, a radical call, indeed, to a new kind of consciousness in which every moment becomes (*is*) eternally momentous.

This becomes the key to understanding how to read Nietzsche and his style, which anticipates postmodernity in its endless games and slippages which 'deconstruct' any attempts to reach conclusion or definition. In the endless attempts fully 'to be' in the eternal movement of recurrence, Nietzsche

10 American 'death of God' theology dates from the early 1960s, particularly in the works of Thomas J. J. Altizer and William Hamilton. Looking back to Nietzsche's challenge to traditional Christian theology, these 'death of God' theologians began the project with the question, 'Is it possible to conceive of a form of Christianity coming to expression without a belief in God?' (Altizer and Hamilton 1968: preface). Altizer continues to publish vigorously, his most recent book being *The Contemporary Jesus* (1998).

emphasizes 'becoming', and it is the superman (*übermensch*) who is the most truly becoming what he is: a figure, frequently misunderstood, who is closer to the biblical prophet or artist than the fearful tyrant or despot. For Nietzsche, the will to power stands over against his dismissal of Christianity and its slave morality, affirming the authentic individual who will oversee the perishing of Christian ethics and their fallacies of good and evil.

Religion is hated for its repressive beliefs and practices, for, as Nietzsche retorts in *The Genealogy of Morals*:

> there is no 'being' behind the doing, acting, becoming; the 'doer' has simply been added to the deed by imagination – the doing is everything . . . our science is still the dupe of linguistic habits; it has never yet got rid of those changelings called 'subjects'.
>
> (1956: 179)

The Genealogy of Morals is not *about* morals, but explores from where their principles, for good and ill, emerge. In the act of writing, and in the act of reading, is played out the 'subject' as a dynamic interaction 'beyond good and evil'. In all his work, Nietzsche sets out not to philosophize or to present an alternative to theology, but to expose the consciousness which, he believed, was dismissed in modern, late Christian, Western culture. In this, like Kierkegaard and Dostoevsky, he anticipates a great deal in twentieth-century *existential* writing with its agonies of self-consciousness: Kafka's *Metamorphosis* (1912), a parable of loathing and self-loathing; or Sartre's novel *La Nausée* (1938), a narrative of absolute alienation and a meditation on the mystery of being.

Nietzsche eventually, perhaps inevitably, went insane. In the last sane year of his life, 1888, he wrote two astonishing works, *Twilight of the Idols* and *The Anti-Christ*. The first, which is subtitled *How to Philosophise with a Hammer*, Nietzsche describes as a 'grand declaration of war' against eternal idols. With apocalyptic fervour (another note taken up by postmodernity), Nietzsche sees himself standing on the edge of history as Christianity perishes, extinguished by its own ethics and encouragement of the 'herd' instinct in humankind. In *Twilight of the Idols* he begins with Socrates, who made a tyrant of reason (1968: 43), and who he describes as a 'misunderstanding'. Indeed, 'the entire morality of improvement, the Christian included, has been a misunderstanding'. On the other hand, Nietzsche celebrates (referring back to his very first work) the tragic artist, for such a one is no pessimist, but rather 'affirms all that is questionable and terrible in existence, he is *Dionysian*' (ibid.: 49). In *The Anti-Christ*, Nietzsche fights his final battle against Christianity and the 'theologian instinct', with a mortal hostility to 'reality'. St Paul, the 'genius of hatred', is the arch-enemy: but what of Jesus himself?

> This 'bringer of glad tidings' died as he lived, as he *taught* – *not to* 'redeem mankind' but to demonstrate how one ought to live. What he bequeathed to mankind is his *practice* . . .
>
> (1895: 157)

And we, as *emancipated* spirits free for the first time from the tyranny of a slave morality and the dire consequences of the Church, alone possess the 'integrity to become instinct and passion', to wage war finally on the 'holy lie'. Nietzsche was, truly, a prophet of the apocalypse.

2.3 Sigmund Freud

At the very end of his life Sigmund Freud (1856–1939) wrote:

> I have not the courage to rise up before my fellow-men as a prophet, and I bow to the reproach that I can offer them no consolation; for at bottom that is what they are all demanding – the wildest revolutionaries no less passionately than the most virtuous believers.
>
> (1953: XXI.145)[11]

And yet, together with Marx and Nietzsche, Freud might justifiably be described as one of the prophets of modernity, his thought and theories casting a huge shadow over the twentieth century and its understanding of selfhood and identity within society. In fact, the term 'Freudian', with certain key ideas on sexuality in the child, the Oedipus complex, dream analysis, the 'Wolf Man', and so on, have long obscured in the popular mind the remarkable and various achievements of Freud himself.

Freud was, like Marx, a Jew, and, like Nietzsche, a convinced atheist. Yet he never ceased to think of himself as Jewish – he once described himself as a 'godless Jew', and despite his loathing of religion, the phenomenon of religion was the subject of a great deal of his writing. Indeed, it might almost be said that his work in psychoanalysis offered a religious alternative to an age which was characterized by the loss of faith in traditional religious certainties. But if for many in the nineteenth century the withdrawal of the sea of faith was a matter for profound regret, Freud regarded religion in a pathological light, suggesting that 'one might venture to regard obsessional neurosis as a pathological counterpart of the formation of a religion, and to describe that neurosis as an individual religiosity and religion as a universal obsessional neurosis' (1953: IX.126–7).[12] Like his fellow prophets, Freud was deeply indebted both to the Enlightenment and to Romanticism. At heart a rationalist (though his thinking is often anything but 'scientific'), Freud was not particularly optimistic as to the triumph of reason. Indeed, his theories of psychoanalysis look back to the Romantic and nineteenth-century obsessions with the darker side of the human mind, and above all the fear of the divided personality with its lurking question, 'Who am I?', the fear of the loss of identity. In literature, this obsessional fear surfaced in novels such as Mary Shelley's *Frankenstein* (1818) and Robert Louis Stevenson's *The Strange Case of Dr Jekyll and Mr Hyde* (1886), but it was Freud who turned this study of the mind and the self-conscious into a matter for scientific discussion in works like *Beyond the Pleasure Principle* (1920) and *The Ego and the Id* (1923).

Although his work began in pathological medicine and neurology, Freud's thinking was essentially a continuation of the interests of men like Herder, Eichhorn and Coleridge as they struggled to meet the need for a modern mythology.[13] In much of his writing on religion he is deeply absorbed in the mystery of origins, and particularly *Beyond the Pleasure Principle* betrays a preoccupation with death in a manner which Freud admitted was 'speculation, often far-fetched speculation' (Gay 1995: 685). However, such a speculative enterprise he regarded as necessary, not least in order to forward the progress of science against the ancient, though eradicable influences of religion. Ultimately, all beliefs which dictate human conduct should be both comprehensible and open to analysis. For, in Freud's words:

11 See also Wollheim 1971: 235.
12 See also Gay 1995: 685.
13 See Shaffer 1975: 32.

In its third function, in which it issues precepts and lays down prohibitions and restrictions, religion is furthest away from science. For science is content to investigate and to establish facts, though it is true that from its applications rules and advice are derived on the conduct of life.

(1953: XXII.162; Wollheim 1971: 220)

Yet despite this somewhat dry claim for science, Freud's persistent interest in religion, and in particular the origins of his own people, remained throughout his life. One of his last works, *Moses and Monotheism* (1938), reveals his preoccupation (it has been suggested identification (Gay 1995: 532)) with Moses as a hero-figure who, he argued, created Judaism and was himself an Egyptian. Such imaginative speculations are not irrelevant, however, to the modern age. In a short work entitled *The Question of Lay Analysis* (1926), Freud concludes by accepting the accusation that a new generation of 'social workers', trained in psychoanalysis, are the equivalent of 'a new kind of Salvation Army'. 'Why not?' he responded: 'Our imagination always follows patterns' (1962: 170).

In Freud, the modern world is ushered in by the dying heroism of ancient, corrupt beliefs and the decaying faith of the nineteenth century. *The Future of Illusion* (1927) is his most articulate psychoanalytic raid on religion within culture, and is a kind of prelude to a small work written two years later under the growing shadow of Nazism, *Civilization and its Discontents*. Freud was no political theorist, and yet this essay stands within a great tradition looking back as far as Plato, which perceives political institutions through the dark prism of human nature. From his lay meditation on the human mind, Freud draws a melancholy conclusion as to the aggressive nature of human society. In 1930, Hitler's NSDAP triumphed in the elections to the German Reichstag. In an addition to *Civilization and its Discontents* written in 1931, for the second edition, Freud wrote:

The fateful question for the human species seems to me whether and to what extent their cultural development will succeed in mastering the disturbance of their communal life by the human instinct of aggression and self-destruction. It may be that in this respect precisely the present time deserves a special interest.

(Gay 1995: 772)

Ten years earlier, in 1921, W. B. Yeats had published his poem, 'The Second Coming', one of the greatest literary monuments to the turn from the modern to the postmodern. Freud, if he ever read it, would have understood Yeats's prophecy:

Turning and turning in the widening gyre
The falcon cannot hear the falconer;
Things fall apart; the centre cannot hold;
Mere anarchy is loosed upon the world . . .
but now I know
That twenty centuries of stony sleep
Were vexed to nightmare by a rocking cradle,
And what rough beast, its hour come round at last,
Slouches towards Bethlehem to be born?

(1921: 210–11)

3 TOWARDS POSTMODERNISM: THE LINGUISTIC TURN

3.1 Ferdinand de Saussure

The painter Georges Braque once remarked, 'I do not believe in things; I believe in relationships' (Culler 1976: 7). This may be a fundamental, perhaps *the* fundamental, claim in the shift towards modernism and eventually postmodernism, its implications within the history of ideas being not only cultural but ultimately also religious. If for Descartes in the seventeenth century the key to how the mind relates to the world and to the sense of being lies in the statement 'cogito ergo sum', for Saussure at the turn of the twentieth century this relationship is grounded in his understanding of the nature of language. The structure of thought is also the structure of language, without which there can be no thinking, and at the heart of language there is no *reference* (whether to the self or to God), but only relationships.

Ferdinand de Saussure (1857–1913) has been called the father of modern linguistics. If Freud's achievement was radically to transform the study of human behaviour through psychology, Saussure's was to do the same thing through his understanding of the nature of language. Rather than focusing on objects or events, Saussure concentrated on the structure of language in its relation to the function and significance of events within society, and in particular the 'essential disjunction between the world of reality and the world of language' (Robey 1986: 47). This differentiation prompted a conceptual shift from object to structures in the world, from which our perceptions of society and culture operate through a series of sign systems, the study of which we now call *semiology*. Such sign systems we may analyse through a linguistic model.

Saussure's own writings, published during his lifetime, are all technical and specialized (his doctoral thesis written for the University of Leipzig was on the use of the genitive case in Sanskrit (1880)), and the work for which he is principally known, the *Cours de linguistique générale*, was only published three years after his death in 1913, edited from his lecture notes in the University of Geneva.[14] Yet the implications of his thinking on the nature of language are immense and broad, as we shall see. In essence, his proposals are really quite simple. We have seen that in his thinking there is an essential disjunction between the world and language. Behind this postulate lies the fundamental postulate that 'languages are *systems* constituted by *signs* that are *arbitrary* and *differential*' (Robey 1986: 47). In Part One of the *Course in General Linguistics*, Saussure quickly dismisses the understanding of language as a 'naming-process only – a list of words, each corresponding to the thing that it names' (Cahoune 1996: 177). Rather, he asserts, 'the linguistic sign unites not a thing and a name but a concept and a sound-image' (ibid.: 178). These two terms he goes on to name the *signified* (*signifié*) and the *signifier* (*signifiant*) respectively: and the whole is designated by the word *sign* (*signe*), 'semiology' being the study of signs.[15]

From here, Saussure states his first principle: that the bond between the signifier and the signified is arbitrary, and that therefore 'the linguistic sign is arbitrary' (ibid.: 179). He illustrates this as follows:

14 The irony here is that 'Saussure' is therefore constructed out of his own unfinished notes. In a sense this 'Saussure' has never existed in the world!

15 For example, we may hold in our minds the concept or image of a tree. This is not any particular tree, but the *idea* of a tree – a large plant with a trunk, branches and leaves. This Saussure calls the 'signified'. Then we may utter, or think, the monosyllable, 'tree'. This he calls the 'signifier'. Relating this idea or concept with this sound-image and the impression which it makes on our senses results in a 'sign' which may be employed to identify a particular tree, an identification which can be refined by adjectives, for example, a 'large tree', a 'spindly tree'.

The idea of 'sister' is not linked by any inner relationship to the succession of sounds *s-ö-r* which serves as its signifier in French; that it could be represented equally by just any other sequence is proved by differences among languages and by the very existence of different languages: the signified 'ox' has as its signifier *b-ö-f* on one side of the border and *O-k-s* (Ochs) on the other.

(ibid.: 179–80)[16]

The consequences of this observation quickly become clear. 'Meaning' emerges from within the structure of language – for example, the word 'dog' is understood not, in the first instance, by its relationship to my furry, four-legged friend (which is an arbitrary relationship), but by the fact that it is *different* from all other words; it is not a cat, or a rabbit. Thus, it is the relationships within the structure of language which are important, such that Saussure can go on to claim:

> *In the language itself, there are only differences.* Even more important than this is the fact that, although in general a difference presupposes positive terms between which the difference holds, in language there are only differences, *and no positive terms.*
>
> (cited in Moore 1994: 16)

If, without language, thought is anarchic, the consequences of Saussure's claim for our understanding of the world are alarming. Can we say anything about anything? We live now in a confusing world of slippages, arbitrariness and 'signs' without natural stability. Language seems to have taken on a life of its own, a fear acknowledged in Saussure's distinction between *langue* (the system of language, common to all specific languages) and *parole* (the actual speech we use to get along with in the world). This distinction is actually somewhat confusing in the *Course of General Linguistics*, but can be reduced to the fundamental issue which lies between system and realization. It is *langue* which is Saussure's primary concern. To explain this a little further, *parole* is the language which is realized in our everyday exchanges with one another, words with which we are generally comfortable by accepted conventions and common use. *Parole* is language validated so that normally 'we know what we mean' by it. *Langue*, on the other hand, designates the underlying structures in human language before it has been simplified by common usage and reference. *Langue* has a mysterious grammatical life of its own, its structures refusing to acknowledge the easy and secure significance of common speech, and its system 'deconstructing' or undermining our conventional meanings and understandings. Nothing seems secure or to be taken for granted. Under the dark shadow of linguistic system, in later structuralist and post-structuralist thought, other certainties crumble. All seems relative, objects crumble before an inevitable, inbuilt deconstructive turn in language; above all, what of that most problematic of signs, *God*?

It has often been observed that Saussure backs away from the most profound implications of his thinking about language. There are no positive terms. Saussure himself quickly recovers himself at this point:

> But to say that in a language everything is negative holds only for signified and signifier considered separately. The moment we consider the sign as a whole, we encounter something which is positive in its own domain . . . although signified and signifier are each, in isolation, purely differential and negative, their combination is in fact of a positive nature.
>
> (ibid.: 16)

16 Born in Geneva, Saussure was French-speaking Swiss, but educated also in Berlin and Leipzig.

But others since have been less cautious and less anxious to arrest the logical slide of Saussure's thinking. Frank Lentricchia, for example, in *After the New Criticism* (1980), races towards the abyss from the view of language as 'a play of differences' to the conclusion that there can be 'no poem in itself'.[17] Is there a text at all, or is it just us, as Stanley Fish's student once famously asked (Fish 1980). Is it all, 'just us'?

But perhaps the sharpest observations emerged in the 1960s, when the French philosopher Jacques Derrida gave his attention to Saussure's lecture notes. In his work *Positions* (1981), Derrida scrutinizes Saussure's 'rigorous distinction' between signifier and signified. We have seen that the term 'signified' replaced the previous term 'concept'. Yet the 'signifier' as 'sound-image' already carries 'the hearer's psychological impression of a sound' (Moore 1994: 17) – itself not far off a concept. And, then, Art Berman and Stephen Moore have observed (Berman 1988: 19),[18] what is left for the signified to do? In *Positions*, Derrida unpicks this anomaly, suspecting a theological reservation which Saussure was unwilling to abandon. For in this question of the actual role of the 'signified' is left open 'the possibility of thinking a *concept signified in and of itself*, a concept simply present for thought, independent of a relationship to . . . a system of signifiers' (Derrida 1981a: 19). The simple point is that language is in danger of losing any anchorage in a particular reference. In other words, it is no longer restrained or disciplined by any actual thing or object, or even idea. Language then has power without restraint. This concept Derrida terms a 'transcendental signified', which might be called more loosely 'God', and this, he suggests, has haunted the entire history of Western thought and consciousness in its 'power, systematic, and irrepressible desire' for ultimate assurance above and beyond all relativities and differences. But this God, Saussure, in spite of himself, had exposed as a fraud in a crisis of and in language. As Derrida wrote at the beginning of his seminal work, *Of Grammatology* (1976),

> Language itself is menaced in its very life, helpless, adrift in the threat of limitlessness, brought back to its own finitude at the very moment when its limits seem to disappear, when it ceases to be self-assured, contained, and *guaranteed* by the infinite signified which seemed to exceed it.
>
> (1976: 6)

But there is nothing beyond, and language will itself always tend to deconstruct such tendencies even within itself.

3.2 Martin Heidegger: 'Letter on humanism'

In a chapter such as this, relatively brief yet with large ambitions, to even begin to do justice to the massive complexity of Heidegger's thought and the paradoxes of his life, is impossible. I will therefore try to do justice to his central place in this discussion of modernity and postmodernity by concentrating on one brief work, the 'Letter on humanism' (1947), which Hannah Arendt called Heidegger's *Prachtstück* – his most splendid effort (Heidegger 1996: 216). George Steiner has suggested that Heidegger did not want to be 'understood' in the normal sense of that word, but 'that he wanted an understanding which would entail the possibility of re-stating his views by means of a more or less close

17 Lentricchia's slippery slide along the knife-edge of Saussurean linguistics is nicely picked apart by Raymond Tallis, 1988: 19–20.
18 See Moore 1994: 17. I am much indebted to Stephen Moore at this point of my argument.

paraphrase' (Steiner 1978: 17). Indeed, reading Heidegger's work is not so much an encouragement to finish the book, and hence to understand its argument, as to engage with the writing – an anticipation of Derrida's meditations on 'the end of the book and the beginning of writing', which will be dealt with in the next section. Furthermore, the tendency of critics to revert to paraphrase, often in a language more quaintly Heideggerian than Heidegger's own, suggests a challenge to hermeneutics and the whole enterprise of interpretation at the very heart of Heidegger's project as a thinker.

From his great early work *Sein und Zeit* (*Being and Time*) (1927), Heidegger's investigation of the meaning of Being (*Dasein*) itself reaches beyond Cartesian subjectivism and finds its roots, among other things, as we shall see, in the mysticism of medievals like Meister Eckhart, but also projects forward particularly to the thought of Derrida, and is therefore crucial in the history of postmodernity. In the recent history of German ideas the two greatest influences on Heidegger were the philosopher Nietzsche and the poet Hölderlin. The former he regarded as the last metaphysical thinker of the West, the latter as the 'poet's poet'. From each Heidegger attempts to move on to a new and radical position within Western humanism and religion, avoiding the collapse of Being[19] into questions of either the divine or the human. Though he denied that he was a theologian, he poses unavoidable questions for all contemporary theologians and religious thinkers. His preoccupation with 'thinking' rather than philosophy itself aligns him closely with Kant, with whom his sedentary life, spent increasingly at his Black Forest retreat, bears much resemblance, and problematizes his notorious allegiance with the Nazi party which resulted in his suspension from teaching by the Allied authorities between 1945 and 1951. 'Thinking', for Heidegger, is a process both necessary and hugely difficult, and is to be distinguished from the systematic discipline of philosophy.

Heidegger's 'Letter on humanism' was written as a response to a letter from the young French philosopher Jean Beaufret in direct repudiation of the existentialism of Sartre. It begins on a note which will now be familiar to us: 'Language is the house of Being. In its home man dwells' (cited in Cahoune 1996: 275). Yet language, as the house of the truth of Being, endlessly denies us its essence (ibid.: 278). Although, in an apocalyptic phrase, language is the 'lighting-concealing advent of Being itself' (ibid.: 284), yet in the hands of human beings it allows itself to become an instrument of domination. How then is it to be recovered as the true home of the essence of beings? (ibid.: 288). In a religious phrase, Heidegger pursues 'the essence of ek-sistence derive[d] existentially-ecstatically from the essence of the truth of Being' (ibid.: 288).

The themes of home and homelessness pervade the essay, anticipating the wandering anxieties of the postmodern. Karl Marx seeks for a home in society, the Christian seeks through the history of redemption for a home with God (ibid.: 279), while Nietzsche is the great example of modern homelessness, a condition that is now 'coming to be the destiny of the world' (ibid.: 292). For Heidegger, the key to understanding this destiny lies with the Romantic poet Hölderlin, and he refers to his own 1943 lecture on Hölderlin's elegy *Homecoming*, though by 1947 Heidegger is eager to deny that Hölderlin seeks 'that essence in the egoism of his nation' (ibid.: 291). In the aftermath of war, 'Homecoming' is not to Germany, but is to be understood in a mystical sense. It is to be reconciled with the self and with what Heidegger calls 'Being', a mystery which he sums up in the phrase 'to exist in the nameless'.

Here we are close to the heart of the Letter, and Heidegger is careful to establish its thinking as continuous with *Sein und Zeit*. Abandoning traditional philosophical thinking which seeks the

---

19 *Dasein* must be carefully distinguished from *beings* or things. Heidegger's primary concern is with *human being* rather than *human beings*.

domination of Being through language, man must now become the shepherd of Being – and at this point Heidegger offers a definition:

> Yet Being – what is Being? It is It itself. The thinking that is to come must learn to experience that and to say it. 'Being' – that is not God and not a cosmic ground. Being is farther than all beings and is yet nearer to man than every being, be it a rock, a beast, a work of art, a machine, be it an angel or God. Being is the nearest. Yet the near remains farthest from man.
>
> (ibid.: 287)

The language is biblical (Exodus 3.14; John 8.58) and deeply religious, also foreshadowing the 'negative theology' and fascination with the 'unsayable' of postmodernity.[20] Towards the end of the Letter, Heidegger returns to this theme in explicitly religious language, asserting that the essence of the holy can only be thought from the truth of Being, and 'only from the essence of the holy is the essence of divinity to be thought' (1996: 300).

Here, as always, Heidegger is thinking about thinking, taking back into metaphysics problems which have been with us specifically since Kant's writings on religion. But the Letter also ushers in conversation which will be central to later thinkers, specifically the distinction between speech and writing. In a passage which anticipates what Derrida would later call 'phonocentrism', that is the privileging of speech over writing, Heidegger writes directly to Beaufret, 'surely the questions raised in your letter would have been better answered in direct conversation' (ibid.: 276). The point is actually one about language, and both Heidegger and Derrida move beyond Saussure, for whom *all* language is finally a system of differences. But for Heidegger, 'speaking remains purely in the element of Being', while in writing 'thinking easily loses its flexibility'.

Sartre, Heidegger's principal opponent in this work, tried to distinguish between the two 'humanisms' of Christianity and Communism. In his concern for Being, Heidegger moves far beyond this distinction and beyond the traditional options of human or divine. With something approaching the mysticism of the later 'death of God' theologians (who also wrote after Nietzsche), to which reference will later be made, Heidegger's thinking opens up radical possibilities, as well as impossibilities, in what are probably the two crucial areas of concern for all postmodern reflection, that is religion and ethics. For him, true humanism involves a final abandonment of the traditional philosophical enterprise, which had, in many ways, been in its death throes throughout the nineteenth century, and a bringing of 'the lighting of the truth of Being before thinking' such that the essence of human beings becomes proximate to Being itself, and man becomes the 'shepherd' of Being.

3.3 Jacques Derrida: 'The end of the book and the beginning of writing'

The French philosopher Jacques Derrida, it could be argued, is the true, though uneasy, heir of both Saussure and Heidegger. But his work has also been described as 'the latest in the line of Jewish heretic hermeneutics' (Handelman 1982: 163), and his recent works have shown an increasing and overt concern to explore the theological implications within postmodernity. As with Heidegger, Derrida's range of writing is enormous and well-documented, and therefore the necessarily brief discussion here will largely focus on the opening pages of his great early work, *Of Grammatology* (1976), which set out many of the central concerns of his later work.

20 See Budick and Iser 1989, especially Jacques Derrida, 'How to avoid speaking: Denials', 3–70.

The structuralist thinking to which Derrida is heir has been described as 'Kantianism without the transcendental subject' (Norris 1982: 3), and it is this trajectory from Kant to Saussure which we have been tracing. Kant's escape from the scepticism of David Hume and others involved the exploration of the divorce between the mind and the 'reality' to which it gives attention, a divorce made absolute in the linguistics of Saussure (ibid.: 4ff.). This incompatibility Derrida pursues further in the realm of textuality and its inevitable 'deconstruction', specifically in the writings of Rousseau.[21] But what Derrida means by 'writing' is not just the black marks made on the page by the pen of Rousseau. It is far more than that. Christopher Norris makes the point succinctly:

> Nor is it opposed to a real world existing outside or beyond the text, at least in the sense that one might draw a clear demarcation between the two realms. This is what Derrida terms *arche-writing*, that which exceeds the traditional (restricted) sense of the word in order to release all those hitherto repressed significations which have always haunted the discourse of logocentric reason.
>
> (1987: 122)

Derrida's repeated attacks on 'logocentricity' are a 'deconstruction' of the insistence in Western thinking of ideas of *origin*, of a primacy in language ('In the beginning was the word', John 1.1), which authentic first instance allows and encourages the establishment of hierarchies through a series of binary oppositions which, he would argue, are repeatedly undermined within textuality itself. With its starting point in the first chapter of St John's Gospel, Derrida's understanding of the centrality of the divine, creative 'word' (in Greek *logos*) already encounters oppositions in the first few verses of the Gospel: light/darkness: will of God/will of man. The word, or language itself, initiates a hierarchy of powers. A good student of Saussure, we have already seen how he goes beyond the master himself. The discourse of logocentricity is marked by a system of oppositions (speech/writing; origin/supplement; etc.) which ultimately break down under the pressure of the 'logic of supplementarity' – for Derrida there are no origins, no first point, and the end of the book merely marks the beginning of the endlessness of writing.[22] Jürgen Habermas shows how Derrida 'compels texts by Husserl, Saussure or Rousseau to confess their guilt, against the explicit interpretations of their authors' (Habermas 1987: 189), by overturning their logic as, for example, philosophical texts and treating them 'as [they] would not like to be' – as *literary* texts. The basic hierarchies of genre are overturned as Derrida breaks the rules – we cannot decide whether he is a philosopher, a literary critic, a theologian, for he is all and none of these.

The implications of this for the *authority* of texts must be clear. And so let us turn to the opening of *Of Grammatology*. We have seen already how Derrida begins with the crisis of language, 'adrift in the threat of limitlessness' (1976: 6). The startling consequences of this crisis are radical for three millennia of Western logocentric metaphysics, based not least upon the trust placed in the authority of one book of books, the Bible, interpreted as the broad history of the beginning and end of all things. For we are now experiencing an exhaustion which is nothing less than 'the death of the civilisation of the book' (Derrida 1976: 8), and a new mutation in the history of writing and in history as writing. With

---

21 See also Derrida's fellow 'deconstructionist' Paul de Man, 1979.

22 A simple illustration of this might be the Gospel of Mark, of which the notoriously 'open' ending at chapter 16, verse 8, invites the reader to return again to the beginning. Assuming that 16.9–19 are the addition of a later, 'logocentric' scribe, the Gospel becomes an endless exercise in writing, without end. A more modern example is James Joyce's *Finnegans Wake*. In other words, these texts always lead us beyond themselves, and are more than we can ever conclude about them. Such is the logic of supplementarity.

the abandonment of the 'logocentric' and its assurances of stability of meaning vanishes also the 'ratio-nality' which underlies European thought from the Enlightenment. And once that is abandoned, the question of the 'signification of truth' (ibid.: 10) itself becomes problematical. As Derrida expresses it:

> All the metaphysical determinations of truth, and even the one beyond metaphysical onto-theology that Heidegger reminds us of, are more or less immediately inseparable from the instance of the logos, or of a reason thought within the lineage of the logos . . .
>
> (ibid.)

Such things are no longer available to us. In a phrase reminiscent of Kant himself, Derrida denies that the 'written signifier' has 'constitutive meaning' – it is merely technical and representative (ibid.: 11).

After the epoch of the logos, writing itself is freed from its earlier debasements and the curse of the 'exteriority of meaning' (ibid.: 13). Language becomes not a matter of prescribed 'meaning', imposed by an authoritative and divine 'logos', but becomes a place of suggestive possibility and openness. To put this another way, the word becomes not denotative but connotative, expansive and many-layered. Words may have many 'meanings'. As meaning is no longer imposed upon writing, always threatening its closure, so we are reminded of another French thinker, Maurice Blanchot, for whom the work of literature is a space within which demands may be made, but upon which nothing is imposed (Blanchot 1989; de Certeau 1992: 4978). Or, to reverse the metaphor of the Fall, so beloved by Derrida, the text may become a garden which encourages the play of endless signification and creativity. As the text becomes a place of play, so Derrida's concern in the first chapter of *Of Grammatology* is to begin to *think* about *writing*, taking as his first mentor Hegel, whom he describes as 'the last philosopher of the book and the first thinker of writing' (Derrida 1976: 26). Focusing also on Heidegger in *Sein und Zeit*, Nietzsche and, as a hidden, ubiquitous presence, Saussure, Derrida's chapter is a deeply theological meditation in which the texts of logocentricity are deconstructed from within, opening up the radical challenge of the postmodern to Western theologies.

We have seen how Derrida unveils the hidden theological investment in Saussure's insistence on the distinction between signifier and signified. He now goes on to unmask 'other hidden sediments' which cling to the 'metaphysical theological roots' (ibid.: 13) that remain within Saussurean linguistics. In a typically Derridean manner he surmises, 'the age of the sign is essentially theological. Perhaps it will never *end*. Its historical closure is, however, outlined' (ibid.: 14). His technique is relentlessly to invert priorities within the understanding of text and writing, to free writing from the chains of logocentricity and the claims of 'literal' meaning so that 'it is not . . . a matter of inverting the literal meaning and the figurative meaning but of determining the "literal" meaning of writing as metaphoricity itself' (ibid.: 15).

Derrida's Jewishness is never far below the surface in his work. He writes as one of the 'people of the Book', and yet he epitomizes a moment in cultural and intellectual history which seeks freedom from 'the book' and its tendency towards totalitarian claims for meaning and completion. Yet within textuality, as all his writings seek to show, 'the movements of deconstruction do not destroy structures from the outside' (ibid.: 24), but inhabit the very structures themselves. And their energy is released in the processes of writing.

> The idea of the book, which always refers to a natural totality, is profoundly alien to the sense of writing. It is the encyclopaedic protection of theology and of logocentricism against the disruption of writing, against its aphoristic energy, and, as I shall specify later, against difference in general. If I distinguish the text from the book, I shall say that the destruction of the book, as it is now

under way in all domains, denudes the surface of the text. That necessary violence responds to a violence that was no less necessary.

(ibid.: 18)

Derrida's writings often seem almost rabbinic – a claim we shall explore in more detail a little later – and his sense of text seems midrashic.[23] Increasingly in his more recent work, he has returned to religious themes, emergent from the suspicions of postmodernity, though they have always been there. Often castigated as the arch-destroyer, the one who leaves us with nothing of our tradition, Derrida nevertheless often appears, with almost touching naivety, as a person of the profoundest faith – after Hegel, after Nietzsche, after Heidegger, and after the trauma of the 'linguistic turn'. In an interview published in *Memoirs of the Blind* (1993), a work which explores the theme of blindness in the visual arts, Derrida plays on the two meanings of tears (as a rent), and tears (as weeping):

Tears that see . . . Do you believe?
I don't know, one has to believe . . .
(1993: 129)

Aways resistant to the colonizing of his work by theologians,[24] Derrida, after Heidegger, poses possibly the greatest challenge to the traditions of Western theology in our postmodern condition. Yet, at the same time, the note sounded is ancient and familiar. For Derrida acknowledges that theology has always been close to the desert and the *via negativa*[25] and the logocentricity of biblical theology has within it a deconstructive moment (Derrida 1992: 283–323). As Valentine Cunningham has expressed it:

From the beginning, from Babel onwards, or from the time when Moses the prophet returned stuttering from encountering the tautologous Deity of the Burning Bush, the 'I am that I am', 'the challenge of deconstruction' has been the challenge of theology. And of course, vice-versa.

(1994: 403; Steiner 1989)

23 'Midrash' is an ancient Jewish practice of interpretation or hermeneutic, characterized not so much by the search of 'the meaning' of a text, but by argument, experiment and debate. For the rabbis, texts thus become an opportunity for debate and discussion – opportunities for expansion rather than contraction into a fixed conclusion or meaning.

24 There have been a number of recent 'theological' studies of Derrida, notably Caputo 1997. Derrida, like Heidegger before himself, strongly resists the title 'theologian'. The point takes us neatly to our next section.

25 Literally, 'negative road'. It is an ancient tradition in Christian theology with roots in Neoplatonism. It recognizes the limits of human language and its capacity to speak of God, who is so far greater than anything we can affirm that we can only use negative terms, no qualities which we can positively ascribe to God being appropriate. The *via negativa* is often associated with mysticism, which has re-emerged in contemporary religious thought under the influence of postmodernity, the subject of the following section.

▌ 4 POSTMODERN THEOLOGIES

4.1 Jean-François Lyotard: 'The postmodern condition'

The theme underlying this chapter from the very beginning has been located in the term 'deconstruction'. Yet that term can actually be located nowhere, and eludes definition, inherent within the instabilities of Saussurean linguistics. Lacking its own planes of argument (it is not a theory or a method) it has been there from the very beginning, an acknowledgement of the ineluctable mystery at the heart of every structure and the excess which overruns all our finite claims to knowledge. In George Steiner's words, 'it embodies, it ironises into eloquence, the underlying nihilistic findings of literacy, of understanding or rather in-comprehension, as these *must* be stated and faced in the time of epilogue' (1989: 132). Deconstruction, perhaps the most deeply religious of postmodern terms, suspends any *assumed* correspondence between mind, meaning and method,[26] and it is this scepticism which characterizes Jean-François Lyotard's seminal work, written as a report on the state of knowledge in the West at the request of Conseil des Universités of the government of Quebec, *The Postmodern Condition* (published in French, 1979, and in English, 1984).

At its simplest, Lyotard defines *postmodern* as 'incredulity toward metanarratives' (1984: xxiv). Metanarratives are the overarching 'stories', myths even, by which we live and seek understanding of ourselves and the world, and such stories may be religious, political, scientific, and so on. For example, if we understand the Bible under the auspices of the Christian theme as a grand narrative from the beginning of all things in creation, through fall and redemption, to the culmination of all things in apocalypse, then this is one of the most powerful metanarratives in the Western tradition. Our contemporary incredulity, says Lyotard, is the result of progress in the sciences, above all the paradigm shift from a Newtonian anthropology (which allowed the rise of structuralist theories: Saussure was a good Enlightenment man!) to twentieth-century relativity and what Lyotard terms 'a pragmatics of language particles' (ibid.). Now the universal gives way to the local and our primary problem is one of legitimation (ibid.: 6–9).

In the reversals of Derridan deconstruction, how can we *know* what in knowledge is legitimate, and what is illegitimate? Within the postmodern both knowledge and decisions about forms of behaviour are thrown into profound crisis. Not only language but all forms of social bondings suffer atomization, and work, if they work at all, not by any legitimizations which they carry within themselves, but by a pragmatics of contract, of which the rules are at best dubious (ibid.: 10).[27] This postmodern 'crisis' has been succinctly described by Maurice Blanchot:

> There is an 'I do not know' that is at the limit of knowledge but that belongs to knowledge. We always pronounce it too early, still knowing all – or too late, when I no longer know that I do not know.

Within technocratic societies, on the cusp of industrial decline, such pragmatism will grant to the 'technocrats', the scientists who run the machines which we no longer understand but without which (we think) we cannot survive, immense power and prestige. And yet anxiety is never far below the

---

26 See Norris 1982:3.

27 For an example of such pragmatism in the practice, see Rorty 1989, which argues that after Nietzsche, Freud and Wittgenstein, societies must be seen as historical contingencies rather than ahistorical or dependent upon universal, suprahistorical goals.

surface.[28] It emerges as a nostalgia for a lost 'presence', identified by Lyotard through an insistent voice in twentieth-century art and literature, in the German Expressionists, in Braque and in Picasso, but above all in literature, and he refers specifically to Proust and Joyce. But it is a voice which carries a high price.

> In Proust, what is being eluded as the price to pay for this allusion is the identity of consciousness, a victim to the excess of time (*au trop de temps*). But in Joyce, it is the identity of writing which is the victim of an excess of the book (*au trop de livre*) or of literature.
>
> (Lyotard 1984: 80)

In the paradoxes of postmodernity there is almost a faint echo of the biblical chiasmus, 'He who finds his life will lose it, and he who loses his life for my sake will find it' (Matthew 10.39), yet buried deep in the crises of identity and legitimation.

There is no easy way back. Lyotard concludes his Report with a warning and an exhortation. The first is anchored in the perceptions of Kant. It is clear, Lyotard admits, that the postmodern condition does not allow us 'to supply reality', but rather 'to invent allusions to the conceivable which cannot be presented' (ibid.: 81). Has not that always been the task of theology? For theology does not speak directly but indirectly and by analogy and metaphor. When it moves towards totalization (as in the 'transcendental illusion' of Hegel) then it tends to outstrip its own faith claims and the inconceivable, the divine is realized in human terms. If that is the case, Kant is there to warn us that the price for such an illusion is terror, and the last two centuries give plenty of evidence of such. In Lyotard's words, 'We have paid a high enough price for the nostalgia of the whole and the one, for the reconciliation of the concept and the sensible' (ibid.: 81–2).

Theologians from Karl Barth to Paul Tillich have gazed upon this terror in the ideological enormities of the twentieth century and sought to retain a theological path through it. We need only reflect upon the new theological language used by Hitler and Stalin to sustain their totalitarian claims to empire. Perhaps now the only options, if options be there, are yet more radical and unthinkable.

> Let us wage war on totality; let us be witnesses to the unpresentable; let us activate the differences and save the honour of the name.
>
> (ibid.: 82)

4.2 Michel Foucault and the question of power

But there is a little way to travel yet before we can begin to speak of the possibilities of 'postmodern theologies'. The writings of Michel Foucault (1926–84) cover a wide variety of disciplines, investigating society from the inside with studies of prisons, schools, hospitals, the military, sexuality and the family. But perhaps his central concerns are best summed up in the title of his last position at the Collège de France as Professor of History of Systems of Thought, and in his two methodological works *The Archaeology of Knowledge* (1969) and *The Order of Things: An Archaeology of the Human Sciences* (1966). I shall concentrate here on two central concepts in Foucault's thinking – truth and power.

---

28 The 1960s foreshadowed the postmodern condition in such works, influential in their time, as those of Theodore Roszak (1968 and 1972).

I began this chapter with a reference to Kant's 1784 essay 'What is Enlightenment?'[29] in which Kant equates enlightenment with maturity attained through reason and its relation to the historical moment. But if Kant equates modernity and maturity, for Foucault they stand in opposition to one another. He goes so far with Kant, agreeing that we bear responsibility for the employment of reason – we cannot simply rest, like children, on guarantees given from outside.[30] But where he diverges from Kant is in his refusal to acknowledge the universal nature of critical reason. For Foucault, Kant is misguided in his attempt to offer a universal solution – modernity must move into postmodernity. From Kant's universalism, Foucault shifts to a responsive reason, a critical ontology issuing in an ethics which neither seeks universal salvation nor proposes, like the early Heidegger, that there is no deep truth, 'so that maturity consists in facing up to the groundlessness of our being-in-the-world' (Dreyfus and Rabinow 1986: 121). In his essay 'What is Enlightenment?', Foucault remarks:

> The critical ontology of ourselves has to be considered not, certainly, as a theory, a doctrine, nor even as a permanent body of knowledge that is accumulating; it has to be conceived as an attitude, an ethos, a philosophical life in which the critique of what we are is at one and the same time the historical analysis of the limits that are imposed on us and an experiment with the possibility of going beyond them.
>
> (Foucault 1984: 50)

Maturity moves beyond the Kantian position, with a certain necessary irony, responding to current and specific problems in human experience and society and identifying the particular instantiations of power and truth in culture and history, and their interrelationships. Foucault neither denies the concept of truth, nor denounces, *per se*, the exercise of power. His ethics are not a reduction to the arbitrary, nor are they dependent on universal claims.

Hence, as he readily admits, the importance of Nietzsche (Foucault 1980: 109–33). Foucault seeks to identify historically the effects of truth within forms of disclosure that are, in themselves, neither true nor false. This is possible given the particular relationship between truth and *power*.

> It is not a matter of emancipating truth from every system of power (which would be a chimera, for truth is already power) but of detaching the power of truth from the forms of hegemony, social, economic and cultural, within which it operates at the present time.
>
> (ibid.: 133)

Such a realignment of truth and power within the specifics of a given historical moment places Foucault in a crucial position in the rethinking of a postmodern ethics,[31] but also in the thinking of theologians, who must also inescapably be concerned with issues of truth and power in the pursuit of maturity after Kant and within the crisis of legitimation of the postmodern condition. Foucault's challenge has been succinctly put by Hubert L. Dreyfus and Paul Rabinow:

29 See p. 290. See also Hubert L. Dreyfus and Paul Rabinow, 'What is Maturity? Habermas and Foucault on "What is Enlightenment?"', in David Couzens Hoy (ed.), *Foucault: A Critical Reader* (Oxford: Blackwell, 1986), pp. 109–21.

30 In Derrida's terms, we cannot simply place our burden on some 'infinite signified' which dispenses with our moral responsibilities.

31 Oddly, this is not always recognized. Foucault is only mentioned three times, and then somewhat disparagingly, in such a standard work as Critchley 1992.

there is a kind of ethical and intellectual integrity which, while vigorously opposing justifications of one's actions in terms of religion, law, science or philosophical grounding, nonetheless seeks to produce a new ethical form of life which foregrounds imagination, lucidity, humour, disciplined thought and practical wisdom.

(Dreyfus and Rabinow 1986: 121)

4.3 The emergence of the French feminists

Toril Moi, editor of *French Feminist Thought: A Reader* (1987) among many other works devoted to feminist theory, once remarked that under the ineradicable patriarchalism of the Western tradition, men will always speak from a different *position* than women, and, with the best of intentions, may be doing the feminist cause a disservice 'by muscling in on the one cultural and intellectual space women have created for themselves within [a] male-dominated discipline' (1986: 208). Perceiving the risk, therefore, I will keep this section fairly short! As with Foucault, the issue is fundamentally a political one, and the French feminists of the early 1970s, following the lead of Simone de Beauvoir,[32] were overtly so, demonstrating in the streets of Paris on such fundamental issues as violence against women, or the right to choose whether to have children. The argument put forward by Arlette Farge and others was that women had systematically been written out of the official history of Western politics and culture and had therefore been granted no 'space' of their own, both literally and in terms of identity and voice. In short, women's history needed to be radically invented.

The debate has taken many forms. The philosopher Michèle le Doeuf, in a remarkable book entitled *Hipparchia's Choice* (1989), presents the history of philosophy as the history of masculine texts and therefore the pursuit of male problems, suggesting that 'in the writings of a man philosopher, "woman" may be no more or less than a word for a foil whose role is to guarantee the philosopher's "greatness" by contrast' (1989: xi). In short, women have no 'voice' or discourse, which must be invented. But from where?

There is no room here for what Toril Moi has disparagingly called 'virtuous neutrality'. Feminists have spoken not with one voice but many in order to be heard. Denied a voice under the dominance of patriarchal oppression, feminists have spoken loudly and clear from a variety of perspectives, whether it be purely political, the attempt to turn Freudian psychoanalysis into an instrument of cultural transformation via the recovery of sexual difference, or, in the case of Hélène Cixous and Luce Irigaray, the adaptation of Derridian strategies of deconstruction (Moi 1986: 206). Not least the recognition of the dominance of patriarchy in our forms of discourse has led feminist critics to give attention to the most patriarchal of all our texts – the Bible.[33] In a series of studies of the Book of Judges, the Dutch feminist Mieke Bal exposes the patriarchal 'politics of coherence' in the reception history of Judges, whereby, in the interests of a powerful theological and political imperative still largely untouched in our reading of the Bible, women remain nameless, powerless and victimized.

As a narratologist, Bal sets out to deconstruct such hierarchies by the exposure of a 'countercoherence' within the very text and its narrative action, throwing down a feminist gauntlet to biblical critics, but

---

32 Simone de Beauvoir's ground-breaking work *The Second Sex* was published as early as 1949.

33 The perception of the Bible as oppressive to women was hardly new. In her 1895 Introduction to *The Women's Bible*, Elizabeth Cady Stanton stated that Scripture was based on the idea of the inferiority of women made subject to man

also to a much wider and more significant readership as well. Her approach to reading is deliberately interdisciplinary and disturbing:

> The analysis of the book [Judges] that I intend to carry out cannot but be interdisciplinary in its scope and method. The two opposing boundaries that the narratalogical analysis will hit are philosophy on the textual side and anthropology and history on the social side.
>
> (Bal 1988a: 39)[34]

This is clearly the language of battle. For some feminists, the war, in one sense, is no longer even worth fighting on the old ground. Daphne Hampson, for example, would discard Scripture and the Christian myth as both untrue and unethical, an impossibility for women, although she would continue to argue for a form of theism which continues to echo with certain overtones of Matthew Arnold's *Literature and Dogma*.[35] Hampson in Great Britain, and others like the more radical Mary Daly in the United States, have found themselves lost in the tradition, in various ways caught, in Matthew Arnold's famous words from his poem 'Stanzas from the Grande Chartreuse' (1855), 'wandering between two worlds, one dead, the other powerless to be born'.

In the more aggressive traditions of French feminism, writers like Irigaray have argued for the revival of a language of sexual difference through the deconstruction of traditional binary oppositions (Father/Mother; intelligence/emotions; etc.) and the employment of a language of the body and its functions. Such a language will begin to resituate our perceptions of boundaries, our understanding of power, indeed rewrite our very metaphors which underlie, not least, religious discourse. Speaking 'from the body', feminism has often willingly taken up a postmodern position on the margins of logocentricity by refusing to buy into those very structures of power, political, theological and textual, which have traditionally excluded women. Indeed, the term 'logocentric' is frequently replaced by more gendered expressions such as 'phallocentric'. For Julia Kristeva, such marginality implies a shift from an essential to a positional understanding of the feminine, so that women begin to share the nature of all marginal and frontier situations – both inside *and* outside, both familiar *and* alien.[36]

Feminist criticism, in its many forms, is a reminder that nothing, least of all religion and theology, can exist in a vacuum. Furthermore, its vigorous deconstruction of texts of power within the Western tradition raises acutely the issue of *textuality* itself, and whether our assumptions about the nature of the texts which underpin our theological thinking are justified and universal.

4.4 Rabbinic interpretation and modern literary theory

Matthew Arnold has had an odd tendency to intrude into our discussions at rather surprising moments. It is strange to find him again as a preface to Derrida's great essay of 1964 on Emmanuel Levinas, 'Violence and metaphysics'. It is a quotation from Arnold's *Culture and Anarchy* (1869):

---

34 See also Bal 1988b.
35 Hampson 1996, esp. ch. 6, 'A future theism', pp. 212–53.
36 See further, Moi 1986.

> Hebraism and Hellenism, – between these two points of influence moves our world. At one time
> it feels more powerfully the attraction of one of them, at another time of the other; and it ought
> to be, though it never is, evenly and happily balanced between them.[37]

Arnold speaks vaguely of a 'balancing', a reconciliation which seeks closure in a single vision, as a book comes to an end in a conclusion which Derrida sees as a death (Derrida 1976: 8). Against that, as we have seen, Derrida sets the endlessness of *writing*, a quite different view of textuality and the nature of text. Christian doctrine has been formed from its earliest day by a Greek understanding of text grounded in logocentricity and the *Logos* as the absolute Word of God. The consequence of this tends to be the paradox that 'the text' – the Bible – becomes absolute and authoritative, to which nothing can be added or taken away, while at the same time *writing* is merely instrumental and a mere means to an end. We move through the text to the ultimate truth which lies beyond it.[38]

Derrida's work on the book and writing exposes his background in a tradition with a very different sense of 'text', however. Significantly he delights in games of signature, calling himself 'Reb Derissa' – the laughing Rabbi. It is no accident that so many of the leading postmodern thinkers have a background, variously expressed, in Judaism; not only Derrida, but also Levinas, Harold Bloom, Geoffrey Hartman – and before them Marx and Freud. Derrida is close to the tradition of *mashal*, the riddle[39] and *midrash*, as commentary or paraphrase breaking down the distinction between text and comment.[40] Just as the political energies of postmodern feminisms prompt a new hermeneutic, so Derrida's frequent references to the methods of talmudic commentary draw our attention to an alternative understanding of the nature of text itself, at once deconstructive and creative, in which 'the Biblical text is not, according to the Rabbinic view, a material thing located in a single space and circumscribed by a quantifiable time' (Handelman 1982: 37). Rather it is of and before all time, nothing less than the divine wisdom itself, preceding the written words which we read. Indeed, it is said, the 'Torah preceded the world',[41] the ink and parchment being the garments of the divine wisdom. As such, the parameters of the text are infinite, endless conversations in writing in which commentary is part of the *process* in text and interpretation which reflects the continuous and endless process of creation itself, without beginning or end. Thus a famous midrash on Genesis reads:

> It is customary that when a human being builds a palace, he does not build it according to his
> own wisdom but according to the wisdom of a craftsman. And the craftsman does not build
> according to his own wisdom, rather he has plans and records in order to know how to make
> rooms and corridors. The Holy One, blessed be He, did the same. He looked into the Torah and
> created the world.[42]

The end of hermeneutics, or interpretation, then, is not to reach conclusion or meaning, nor is it conceptualizing or totalitarian. It is, instead, a kind of continuous revelation, and in these Rabbinic

---

37 Matthew Arnold, quoted in Derrida 1981b: 79.
38 A good example of this in recent biblical criticism is Rudolf Bultmann's programme of demythologizing.
39 See, for example, Judges 14.10–20, the 'riddle' of Samson at his feast.
40 For a succinct definition of *midrash*, see Neusner 1987. See further, and for the contemporary relevance of midrash, Hartman and Budick 1986. Talmud (literally, Teaching, Learning) is a compilation of the oral Torah. The Babylonian Talmud dates from the fifth century CE.
41 Talmud (Babylonian), *Shabbat* 886.
42 *Bereishit Rabbah* (on Genesis). See also Handelman 1982: 38.

processes can be found many of the major concerns of Derridean deconstruction – the opposition between text and writing, the privileging of speech over writing ('phonocentrism'), and theology as aporetic. It is against this background that we must read such important reflections on postmodern theology as Mark C. Taylor's *Erring: A Postmodern A/theology* (1984) with its endless word-plays after the death of God, an event of the most profound significance in the liberation of theology:

> The time and space of graceful erring are opened by the death of God, and the loss of self, and the end of history. In uncertain, insecure, and vertiginous postmodern worlds, wanderers repeatedly ask: 'Whither are we moving? . . . Are we plunging continually? backward, sideward, forward, in all directions? Is there still any up or down? Are we not erring as through an infinite nothing?' while the death of God is realised in the play of the divine Milieu and the disappearance of the self is inscribed in markings and traces, history 'ends' when erring 'begins', and erring 'begins' when history 'ends'.
>
> (Taylor 1984: 150–1)

The language here coincides with a moment in Western philosophy when Hegel, reacting against the timeless, a priori claims of Kantian reason (Norris 1987: 232), conceptualizes history on the principle of endless return to its own beginnings – in effect, the end of history. Hegel's circularity implies a total self-presence from which there is no escape, an impasse which Emmanuel Levinas exposes in his great work *Totality and Infinity* (1979), in which he confronts philosophy developed as *epistemology*, a form of knowing which regards as primary the relationship between the mind and the object, the knower and the known. The alternative to this impasse, freed only in the 'mazing' discourse of Taylor or Rabbinic conversation, is the different kind of encounter between the self and the other in a mode of endless ethical obligation to the other in a fraternal discourse which refuses totalization (Hand 1989). Levinas seeks to sustain an ethics which is not subject to the governing demands of epistemology, concluding thus:

> The face to face is not a modality of coexistence nor even of the knowledge (itself panoramic) one term can have of another, but is the primordial production of being on which all the possible collocations of the terms are founded.
>
> (1979: 305)

In the move beyond epistemology, 'goodness' is never anonymous and morality precedes philosophy. Levinas, as a profound reader of the Talmud (1990), translates an art of reading into reflections on contemporary issues and problems within the radical tradition of Rabbinic interpretation. Abandoning linearity, texts interact in an endless *intertextuality* and a visual *textuality* in which commentary literally surrounds, and is surrounded by, text.[43] Such texts are not so much read from beginning to end, but are read against each other, and are *seen* in complex layouts on the page, the eye following patterns of words almost like a picture.

Derrida and Levinas do not always agree. Indeed, it is of the nature of such discourse that they should argue. But Levinas remains a profound influence on Derrida's thinking in its move beyond logocentricity, its deconstruction of rationality, its deep ethical motives, and its theological awareness.

---

43 See the format of Derrida 1986.

4.5 The apocalypse of Thomas J. J. Altizer

Much could be said about 'the postmodern God' which will, for want of space, be omitted here. However, a recently published *Reader* on the subject moves a little further beyond the thinkers and issues with which we have so far been concerned (Ward 1997). As we draw towards a conclusion (though by now this must be considered only as a beginning!), therefore, it might be most appropriate to pause for a moment with the writings, still unfinished, of one of the most original and misunderstood theologians of our day, and not least because he picks up precisely on the point in Hegel which we identified in our glance at Levinas's *Totality and Infinity*.

Altizer comes out of the tradition of preachers in the southern States. He speaks with a rhetoric that is passionate and frequently almost mystical. Yet it is also impossible to understand his work without acknowledging his immersion in Hegel and Nietzsche, in Dante, Milton and Joyce, in the Bible, and finally in the aporias of the postmodern. He became known in the 1960s as the theologian, *par excellence*, of the death of God.[44]

Since then, in numerous books and articles, his thought has been a consistent and ever more profound reflection on his initial question, 'Is it possible to conceive of a form of Christianity coming to expression without a belief in God?' (ibid.: 9). Altizer's unequivocal answer is 'Yes', although his attitude towards the Church and Christendom is equally persistently negative. Early in his career he wrote:

> [William] Blake belongs to a large company of radical or spiritual Christians, Christians who believe that the Church and Christendom have sealed Jesus in his tomb and resurrected the very evil and darkness that Jesus conquered by their exaltation of a solitary and transcendent God, a heteronomous and compulsive law, and a salvation history that is irrevocably past. Despite its great relevance to our situation, the faith of the radical Christian continues to remain largely unknown, and this is so both because that faith has never been able to speak in the established categories of Western thought and theology and because it has so seldom been given a visionary expression.
>
> (ibid.: 182)

Altizer has little time for the traditional 'theologian', though his own vocation is deeply theological. He is highly sensitive to postmodernity, as we have reviewed it, to Derrida's belief in modernity as the closure of history – and, at the same time, insists that we have been brought to a moment in which only the visionary imagination of the poet can take us to the next, constructive, stage. Thus, as we shall see, Altizer's characteristic tone is an apocalyptic one, and one also deeply at one with the mystical tradition which has also haunted these pages.[45]

Hegel's conceptualization of history proposed the equation of truth with self-presence. Literally one stands *in* the presence. This self-presence is inverted by Altizer to realize the absolute self-embodiment of God, a total presence only made possible in the death of God. Altizer thus stands as the radical alternative to the Enlightenment project of modernity, a true postmodern who is also rooted in a profound archaism. His roots in the most ancient strands of Christian theology, Altizer sees God most profoundly present in the moment of negation, that is, Christ's death on the cross. God is most deeply embodied

---

44 See Altizer and Hamilton 1968. The book is dedicated to the memory of Paul Tillich.
45 Compare Jacques Derrida, *D'un ton apocalyptique adopté naguère en philosophie* (Paris: Galilée, 1983).

and present to us in the moment of cancellation and absence, and this paradox is at the heart of Christian truth. In his most intense and personal book, *The Self-Embodiment of God* (1977), Altizer immediately recognizes that 'theology today is most fundamentally in quest of a language and a mode whereby it can speak' (1977: 1). Yet if he realizes what in the present chapter has been termed the crisis of the 'linguistic turn' in the twentieth century, Altizer's pursuit of a language for theology takes a very different course. For he asserts that theology can now only pursue a radical path towards language which moves precisely through the desert experience and the *via negativa*, beyond postmodernity to a condition in which language is only fully realized in silence, for only then can the disjunctions of speech and language finally be overcome in an enactment which 'does not simply make silence presence, it brings an end to all that distance established by speech, and now that distance is resurrected in the immediate and total presence of speech, a presence which can be present only in silence' (ibid.: 94). As all the poets know, language leads ultimatley to silence, an absence of speech which is embraced by the word. It was this profound silence which drove the early saints of the Church into the desert, to meet God in absence and negation.

For Altizer this is the true apocalypse – a revelation of that which remains utterly hidden. It is the genesis of God[46] made possible only by the death of God. Initially, at least, Altizer seems to hold some affinity with the Karl Barth of *Der Romerbrief*, which was first published in 1918 in the aftermath of the Great War and Germany's defeat, and in which Barth affirms 'the new (impossible) possibility which constitutes a real nearness to God [which] can be discerned only in the likeness of death'.[47] Altizer, however, moves far beyond Barth and indeed specifically diverges from him on one major issue. For if Barth, together with other major theologians of the twentieth century like Bultmann, Tillich and Rahner, represents a deep negation of Hegelian thinking, then Altizer, in a typical *coincidentia oppositorum*, returns to Hegel as one who 'gave birth to a uniquely modern theological thinking' through his affirmation of an absolute *kenosis* – the idea of self-emptying which is fundamental for Altizer.[48]

Here for 'modern' we may perhaps read 'postmodern'. For this *kenosis* is the final realization for history as apocalypse, a radical self-emptying even to death, so that God is only realized in his absolute opposite. For the Christian, and Altizer is most profoundly a Christian, albeit a postmodern one, this apocalypse moves beyond history 'in the totality of its historical enactment' in Christ,

> And a divine abyss that is cosmic and historical at once, interior and exterior at once, thereby embodying an anonymity of Jesus that is an abysmal but nevertheless a truly universal anonymity? A truly universal body and a world that is precisely thereby a total *coincidentia oppositorum* of Satan and Christ?
>
> (Altizer 1998: 204)

46 *The Genesis of God: A Theological Genealogy* is the title of a book which Altizer published in 1993.
47 Barth 1968: 206. There have been two major claims for the close affinity between Barth and forms of postmodern thinking: Ward 1995 and Lowe 1993.
48 Altizer 1993: 37. The Greek word *kenosis* is taken here from Philippians 2.7, '[God] emptied himself, taking the form of a servant, being born in the likeness of men' (RSV).

5 POSTMODERN A/THEOLOGIES: THE FUTURE OF THEOLOGICAL THINKING

We have come far and much more could have been said and remains to be said. I am left at Hebrews 11.32, 'And what more shall I say? For time would fail me to tell of . . .'. The trajectory that has been traced from the origins of modernity in Descartes and the Enlightenment to our present postmodern condition is essentially a simple one – perhaps as simple as the rise and fall of 'reason' – and yet, for that very *reason*, one should be suspicious of it as yet another grand metanarrative, doomed to be deconstructed by countless critics. And if we now live in a time of suspicion, how confident can we be of our future, or even that there will be a future for theology and for theological thinking?

There is no shortage of those who would direct us on the way, impatient of any simple assumption that contemporary thought is enslaved to varieties of nihilism. As just one example, a conference held in Cambridge in 1990 has resulted in a volume of essays edited by Philippa Berry and Andrew Wernick entitled *Shadow of the Spirit: Postmodernism and Religion* (1992), offering a wide variety of readings in the 'sacred' and the 'divine' in current thought and culture. In the end, perhaps, they amounted to very little, and levelled against these somewhat empty claims, the larger questions remain – is there life after postmodernism? Is there simply the fascination with the 'thrill of catastrophe . . . the ecstatic implosion of postmodern culture into excess, waste, and disaccumulation'? (Kroker and Cook 1988: 1).[49]

I have suggested a more serious and visionary theological voice after postmodernism in Thomas Altizer. I have focused upon him because, with his interest in literature and the poets even more than in the theologians, Altizer represents part of the necessary shift from 'theology' to the more dynamic environment of 'theological thinking', which is perhaps more appropriate to our present condition. Carl Rashke, in his book *Theological Thinking: An In-quiry* (1988), describes this activity as follows:

> It is our task here not to be concerned simply with thinking, but with *theological thinking*. The inquiry that amounts to thinking theologically may be regarded as a kind of 'inquest' into the mysterious contention that 'God is dead' for which the corollary is that theology has 'ended'.
>
> (1988: vii)

Not just thinking, but theological thinking, and not just theology either. One of the problems for 'theology' is that it remains encased in a set of paradigms which science, for one, has long abandoned under the pressure of relativity theory and quantum physics. To put it very briefly, theology has never experienced the paradigm shift which is represented by the explosion of Newtonian physics under the blows of Max Planck and later Einstein's theory of special relativity. Theology, there, has never been equipped to acknowledge fully the world of the postmodern, and, in spite of all those who have prepared a way for the theologian from Heidegger to Derrida, remains in the shadows of crumbling institutions, lamenting past glories.

Altizer holds an apocalyptic vision after Blake, Hegel and Nietzsche. There are a few others. Mark C. Taylor has now abandoned the enterprise after the early promise of *Erring*, preferring the virtual reality of his later works like *Imagologies* (1994), conceived, rather than written, with Esa Saarienen. The French philosopher Jean-Luc Marion has thrown a new light on metaphysics and phenomenology for theologians (Marion 1997: 279–96) and, in his widely discussed book *God without Being* (1982), looks beyond metaphysics, beyond Heidegger and even Nietzsche, to a God outside all categories of

49 For a more positive view see Fekete 1988.

being. But from the postmodern, Marion returns to the more familiar arena of *agapē* – God as love. In the end he seems not so very far from the post-Christian Daphne Hampson – extremes, perhaps, may always meet. Or again there is the finely philosophical American theologian Robert P. Scharlemann, whose underrated, though admittedly difficult, book *The Reason of Following* (1991) returns to a Christology which seeks to link the biblical 'I am' with contemporary understandings of the self and identity, though he is heavily indebted to the now somewhat dated hermeneutics of Rudolf Bultmann.

So, the future for theological thinking within the primarily Christian West, which has been our principal concern, is unclear though far from dead, though some would regard it as such within the incoherent, distraught world of the postmodern, a world of illusion and hyper-reality. Yet perhaps its very impossibilities, far beyond the reach of reason, are themselves reasons for hope. As Robert Detweiler has said, in an essay on apocalyptic fiction, 'over much of the globe we are already living the unthinkable, to the extent that my freedom to think the unthinkable . . . is a First-World luxury' (1990: 181). If the concern with apocalyptic, which we have already noted as a characteristic of our condition, marks the end, finally, of Western traditions of realism (note the vitality of apocalyptic narratives in postmodern fiction[50]), then perhaps we are being freed to think beyond realism, and beyond mimesis to a new theological thinking of how the world 'is'. We have learnt since Kant, and through Kierkegaard, Heidegger, Derrida, Levinas and others, how to begin to think about thinking, beyond epistemological categories, and may therefore be beginning to be able to 'think' within the apocalyptic mode within which we are already living.[51] If that is so then there remains hope for the definition from the future of new kinds of realism, and the traumatic and extended anxieties from the Enlightenment, through modernity and postmodernity, will not have been in vain. In the alchemy of the word, theology may yet be reborn.[52] It may be said that all that has been reviewed in this chapter constitutes the decline of the possibility of traditional theological language and thinking in the West. Yet, at the same time, the radical world of postmodernity, and the terrifying prospect of a world capable of bringing about its own end in an apocalypse of nuclear holocaust and genocide, carries within it, paradoxically, the seeds of new kinds of theological thinking and new kinds of language to reunite us with the divine wisdom.

BIBLIOGRAPHY

Adorno, T., and M. Horkheimer (1944) *Dialectic of Enlightenment*, trans. John Cumming, 1996. New York: Continuum Press.

Altizer, T. (1977) *The Self-Embodiment of God*. New York: Harper & Row.

Altizer, T. (1993) *The Genesis of God: A Theological Genealogy*. Louisville: Westminster/John Knox Press.

Altizer, T. (1998) *The Contemporary Jesus*. London: SCM Press.

Altizer, T., and W. Hamilton (1968) *Radical Theology and the Death of God*. London: Penguin.

Arnold, M. (1855) 'Stanzas from the Grande Chartreuse'.

Arnold, M. (1867) 'Dover Beach', in *New Poems*. London: Macmillan.

Arnold, M. (1873) *Literature and Dogma*, ed. James C. Livingston. New York: Frederick Uingar, 1970.

Aronson, R. (1983) *The Dialectics of Disaster: A Preface to Hope*. Thetford: Thetford Press.

Bal, M. (1988a) *Death and Dissymmetry: The Politics of Coherence in the Book of Judges*. Chicago: University of Chicago Press.

50 For example, Ballard 1970; Hoban 1980. One could go on almost *ad infinitum*.

51 See Aronson 1983: 7–8.

52 See Rashke 1979.

Bal, M. (1988b) *Lethal Love: And Murder and Difference: Gender, Genre and Scholarship on Sisera's Death*. Bloomington: Indiana University Press.

Ballard, J. G. (1970) *The Atrocity Exhibition*. London: HarperCollins, 1993.

Barth, K. (1968) *The Epistle to the Romans*, trans. from the 6th edn Edwin C. Hoskyns. Oxford: Oxford University Press.

Beauvoir, S. de (1949) *The Second Sex*, trans. H. H. Parshley, 1953. Harmondsworth: Penguin, 1972.

Berman, A. (1988) *From the New Criticism to Deconstruction: The Reception of Structuralism and Post-Structuralism*. Urbana: University of Illinois Press.

Berry, P., and A. Wernick (eds) (1992) *Shadow of Spirit*. London: Routledge.

Blanchot, M. (1989) *The Space of Literature*, trans. Ann Smock. Lincoln, NE: University of Nebraska Press.

Blumenberg, H. (1983) *The Legitimacy of the Modern Age*, trans. Robert M. Wallace. Cambridge, MA: MIT.

Budick, S., and W. Iser (eds) (1989) *Languages of the Unsayable: The Play of Negativity in Literature and Literary Theory*. New York: Columbia University Press.

Butler, C. (1994) *Early Modernism: Literature, Music and Painting in Europe, 1900–1916*. Oxford: Clarendon Press.

Cahoune, L. (1996) *From Modernism to Postmodernism: An Anthology*. Oxford: Blackwell.

Caputo, J. (1997) *The Prayers and Tears of Jacques Derrida: Religion without Religion*. Bloomington: Indiana University Press.

Chadwick, O. (1975) *The Secularisation of the European Mind in the Nineteenth Century*. The Gifford Lectures for 1973–4. Cambridge: Cambridge University Press.

Coleridge, S. T. (1817) *Biographia Literaria. The Collected Works*, vol. 7, ed. James Engell and W. Jackson Bate. Princeton: Princeton University Press, 1983.

Coleridge, S. T. (1840) *Confessions of an Inquiring Spirit*. London: William Pickering.

Conquest, R. (1972) *Lenin*. London: Collins.

Critchley, S. (1992) *The Ethics of Deconstruction*. Oxford: Blackwell.

Culler, J. (1976) *Saussure*. London: Collins.

Cunningham, V. (1994) *In the Reading Gaol: Postmodernity, Texts and History*. Oxford: Blackwell.

de Certeau, M. (1992) *The Mystic Fable*, trans. M. B. Smith. Chicago: University of Chicago Press.

de Man, P. (1979) *Allegories of Reading: Figural Language in Rousseau, Nietzsche, Rilke and Proust*. New Haven and London: Yale University Press.

Derrida, J. (1976) *Of Grammatology*, trans. G. C. Spivak. Baltimore: Johns Hopkins University Press.

Derrida, J. (1981a) *Positions*, trans. Alan Bates. Chicago: University of Chicago Press.

Derrida, J. (1981b) 'Violence and metaphysics: an essay on the thought of Emmanuel Levinas', in *Writing and Difference*, trans. Alan Bass. London: Routledge.

Derrida, J. (1986) *Glas*, trans. John P. Leavey, Jr., and Richard Rand. Lincoln, NE: University of Nebraska Press.

Derrida, J. (1992) 'Post-scriptum: aporias, ways and voices', in Harold Coward and Toby Fashy (eds), *Derrida and Negative Theology*. Albany: State University of New York Press.

Derrida, J. (1993) *Memoirs of the Blind: The Self-Portrait and other Ruins*, trans. Pascale-Anne Brault and Michael Naas. Chicago: University of Chicago Press.

Descartes, R. (1996) *Meditations on First Philosophy* (1641), in Lawrence Cahoone (ed.), *From Modernism to Postmodernism: An Anthology*. Oxford: Blackwell.

Detweiler, R. (1990) 'Apocalyptic fiction and the end(s) of realism', in David Jasper and Colin Crowder (eds), *European Literature and Theology in the Twentieth Century*. London: Macmillan.

Dreyfus, H. L., and P. Rabinow (1986) 'What is maturity? Habermas and Foucault on "What is Enlightenment?"', in David Couzens (ed.), *Foucault: A Critical Reader*. Oxford: Blackwell.

Engels, F. (1956) *Anti-Dühring*, Part I, in Henry D. Aiken, *The Age of Ideology: The Nineteenth Century Philosophers*. London: The New English Library.

Fekete, J. (ed.) (1988) *Life after Postmodernism: Essays on Value and Culture*. London: Macmillan.

Fish, S. (1980) *Is There a Text in this Class? The Authority of Interpretive Communities*. Cambridge, MA: Harvard University Press.

Foucault, M. (1980) 'Truth and power', an interview with Alessandra Fontana and Pasquale Pasquino, in Colin Gordon (ed.), *Power/Knowledge: Selected Interviews and Other Writings*. New York: Pantheon.

Foucault, M. (1984) 'What is Enlightenment?', in Paul Rabinow (ed.), *The Foucault Reader*. Oxford: Blackwell.

Freud, S. (1953) *Standard Edition of the Complete Psychological Works*. London: Hogarth Press.

Freud, S. (1962) *Two Short Accounts of Psycho-Analysis*. London: Penguin.

Gay, P. (ed.) (1995) *The Freud Reader*. London: Vintage.

Greene, T. M. (1960) 'The historical context and religious significance of Kant's *Religion*', an Introduction to *Religion Within the Limits of Reason Alone*. New York: Harper.

Habermas, J. (1987) 'Excursus on leveling the genre distinction between philosophy and literature', in *The Philosophical Discourse of Modernity*. Cambridge: Polity Press.

Hampson, D. (1996) *After Christianity*. London: SCM Press.

Hand, S. (ed.) (1989) *The Levinas Reader*. Oxford: Blackwell.

Handelman, S. (1982) *The Slayers of Moses: The Emergence of Rabbinic Interpretation in Modern Literary Theory*. Albany: State University of New York Press.

Hartman, G., and S. Budick (1986) *Midrash and Literature*. New Haven and London: Yale University Press.

Heidegger, M. (1996) *Basic Writings*, rev. edn, ed. David Farrell Krell. London: Routledge.

Hoban, R. (1980) *Ridley Walker*. London: Picador, 1982.

Kant, I. (1960) *Religion Within the Limits of Reason Alone*. New York: Harper.

Kant, I. (1991) *Political Writings*, ed. Hans Reiss, trans. H. B. Nisbet, 2nd edn. Cambridge: Cambridge University Press.

Kroker, A., and D. Cook (1988) *The Postmodern Scene: Excremental Culture and Hyper-Aesthetics*. London: Macmillan.

le Doeuf, M. (1989) *Hipparchia's Choice: An Essay Concerning Women, Philosophy, etc.*, trans. Trista Selous. Oxford: Blackwell, 1991.

Levinas, E. (1979) *Totality and Infinity: An Essay on Exteriority*, trans. Alphonso Lingis. The Hague: Martinus Nijhoff.

Lowe, W. (1993) *Theology and Difference: The Wound of Reason*. Bloomington: Indiana University Press.

Löwith, K. (1949) *Meaning in History: The Theological Implications of the Philosophy of History*. Chicago: University of Chicago Press.

Lübbe, H. (1965) *Säkularisierung, Geschichte einen ideenpolitischen Begriffs*. Freiburg: Alber.

Lyotard, J.-F. (1984) *The Postmodern Condition: A Report on Knowledge*, trans. Geoff Bennington and Brian Massuni. Manchester: Manchester University Press.

Magnus, B., S. Stewart and J. P. Mileur (1993) *Nietzsche's Case: Philosophy as/and Literature*. New York: Routledge.

Marion, J.-L. (1982) *God Without Being*, trans. T. A. Carlson. Chicago: University of Chicago Press.

Marion, J.-L. (1997) 'Metaphysics and phenomenology: a summary for theologians', in Graham Ward (ed.), *The Postmodern God*. Oxford: Blackwell.

Marx, K. (1888) 'Theses on Feuerbach', in *Marx and Engels: Basic Writings on Politics and Philosophy*, ed. Lewis S. Feuer. London and Glasgow: Collins, 1969.

Marx, K., and F. Engels (1888) *The Manifesto of the Communist Party*, English edn of 1888, in *Marx and Engels: Basic Writings on Politics and Philosophy*, ed. Lewis S. Feuer. London and Glasgow: Collins, 1969.

Moi, T. (ed.) (1986) *The Kristeva Reader*. Oxford: Blackwell.

Moore, S. D. (1994) *Poststructuralism and the New Testament: Derrida and Foucault at the Foot of the Cross*. Minneapolis: Fortress Press.

Neusner, J. (1987) *What is Midrash?* Philadelphia: Fortress Press.

Nietzsche, F. (1895) *The Anti-Christ*, trans. R. J. Hollingdale. London: Penguin Classics, 1968.

Nietzsche, F. (1956) *The Geneaology of Morals*, trans. Francis Golffing. New York: Doubleday.

Nietzsche, F. (1968) *Twilight of the Idols*, trans. R. J. Hollingdale. London: Penguin Classics.

Norris, C. (1982) *Deconstruction: Theory and Practice*. London: Methuen.

Norris, C. (1987) *Derrida*. London: Collins.

Rabinow, P. (ed.) (1984) *The Foucault Reader*. New York: Pantheon.

Rashke, C. (1979) *The Alchemy of the World: Language and the End of Theology*. Missoula: Scholars Press.

Rashke, C. (1988) *Theological Thinking: An In-quiry*. Atlanta: Scholars Press.

Reventlow, H. G. (1984) *The Authority of the Bible and the Rise of the Modern World*, trans. John Bowden. London: SCM Press.

Robey, D. (1986) 'Modern literature and the language of literature', in Ann Jefferson and David Robey, *Modern Literary Theory: A Comparative Introduction*, 2nd edn. London: Batsford.

Rorty, R. (1989) *Contingency, Irony and Solidarity*. Cambridge: Cambridge University Press.

Roszak, T. (1968) *The Making of a Counter-Culture: Reflections on the Technocratic Society and Its Youthful Opposition*. London: Faber, 1970.

Roszak, T. (1972) *Where the Wasteland Ends: Politics and Transcendence in Post-Industrial Society*. London: Faber, 1974.

Saussure, F. de (1911) *Course in General Linguistics*, trans. Wade Baskin, 1960. London: Peter Owen.

Scharlemann, R. P. (1996) *The Reason of Following*. Chicago: University of Chicago Press.

Shaffer, E. (1975) *'Kubla Khan' and The Fall of Jerusalem: The Mythological School in Biblical Criticism and Secular Literature 1770–1880*. Cambridge: Cambridge University Press.

Shelley, P. B. (1821) 'A defence of poetry', in Edmund D. Jones (ed.), *English Critical Essays* (*Nineteenth Century*). Oxford: Oxford University Press, 1916.

Stanton, E. C. (1895) *The Woman's Bible*. Seattle: Coalition Task Force and Women and Religion, 1974.

Steiner, G. (1978) *Heidegger*. London: Collins.

Steiner, G. (1989) *Real Presences*. London: Faber.

Tallis, R. (1988) *Not Saussure: A Critique of Post-Saussurean Literary Theory*. London: Macmillan.

Taylor, C. (1989) *Sources of the Self: The Making of the Modern Identity*. Cambridge, MA: Harvard University Press.

Taylor, M. C. (1984) *Erring: A Postmodern A/theology*. Chicago: University of Chicago Press.

Taylor, M. C. (1986) *Deconstruction in Context: Literature and Philosophy*. Chicago: University of Chicago Press.

Taylor, M. C. (1994) *Imagologies*. London: Routledge.

Trollope, A. (1866) *Clergymen of the Church of England*. Leicester: Leicester University Press, 1974.

Vattimo, G. (1988) *The End of Modernity*, trans. John R. Snyder. Cambridge: Polity Press.

Ward, G. (1995) *Barth, Derrida and the Language of Theology*. Cambridge: Cambridge University Press.

Ward, G. (1997) *The Postmodern God: A Theological Reader*. Oxford: Blackwell.

Willey, B. (1956) *Nineteenth Century Studies: A Group of Honest Doubters*. London: Chatto & Windus.

Wollheim, R. (1971) *Freud*. London: Collins.

Yeats, W. B. (1921) 'The Second Coming', *Collected Poems*. London: Macmillan, 1969.

Religious fundamentalism and politics

Jeff Haynes

One of the most pivotal ideas about societal development during the twentieth century – that nations would inevitably secularize as they modernized – was misplaced. After World War II, apparent decline of religious faith and growing secularization in Western Europe fitted neatly with the idea that technological development and the application of science to overcome perennial social problems of poverty, hunger and disease would result in sustained progress for all. And in this process, it was believed, religion would be an inevitable casualty.

One of the main tenets of modernization theory was that societies would secularize as they modernized and industrialized. Harvey Cox (1965) argued that (Western, Christian, urbanized) theologians were fighting a losing battle in trying to swim against the tide of secularization which accompanied the growth of industrial cities; their best chance of retaining any popular relevance and significance was to seek to influence the burgeoning secular movements of social change then common in the Americas and Western Europe. One practical result of the melding of spiritual and political concerns was the involvement of left-leaning theologians in the neo-Marxist-influenced liberation theology movements which emerged in parts of Latin America, the Far East, and the Caribbean in the 1960s.

More than thirty-five years after the publication of *The Secular City*, it is no longer even slightly controversial to claim widespread links between religion and politics in the contemporary world. Over the last twenty years attention has focused, *inter alia*, on: the Iranian revolution of 1978–80, and more widely on Islamic militancy; Christian fundamentalism and the rapid growth of politically quietist Protestant evangelical sects in Africa and the Americas; Hindu and Buddhist 'fundamentalist' groups in India and Southeast Asia; and Jewish 'fundamentalists' in Israel and elsewhere.

To many observers and 'ordinary' people, religious fundamentalism is always socially and politically conservative, backward-looking, inherently opposed to change. But if this is the case how can we explain the activities of militant Islamic groups around the world – often dubbed 'fundamentalist' – who strive to overthrow regimes with which they disagree? Other groups which have been labelled fundamentalist – such as 'born again' Christians in the United States or Orthodox Jews in Israel – seem to fit more closely the conventional wisdom, as they are often linked to very conservative political forces who seek to roll back what they perceive as an unwelcome liberalization and relaxation of social and moral mores.

The nature of the interaction between religion and politics has long posed problems for analysis. The main issue is how to analyse the phenomenon when until recently the consensus was that secularization and modernization would inexorably displace religion from most people's concerns? Even a highly materialist strand of analysis, neo-Marxist thought, came eventually to recognize that politics was not merely concerned with economic structures and processes, but also with attitudes and values formed in part by religious considerations. In other words, class-based analysis on its own was no longer a defensible form of political analysis without concern with other, non-materialist issues, including religion. In addition, advocates of another strand of political analysis – rational choice theory – were also obliged to amend their analytical frameworks; it was necessary, henceforward, to break out of their 'reductionist microrational quandary' by admitting that rational self-interest models must be set in a multifaceted context involving laws, rules, ideas, beliefs and values in order to add to explanatory models (Almond 1993: xi)

Both analytical frameworks – neo-Marxist and rational choice theory – were in effect obliged to take into account political culture issues. Since Almond and Verba's (1963) groundbreaking work nearly 40 years ago, the genre had become somewhat passé over time with the emergence of other, partially economistic forms of analysis from the 1960s and 1970s. Yet, over time, the perceived resurgence of religion in politics, sometimes linked to nationalist or ethnic concerns, could clearly not be explained by economic or class issues alone. The consequence was that political culture, reflecting important underlying beliefs, values and opinions, including religious concerns, had returned to the analytical centre stage after years of declining interest. Moyser posed two important analytical questions in this respect (1991: 8). First, to what extent are religious orientations linked to a national political culture and/or given subcultures? Second, are religious belief systems, such as they are at the mass level, systematically associated with ideological dispositions in the political realm? He suggests that in many 'developed' and 'developing' countries, religion and politics do seem to 'connect' in this way. For example, there appear to be connections between, on the one hand, religion and nationalism/ethnicity and, on the other, at least in some cases, between religious fundamentalism and political conservatism.

In this chapter I will focus upon two issues: (1) discussing what religious fundamentalism is; and (2) examining examples of fundamentalist groups' involvement with political issues. I shall draw my examples from among Christian, Muslim, Jewish, Hindu and Buddhist fundamentalists.

1 WHAT IS RELIGIOUS FUNDAMENTALISM?

Religious fundamentalism is often seen as a 'distinctively modern twentieth-century movement', albeit with 'historical antecedents' (Woodhead and Heelas 2000: 32). As a concept, 'religious fundamentalism' has been widely employed since the 1970s, especially by the mass media, to describe and account for numerous, apparently diverse, religious and political developments around the globe (Caplan 1987). While the designation 'religious fundamentalist' was first applied to themselves by conservative evangelicals inside the mainstream Protestant denominations in the early years of the twentieth century, as a generic term, it is now widely applied additionally to a multitude of groups outside the corpus of Christianity; especially, but not exclusively, to Judaist and Islamist entities.

Generally speaking, the character and impact of fundamentalist doctrines is located within a nexus of moral and social issues revolving, in many contemporary countries and religions, around state–society interactions. In some cases, the initial defensiveness of beleaguered religious groups developed into a political offensive which sought to alter the prevailing social and political realities of state–society relations. Often encouraging this was a perception that rulers were performing inadequately and/or corruptly, with religious fundamentalists often (but not always, Buddhist and Hindu 'fundamentalisms' are exceptions) relating contemporary developments to critical reading of religious texts. The significance of this from a political perspective was that it could serve to supply an already restive group with a ready-made manifesto for social change. Religious leaders used religious texts both to challenge secular rulers and to propose a programme for radical reform. Under these circumstances it was often relatively easy for fundamentalist leaders to gain the support of those who felt that in some way the development of society was not proceeding according to God's will or the community's interests. In sum, various manifestations of what might be called religious fundamentalism seem to appeal to different groups for different reasons at different times.

The point is that in many cases contemporary religious fundamentalism is rooted in the failed promise of modernity, reactive against perceived unwelcome manifestations of modernization, such as declining morals. To many fundamentalists the current era is one where God is in danger of being superseded by a gospel of technical progress accompanying sweeping socio-economic changes. The pace of change, especially since World War II, strongly challenged traditional habits, beliefs and cultures which were under considerable pressure to adapt. In an increasingly materialist world one's individual worth was increasingly measured according to standards of wealth and status, with religion ignored or belittled. Such cultural and economic changes were regarded by many as the root cause of a perceived, generalized decline of the societal salience of religion. And it was this development which led to the growth of religious militancy and accounts in general terms for the recent rise of what is widely – if loosely – known as religious fundamentalism.

But there is a major analytical problem to confront: it is suggested that 'religious fundamentalism' is an empty and therefore meaningless term, erroneously and casually employed 'by western liberals to refer to a broad spectrum of religious phenomena which have little in common except for the fact that they are alarming to liberals!' (Woodhead and Heelas 2000: 32). Critics contend that the range of groups that have been called 'fundamentalist' is so wide – for example, resurgent Islam in Iran and Latin American Pentecostalism – that the term has no meaning; while it is often insulting for those people described as 'fundamentalists'. Not least among the differences between such groups is that some wish to influence or even control the public and political arena while others actively work to disengage from social and political issues. As a consequence, it is argued, the

> broad use of the term has become increasingly irrelevant. In sum, viewed as a derogatory concept, tied to Western stereotypes and Christian presuppositions, the casual use of the term easily causes misunderstandings and prevents the understanding of the dynamics and characteristics of different religious groups with explicit *political* objectives.
>
> (emphasis added; Hallencreutz and Westerlund 1996: 4)

However, as already noted, and despite such criticisms, the term 'religious fundamentalism' has become increasingly common, in both academic and popular discourse since the 1970s. Numerous journal articles and books on the topic, including volumes by Marty and Appleby (1991–5) and Lawrence (1995), have appeared in recent years. Those accepting the analytical relevance of the term do so because they perceive contemporary movements of religious resurgence – albeit encompassing different religious traditions around the world – as having various features in common which denote a shared concern with 'fundamentalism'. Woodhead and Heelas (2000: 32) identify the following features of religious fundamentalism:

- a desire to return to the fundamentals of a religious tradition and strip away unnecessary accretions
- an aggressive rejection of Western secular modernity
- an oppositional minority group-identity maintained in an exclusivist and militant manner
- attempts to reclaim the public sphere as a space of religious and moral purity
- a patriarchal and hierarchical ordering of relations between the sexes.

Drawing on data from a large variety of fundamentalist movements, Marty and Scott Appleby define religious fundamentalism as a 'set of strategies, by which beleaguered believers attempt to preserve their distinctive identity as a people or group' in response to a real or imagined attack from those who, it appears, want to draw the religious believers into 'syncretistic, areligious, or irreligious cultural milieu[s]' (1993c: 3). This defensiveness may develop into a political offensive aiming to alter prevailing socio-political realities.

From the list of characteristics noted, it would appear that what religious fundamentalists have in common is a fear that their religiously orientated way of life is under threat from unwelcome alien influences, especially secular-orientated governments. As a result, religious fundamentalists, believing themselves threatened by 'modernization', which implies secularization, have sought to reform society in accordance with what they believe are suitable religious tenets and to change the laws, morality, social norms and – if necessary – the political configurations of their polity. In other words, such people seek to create a traditionally orientated, less modern(ized) society, willing in some cases to fight governments if the latter's jurisdiction appears to be encompassing areas which the fundamentalists believe are integral to the building of an appropriate society: education, gender relations and employment policy, and the nature of society's moral climate. Fundamentalists may also struggle against those they see as 'nominal' or 'backsliding' co-religionists – whom they perceive as lax in their religious duties – and against members of opposing religions – whom they may perceive as evil or even satanic.

Those who reject blanket use of the term 'fundamentalism' might however allow that it has relevance in one specific context: self-designated, fundamentalist Christians in the United States. Such people wrote their declarations more than a hundred years ago, anxious to defend what they saw as fundamental doctrines of their faith. These included both the inerrancy of the Bible as well as a determination to fight back against what they saw as the unacceptable inroads of secular modernity. While such people were normally apolitical for decades – from the 1910s to the 1970s – American Christian fundamentalists began to realize that retreating from the world was a self-defeating strategy. This was because in so doing they were unable to alter what they saw as catastrophically unwelcome developments linked to the progress of modernization. The consequence was that from the 1970s American Christian fundamentalists became an increasingly vociferous political constituency. Well-known examples include Jerry Falwell and his organization Moral Majority, formed in 1979, as well as recent presidential candidates, Pat Robertson and Pat Buchanan. In sum, Christian fundamentalism in the United States is closely linked to conservative political forces seeking to reverse what they perceive as excessive liberalization and relaxation of social and moral mores, believed to be the root cause of what has gone wrong in American society since the 'swinging Sixties'.

Drawing on the example of American Christian fundamentalists, many analysts who employ the term fundamentalism suggest that it is only properly applicable to Christianity and other Abrahamic religions of the 'book': Islam and Judaism. This is because, like fundamentalist Christians, Muslim and Jewish fundamentalists also take as their defining dogma what is believed to be the inerrancy of God's own words set out in holy books like the Bible. In other words, in these three religions, singular scriptural revelations are central to each set of fundamentalist dogma. The inference is that, because neither Hinduism nor Buddhism have central tenets of political, social and moral import conveniently accessible in holy books, then it is not logically possible for there to be Hindu or Buddhist fundamentalism. However, somewhat confusingly, as we shall see later, in recent years popular 'fundamentalist' movements within both Hinduism and Buddhism have emerged in pursuit of demonstrably political goals. Such groups are not defined by their absolutist insistence upon the veracity of God's revealed will, but by a desire to recapture elements of national identity which are perceived as being lost either by dint of cultural dilution or mixing or by perceived deviations from the religious philosophy and/or teachings (Ram-Prasad 1993: 288).

I will argue in this chapter that the growth of religio-political fundamentalist movements is linked both to modernization and to secularization. These closely related developments served seriously to undermine or threatened to undermine the social importance of religion in many parts of the world, among both 'developed' and 'developing' countries. I will suggest that what is happening in the sphere of religion and politics is the consequence of a widespread 'deprivatization' of previously privatized religions in the Western world: Europe (including Israel) and North America. These are regions where there is a more or less clear tripartite division of democratic polities into state, political society and civil society. According to conventional social science wisdom such an arrangement should – inevitably – lead to religion's privatization and corresponding decline in social and political importance. On the other hand, where the process of religious privatization is not so far advanced – that is, in most 'developing' countries – it is *fear* of imminent or creeping privatization which, I believe, provides a stimulus for religious actors to act in the political sphere in order to try to prevent what they see as the social marginalization of their religion. Secular political ideologies – for example, liberal democracy and capitalism, socialism, or social democracy – have been tried and, in many cases, been seen to fail. A consequence is that, in many countries, the growth and emergence of religious fundamentalism, sometimes allied with nationalism, ethnicity or communalism, can function as a mobilizing ideology to focus opposition to the status quo (McGreal 2000). I should make it clear that I am *not* suggesting that religio-political movements were necessarily unimportant in the past; the growth and eventual politicization of Christian fundamentalism in the United States and the emergence of successive waves of Islamic reformists over the last two centuries in West Africa and elsewhere would belie that argument. What I am proposing is that the overtly politicized goals of contemporary fundamentalist movements are best understood in relation to the insecurities of the postmodernist era and the continual accretions of power sought by states as a function of the secularization of state and society.

While I shall focus explicitly on various kinds of religious fundamentalism later, I will continue with a brief survey of some of their main socio-political characteristics.

1.1 Islamic fundamentalism

A defining character of religious fundamentalism is that it is always socially but not necessarily politically conservative. For example, some Islamic fundamentalist (or, as I prefer, *Islamist*) groups seek an overthrow of the current socio-economic and political order by the use of various means, including: violence or terrorism, incremental reform of existing political regimes or by winning elections through the mobilization of a political party. Islamists, like their Jewish and Christian counterparts, take as their defining dogma what are believed to be God's words written in their holy book, the Qur'an. In other words, singular scriptural revelations are central to Islamic fundamentalist dogma.

Modern Islamic resurgence dates from the 1920–40 period. This was a time when growing numbers of countries in the Middle East were demanding – and in some cases receiving – political freedom from colonial rule. The main point of contention was how far should these predominantly Muslim states employ the tenets of shariah law in their legal systems. This example of a desire to islamicize polities had its precedents in the Muslim world in anti-imperialist and anti-pagan movements (*jihads*) which periodically erupted from the late nineteenth century, especially in parts of West Africa and East Asia (Haynes 1993). These were regions where the conflict between tradition and modernization, and between Islam and Christianity, was often acute.

Going even further back, to the beginning of Islam over 1,300 years ago, religious critics of the status quo periodically emerged in opposition to what they perceived as unjust rule. Contemporary Islamic fundamentalists are the most recent example of such a phenomenon. They characterize themselves as the 'just' involved in a 'holy war' against the 'unjust'. The dichotomy between 'just' and 'unjust' in the promotion of social change throughout Islamic history parallels the tension in the West between 'state' and 'civil society'. In other words, 'just' and 'unjust', like 'state' and 'civil society', are mutually exclusive concepts where a strengthening of one necessarily implies a weakening of the other. The implication is that the 'unjust' inhabit the state while the 'just' look in from the outside, aching to reform the corrupt political system. The Islamic 'just' strive to achieve their goal of a form of direct democracy under the auspices of shariah law. The ruler uses his wisdom to settle disputes brought before him by his loyal subjects. The Islamic concept of *shura* (consultation) does not by any means necessarily imply popular sovereignty, that is with God alone; 'rather it is a means of obtaining unanimity from the community of believers, which allows for no legitimate minority position' (Dorr 1993: 151–2). The goal of the 'just' is an Islam-based society; at the current time in many countries, Islamist groups are the vehicle to achieve this end. To some Muslims, liberal democracy is fatally flawed and compromised, a concept of relevance only to secular, Western(ized) societies which often appear to many Muslims unacceptably morally deficient. As a young Algerian graduate of the Islamic Science Institute of Algiers averred, 'The modern world is going through a major moral crisis which can be very confusing to young people. Just look at what is happening in Russia. Personally I have found many of the answers and solutions in Islam' (quoted in Ibrahim 1992).

The global Muslim community, the *ummah*, is a good example of a transnational civil society (the Roman Catholic Church is another), which contains the seeds of both domination and dissent. Shared beliefs, relating especially to culture, sentiments and identity, link Muslims. For this reason it is unsurprising that international manifestations of Islamic resurgence appeared after the humbling defeat of Arab Muslims by Israeli Jews in the Six-Day War (June 1967). Since then a combination of poor government, growing unemployment and generalized social crisis together have produced Islamist movements throughout the Muslim world. These developments have also been the result of failed modernization. Where possible, rulers have generally been content to gain rents accrued from their control of the sale of oil for hard currency. Little has been done to develop more representative polities, plan successfully for the future, or seek means to reduce un- and underemployment. In short, there has been a skewed modernization, with urbanization and the development of strong, centralized states proceeding while many people became increasingly dissatisfied with the way that their rulers rule.

1.2 Christian fundamentalism

For many Muslims, poverty and a declining faith in the development abilities of their governments has led to their being receptive to fundamentalist arguments. Poverty and a feeling of hopelessness may be exacerbated by a withering of community ties as people move from the countryside to the town in a search for paid employment. And when traditional communal and familial ties are seriously stretched or sundered, religion-orientated ones may replace them. In the United States, on the other hand, Christian fundamentalists are often found among affluent, successful people (Wald 1991: 271). Clearly, it would be absurd to argue that alienation explains the existence of such people in the United States.

Christian fundamentalism, after achieving social and political prominence in the early decades of the twentieth century, re-emerged as a legitimate vehicle for political ideas in the United States from the 1970s, a period of political, social and economic upheaval in America. Less legitimate manifestations of what purported to be religiously inspired groups, such as the Ku-Klux Klan, had developed from the time of the American Civil War (1861–5), but they were hardly a part of the political mainstream except in areas of the southern United States, where white Protestant hostility to Jews, Catholics and Black Americans surfaced after World War I. Instead, most Christian fundamentalists were concerned with allegedly high levels of amorality in the United States. Their success in terms of gaining recruits can be judged by the fact that, in the late 1980s, there was estimated to be around 60 million fundamentalist Christians in the USA, that is, over 20 per cent of the total population (Hertzke 1989: 298–9). And many were political: Christian fundamentalists provided the core support for Pat Robertson's unsuccessful 1988 presidential campaign, and for Pat Buchanan's in 1992, 1996 and 2000.

1.3 Jewish fundamentalism

The third religion of the book, Judaism, also has its religious fundamentalists; one of them, Yigal Amir, assassinated Yitzhak Rabin, then Israeli prime minister, in November 1995. Rabin's 'crime' was negotiating with the Palestine Liberation Organization (PLO) leader, Yasser Arafat, with the goal of allowing Palestinians a large measure of self-government, premised upon a reduction in the physical size of Israel. It was this – a proposed reduction in the size of the God-given state of Israel – which incurred the wrath of Amir and other Jewish fundamentalists. In sum, Jewish fundamentalist groups in Israel, including the largest, Gush Emunim (Bloc of the Faithful), are characterized by an utter unwillingness to negotiate with Palestinians over what they see as holy land.

Gush Emunim was founded after the 1978 Camp David agreement between Israel and Egypt, which resulted in the handing back of the Sinai desert to the latter. Other fundamentalist groups, such as the late Rabbi Meir Kahane's organization, Kach, also fulminate against the return of territory to Egypt or any other non-Jews. The biblical entity, Eretz Israel, they argue, was significantly larger than the contemporary state of Israel. To hand back any territory to Arabs is tantamount, they argue, to going against God's will as revealed in the Old Testament of the Bible. Simmering religious opposition to the peace plan with the PLO, involving giving autonomy to the Gaza Strip and to an area around Jericho, reached tragic levels in February 1994 when a religious zealot, Baruch Goldstein, linked with militants of both Kach (Thus) and Kahane Chai (Kahane Lives), murdered a number of people during a dawn attack on a mosque in the occupied West Bank town of Hebron. After the massacre both Kach and Kahane Chai were banned by the Israeli government, a sign of its commitment to crush religious extremist groups which systematically used violence to gain their ends. However, the banning of such extremist groups did little to diminish the growing political influence of Jewish fundamentalist groups in Israel.

1.4 Hindu fundamentalism

While Hindu fundamentalism is rooted in cultural chauvinism it is by no means *sui generis*. Like Rabin, Mahatma Gandhi, the leading Indian nationalist and a committed Hindu, was assassinated by a religious extremist in 1948 for the 'crime' of appearing to condone the creation of a bifurcated homeland for India's Muslims, East and West Pakistan. More recently, simmering Hindu fundamentalist suspicion of India's largest religious minority – Muslims, comprising about 11 per cent of the population, more than 100 million people – was manifested in the destruction in 1992 of an historic mosque at Ayodhya in Uttar Pradesh. This mosque, according to militant Hindus, was built on the birthplace of the Hindu god of war, Rama. As long ago as 1950, the mosque was closed down by the Indian government, as militant Hindus long sought to build a Hindu temple in place of the mosque.

In a further example of the fanning of communal flames, the late prime minister, Indira Gandhi, paid with her life in 1984 by appealing to Hindu chauvinism to take on Sikh militancy in the Punjab. Her son, Prime Minister Rajiv Gandhi, was probably assassinated by a Tamil Hindu in 1991 because of his sending Indian troops to try to resolve the civil conflict in Sri Lanka between Hindu Tamils and Buddhist Sinhalese. Since then, the Hindu-chauvinist Bharatiya Janata Party (BJP) has been an increasingly important political player, with a role in government since the mid-1990s.

1.5 Buddhist fundamentalism

In Thailand, a neo-Buddhist movement, Santi Asoke, made a unilateral declaration of independence from the orthodox Thai *sangha* (body of monks) in 1975. One of its most prominent followers, a former governor of Bangkok, Major-General Chamlong Srimaung, formed a political party in the late 1980s, called Palang Tham (*tham* means both 'moral' and 'dhamma' in the teachings of Buddhism). Some have argued that Palang Tham's ultimate goal is the creation of a radical Buddhist state in Thailand (McCargo 1992). What this would entail, it would appear, is a corruption-free political environment with the role of the military downplayed and with state ideology rooted in Buddhist ideals and teaching. However, despite some initial political success, for example, winning fourteen parliamentary seats in the 1988 elections, Palang Tham's Buddhist fundamentalist message generally failed to influence Thais.

▌2 RELIGION AND POLITICS: WHAT IS THE CONNECTION?

I have suggested that religious fundamentalism may be divided into two broad categories: one, pertaining to religions of the book, with scriptural revelations relating to political, moral and social issues forming the core of fundamentalist belief, and often informing programmes of political action. The second comprises Hindu and Buddhist fundamentalisms. In this case, absence of definitive scriptures encourages fundamentalist dogma to move into nationalist and/or chauvinist dimensions. It should be noted, however, that, despite intermittent political importance, normally, religious fundamentalist groups – India is an exception – remain relatively marginal to national political processes and outcomes.

Given the political foci of many religious fundamentalist groups it is useful to spend some time on the following issue: *How* do religious values, norms and beliefs stimulate and affect socio-political developments and vice versa?

It seems uncontroversial to note that belief – of some kind – is at the core of all religions. However, as Bellah noted more than 35 years ago, it has proved extremely difficult to come up with a 'brief handy definition of religion'; nothing has changed since then to make the task any easier. Bellah defines religion as 'a set of symbolic forms and acts which relate man [*sic*] to the ultimate conditions of his existence' (1964: 359). In this chapter, I use the term religion in two distinct, yet related, ways. First, religion refers – in a material sense – to religious establishments (that is, institutions and officials), as well as to social groups and movements whose main *raison d'être* is to do with religious concerns. Examples of the latter include the conservative Roman Catholic organization Opus Dei and various fundamentalist movements, such as Algeria's Islamic Salvation Front (FIS) and the Hindu-chauvinist Bharatiya Janata Party (BJP) of India.

Second, in a spiritual sense, religion pertains to models of social and individual behaviour that help believers to organize their everyday lives. Thus, religion is to do with: the idea of *transcendence*, that is, it relates to supernatural realities; with *sacredness*, that is, as a system of language and practice that organizes the world in terms of what is deemed holy; and with *ultimacy*, that is, it relates people to the ultimate conditions of existence (Moyser 1991). In sum, I approach the issue of religion in politics from three linked perspectives: (1) a body of ideas and outlooks (that is, as theology and ethical code); (2) as a type of formal organization (for example, the ecclesiastical Church); (3) as a social group (for example, religious movements).

Therborn argues that there are two basic ways 'in which religions can affect this world': (1) by what they say, and (2) by what they do (1994: 104). The former is the doctrine or theology. The latter refers to religion as a social phenomenon working through variable modes of institutionalization, including political parties and church–state relations, and functioning as a mark of identity for members of self-identified groups. In other words, in this conception religion does not simply have meaning at the individual level. That is, like politics, it is also a matter of group solidarities and often of inter-group tension and conflict, focusing on shared or disagreed images of the sacred. To complicate matters, '[t]hese . . . influences . . . tend to operate differently and with different temporalities for the same theologically defined religion in different parts of the world' (Moyser 1991: 11). And, in addition, to assess 'the political impact of religion depends greatly on what facet of religion is being considered and which specific political arena is under investigation' (Wald 1991: 251).

The issue of church–state relations has been of pivotal importance for political analysis in many countries for a long period. (In this chapter, the term 'church' refers to *any* established form of religion; it is not restricted to the *Christian* church.) Therborn argues that 'the more close the relationship [of the church] to the state, the less resistance to adaptation [to modernity]' (1994: 105). For example, over time, especially in the industrialized West, mainline churches, that is, mainstream religious organizations, generally developed an empathetic relation with political power, even when they ideologically opposed it (for example, the Russian Orthodox Church during the Communist era).

Reflecting this affinity between temporal and spiritual power, most typologies of church–state relations underscore the mutual synergy between these actors. Weber identified three types of relations between secular and ecclesiastical power: *hierocratic*, that is, secular power is dominant but cloaked in a religious legitimacy; *theocratic*, that is, ecclesiastical authority is pre-eminent over secular power; and *caesaro-papist*, that is, secular power holds sway over religion itself (1978: 1159–60). More recent typologies often take into account growing separation between church and state, assumed to be a function of Western-style modernization, a process that, typically, leads to increasing secularization within nations. Reflecting on the creation of anti-religion states in the USSR, Albania and elsewhere, Parsons (1960) notes that a church may have a symbiotic relationship with the state at one extreme or be totally separate from it at the other; the latter position is not reflected in Weber's tripartite typology.

Medhurst (1981) extends the range of types of state–church relationship from three to four, proposing: (1) 'The Integrated "Religio-political System"' (IRS); (2) 'The Confessional Polity (or State)'; (3) 'The Religiously Neutral Polity (or State)'; and (4) 'The Anti-Religious Polity (or State)'. The IRS is a type of theocracy, virtually extinct (Saudi Arabia is Medhurst's only extant example) that pertains to pre-modern political systems where religious and spiritual power converge in one dominant figure. Historical examples of the IRS include pre-1945 Japan and ancient Mesopotamia. Medhurst argues that the IRS is contemporarily rare because one of the most consistent, global effects of modernization is to separate religious and secular power. However, this should not be taken too far: the demise of the hardline Marxist states of Eastern Europe, such as Albania or the Soviet Union, where religion was 'throttled', meant that Medhurst's fourth category – the 'Anti-Religious Polity' – also became practically extinct in recent times (with the exception of the last of the hardline Communist states: North Korea).

The remaining two categories of church–state relationship highlighted by Medhurst are, in contrast, common at the present time. The 'Confessional Polity' emerges when the 'traditional "religio-political system" begins to crumble and gives way to a new situation of religious or ideological pluralism' (Medhurst 1981: 120). In other words, this is a situation characterized by a (more or less) formal separation of state and a (dominant) religion, although in practice close links between the two actors often endure. Examples of the Confessional Polity include Ireland, Colombia and post-revolutionary Iran. Finally, the category of 'Religiously Neutral Polity' includes constitutionally secular states, such as India, the USA and the Netherlands. In such countries, no religion is privileged over others.

Writing in the early 1990s, and hence reflecting the demise of the Eastern European Communist bloc, Mitra offers four different categories of church–state relations: (1) *hegemonic*, that is where one religion dominates, but other religions are tolerated, as in Britain (this category corresponds closely to Medhurst's 'Confessional Polity'); (2) *theocratic*, for example in Iran, or Israel – in this categorization, unlike Medhurst's IRS formulation, state power is dependent upon a close relationship with the dominant religion; (3) *secular*, corresponding to Medhurst's 'Religiously Neutral Polity', for example in France, USSR and the United States; and (4) *neutral*, for example, in India, where government is constitutionally obliged to be even-handed in its approach to all religions (Mitra 1991: 758–9).

For Mitra, religion provides the moral basis of the state's authority, as well as an institutional and metaphysical structure for social transactions. Yet, religion is affected by the dispositions of temporal power and by changing social norms and attitudes, especially secularization. In the context of church–state relations, the 'specific role attributed to religion at a given time and place depends primarily upon the status of religion in the constitutional framework and the social meaning attached to it' (Mitra 1991: 758). The constitutional position of religion is reflected in his typology. The social meaning, on the other hand, may alter, perhaps radically, as a result of changing circumstances.

It has long been assumed that the connection between politics and religion is only a problem in countries which are not religiously homogeneous. (Most political thinkers since Aristotle have taken it for granted that religious homogeneity is a condition of political stability within a polity.) Alford puts it thus: when opposing beliefs about 'ultimate values enter the political arena, they exacerbate struggles by preventing compromise' (1969: 321). Such is clear in relation to India, upon which Mitra focuses, where communal strife between Hindus and Muslims is increasingly common, encouraging Hindu fundamentalism. The wider point is that, while the relationship between state and church within a country may well be of importance politically, the sociopolitical position of a religion cannot only be dependent on the constitutional position.

As Figure 7.1 shows, Mitra views the relationship between state, society and religion as triadic. That is, in national settings, religion's role in politics is 'influenced by the specific kind of state and society relation that obtains in a given historical conjuncture . . . A particular historical conjuncture may be conducive towards the growth of a particular form of religious movement' (Mitra 1991: 757).

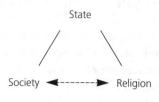

Figure 7.1 The triadic relationship of state, society and religion

This point can be illustrated by reference to India. Following independence from British colonial rule in 1947, the postcolonial political elite who took power via the Congress Party expected that there would be a 'natural' process of modernization which would, as in the West, 'inevitably' lead to the downgrading of religion in public life and its replacement by a more secular terrain. However, such expectations turned out to be misplaced: democratization and secularization worked at cross-purposes, with increasing participation in the political arena drawing in new social forces that demanded greater formal recognition of particular religions – especially Hinduism and Sikhism. The result was that, by the 1980s, far from receding as a political issue, religion assumed a centrality that was certainly not envisaged by nationalist leaders at independence.

3 SECULARIZATION AND RELIGIOUS FUNDAMENTALISTS' POLITICAL INVOLVEMENT

India is not an isolated example. Woollacott (1995) notes that '[a]nybody who had prophesied thirty years ago that the twentieth century would end with a resurgence of religion, with great new cathedrals, mosques, and temples rising up, with the symbols and songs of faith everywhere apparent, would, in most circles, have been derided'. For some observers, the rise of religious fundamentalisms is but one facet of a general religious resurgence around the world since the 1970s (Hadden 1987; Shupe 1990; Thomas 1999, 2000). Others argue, however, that, except under certain limited circumstances and conditions, secularization is generally continuing (Wallis and Bruce 1992; Wilson 1992; Bruce 1993). The point here is that religious fundamentalism can be seen as a counter-movement to the onwards march of secularization, a process which ultimately leads to the political and public marginalization of religion.

Secularization, implying a significant diminishing of religious concerns in everyday life, has been one of the main social and political trends in Western Europe since the Enlightenment (1720–80). It was long believed that as a society modernizes it inevitably secularizes – that is, in becoming more complex, a division of labour emerges whereby institutions become more highly specialized and, as a consequence, are increasingly in need of their own technicians. To many, secularization was one of the most fundamental structural and ideological changes in the process of political development, a global trend, a universal facet of modernization. Everywhere, as societies modernized there would be a demystification of religion positing a gradual, yet persistent, erosion of religious influence. The end result of secularization is a secular society, that is, where the pursuit of politics and public policy takes place irrespective of what religious actors do or say.

In many cases, secularization has gone hand in hand with separation of power between church and state. In much of Europe this situation developed over time, with an important symbolic starting point the Treaty of Westphalia (1648). This agreement not only brought to an end the Thirty Years War between Protestants and Catholics, but also saw the end of religious wars which had followed in the wake of the Reformation. The Westphalian settlement established the rule that it was for secular political leaders to decide which religion would be favoured in their polity. What this amounted to was that the emerging states of Western Europe tended to be more or less religious monopolies of one religion or another, as well as increasingly the homes of self-conscious national groups. Autocratic rulers saw religious conformity as an essential underpinning of their rule, necessary to maintain the existing social political order in their favour.

The tendency towards rulers' absolutism and the growth of nationalism were both greatly affected by the French Revolution of 1789. In France itself, the Catholic Church, which had retained much of its wealth, social influence and political power after the 1648 Treaty, came under attack from radicals and revolutionaries. The division between them and the Church was not bridged during the nineteenth century: by its end the rise of socialism and communism helped to diminish further the Church's influence in the political battles fought between socialists, social democrats, liberals and conservatives. While this necessarily simplifies a complex situation (for example, the Catholic Church retained much power in some cases, such as Italy and Ireland), the overall effect of the growth of nationalism and secular political mobilization in Europe was effectively to diminish the Church's political power in relation to secular rulers.

The decline in the social and political importance of religion in the West is solidly grounded in mainstream social science (but see Dark 2000 for an alternative view). Shupe notes that '[t]he demystification of religion inherent in the classic secularisation paradigm posit[s] a gradual, persistent, unbroken erosion of religious influence in urban industrial societies' (1990: 19). Secularization implies a unidirectional process, whereby societies move from a sacred condition to an increasingly areligious state until the sacred eventually becomes socially and politically marginal. Under secularization, societies gradually move from being focused around the sacred and the divine, with religious professionals enjoying much power and authority, to the opposite: a steep decline in religious power and authority and the eventual result, a fundamental transformation in the traditional relationship between religion and politics. While having distinctive ideological positions, commanding figures of nineteenth-century social science – such as Emile Durkheim, Max Weber, Karl Marx – all concurred that secularization was an absolutely integral facet of modernization, a global trend of importance in all societies as they moved from 'tradition' to 'modernity'. As a result of secularization religion is privatized, losing its grip on culture and society, and becoming instead a purely personal matter of private belief. Consequently, religion would no longer be a collective force with mobilizing potential for social change. In sum, secularization was 'the most fundamental structural and ideological change in the process of political development' (Smith 1970: 6).

The processes of secularization encompass a number of discrete areas that can be summarized as follows: (1) *constitutional secularization* Religious institutions cease to be given special constitutional recognition and support. (2) *policy secularization* The state expands its policy domains and service provisions into areas previously reserved to the religious sphere. (3) *institutional secularization* Religious structures lose their political saliency and influence as pressure groups, parties and movements. (4) *agenda secularization* Issues, needs and problems deemed relevant to the political process no longer have an overtly religious content. (5) *ideological secularization* 'The basic values and belief-systems used to evaluate the political realm and to give it meaning cease to be couched in religious terms' (Moyser 1991: 14).

Secularization is clearest in the industrialized West, where falling income levels for mainline churches, declining numbers and quality of religious professionals, and diminishing church attendance collectively point to 'a process of decline in the social significance of religion' (Wilson 1992: 198). In many Western countries, religion has lost many of the functions it once fulfilled for other social institutions: providing 'legitimacy for secular authority'; endorsing – even sanctioning – public policy; sustaining with 'a battery of threats and blandishments the agencies of social control'; claiming to be the font of 'true' learning; socializing the young; and 'sponsoring a range of recreative activities' (Wilson 1992: 200).

It is suggested that secularization will make progress *except when religion finds or retains work to do other than relating people to the supernatural.* As Bruce puts it, '[o]nly when religion does something other than mediate between man and God does it retain a high place in people's attentions and in their politics' (1993: 51).

Put another way, under the influence of secularization, religion shrinks in social significance except in two important ways. First, it may be a component of *cultural defence*, that is, 'when culture, identity, and a sense of worth are challenged by a source promoting either an alien religion or rampant secularism and that source is negatively valued'. Second, it may be an aspect of *cultural transition*, that is, where 'identity is threatened in the course of major cultural transitions' (Wallis and Bruce 1992: 17–18). In both cases, religious belief can furnish the resources for attempting to deal with such circumstances by helping religious groups to assert their claim to a sense of worth in a secularizing society where the value and status of religion is perceived to be seriously declining.

Opponents of the secularization thesis assert that the current era is characterized, not by the decline of religion, but by its widespread resurgence; that is, the secularization thesis is simply wrong (Shupe 1990; Sahliyeh 1990a, 1990b; Thomas 1995; Woollacott 1995; Dark 2000). Thomas argues that 'the global resurgence of religious ideas and social movements is one of the most unexpected events at the end of the twentieth century . . . taking place at the same time among diverse cultures, in different countries, and in states at different levels of economic development' (1995: 1). Sahliyeh claims that over the last two decades or so, 'a number of highly politicized religious groups, institutions and movements, surfaced in different parts of the world. Although of different faiths and sects, these groups shared a common desire to change their societies and even to change the international order.' Some confine their activities to the realm of political protest, reform or change through the ballot box, others resort to violence in pursuit of their objectives (Sahliyeh 1990a: vii). In the many 'developing' countries, it is argued, religion has retained a high level of social importance, even in swiftly modernizing societies.

Sahliyeh argues that there are three broad reasons explaining what he sees as global resurgence of religion. First, there is the destabilizing impact of modernization. Rather than leading to secularization, the social upheaval and economic dislocation associated with modernization leads to a renewal of traditional religions (Sahliyeh 1990b: 15). Second, religious resurgence is a response to a general 'atmosphere of crisis', with its origins in a range of factors, including

> the inconclusive modernizing efforts of secular elites in the Third World, growing disillusionment
> with secular nationalism, problems of legitimacy and political oppression in many developing
> countries, problems of national identity, widespread socio-economic grievances, and the erosion

of traditional morality and values both in the West and in the Third World. The coterminous existence of several or all of these crises in much of the contemporary world provides a fertile milieu for the return to religion.

(Sahliyeh 1990b: 6)

The third factor is the political activism of contemporary religious groups and movements said to be accountable by reference to what Sahliyeh calls a 'resource mobilization model'. Three elements of this model are analytically important. Religious groups (1) must have the opportunity to form political movements; (2) should exhibit political vitality, a result of adequate financial resources, political leadership, organizational structures, communications networks, manpower and a suitable mobilizing ideology; and (3) need 'incentives, reasons, and motives' before they can successfully organize and endure (Sahliyeh 1990b: 10–11). In short, to be successfully politically active, religious groups must have: a political *raison d'être*, leaders, cadres, resources and ideology.

A second viewpoint is that, rather than religious resurgence, what is happening is that political religion is now simply more visible as a consequence of the communications revolution. Thus politicized religion is persistent rather than resurgent. Shupe argues that, throughout the world, 'organized religion is a stubbornly persistent and . . . integral factor in . . . politics' (1990: 18). Smith claims that '[w]hat has changed in the present situation . . . is mainly the growing awareness of [global manifestations of political religion] by the Western world, and the perception that they might be related to our interests' (1990: 34). Thus, what is said to be happening in many 'Third World' countries is merely the latest manifestation of *cyclical* religious resurgence, made highly visible (and to many alarming) by advances in communications technology and availability. Smith points to various religions – especially Hinduism, Buddhism and Islam – which experienced periods of intense political activity during the first half of the twentieth century (Haynes 1993, 1996).

Between the world wars (that is, in the 1920s and the 1930s), religion was frequently used in the service of anti-colonial nationalism, a major facet of emerging national identity in opposition to alien rule (Haynes 1996: 55–6). For example, in some Muslim countries – including, Algeria, Egypt and Indonesia – Islamic consciousness was the defining ideology of nationalist movements. In 1947, immediately after World War II, Pakistan was founded as a Muslim state, religiously and culturally distinct from India, 80 per cent Hindu. A decade later, Buddhism was politically important in, *inter alia*, Burma, Sri Lanka and (South) Vietnam. In the 1960s in Latin America, both Christian democracy – the application of Christian precepts to politics – and liberation theology – a radical ideology using Christianity as the basis of a demand for more equality for the poor – were politically consequential. Ten years later, in Iran and Nicaragua, religion also assumed an important political role. During the 1980s and 1990s, religion was active in a number of contexts, including the demise of communism in Eastern Europe, neo-Buddhist movements in Southeast Asia, Hindu-chauvinist parties in India, and Algeria's civil war. In sum, opposition is the traditional forte of political religious groups, and has been since the early years of the twentieth century. Current manifestations of political religion, including religious fundamentalism, should be seen in this historical context, and exemplify continuity rather than integral change.

4 POSTMODERNISM AND RELIGIOUS FUNDAMENTALISM

At first glance, interconnections between various manifestations of religious fundamentalism, such as the 'new political activism of American [fundamentalist] clergymen . . . the growth of Islamic funda-mentalism . . . [and] Sikh separatism in India', may seem 'weak or non-existent. Liberation theologians and revolutionary ayatollahs may be aware of each other's existence but have not influenced each other very much' (Smith 1990: 33). What, if anything, do these manifestations of political religion have in common, other than that they all occurred from the 1970s?

As already discussed, secularization has made sustained progress *except when religion finds or retains work to do other than relating individuals to the supernatural*. Those who argue that there is conclusive evidence of a *global* resurgence of political religion, many of whom are religious people, are, in my opinion, indulging in wishful thinking. On the other hand, it cannot be gainsaid that examples of political religion abound and Smith's (1990) argument that we are more aware of them than previously certainly has merit. I doubt, however, that this is the whole story. Sahliyeh's (1990a) allusion to 'social crisis', the importance of communications networks, and social upheaval and economic dislocation, are all characteristic of the postmodern condition, and it is these concerns which, I will argue, inform most contemporary manifestations of religious fundamentalism with political concerns.

Examples of political religion noted above relate emphatically to the mundane, rooted in perceptions of a group feeling that the status quo is not conducive to long-term well-being. In the case of Sikh fundamentalism, the mobilizing issue is cultural defence against the perceived hegemonic designs of the Indian (Hindu) state, itself challenged for being 'too secular' (read: pro-Muslim) by resurgent Hindu separatists (Ram-Prasad 2000). In the other examples Smith employs – that is, American fundamentalist clergymen and Islamic radicals – the rigours of cultural transition threaten their identity and underpin and galvanize their religio-political reaction.

Postmodernism, said to have been coined by J.-F. Lyotard (1979), is defined as: incredulity towards metanarratives, that is, a rejection of absolute ways of speaking truth. However, postmodernism is an enigmatic concept, whose ambiguity nevertheless reflects the confusion and uncertainty inherent in contemporary life for many people. The term has been applied in and to many diverse spheres of human life and activity. It is important for politics and political analysis as it decisively reflects the end of belief in the Enlightenment project, that is, an assumption of universal Progress based on Reason, and in the 'modern Promethean myth of humanity's mastery of its destiny and capacity for resolution of all its problems' (Watson 1994: 150). Socially, postmodernism is related to 'changes in the everyday practices and experiences of different groups, who . . . develop new means of orientation and identity structures . . . Postmodernism . . . directs our attention to changes taking place in contemporary culture' (Featherstone 1988: 208). According to Simpson, 'the postmodern factor is defined by a sociopolitical dimension, a cultural/interpretative dimension, and a human rights dimension' (1992: 13).

Concerns captured by the term postmodernism are, I will argue, of importance in understanding the significance for political religion, including religious fundamentalism. (For a discussion of post-modernism and Christianity, see Simpson 1992; and of postmodernism and Islam, see Ahmed 1992.) Ahmed argues that postmodernism 'encourages the rejection of centres and systems, engenders the growth of local identity, makes available information and thus teaches people to demand their rights, . . . fosters ideas of freedom and eclecticism, [and] challenges the state' (1992: 129). Rosenau stresses the fragmentation and voluntarism inherent in postmodernism.

> Consistent with the decentralizing tendencies that have disrupted authority relations at all levels is the diminishing hold that all-encompassing systems of thought exercise over their adherents.

This decay can be discerned in the pockets of disaffection with the scientific rationalism of Western thought – with what is considered to be the end of 'progress' as defined by the 'modernity project' – represented by postmodernist formulations . . .

(1990: 414)

De Gruchy also stresses both the opportunities and the destabilization which postmodernism is thought to represent: it is 'turbulent, traumatic and dislocating, yet it is also one which is potentially creative' (1995: 5). Finally, various manifestations of religious fundamentalism are said to be representative of the cultural/interpretative dimension of postmodernism (Simpson 1992; Cox 1984).

For many people, the epochal fall of the Berlin Wall in 1989, followed by the sudden, completely unexpected demise of Communist systems in the Soviet Union and Eastern Europe in 1990–1, exemplified the sociopolitical and human rights dimensions of the postmodern era. That is, these events symbolized a fundamental change from one epoch to another, helping to fuel widespread, yet transitory, optimism that a more benign 'New World Order' would follow the ideological divisiveness and malignity of the Cold War. Western optimism, in particular, was premised upon the spread of liberal democracy, pluralism and human rights to countries not previously enjoying these benefits. And liberal democracy – with its implicit or explicit acceptance of religious pluralism – 'found itself without enemies or viable alternatives' after the Cold War (Hyden 1992: 4).

Religious fundamentalism is nearly always premised – some would say by definition – on a rejection of the values associated with liberal democracy. Shupe suggests that endeavours 'to salvage the secularisation model have interpreted evidence of burgeoning religiosity in many contemporary political events to mean that we are witnessing merely a fundamentalist, antimodernist backlash against science, industrialization, and liberal Western values' (Shupe 1990: 19). Wald avers,

The political lines have increasingly been drawn between those in all major religious communities who remain deeply enmeshed in religious cultures and persons who wear their religious loyalty rather more lightly. The former inhabit subcultures that stress moral traditionalism and encourage its application to public policy while the latter, freed of exposure to traditional rules of conduct, are more disposed to accept a libertarian ethic in what is called 'lifestyle choice'. By virtue of their encapsulation in organizations which transmit political norms, the strongly religious exhibit greater political cohesion than the unchurched who divide according to other criteria.

(Wald 1991: 279–80)

As these quotations suggest, religious fundamentalists, feeling their way of life under threat, aim to reform society in accordance with religious tenets.

5 RELIGIOUS FUNDAMENTALISM AND ETHNICITY

The aggregate trend in the West seems to be that, under conditions of democratic pluralism, secular materialism turns attention away from traditional forms of religiosity. Institutionalized political competition gives at least partial vent to nationalist aspirations, funnelling communal conflict from 'potentially virulent combinations of God and nation' (Johnston 1992: 73).

In many 'developing' countries, in contrast, democratic pluralism is often either non-existent or bogus, while both ethnicity and religion are often of great social and political salience (Haynes 1998). Interaction of ethnic and religious concerns often lead to political conflicts that have their roots in what are known as 'cultural' concerns. The main reason why this is a live issue in so many 'developing' countries, unlike in most Western nations, is because 'the basic political issues of national sovereignty and the alignment of ethnic and national boundaries have not been settled' (Bruce 1993: 65). This will affect the underlying beliefs, values and opinions which a people holds dear.

There may be close links between religion and ethnicity, while the political culture of such groups will be an important variable in understanding why they act politically in certain ways and not others. Sometimes, indeed, it is practically impossible to separate out defining characteristics of a group's cultural composition when religion and ethnicity combine to form an integral aspect of culture. In other words, both can be highly important components of a people's self-identity. For example, it would be very difficult – if not impossible – to isolate different cultural components – religious and non-religious – of what it means to be a religiously committed Sikh, Jew, Tibetan Buddhist, Muslim Somali, Christian East Timorese, or a Protestant 'loyalist' or a Roman Catholic 'nationalist' in Northern Ireland.

It is important to note, however, that not all ethnic groups are also collectively followers of one particular religion nor employ an ideology of mobilization that includes concerns that might be labelled 'fundamentalist'. For example, the Yoruba of south-west Nigeria are divided roughly equally between followers of Islam and adherents of various Christianities. But Yoruba group self-identity is tied closely to identification with certain geographically specific areas; religious differentiation is a more recent accretion, traceable in part to the impact of British colonialism. It does not define 'Yoruba-ness' in relation to other ethnic groups. The Ibo of eastern Nigeria, on the other hand, are predominantly Christian; very few are Muslim. While this singular religious orientation is also largely a result of the effects of colonialism, Christianity developed into an integral facet of Ibo identity, particularly in relation to Nigeria's Muslims, predominant in certain parts of the country, especially the north. Ibos came into contact (and conflict) with northern Muslims as a result of the migration of many of the former to the north of Nigeria in pursuit of economic rewards in the 1950s and 1960s. In Nigeria's civil war (1967–70), Ibo secessionists used hatred of Islam, and championing of Christianity, as part of their nationalist rallying propaganda. Ibo nationalists sought to depict the north of the country as exclusively, and aggressively, Muslim, determined to impose an Islam on Ibos and other non-Muslim Nigerians. In sum, the rise in religious conflict in Nigeria since the 1960s is linked to a feeling of nationalism among some of the country's ethnic groups (Haynes 1996).

The Nigerian Civil War is but one example of a discernible trend – religio-ethnic civil conflict in many countries – which became clear from the late 1960s. Until that time, scholars tended to argue that – like religion – ethnicity would gradually wither away as an important political and public issue as societies modernized. When this manifestly failed to occur, academic theories had to be turned on their head to posit a radically different interpretation of the continuity of ethnicity and religion in political conflict. The new approach was to suggest that what was known as 'conflictual modernization' was a result of social, political and economic activity between groups. It did not necessarily lead to growing cooperation between groups as formerly expected, but instead could make inter-group conflict likely (Newman 1991). In short, modernization was a likely condition for the emergence of ethnic and/or religious conflict. The growth of ethno-regional parties in 'developed' countries, such as the Parti Québecois (Canada), the Scottish National Party, Plaid Cymru (Wales), and various Belgian and Spanish groups, indicated that the continuing political salience of cultural issues was not confined to 'developing' countries. In the 1980s and 1990s, serious political conflicts between cultural groups in Eastern Europe, for example in the erstwhile Soviet Union and former Yugoslavia, underlined further the potentials for conflict in multi-ethnic and multi-religion states. As the Soviet Union collapsed, conflict – involving religio-ethnic issues – erupted, involving, for example, Christian Armenia and Muslim Azerbaijan. In the former Yugoslavia, there was a three-way struggle in the 1990s between (Christian)

Serbs, (Christian) Croats, and Muslims in Bosnia-Herzegovina. Each constituency has its international support: the Muslims, Arab states and Islamist groups; the Christians – Armenians, Serbs and Croats – looked to co-religionists in Russia, Germany and Greece.

But it was not only religious conflicts between states which helped focus international attention on religious and ethnic conflict. The assassination of India's prime minister, Indira Gandhi, in October 1984, followed an assault – 'Operation Bluestar' – by Indian security agents and the army on the most holy site for Sikhs: the Golden Temple, Amritsar. The aim was to end its occupation by a Sikh fundamentalist, Jernail Singh Bhindranwale, and hundreds of his followers. This was accomplished – but at the cost of more than 2,000 people, mostly Sikhs, killed in the attack. This catastrophic event helped focus Sikh attention on the demand for an independent state, Khalistan, to be carved out of the pre-existing Indian state of Punjab. Over time, however, Sikh unity fractured, with competing groups and ideologies that ranged along a spectrum from the 'ultra-zealous' at one extremity, willing to use terrorism and political violence in pursuit of their political aims, to the 'moderate' at the other end, using negotiation with the Indian state as their chief tactic. Sikhs failed to gain their state, but their exemplary opposition to what they perceived as India's creeping 'Hinduization' helped encourage other religio-ethnic separatist movements in India. For example, Muslim radicals in the state of Jammu-Kashmir also used appeals to cultural solidarity to focus opposition to the central government in the 1990s and early 2000s.

The defensive nature of the Jammu and Kashmiri Muslim and Sikh mobilizing ideologies is a common feature of cultural groups who perceive themselves under threat from hostile forces. In this respect, the emergence of putative unitary states in the 'developing' world as a result of decolonization after World War II is closely linked to the process of modernization which implies, among other things, the development of strongly centralized government, often along the lines bequeathed by former colonial administrations. The development of a centralized government, often dominated by ethnic, cultural, religious or other particularistic groups, frequently exacerbates previously latent tensions into overt conflict.

For example, in Sudan, southern Sudanese Christian peoples, including the Dinka and the Nuer, have fought a civil war against northern Muslims on and off since independence in 1956. The latter, aided by the government of Iran, seek to found an Islamic state throughout the country. Even though northern Sudanese leaders have claimed that shariah law would not be introduced in non-Muslim areas of the country, it is clear that their aim, involving forced conversion of Christians and pagans to Islam, is eventually to 'arabize' and Islamize the entire country. Culturally and religiously distinct southern Sudanese regard this as an assault upon their way of life, perhaps their very survival.

It is not only the case that religious and cultural conflict arose as a result of the political arrangements left by colonization, as in India and Sudan. While China was never formally colonized by an external power, the development of a Chinese unitary state was not complete by the time of the triumph of the Communists in 1949 following a civil war. One of the foremost aims of the new Chinese government was to extend its writ throughout all the lands claimed to be integral parts of the country – including those with distinctive cultural and religious attributes. In one region, Tibet, the westernmost outpost of the Chinese state, a Buddhist theocracy had developed over centuries with minimal influence from Chinese control. Instead, Tibet was ruled by the supreme religious figure – the Dalai Lama, an individual thought by his followers to be endlessly reincarnated over a long period – until the Chinese army invaded in 1952. When the Chinese tried to impose their culture and religion on the Tibetans, Buddhist monks were in the forefront of Tibetan resistance (Haynes 1995). The Chinese tried to turn Tibet into a province of China, a process of enforced modernization which, over time, resulted in a serious diminution of Tibetan Buddhist culture, due to an influx of non-Buddhist settlers from outside. Serious outbreaks of anti-Chinese resistance began to occur, especially during the 1980s and early 1990s, and intermittent opposition thereafter. By this time, Tibet, home to fewer than 10 million people, contributed more political prisoners than the rest of China's provinces combined. More than 100 Tibetans were arrested and detained in the mid-1990s for demanding Tibet's freedom from Chinese rule. Political unrest, linked to religion, also increased in other 'national minority' areas of China at this time. What the authorities referred to as 'gang fighting' (almost certainly with a religious and cultural component) broke out in 1993 in the Muslim Ningxia Hui Autonomous Region (Asia Watch 1994).

Attempts forcibly to engineer mass cultural and/or religious change also characterized the situation in East Timor, a province of Indonesia until 1999. Like in China, the aim was to change the cultural and religious distinctiveness of an area in the pursuit of a unitary state. East Timor had been annexed by Indonesia in 1975, following the sudden end, after centuries, of Portuguese colonialism and a short-lived civil war won by the main liberation movement, Fretilin (*Frente Revolucionario de Timor Leste Independente*). Indonesia spent the next twenty-five years trying to crush a low-profile resistance movement in order to change East Timor from a culturally distinct nation into a province of Indonesia conforming to that country's religious (Islamic) and linguistic (Indonesian) norms. However, rather than engendering mass conversion to Islam, Indonesia's efforts served to effect mass conversions among the East Timorese from traditional religions to Roman Catholicism. Whereas in the mid-1970s there were an estimated 250,000 Catholics, by the mid-1990s there were around three times as many. The point is that over time East Timor's struggle for independence had become an inter-religious conflict, pitting Indonesian Muslims against East Timor's Christians.

It is not only in the 'developing' world that religio-ethnic solidarity has taken a cultural form in recent years. Radical cultural groups gained prominence among disadvantaged black Americans and within Britain's culturally distinct Muslim communities in recent years. Sometimes such organizations were linked to religious fundamentalist concerns. For example, various Islamist groups – including the Young Muslims, Al Muntada al Islami, Muslim Welfare House and Hizb ut Tahrir (Liberation Party) – emerged in the 1980s and 1990s. Their activists advocated separation from British society and made clear their hatred of Jews.

The Nation of Islam, based in Chicago, was founded in the 1930s by Elijah Muhammad. During the 1980s and 1990s the organization, led now by the fiery Louis Farrakhan, became an important focal point for alienated African-Americans. Preaching a virulent mixture of anti-Semitism, anti-corruption, pro-community, self-help and black separatism, Farrakhan sought to mobilize frustrated African-Americans. Estimates of numbers of members of the Nation of Islam range from 10,000 to 30,000, with up to 500,000 additional 'sympathizers' (Fletcher 1994). Farrakhan's main idea was for African-Americans to work together in common pursuit of group self-interest and solidarity. In addition, the Nation of Islam organizes welfare agencies and a number of successful businesses in pursuit of the goal of emancipation from perceived Jewish and white domination. However, the relationship of Islam as a set of religious precepts to the rationale of the Nation of Islam is perhaps rather tenuous. The group's ideology reflects a dissatisfaction with mainstream American culture rather than reflecting adherence to the idea of building an Islamic state. The choice of a name redolent of religious symbolism – the Nation of Islam – reflects the emergence of Islamism in many Muslim countries as a potent symbol of anti-Westernism and anti-Americanism.

To summarize, cultural groups may, under certain circumstances, rise up against groups perceived as their oppressors. Such a development is very often driven by the apparent dominance of the machinery of state by a specific religious or ethnic group – in India, by Hindus, in Sudan, by northern Arab Muslims, in Tibet, by Han Chinese, in East Timor, by Indonesians, and so on. Such conflicts are common in many countries where the process of building nation-states is still unfinished after colonization. However, as events in former Yugoslavia and Soviet Union make plain, it is not the newness of states *per se* which is necessarily the chief cause of cultural friction. Rather it is incomplete state formation and abortive attempts at modernization. In states with a longer history – such as Britain and the United States – groups which perceive themselves as ignored or threatened by the state may seek to highlight cultural and religious singularities in order to increase solidarity and to press political claims against the centre.

In conclusion, religious fundamentalism can offer community solidarity, which may be especially welcome for many in a period of serious social upheaval and perceived crisis, while also fulfilling followers' spiritual needs. In other words, religious fundamentalism can offer a means of coming to terms with multifaceted changes by offering spiritual well-being and group solidarity through the application of community-focused efforts. However, the connection between religious fundamentalism and political protest is not fixed but variable. For example, Moyser discovered that in Britain, a country characterized by both secularization and popular adherence to mainline religion for the most part, 'religious adherence generally reduced the propensity for protest' (1991: 8). In sum, religion, especially in the guise of fundamentalism, may serve to encourage rejection of unwelcome state policies which seem to threaten believers' religious worlds.

6 FUNDAMENTALISMS: CHRISTIANITY, ISLAM, JUDAISM, HINDUISM, BUDDHISM

In order to exemplify the points already made, in the remainder of the chapter I will focus upon various kinds of religious fundamentalist groups in a number of case studies which have a range of religious and political concerns. I start with Christian fundamentalism in Africa, and seek to ascertain what are the socio-political goals of such groups and how they try to achieve them. Second, I turn to Islamist groups and seek to assess their political *raisons d'être* and goals. Third, I focus upon Jewish fundamentalism, while fourth, the emphasis shifts to India and its Hindu fundamentalism. Finally, I turn to an assessment of the political clout of Buddhist fundamentalism in Thailand.

6.1 Christian fundamentalism and politics in Africa

Contemporary Christian fundamentalism is quintessentially modern, offering a response to contemporary conditions and events, including, perhaps, perceived threats from rival religions. In Africa, for example, contemporary Christian fundamentalism is sometimes seen to have its roots and *raison d'être* in the failed promises of independence: reactive against unwelcome manifestations of modernization – poverty, marginalization and insecurity – and, in some cases, for example in Nigeria, the perceived growth and combativeness of Islam (Haynes 1996).

Recent growth of evangelical, 'born again' Christianity in various parts of the world, notably Latin America and Africa, is the result of a merging of two strands of Christian belief – pentecostalism and fundamentalism (Gifford 1990). American television evangelists, such as Pat Robertson, Jim and Tammy Bakker, Jimmy Swaggart and Oral Roberts, were instrumental in bringing together the two strands in the 1970s and 1980s. The appellation 'born again' is given variously to those who may remain either in the mainline Protestant denominations (for example, Episcopalian, Presbyterian, Methodist, Baptist and Lutheran), or in the Catholic Church (where they are known as 'charismatics'), or to those who worship in their own denominational churches (Gifford 1991).

Generally, 'born again' Christian evangelicals stress religious elements associated with pentecostalism: that is, experiential faith, the centrality of the Holy Spirit, and the spiritual gifts of glossolalia ('speaking in tongues'), faith healing and miracles. Such people are 'fundamentalist' in the sense of wishing to get back to the fundamentals of the faith as they see them. The 'born again' worldview is embedded in certain dogmatic fundamentals of Christianity, with emphasis placed on the authority of the Bible in all matters of faith and practice; on personal conversion as a distinct experience of faith in Christ as Lord and Saviour (being 'born again' in the sense of having received a new spiritual life); and, evangelically, in helping others have a similar conversion experience.

To this end, 'born again' churches sponsor missionaries who are required to look to 'God alone' (by way of followers' contributions) for their financial support. They believe that their church is a lone force for good on earth, locked in battle with the forces of evil; the latter may even manifest itself in the form of Christians who do not adhere to the 'born again' worldview. Unsurprisingly, such 'born again' conservatives are opposed to the ecumenical movement because of the liberal theological views associated with it, which include a concern for social action in tandem with spiritual concerns. To them the proclamation of the gospel of redemption (often in tandem with the self-interest of the 'gospel of prosperity') is paramount.

'Born again' Christians typically seek God through personal searching rather than through the mediation of a hierarchical institution. The aim is to make beneficial changes to one's life spiritually and to life chances through communion and other interaction with like-minded individuals. To this end, groups may come together to pray and to work for both spiritual redemption and material prosperity, sometimes perceived as inseparable from each other. When the latter goal – that of material prosperity – is seen as paramount, this can lead to charges that it is in fact little more than a 'mindless and self-centred appeal to personal well-being' (Deiros 1991: 149–50). In sum, 'born again' Christians may see themselves as offering converts two main benefits: worldly self-improvement and ultimate salvation.

Some accounts suggest that members of such 'born again' groups are politically more conservative than those in the mainstream churches and that such people are willing to submit, rather unquestioningly, to those in authority (Moran and Schlemmer 1984; Roberts 1968). In addition, they are said to assimilate easily to the norms of consumer capitalism which helps further to defuse any challenges to the extant political order (Martin 1990: 160). In addition, in theological and academic debates they are often judged in relation to two other issues: their contribution to personal, social and political 'liberation', and their potential or actual role as purveyors of American or other foreign cultural dogma in non-Western parts of the world. It is also claimed that the 'born again' doctrine may offer converts hope – but it is a hope without practical manifestation in the world of here and now; it does not help with people's concrete problems nor in the creation of group and class solidarities essential to tackle socio-political concerns (Martin 1990: 233). The reason for this political conservatism, it is alleged, is that conservative evangelical churches collectively form an American movement of sinister intent (Gifford 1991).

Cognizant of such concerns, the spread of American-style 'born again' churches to Africa, Latin America and elsewhere was greeted with concern by leaders of the mainline churches, who saw their followers leaving for the new churches in large numbers. Often sponsored by American television evangelists and local churches, thousands of born again foreign crusaders were seen to promote American-style religion and, in some cases, conservative politics from the 1980s. Ardently anti-communist, they worked to convert as many ordinary people as possible to a conservative Christian faith and in the process, it is argued, to promote America's political goals (d'Antonio 1990).

It was also alleged that a new religio-political hegemony emerged as a result of the impact of American fundamentalist evangelicals. Pieterse asserts, for example, that the so-called 'faith' movement gained the cultural leadership of Christianity in many parts of the 'developing' world, because of its social prestige and ideological persuasiveness (Pieterse 1992: 10–11). Norms, beliefs and morals favourable to the American interests were said to be disseminated among the believers as a fundamental part of the religious message. What this amounts to is that individuals who converted to the American-style evangelical churches were claimed to be victims of manipulation by the latest manifestation of neo-colonialism; the objective was not, as in the past, to spirit away material resources from colonial areas, but rather to deflect popular efforts away from seeking necessary political and economic structural changes, in order to serve American strategic interests and those of American transnational corporations. In order to examine such concerns, I focus on Christian fundamentalism in Africa.

Observers have noted that something important seems to have been happening in African Christianity since the late 1970s. Crowds of up to half a million at a time were in attendance during the 'Christ for All Nations' crusade in Kenya in 1986, an event which resulted in mass conversions from mainline churches. The 1980s and 1990s also saw the emergence of thousands of new – mostly fundamentalist – Christian churches. From small beginnings, some of them reached an impressive size. An American, Kenneth E. Hagin, head of the Rhema Bible Church, founded 'daughter' churches in South Africa, Zimbabwe, Swaziland and Malawi. Benson Idahosa's Church of God Mission in Nigeria had more than 2,000 branches, while others, including Andrew Wutawunashe's Family of God Church, Ezekiel Guti's Zimbabwe Assemblies of God Africa (both Zimbabwe), Mensa Otabil's International Central Gospel Church, and Bishop Duncan-Williams's Action Faith Ministries (both Ghana), also grew swiftly in terms of both numbers of churches and members.

In sum, there were over 20,000 new churches in Africa of both indigenous and foreign origin by the mid-1990s; many of them could be described as fundamentalist (Gifford 1994). It has been estimated that more than 10 per cent of Africans – over 50 million people – now belong to such churches. In several African countries – including Nigeria, Kenya, South Africa, Ghana, Zimbabwe, Liberia, Malawi and Zambia – Christian fundamentalists form at least 10 per cent of the population. It is believed that a large proportion of the estimated 6 million Africans a year who become Christians join fundamentalist churches.

But these churches are not all the same, although they may share certain characteristics. Most of their members formerly belonged to the mainline Christian churches – that is, the Roman Catholic Church and various traditional Protestant denominations. While many of the adherents of the new churches were young or younger people, the class component of their memberships was by no means clear-cut: they were not simply ministering to the poor or the middle classes or some other identifiable societal group. Many of the new churches proclaimed 'the faith gospel of health and wealth', originally an American doctrine devised in the 1950s and 1960s. It was not clear, however, to what extent such a gospel remained an identifiably American doctrine or whether it had become Africanized.

What types of Christianity in Africa can be labelled fundamentalist? While there are no definitive yardsticks for judgement, the following are often judged to be within the fundamentalist grouping. First, there are the evangelicals who accept the Bible as the word of God but who incorporate a relatively flexible attitude towards its interpretation. Pentecostalism, on the other hand, is the product of a revival that developed in Africa from the early years of the twentieth century. While Pentecostalists tend to be 'fundamentalist' in their attitude towards the Bible, they also stress the possibility of gaining the gifts of the Spirit such as 'speaking in tongues'. In general, it might be said that an African 'Christian fundamentalist' is typically informed by: personal conversion as a distinct experience of faith in Christ as Lord and Saviour (being 'born again' in the sense of having received a new spiritual life), and helping others have a similar conversion experience. Rather than relying on foreign donations, as many of the former mission churches do, fundamentalist churches in Africa are often largely reliant upon donations from their members.

Millions of Africans are said to have joined fundamentalist churches because of the intensity of the prayer experience they offer, the attraction of a simple and comprehensible message that seems to make sense out of the chaos which many followers perceive all around them, a moral code that offers guidance and the resuscitation of community values and a sense of group solidarity exemplified in the way that individual followers often call each other 'brother' and 'sister'. In addition to spiritual and social objectives, members of the fundamentalist churches often additionally seek more material goals. In other words, the hope and expectation of increased prosperity may be for some one of the main attractions of the churches, leading to the charge that their message of hope is little more than a mindless and self-centred appeal to personal material well-being. However, preachers in such churches claim they offer their followers two interlinked benefits: worldly self-improvement and ultimate salvation.

In sum, in Africa, many fundamentalist churches function as welcome alternatives for those seeking religious and social experiences that the mainline churches appear for many increasingly unable or unwilling to offer. To many African fundamentalist Christians, religion is concerned with social issues in the context of the creation of a counter-culture involving a communal sharing of fears, ills, jobs, hopes and material success. Earthly misfortune is often perceived to be the result of a lack of faith; God will reward true believers. Such believers appear to estimate that people's redemption is in their own hands (or rather in both God's and the individual's hands), and that expectations that government could or should supply all or even most of people's needs and deal with their problems is misplaced.

The fundamentalist churches challenge mainline Christianity both intellectually and materially. Such is the concern with the haemorrhaging of followers, that the mainline Christian churches make two main lines of attack. On the one hand, the fundamentalist churches are accused of being little (if anything) more than American Trojan horses, while at the same time they rush to incorporate evangelical and pentecostal elements (glossolalia, faith healing, copious biblical allusions) into their services. Yet, the fact that millions of Africans – in common with their fellows in Latin America, East Asia and the Pacific Rim – have converted to fundamentalist Christianity over the last two decades suggests strongly that such people find something in their churches that they do not in what their mainline rivals offer. At the same time, the dominance of some fundamentalist churches by wealthy foreign (especially North American) pastors, may help to confirm the association between religion and personal prosperity. Many appear to offer visions of Western consumerist success that serve as a sometimes powerful inducement for less materially successful people to join.

CHRISTIAN FUNDAMENTALISM IN AFRICA: POLITICAL ISSUES

Despite many fundamentalist churches' claims to political indifference or quietism, their political concerns often surface in a variety of ways. It is suggested that followers often have no problem in endorsing their (American or Westernized) leaders' aversion to socialism. Quite apart from the fact that to many socialism defines itself as a negation of the very existence of God, further distrust is born of a first-hand experience with variants of 'African socialism' – as practised until the 1990s in Tanzania, Zambia, Kenya, Senegal, and so on – which for many people is still irrevocably associated with bureaucratization, elitist power concentration, waste and ideological inflexibility.

It is sometimes argued that, generally speaking, African fundamentalist Christians do not join political parties or movements to pursue their political and economic aspirations; many are said to believe in the biblical idea that political leaders should rule, religious professionals and followers should stick primarily to spiritual matters. What this implies is that such people do not ordinarily involve themselves in the cut and thrust of political competition. It does not mean, however, that when a clearly political issue – that is, a 'trigger' issue – arises of significance for fundamentalist Christians they will necessarily remain silent. For example, fundamentalist Christians in Nigeria – and to an extent also in Ghana and Kenya – have become a significant political voice against the perceived Islamicization of their countries.

It is difficult to know whether members of fundamentalist churches are more politically conservative than those who do not join them; it is debatable whether Western conceptions of political preferences have all that much relevance in Africa where many people's view of politics and political change is coloured by different experiences from those in the West. What does seem clear, however, is that the fundamentalist churches can create a kind of counter-society among their followers, with several ramifications for social order. First, they often have rigid conceptions of morality: lying, cheating, stealing, bribing (or being bribed), adultery and fornication are all anathema. In short, fundamentalist Christians usually have strongly moralistic worldviews and a strong sense that the well-being of society is highly dependent upon good standards of personal morality. Second, fundamentalist church members may also be concerned to increase collective material benefits. In Lagos, Nigeria, fundamentalists run their own catering companies, hospitals, kindergartens and record companies. Employment is offered first to co-religionists because they are considered to be honest and to work hard. Third, the nature of social interactions within the fundamentalist churches may help to reorientate traditional gender relations and, in the process, transform sexual politics. While some of the churches continue to promote a doctrine of female submissiveness, many do not. This is one of the main attractions of the churches for young, urban women in south-west Nigeria, and it is particularly in the spheres of marriage, family and sexuality that one finds born-again doctrines and practice transforming gender relations quite dramatically. Fourth, because members of the churches conceive of a clear division between what is right and what is wrong, they tend to be opposed to public corruption.

Despite these impacts upon morality and social interactions, it is often suggested that the growth of Christian fundamentalism in Africa is the result of foreign influence (Pieterse 1992; Gifford 1994). It is certainly true that fundamentalist Christianity in Africa has its roots in the United States and Western Europe. Two waves of foreign proselytization occurred, the first between the 1920s and the 1950s, the second from the 1970s. During the first wave, Seventh Day Adventists had an estimated 2,000 missionaries in the field by the 1950s, while the American Assemblies of God had about 750. By the early 1960s the Full Gospel Businessmen's Fellowship International, founded in 1952 and with headquarters in Los Angeles, had established international chapters throughout Southern and West Africa. It aimed, along with other groups, such as Campus Crusade, Youth With A Mission, and Christ for the Nations, to focus a fundamentalist message of redemption to higher education campuses, where mass conversions took place. A second wave of foreign evangelical penetration of Africa occurred from the 1970s, led by American television evangelists – including Pat Robertson, Jim and Tammy Bakker, Jimmy Swaggart and Oral Roberts – who saw sub-Saharan Africa as a benighted region crying out to be saved.

The spread of American fundamentalist churches in Africa was greeted with understandable concern by leaders of mainstream churches, who often saw their followers leaving for the foreign sects. Sponsored by the American television evangelists and local allies, thousands of fundamentalist foreign crusaders promoted American-style conservative Christianity. Ardently anti-communist, they worked to convert as many Africans as possible to their type of Christianity, and in the process, it is argued, to promote adherence to American values. The result, it is alleged, is that a new religio-political hegemony has emerged in Africa, which has gained the cultural leadership of Christianity because of its practitioners' social prestige and personal persuasiveness. As a result, norms, beliefs and morals favourable to American interests are said to be disseminated among believers as a principal aspect of the religious message. What this amounts to is the claim that Africans converting to American-style Christian fundamentalism are victims of manipulation by the latest manifestation of neo-colonialism; the objective is not to spirit away Africa's material resources, but rather to deflect popular political mobilization away from seeking structural change of the society and the economy, in order to serve American strategic interests and/or the financial objectives of US transnational corporations.

I believe we should treat such claims with a degree of scepticism. This is because successive waves of foreign Christian proselytization in sub-Saharan Africa have resulted in gradual religious indigenization rather than replication along Western lines. Colonial-era Christianity tried unsuccessfully to appropriate the richness of the autochthones' imagination and beliefs, in order better to convert and to dominate (Haynes 1996). Colonial and post-colonial anti-establishment religious entrepreneurs related their messages to the uncaptured store of paganism which existed side by side with the orthodox Christian beliefs; their work resulted in the birth of African independent churches as well as Africanization of the former mission churches. Generally, they rehabilitated certain central givens of orthodox Christianity and added to the structure elements adapted from local traditions and beliefs. The same process occurred in the post-colonial period in relation to Christian fundamentalism: preachers attract followers in part because they offer the same kinds of material benefits that the mission churches did a hundred years ago. Then, physical well-being was derived from the missions' control of health care systems, while prosperity was believed to be a function of education, which they also controlled. Over the last twenty years, health and education facilities have faltered in many African states, in part as a result of the effects of economic reform programmes. As an alternative to a declining state, material benefits may be found through membership of Christian fundamentalist churches, whose attractions may well be enhanced because they are seen to be closely linked with wealthy foreign figures. But this is not the same as saying that the churches' members blindly follow the dictates of their American leaders.

On the other hand, it would be naive to claim that American fundamentalists' tactics have not been successful. Personal 'crusades' are popular, in tandem with radio and television broadcasts. Radio stations controlled by foreign fundamentalists broadcast throughout Africa. For example, the Sudan Interior Mission's radio station, known as ELWA, broadcasts from Monrovia, Liberia, transmitting programmes in about forty languages across West Africa. Trinity Broadcasting Network (TBN) broadcasts to an appreciative audience in South Africa, also providing the Swazi television network with programmes. In 1988 TBN hosted three evangelical rallies in Ciskei (formerly a 'homeland' in South Africa) which each attracted crowds of over 10,000 and which resulted in a reported '6,000 decisions for Christ' – a conversion rate of one in five of those attending. There is also the Christian Broadcasting Network, the fourth largest cable network in the United States, which broadcasts programmes to some twenty-five African countries, including Egypt, Kenya, Uganda, Nigeria, Zimbabwe and South Africa.

Critics of the foreign fundamentalists argue that their message is inappropriate in the current phase of economic and political upheaval in Africa, for reasons to do with the nature of the purveyors of the message, the social effects of the message, and the (not so) hidden agenda of the message. First, the churches are said to be spiritually fraudulent, little more than money-making machines taking advantage of the naivety of their followers. Second, they are said to encourage a passive acceptance of disasters, misfortune and a lack of social responsibility, leading to the absence of any commitment to development. Finally, American-promoted Christian fundamentalism has as its primary aim, critics argue, a decidedly non-spiritual concern for the promotion and pursuit of America's anti-communist foreign policy goals. In sum, the alliance of capitalism and foreign fundamentalism are said to work together to limit severely the impact of progressive Christianity in Africa.

Two questions suggest themselves in relation to these issues. First, is there a distinctively *African* Christianity? And, if so, is it being subverted – and with what results – by the influence of the foreign fundamentalist preachers? As already noted, Africans were never fully appropriated by mission Christianity with its tendency, especially pronounced in Catholicism, to proclaim one narrow set of spiritual and theological concerns as the 'truth'. Arguably, a primary aim of many Africans who adopted Christianity was to benefit materially in some way. In the post-colonial era, many Africans have continued to regard Christianity as a means to attain material as well as spiritual goals; many preachers have emerged in response to social needs, as the material quality of life diminished.

Many of those who regard themselves as socially progressive Christians appear to assume that the impact of foreign fundamentalists is to prevent the development of appropriate religious vehicles of community advancement, such as Base Christian Communities (BCCs). Yet, even in Latin America where BCCs have traditionally been strong, their numbers and dynamism appear to be diminishing, with hundreds of thousands of former Catholics converting to fundamentalist Protestantism in recent years (Haynes 1995). Progressive Catholicism, standing for solidarity and collective commitment, for a reading of the Bible through the eyes of the poor, and for the pursuit of the Kingdom of God on earth and in society, rather than in heaven and in individual isolation, is seen to be lacking as an ideology of community development in many social environments. Given that the nature of African society has – like Latin America – changed greatly over the last thirty years or so, then we might well expect that the types of churches which people want would reflect this development.

African societies, often riven by ethnic schisms, are inherently unlikely to develop a set of religious beliefs which are orientated towards the amelioration of structural deficiencies. It is far more likely that people will be attracted to a religion which puts the individual and his or her family first. By giving money to the church the individual will become richer, conversion will solve the individual's problems and those of his or her family. Salvation comes through faith. Fundamentalist churches in Africa, as in Latin America, are largely urban phenomena, they are products of modernization. Their followers come both from the ranks of the poor and from the urban middle classes. Their churches reflect the social changes that accompany modernization as well as a globalization of ideas whereby a faith concocted in one place – the United States – can be adopted and adapted elsewhere – for example, Africa – to satisfy the religious needs of millions of people.

Rather than seeing the fundamentalist churches of sub-Saharan Africa as an indication of the negative impact of American cultural and spiritual hegemony, they should be regarded as manifestations of both individual and community self-interest. They may acquire political interests and have an important role as mobilizing agents. Churches will interact with public authority when they seek to diversify into other activities – such as education, health care or business – because they will be subject to governmental regulation. Given that the standard procedure for dealing with drawbacks, i.e. the bribe, is not (or not so readily) open to fundamentalist Christians, then the religious community as a whole may be mobilized to achieve desired results.

CONCLUSION

Fundamentalist Christianity in Africa is a distinctive reinvention of an externally derived innovation. Just as 'orthodox' Christianity and 'orthodox' Islam have taken on African characteristics, so too is American-style Christian fundamentalism being transformed into something recognizably African. The original (American) religion is being indigenized, appropriated and reconstructed to serve popular aims and objectives – moulded and adapted to offer spiritual rebirth, potentialities for material improvements, and an urban community spirit. Sometimes, in addition, it informs political issues.

6.2 Islamic fundamentalism

To many people, Bealey notes, religious fundamentalism is a

> religious position claiming strict adherence to basic beliefs. This frequently results in intolerance towards other beliefs and believers in one's own creed who do not strictly observe and who do not profess to hold an extreme position. Thus Protestant fundamentalists scorn Protestants who fail to perceive a danger from Catholicism; Jewish fundamentalists attack Jews with secularist leanings; and Muslim fundamentalists believe that they have a duty to purge Islam of any concessions to cultural modernisation. *A political implication is the tendency of fundamentalists to turn to terrorism.*
>
> (emphasis added; 1999: 140)

While the Muslim world, like the Christian universe, is divided by religious disputes, it is also the case that many Muslims accept they are linked by belief, culture, sentiments and identity. International manifestations of Islamic resurgence appeared after the humbling defeat of the Arabs by Israel in the Six-Day War of June 1967. In addition, the Iranian revolution of 1979 was also a formative experience for many Muslims.

It was the latter event which for many non-Muslims, ordinary citizens and academic observers alike, suggested that Islamic 'fundamentalism' posed a serious threat to political stability at both the global and domestic levels (Huntington 1993). It should be noted, however, that there are numerous different kinds of Islamic 'fundamentalist' groups. Some propose (and/or practise) armed struggle to wrest power from governments that are seen to be ruling in un-Islamic ways; some believe in incrementalist change through the ballot box; some seek to achieve their goals by way of a combination of extra-parliamentary struggle, societal proselytization and governmental lobbying. But despite differences in strategy and tactics, what such groups have in common is twofold: (1) that politics and religion are inseparable; and (2) that shariah law should be applied to all Muslims. Many also share a concern that Muslims as a group are the focal point of a conspiracy involving Zionists and Western imperialists aiming to take over Muslim-owned lands and resources (notably oil). Such a concern is underlined by American transnational corporations' control over Arab oil, as well as by Israel's implacable denial of political and civil rights for its (largely Muslim) Palestinian constituency. These issues provide grist to the mill of Islamic fundamentalists' claims of conspiracy to belittle and deprive Muslims. In sum, 'Islamic fundamentalists' or, as I call them, Islamists, have two sets of enemies: backsliding governments and aggressive, alien foreign interests and governments.

Islam is often regarded by Western liberals as a reactionary, decidedly undemocratic, set of ideas. Indeed, the very concept of the Islamic state suggests to many the clear antithesis of democracy. In December 1991 Algeria held legislative elections which most independent observers characterized as among the freest ever held in North Africa or the Arab Middle East. The following January, however, Algeria's armed forces seized power to prevent an overwhelming victory in the elections by the radical Front Islamique du Salut (FIS), an act generally welcomed in the Western media. The assumption was that if the FIS achieved power it would summarily close down Algeria's newly refreshed democratic institutions and political system. A respected London-based weekly news magazine, *The Economist*, posed a question on many people's lips at the time: 'What is the point of an experiment in democracy if the first people it delivers to power are intent on dismantling it?' (*The Economist*, 2.1.1992: 3). The answer might well be: this is the popular will, it must be respected whatever the outcome. Algeria's army nevertheless had its own ideas. The FIS was summarily banned, thousands of supporters were incarcerated from 1992, and a civil war ensued which led to 80,000–100,000 deaths.

How best are we to perceive such a development? Is it simply a backlash by dangerous religious conservatives, determined to prevent the modernization of their societies? Or is Islamism more to do with a religiously-orientated socio-political movement seeking what proponents regard as necessary improvements in how societies are led and run? Mardin reminds us that since the beginning of Islam, over 1,300 years ago, critics of the status quo in Muslim-led polities periodically emerged to oppose what they perceived as unjust rule (S. Mardin, cited in Dorr 1993: 151). Contemporary Islamists can be seen as an example of this tradition, people who characterize themselves as the 'just' fighting against their 'unjust' rulers, anxious to reform the corrupt system. The dichotomy between 'just' and 'unjust' in the promotion of social change throughout Islamic history, according to Mardin, parallels the historic tension in the West between 'state' and 'civil society'.

Historically, the goal of the Islamically 'just' was to form popular consultative mechanisms so that the ruler would be compelled to listen to what the mass of ordinary people had to say on important issues. However, this concept – *shura* (consultation) – should not be equated closely with the Western notion of popular sovereignty because sovereignty, according to Islam, resides with God alone. Instead, *shura* is a way of ensuring unanimity from the community of Muslims, 'which allows for no legitimate minority position. The goal of the "just" is an Islamically based society' (Dorr 1993: 151). The consequence of this is that most Islamists would *oppose Western interpretations of democracy, where sovereignty, at least theoretically, resides with the people, because such a system would inevitably negate God's own sovereignty.* It is largely for this reason that Islamists have been conspicuous by their absence in current demands for Western-style democratic changes in their countries. However, despite an unwillingness to accept any sovereignty other than God's, some Islamic radicals nevertheless accept the need for earthly rulers to seek a mandate from their citizens. For example, Dr Abdeslam Harras, leader of the Moroccan radical Islamic movement, *Jama'at al-Da'wa al-Islamiyah*, asserted that the ruler of an Islamic country should be elected by a majority of the people (Harras, quoted in Dorr 1993: 152). More often, however, Islamists perceive liberal democracy as fatally flawed and compromised, of relevance only to secular, Western(ized) societies which often appear to them morally deficient.

Governing regimes in Muslim countries often seek to utilize Islam as a facet of national identity and state power, and to bolster autonomy and influence in the international Muslim community. The state aims to dominate all international Muslim transactions; it strives to be the interlocutor, the negotiator and the beneficiary of all relations and communications that its national Muslim community maintains with the wider Islamic world; the state seeks to make use of Islam as an ideology of national unity. In many cases, state-controlled national Muslim organizations seek to channel the faith of the Prophet into specific organizations which help to integrate a putative counter-elite of reformists into the state framework (Bayart 1993).

However, at the root of the rise of the Islamists in many Muslim countries is the failure of government-propelled modernization to deliver its promises of improvement to the mass of ordinary people. Etienne and Tozy argue that Islamic resurgence in Morocco carries within it 'the disillusionment with progress and the disenchantments of the first 20 years of independence' (1981: 251). This argument can be extended. Faced with state power which apparently seeks to destroy or control communitarian structures and to replace them with an idea of a national citizenry based on a systematic link between state and individual, popular (as opposed to state-controlled) Muslim groups emerged as a vehicle of political aspirations. Put another way, the Muslim awakening should be seen in relation to its capacity to oppose the state. 'It is primarily in civil society that one sees Islam at work' (Coulon 1983: 49). Opposition groups seek to appeal to differing ideological constructs, bolstering and justifying campaigns against incumbent political and religious elites, functioning in many cases as conduits of opposition and anti-regime solidarity. In other words, the state does not necessarily have a monopoly of control of social organizations. As Fossaert notes: 'men-in-society [sic] are organized in and by the state, but they are also organized in families, in village communities, in provinces, in workplaces, in factories in which the state is not always the proprietor, in trade unions, in parties and in associations and in other ways which the state does not necessarily control' (1978: 149). The point to underline is that Islam is the expression of community, a system of relations between individuals; at local and community level it may well be an 'anti-structure' expressing what Turner (1969) refers to as 'the powers of the weak'; in its own way, it is a counter-society. In urban surroundings, manifestations of Muslim community, outside of the state's control, include Islamist associations (such as the Hamadiyya Shadhiliyya of urban Egypt) and the growing network of 'community' – that is, not state controlled – mosques.

However, Muslim civil society is not only the product of universalist Muslim cultural currents. Although it is characterized by certain unchanging cultural referents, the latter are still moulded by discrete, even unique, social and political situations which serve to alter the original 'arabist' significance. Popular Islam, often leaning towards a 'fundamentalist' perspective, is present in civil society to an extent which is only matched, perhaps, in religious terms, by the 'born again' Christian churches which, as noted above, have grown rapidly in Africa and elsewhere in recent times. It is the political potentialities which such Islamic organizations contain which makes the state both suspicious and wary of them. The state seeks to dislocate Islamic resentment by controlling and defusing it. While the state must 'put "its nose" into the life of the Muslim community' where Islam is the main ideological referent, it will be aware that its 'secular discourse and secularity is scarcely effective as a mobilizer' among devout Muslims (Coulon 1983: 50).

Popular Islamic political modes are often subversive to elites' interests. Three ideal types can be identified. There is the 'Islam of the social activists', for example, associations of Muslim women, which are sometimes described as 'apolitical' (Peil with Sada 1984: 199). However, such organizations, which focus their activities on helping poor females and spreading education among girls, are actually highly political at the level of gender politics, working as they do towards women's liberation. Growing numbers of female Muslims find employment in the modern sector – for example, as teachers and secretaries – as a direct result of the spread of education to areas previously isolated. Second, there are the millenarian or utopian movements, for example that associated with the Cameroonian, Muhammad Murwa, in and around Kano in northern Nigeria in the late 1970s and 1980s. Third, there are the counter-elites that utilize Islam as a revolutionary ideology. They offer a programme aiming to unify the restless ambitions of a counter-elite and the ever-present material grievances of the Muslim masses. Examples include FIS in Algeria, the Egyptian Muslim Brotherhood and their counterparts elsewhere in the Arab Middle East, Balukta in Tanzania, and the Islamic Party of Kenya (Haynes 1996).

CONCLUSION

The politics of the secularization of society, that is, the determination of rulers to mobilize the people in 'mass' parties, have often been unsuccessful in their aims of subjugating autonomous forms of collective life to state control. In urban settings, replacing former social solidarity networks focused on kinship structures, clan and age groups, there is a sense of Muslim community which offers a welcome structure of solidarity. It seeks to transcend ethnic division in the same way that Christian 'born again' churches often do. Such religious organizations offer important ways of affirming the autonomy and the identity of a community in a new type of social surrounding, the city.

6.3 Jewish fundamentalism

Since the establishment of the state of Israel as a homeland for the Jews in 1948, there has been intense controversy in the country over whether the state should be a modern, Western-style country – where normally religion would be privatized – or a *Jewish* state with Judaist law and customs taking precedence over secular ones. Luckmann noted more than thirty years ago that the state of Israel was characterized by a process of bureaucratization along rational business lines, reflecting for many Jewish Israelis, he argued, accommodation to an increasingly 'secular' way of life (1969: 147). According to Weber's classificatory schema (1978: 56), Israel would be judged a 'modern' state, that is, with a powerful legislative body (the Knesset) enacting the law; an executive authority – government – conducting the affairs of the state; a disinterested judiciary enforcing the law and protecting the rights of individuals; an extensive bureaucracy regulating and organizing educational, social and cultural matters; and with security services – notably the police and the armed forces – protecting the state from internal and external attack.

Yet, to many, Israel is not 'just' another Western state. This is largely because in recent years religion seems to have gained an increasingly central public role. Religious Jews warn of the social catastrophes that they believe will inevitably occur in secular, 'godless', societies, while many non-religious Jews see such people as intolerant religious fanatics. Then, in November 1995, the then prime minister, Yitzhak Rabin, was assassinated by Yigal Amir, a 25-year-old religious Jew because of Rabin's willingness to negotiate with the Palestine Liberation Organization (PLO) to end the conflict between Israel and the PLO. The murder led some Israelis to fear that violence would increasingly characterize the already tense relationship between religious and secular Jews. Yet what appeared initially to some observers to be the onset of a religious war among the Jews seems so far to have had little impact in a setting where, despite much intense political and social conflict, religious interests have never emphatically been able to determine major issues of public policy.

On the other hand, the murder of Rabin by a Jewish fundamentalist appeared to be a clear manifestation of the willingness of 'Jewish fundamentalists [to] attack Jews with secularist leanings' in pursuit of their religio-political agendas (Bealey 1999: 140). The killing of Rabin served to focus attention on the growing polarization in Israel between, on the one hand, non-religious or secular Jews, and, on the other, highly religious or 'fundamentalist' Jews. The latter are characterized by a determination personally to follow the 'fundamentals' of Judaism and to work to get them observed in public and private life (Silberstein 1993). Contemporary Jewish fundamentalism – manifested by organizations such as *Gush Emunim* – is believed, in part, to be a result of the impact of Israel's victory over the Arabs in the 1967 war (Sprinzak 1993). For many religious Jews this was a particular triumph as it led to the regaining of the holiest sites in Judaism from Arab control, including Jerusalem, the Temple Mount, the Western Hall, and Hebron. This was taken as a sign of divine deliverance, an indication of impending redemption. Even some secular Jews spoke of the war's outcome in theological terms.

Jewish identity has long been understood as an overlapping combination of religion and nation. Put another way, the Jews of Israel tend to think of themselves as a nation inhabiting a *Jewish* state created by their covenant with God. The interpretation of the covenant and its implications gave rise to the characteristic beliefs and practices of the Jewish people. Vital to this covenant was the promise of the land of Israel. Following their historical dispersions under first the Babylonians and then Romans, Jews had prayed for centuries for the end of their exile and a return to Israel. However, except for small numbers, Jews lived for centuries in exile, often in separate communities. During the diaspora, while awaiting divine redemption to return them to their homeland, many Jews' lives were defined by *halakhah* (religious law), which served as a national component of Jewish identity. The Jews' historical suffering during the diaspora was understood as a necessary continuation of the special dedication of the community to God.

POLITICAL JUDAISM

While monotheistic, Judaism lacks the universalist and proselytizing tendencies of both Islam and Christianity. As former Chief Rabbi Epstein put it: 'when paganism gave place to Christianity and later also to Islam, Judaism withdrew from the missionary field and was satisfied to leave the task of spreading the religion of humanity to daughter faiths' (quoted in Parrinder 1977: 67). In addition, Jews have a different view of revelation from Christians. For the latter, the proclaimed Messiah – Jesus Christ – has already come; Jews, however, look forward to the arrival of their *Mashiah* at some future date.

There are two main strands of the Jewish faith: Orthodox and Reform Judaism. The division between them is ostensibly on the question of whether tradition can be changed in the face of new situations. In other words, is the Torah, the Jewish holy book (essentially the first five books of the Hebrew Bible), theoretically totally immutable? While still a highly important issue for many Jews, it would be fair to say that, over time, the hegemony of Orthodoxy has declined. Earlier, in medieval times, Jewish ritual life was highly elaborated, the result of the dominance of the Rabbis, both spiritual counsellors and teachers of the traditions of the Torah. Various injunctions of the Torah controlled nearly all acts of everyday life in both the home and the synagogue, serving constantly to remind Jews that they were God's chosen people (Smart 1989: 265). Ethically and morally, Jews were expected to keep to the high standard of the Ten Commandments and other injunctions promulgated by the Rabbis, such as monogamy. Regarding doctrine, the insistence on strict monotheism was absolute.

The traditional view of Judaism as a revealed religion governing every aspect of life began to face increasingly serious challenges at the end of the eighteenth century following the French and American Revolutions. Henceforward, Jews in growing numbers began to participate fully in the life of their wider societies and, in many cases, increasingly to share many of their values 'in contradiction to traditional Jewish life and values' (Jacobs 1992: 31). A consequence was the emergence of the *Haskalah* (Enlightenment) movement, led by a German Jew, Moses Mendelssohn. The Haskalah aimed to influence Jewish intellectuals towards a greater appreciation of the need to adapt to the new order. They did not necessarily seek to reject tradition, but to promote a new approach whereby traditional practices could live side by side with new learning and social forms. Essentially, the Haskalah was a Jewish Renaissance whereby the Jewish Middle Ages came to an end. It spread to Eastern Europe, where it met with considerable hostility on the part of traditional Rabbis, but its impact was such that no Jew could be impervious to its influence (Jacobs 1992: 31).

The ideology of Zionism – that is, the political endeavour to create a national home for the Jews – emerged in the second half of the nineteenth century. Fundamental to Zionism is the recognition of the national identity of the Jews, the rejection of the exile and a belief in the impossibility of assimilation. While the Bible is central to secular Zionists as a 'historical' document, many seem to be unclear concerning the centrality of religious elements in Jewish cultural history and the rejection of Orthodox practice. The 'political' Zionism of Theodor Herzl's World Zionist Organization (WZO), founded 1897, was condemned as 'idolatry' by many Orthodox Jews, who felt it replaced reverence for God and the Torah by secular nationalism and the 'worship' of the land. Orthodox Jews were instrumental in founding the *Mizrahi* party (*Merkaz Ruhani* or Spiritual Centre) in 1902 and *Agudat Israel* (Association of Israel, founded 1912), although many supported Zionist efforts to establish a Jewish state. Although by the 1930s there was growing support for the idea of Israel from many Orthodox Jews, the Holocaust in Nazi-controlled Germany – when some six million Jews were killed – was actually pivotal in the founding of the state of Israel in 1948.

In the next section I want to examine the interaction of religion and politics in Israel, where historically religious Jews and more recently various fundamentalist groups have been significant political actors in recent years.

JUDAISM AND POLITICS IN CONTEMPORARY ISRAEL

Aiming to exploit divisions between secular and religious Jews, governmental policy has traditionally favoured the political centre ground; consequently, neither religious nor anti-religious extremes has been able to dominate the political agenda. Increasingly, however, religious Jews have become an important political voice, although, like Christian fundamentalists in the USA, they are not strong enough normally to determine electoral outcomes. However, as they are particularly vocal on the issue of conceding parts of biblical Israel for the sake of peace with the Palestinians, a subject of intense controversy profoundly dividing the country, as that issue has dominated the political agenda so the political influence of the religious Jews has increased. In addition, the issue of the state's role in determining what are traditionally religious concerns – Sabbath observance, kosher food, secular marriage, divorce, burial, abortion and other medical matters, the definition of who is a Jew, and the rights of non-Orthodox congregations and their Rabbis – is of growing public concern.

The public face of religion in Israel is expressed through a number of religious parties. Traditionally, the National Religious Party (NRP) and Agudat Israel were the most important, although others have more recently emerged. Normally in elections religious parties achieve about 15 per cent of the vote – about 20 per cent of the Jewish population of Israel is strictly religious-observant – and between 15–18 seats in the 120-seat Knesset. However, in elections since the mid-1990s the religious parties collectively gained around 25 seats (21 per cent of the total), making them crucial elements in both the Likud government headed by Binyamin Netanyahu and its successor Labour-dominated regime, led by Ehud Barak.

The predecessor of the NRP, Mizrahi, won 16 seats in the first general election in 1949, before becoming the NRP in 1956 after a merger of several parties. Its success in 1949 meant that it was able to force a series of compromises from the then national president, David Ben-Gurion, despite the fact that the latter regarded the new secular Israeli state – rather than religion *per se* – as the focal point of popular allegiance. Under pressure from the NRP, Ben-Gurion agreed: (1) to set up a ministry of religious affairs with formal authorization over many aspects of Jewish life and (2) not to formulate a permanent constitution. This was because NRP leaders feared that the status of halakhah (religious law) would be diminished if a constitution was written.

From the 1950s to the 1970s the NRP held at least two cabinet posts under successive Labour governments. Through control of the Ministry of Religious Affairs, it had wide-ranging control over the Rabbinical establishment and the religious councils operating in both the urban and rural areas, providing religious services to the citizenry. It also periodically had authority over the Ministries of the Interior and Social Welfare, giving it, by control of the latter, patronage abilities in relation to the social-welfare allowances of the underprivileged. This power enabled it 'generally' to get such people's electoral 'support as a token of gratitude' (Dieckhoff 1991: 10–11). In the 1980s, however, the NRP saw its electoral support fall away dramatically as erstwhile supporters perceived it as not radical enough (Morris 1989: 129).

Agudat Israel, with, typically, four or five seats after each parliamentary election, was the second largest religious party until the late 1980s, when it was overtaken by Shas. Agudat traditionally represented a section of the ultra-Orthodox community but only rarely sought cabinet posts in the Labour govern-ments. In 1977, however, when Likud ousted Labour, it became a regular feature in government. Between 1977 and 1984, Agudat had the chairmanship of the important Finance Commission as well as the vice-speakership of the Knesset. It was able to introduce and strengthen religious legislation in various areas, including abortion, autopsy, and national airline flights on the Sabbath. In the national unity governments between 1984 and 1988, its role diminished as the Labour–Likud coalition could function without it. However, it returned to prominence following the Likud election victory of 1990, gaining several cabinet seats. It was behind several pieces of religious legislation in the early 1990s, such as the banning of 'offensive' advertisements (displaying parts of the body of a man or a woman) and the sale of pork, the closing of businesses on the Sabbath, and further restrictions on abortion rights. The party's political influence in the 1990s reflected the fact that many religious Jews were coming to the conclusion, like Christian fundamentalists in the USA at the same time, that the defence of their interests was best pursued via involvement in the decision-making process rather than by a holy separatism.

Also understanding the importance of political involvement rather than standing aside was *Shas* (Sephardi Torah Observance), an Orthodox Jewish party representing the interests of the Sephardi constituency. It was founded in 1984, gaining six seats in both the 1988 and 1992 general elections, before rising to 10 in 1996. Like the NRP and Agudat, it held various ministerial posts – Absorption, Communications, and the Interior. Closely linked to Shas is yet another religious party – *Degel Torah* (Torah Flag), an ultra-Orthodox party which gained two seats in the 1988 election. In the 1996 election – as United Torah Judaism – it increased its representation to four seats.

The presence of religious parties in government since 1949 was both to protect the interests of the religious community and to increase its influence in a variety of social areas. But until 1967 such groups remained a decidedly subordinate trend in the political life of Israel. It was Israel's decisive victory in that conflict which for many religious Jews ushered in the messianic age and the recreation of the kingdom of Israel and provided an important incentive for new religious movements, including: *Edah Haredit* (God Fearful Community), *Neturei Karta* (Guardians of the City) and *Gush Emunim* (Bloc of the Faithful). The most important, Gush Emunim, was from its founding in 1974 committed to establishing Jewish settlements in the West Bank and, until its handing over to the Palestinians in the mid-1990s, the Gaza Strip, judged to be integral parts of the biblical land of Israel (Sprinzak 1993: 247). The general point is that such groups – mouthpieces of the mostly Orthodox settlers – had a major and direct influence on Israeli politics in addition to that wielded by the traditional religious parties.

Gush Emunim was formed in early 1974 in the West Bank settlement of Kfar Etzion. Its main concern was the conquest and settlement of the whole land of Israel. Between the mid-1970s and mid-1980s, Gush grew rapidly, especially after the 1978 Camp David agreement led to the return of the Sinai desert – grabbed by Israel in the 1967 war – to Egypt. Gush Emunim and other fundamentalist groups, such as the late Rabbi Meir Kahane's organization, *Kach* (Thus), argued strongly, on religious grounds, against giving back territory to Egypt. This was because the biblical entity, Eretz Israel, they argued was significantly larger than today's Israeli state. To hand back any territory to Arabs, non-Jews, was tantamount to going against God's will. Simmering religious opposition to the peace plan with the PLO, involving giving autonomy to the Gaza Strip and to an area around Jericho, reached tragic levels in February 1994 when a religious zealot, Baruch Goldstein, who had links with militants of both Kach and *Kahane Chai* (Kahane Lives), murdered 15–20 people in a dawn attack on a mosque in the West Bank town of Hebron. After the massacre both Kach and Kahane Chai were banned by the Israeli government, a sign of its commitment to crush religious extremist groups systematically using violence to gain their ends.

But this was not to be the end of political murders in Israel. Less than two years after the Hebron massacre, Israel suffered another destabilizing blow when Prime Minister Rabin was assassinated. After the killing, the 1996 general election was widely assumed to be a likely win, because of the expected huge 'sympathy vote', for Labour, then the governing party. As the election campaign progressed, however, it began to dawn on many Israelis that the Labour government's undeclared aim was to assist in the creation of an independent Palestinian state in the West Bank and Gaza Strip. 'Labour's coalition partner, Meretz, was open about these objectives; Labour was more cautious' (Bhatia 1996). As far as the Israeli secular right-wing and the ultra-Orthodox were concerned this meant the slow dismemberment of the Jewish state. Their leaders were not prepared to accept the PLO leader, Yasser Arafat's, assertion that his people finally recognized Israel's right to exist within its pre-1967 borders. When the Labour government began to discuss the issue of Palestinian refugees returning home, the religious and right-wing disquiet grew. 'They were not only worried about the fate of 150,000 Jewish settlers in the West Bank and the Gaza Strip, but they were also concerned at the prospect of hundreds of thousands of Arab refugees converging on the [Israeli] homeland' (Bhatia 1996).

Such concerns were important in the Likud (Unity) party's victory in the 1996 elections, achieved under the flamboyant leadership of Binyamin 'Bibi' Netanyahu. Likud and its secular allies won 45 seats, while religious parties gained 23 seats in the 120-seat parliament – giving the Netanyahu government a clear majority. The religious parties' 23 seats meant that they could hope to occupy some very important ministries, including Education, Housing and the Interior. Control of the Ministry of Education would allow a new stress on the importance of Jewish religious traditions and culture in the country's schools, while management of Housing would almost certainly lead to increases in funding for Jewish settlements in Palestinian areas. Domination of the Interior would allow them to 'reward' those municipalities – like Jerusalem – controlled by like-minded politicians and allow the religious new influence to impose edicts, such as that all shops, pubs, restaurants and night clubs would have to close on the Sabbath (Saturday).

There was speculation that the rise in the religious parties' share of the vote heralded a crisis in Israel's politics. Like in 1988, when the religious parties' share of seats increased to 18, the outcome of the 1996 election prompted commentators to write of impending 'war' between the religious and non-religious. Many secular Jews appeared to fear that the religious constituency would attempt to create a theocratic state by using their new strength to lever substantial religious concessions as the price for their support in Netanyahu's government (Black 1996; Bhatia 1996; Oz 1996). While almost certainly not heralding a theocratic state, the rise in the share of the vote of the religious parties did reflect the period of intense self-questioning as to Israel's identity as a nation in the late 1990s. The self-scrutiny took many forms – for example, the meaning of 'Jewish' in the phrase 'the Jewish State', as formulated in Israel's Declaration of Independence (1948), to the adherence to the democratic values also enshrined in the same Declaration, in the light of an anticipated Arab majority at some stage in the future.

Given the maintenance of the religious parties' vote in the 1999 elections which saw the election as prime minister of Ehud Barak, and the poll of 2000 that led to the accession to power of the hardline Likud leader Ariel Sharon, there are several good reasons why the political impact of Jewish fundamentalist parties and movements in Israel is unlikely to diminish significantly. First, the basis of both nationality and the creation of the state of Israel is religious identity. This makes it highly vulnerable to the claims of the religiously observant militants. Second, there has been a spectacular growth of Orthodox Jewry since the early 1970s. In the late-1990s, it was claimed that one in three Jews in Israel 'respects the religious commands' and one in ten belongs to the *haredi* (ultra-Orthodox) community. Sixty per cent of the *haredi* population is under 25 years – and the proportion of Orthodox is likely to grow because many have large numbers of children (Bhatia 1996). Such people are highly likely to be impressed by the arguments of the religious movements and third parties. Third, the latter will continue to have major political influence because of the nature of the country's political system. As in the past, they have a capacity to gain numerous benefits in return for support of either Likud or Labour. Finally, a dovetailing of secular right-wing concerns (security) and religious interests (fear of secularization) produces a powerful coalition likely to endure until – or if – the issue of the Palestinians is finally settled.

6.4 Hindu fundamentalism

We have seen that, since the 1970s, Christian, Muslim and Jewish fundamentalists have all exhibited 'refusal to be restricted to the private sphere of religious traditions' (Casanova 1994: 6). Until recently, less noticed was the contemporaneous resurgence of Hindu fundamentalism in India. Hindu fundamentalism, like its counterparts in other religions, reacted intensely against the secular visions of modern nationalism, using a number of strategies for change, including targeting the traditional secular parties, India's Muslim minority, the political process itself and the country's secular political culture that underpinned it. What is striking about the Indian case is how consistently Hindu fundamentalists aimed at political targets in order to solve religious problems or to bring about a consolidation of religious identities and values. The level of violence associated with the Hindu fundamentalist movement became intense in the 1990s, with frequent political assassinations. The Indian case is useful for understanding the variety of ways in which religious militants seek to achieve their objectives from political violence to electoral politics. Both strategies have at their heart a total rejection of India's secular state, a notion at the heart of the country's political culture since independence.

India's secular state emerged out of the trauma of a communal holocaust, leading – in 1947 – to partition along communal lines, with (East and West) Pakistan as the designated homeland for Muslims. Since then, it has been impossible in India to replicate a Western version of secularism through a strict institutional separation between church and state. This is partly because Hinduism, the religion of most of the population, does not have an institutionalized hierarchy – hence, no 'church' – and partly because of the historically short time since the founding of India. Comparable attempts at building secular states in Western Europe, it should be remembered, took up to four centuries.

The rise of the politics of religious identity underlines a central problem: how can religiously plural India survive the creation of a powerful sense of identity based upon religion? Eighty-two per cent of the more than one billion Indians are Hindus, 11 per cent are Muslim, 2.5 per cent are Christians, and 1.6 per cent are Sikhs. There are also small numbers of Buddhists, Parsis, Jains and followers of traditional religions. Because of such diversity it was central to the concept of the Indian state at independence that its leaders would pursue a development path firmly located within a secular socio-political and cultural milieu. The core of Indian secularism was tolerance towards religious plurality – denoted in the Sanskrit phrase *sarva dharma sambhava* ('equal treatment for all religions').

Perhaps the most significant implication of the recent electoral success of Hindu extremism at the polls was not the likelihood of the formal founding of a Hindu state, which may never come about, but the general stimulation it provided for extremists from other cultural groups. It appears to many observers that the secular features of the existing state are weakening, helping fuel political campaigns, not only by Hindu extremists, but also from regional Muslim, Christian and Sikh groups. However, this is not necessarily Hindu *fundamentalism* – which would for many observers be rooted in a common understanding linked to the revealed words of God in a holy book as a set of socio-political aspirations and goals – but rather a *nationalist* project with the goal of the projection of a wider Hindu *identity* at its core.

Various theories have been offered to explain the resurgence of political religion in India; many see the 1980s as a crucial period. But why the 1980s? It was not a decade when India's government overtly sought to privatize religion, but it was a period of pronounced economic instability and of 'new distortions of the homogenised Western menu of modernity and its consumerist culture peddled through its multinationals' (Ray 1996: 10). This coincided with the re-emergence of the question of both Hindu and Sikh national identity, issues which quickly became central to India's political scene.

Explanations for the religio-political resurgence of Hindu nationalism can be roughly divided into political, psychological, socio-economic, cultural and 'the impact of modernization' theories. However, it is important to note that they are not mutually exclusive – none can claim to be exclusively 'correct' – but that taken together they may explain reasonably well the rather unexpected resurgence of religion in politics in India in recent times.

Arguing for a political explanation, Juergensmeyer asserts that the secular Congress Party government, which ruled from independence until the mid-1970s, became a target for the wrath of Hindu nationalists because it was perceived to be favouring Muslims, Sikhs, Christians and other religious minorities (1989: 100). While 'the rise of Sikh fundamentalism in the Punjab especially played on Hindu nerves' (Copley 1993: 57), increased Muslim assertiveness – following the Iranian revolution – seemed to many Hindus also to threaten them.

Psychological theories stress high-caste alarm at the conversion to Islam of *Dalits* (erstwhile 'untouchables') in various parts of India, especially the well-publicized case of the Tamil Nadu village of Meenakshipuram in 1984 (Copley 1993: 57). This incident is thought to have led many Hindus to vote for the leading Hindu nationalist party, the Bharatiya Janata Party (the BJP, or Indian People's Party) in following elections. More generally, Chiriyankandath (1996) notes that many conservative Hindus were incensed over the government's protection of mosques built over Hindu sacred sites during the Mughal period. In 1984 the Vishwa Hindu Parishad (VHP) called for a reassertion of Hindu control over a dozen such sites. Observers point out that many Muslims would have consequently seen themselves as the focus of Hindu attacks, perhaps in turn encouraging Islamic radicalism (Sisson 1993: 58–9; Talbot 1991: 149–51).

Also encouraging communal friction was political instability caused by economic uncertainty, the third factor. In the 1980s, Callaghy notes, the Indian economy was suffering serious problems: 'the balance of payments and inflation moved beyond control; foreign exchange reserves dropped; a debt crisis loomed; and pervasive statism and bureaucratic controls were having increasingly negative consequences . . .' (1993: 194–5). The government attempted (initially timidly) to liberalize the economy; the main impact, however, was probably unintended: the creation of a tiny group of super rich and a growing stratum of extremely poor people. Many urban middle-class Hindus were unsettled by the economic reforms and, like many poor Hindus, looked to a party – notably the BJP – promising that Hindus would be privileged over other groups. In sum, economic changes were probably an important factor in the growing appeal of Hindu nationalism among both the poor and the rapidly expanding sector of urban middle-class producers and consumers.

Fourth, Hindu nationalism received a cultural boost when the immensely popular Hindi serializations of the *Ramayana* and *Mahabharatha* appeared on state television in the early 1990s. Observers assert that these television programmes helped to foster an all-India Hindu self-consciousness.

Fifth, it is in the context of cultural change that the final set of theories – those linked to the impact of modernization – are located. As Chiriyankandath notes, 'much of the recent electoral success of the neo-religious parties can be ascribed to their endeavour to provide those uprooted from their traditional environment with a bridging ideology' (1994: 36–7). What he is referring to is the Hindu nationalist appeal, which not only offered an intensely needed emotional tie with the past, but also claimed to provide a 'philosophical and practical framework for coping with, and regulating change'. The BJP aim, according to K. R. Malkani, a vice-president of the party and its chief theoretician, was to 'remain anchored to our roots as we modernise so we don't lose ourselves in a tidal wave of modernisation' (quoted in ibid.). In sum, the BJP and other Hindu nationalist groups expressed their political programmes in the form of reinterpretive responses to the impact of Western expansion and accompanying technological modernization within the historically well-established Hindu religious traditions.

These five factors collectively helped to facilitate the rise of the Hindu nationalists – while leading to an increase in minorities' self-awareness. In the 1980s, movements such as the VHP attempted to contrive a semitised 'fundamentalist' version of Hinduism, while Hindu nationalist political parties – notably the BJP – fought for political power via the ballot box. Unlike Sikh nationalists, who, because of their small numbers and intra-group schisms, cannot plausibly achieve their objective – independent Khalistan – through the electoral process, Hindu nationalists progressed electorally. From the late 1980s, the BJP made an increasingly effective showing in the electoral battle against what its leader, Lal Krishna Advani, called the 'pseudosecularism' of secular politicians (Juergensmeyer 1993: 81). From two seats in 1984, rising to 85 in 1989, the BJP won 119 seats in 1991, making it the largest opposition party in the Lok Sabha, India's national parliament (Hellman 1996: 237). Five years later, the party secured 188 seats, making it the largest single party, before achieving power in a coalition government in 1998.

Juergensmeyer notes that 'one of the reasons why India has been vulnerable to the influence of Hindu nationalists is that Hinduism can mean so many things' (1993: 81). Before continuing it may be useful to describe briefly, first, the essential characteristics of Hinduism and, second, the traditional relationship between Hinduism and politics in India. After that I will trace the electoral rise of the BJP.

WHAT IS HINDUISM?

The term 'Hindu' has been used to refer to what has been believed and practised religiously for around 5,000 years by many people living in present-day India. Taken as a whole, the Hindu tradition is one of the oldest religious traditions in the world. But it is exceedingly difficult to take as a whole, for it is also one of the most diversified extant religious traditions. There is no single teacher acknowledged by all nor any one creed recited by all. As Lewis and Slater put it, Hinduism 'is a great Ganges River of religious beliefs and practices fed by many streams' (1969: 31). Chiriyankandath asserts that the 'plural religious culture of Hinduism . . . renders it meaningless to try to discern any singular religion or "faith"' (1996: 45).

Perhaps all that can be stated with confidence when referring to this great tradition is that we are dealing with a cluster of practices arising on Indian soil and largely, but by no means entirely, confined to India. Religiously, the Hindu tradition is notable for the following: It has no central church; it has no historical basis and stands in contrast to the West-Asian Judaic tradition; it has a cyclical vision of universal evolution: creation, maintenance, and destruction are the processes that recur over macro-time spans called *yugas* or epochs; its beliefs and practices are a compendium of animistic, polytheistic and monotheistic principles; the caste system; the concept of Absolute Brahminism (Venugopal 1990: 78). Hindus share a basic idea with Buddhism – that of *karma*, denoting the conception of moral causation, that is, the idea that what a person is and where they are today is largely determined by what they have done in past lives (moral responsibility). *Moksha* is the notion of salvation, signifying emancipation from the bonds of present existence. To attain this it is necessary to transcend *avidya* (ignorance) or *maya* (illusion) (Lewis and Slater 1969: 32).

Hinduism caters to a variety of groups. In general, most ordinary people follow a mixture of animistic and polytheistic beliefs, while those belonging to the reformed sects have a monotheistic base. A notable dimension of Hinduism is its immanentism – that is, the belief that gods are pervasive and easily accessible to the people. The Hindu notion of *avataras* implies that gods take birth in animal or human form to redeem mankind. Hindu soteriology – that is, the way to achieve salvation – rests on the renunciation of worldly ties and the attainment of *moksha*, wherein the cycle of births and deaths no longer operates.

Hinduism rests on a stable social organization, the caste system. In this ascriptive stratification system some castes are placed higher than others in order of ranking. The higher castes are believed to be purer in ritual terms than the lower ones. People are expected to follow the traditional practices and rites prescribed by their caste. For most ordinary Hindus the final goal is not *moksha* but simply a scrupulous observance of rites prescribed by the sacred texts. Two widely used Indian terms may be mentioned in this connection. These are the *Varnas* (originally meaning colour), the four basic caste divisions, which are notional rather than empirical. There are four *Varnas* – *Brahmin, Kshatriya, Vaishya*, and *Sudra* – arranged hierarchically. Empirically, however, there are numerous castes, high or low, which are concrete constituents of *Varnas*, called *Jatis*. No-one is born into a *Varna*, but everyone is born into a *Jati* (Venugopal 1990: 79).

The Hindu sacred literature, written in the ancient language of Sanskrit, consists of four *Vedas*, collections of hymns, prescriptive rites and procedures for five sacrifices, believed to bring prosperity or victory to the performers. Today, however, Vedas are read almost solely as sacred verses. The Vedas reflect changes of thought over time. Many of the gods mentioned in one of the early Vedas, the *Rig Veda*, disappear from view by the end of the Vedic period. In the later Vedic texts the main trend of thought is neither polytheistic nor theistic but in the direction of a pantheistic monism. In the epic scriptures, however, the trend is theistic. References abound to the high gods, Vishnu and Shiva. They, together with the god Bramah, later constitute what is sometimes called the Hindu trinity (Lewis and Slater 1969: 33). Second, there are the *Upanishads*, philosophical, speculative discourses usually held between master (*guru*) and pupil. Third, there are the *Puranas* (myths), held in high popular esteem. Immanentism is central to the Puranas because gods and goddesses arrive on earth to redeem humans from their tormentors. Fourth, there is the *Bhagavad Gita* ('Song of the Lord'). The *Bhagavad Gita* is part of the epic *Mahabharata*, which, along with the *Ramayana*, discusses the dynastic struggles of antiquity. Both were written down in their present literary forms around the first century CE. It is generally agreed that the *Bhagavad Gita*, more than any other sacred text, informs contemporary Hindu thought and conduct. Many scholarly Hindus believe that the *Bhagavad Gita* brings together all that is the most significant in the Hindu tradition. For many Hindu nationalists it is the most sacred text (Jaffrelot 1995).

HINDU NATIONALISM AND POLITICS

Although officially secular, nationalist leaders in India drew much of their 'inspiration from religious faith. Religious appeals and symbolism popularised the nationalist message' (Talbot 1991: 143). In the 1940s, India's independence movement couched its message in recognizably Hindu terms, referring not only to the notion of dharmic obligation, but also to the idea of Mother India with the characteristics of a Hindu goddess. Breaking with what they saw as the Hinduized nationalist movement, Mohammad Ali Jinnah and the Muslim League demanded a separate state for Muslims. After bloody civil conflict, the goal was achieved in 1947. Although 'Mahatma' Mohandas Gandhi, the leader of India's nationalists, strongly protested against the partition of India and the communal hatred it involved, militant Hindus considered that he had capitulated to Muslim pressure. He paid the ultimate price – a member of the extremist Rashtriya Swayamsevak Sangh assassinated him in 1948.

In the first years after independence, with the murder of Gandhi no doubt fresh in many people's minds, religion as a source of political tensions appeared to be a spent force (Parrinder 1977: 69–70, 105–7). India's first post-colonial prime minister, Jawaharlal Nehru, stressed the themes of economic modernization and secularism, which were enshrined in the 1950 constitution. The Preamble to the Constitution states, 'We the people of India, having solemnly resolved to constitute India into a sovereign socialist, secular democratic republic . . . in our constituent assembly . . . do hereby adopt, enact, and give to ourselves this constitution.' The constitution itself sought to remove the threat of the disruptive potential of religion in two ways. First, it employed an intentionally unclear concept of secularism that was however widely interpreted as according equal respect to all religions, while protecting religious minorities. Second, the 25-state, linguistically-based federal structure would, it was hoped, prove to be sufficiently flexible to allow for the cognizance of ethnic plurality.

However, it seems very likely that the absence of an accepted role for religion in politics made for an unworkable situation in post-colonial India: 'as a generally shared credo of life' secularism in India 'is impossible, as a basis for state action impracticable, and as a blueprint for the foreseeable future impotent' (Madan 1987: 748). Democratization and secularization would, it was feared, work at cross purposes. Increasing participation in the political arena drew in new social and religious forces whose demands for greater formal recognition of Sikhism, Islam, Christianity and Hinduism were partly 'responsible for making religion the dominant issue in Indian politics today' (Mitra 1991: 759).

There was a relative – albeit short-lived – religious calm in the first decade and a half after independence. However, the year of Prime Minister Nehru's death, 1964, saw a sharp increase in communal incidents. Two thousand lives were lost that year to fighting between Muslims and Hindus (Sisson 1993: 58). In the 1970s and 1980s communal violence continued. The average annual number of deaths during the former decade was 111, while in the latter it was four times higher at 454. At the heart of the matter lay the question of the role that religion should play in a modernizing society. Nehru and his fellow secularists believed that the only way forward was steady reduction of religion's influence and creation of a more secular culture, to be achieved primarily via a progressively more prosperous society. To this end, Nehru sought to promote the existence of an inclusive political community within which groups were differentiated by economic and social interests rather than by ties based on religion, language, ethnicity or locality. However, this glossed over the glaring paradox at the core of the state: India's secular constitution gave no role for religion in public affairs; this situation was to be superimposed on a society where religion was a vital interpersonal bond for hundreds of millions of people. It would have been miraculous if religion did not at some stage become central to politics. In the 1980s, it did.

As we have seen, the selective adaptation of tradition is indispensable to Hindu nationalism. The long campaign to construct a temple upon the site of a mosque at the supposed birthplace of the deity Rama (or Ram), the Hindu god of war, in Ayodhya, had a dramatic influence upon the pattern of politics of some Indian states (such as Uttar Pradesh, Gujarat) but not others. Reference to popular regional religious and cultural traditions might help explain the differential response to the contemporary Hindu nationalist evocation of tradition. However, because of the potential repercussions for the country's more than 100 million Muslims and other minority groups, Hindu nationalism – focused by the violence surrounding the destruction of the Babri mosque at Ayodhya in December 1992 – is widely thought to threaten seriously India's ultimate survival as a pluralist democracy. This event conclusively destroyed the democratic, secular consensus envisaged by the architects of the Indian Constitution.

What religious edifice would take pride of place at Ayodhya has long been a contentious issue. In 1949, following riots, the mosque was closed down by the government. Forty years later, *The Times of India* claimed presciently that the 'laying of the foundation stone of the Rama temple in Ayodhya can be seen to be a dangerous turning point in the history of independent India' (quoted in Copley 1993: 47). However, the wider significance of the Ayodhya incident was that it threw into the open an issue ignored for a long time, that is, 'the relationship between religion and politics, and, more darkly, its seemingly inevitable concomitant relationship with communalism' (ibid.).

But Ayodhya did not come out of the blue. More than thirty years ago, anti-Muslim rhetoric informed the ideology of the Bharatiya Jana Sangh (BJS), the forerunner of the BJP (Chiriyankandath 1996: 53). But the BJS did not enjoy anything like the same electoral success as the BJP. Part of the reason was historical. Because overt Hindu communalism was discredited in the backlash following Gandhi's assassination, the BJS had to narrow its sights. It had to be content with sniping at the Muslim way of life shored up by the Urdu language and loyalty to shariah law. But this was not electorally successful. In addition, in Uttar Pradesh, the focus of the BJS's linguistic anti-Urdu campaign in the 1960s, the Congress government was itself staunchly pro-Hindi – and the BJS made little headway. Nationally at this time, the BJS was only able to identify itself as a 'narrow, northern, regional, Hindi, imperialist party', without wider appeal (Copley 1993: 56).

The picture changed in the 1980s. From being just one of the diverse currents in the ebb and flow of Indian politics in the 1960s and 1970s, the Hindu nationalists, by now focused in the BJP, began to project themselves as the party of the future. Between 1989 and 1991 its share of the vote tripled to 20 per cent. By 1991, it had become 'the strongest official parliamentary opposition to the Congress Party since independence' (Chiriyankandath 1994: 31). Between 1990 and 1995 the BJP won power in the National Capital Territory of Delhi and in six of India's twenty-five states – four in the Hindi-speaking belt of north India and two on the west coast. Of the 119 BJP members in the 545-seat Lok Sabha in 1995, 106 came from these areas, while only eight of the 220 seats in the eastern and southern regions of India were held by the party. Yet, in the 1996 general election the BJP's share of the vote did not increase much above the 1991 figure, only to 23.5 per cent. But this was enough to give it and its allies 188 seats, that is, more than a third of seats on less than a quarter of the vote. The geographical unevenness of the Hindu nationalist support reflects the plural character of the Indian political scene. The challenge for Hindu nationalism is 'to overcome the centrifugal trends that arise from this heterogeneity, based both on vertical (caste and class) and horizontal (language and region) distinctions' (Chiriyankandath 1995: 1).

However, the 1996 result also confirms the steady polarization of Indian society. The Congress Party, the traditional ruling party, lost seats heavily in the north, west and south, although it managed to maintain its position in the east of the country, hanging on to 36 seats. The share of the vote for Congress declined from 48 per cent in 1984 to just over 28 per cent in 1996. The fading of Congress in the first three regions was hastened because of the failure of India's Muslims to do what they traditionally have done: vote for the Congress Party. In the 1995 round of state elections, it is reckoned that most Muslims voted against both the BJP and Congress in favour of candidates or parties with secular credentials (Bhatia 1995). This helps explain the rout of the ruling Congress Party in 1996. Many Muslims identified the party with pro-Hindu sentiments, particularly because of the demolition of the mosque in Ayodhya four years earlier. More widely, the Ayodhya incident also had a dramatic influence upon the pattern of politics of several states – Uttar Pradesh, Gujarat, Maharashtra, where the BJP or its allies made huge gains – but not in others – Kerala, Tamil Nadu – where the Hindu nationalist message was received with coolness.

However, partial scepticism was not enough to prevent the BJP's relentless electoral progress. But the BJP was not able to achieve power on its own. The BJP's chief difficulty lay in persuading those unimpressed by its nationalistic agenda that its political aims had a wider applicability in India's pluralist society. The BJP did not manage to convince non-nationalist politicians following its failure to stitch together a government; the second largest party – Congress – was able to put together a ruling coalition that managed to survive into 1997. Later, from 1998, the BJP achieved power at the head of a coalition government, and managed to stay there for the next three years.

The BJP now dominates the political landscape of north and west India; however, it has found the south and west of the country a tougher nut to crack. This is because it is regarded as a northern-dominated party, intent on imposing its narrow version of the Hindu tradition, at the expense of alternative regional traditions. In the 1996 and 1998 elections the BJP and its allies only managed to acquire a handful of seats in the south and east. Compare this to the 180 it gained – of the 323 on offer – in the north and west in 1996. In these regions, its communistic programme, perceived by many Indian secular intellectuals as the expression of primordial sentiments indicative of the underdeveloped nature of the people concerned, was obviously highly appealing to millions of Indians. Why does the BJP – and Hindu nationalism more generally – appeal? Why in some regions and not others?

Recent Hindu attacks on the status quo in part reflect the absence of a religious hierarchy and organization which engages with the state at the institutional level. Hindu-chauvinist anger is directed at a modernization that failed to benefit all groups in society; it reflects the existence of enduring and deepening societal crisis and the apparent inability of secular government to correct matters. Whereas in different ways Christian and Islamic notables reacted to issues of democratization by either attacking governments or closing ranks with them, it is significant for political culture issues that religious resurgence tended to be at the level of *popular* political culture. Political and religious elites, especially in the Abrahamic religions, generally profess adhesion to religious precepts of *equality* at the same time as they act – and are seen to act – self-interestedly.

Conclusion

As with Christianity and Islam, the processes of global modernization through electronic media have not only diminished the state as a source of identity for many people, but have also stimulated the spread of radical religious ideas. Hinduism is no exception to this trend. Even though Hindu doctrine separates people into a 'complex series of castes that defines their rights, privileges, and ways of life . . . (it) has not posed (until recently) much of an obstacle to the practice of liberal politics in India' (Fukuyama 1992: 228). As already noted, several mass organizations have emerged or re-emerged as significant political players. Among these are the RSS, one of whose members assassinated ('Mahatma') Mohandas Gandhi in 1948, the *Vishwa Hindu Parishad* (VHP 'All Hindu Conference') and the BJP. By the late 1980s the VHP had more than 3,500 branches throughout India and over a million dedicated workers. The context of the rise of these organizations is not only disquiet at the effects of modernization, but also the historic clash between Muslim and Hindu in the region. Internationally, rivalry is manifested between India and Pakistan, while local Muslims in Kashmir (backed by the latter in a proxy war against the former) fight against Indian troops. Intensifying religious strife in India also manifests itself in conflict between the state and militant Sikhs fighting for Khalistan. The destruction of the Ayodhya mosque in December 1992 brought to the fore the issue of whether India would remain a secular democratic state or become a Hindu-dominated one. The issue in essence reduces itself to the question of whether India would remain committed to the principles of modernity and secularism, with no religion receiving especial treatment, or whether Hindu chauvinism would triumph. Certainly, India's middle class would defend the status quo to keep its own position in the state and India's in the world. As Ajami notes, 'A resourceful middle class partakes of global culture and norms' (1993: 3). He argues that as a result of the long struggle to overturn British rule and the struggle against 'communalism', the champions of national unity constructed a large yet durable state they would not give up lightly, especially for 'a political kingdom of Hindu purity' (Ajami 1993: 3). While this is a decidedly optimistic and touching demonstration of belief in the incipient good sense of India's middle class, much will rely upon the ability of central government to deliver sufficient economic growth, relatively equitably spread, to head off Hindu chauvinism and allay Muslim fears. Only time will tell whether international-orientated political culture will triumph over the local brand of intolerance rooted in India's past which the BJP and other militant Hindu groups represent.

6.5 Buddhist 'fundamentalism' in Thailand

Buddhism in Thailand provides the state with an ideological basis and political legitimacy and is widely used to facilitate government policies and to maximize its legitimacy. In Thailand, where over 90 per cent of the people are Buddhists, there is a traditionally close political connection between Buddhist professionals and political rulers. The links between religious and temporal power are reflected in the fact that the present monarch, King Bhumipol Adulyadej, must profess and defend both the Buddhist dharma and the sangha (the body of monks). However, reflecting the prevailing power arrangements he must also reach a *modus vivendi* with the most powerful social group – the military – because of its traditional political role as power broker (Chai-Anan Samudavanija 1993).

The interaction between Buddhism and political rulers in Thailand is taken as a case of reference because, first, since the formation of the Thai state, Buddhism has uninterruptedly been the dominant religion of a great majority of its people. Second, unlike, for example, Laos, Burma or Cambodia, Thailand did not experience the effects of colonial rule. Third, as a result, its traditional mode of government has recognizably continued for many centuries (Somboon Suksamran 1993: 109–10). The general point is that the mobilization of traditional institutions, notably Buddhism and the monarchy, in aid of political stability in Thailand, has been remarkable. In other words, Buddhism and the monarchy have together functioned traditionally as the most visible symbol of national unity.

However, as Swearer notes, while 'the national monastic order strongly supports the state, there have been instances of charismatic monks . . . who have resisted pressures by the state towards standardisation of monastic education and practice' (1987: 64). This points to what Somboon Suksamran has described as a 'continuous dialogue' between the country's Buddhist order and the state (1982: 7). At the heart of the interlocution is the question of whether Buddhism is, or is not, the state religion. Buddhism is known in Thailand as the *sasana pracham chat*, that is, the 'inherent' national religion. However, no Thai constitution has ever specified that Buddhism is actually the state religion, although all have stated that the King must profess the Buddhist faith. Thus the constitutional position of Buddhism is open to interpretation and its public role open to debate.

Historically, a number of measures have highlighted attempts by the secular authorities to bring Buddhism under firm control. This was well expressed in the 1962 Sangha Act which sought to make direct use of Buddhist monks in the service of the state. Henceforward, monks were enlisted in various programmes combining Buddhist proselytizing with combating communism and spreading state ideology to Thailand's minority (non-Buddhist) tribal peoples with the goal of assimilating them into mainstream society. Since the early 1970s, however, not all interaction between monks and the state has been mutually supportive. The catalyst for change was the so-called 'October Revolution' of 1973 when student- and monk-led demonstrations succeeded in toppling the military dictatorship of Field

Marshals Thanom Kittikachorn and Praphat Charusathien. The result of the monks taking the side of the opposition in 1973 was that henceforward the traditional pattern of a subservient sangha legitimating an authoritarian government was emphatically broken. From this time, monks openly and regularly took political sides, some on the side of political liberalization and reform, while others were opposed. Many among those against expressed the view that the post-1973 regime was dangerously liberal, seriously undermining traditional state–sangha relations and, consequently, Buddhism itself.

The most radical monks tended to look beyond the confines of state–sangha concerns, and some openly supported a reformist student movement campaigning for a modern democratic system while others canvassed for the avowedly secular Socialist Party in the 1975 elections. Both professed to see a clear parallel between the inequality and authoritarianism of the sangha hierarchy, and wider socio-economic injustices in Thailand. However, monks whose politics challenged the power of the state were not easily tolerated. Many were severely disciplined (Somboon Suksamran 1982: 56–61, 84–90, 103–5). At the other end of the political spectrum, an outspoken right-wing monk, Kittiwuttho, founded an extreme nationalist movement, Nawaphon, declaring a 'holy war' on communism, proclaiming that 'killing communists is no sin' (McCargo 1992: 11). Despite such inflammatory statements, his organization was permitted to pursue its activities unhindered, while Kittiwuttho himself established close ties with a group of right-wing military officers. This seeming double standard serves to underline the sometimes rather ambiguous nature of the 'dialogue' between religious and political authorities in Thailand.

The general point is that the 1962 Sangha Act was the product of a period of Thailand's political history characterized by a rather crude authoritarianism. As a result of the Act, a handful of elderly and extremely conservative monks were able to rule the sangha with a dictatorial hand. Yet, they conspicuously failed to address such urgent problems as poor internal discipline and declining numbers of long-term ordinations. It is scarcely surprising that, by the very nature of the system which selected them, such senior monks tended to be strongly supportive of the political status quo.

As already noted, however, since the 1970s challenges emerged from within the collectivity of monks which not only focused upon the nature of the state policies but increasingly upon the nature of the sangha regime itself. Since that time, a new generation of monks has emerged. Such individuals aimed to teach a contemporary Buddhism relevant to a rapidly changing society. In some ways they resembled Latin America's Catholic priests animated by the concerns of liberation theology that were such an important feature of the religio-political scene in the 1970s and 1980s. In Thailand, such 'progressive' monks were similarly engaged in development work, including environmental, conservation and community projects and moral education, largely for the same reasons as their Catholic counterparts. The monks believed that the pre-eminent place and relevance of Buddhism in Thai society – like that of Catholicism in Latin America – must be ensured by its evolution in the context of changing circumstances. They must achieve an *active* engagement with society, rather than being satisfied with a ritual legitimation of the state alone. However, most were no more or less 'political' than their titled superiors; the point is that the former worked for socially progressive goals while the latter were, for the most part, strongly conservative. It is this schism that led McCargo to contend that the 'existing edifice of the Thai Buddhist *sangha*, for all its traditional centrality in the rituals of the state, contains dangerous cracks' (1992: 12).

The division within the sangha is not, however, the only recent development within Thai Buddhism with political resonance. Another is the emergence of a number of 'new Buddhist movements', including Phuttathat Bhikku's Suan Moke, Wat Phra Dharmakaya, and Photirak's Santi Asoke. All have been beneficiaries of the mainstream sangha's high-level paralysis and indirection. In their different ways, each movement is concerned with Buddhism's quest for modern relevance; broadly, they are society-oriented. Santi Asoke, uniquely, has openly entered the political arena. In sum, their emergence may well reflect a general shift in Thailand's political power, that is, away from traditional – and conservative – state institutions such as the military and the orthodox sangha, and towards a stronger and more diverse civil society (Hewison 1993: 180–1). Before analysing such groups and their contribution to an emerging Buddhist 'fundamentalism' in Thailand it may be appropriate to describe the fundamentals of Buddhism, as these seem relatively little known.

THE FUNDAMENTALS OF BUDDHISM

While sharing many features of Hinduism, Buddhism broke away more than two thousand years ago owing to dissatisfaction with the former's ritualism and the dominance of the priestly class. It developed as a separate religious tradition, both rationalistic and atheistic: there is no all-powerful God believed to be presiding over people's destiny. However, Buddhism is a thoroughgoing *ethical* system; its followers believe that people prosper or not according to the Buddhist law of karma, that is, what has been enacted in some distant past affects what is possible in the present. Every individual goes through a series of births, with salvation eventually attained through cessation of the cycle of births and deaths.

For lay people to define themselves as 'Buddhist', it is often sufficient for them to declare that they go to the Three Refuges: the Buddha, the Dharma (the Buddha's doctrine) and the body of monks and nuns (the sangha), and that they will abide by the Five Precepts (not to kill, steal, be unchaste, lie, or take intoxicants). There are days in the lunar month of intensified observance (*uposatha* days) when, ideally, a lay person takes the Eight Precepts – that is, the basic five, plus all sexual activity to be excluded, not to watch entertainments or use adornments nor use luxurious beds. This is close to lower ordination (*pabbajja*) entailing taking the Ten precepts. This is like the Eight, except the strictures against adornments and entertainments are separated, while the use of money is forbidden.

Theoretically, the single aim of Buddhist practice is to achieve nirvana, the extinction of desire and the end to rebirth and suffering. Traditionally, the way to attain the goal is to progress via moral purity, self-restraint and the practice of meditation to the acquirement of wisdom, a path which only a monk or nun can hope to tread successfully. Practically, however, the religious goal of nirvana is either too remote or too difficult to understand to be attractive to the vast majority of ordinary people. In addition, the Buddhist teaching that existence is 'unsatisfactory' or 'suffering' (*dukkha*) is probably only partially accepted by many people. This is because they can see or imagine states of wealth and power where suffering is outweighed by happiness and pleasure. These states, even if impermanent, still seem desirable. Thus the ideal goal for many becomes, practically, not nirvana but a better rebirth, probably as a wealthy person.

To achieve the diminished goal of a better rebirth it is necessary to acquire merit. As a result, virtually all Buddhist religious practice, whether by monks or laity, has merit as its aim. Merit-making is compatible with doctrine, since it all contributes – ultimately – to attaining nirvana. To attain merit, which in turn will help achieve a better rebirth, it is essential not to do bad actions. The latter produce karmic retribution in the form of a worse rebirth. Merit is perceived by many Buddhists as a kind of intangible spiritual 'currency' which can be reckoned and 'transferred', increasing in proportion to the amount 'invested' (Johnson 1988: 734). There are ten ways of earning merit, the most rewarding activity: generosity, especially giving food and other goods to monks in exchange for various religious services, plus observing the precepts, meditation, transferring merit, empathizing with merit, serving one's elders, showing respect, preaching, listening to preaching, and holding right beliefs. For the layperson, the most important function of the sangha is to provide the individual with the opportunity to make merit by giving to the monks. As a result, most monks spend much of their time performing merit-making rituals – especially sermons and readings from the texts – for laypeople. Since few monks consider nirvana to be a realistic goal, such activity is in fact beneficial for them as well as laypeople. This is because preaching and propagating the dharma is one of the ways in which they acquire merit and thus the chance of a better rebirth. Thus there is a symbiotic relationship between laypeople and monks: each benefits from merit-making, while overall the store of merit goes on increasing (Johnson 1988: 735).

BUDDHISM AND POLITICS IN THAILAND

In Thailand, a Buddhist 'fundamentalist' group, Santi Asoke, was accused in the early 1990s of trying to create a model society, a 'Thai Buddhist utopia' (McCargo 1992: 2). Even though Thailand is a strongly Buddhist country (Buddhism is one of the three foundations of the state along with loyalty to king and country), Buddhism has played a fairly minor overt role in Thai national politics. The sangha (monkhood) remains relatively apolitical, as it is well organized in a hierarchical structure under the leadership of the king. One of the most significant aspects of Thailand's politics is the traditional political importance of the military. The absence of colonialism in Thailand served to create a Thai military unaffected by anti-colonial aspirations. Whereas most military structures were strongly anti-colonial in many colonies, the role of the military in Thailand was traditionally strongly in support of the status quo, especially in the context of regional attempts to impose communist regimes. Indeed, in the 1960s when fear of communist insurgency in the country was at its height, members of the sangha were involved in policies emphasizing development, national unity and anti-communism, the values which the military in Thailand appeared to hold most dear. However, in recent years Thailand has been striving to become more democratic.

What this amounts to is that in Thailand the political orientations of the elites were often shaped not so much by religious concerns as by fear of radical political change which might overthrow them all, including the powerful military leaders. An ideology of development had as its rationale and centre-piece a requirement for an effective political authority rather than one that was necessarily democratically accountable. The idea of stability as more important than democracy was not undermined by strong challenges from Buddhist sources. This was in part because Thai Buddhism was not plugged into a universal religious structure, unlike Islam or Christianity, which could sometimes transcend the effects of local political cultures. In part this was because of the fact that the relationship between state and society (in Thailand, as elsewhere in Asia) was more intricate, even 'multidimensional', than in many Western countries (Chai-Anan Samudavanija 1993: 270).

On the other hand, the image of a quiescent, even passive Buddhist population was strongly shaken by two events in recent times in Thailand. The first was the founding of a Buddhist-orientated political party, the Palang Tham Party, whose main figure, Major-General Chamlong Srimaung, initially enjoyed some political success. The second was the probably unprecedented outbreak of popular political rebellion in May 1992 against the appointment of a non-elected prime minister. What was of significance was the international diffusion effects of pro-democracy agitation which reached Thailand via the electronic media. In the ensuing political violence, hundreds of demonstrators were killed, and thousands injured (Chai-Anan Samudavanija 1993: 286). In the resulting elections in September 1992 the civilian-led, modernizing Democratic Party won the poll and its leader took the post of prime minister in the new government.

New Buddhist movements and politics

Since the 1930s, Thai politics has been a situation where the interests of civilian and military elites have been privileged, enjoying a monopoly of real political power. While procedural elements of democracy (political parties and elections, more or less democratic constitutions) have been – intermittently – present, representative democracy has not developed to any great extent. There has been little room for countervailing forces of civil society – socially progressive monks, reformist business groups, trade unions, environmental protection groups, pro-democracy organizations, new political parties, the mass media, and so on – to pursue essentially reformist goals. In short, until recently politics has been understood primarily as the domain of elite interests, while those challenging the status quo have been marginalized (Chai-Anan Samudavanija 1993: 282–7; Hewison 1993: 167–84). The emphases and directions of new Buddhist movements in Thailand are basically reformist and should be understood in relation to the foregoing. They are attempts to make the religion meaningful to modern life, as both critique and affirmation (Satha-Anand Suwanna 1990: 405). Put another way, they should be understood in the context of Thailand's changing political system.

Various scholars have argued that the rise of new social forces in civil society has served to invalidate the conventional elite-centred conception of Thai politics (Swearer 1987; Hewison 1993; Somboon Suksamran 1993). This has occurred because, whereas in the past the elites were normally able to co-opt any challengers to the status quo, recent rapid socio-economic change has shifted power especially towards a new business class. Such business interests have worked with some of the emerging civil society groups to wrest a degree of economic power from the hands of state officials and the military. But the impact has been felt not only in the economic sphere, but also in those of religion and politics.

According to temple statistics, most members of one of the new Buddhist movements – the Wat Dharmakaya – are from the middle class. Forty-one per cent are said to be university students and 22 per cent private business owners. They 'seem to represent a segment of the emerging middle class that is keen on achieving both worldly pleasure and peace of mind in religious form' (Satha-Anand Suwanna 1990: 407). In short, an area of democratic 'space' has opened up where new political and religious forces operate with greater freedom and effectiveness, challenging not just the religious, but also the wider, socio-political, status quo.

The rise of the new Buddhist movements is an important part of this process of political change because they offer emergent social groups the ability to develop religious practices – broadly within the Buddhist tradition – which, crucially, are not subject to the direct day-to-day control of senior monks or the Thai state. As McCargo (1992: 19) notes, 'orthodox Thai Buddhism amounts to an extension of bureaucratic dominance into the religious and personal life of ordinary citizens'. There is also a widening social gulf between most ordinary monks – over 90 per cent hail from the rural uneducated populace – and the emerging middle class of Bangkok and other population centres (Satha-Anand Suwanna 1990: 407). While many orthodox monks offer ritualistic services and give occasional sermons to the urban middle class, a widening gap exists between the two groups which the new Buddhist movements help to fill. By adopting new modes of Buddhist practice and belief, members of key civil society groups are able to define for themselves a distinct identity which is no longer subservient to state concerns. Yet, changing class structure and an emerging civil society is not the only explanation for the rise of the new Buddhist movements. They are also, it is argued, a fundamental part of what has been called Thailand's 'individualistic revolution' (Keyes 1989; Taylor 1990).

CONCLUSION

New Buddhist movements in Thailand are difficult to account for definitively because, so far, they have not been fully quantified, nor adequately classified. It is nonetheless fairly clear that they are the result of social change, of urbanization and of resulting spiritual dislocations. Reflecting the impact of modernization, Thailand's new Buddhist movements are part of a global pattern of religious resurgence – a development which cannot wholly be correlated with country-specific patterns of socio-economic change and which, in some contexts, has seen the emergence of religious fundamentalist groups. However, the increased pluralism of Buddhist teaching and practice offered by the new movements testifies to the emergence of a less homogeneous society and religion, and a reduction of the capacity of the state to impose religious, social and political values upon middle-class Thais. It is less clear that they reflect manifestations of Buddhist fundamentalism.

6.6 Overall conclusion

The concept of popular religious interpretations, including religious fundamentalist ones, is not new; there have always been opponents of mainline religious interpretations. What is novel, however, is that in the past manifestations of popular religion were normally bundled up within strong frameworks that held them together, serving to police the most extreme tendencies, as in the Christian churches, or were at least nominally under the control of the mainline religion – as with popular sects in Islam and Buddhism. In the contemporary era, however, it is no longer possible to keep all religious tendencies within traditional organizing frameworks. This is primarily a consequence of two developments: (1) widespread, destabilizing change after World War II – summarized as postmodernism – leading many people to question what were once their most unshakeable convictions; and (2) religious privatization, especially in the increasingly secular West.

In the past, popular religious groups functioned in isolation. This is no longer the case. Paralleling, and in some ways reinforcing, the impact of postmodernism, is that of globalization. In the context of the spread of ideas, especially religious views, globalization – particularly the impact of the spread of communications to all parts of the world – means that groups are no longer isolated as in the past. Historically, when there were breaks in religious traditions, the breakaways were either recaptured or, if they stayed independent, came in time to reflect again the diversity from which they wished to escape.

It seems clear that – under certain circumstances of cultural defence and transition – religion has had increasingly political impacts in many parts of the world. Confidence that the growth and spread of urbanization, education, economic development, scientific rationality and social mobility would combine to diminish significantly the sociopolitical power of religion was not well founded, with various 'fundamentalist' groups emerging in many countries as vehicles of popular opposition to the status quo. Threats emanating either from powerful outsider groups or from unwelcome symptoms of modernization (breakdown of moral behaviour, perceived over-liberalization in education and social habits) helped galvanize such religion-based reactions.

Religious fundamentalism can be divided into two categories: the 'religions of the book' and nationalist-oriented Hinduism and Buddhism. Scriptural revelations relating to political, moral and social issues form the corpus of fundamentalist demands. Sometimes these are deeply conservative (American Christian fundamentalists); sometimes they are reformist or revolutionary (some Islamist and Buddhist groups); and sometimes they are xenophobic, racist and reactionary (some Jewish groups, such as Kach and Kahane Chai, and various Islamist groups). Hindu 'fundamentalism', on the other hand, assumed a nationalist dimension when it sought a rebirth of national identity and vigour denied in the past, zealots considered, by unwelcome cultural dilution and inadequate government.

While secularization seems the 'normal' – and continuing – state of affairs in most Western societies, the various religious groups examined in this chapter tend to share a disaffection and dissatisfaction with established, hierarchical, institutionalized religious bodies; a desire to find God through personal searching rather than through the mediation of institutions; and a belief in communities' ability to make beneficial changes to their lives through the application of group effort. The desire to 'go it alone', not to be beholden to 'superior' bodies, tends to characterize any of the groups we have examined. Religion offers a rational alternative to those for whom modernization has either failed or is in some way unattractive. Its interaction with political issues over the medium term is likely to be of especial importance, carrying a serious and seminal message of societal resurgence and regeneration in relation to both political leaders and economic elites.

BIBLIOGRAPHY

Ahmed, A. (1992) *Postmodernism and Islam: Predicament and Promise*. London: Routledge.
Ajami, F. (1993) 'The summoning', *Foreign Affairs* 72(4): 2–9.
Alford, R. R. (1969) 'Religion and politics', in R. Robertson (ed.), *Sociology of Religion*. Baltimore: Penguin, pp. 321–30.
Almond, G. (1993) 'Foreword: The return to political culture', in L. Diamond (ed.), *Political Culture and Democracy in Developing Countries*. Boulder and London: Lynne Rienner, pp. ix–xii.
Almond, G., and S. Verba (1963) *The Civic Culture. Political Attitudes and Democracy in Five Nations*. Princeton: Princeton University Press.
d'Antonio, M. (1990) *Fall from Grace: The Failed Crusade of the Christian Right*. London: Deutsch.
Asia Watch (1994) *Detained in China and Tibet*. London: Asia Watch.
Bayart, J.-F. (1993) *The State in Africa*. London: Longman.
Bealey, F. (1999) *The Blackwell Dictionary of Political Science*. Oxford: Blackwell.
Bellah, R. (1964) 'Religious evolution', *American Sociological Review* 29(3): 358–74.
Bhatia, S. (1995) 'Bombay's McCarthyite terror', *The Observer*, 23 April.
Bhatia, S. (1996) 'A dark shadow descends on Israel', *The Observer*, 2 June.
Black, I. (1996) 'The hard noes [sic] leader', *The Observer*, 2 June.
Bruce, S. (1993) 'Fundamentalism, ethnicity and enclave', in M. Marty and R. Scott Appleby (eds), *Fundamentalisms and the State: Remaking Polities, Economies, and Militance*. Chicago: University of Chicago Press, pp. 50–67.
Callaghy, T. (1993) 'Vision and politics in the transformation of the global political economy: lessons from the second and third worlds', in R. Slater, B. Schutz and S. Dorr (eds), *Global Transformation and the Third World*. Boulder and London: Lynne Rienner, pp. 161–258.
Caplan, L. (ed.) (1987) *Studies in Religious Fundamentalism*. Albany: State University of New York Press.
Casanova, J. (1994) *Public Religions in the Modern World*. Chicago and London: University of Chicago Press.
Chai-Anan Samudavanija (1993) 'The new military and democracy in Thailand', in L. Diamond (ed.), *Political Culture and Democracy in Developing Countries*. Boulder: Lynne Rienner, pp. 269–94.
Chiriyankandath, J. (1994) 'The politics of religious identity: a comparison of Hindu nationalism and Sudanese Islamism', *Journal of Commonwealth and Comparative Politics* 32(1): 31–53.

Chiriyankandath, J. (1995) 'Hindu nationalism and Indian regional political culture: a study of Kerala'. Paper prepared for the workshop 'Political culture and religion in the Third World', European Consortium for Political Research Joint Sessions of Workshops, Bordeaux, April–May.

Chiriyankandath, J. (1996) 'Hindu nationalism and regional political culture in India: a study of Kerala', *Nationalism and Ethnic Politics* 2(1): 44–66.

Copley, A. (1993) 'Indian secularism reconsidered: from Gandhi to Ayodhya', *Contemporary South Asia* 2(1): 47–65.

Coulon, C. (1983) *Les Musulmans et le Pouvoir en Afrique Noire*. Paris: Kartala.

Cox, H. (1965) *The Secular City*. London: Collier.

Cox, H. (1984) *Religion in the Secular City: Toward a Postmodern Theology*. New York: Simon & Schuster.

Dark, K. (2000) 'Large-scale religious change and world politics', in K. Dark (ed.), *Religion and International Relations*. Basingstoke: Macmillan, pp. 50–82.

De Gruchy, J. (1995) *Christianity and Democracy: A Theology for a Just World Order*. Cambridge: Cambridge University Press.

Deiros, P. (1991) 'Protestant fundamentalism in Latin America', in M. Marty and R. Scott Appleby (eds), *Fundamentalisms Observed*. Chicago: University of Chicago Press, pp. 142–96.

Dieckhoff, A. (1991) 'The impact of Jewish religious parties in the State of Israel'. Paper prepared for the workshop 'Religion and international politics', European Consortium for Political Research Joint Sessions of Workshops, University of Essex, March.

Dorr, S. (1993) 'Democratization in the Middle East', in R. Slater, B. Schutz and S. Dorr (eds), *Global Transformation and the Third World*. Boulder and London: Lynne Rienner, pp. 131–57.

Etienne, B., and M. Tozy (1981) 'Le Glissement des Obligations Islamiques Vers le Phénomène Associatif à Casablanca', in Centre de Recherches et d'Etudes sur les Sociétés Méditerranéennes, *Le Maghreb Musulman en 1979*. Paris: Editions du centre national de la recherche scientifique, pp. 235–51.

Featherstone, M. (1988) 'In pursuit of the postmodern: an introduction', in M. Featherstone (ed.), Special Issue of *Theory, Culture and Society* 5(2–3): 195–216.

Fletcher, M. (1994) 'Mullah of Chicago's mean streets', *The Guardian*, 17 February.

Fossaert, R. (1978) *La Société*, vol. 5: *Les Etats*. Paris: Seuil.

Fukuyama, F. (1992) *The End of History and the Last Man*. Harmondsworth: Penguin.

Gifford, P. (1990) 'Prosperity: a new and foreign element in African Christianity', *Religion* 20(3): 373–88.

Gifford, P. (1991) *The New Crusaders: Christianity and the New Right in Southern Africa*. London: Pluto Press.

Gifford, P. (1994) 'Some recent developments in African Christianity', *African Affairs* 93(373): 513–34.

Hadden, J. (1987) 'Towards desacralizing secularization theory', *Social Forces* 65: 587–611.

Hallencreutz, C., and D. Westerlund (1996) 'Anti-secularist policies of religion', in D. Westerlund (ed.), *Questioning the Secular State: The Worldwide Resurgence of Religion in Politics*. London: Hurst, pp. 1–23.

Haynes, J. (1993) *Religion in Third World Politics*. Buckingham: Open University Press.

Haynes, J. (1995) 'Religion, fundamentalism and identity: a global perspective', Discussion Paper 65. Geneva: United Nations Research Institute for Social Development.

Haynes, J. (1996) *Religion and Politics in Africa*. London: Zed Books.

Haynes, J. (1998) *Religion in Global Politics*. Harlow: Longman.

Hellman, E. (1996) 'Dynamic Hinduism towards a new Hindu nation', in D. Westerlund (ed.), *Questioning the Secular State: The Worldwide Resurgence of Religion in Politics*. London: Hurst, pp. 237–58.

Hertzke, A. (1989) 'United States of America', in S. Mews (ed.), *Religion in Politics: A World Guide*. Harlow: Longman, pp. 298–317.

Hewison, K. (1993) 'Of regimes, states and pluralities: Thai politics enters the 1990s', in K. Hewison, R. Robison and G. Rodan (eds), *Southeast Asia in the 1990s*. St Leonards: Allen & Unwin, pp. 161–73.

Huntington, S. (1993) 'The clash of civilisations?', *Foreign Affairs* 72(3): 22–49.

Hyden, G. (1992) 'Governance and the study of politics', in G. Hyden and M. Bratton (eds), *Governance and Politics in Africa*. Boulder and London: Lynne Rienner, pp. 1–26.

Ibrahim, Y. (1992) 'Islamic plan for Algeria on display', *The New York Times*, 7 January.

Jacobs, L. (1992) 'Contemporary Judaism', in I. Harris, S. Mews, P. Morris and J. Shepherd (eds), *Contemporary Religions: A World Guide*. Harlow: Longman, pp. 31–8.

Jaffrelot, C. (1995) 'The Vishva Hindu Parishad: structures and strategies'. Paper prepared for the workshop 'Political culture and religion in the Third World'. European Consortium for Political Research Joint Sessions of Workshops, Bordeaux, April–May.

Johnson, W. (1988) 'Theravada Buddhism in South-East Asia', in S. Sutherland, L. Houlden, P. Clarke and F. Hardy (eds), *The World's Religions*. London: Routledge, pp. 726–38.

Johnston, H. (1992) 'Religious nationalism: six propositions from Eastern Europe and the Former Soviet Union', in B. Misztal and A. Shupe (eds), *Religion and Politics in Comparative Perspective*. Westport and London: Praeger, pp. 67–78.

Juergensmeyer, M. (1989) 'India', in S. Mews (ed.), *Religion in Politics: A World Guide*. Harlow: Longman, pp. 98–107.

Juergensmeyer, M. (1993) *The New Cold War? Religious Nationalism Confronts the Secular State*. Berkeley and London: University of California Press.

Keyes, C. (1989) 'Buddhist politics and their revolutionary origins in Thailand', *International Political Science Review* 10(2): 121–42.

Lawrence, B. (1995) *Defenders of the Faith: The International Revolt Against the Modern Age*. Columbia, SC: University of South Carolina Press.

Lewis, H. D., and R. L. Slater (1969) *The Study of Religions*. Harmondsworth: Penguin.

Luckmann, T. (1969) 'The decline of Church-oriented religion', in R. Robertson (ed.), *The Sociology of Religion*. Baltimore: Penguin, pp. 141–51.

Lyotard, J.-F. (1979) *The Post-Modern Condition: A Report on Knowledge*. Manchester: Manchester University Press.

Madan, T. (1987) 'Secularism in its place', *Journal of Asian Studies* 46(4): 740–53.

Martin, D. (1990) *Tongues of Fire: The Explosion of Protestantism in Latin America*. Oxford: Blackwell.

Marty, M. E., and R. Scott Appleby (eds) (1991) *Fundamentalisms Observed*. Chicago: University of Chicago Press.

Marty, M. E., and R. Scott Appleby (eds) (1993a) *Fundamentalisms and Society*. Chicago: University of Chicago Press.

Marty, M. E., and R. Scott Appleby (eds) (1993b) *Fundamentalisms and the State*. Chicago: University of Chicago Press.

Marty, M. E., and R. Scott Appleby (eds) (1993c) 'Introduction', *Fundamentalisms and the State: Remaking Polities, Economies, and Militance*. Chicago: University of Chicago Press, pp. 1–9.

Marty, M. E., and R. Scott Appleby (eds) (1994) *Accounting for Fundamentalisms*. Chicago: University of Chicago Press.

Marty, M. E., and R. Scott Appleby (eds) (1995) *Fundamentalisms Comprehended*. Chicago: University of Chicago Press.

McCargo, D. (1992) 'The political ramifications of the 1989 "Santi Asoke" case in Thailand'. Paper presented at the Annual Conference of the Association of South-East Asian Studies, School of Oriental and African Studies, University of London, 8–10 April.

McGreal, C. (2000) 'Islamic law advances in Nigeria', *The Guardian*, 28 November.

Medhurst, K. (1981) 'Religion and politics: a typology', *Scottish Journal of Religious Studies* 2(2): 115–34.

Mitra, S. K. (1991) 'Desecularising the state: religion and politics in India after Independence', *Comparative Studies in Society and History* 33(4): 755–77.

Moran, E., and L. Schlemmer (1984) *Faith for the Fearful?* Durban: Centre for Applied Social Studies.

Morris, P. (1989) 'Israel', in S. Mews (ed.), *Religion in Politics: A World Guide*. Harlow: Longman, pp. 123–37.

Moyser, G. (1991) 'Politics and religion in the modern world: an overview', in G. Moyser (ed.), *Politics and Religion in the Modern World*. London and New York: Routledge, pp. 1–27.

Newman, S. (1991) 'Does modernization breed ethnic political conflicts?', *World Politics* 43(2): 451–78.

Oz, A. (1996) 'A fantasy returns', *The Observer*, 2 June.

Parrinder, G. (1977) *Comparative Religion*. London: Sheldon.

Parsons, T. (1960) *Structures and Process in Modern Societies*. Chicago: University of Chicago Press.

Peil, M., with P. Sada (1984) *African Urban Society*. Chichester: John Wiley.

Pieterse, J. (1992) 'Christianity, politics and Gramscism of the Right: Introduction', in J. Pieterse (ed.), *Christianity and Hegemony: Religion and Politics on the Frontiers of Social Change*. Oxford: Berg, pp. 1–31.

Ram-Prasad, C. (1993) 'Hindutva ideology: extracting the fundamentals', *Contemporary South Asia* 2(3): 285–309.

Ram-Prasad, C. (2000) 'Hindu nationalism and the international relations of India', in K. Dark (ed.), *Religion and International Relations*. Basingstoke: Macmillan, pp. 140–97.

Ray, A. (1996) 'Religion and politics in South Asia', *Asian Affairs* 1(1): 9–12.

Roberts, B. (1968) 'Protestant groups and coping with urban life in Guatemala City', *American Journal of Sociology* 73(3): 753–67.

Rosenau, J. (1990) *Turbulence in World Politics: A Theory of Change and Continuity*. Princeton: Princeton University Press.

Sahliyeh, E. (1990a) 'Foreword', in E. Sahliyeh (ed.), *Religious Resurgence and Politics in the Contemporary World*. Albany: State University of New York Press, pp. vi–ix.

Sahliyeh, E. (1990b) 'Religious resurgence and political modernization', in E. Sahliyeh (ed.), *Religious Resurgence and Politics in the Contemporary World*. Albany: State University of New York Press, pp. 1–16.

Satha-Anand Suwanna (1990) 'Religious movements in contemporary Thailand', *Asian Survey* 30(4): 395–408.

Shupe, A. (1990) 'The stubborn persistence of religion in the global arena', in E. Sahliyeh (ed.), *Religious Resurgence and Politics in the Contemporary World*. Albany: State University of New York Press, pp. 17–26.

Silberstein, L. (1993) 'Religion, ideology, modernity: theoretical issues in the study of Jewish fundamentalism', in L. Silberstein (ed.), *Jewish Fundamentalism in Comparative Perspective: Religion, Ideology, and the Crisis of Modernity*. New York and London: New York University Press, pp. 3–26.

Simpson, J. (1992) 'Fundamentalism in America revisited: the fading of modernity as a source of symbolic capital', in B. Misztal and A. Shupe (eds), *Religion and Politics in Comparative Perspective: Revival of Religious Fundamentalism in East and West*. Westport and London: Praeger, pp. 10–27.

Sisson, R. (1993) 'Culture and democratization in India', in L. Diamond (ed.), *Political Culture and Democracy in Developing Countries*. Boulder and London: Lynne Rienner, pp. 37–66.

Smart, N. (1989) *The World's Religions*. Cambridge: Cambridge University Press.

Smith, D. E. (1970) *Religion and Political Development*. Boston: Little, Brown.

Smith, D. E. (1990) 'Limits of religious resurgence', in E. Sahliyeh (ed.), *Religious Resurgence and Politics in the Contemporary World*. Albany: State University of New York Press, pp. 33–44.

Somboon Suksamran (1982) *Buddhism and Politics in Thailand: A Study of Socio-Political Change and Political Activism of the Thai Sangha*. Singapore: Institute of Southeast Asian Studies.

Somboon Suksamran (1993) 'Buddhism, political authority, and legitimacy in Thailand and Cambodia', in T. Ling (ed.), *Buddhist Trends in Southeast Asia*. Singapore: Institute of Southeast Asian Studies, pp. 101–53.

Sprinzak, E. (1993) 'Fundamentalism, ultranationalism, and political culture: the case of the Israeli radical right', in L. Diamond (ed.), *Political Culture and Democracy in Developing Countries*. Boulder and London: Lynne Rienner, pp. 247–78.

Swearer, D. (1987) 'The Buddhist tradition in today's world', in F. Whaling (ed.), *Religion in Today's World*. Edinburgh: T. & T. Clark, pp. 55–75.

Talbot, I. (1991) 'Politics and religion in contemporary India', in G. Moyser (ed.), *Politics and Religion in the Modern World*. London: Routledge, pp. 135–61

Taylor, J. L. (1990) 'New Buddhist movements in Thailand: an "individualistic revolution", reform and political dissonance', *Journal of Southeast Asian Studies* 21(1): 130–43.

Therborn, G. (1994) 'Another way of taking religion seriously: comment on Francis G. Castles', *European Journal of Political Research* 26(1): 103–10.

Thomas, S. (1995) 'Religion and international society'. Paper prepared for the workshop 'Political culture and religion in the Third World', European Consortium for Political Research Joint Sessions of Workshops, Bordeaux, April–May.

Thomas, S. (1999) 'Religion and international society', in J. Haynes (ed.), *Religion, Globalization and Political Culture in the Third World*. Basingstoke: Macmillan, pp. 28–44.

Thomas, S. (2000) 'Religion and international conflict', in K. Dark (ed.), *Religion and International Relations*. Basingstoke: Macmillan, pp. 1–23.

Turner, V. (1969) *The Ritual Process: Structure and Anti-Structure*. Ithaca: Cornell University Press.

Venugopal, C. N. (1990) 'Reformist sects and the sociology of religion in India', *Sociological Analysis* 51 (Summer): 77–88.

Wald, K. (1991) 'Social change and political response: the silent religious cleavage in North America', in G. Moyser (ed.), *Religion and Politics in the Modern World*. London: Routledge, pp. 239–84.

Wallis, R., and S. Bruce (1992) 'Secularization: the orthodox model', in S. Bruce (ed.), *Religion and Modernization*. Oxford: Clarendon Press, pp. 8–30.

Watson, M. (1994) 'Christianity and the Green option in the New Europe', in J. Fulton and P. Gee (eds), *Religion in Contemporary Europe*. Lewiston: Edwin Mellen, pp. 148–59.

Weber, M. (1978) *Economy and Society*. Berkeley: University of California Press.

Wilson, B. (1992) 'Reflections on a many sided controversy', in S. Bruce (ed.), *Religion and Modernization*. Oxford: Clarendon Press, pp. 195–210.

Woodhead, L., and P. Heelas (eds) (2000) 'Introduction to Chapter Two: Religions of Difference', in *Religion in Modern Times*. Oxford: Blackwell, pp. 27–33.

Woollacott, M. (1995) 'Keeping our faith in belief', *The Guardian*, 23 December.

SUBJECT INDEX

Abhidarma 71–3, 78–79, 82, 98, 104, 105
   see also Amida
ablutions 239
acquisition 235
Adam Kadmon 153–4
Advaida Vedanta 13, 28, 53–4
Agudat Israel 354–6
Ajivikas 35
Alaya consciousness 83, 91
alms-tax *see zakat*
American University of Cairo 255
Amida 106–8
Amoraim 140, 144, 146
Amritsar Golden Temple 341
anti-Semitism 119, 121, 163, 165–8, 170
apostasy: in Judaism 156
Arahat 73
Arya/s 16–18, 42, 44, 46
Arya Samaj 28, 32, 48
Aryans 16–17
Ashkenazi Jews 161
atheism 292, 296, 300
atman 34, 53
avidya 360
Awakening of Faith 87, 91–2, 102
ayd al-fitr 247
Ayodhya 31, 331, 362–3
al-Azhar University 255, 275

Babri masjid 31, 33
Bahais 268
Balfour Declaration 172
Bangladesh 14
Barelvis 284
Base Christian communities 349
Berlin Wall 339
Bengal 21, 29
Bhagavad Gita 19, 23, 28–9, 33–4, 36, 67, 361

Bhakti/s 23–4, 26
Bharata-varsha 19
Bharatiya Janata Party (BJP) 31, 331–2, 359–60, 363–5
Bible 178, 180
Bodhisattva 73, 76, 80, 86, 108
Brahma sutra 19
brahman 16, 26, 53
Brahmanas 16
Brahmaputra 14
Brahmins 12, 18, 20–1, 23, 30–1, 35, 45
Brahmo-Samaj, 27
Brihad-Aranyaka 34, 43, 49
Brihat-Samhita 23
Buddha 20, 60
Buddha-nature 87, 89–91, 99
Buddhism 14, 18–19, 21–2, 33, 45, 47;
   Buddhist canon 60; Buddhist fundamentalism 365–70

Camp David 330, 356
caste 27, 29–30, 43–5, 47
Chabad-Lubavitch 160–1
chakra-varti 18, 23
Chalcedon 182, 196
Chalukyas 22, 25
Chasidic movement 154
Chera kings 46
Chola Kings 22–3, 46
Christian church 192; canon 179, 181; relations with state 332–3
Christians: born-again 344; fundamentalists 330; fundamentalists in USA 327
Christianity beyond Europe 218–28; in Africa 343–49; in India 219–28; in Ethiopia 221; Western 205–18
Church of St. Thomas 219–20
civil society 329, 351, 369

INDEX OF PERSONS AND DEITIES